A RESOURCE GUIDE FOR TEACHING K–12

SIXTH EDITION

A RESOURCE GUIDE FOR TEACHING K–12

RICHARD D. KELLOUGH
Emeritus, California State University at Sacramento

Boston   Columbus   Indianapolis   New York   San Francisco   Upper Saddle River
Amsterdam   Cape Town   Dubai   London   Madrid   Milan   Munich   Paris   Montreal   Toronto
Delhi   Mexico City   Sao Paulo   Sydney   Hong Kong   Seoul   Singapore   Taipei   Tokyo

Acquisitions Editor: Kelly Villella Canton
Editorial Assistant: Annalea Manalili
Vice President, Director of Marketing: Quinn Perkson
Senior Marketing Manager: Darcy Betts
Project Manager: Renata Butera
Operations Specialist: Renata Butera
Creative Art Director: Jayne Conte
Cover Designer: Suzanne Duda
Manager, Interior Permission Coordinator: Kathy Gavilanes
Manager, Cover Visual Research & Permissions: Karen Sanatar
Cover Art: Bob Daemmrich Photography, Inc.
Full-Service Project Management: Aparna Yellai
Composition: GGS Higher Education Resources, PMG
Printer/Binder: Bind-Rite Graphics/Robbinsville
Cover Printer: Lehigh-Phoenix, Hagerstown
Text Font: New Baskerville

For related titles and support materials, visit our online catalog at www.pearsonhighered.com.

Between the time website information is gathered and then published, it is not unusual for some sites to have closed. Also, the transcription of URLs can result in typographical errors. The publisher would appreciate notification where these errors occur so that they may be corrected in subsequent editions.

Photo Credits: Cover: Bob Daemmrich/Bob Daemmrich Photography, Inc., Laura Bolesta/Merrill, p. 1; Scott Cunningham/Merrill, p. 4; Todd Yarrington/Merrill, p. 8; Scott Cunningham/ Merrill, p. 21; Anthony Magnacca/Merrill, p. 26; Bob Daemmrich/Bob Daemmrich Photography, Inc., p.32; Scott Cunningham/Merrill, p. 41; Scott Cunningham/Merrill, p. 73; Anne Vega/Merrill, p. 92; Ryan McVay/Getty Images, Inc., Photodisc./Royalty Free, p. 121; Barbara Schwartz/Merrill, p. 125; Frank Siteman/Frank Siteman, p. 171; Scott Cunningham/Merrill, p. 178; Anthony Magnacca/Merrill, p. 182; Barbara Schwartz/Merrill, p. 183; Scott Cunningham/ Merrill, p. 204; Kristian Sekulic/Shutterstock, p. 212; Scott Cunningham/Merrill, p. 220; Pearson Learning Photo Studio, p. 233; Robert Vega/Merrill, p. 244; Anne Vega/Merrill, p. 248; Jupiter Unlimited, p. 259; Lloyd Lemmerman/Merrill, p. 260; Barbara Schwartz/Merrill, p. 283, Patrick White/Merrill, p. 284; Scott Cunningham/Merrill, p. 315; Jupiter Unlimited, p. 351; Scott Cunningham/Merrill, p. 352; G. Walts/The Image Works, p. 357.

Library of Congress Cataloging-in-Publication Data

Kellough, Richard D. (Richard Dean)
  A resource guide for teaching K–12 / Richard D. Kellough. — 6th ed.
    p. cm.
  Includes bibliographical references and index.
  ISBN-13: 978-0-13-705017-8
  ISBN-10: 0-13-705017-8
  1. Teaching—Problems, exercises, etc.   2. Classroom management—United States—Problems, exercises, etc.   I. Title.
LB1025.3.K45 2011
371.102—dc22

                               2009047533

Printed in the United States of America

10 9 8 7 6 5 4 3 2 1 BRG 14 13 12 11 10

www.pearsonhighered.com

ISBN-13: 978-0-13-705017-8
ISBN-10:   0-13-705017-8

DEDICATION

I proudly dedicate this book to the following persons who in their individually unique ways were major contributors to the concrescence of my life as a teacher, writer, and person.

Rodger O. Borror
Kay Borton
Art Costa
Noreen Kellough
Stanley Kellough
Eugene C. Kim
Al Miller
Van Richards
Patti Roberts
Bob Sabin
Esther Williams
Jack Zweig

BRIEF CONTENTS

CONTENTS

PREFACE

My intent for this sixth edition of *A Resource Guide for Teaching K–12* is to provide a contemporary source of appropriate and relevant pedagogy, learning activities, and resources for those who are preparing to teach young people of grades K–12.

WHAT'S NEW TO THIS SIXTH EDITION

Exemplary K–12 educational programs are rooted in celebrating and building upon the diverse characteristics and needs of America's youth. To become and to remain exemplary, teachers in such programs must be in a continual mode of inquiry, reflection, and transformation. It is no different for me as author of this book. In a continuing effort to prepare a comprehensive and exemplary book for teaching grades K–12, I find myself in a *continual mode of inquiry* into the latest findings in research and practice, *in constant reflection* as I listen to and assess the comments from practitioners in the field and from users and reviewers of previous editions of the book, and in *steady transformation* as I respond to the challenge of continuing to provide relevant and appropriate coverage for integrating methods and resources.

While still providing comprehensive coverage of methods of instruction enhanced with exercises for active learning, both continuing hallmarks of this resource guide, for this sixth edition I have:

- Updated all research support throughout the book, as I reviewed every word of every sentence, and rewrote, deleted, or added material as necessary. In addition, references are now listed at the end of the book, rather than at the end of each chapter.
- Reorganized and rewritten former Chapters 7 and 8 into three chapters, so Chapter 7 is now about the thinking curriculum: using teacher talk, demonstrations, inquiry, and games (former Chapter 8) while Chapter 8 is about mastery learning and differentiated instruction (part of former Chapter 7), and Chapter 9 is about organizing and guiding student learning in groups (part of former Chapter 7) with additional coverage in each.
- By popular request, brought back the exercise on the development of a self-instructional module (SIM)

that had been in the first four editions of this book, a hallmark of the book since its first edition, and is included here in Chapter 8.
- Considerably enhanced and updated the content coverage regarding the latest media technology used in teaching (Chapters 2, 7, 8, and 9).
- Enhanced content on dealing with anxiety and stress, both student and teacher varieties (primarily in Chapters 10 and 11).
- Enhanced and updated content coverage throughout about culturally responsive teaching and literacy (Chapters 2–10) and about assessment practices (Chapters 5 and 10).
- Moved all exercises to the end of their relative chapters, something many users in the past have asked for so that the exercises do not interrupt flow of narrative portion of the text.
- In a continuing effort to maintain a reasonable length to the book, for this edition I reduced the number of Questions for Discussion at chapter ends to 5 rather than 10. This was done by eliminating the less useful questions as indicated by reviewers of the previous edition.

Other changes are indicated in the paragraphs that follow.

AN OVERVIEW OF THIS EDITION

Represented by Chapters 1–5, the *planning phase of teaching* consists of all those intellectual functions and decisions the teacher makes prior to actual instruction. This includes decisions about content selection, goals and objectives, homework assignments, what students already know or think they know and can do, appropriate learning activities, questions to be asked, and the selection, collection, and preparation of instructional materials.

Represented by Chapters 6–9, the *interactive phase of teaching* includes all the decisions made during the immediacy and spontaneity of the teaching act. This includes obtaining and maintaining student focus, questions asked by the teacher, types of feedback given to the students, and ongoing assessments and adjustments to the instructional plan.

Chapter 10 focuses on the *analyzing and evaluating* or *reflective phase of teaching*. This is the time taken by the teacher to reflect on, analyze, and judge the decisions and behaviors that occurred during the interactive phase. It is during reflection that the teacher makes decisions about student learning, student grades, feedback given to parents and guardians, and adjustments on what and how next to teach. With the latter the teacher has moved into the application and projective phase, that is, abstracting from the reflection and preparing to project his or her analysis into subsequent teaching acts.

Chapter 11, the final chapter of the book, takes the reader into the *projective phase of teaching*, where the teacher is in process of evaluating the effects of his/her choices and actions on others in the learning community and continues to actively seek out opportunities to grow professionally.

Beginning with an introductory chapter that orients the readers to today's schools and students, the resource guide progresses in a natural sequence. It provides information on basic teaching responsibilities and behaviors and on the establishment and maintenance of an effective classroom learning environment (*classroom management*), and then moves into how to plan efficiently for optimal learning experiences (*content management*). It concludes with strategies for teaching, further resources, assessment, and suggestions for finding a teaching job.

As teacher candidates proceed through these chapters and begin the development of an instructional plan (in Chapter 5), from time to time they will want to refer to particular topics in both preceding and subsequent chapters. *Becoming a competent teacher is not nearly so linear a process as might be implied by a chapter-to-chapter arrangement.*

FEATURES OF THE TEXT

While there has been some reorganization for this edition, previous users will be familiar with most of its features, including its comprehensiveness, reader friendly narrative, vignettes, and examples, and engaging exercises. Some of the features that have become synonymous with *A Resource Guide for Teaching K–12* include:

- **Exercises for active learning.** Found throughout are exercises that require teachers and teacher candidates to deal in some descriptive, analytical, or self-reflective manner with text concepts and real practice. Certain exercises build upon previous ones, whereas others necessitate a school visit or suggest that assistance be obtained from teachers in the field. It is unlikely that all exercises could be (or should be) completed in a one-semester course; an early review of the exercises is advised so instructor and students can collaborate in planning school visits and the exercise work schedule.

- **Exercises for inclusion in the developing professional portfolio.** Some exercises might be suitable for inclusion in the student-user's developing professional portfolio. As starters, I recommend Exercises 3.3, 5.3, and 8.1.
- **Chapter Objectives.** Learning outcomes for the reader appearing near the start of each chapter.
- **Questions for class discussion.** At the conclusion of each chapter, Questions for Class Discussion offer ideas for reviewing and discussing the concepts covered.
- **Situational case studies, teaching vignettes, classroom scenarios.** Situational case studies are presented in Chapter 3, and teaching vignettes and scenarios are distributed throughout the text, all of which are designed to stimulate discussion and reflective thinking.
- **Performance assessment.** Assessment of developing teacher competencies is encouraged by the inclusion of three micro peer teaching exercises (6.7, 7.2, & 11.1), lesson plan (5.2) and unit plan (5.3), and a self-instructional module (8.1).
- **Related web sites.** Throughout each chapter are sites and Internet references that I can recommend. Each site was visited and checked personally by me in 2009.
- **Outstanding teaching practices and exemplary educational programs.** Many such practices and programs are recognized and identified by name throughout the text.
- **Perforated pages.** Pages of the book are perforated for easy removal and /or photo copying of the exercises and other figures.
- **Glossary, references, and index.** References are listed at the conclusion of the book. The text concludes with a glossary of terms and a name and subject index.

MYEDUCATIONLAB

"Teacher educators who are developing pedagogies for the analysis of teaching and learning contend that analyzing teaching artifacts has three advantages: it enables new teachers time for reflection while still using the real materials of practice; it provides new teachers with experience thinking about and approaching the complexity of the classroom; and in some cases, it can help new teachers and teacher educators develop a shared understanding and common language about teaching...."[1]

As Linda Darling-Hammond and her colleagues point out, grounding teacher education in real classrooms—among real teachers and students and among

---

[1]Darling-Hammond, l., & Bransford, J. (Eds.). (2005). Preparing teachers for a changing world. San Francisco, CA: Wiley.

actual examples of students' and teachers' work—is an important, and perhaps even an essential, part of training teachers for the complexities of teaching in today's classrooms. For this reason, we have created a valuable, time-saving web site—MyEducationLab—that provides you with the context of real classrooms and artifacts that research on teacher education tells us is so important. The authentic in-class video footage, interactive skill-building exercises, and other resources available on MyEducationLab offer you a uniquely valuable teacher education tool.

MyEducationLab is easy to use and integrate into both your assignments and your courses. Wherever you see the MyEducationLab logo in the margins or elsewhere in the text, follow the simple instructions to access the videos, strategies, cases, and artifacts associated with these assignments, activities, and learning units on MyEducationLab. MyEducationLab is organized topically to enhance the coverage of the core concepts discussed in the chapters of your book. For each topic on the course you will find most or all of the following resources:

Connection to National Standards

Now it is easier than ever to see how your coursework is connected to national standards. In each topic of MyEducationLab you will find intended learning outcomes connected to the appropriate national standards for your course. All of the Assignments and Activities and all of the Building Teaching Skills and Dispositions in MyEducationLab are mapped to the appropriate national standards and learning outcomes as well.

Assignments and Activities

Designed to save instructors preparation time, these assignable exercises show concepts in action (through video, cases, or student and teacher artifacts) and then offer thought-provoking questions that probe your understanding of theses concepts or strategies. (Feedback for these assignments is available to the instructor.)

Building Teaching Skills and Dispositions

These learning units help you practice and strengthen skills that are essential to quality teaching. First you are presented with the core skill or concept and then given an opportunity to practice your understanding of this concept multiple times by watching video footage (or interacting with other media) and then critically analyzing the strategy or skill presented.

General Resources on Your MyEducationLab Course

The *Resources* section on your MyEducationLab course is designed to help you pass your licensure exam, put together an effective portfolio and lesson plan, prepare for and navigate the first year of your teaching career, and understand key educational standards, policies, and laws. This section includes:

- *Licensure Exams:* Access guidelines for passing the Praxis exam. The *Practice Test Exam* includes practice questions, *Case Histories,* and *Video Case Studies.*
- *Portfolio Builder and Lesson Plan Builder:* Create, update, and share portfolios and lesson plans.
- *Preparing a Portfolio:* Access guidelines for creating a high-quality teaching portfolio that will allow you to practice effective lesson planning.
- *Licensure and Standards:* Link to state licensure standards and national standards.
- *Beginning Your Career:* Educate yourself—access tips, advice, and valuable information on:
  - Résumé Writing and Interviewing: Expert advice on how to write impressive résumés and prepare for job interviews.
  - Your First Year of Teaching: Practical tips to set up your classroom, manage student behavior, and learn to more easily organize for instruction and assessment.
  - Law and Public Policies: Specific directives and requirements you need to understand under the No Child Left Behind Act and the Individuals with Disabilities Education Improvement Act of 2004.
- *Special Education Interactive Timeline:* Build your own detailed timelines based on different facets of the history and evolution of special education.

Visit www.myeducationlab.com for a demonstration of this exciting new online teaching resource.

INSTRUCTOR RESOURCES

The text has the following ancillary materials for instructors located on the password-protected Instructor Resource Center at www.pearsonhighered.com. Please contact your Pearson representative if you need assistance with downloading the supplement.

Instructor's Manual and Test Bank

The Instructor's Resource Manual/Test Bank provides concrete chapter-by-chapter notes for each section and exercise. Each chapter includes chapter objectives, teaching suggestions, supplemental readings, and test questions.

MY BELIEFS WITH WHERE AND HOW THEY ARE REFLECTED IN THIS BOOK

In preparing this book, I saw my task not as making the teaching job easier for you—effective teaching is never easy—but as improving your teaching effectiveness and providing relevant guidelines and current resources.

You may choose from these resources and build upon what works best for you. Nobody can tell you what will work with your students; you will know them best. I share what I believe to be the best of practice, the most useful of recent research findings, and the richest of experiences. The boldface italic statements present my beliefs, each followed by an explanation of how they are embraced in this book.

Effective teaching doesn't just happen. Certain understandings and behaviors are absolutely fundamental for the most effective teaching and learning to occur. Fundamental understandings include the nature of the subject matter taught (learned in your content-centered courses), the nature of today's challenge (reviewed in Chapter 1), how young people best learn (learned in your educational psychology class and reviewed throughout this resource guide). Fundamental teacher behaviors (Chapters 2 and 3) create the conditions needed to enable students to think and to learn, whether the learning is a further understanding of a concept, the internalization of attitudes and values, the development of cognitive processes, or the actuating of the most complex behaviors. Clearly, at least some of the fundamental teacher behaviors are also instructional strategies. Questioning (Chapter 6) is one example. The difference is that the behaviors must be in place for the most effective teaching to occur, but strategies (Chapters 7, 8, and 9) are more or less discretionary; that is, they are pedagogical techniques from which you may select but are not obligated to use. For example, questioning and the use of silence are fundamental teaching behaviors (discussed in Chapter 2), whereas lecturing (Chapter 7) and taking children on a field trip (Chapter 2) are not. Therefore, you see, your task is twofold: (1) develop your awareness of and skills in using the fundamental teaching behaviors, and (2) develop your repertoire and skills in selecting and using appropriate instructional strategies for facilitating student's learning. Only beginning now, your understanding and development of these skills will continue throughout your teaching career. [Note: Chapter 2 reflects the teacher behaviors and responsibilities necessary to be a competent classroom teacher. You are encouraged to compare the categories of responsibilities and the 22 competencies identified in that chapter with the teacher competency standards used by your own state for teacher licensing.]

Teaching skills can be learned. In medicine, certain knowledge and skills must be learned and developed before the student physician is licensed to practice with patients. In law, certain knowledge and skills must be learned and developed before the law student is licensed to practice with clients. So it is in teacher preparation—knowledge and skills must be learned and developed before the teacher candidate is licensed to practice the art and science of teaching young people. I would never allow just any person to treat my child's illness; the professional education of teachers is no less important! Receiving a professional education on how to teach young people is absolutely necessary, and certain aspects of that education must precede any interaction with students if teachers are to become truly competent professionals.

The best learning occurs when the learner actively participates in the process, and that includes having ownership in both the process and the product of the learning. Consequently, this book is designed to engage you in hands-on and minds-on learning about effective classroom instruction. For example, rather than simply reading a chapter devoted to the important topic of cooperative learning, in each chapter you will become involved in cooperative and collaborative learning. In essence, via the exercises found in every chapter, you will practice cooperative learning, talk about it, practice it some more, and finally, through the process of doing it, learn a great deal about it. While specifically discussed in several locations, and to a large degree in Chapter 9, throughout this book you are *involved in* cooperative learning.

The best strategies for learning about teaching young people in the classroom are those that model the strategies used in exemplary teaching of young people. As you will learn, I agree fully that *integrated learning* is the cornerstone of the most effective teaching, and that is a premise upon which this resource guide continues to be designed. Like living, the reciprocal process of teaching and learning is a multifaceted, eclectic process. The job of the teacher is to help learners bridge the facets, understand and make sense of the process—to help them connect various aspects of learning and living by modeling the very skills necessary to make sense of the connections.

To be most effective a teacher must use an eclectic style in teaching. Rather than focus your attention on particular models of teaching, I emphasize the importance of an eclectic model—that is, one in which you select and integrate the best from various instructional approaches. For example, sometimes you will want to use a direct, expository approach, perhaps through a minilecture; more often you will want to use an indirect, social-interactive, or student-centered approach, perhaps through project-based learning. This book not only provides guidelines to help you decide the approach to use at a particular time but also develops your skill in using specific approaches. Equally important, you will learn of the importance of being able to combine both direct and indirect approaches, of using what I refer to as *multilevel instruction.*

Learning should be active, pleasant, fun, meaningful, and productive. My desire is to present this book in an enthusiastic, positive, and cognitive-humanistic way, in part by providing rich experiences in social-interactive learning. How this is done is perhaps best exemplified by the active learning exercises found not isolated on some remote and separate CD or Internet location, but rather at the conclusion of each chapter. Exercises were developed to ensure that you become an active participant in learning the methods and procedures that are most appropriate in facilitating the learning of active, responsive students.

Regardless of their individual differences, students must have equal opportunity to participate and learn in the classroom. Beginning in the first chapter, this belief is reflected throughout this book, sometimes in a very direct fashion and other times indirectly. This overall sensitivity to diversity models not only my belief but also how to be inclusive to people of diverse backgrounds in many ways. My agenda here is not hidden: *cultural and language diversity in our country and in K–12 classrooms is a good thing!*

Effective teaching is performance based and criterion referenced. From its inception this book continues to be constructed in this manner. Because I believe that teaching, indeed living, must allow for serendipity, encourage the intuitive, and foster the most creative aspects of one's thinking, I cannot always be specific about what students will learn as a result of our instruction, and hence the occasional ambiguity must be expected. Most directly reflecting this belief are Chapters 4 and 5, chapters that will be a primary focus of your time and attention as you use this book as one important guide toward becoming a competent teacher.

To teach young people most effectively, you must recognize, appreciate, and understand them and be able to establish and operate a safe and supportive classroom learning environment. Connecting with the content of Chapter 2, specific guidelines for accomplishing that are presented in Chapter 3.

Chapter 4 focuses on the curriculum and programs that comprise it; on the rationale for planning and selecting the content of the curriculum; on the national, state, and local documents that provide benchmarks for learning and that guide content selection; and on preparing goals and learning targets and using them in planning for and assessing student learning.

Chapter 5 presents detailed information and step-by-step guidelines for integrating students' learning, selecting developmentally appropriate learning activities, and preparing various types of instructional units with lessons. As I will be reminding you, while separated in this book for reasons of organizational clarity, it is impossible to satisfactorily complete the work in instructional planning (both unit and lesson planning)

expected in Chapter 5 without becoming knowledgeable of content in Chapters 6–10.

Although it is very difficult to predict what 5- to 18-year-olds of today will need to know to be productive citizens in the middle of this century, I believe *they will always need to know how to learn, how to read, how to think productively, and how to communicate effectively and work together cooperatively.* I believe that children need to acquire skills in how to gain knowledge and how to process information, and they need learning experiences that foster effective communication and productive, cooperative behaviors. I hope all children feel good about themselves, about others, and about their teachers, schools, and communities. I emphasize the importance of helping students to develop those skills, feelings, and attitudes. Teachers of all children share in the responsibility for teaching skills in reading, writing, thinking, working cooperatively, respecting self and others, and communicating effectively. This responsibility is reflected clearly throughout this book.

The appropriate teaching methods for reaching these goals incorporate thoughtful planning, acceptance of the uniqueness of each individual, honesty, trust, sharing, risking, collaboration, communication, and cooperation. Furthermore, I believe that students of all ages best learn these skills and values from teachers who model the same. This resource guide is faithful to that hope and to that end.

Chapter 6 focuses your attention on one significantly important teaching and learning strategy—questioning—with an emphasis on the encouragement of questions formulated and investigated by students. The chapter includes the first of three micro peer teaching exercises found in the book.

Chapter 7 presents guidelines for using formal and informal teacher talk, demonstrations, direct teaching of thinking, discovery and inquiry, and educational games. Chapter 7 includes the second micro peer teaching exercise found in the book.

Chapter 8 focuses your attention to the topic of teaching toward mastery, ways of differentiating the instruction so each and every child achieves quality learning. The one exercise in this chapter is designed to guide you through the inception and completion of the most perfect and highly differentiated and individualized lesson you may ever create—one that can guarantee a student's mastery of the anticipated learning.

Chapter 9 presents guidelines for grouping students, using project-centered teaching, assignments and homework, ensuring classroom equity, and writing across the curriculum. Chapter 9 ends with a section you may find useful for years to come—a popular and updated annotated listing of 130 motivational strategies and ideas for lessons, interdisciplinary teaching, transcultural studies, and student projects for all grade levels and subject areas. As said by one reviewer/user of the previous edition, "that list alone is worth the price of this book." The resource guide is intended to be useful to you not only while you are in phases of teacher preparation but well into your initial years of teaching.

Although separated in this book for reasons of organizational clarity, the assessment component of teaching and learning is an integral and ongoing component of the total curriculum. Chapter 10 focuses attention on the assessment of what students know or think they know and can do preceding, during, and following the instructional experience. Chapter 10 also provides practical guidelines for parent/guardian and teacher collaboration and for grading and reporting student achievement.

Chapter 11, the final chapter, focuses on how well you are doing—the assessment of teaching effectiveness. In addition, it provides guidelines that you will find useful during your student teaching or during intern teaching, for finding a teaching position, and for continued professional growth. And, the chapter concludes with the final micro peer teaching exercise.

ACKNOWLEDGMENTS

Although teaching and learning have become increasingly complex—with many new and exciting things happening as schools continue to restructure their efforts to provide the best learning for today's youth—I strive to keep the text at a reasonable length and to keep it user friendly. I thank all the persons who helped in its development, most especially Kelly, Renata, Aparna, and Kathy. I thank those who contributed and who are acknowledged at appropriate places throughout, and my friends and highly competent professionals at Pearson Allyn & Bacon who have maintained their belief in and support for this resource guide.

While I take full responsibility for any errors or omissions in this book, I am deeply grateful to others for their cogent comments and important contributions that led to the development of this sixth edition. I express my appreciation to the reviewers: S. Joseph Marie Carter, Immaculata University; Simin L. Cwick, Southeast Missouri State University; and Dixie K. Keyes, Arkansas State University.

I am indeed indebted and grateful to all the people in my life, now and in the past, who have interacted with me and reinforced what I have known since the day I began my career as teacher: Teaching is the most rewarding profession of all.

R.D.K.

Teaching Then, Teaching Now

Personal and Shared Thoughts of the Author

I can imagine what teaching must have been like for Stan Kellough, my father, who after just two years of college began his career teaching in the early 1930s, (more than 15 years and a world war later he completed a master's degree at Columbia University), during a serious national economic depression, with a bunch of children of all grades in a small one-room schoolhouse in Southern Ohio.

Shortly before his death in 2002 I was fortunate to be able to find that place and to take him to it, a small brick building still standing (built to last!) although deserted as a school in 1934, now on private land and used by a farmer for equipment storage. A never-to-be forgotten and most cherished moment of my life is that of my father and I standing there together in that room, on its dirt floor, with its slate blackboards still mostly intact on the walls (nearly 70 years later!), with chalk trays now brimming with rat feces. I quietly watched my father while he gazed at the walls and the boards, and out the school's single window (no longer with glass), as with a slight smile he obviously was reliving precious memories of those days when the room was full of busy children, and he was a very young beginning teacher.

I don't know whether teaching today is any more difficult than when Stan Kellough first began his 37 year career as a classroom teacher, but in many respects it must be quite different. However, as you will see, some things have remained the same.

Today's Schools:

Recognizing and

Understanding the Challenge

Welcome to the exciting and ever-changing world of teaching. Whether you are in your early 20s and starting your first career or older and returning or beginning a new career, this book is for you—that is, for any person interested in becoming a competent classroom teacher.

The bell rings and the students enter your classroom, a kaleidoscope of personalities, all peerless and idiosyncratic, each a bundle of energy with different focuses, experiences, dispositions, learning styles, learning capacities, and proficiencies in use of the English language—different challenges. What a formidable task it is to understand and teach 30 or so unique individuals, all at once, and do it for 6 hours a day, 5 days a week, 180 days a year! What a challenge it is today to be a public school classroom teacher. To prepare yourself for this challenge, consider the information provided in this chapter about schools and about the diverse characteristics and needs of youth, for it is well known that their academic achievement is greatly dependent upon how well their other developmental needs are understood and satisfied. We must begin this journey somewhere, so let's do it with the following clarification of terms and purpose. I hope you enjoy your quest.

Let's begin with a few definitions. What is referred to as the **elementary school** sometimes includes students from kindergarten through grade 8, although more often it stops with grade 5 or 6. An **intermediate grades school** commonly houses children of grades 4–6. **Middle-level schools** most often house children of grades 6–8. A **high school** houses students of some combination of grades 9–12. There are other arrangements. Regardless of where or how students are housed and regardless of the cognomen of the school in which they

are housed, this resource guide is about preparing you to teach students in the classroom.

If you are now in a program of teacher preparation, then perhaps near the completion of the program you likely will be offered your first teaching contract. I use the optimistic "likely" because there is within the profession a general agreement and concern that for the next several years in the United States there will be an acute shortage of teachers. You will be excited and eager to sign the contract and begin your new career. Yet after the initial excitement, you will have time to reflect. Many questions will then begin forming in your mind. If in a multiple-school district, to which school will I be assigned? Will it be a traditional school or will it be a **magnet** school or **theme school**, that is, a school that specializes in a particular area of the curriculum, such as the visual and performing arts, or science, mathematics, and technology, or international studies? Or a school might be a **charter school**, that is, a public school that is freed from many of the usual rules while still accountable for results (Weertz, 2002). Or a **full-service school**, a school that serves as a hub for quality education and comprehensive social services all beneath one roof (Black, 2004; Dryfoos, 2002). Or an **International Baccalaureate School**, that is, one with a curriculum approved by the International Baccalaureate Organization (IBO), a worldwide nonprofit educational foundation that is based in Switzerland. In addition to its Primary Years Program (for children ages 3 to 12), IBO offers a Middle Years Program (for students ages 11 to 16) and a Diploma Program (for students in the final two 2 years of high school). The IBO is currently working with more than 2,500 schools in at least 132 countries, and more than 900 of those schools are in the United States (www.ibo.org). Or will it be an **alternative school**, a school for students who for some reason or another need something different than what is offered in regular school. See, for example, the story of the New Orleans (LA) Center of Science and Mathematics (MacPhee & Dempsey, 2003) and websites such as that of the Eagle Rock School and Professional Development Center in Estes Park, Colorado (www.eaglerockschool.org). Or perhaps it might be another type or combination of these, for example, a charter-magnet school such as Pro-Vision Charter School (www.provision-inc.org), an all-male public school (Houston, TX), or the Irma Rangel Young Women's Leadership School, an all-female public school (Dallas, TX). Although in different ways and with varying terminology, the historical practice of providing different routes for students with different needs and different vocational and academic aspirations continues.

Will your teaching placement be in a school that has its start in the fall, as is traditional, or will it be an **extended-year school** (one that extends longer than the usual 180 days) or a **year-round school**? Although considered to be 180 in the United States, the actual length of the school year varies slightly from state to state. Additionally, what is officially called the **school year** must accommodate schoolwide assemblies, inservice training for teachers, field trips, and a variety of other things that need doing, reducing the real number of days of classroom instruction to something considerably less than 180. At least 27 countries have longer school years than the standard 180 days of the United States, topping out with Japan's 243 days, South Korea's 220, Israel's 216, Russia's 211, Germany's 210, Holland, Scotland and Thailand's 200, Swaziland's 191, England and Hungary's 192, and France's 185 as examples. For the United States, many educators and politicians would like to extend the school year from 180 days to perhaps as many as 200 days. However, at this time the political and financial realities would indicate that an extension of the school year doesn't seem feasible. Two things that are likely are that individual schools and districts (1) will continue searching for and finding ways of increasing the instructional efficiency and effectiveness with the time that now exists and (2) will gradually increase the number of days and weeks in the school year.

Which courses or subjects will I be assigned to teach? What specific grade levels will I have or what will be the range of ages, cultural diversity, reading abilities, and intellectual capacities of my students? How many preparations will I have? Will I be a member of a teaching team? Will I have core curriculum teaching responsibilities? What advisory and supervision responsibilities might I have? What will the students be like? What will their parents or guardians be like? How will I be able to get along with the rest of the faculty? What textbooks, media, and curricular materials will I use, will I know how to use them, and when can I expect to see them?

How should I prepare? How can I prepare when there are so many unanswered questions? What school district policies do I need to learn about now? What support services can I expect? How extensive are the school's rules and regulations? Will there be an orientation and an induction program for new and beginning teachers? How can I prepare for students I know nothing about?

These questions, and many others, are often the concerns of beginning teachers. To guide you through this initial experience and help answer some of your questions, this chapter offers a first glimpse into today's world of public school teaching. This chapter provides an orientation and basis for your planning and selecting learning activities presented in subsequent chapters.

Specifically, upon completion of this chapter you should be able to:

1. Define and differentiate between *elementary school, middle school, junior high school,* and *high school.*
2. Describe key characteristics that identify a school as being exemplary.
3. Describe the purposes and characteristics of the small learning community concept.
4. Describe the meaning of the phrase "quality education for each and every student."
5. Describe the meaning of "teacher as a reflective decision maker."
6. Describe current trends, problems, and issues in public K–12 education.
7. Describe key principles of today's *No Child Left Behind Act* and how that act is likely to affect your work as a classroom teacher.
8. Describe efforts made by today's schools to involve parents, guardians, and the community in the children's education. Enjoy your quest toward becoming the best teacher you can be.

THE CLASSROOM IN A NATION OF DIVERSITY AND SHIFTING DEMOGRAPHICS

Central to your challenge as a classroom teacher is the concept of multicultural education, the recognition and acceptance of students from a variety of backgrounds. As stated by Banks (1999, pp. 8–10), an important goal of this concept

is to educate citizens who can participate successfully in the workforce and take action in the civic community to help the nation actualize its democratic ideals. . . . Schools should be model communities that mirror the kind of democratic society we envision [where] the curriculum reflects the cultures of the diverse groups within society, the languages and dialects that students speak are respected and valued, cooperation rather than competition is fostered among students and students from diverse racial, ethnic and social-class groups are given equal status.

There is increasing emphasis today on the need for **culturally responsive teaching** to help bring diverse school communities together to make learning most meaningful. Unlike multicultural education, which is important for bringing the world's cultural and ethnic diversity into the curriculum, teaching that is culturally responsive draws on the experiences, understanding, views, concepts, and ways of knowing of the students who are in a particular classroom (Saifer & Barton, 2007; Stairs, 2007).

Skill Areas Around Which This Resource Guide Is Centered

The variety of individual differences among students in today's schools requires classroom teachers to use teaching strategies and tactics that accommodate those differences. To most effectively teach students who are different from you, you need skills in the following:

1. Establishing a classroom climate in which all students feel welcome, can learn, and are supported in doing so—that is, one that is student centered (Chapters 2 and 3).
2. Using techniques that emphasize cooperative and social–interactive learning and deemphasize competitive learning (Chapters 3, 5, and 9).
3. Using strategies that encourage the development of thinking skills, that build a sense of community, and that incorporate assessment and reflection (Chapters 5, 6, and 8).
4. Building upon students' learning styles, capacities, and modalities (Chapters 5, 8, and 9).
5. Using strategies and techniques that have proven successful for students of specific characteristics and differences (Chapter 5, 8, and 9).
6. Building a curriculum that is connected and integrated (Chapter 4).

This sixth edition of this resource guide has been prepared with the purpose of assisting you in your understanding and development of skills in those six areas, areas that incorporate the theory of culturally responsive classroom teaching.

To help you meet the challenge, a wealth of information is available. As a licensed and highly qualified teacher, you are expected to know it all or at least know where you can find all the necessary information and review it when needed. Certain information you have stored in memory will surface and become useful at the most unexpected times. While concerned about all students' safety and physical well-being, you will want to remain sensitive to each student's attitudes, values, social adjustment, emotional well-being, and cognitive development. You must be prepared not only to teach one or more subjects, but also to do it effectively with students of different cultural backgrounds, diverse linguistic abilities, and varying learning styles, as well as with students who have other educationally relevant differences, such as students with disabilities, students who live in extreme poverty, and those who are significantly influenced by variations in religion or gender. It is, indeed, a challenge, as the following statistics make even clearer. As author of this resource guide, my goal is to prepare you well for the challenges of today's teaching. I want you to be prepared well so that you are neither shocked nor discouraged during your initial years of employment. To the extent possible, I want you to be realistically prepared for that which can become for you a long and satisfying career in the wonderful profession of teaching.

Perhaps as many as 20 percent of today's youth in the United States live in poverty, a statistic that with the economic crisis that began appearing in 2007, may be steadily increasing as I write this edition of the resource guide. Approximately one-half of today's children will spend some years being raised by a single parent, or a grandparent. Perhaps as many as one-third of young people go home or other places after school that are devoid of any adult supervision. And on any given day, some young people have no place at all to call home. And, although homelessness may be more apparent in large cities, it is far from just an urban problem: a significant number of today's homeless live in the suburbs, rural areas, and small towns throughout our country. And, lastly, although accurate statistics are difficult to come by, it is estimated that the nation's largest cities have school dropout rates of approximately 50 percent. These are just a few of the realities of the world of young people today.

The Realities of Public School Teaching Today

As you undoubtedly are well aware, the United States is truly a multilingual, multiethnic, and multicultural country—perhaps the most diverse nation in the world. In 2007, more than 40 percent of all students in grades K–12 were minorities. Approximately one-fourth of the nation's kindergartners, and about one-fifth of all K–12 students are Hispanic. In many large urban high schools, as many as 100 or more languages are represented, with as many as 20 or more different primary languages found in some classrooms. Many of those students have only limited proficiency in the English language (i.e., conversational speaking ability only), or perhaps absolutely no proficiency.

The term **English language learner (ELL)** is used to refer to students who are non- or limited-English proficient (also known as NEP and LEP, respectively). Although more than half of all ELLs speak Spanish as their first language, there are millions of ELLs in U.S. public schools who altogether speak more than 400 different languages. An increasing ethnic, cultural, and linguistic diversity is quickly and strongly affecting schools all across the country—not only the large urban areas, but

While there is probably no organizational or academic shoe that fits all children in all schools in all communities, one fact does remain clear: students of all ages need teachers who are well organized and who know how to establish and manage an active and supportive learning environment.

also traditionally homogeneous suburbs and small rural communities.

> Though at one time it was believed that the United States was a "melting pot" in which ethnic cultures would melt into one, ethnic and cultural differences have remained very much a part of life in the United States.
>
> Forrest W. Parkay, Glen Hass, & Eric J. Anctil (2010, p. 51)

The overall picture that emerges is an increasingly diverse student population that challenges teaching skills. Teachers who traditionally have used direct instruction (such as by whole-class discussions and lecturing) as the dominant mode of instruction have done so with the assumption their students were relatively homogeneous in terms of experience, background, knowledge, motivation, and facility with the English language. However, no such assumption can be made today in classrooms of such diversity. *As a classroom teacher today, you must be knowledgeable and skilled in using teaching strategies that recognize, celebrate, and build upon that diversity.* In a nutshell, that is your challenge. While some guidelines to start your thinking process are presented in Figure 1.1, others are presented throughout this book.

A Rather Recent and in My Opinion Unfortunate Addition to the Challenge

In the years since first enactment of the **No Child Left Behind Act**, signed into law in January 2002, we increasingly read and hear of teachers being expected, even instructed, by their supervisors to do more rather than less direct instruction in order to help students score well on the state's standardized achievement tests. Although increasing the amount of direct instruction may or may not help learners score well on tests, it is, as you will learn as you work your way through this resource guide, an unfortunate inconsistency with what is known about instilling meaningful, longest lasting learning.

The foregoing represent the realities that confront beginning teachers in varying degrees of intensity in virtually every school district in the United States. To succeed, you must perceive these realities as challenges and opportunities. Your challenges lie in seeing that every student succeeds in school, so that none is left behind. Your opportunities can be found in making sure that the lives of *all* your students are enriched through contact with classmates whose cultural and ethnic backgrounds may be quite different from their own. Responding to these challenges and grasping these opportunities underscore the idea that teaching is basically a call to social service.

ORIENTATION: NO SINGLE SHOE FITS ALL

The rapid and dramatic changes occurring throughout modern society, as well as what has been learned in recent years about intelligence and learning, are reflected in the equally rapid and dramatic changes occurring in today's schools. The school in which you are or soon will be teaching may bear little resemblance to one that you

Figure 1.1 Ways for teachers to support multiracial youth and to counter racism. (*Source:* W. Schwartz, *The Schooling of Multiracial Students,* ERIC/CUE Digest, Number 138 (New York: ERIC Clearinghouse on Urban Education, 1998)).

Within the subject fields and grade level that you teach, make an effort to

- Address directly the history of and reasons for racism against groups of people, including the multiracial population.
- Celebrate many different heritages, stressing their interplay in life and the ways that different cultures have similar commemorations.
- Demonstrate how people in the United States have successfully mixed languages, cultures, and religions throughout the nation's history, and how the country has always been a home to multiethnic people.
- Discuss the current status of multiracial people around the world, such as Mestizos, Creoles, and Brazilians.
- Encourage the development and sharing of family trees.
- Facilitate age-appropriate discussions that foster open and supportive questioning about race in ways that build student self-concepts and educate the questioner.
- Identify multiracial historical heroes such as Frederick Douglass and James Audubon and cultural figures like ballerina Maria Tallchief, singer and *American Idol* star Paula Abdul, and President Barack Obama.
- Include curriculum study units in art, music, and literature that transcend ethnic boundaries instead of focusing on specific groups, such as "Indians."
- Include multiracial persons as role models when selecting guest speakers and resource persons.
- Provide students with information and photos of people of many racial and ethnic groups, including those of mixed heritage.
- Study monoracial groups to promote an understanding of the role of race in society by exploring why some people need to belong to an exclusive group or need to feel superior to others, and what the societal and personal consequences of such attitudes may be.
- Use books and resources that depict multiracialism.

ENGAGING A NEW GENERATION OF CITIZENS

Immigrant students might find the U.S. concept of democracy difficult to grasp. How can a school make students with different languages, ethnicities, races, and complex personal histories understand the importance of the democratic tradition even as they pursue individual dreams of achievement? The answer: Make learning student centered and activity and project based. Allow immigrant students to communicate in both English and native languages and work in small groups to create a play, collaborate on a work of art, or hash out a mathematical concept.

Rick Allen (2003, p. 8)

attended—in its curriculum, its student body, its methods of instruction, its size, or its physical appearance. Two things seem clear:

- Regardless of organizational patterns, to become and to remain an exemplary school, the school must be in a continual mode of inquiry, reflection, and change.
- The advantage of utilizing a combination of practices concurrently is usually greater in helping all students succeed in school than is the gain from using any singular practice by itself.

The bottom line? Schools and the teachers must constantly change; there is no single shoe that best fits all children in all neighborhoods. Our country is too large and too diverse for that to ever be the case.

So, what does this mean for you? It means that from the moment you set foot onto a school campus, you will want to keep your sensory input channels broadly open, learning as much as you can about the school, its organization, its students, the administration, and its support staff. It means establishing a collegial relationship with colleagues (an important topic to which I return in the final chapter of this resource guide). Although it is perhaps only the beginning to your learning about teaching, this resource guide does offer information and resources that you will want to refer to time and again, perhaps long after the passing of the initial purpose for its use.

Start of the School Year Orientation

As a beginning teacher, you will likely be expected to participate in orientation meetings. When not in meetings you will have time to prepare your assigned classroom(s) for instruction.

Some school districts start the school year with a districtwide orientation, whereas others schedule on-site orientations at each school. Many school districts do

Teaching in Practice

Teach But Don't Touch

Pat Jacobson, attorney for the local teachers' professional association, is addressing the teachers at their fall preschool meeting:

Last year in this country, we had an alarming number of cases of parents and school officials taking teachers to court for touching children in ways considered inappropriate. A music teacher with 16 years' experience faced charges of sexual harassment and unprofessional conduct and a recommendation of dismissal because of a hugging incident. For the past three decades, this society has given social approval to hugging and other forms of physical contact for purposes of comfort and support. We say to people in distress, "Is there anything I can do?" And the reply could very well be, "I need a warm and fuzzy hug."

On Sunday in church you might hug your neighbor and her 10-year-old daughter and wish them "peace," but don't try it the next day in school without putting yourself in jeopardy! My advice to you is to teach but don't touch. Don't hug kids. Don't put your arms around them. Don't hold hands with them on the playground. Don't pat them on the back. Don't have any physical contact with them in any way. Period.

1. Discuss with your classmates whether you think this attorney's advice is sound or extreme.
2. Can teachers do their jobs without having *any* physical contact with their students?
3. How can teachers project feelings of affection and genuine caring without touching students?
4. Research shows that physical contact with other human beings is a critical requirement for children's normal development. If children are caressed neither at home nor at school, how can we expect them to develop normally? Does this fall within the realm of a teacher's responsibility?
5. Does it matter the grade level? the type of school (such as private or public)?
6. Using a selected specific occurrence, discuss this issue with others in your class in terms of *context* variables such as the following: (a) the age of the student; (b) the gender of the teacher and the child; (c) whether the contact is in a public, open place with others around or in an isolated area; (d) whether the contact is a pattern of the teacher's behavior; and (e) the *intent* of the teacher's behavior.

both, with perhaps a districtwide morning meeting followed by on-site school meetings in the afternoon. Such meetings provide you with the opportunity to meet other teachers and establish new collegial friendships and professional relationships. Many school districts sponsor beginning teacher induction programs that provide special assistance to new teachers (discussed in the final chapter of this resource guide). Of course, the scheduling and planning of orientation meetings will vary by district and by school. The objectives for all orientation meetings, however, should be similar to those discussed in the following paragraphs.

You should become familiar with the district's (or school's) written statement of its unique beliefs and goals—its statement of mission (or philosophy or vision)—and what that statement means to people affiliated with the district or school. [Note: Although the terms **mission statement**, **philosophy statement**, and **vision statement** are often used interchangeably, and although in my opinion the first two are synonymous, the vision statement is or should be a statement of intention that goes beyond the immediate mission of the school and gives future direction to the school's stated mission.] Sample mission statements, some very brief while others are detailed and lengthy, can be found online by going to school websites.

You will be encouraged to become knowledgeable about policies of the school and its district. Numerous policies usually cover a wide range of subjects. There are policies for procedures relating to students who are injured at school; for what to do during disasters whether natural, such as earthquakes, flooding, and severe storms, or those caused by humans, such as terrorist attacks; regarding students who need to take prescribed medications; for finding illegal drugs and weapons; for campus intruders; for parking on campus; for leaving campus during the school day; for classroom conduct; for school programs, field trips, and parties in the classroom; for mandatory testing and grading practices; for completing absentee and tardy forms; for sending students to the office; and for chaperoning and sponsoring student activities. And these examples are just the beginning.

You will learn about the myriad forms that teachers must fill out. There are forms for injuries that occur while at school, textbook loans, equipment loans, key loans, attendance, student academic deficiencies and achievements, working with English language learners, working with students with special needs, sponsoring student activities, field trips, and referrals of students for inappropriate behavior, to name just a few.

You will learn about the approved curriculum that defines what teachers are mandated to teach and what students are expected to learn. This means that you must familiarize yourself with the curriculum frameworks and learning benchmarks, courses of study, curriculum guides, resource units, teacher's manuals, student textbooks, media programs, assessment strategies and testing schedules, and supplementary materials—all of which should reflect the school's mission statement and approved curriculum. You will learn about the school or district plan for monitoring, assessing, and supervising implementation of the curriculum and about available resource materials and equipment.

You will learn about the school library/media resource center, its personnel, and its procedures, and you will meet district and school personnel and become familiar with the many services that support you in the classroom. You will meet campus security personnel, resource officers, and other ancillary personnel and learn about their functions and locations.

As a student in a program for teacher preparation, you may be expected to participate in an orientation meeting at your college or university. The meeting may be held at the beginning of the program, just before the beginning of your field experiences, or both times. Perhaps this meeting will be a function of one of your college or university courses. You will receive your school assignment, the name of the school and the school district, the school's location, the date when you should report to that assignment, the name of your co-operating teacher(s), the grade level(s), the subject(s), and perhaps the name of your college or university supervisor. You will probably be encouraged to follow many of the objectives just discussed as well as to meet other teacher candidates.

When you arrive at your assigned school and after introductions have been made, you should begin to familiarize yourself with the school campus and the way the school is organized. Walk around the campus, perhaps with a copy of the school map, and learn the location of your classroom(s). Also locate the nearest restrooms for girls, boys, adult men, and adult women. You may be loaned one or several keys—one for the classroom, one for a restroom, and perhaps one for a faculty workroom. Become familiar with such areas as the teachers' workroom, the faculty room, and the faculty lunchroom (which may or may not be a single area—a large high school, for example, may have several faculty rooms scattered about the campus).

Thoroughly investigate this campus environment. Where do students eat their lunches? Is there a multi-purpose room—a room used for lunch as well as for educational purposes? Is there a school nurse? Where is the nurse's station? When is the nurse available? Where is the nearest first aid and emergency equipment? How do you notify maintenance and security personnel quickly and efficiently? Where are the written procedures for fire drills and other emergencies? Where is information about the school's crisis preparedness plan and its emergency warning system (Porterfield, 2006)? Is there a plan posted in a conspicuous place for all to see? Where are the various administrative offices? Where are the counseling and guidance offices? Is there an office of student activities? Where are the library, media center, resources room, gymnasium(s), and the auditorium? Where are textbooks stored and how are students expected to use them? Are they to be checked out and distributed? If so, how? Where is the attendance office? Are there resource specialists, and if there are, what are their functions and where are their offices located?

At an orientation session, you may meet the grade-level or department chairperson or the team leader and members of that team. How can you find out where those persons are located at various times during the school day? Where are teaching materials and laboratory supplies kept and how do you obtain them? Have you located your faculty mailbox and the place to check in or out when you arrive at school or leave at the end of the day? What procedures do you follow if you are absent because of illness or if you know you are going to arrive late? Do you have the necessary phone numbers of relevant contact information? Is there a school web site? If there is, how extensive and current is it? Not least in importance, if you drive a vehicle to school, where do you park? Otherwise, what is the best local transportation available for getting to and from school each day?

After becoming familiar with the school campus and obtaining answers to some of your more urgent questions, you will want to focus your attention on the various school schedules, especially your own teaching schedule.

The School Year and Teachers' Schedules

School years vary from state to state, district to district, and school to school. Most school years begin in August and continue through late May or mid-June. However, to accommodate more students without a significant increase in capital costs and to better sustain student learning, some schools have eliminated the traditional long summer break by switching to year-round education (YRE). Some schools that are called year-round simply start just a week or two earlier than is traditional and end only a week or two later and still have a summer break of two or more months. As said earlier in this chapter, for most teachers and students in the United States the school year still approximates 180 days.

In a school with year-round operation, a teacher might teach for three-quarters of the year and be off for one-quarter or teach in a 45/15 program, which means 9 weeks of school (45 days) "on track" followed by 3 weeks of school (15 days) "off track" throughout the year. In a 45/15 arrangement, teachers and students are on tracks, referred to as A Track, B Track, and so on, with starting and ending times that vary depending on the track and time of year. At any one time there is usually at least one track that is on vacation. Intersession programs may be held during off-track time, at which time students might participate in classes designed for remediation, exploration, or enrichment.

Beginning about 8:00 A.M. the school day lasts until about 3:00 P.M. During hot summer months, some schools begin earlier, say at 7:15, and end around 2:00. District and state laws vary, but generally teachers are expected to be in the classroom no less than 15 minutes prior to the start of school and to remain in their classrooms no less than 15 minutes after final dismissal of students. Some schools use what is commonly called a **freeze time**, a scheduled time each week, such as 2:30–3:30 P.M. every Monday, when all teachers are in their classrooms to help students and meet with parents/guardians. Typically, no other activities, such as athletic practices or club meetings, are supposed to be scheduled at that time.

Drawing upon studies of adolescent sleep patterns as well as the need to find ways to deal with crowded schools or to cut transportation expenses by reducing the number of busses and drivers needed, some schools are experimenting with later-than-usual starting times, or because no single schedule can accommodate the desires and needs of everyone, with multiple starting times.

Teaching Teams

Traditionally, elementary school teachers taught their groups of children in their self-contained classrooms for most of the school day, and junior high and senior high school teachers taught their subject disciplines as often as seven or eight times (periods) each day to as many groups of students. At all levels, teachers taught in their assigned classrooms while fairly isolated from other teachers and school activities—not unlike the parallel play of preschool children, that is, playing side by side but not really together. In some schools, unfortunately, that is still the case. Increasingly, however, teachers are finding themselves members of a collaborative teaching team in which several teachers work together to reflect, plan, and implement a curriculum for a common cohort of students. [Note: A distinction must be made between **teaching teams** and **team teaching**; team teaching refers to two or more teachers simultaneously providing instruction to students in the same classroom. Members of a teaching team may participate in team teaching.]

For a teaching team to plan effectively and efficiently, members must meet together frequently. This is best accomplished when they share a common planning time where they can plan curriculum and discuss the progress and need of individual students within the cohort.

The teaching team may consist of only a few teachers, for example, all third-grade teachers of a particular elementary school, all the teachers who teach the same cohort of sixth-grade students at a particular middle school, or all 11th-grade teachers of history and English who team for one semester on a Renaissance theme at a particular high school. They may meet regularly to plan curriculum for the particular cohort of students, or they may meet periodically to plan a curriculum and learning activities around a common theme.

Sometimes teaching teams consist of one teacher each from the curriculum areas of English/reading/language arts (known also as **literacy**), history/social studies/geography, mathematics, and science. In addition, other teachers may be part of the team, including teachers of physical education, the visual and performing arts, and even special education teachers and at-risk specialty personnel or school counselors. As a visiting or continuing member of this **interdisciplinary team organization (ITO)**, a team may invite a community-resource person. These teams are commonly called **interdisciplinary teaching teams** or simply **interdisciplinary teams**.

The Community of Learners Concept

An interdisciplinary teaching team and its common cohort of students is sometimes referred to as the community of learners, or **learning community** (also called **school-within-a-school**, **village**, **pod**, **academy**, **family**, **neighborhood**, **house**, or just plain **team**) concept, where each team of teachers is assigned each day to the same cohort of students for a common block of time. Within this block of time, teachers on the team are responsible for the many professional decisions necessary, such as how school can be made developmentally responsive (i.e., most meaningful) to students' lives, what specific responsibilities each teacher has each day, which students need special attention, and how students will be grouped for instruction. Members of such a team become "students of their students" and thereby build the curriculum and instruction around their students' interests, perspectives, and perceptions. The team and their students truly become a community of learners, such as, for example, *The Met High School* that began in Providence, Rhode Island, and that now has grown to approximately 50 similar schools scattered around the country (http://www.themetschool.org).

The community of learners concept helps students make important and meaningful connections among disciplines. It also provides them with both peer and adult group identification, which provides an important sense of identity and belonging. In some elementary schools in particular, using an arrangement called **looping** (also referred to variously as **banding, family-style grouping, multiyear grouping, multiyear instruction, multiyear placement, persisting groups**, and teacher-student progression), the cohort of students and teachers remain together as a group for several or all the years a student is at that school. Spending more than the usual one school year with a group of students allows their teacher or the teaching team to acquire greater knowledge of the students' personalities, their learning styles and capacities, and their needs.

The advantages to being a member of a teaching team in a learning community environment are numerous. For example, the combined thinking of several teachers creates an expanded pool of ideas, enhances individual capacities for handling complex problems, and provides intellectual stimulation and emotional support. The combination of talents produces an energy that has a positive impact on the instructional program. A beginning teacher who joins a team has the benefit of support from more experienced teammates. When a team member is absent, other members of the team work closely with the substitute, resulting in less loss of instructional time for students. More and better planning for students occurs as teachers have discourse and reach agreement on behavioral expectations, curriculum emphasis, instructional approaches, and materials.

For a teaching team to plan effectively and efficiently, members must meet together frequently. This is best accomplished when they share a **common planning time**. This means in addition to each member's daily planning time, members of a team share a common time to plan curriculum and discuss the progress and needs of individual students within the cohort.

Each team assigns a member to be team facilitator, or **lead teacher**. This person organizes the meetings and facilitates discussions during the common planning time. Usually, this lead teacher also acts as a liaison with the administration to ensure that the team has the necessary resources to put its plans into action. A team's lead teacher (or another member designated by the team) may also serve on the school leadership (management) team, a group of teachers and administrators and sometimes students (Fiscus, 2005), designated by the principal or elected by the faculty (and student body) to assist in the leadership of the school (Kellough, 2008).

Nontraditional Scheduling

To maximize the learning time, to allow for more instructional flexibility, and to accommodate common planning time for teachers, since the late 1960s schools have tried and continuing trying a variety of forms of nontraditional scheduling.

Some schools use some form of **block scheduling**. Block scheduling means, for at least a portion of the school day or of the week, blocks of time ranging from 70 to 140 or more minutes replace the traditional structure of 50-minute-long instructional periods. The possible variations are nearly limitless.

Also, the reduction of bells ringing from as many as eight times a day to perhaps only two or three times a day or not at all creates less disturbance. Many schools use no passing bells or signals at all.

Because students are not roaming halls for 3 to 5 minutes five or six times a day, teachers can more easily supervise unstructured time and thereby have improved control over portions of the subtle message systems within schools referred to as the **hidden** (aka **covert, informal**) **curriculum**. The messages of the hidden curriculum are the school climate, the feelings projected from the teachers and other adults to students and from the students to one another, not only in classrooms but before and after school, at social events, school programs, club meetings, and in the halls, restrooms, lunch areas, and other places on the school campus not monitored as closely as are classrooms. Exercise 1.1, *What Message Is Being Conveyed?* (found at end of this chapter), which you should do now if so expected by your course instructor, shows how the hidden curriculum can impact students even though the teacher may not be aware of his or her actions.

Nontraditional school schedules are not without their problems. Problems that sometimes arise from block scheduling are as follows: There may be a mismatch between content actually covered and that expected by state-mandated tests and the dates those tests are given to students; content coverage for a grade level or in a course may be less than that which was traditionally covered (certainly neither of these first two is an unimportant issue in this day of high-stakes exterior-developed academic achievement testing); teachers may be unhappy, if classes meet less frequently than in the traditional once-a-day, 5-days-a-week schedule; and when the instructional strategy is developmentally inappropriate, students are likely to become bored, restless, frequently late to class or absent, and mischievous, that is, the students become turned-off to learning.

Using a **modified block schedule**, some schools have successfully combined schedules, thus satisfying teachers who prefer block scheduling and those who prefer the traditional schedule. A modified block schedule can provide both traditional 40-minute periods (sometimes called **split-block periods**) that meet daily and longer blocks. A modified block schedule centers on a day consisting of seven or eight 45- or 40-minute periods along with alternate longer blocks. In a modified block schedule all students might start the day with a 30- or 40-minute-long first period that serves as an advisory time (known also as **homeroom, home base**, or **advisor–advisee**). From there, some students continue the morning attending traditional-length periods, whereas others move into a morning block class. Throughout the day, teachers and students may pass from block classes to those of traditional length or vice versa.

Some schools use a **flexible block schedule**. The daily schedule is a seven-period day with all seven classes meeting on Monday. Periods one through four meet for 75 minutes, and periods five through seven meet for 30 minutes. Periods one through four meet for 105 minutes each on Tuesdays and Thursdays, and periods five through seven meet for 120 minutes each on Wednesdays and Fridays. A 30-minute advisory period is held at the same time each day, perhaps the first thing in the morning or immediately after lunch.

In short, there is little doubt that longer blocks of instructional time can be a positive factor contributing to students' meaningful learning, especially when combined with year-round education, curriculum integration, differentiated instruction, interdisciplinary thematic instruction, and project-based learning.

Today, perhaps because of what is known about student learning and perhaps due to the diversity of students in schools, there is a continuing interest in nontraditional scheduling, as schools continue the never-ending pursuit to find the most effective ways of providing quality education for each and every student.

Quality Education for Every Student

Smaller learning communities and nontraditional scheduling are efforts to organize schools in ways that will deliver quality education for every student. *The curriculum of a quality education school is one seen by students as having meaning and usefulness in their lives and is delivered via activity-oriented instruction that is differentiated to meet the diverse needs of the students.*

Instruction That Is Differentiated

Differentiated instruction provides opportunities for students to access the same curriculum but via varying entry points, learning activities, and learning outcomes that are to a great degree tailored to individual students' needs. Rather than dictating procedures, ordering students to work, and berating them when they do not, in a quality school the teachers provide a stimulating learning environment and are seen by the students as being positive, encouraging, respectful, and supportive. Teachers who are successful differentiators are able to use student diversity as an asset rather than deterrent to student learning (Carolan & Guinn, 2007).

> Today's movement to transform all schools into caring and responsive learning communities has as its sole purpose helping each and every student to make the transitions necessary to succeed in school and in life. Perhaps as we move closer to accomplishing that purpose we will greatly reduce the number of school dropouts.

Responsive Practices for Helping Each Student Succeed

Because of the enormous diversity of students, the advantage from utilizing a combination of practices concurrently is usually greater in helping all students succeed in school than is the gain from using any singular practice by itself. School reorganization, the restructuring of schedules, and efforts to differentiate and individualize instruction, then, represent three important transformation efforts to help all students make successful transitions.

Other important responsive practices, most of which are discussed in various ways throughout this resource guide, include the following:

- A perception, shared by all teachers and staff, that each student can learn when given adequate support, although not all students need the same amount of time to learn the same thing
- Attention to the emotional development and the coping skills of each student
- Engagement of parents and guardians as partners in their child's education
- High, although not necessarily identical, expectations for all students
- Highly qualified teachers, specialist teachers, and smaller schools with smaller classes
- Peer tutoring and cross-age coaching
- Personal attention, adult advocacy, scheduling, and learning plans to help students learn in a manner by which they best learn
- Time and guided attention to basic skills—especially those of literacy, thinking, and social—rather than solely on rote memory

ELEMENTARY SCHOOLS

That referred to as the elementary school usually enrolls children between the ages of 5 and 11; converting these ages to grades, we get kindergarten (K) through 6. In some places, the elementary school is a primary school, with grades K–4, followed by a 4-year middle school, and then a high school. In some places, the elementary-school grade ranges are K through 8, an arrangement in which there is a rekindled interest in the United States (discussed below, under "middle-level school"). The K–8 elementary schools ordinarily are followed by a 4-year high school (K–8–4). The K–6 elementary schools are usually followed by a 3-year junior high school, or a middle school, followed by a 3-year senior high school (K–6–3–3). However, a K–6 elementary school with a 2-year middle school and a 4-year high school is not uncommon.

The Graded School Concept

Schools in colonial America and those of the early national period did not use the age-sorting system we call **grades**. At that time in our history, children of varying ages were assigned to one teacher, most often an unmarried female, who tutored them individually or taught them in small cross-age groups. It was not until the middle of the 19th century that the practice of grouping children according to age (i.e., age grading) became common.

Following the Civil War, there was rapid acceptance of the practice of grouping children of a similar age and keeping those groups intact from one year to the next as they progressed through school. Schools were therefore *graded* by age, and communities and states used that term in curriculum documents and school regulations and names. The expression *grade school* is the term commonly used when speaking of the elementary school. However, as shown in Figure 1.2, not all are in favor of the practice today.

SELF-CONTAINED CLASSROOM

The most common arrangement for at least the primary grades, that is, the K–3 level organization, is the self-contained classroom. A **self-contained classroom** is one in which one teacher is assigned to a group of children of approximately the same age (leftover from the "graded school" concept) for an academic year, and that teacher has primary responsibility for implementing the program of instruction for those children. That teacher is the teacher of record for those children for an entire school year, even though other teachers of special subjects, such as music, art, physical education, or computers, may work with them part of the time. Within the self-contained classroom, we can find incorporated many if not all the characteristics common to research findings on exemplary teaching, most of which as noted are discussed later in this resource guide:

- Classrooms rich in materials for children to experience choices, challenges, social interaction, and success (especially Chapters 2, 3, and 9)
- Classrooms with provisions for a variety of types of group settings, including one-on-one, dyad, small-group, and large-group instruction (Chapters 8, 9 and others)
- Climate of community, respect, and cooperation (especially Chapters 3 and 9)
- Climate of expectations for work and achievement (especially Chapters 8 and 10)

Figure 1.2 Arguments for and against the concept of graded school.

Proponents of the graded-school concept argue the following:

- It reduces variability within instructional groups by keeping the age of children constant within the groups.
- It equalizes educational opportunity by exposing all children to the same curriculum.
- Textbooks, instructional materials, and achievement tests can be constructed on the basis of age-grade norms.
- Children's social development, to some extent, relates to age, and therefore, age groups tend to be natural social groups.
- It is an efficient way to accommodate the large number of children who are required to attend school.
- It allows teachers to specialize their teaching skills in terms of the age of the children with whom they work best.
- It is possible to require set standards of achievement for the various grades.

Opponents of the graded-school concept argue the following:

- It is too lockstep, encouraging teachers to disregard individual differences in children and in their developmental patterns.
- It sets unrealistic standards for children and is especially unfair to low achievers.
- It encourages mechanical teaching, analogous to assembly-line production in industry.
- It encourages traditional recitation-response teaching practices, ignoring what has been learned in recent years about learning.
- It encourages a rigid and undifferentiated curriculum.
- The competitive and comparative system of determining grades (marks of achievement) and promotion are educationally dysfunctional and psychologically unsound.
- It encourages an authoritarian classroom atmosphere that is antagonistic to what is now known about how children best learn.

- Emphasis on skill development (especially Chapters 3, 4, 5, and 6)
- Instructional experiences designed to foster the construction of meaning (especially Chapters 2, 3, and 6)
- Interdisciplinary thematic instruction (especially Chapters 5 and 8)
- Multilevel (differentiated) instruction (Chapter 8 and throughout)
- Opportunities for peer tutoring and cross-age mentoring (Chapter 9)

MIDDLE-LEVEL SCHOOLS

When you receive your teaching credential, you may or may not be certified to teach at the middle school level. In some states an elementary school credential certifies a person to teach in any grade, kindergarten through grade 8. In some states a secondary school credential certifies a person to teach a particular subject at any grade level, kindergarten through grade 12. In other states such a credential qualifies a person to teach only grades 7 through 12. At least 33 states provide a middle school teaching credential to candidates who have successfully completed a program specifically designed to prepare teachers for that level.

There are two sometimes quite different types of schools, both of which may be called middle schools. One is the traditional junior high school with perhaps a few minor changes, such as changing its name to "middle school." The second is the exemplary middle school,

which is, as shown in Table 1.1, quite different from the traditional junior high school.

Used historically from about 1880, the term **junior high school** most commonly refers to schools having grades 7 and 8 or grades 7, 8, and 9, in which a program is designed to approximate the type of education commonly found in traditional high schools. Thus, historically a junior high school might be considered a "not-quite-yet-but-trying-to-be" high school. Students graduating from a junior high school often would then move on to a senior high school.

Beginning in the 1960s, the term **middle school** gained favor as a result of the movement away from the concept of "junior" high school. Reasons for the reorganization away from the concept of junior high school and the adoption of a middle school education included: (a) to provide a program specifically designed for young adolescents, (b) to set up a more effective transition between the elementary school and the high school, and (c) to move ninth-graders to the high school or, as has happened in some school districts, to a location designed solely for ninth-graders. Proponents of the separate facility for ninth-graders argue that having a separate school improves their academic and social transition to high school (Reents, 2002).

Although any combination of grades 5 through 9 may be included in a middle school, the most common configuration is grades 6 through 8. Including sixth-graders and excluding ninth-graders is a reflection of the recommendation of the National Middle School

Table 1.1   Summary of Differences Between Middle and Junior High Schools

	Junior High School	*Middle School*
Most common grade span	7–8 or 7–9	6–8
Scheduling	Traditional	Flexible, usually block
Subject organization	Departmentalized	Integrated and thematic; interdisciplinary; usually language arts, math, science, and social studies
Guidance/counseling	Separate advising by full-time counselor on individual or "as-needed" basis	Advisor–advisee relationship between teacher and student within a home base or homeroom
Exploratory curriculum	Electives by individual choice	Common "wheel" of experiences for all students
Teachers	Subject-centered; grades 7–12 certification	Interdisciplinary teams; student-centered; grades K–8 or 6–8 certification
Instruction	Traditional; lecture; skills and repetition	Thematic units; discovery techniques; "learning how to learn" study skills
Athletics	Interscholastic sports emphasizing competition	Intramural programs emphasizing participation

Association in its official position paper, *This We Believe* (NMSA, 1982, rev. 1995).

The term **middle-level education** identifies school organizations based on a philosophy that incorporates curricula and instructional practices specifically designed to meet the developmental needs of young adolescent students, that is, of students "between the ages of 10 and 15." This philosophy is referred to as the **middle school concept** (NMSA, 1995).

In recent years, many school districts, especially large, urban school districts, perhaps from equating low achievement test scores with the middle school concept, have searched for ways to more effectively improve the academic achievement of its young adolescent students, such as closing middle schools and returning to the neighborhood K–8 elementary school concept. [Note: Schools with the grades K–8 inclusion are sometimes referred to as **elemiddle schools**.]

The reasoning for returning to the K–8 configuration includes: (a) a belief that teachers get to know children better and can more effectively share important information about the children and about the curriculum when children are at the same school for 8 or 9 years rather than just 3 or 4 years, (b) children in a K–8 school can be continuously assessed and will therefore progress more smoothly and successfully through the curriculum than when there is a break due to their having to change schools, (c) more effective modeling behaviors occur as the young adolescents realize their responsibility resulting from the younger children adulating them, and (d) the stress of early adolescence is less magnified than when only young adolescents are together in a school (Arth et al., 2004; Herman, 2004; Pardini, 2002).

HIGH SCHOOLS

If you are intending to teach high school, the high school from which you graduated was probably a large comprehensive high school, perhaps with a student population of 2,000 or more. In the United States the high school is a relative newcomer to public education and, much like middle-level schooling, the concept of high school is still a work in progress. Although it has been in existence for about 100 years, the contemporary large and comprehensive high school, designed to provide something for every student, is at risk. As I emphasized at the start of this chapter, the rapid and dramatic changes occurring throughout modern society, as well as what has been learned about intelligence and learning, are reflected in the equally rapid and dramatic changes occurring in today's schools. Major changes to the large comprehensive high school perhaps are only beginning to happen, although changes needed were clearly stated in the more than 80 recommendations made more than a decade ago in *Breaking Ranks: Changing an American*

Institution, the 1996 publication of the National Association of Secondary School Principals (NASSP).

There is mounting concern that the nation's large comprehensive high schools, usually housing from 2,000 to 3,000 or more students, especially those in the large urban school districts, are failing to support the academic success of an increasingly larger percentage of their students. Although the concern is far from ubiquitous (although one of the main themes emphasized in *Breaking Ranks* is that high schools should be divided into units of no more than 600 students each), as a new teacher you may be at the forefront of a true reinvention of the American high school. For example:

- Active in more than a dozen school districts across the country *Project Grad* is a K–16 reform model with the mission of ensuring a quality public education for all children in economically disadvantaged communities to increase high school graduation rates and prepare graduates to be successful in college. (www.projectgrad.org)
- Having begun in 2002 and now with more than 160 high schools in 24 states participating, *Early College High Schools* are small schools where students earn not only a high school diploma but also 2 years of college credit toward a bachelor's degree. (www.earlycolleges.org)
- *Hope High School* (Providence, Rhode Island), with a population of approximately 1,500 students in grades 9–12, was recently reorganized into three smaller, semi-independent learning communities, each with its own principal, although housed in the same building. Under this "triune" system, each learning system offers its own distinct curriculum: Hope Leadership School offers emphasis in business, law and government, and junior ROTC; Hope Information Technology School offers emphasis in television production and in computer technology; and, Hope Arts offers courses in theater, music, dance, and fine arts.
- In Chicago, the Board of Education introduced its *Renaissance 2010* plan, bringing closure to many of the district's large schools and the creation of approximately 100 new ones, with only about a third of the new schools run by the district, while others are to be operated as charters or as contract schools. With an emphasis on **personalized learning**, most of the new schools will house no more than 500 students each. By fall 2008, 76 new schools had opened and the program is reportedly on track to have opened 100 new schools by 2010. (www.ren2010)
- In Ohio, the *High School Transformation Initiative* has been undertaken to assist school districts from 21 large urban areas in transforming large high schools into autonomous smaller learning communities of approximately 100 students per grade level, or 400 within each learning community.

CYCLE OF CHANGING SCHOOL SIZE IN PAST HALF CENTURY

You may be unaware of how school size in this country has cycled. For example, in the 1950s many of the nation's high schools were small township high schools, often with far fewer than 500 students. Then, in the 1960s, began the process of closing the small schools in favor of opening new and larger high schools. The process continued for the next half-century until the current trend, a return to smaller (less than 500) schools.

- Lebanon (Oregon) High School, formerly a school of approximately 1,400 students, opened in 2004 with the building divided into four academies or "small schools," each one specializing in a different academic area, and each with roughly 300 students. The four academies are information systems, living systems, physical systems, and social systems, each with its own principal and counselor. In each academy the students remain together through all 4 years of high school with the same team of teachers.
- The *New Century High Schools Initiative* (NCHSI) is providing New York City's students with smaller high schools intended to help them meet high standards of academic and personal success. (www.newvisions.org/schools)

Indeed, whether it is to teach elementary, middle-level or high school, this is an exciting time to begin your career in public school teaching.

THE FUNDAMENTAL CHARACTERISTIC OF QUALITY EDUCATION

Wherever and however the students are housed, and regardless of other responsive practices, in the end it is the dedication, commitment, and nature of the understanding of the involved adults—the teachers, administrators, bus drivers, cooks, grounds crew, security staff, custodial staff, and support personnel—that remains the incisive element. That, in my opinion, is the fundamental characteristic of quality public education—that is, to celebrate and build upon the diverse characteristics and needs of students. As from its inception this resource guide continues in its commitment to that premise.

Committed Teachers

Public school teachers represent myriad individual personalities—perhaps impossible to capture in generalizations. Let us imagine a teaching colleague mentions that Andi Rogers, in Room 17, is a "fantastic teacher," "one of the best teachers in the district," "super," and "magnificent." What might be some of the characteristics you would expect to see in Andi's teaching behaviors? (A detailed presentation of teacher responsibilities and behaviors is the topic of Chapter 2.)

Perhaps foremost is that Andi constructs positive, accepting, respectful, and trusting relationships with students and their families. Additionally, we can expect Andi to

- be knowledgeable about the developmental characteristics of the age of students under Andi's supervision;
- be understanding of and committed to the school's statement of philosophy or mission;
- know the curriculum and how best to teach it;
- be enthusiastic, motivated, positive, and well organized;
- demonstrate effective communication and interpersonal skills;
- be willing to listen to the students and to risk trying their ideas;
- acknowledge students' strengths, not their limitations;
- be a reflective and responsible decision maker.

Students of all ages need teachers who are confident, are well organized, and know how to establish and manage an active and supportive learning environment, even with its multiple instructional demands. Students respond best to teachers who provide leadership and who enjoy their function as role models, advisors, mentors, and reflective decision makers.

Reflective Decision Making

During any school day you will make hundreds of nontrivial decisions, many of them instantaneously. In addition, you will have already made many decisions in preparation for the teaching day. During one school year a teacher makes literally thousands of decisions, many of which can and will affect the lives of students for years to come. As in the nearly poetic words of Brown and Moffett (1999, p. 24), "We [teachers] influence students in myriad, unperceived ways that affect them and the lives of people with whom they interact like the widening circles extending from a stone tossed into a tranquil pond." This may seem to be an awesome responsibility; indeed it is!

Initially, of course, you will make errors in judgment, but you will also learn that your students are resilient and there are experts available who can guide you to help ensure that the students are not harmed severely by your mistakes. You can and should learn from your errors. Keep in mind the sheer number of decisions you make each day will mean not all will be the best decisions you could have made had you had more time and better resources for planning.

Whereas pedagogy is based on scientific principles, good classroom teaching is as much an art as it is a science. Few rules apply to every teaching situation. The writers of published curriculum programs wrote for students of a particular age in general; they did *not* know your students specifically. In fact, real decisions about the selection of content, instructional objectives and materials, teaching strategies, a teacher's response to student misbehavior, and the selection of techniques for assessment of the learning experiences are all the result of subjective judgments.

Although many decisions are made at a somewhat unhurried pace when you are planning for your instruction, many others will be made intuitively and *tout de suite*. Once the school day has begun, there is rarely time for making carefully thought-out judgments. At your best, you base your decisions on your teaching style, which, in turn, is based on your knowledge of school policies, pedagogical research, the curriculum, and the unique characteristics of the young people in your classroom. You will also base your decisions on instinct, common sense, and reflective judgment. The better your understanding and experience with schools, the curriculum, and the students and their home lives, and the more time you give for thoughtful reflection, the more likely it will be that your decisions will result in students meeting the educational goals. You will reflect upon, conceptualize, and apply understandings from one teaching experience to the next. As your understanding about your classroom experiences accumulates, your teaching will become more routinized, predictable, and refined. This discussion of reflective decision making, a basic concept about which this book is designed, is continued at the beginning of the next chapter.

Now, as instructed by your course instructor, to learn more about the reality of teaching do Exercise 1.2, *Conversation with a Classroom Teacher*, found as the end of this chapter.

School Leadership

As a new or visiting member of the faculty, one of your tasks is to become familiar with the administrative organization of your school and district. The roles of principals, superintendents, and other educational leaders have changed significantly in recent years, with a much larger focus today on teaching and learning, professional development, achievement testing, and accountability.

> Schools should focus not only on the traditional three R's (reading, writing, and arithmetic) but also the other three R's (reasoning, resilience, and responsibility.
>
> Robert Sternberg (2008)

One person significantly responsible for the success of most any school is its principal. What are the characteristics of an effective school principal? Perhaps foremost is that the principal has a vision of what a quality school is and strives to bring that vision to life. Improvement of student learning is the effective school principal's constant theme. Because exemplary educators today believe in the innate potential of every student, rather than in the dumbing down of standards and expectations, they modify the key variables of time, grouping, and instructional strategies to help individual students achieve quality learning, nearly impossible to do without a supportive, forward- and positive-thinking school principal.

In addition to the school principal there may be vice- or assistant principals, persons with specific responsibilities and oversight functions, such as student activities, school discipline and security, transition programs, and curriculum and instruction. A school might also employ a school administration manager (SAM), a person with specialized training in business management who assumes a variety of administrative tasks to free the principal to focus on education (Kellough, 2008).

Sometimes teachers who are department or grade-level chairs, designated team leaders, or staff-development teachers may also serve administrative functions. Blurring the traditional lines that separated administrators and teachers, for the purposes of improving instruction and ultimately the scores of students on high-stakes assessments, more and more school districts are giving select teachers leadership roles beyond their own classrooms. But the principal is (or should be) the person with the final responsibility for everything that happens at the school.

Effects of No Child Left Behind Legislation

Today's educators are making major efforts to enhance the connections between the home, school, and local and global communities to promote the success of every child. Indeed, enhanced connections between home and school is a key provision of the *No Child Left Behind Act of 2001*, a massive federal education policy initiative (a revised version of the Elementary and Secondary Education Act, the central federal law in precollegiate education first enacted in 1965) that impacts nearly all aspects of public education. NCLB (www.nochildleftbehind.gov) has been called the most significant and controversial change in federal education policy since the federal government assumed a major role in American education more than 40 years ago (Cobb & Rallis, 2008; Sunderman & Kim, 2004). Signed into law by President Bush in January 2002, NCLB is based on the "four pillars" of stronger accountability for results, more freedom for states and communities, proven education methods, and more choices for parents. Some highlights of the legislation are shown in Figure 1.3.

NCLB is the latest federal legislation (a previous one was Goals 2000), which enacts the theories of **standards-based education** reform, formerly known as **outcome-based education**, and based on the belief that setting high standards and establishing measurable goals leads to an improvement in individual student learning outcomes. The act requires that in order for states to receive federal funding for schools, they must develop assessments in basic skills to be given to all students in specified grades. In keeping with the principle of local control of schools as established by the Tenth Amendment of the

Figure 1.3   Some highlights of the No Child Left Behind Act.

- All students are to be brought up to the "proficient" level on state tests by the year 2013–14.

- Along with the requirement to have had content standards in science in place by the 2005–06 school year, beginning in the 2007–08 school year, students are tested in science once in each of three grade spans, 3–5, 6–9, and 10–12.

- Annual reporting of school-by-school data that show a range of information.

- Annual testing demonstrating all groups of disadvantaged children making substantial progress every year in every school, thus narrowing the gap between advantaged and disadvantaged students and between all subgroups of students.

- Dialogue between schools and families, especially in low-income communities, and for states, districts, and schools to notify parents/guardians about their children's progress and about their options for transferring out of low-performing schools.

- Highly qualified teachers in core content areas. [Note: As defined by NCLB, core content areas are English, reading or language arts, mathematics, science, foreign languages, civics and government, economics, art, history, and geography. Although each state can determine its own definition of "the arts," it most likely will include music, visual arts, and dance. As defined by NCLB, "highly qualified" means the teacher has (1) full state certification, which can be "alternative certification," as defined by a state, (2) at least a bachelor's degree, and (3) demonstrated subject matter competence in the core academic subjects taught.]

- Paraprofessionals hired with Title I funds with at least 2 years of college, an associate's degree or higher, or an evaluation to demonstrate knowledge and teaching ability.

- States must classify schools based on students meeting the state's academic standards.

U.S. Constitution, NCLB does not assert a national achievement standard; standards are set by each individual state.

Because the effectiveness and desirability of NCLB's measures have been hugely questionable, something of a rebellion has occurred to certain aspects of NCLB and to its cost, with some school districts refusing federal funding rather than complying with NCLB mandates. Several states have requested federal waivers on certain requirements. It is probably reasonable to expect modifications to NCLB to continue for years to come. Indeed it must occur because as many educators agree, the initial act was flawed and ill-funded, perhaps actually leaving more students, teachers, and schools behind than was so prior to its enactment (Gibboney, 2008; Mathews, 2008; Smyth, 2008; Walden & Kritsonis, 2008; Zhao, 2008).

Since 2003, all 50 states, plus the District of Columbia and Puerto Rico, have had *No Child Left Behind (NCLB) Act* accountability plans in place; those will be areas of major focus, particularly as President Obama and legislators grapple with revisions and reauthorization of NCLB, which may have occurred by the time you are reading these words.

PARENTS, GUARDIANS, AND THE COMMUNITY

It is well known that parental and family involvement in a child's education can have a positive impact on the student's achievement at school. When parents or guardians of students who are not doing well in school get involved, the student benefits with more consistent attendance at school, more positive attitudes and actions, better grades, increased motivation, and higher test scores.

Although not all schools have a parent/guardian organization, many schools have adopted formal policies about home and community connections. These policies usually emphasize that parents/guardians should be included as partners in the educational program and that teachers and administrators will make concerted effort to inform parents/guardians about their child's progress, about the school's family involvement policy, and about any programs in which family members can participate. Schools' efforts to foster parent/guardian and community involvement are as varied as the people who participate, and include those as shown in Figure 1.4.

Community Service Learning

Through service learning, students learn and develop during active participation in thoughtfully organized and curriculum-connected experiences that meet community needs. Community members, geographic features, buildings, monuments, historic sites, and other places in a school's geographic area constitute one of the richest instructional laboratories that can be imagined. To take advantage of this accumulated wealth of resources, as well as to build school–community partnerships, once hired by a school district, you should start a file of community resources related to subject

Figure 1.4 Examples of ways schools encourage home–school–community partnerships and involvement.

- Activities at school that involve families, such as family math night, meetings where food is served, where students perform (band or choir) or demonstrate their art work or science projects, where door prizes are offered, and parent volunteer luncheons with the presentation of awards for participants

- Enrollment of not only students but also entire families as participating members of a learning team

- Home visitation programs

- Homework hotlines

- Involvement of members of the larger community into the classroom as mentors, aides, and role models

- Involvement of students in community service learning (see examples in the list of motivational strategies in Chapter 9)

- Newsletters, workshops, and electronic hardware and software for parents/guardians to stay in touch with a child's progress at school and to help their children

- Parent/guardian volunteers as "co-teachers" in the classroom

- Regular phone calls or emails and personal notes home about a student's progress

- Student–teacher–parent/guardian contracts and assignment calendars, oftentimes posted on the school's web site

- Use of adult coordinators as liaisons between home and school

content areas in which you work. For instance, you might include files about the skills of the students' parents and other family members, noting those that could be resources for the study occurring in your classroom. You might also include files on various resource people who could speak or present to the class, on free and inexpensive materials, on sites for field trips, on sources of virtual field trips, and on what other communities of teachers, students, and adult helpers have done.

It is a useful idea to start your professional resources file now and to maintain it throughout your professional career; for that, see Figure 1.5. Many specific resource ideas and sources are mentioned and listed throughout this resource guide.

THE EMERGENT OVERALL PICTURE: CURRENT ACTIONS, TRENDS, PROBLEMS, AND ISSUES

Certainly no facet of education receives more attention from the media, causes more concern among parents and teachers, or receives larger headlines than that of a decline (factual or fanciful) in students' achievement in the public schools. Reports are issued, polls are taken, debates are organized, blue ribbon commissions are formed, and legislation is enacted. Community members write letters to local editors about it, news editors devote editorial space to it, blogs about it are created, television anchors comment about it, and documentaries and television specials focus on it in full color. We read, "Schools put in program for failing academic standards," "30,000 facing summer school: Student failures push city to costly remedial program," "In a global test of math skills, U.S. students behind the curve," "We have let our grades slip, our school crumble, our teacher quality fall

Figure 1.5 Beginning my professional resources file.

A professional resources file is a project you could begin now and continue throughout your professional career. Begin your file either on a computer database program or on color-coded file cards listing (1) name of resource, (2) how and where to obtain the resource, (3) description of how to use the resource, and (4) evaluative comments about the resource.

Organize the file in a way that makes sense to you. Cross-reference or color code your system to accommodate the following categories of resources:

- CD/DVD titles
- Community resources
- Free/inexpensive materials
- Games
- Guest speakers/presenters
- Internet resources
- Media sources
- Print resources

- Printed visuals
- Resources to order
- Software titles
- Student worksheets
- Test items
- Unit/lesson plans & ideas
- Video titles
- Miscellaneous/other

short, and other nations outpace us," and so on. What initiated this attention that began at least four decades ago and continues today? I am not sure, but it has affected and continues to affect both the public schools and programs in higher education that are directly or indirectly related to teacher preparation and certification. And, now, as I prepare this sixth edition of this resource guide, hard-to-come-by dollar amounts appear to be forcing even greater cuts in education at this time when the cost of operations and programs is increasing and the demands of the NCLB Act appear increasingly greater over states and schools.

In response to the reports, educators, corporations and local businesspersons, and politicians acted and continue acting. Around the nation, their actions have resulted in the following:

- Changes in standards for teacher certification
- Emphasis on education for cultural diversity and ways of teaching and working with English language learners
- Emphasis on helping students make connections between what is being learned and real life, as well as connections between subjects in the curriculum and between academics and vocations
- Emphasis on helping students make effective transitions from home to school, from one level of schooling to the next, and from school to life
- Emphasis on rising test scores, increasing quality instructional time, and changing curricula
- Emphasis on standards-based education, with frequent testing for achievement
- Improvement of school–home–community connections
- Inclusive classrooms
- Recognition that the nation has a school dropout crisis, with highest dropout rates occurring from African American and Latino youth, students with behavioral or emotional problems, and students from low-income families (McNeil, Coppola, Radigan, & Heilig, 2008; Stanley & Plucker, 2008)
- School reorganization to provide improved learning

Key Trends and Positive Practices

Listed here are key trends and positive practices in education today, many of which are discussed in subsequent chapters (see index for topic locations), however, by the time you read these words many if not all of which will to some degree be affected, perhaps even temporarily curtailed, by the current economic crisis the country is experiencing. Perhaps you and members of your class can identify other trends and practices.

- Increasing the use of new media such as podcasts and electronic books
- Broadening the definition of what it means to be "literate," especially in response to continuing

development of technologies, globalization, and rapid societal changes, with a concomitant development of the term *multiliterate*

- Continuing the influx of immigrant and language-minority students throughout the United States, rural, suburban, and urban
- Continuing the interest in finding the most effective school scheduling
- Continuing the interest in integrating the subjects of the curriculum
- Creating global classrooms via the development and use of international projects and communications using online resources and more globally focused social studies curriculum with students learning to think critically about other nations and about how people in other countries interact
- Differentiating the instruction
- Dividing the student body and faculty into smaller cohorts or learning communities
- Eliminating "F" grades, sometimes substituting the "I" (incomplete) grade, focusing on providing students with continuing and additional opportunities to succeed
- Combining the use of online and face-to-face approaches—known as **blended learning**—as a new tool in the educational tool kit, thus enabling classroom teachers to increase student learning opportunities beyond the school day and school year
- Encouraging the practices of reflective thinking and self-discipline
- Establishing partnerships with lower grades and high schools to ease the transition for students into the ninth grade
- Facilitating the students' social skills as they interact, relate to one another, identify and solve meaningful problems, develop skills in conflict resolution, and foster peaceful relationships and friendships
- Finding ways of providing hands-on learning activities to students who are in distance learning
- Finding ways of providing high-quality instruction through a steady monitoring of student progress with an analysis of the student's need and behavior, a practice most common to elementary school and middle schools, known as response to intervention (RtI), a tiered approach for helping students, especially those who are struggling academically and who exhibit at-risk behaviors
- Finding ways to reduce the so-called summer regression, which is the loss of students' skills and content knowledge due to the traditional summer layoff. (One such move is away from the traditional "agrarian school calendar" to a 45/15 year-round or modified year-round calendar, and another is through the use of looping and assigning of summer homework.)
- Holding high expectations, although not necessarily identical expectations, for all students by establishing

benchmark academic standards, teaching toward those standards, and frequently assessing student achievement against those standards and adjusting instruction accordingly

- Improving literacy skills via reading and writing email, blogs, and other telecommunications

> Being able to read and write multiple forms of media and integrate them into a meaningful whole is the new hallmark of literacy.
>
> Jason Ohler (2009, p. 9)

- Incorporating electronic media and games as instructional tools
- Increasing requirements for high school graduation; for example, an increasing number of states (at least 21) require students to pass algebra to graduate, and an increasing number are requiring exit examinations
- Increasing the use of virtual field trips rather than traditional off-campus field trips
- Increasing the interest in allowing some high school students to graduate after the equivalent of the traditional sophomore year
- Increasing the interest in hand gesturing and its relevance to learning
- Inviting students to participate in traditional parent/guardian–teacher conferences
- Involving parents/guardians and communities in the education of the children
- Involving students in the self-assessment of their learning
- Moving to a grades K–8 and 9–12 school organization, that is, to a two-school (elementary and high school) rather than a three-school organization (elementary, middle school, high school)
- Posting school papers and notices online rather than by the paper flyers as previously sent home with students
- Providing students with the time and the opportunity to think and be creative, rather than simply memorizing and repeating information
- Providing meaningful curriculum options with multiple pathways for academic success and for high school graduation
- Revamping the displays and programs in public museums to adjust to state curriculum standards in order to reattract school field trips
- Redefining giftedness to include nonacademic as well as traditional academic abilities
- Renewing an interest in eliminating grade levels and grouping students more on what they know, that is, by their advancing levels of proficiency rather than by age
- Replacing traditional writing boards, and TVs previously rolled into classrooms on carts, with wireless

laptop computers, electronic whiteboards, remote controls, and large LCD screens

- Using school-based community learning centers that also provide social services
- Incorporating statewide accountability systems for all students
- Teaching and assessing for higher-order thinking skills
- Using heterogeneous small-group learning, peer coaching, and cross-age tutoring as classroom instructional strategies
- Using the Internet as a communication tool and learning resource

> Considering they barely existed just five years ago, online networks have quickly changed the landscape in terms of how we connect with others around the world.... Learning is no longer fixed in time and space; it can happen anytime and anywhere that we are connected.
>
> Will Richardson (2009, pp. 28–29)

Major Problems, Concerns, and Issues

Major problems, concerns, and issues plague our nation's schools. Some of the most pressing include the following:

- Concern about child abuse and neglect (e.g., physical abuse, incest, malnutrition, being improperly clothed, and inadequate dental care)
- Concern about the anxiety shown in youth, with the concomitant knowledge that anxiety is counterproductive to positive academic performance
- Concern for the declining focus on teaching handwriting and the growing inability to read cursive writing [Note: For an eloquently written discussion, see David Mehegan's article "Cursive, foiled again," in the January 19, 2009, edition of *The Boston Globe.*]
- Concern over low-performing schools that have not shown significant improvement even after years of effort and expenditure of large amounts of tax dollars
- Concern that increased focus on assessments in English classes is causing a reduction in the use of assigned reading of full-length novels
- Concern that schools have recently become more racially segregated than at any time since the civil rights era
- Concern that time given to standardized testing is causing schools and teachers to change their focus from teaching to whether students are learning
- Concern that while schools are spending more time on reading and mathematics, implementation of NCLB legislation is causing less time being spent on students' learning of other subjects of the curriculum
- Concern that with the increased emphasis in mathematics on critical and conceptual thinking and practical

problem solving, there has been a corresponding de-emphasis on skills of arithmetic and calculation, a trend that weakens math performance in general and makes math less useful for students who go on to college

- Continuing concern about the "digital divide," that is, inequitable differences between schools of high and low socio-economic status (SES) in terms of their provision of supports for their students in their achievement of information communication technology (ICT) literacy (Hohlfeld, Ritzhaupt, Barron, & Kemker, 2008)
- Continuing controversy and concern over the value and effects of the NCLB Act and the concomitant high-stakes standardized testing
- Continuing debate on national music assessment, with some arguing for national testing of music students, while others argue that assessment within music education will have negative effects on music education (Fisher, 2008)
- Controversy over what is the actual percentage of students who complete high school and the concomitant concern that the percentage is decreasing, especially among Latinos and African Americans (Walden & Kritsonis, 2008)
- Controversy over whether charter schools are doing as well as had been expected
- Development of a school-based work readiness credential and the ensuing debate about whether such a credential would weaken the incentive for a student to complete high school
- Difficulty in ensuring that no child is left behind when children move from one school district to another, sometimes many times before completing high school
- Economic and educationally productive ways of bringing blogging, podcasting, online video, and social networking into the classroom
- Education of teachers to work effectively with young people who may be too overwhelmed by personal problems to focus on learning and to succeed in school
- Finding alternatives to grade retention and social promotion
- Growing concern over the nation's current economic woes and the effect on public schools; for example, at the time of preparation of this edition of the resource guide there are (1) discussions about reducing the number of school districts in any given state by merging existing districts, thereby saving on district administration costs, (2) preparation for the reduction in classified and nonclassified staffs within existing districts, (3) reductions in the service provided by school busing, and (4) concern about the funding problem and gap in many states, with a nationwide per-student expenditure disparity between high-poverty and low-poverty school districts
- Impedance of immigrant parental/guardian involvement in school activities due to the school's difficulty in bridging cultural and communication barriers

- Increasing concern that higher-performing students (and schools) are being shortchanged because of increased attention being given to lower-performing students (and schools)
- Increasing number of schools that are without libraries or have a library but no library staff
- Increasing number of students arriving to the United States, especially in some large cities such as New York, who have had what is known as an Interrupted Formal Education (IEF), that is, who have arrived from other countries where they did not attend school at all and consequently who are illiterate even in their native language
- Interest in the development of a mandated national curriculum, or even an international curriculum
- Interest in the development of a national curriculum for technology education
- Number of youth at risk of dropping out of school and who are, in fact, dropping out
- Potential misdiagnosis of children as intellectually or behaviorally challenged
- Potential need to include the topic of critical media literacy in the K–12 curriculum
- Recruiting and retaining the best teachers and school administrators
- Rush to mainstream students identified as limited English proficient
- Scarcity of male teachers, currently at the lowest percentage in four decades
- Scarcity of minority teachers to serve as role models for youth
- School buildings and facilities that are outdated, needing upgrading and repairs
- Security and the related problems of bias, bullying, cyberbullying, crime, drugs, harassment, prejudice, violence, and weapons on school campuses and in school neighborhoods, and the prevalence of criminal youth gangs, not just in large cities but rural areas as well
- Use of standardized test scores and statistics to judge and reward the performance of schools and teachers, thereby creating a disincentive for teachers and administrators to work with particular groups of students

Perhaps you and your classmates can identify and describe other concerns, issues, and problems faced by our nation's schools, particularly for those in your immediate geographic area. In any case, as you can see your work ahead is clearly cut out for you.

MEETING THE CHALLENGE: INITIAL GUIDELINES FOR RECOGNIZING AND PROVIDING FOR STUDENT DIFFERENCES

To provide learning experiences that are consistent with what is known about ways of learning and knowing, consider the following general guidelines, which will be the

A critical problem in schools today is the scarcity of minority teachers to serve as effective role models for an increasing percentage of minority students.

main focus of subsequent content of this resource guide. If you haven't begun already, then begin now making notes to yourself as you read on.

- As frequently as is appropriate, and especially for skills development, plan the learning activities so they follow a step-by-step sequence from concrete to abstract.
- Communicate with each student in a clear, direct, respectful, and consistent manner.
- Establish multiple learning centers within the classroom. (As emphasized in Chapter 9, learning centers are not the sole propriety of elementary school teachers!)
- Even when teaching a mandated and even scripted curriculum, to the extent possible concentrate on the use of student-centered instruction by using project-centered learning, discovery and inquiry strategies, and simulations and role-playing.
- Maintain high expectations, although not necessarily identical, for every student; establish high standards and teach toward them without wavering, assessing frequently to see how you and each student are doing, making instructional adjustments as necessary along the way.
- Plan interesting activities to bridge learning, activities that help students connect what is being learned with their real world as it exists to them now.
- Provide a structured learning environment with well-understood and frequently rehearsed procedures.
- Provide tiered assignments, with optional due dates, that are based on individual student abilities, understandings, and interests.
- Use direct instruction to teach to the development of observation, generalization, and other thinking and learning skills.

- Use interactive computer programs, an electronic whiteboard, and other modern media.
- Use interdisciplinary thematic instruction.
- Use multilevel instruction.
- Use reciprocal peer coaching and cross-age tutoring.
- Use self-instructional modules.
- Use small-group and cooperative learning strategies.
- With students, collaboratively plan challenging and engaging classroom learning activities and assignments.

SUMMARY

Despite the many commissions, writers, and politicians who have and continue to vilify the failures of public education, thousands of committed teachers, administrators, parents and caregivers, and members of the community struggle daily, year after year, to provide our youth with a quality education. Regardless of all the legislation and other responsive school practices, in the end it is the dedication, commitment, and understanding of the involved adults—the teachers, administrators, bus drivers, cooks, grounds crew, security staff, custodial staff, and support personnel—that remain the incisive elements in our youth's learning. And, from the work of many researchers, it has been made clear that teachers' actions in their classrooms can have a far greater impact on student achievement than do school matters of curriculum, assessment, staff collegiality, and community involvement (Marzano & Marzano, 2003).

This resource guide is designed to help you with your understandings and to develop your teaching competencies. You have read an overview of today's schools, and of the characteristics of some of the adults who work in the schools, of trends and practices, and of problems, issues, and challenges that continue to plague our nation's schools. That background of knowledge will be useful in your assimilation of the content explored in the chapters that follow, beginning in the next chapter with descriptions of teacher behaviors and specific responsibilities necessary for meeting the challenges.

QUESTIONS FOR CLASS DISCUSSION

1. Describe clues that would suggest that you were likely at an exemplary school.

2. Describe the major ethnic, racial, and cultural groups that live in the geographic area in which you plan to teach. Have the percentages of represented groups changed in the past 15 years? What implications are there in these social realities for your work as a public school teacher?

3. Some experts fear that using test scores as the sole indicator of students' and teachers' knowledge and skills is harming students and causing students to drop out of school and driving the best teachers from the profession. What is your opinion on this issue? Find support for your opinion and share your findings with your classmates.

4. Assume that you are a high school teacher and that your teaching schedule includes three sections of U.S. History. Furthermore, assume that students at your school are tracked and that one of your classes is a so-called college prep class with 30 students; another is a regular education class with 35 students, 3 of whom have special needs because of disabilities;

and the third is a sheltered English class with 13 students, 7 of whom are Hispanics with limited proficiency in English, 3 of whom are from Russia with very limited proficiency in English, and 4 of whom are Southeast Asians, 2 with no ability to use English. Will one lesson plan using direct instruction (such as by lecture, discussion, and worksheets) as the primary instructional strategies work for all three sections? If so, explain how. If not, explain what you will need to do and why. [Note: Save your response to this question, as you will be returning to it later.]

5. As is being and recently has been discovered by those involved, dividing a large school, such as a high school of 2,000 students, into smaller learning communities of no more than 400 students each is far from being an uncomplicated task that automatically solves the problems experienced when and because the school was larger. For example, when implementing the learning community, urban areas often have difficulty finding suitable locations for the new smaller schools and finding teachers with the required qualifications. Also, smaller schools may have a more limited range of course offerings. When the smaller learning communities are learning academies that are centered on a particular subject area, such as biological sciences, students may feel prematurely career tracked. Discover whether there are schools in your area making the transition from large to smaller learning communities and inquire about problems they have encountered and steps they have taken to resolve those problems. Share your findings with your classmates.

Now go to Topics #1 and 15: **Schools and Teaching Today** and **Collaborating with Colleagues and Families** in the MyEducationLab (www.myeducationlab.com) for your course, where you can:

- Find learning outcomes for these topics along with the national standards that connect to these outcomes.
- Complete Assignments and Activities that can help you more deeply understand the chapter content.
- Apply and practice your understanding of the core teaching skills identified in the chapter with the Building Teaching Skills and Dispositions learning units.

EXERCISE 1.1   WHAT MESSAGE IS BEING CONVEYED?

INSTRUCTIONS: Although it is seldom planned and almost never assessed, children do learn through the hidden or covert curriculum. For this exercise your task is two-fold. First, identify what you believe to be the hidden message, if any, that is conveyed to the students by behaviors of each of the following teachers. Then, share and discuss your responses with your classmates. Later in the course, you might like to revisit this exercise and think about what, if anything, in each instance would have been a more appropriate teacher behavior.

1. Ms. Wong is a first-year teacher. After visiting her classroom, the principal suggested that she brighten the classroom and decorate its walls with a display of student work. When the principal returned to the classroom 2 weeks later, Ms. Wong had put up a display—a chart of the homework and test records of students.

   Hidden message sent by Ms. Wong: _____

   _____

   _____

2. Mr. Lever has decorated one wall of his classroom with pictures and stories of famous scientists, all of whom are men.

   Hidden message sent by Mr. Lever: _____

   _____

   _____

3. While Ms. Gushé is talking to her classroom of students, the school principal walks into the room. Ms. Gushé stops her talk and walks over to greet the principal and find out what the principal wants.

   Hidden message sent by Ms. Gushé: _____

   _____

   _____

4. Mr. Latte is nearly always late in arriving to his class that meets right after lunch, seldom beginning class until at least 5 minutes past the scheduled start time.

   Hidden message sent by Mr. Latte: _____

   _____

   _____

5. Three minutes into the planned 10 minutes of silent reading, Ms. Silencia asks for everyone's attention, verbally reprimands two students for horsing around, and then writes out a referral for each of the two students.

   Hidden message being sent by Ms. Silencia: _____

   _____

   _____

EXERCISE 1.2   CONVERSATION WITH A CLASSROOM TEACHER

INSTRUCTIONS: The purpose of this exercise is to interview one or more teachers, perhaps one who is relatively new to the classroom and one who has been teaching for 10 or more years. Use the following questions. You may duplicate blank copies of this form. Share the results with others in your class.

1. Name and location of school

_____

_____

2. Total enrollment

_____

_____

3. Grade span of school

_____

_____

4. Date of interview

_____

_____

5. Name and grade level (and/or subject) of interviewee

_____

_____

6. In which area(s) of the school's curriculum do you work?

_____

_____

7. Tell me one or two factors in your life or in your education that led you to choose teaching as a career.

_____

_____

_____

8. What were the circumstances that led you to teach at this grade level?

_____

_____

_____

9. Please describe the preparation or training that you had for this teaching.

_____

_____

_____

EXERCISE 1.2 *(continued)*

10. What do you like the most about your work?

_____

_____

_____

11. What do you like the least about your work?

_____

_____

_____

12. What would you say is the most important thing for me to know in order to be an effective classroom teacher?

_____

_____

_____

13. What advice about preparation can you offer me?

_____

_____

_____

14. Is there any other advice you have for us who are entering the teaching profession?

_____

_____

_____

2 Teacher Professional Responsibilities

The primary expectation of any teacher is to facilitate student learning. As a competent classroom teacher, you will have professional responsibilities that will extend well beyond the ability to work effectively in a classroom from early morning until late afternoon. In this chapter, you will learn about the many responsibilities you will assume and the competencies and behaviors necessary for fulfilling them. Four categories of responsibilities and 22 competencies are identified.

The four categories are (1) responsibility as a reflective decision maker, (2) commitment to young people and to the profession, (3) noninstructional responsibilities, and (4) instructional responsibilities and fundamental teaching behaviors. As these categories and the 22 competencies are presented, you are guided through the reality of these expectations as they exist for today's classroom teacher.

Specifically, upon completion of this chapter you should be able to:

1. Describe the four decision-making and thought-processing phases of instruction and the types of decisions you must make during each.
2. Describe an operational awareness of the variety of materials, tools, and resources for use in your teaching.
3. Demonstrate knowledge of copyright laws for using printed and media materials for teaching.
4. Demonstrate an understanding about using community resources, speakers, and field trips.
5. Demonstrate competence in using standard classroom tools for teaching.
6. Describe the importance of the concept of *locus of control* and its relationship to your professional responsibilities.

7. Demonstrate your understanding of the depth and breadth of the *instructional* and the *noninstructional responsibilities* of being a classroom teacher.
8. Demonstrate knowledge of certain basic safety and legal guidelines for the classroom teacher, both those that are general for all teachers and also any that may be specific for your subject field.
9. Contrast teacher use of *praise* and of *encouragement* and describe situations in which each is more appropriate.
10. Compare and contrast teacher *facilitating behaviors* with *instructional strategies*.
11. Demonstrate your growing understanding of the concept of *teaching style* and its relevance to classroom instruction.
12. Describe the importance of *reflection* to the process of constructing skills and understanding.
13. Demonstrate your growing understanding of the concept of *multilevel instruction* and describe how you would use multilevel instruction in your teaching.

THE TEACHER AS A REFLECTIVE DECISION MAKER

During any single school day you will make hundreds of decisions. Some decisions will have been made prior to meeting your students for instruction, others are made during the instructional activities, and yet others will be made later as you reflect on the instruction for that day. *It is this decision-making obligation and privilege that defines the teacher as an artist and classroom teaching as a profession.*

Decision-Making Phases of Instruction

Instruction can be divided into four decision-making and thought-processing phases: (1) the planning or preactive phase, (2) the teaching or interactive phase, (3) the analyzing and evaluating or reflective phase, and (4) the application or projective phase (Costa, 1991).

The planning or preactive phase consists of all those intellectual functions and decisions you make prior to actual instruction. This includes decisions about content selection, goals and objectives, homework assignments, what students already know and can do, appropriate learning activities, questions to be asked (and possible answers), and the selection and preparation of instructional materials.

The teaching or interactive phase includes all the decisions made during the immediacy and spontaneity of the teaching act. This includes the maintaining of student focus, questions asked by the teacher, feedback given to the students, and ongoing adjustments to the lesson plan. Decisions made during this phase are likely to be more instinctive and routine than those made during the planning phase.

The analyzing and evaluating or reflective phase is the time you take to reflect upon, analyze, and judge the decisions and behaviors that occurred during the interactive phase. (See questions for self-reflection in Figure 2.1.) It is during reflection that you make decisions about student learning, student marks and grades, feedback given to parents and guardians, and adjustments on what and how next to teach.

As emphasized by Schon (1983) nearly three decades ago, *it is not that we learn so much from our experience, but from our reflection on our experience.* As a result of teacher self-reflection, decisions are made to use what was learned in subsequent teaching actions.

The application or projective phase consists of abstracting from your reflection and projecting your analysis into subsequent teaching behaviors. It is suggested that one reason some teachers are not as effective as they might be is because of their lack of attention to any sustained self-reflection (Danielson & McGreal, 2000). What is the characteristic of a "sustained self-reflection"? It is when a teacher asks questions like those of Figure 2.1, thoughtfully answers the questions, and then acts accordingly.

Reflection, Locus of Control, Sense of Self-Efficacy, and Teacher Responsibility

During the reflective phase, teachers have a choice of whether to assume full responsibility for the instructional outcomes or to assume responsibility only for the positive outcomes of the planned instruction while placing the blame for the negative outcomes on outside forces (e.g., district, state or federal requirements, parents and guardians, or society in general, colleagues, administrators, or textbooks or lack thereof). Where the responsibility for outcomes is placed is referred to as **locus of control**. A person with an internal locus of control typically is more likely to persist against formidable odds (see "intelligent behaviors" in Chapter 7). Teachers who have a strong sense of **self-efficacy** (feeling of "I can") are more likely to instill in their students the same sense of empowerment (Ashton & Webb, 1986).

Figure 2.1 Questions for self-reflection.

- Did the objectives seem to be met? What evidence is there?

- What is my overall opinion about today's lesson—good, fair, or bad? What specifically made me feel this way?

- Did students seem to enjoy the lesson? What specifically makes me think so?

- Were I a student in my class today, would I look forward to returning tomorrow? Why?

- What aspects of the lesson went well? What makes me believe so?

- Were I to repeat the lesson, what changes might I make?

- Which students seemed to do well? Which ones didn't? What should I do about that?

- To what extent was this lesson personalized for the students? Could I do more in this regard? If so, what? If not, then why not?

- To what extent did this lesson engage various learning modalities? Should more have been done in this area? Why or why not?

- Did the students seem to have sufficient time to think and apply? Why or why not?

- Would I have wanted my own child present as a student in this class? Why or why not?

- Would I have been proud had the school district superintendent been present to observe this lesson? Why or why not?

Teaching in Practice

Once upon a time there was a high school biology student teacher who always, to teaching colleagues and the university supervisor, seemed to be complaining. "Too many students in the class." "Not enough microscopes." "Textbooks are outdated." "Half the students in this class shouldn't be in here." "Their parents don't care; the kids don't care!" "Supply budget is inadequate." "I can't get any help from my cooperating teacher; I never even see him." Finally, one day, out of frustration, the student teacher's university supervisor said, "For crying out loud, stop complaining. You now have the one thing you have been working for—a class of high school biology students. If you are a teacher, then for Pete's sake teach them!"

Questions for Discussion

1. What thoughts came to you from reading this brief scenario?
2. From what little you know, was the supervisor out of line?
3. Have you ever heard stories of teachers who had their students make their own textbooks? Make their own microscopes with bamboo rods and a drop of water in each end? Litmus indicators using petals of flowers? What are your thoughts about such teacher actions?
4. Do you have additional thoughts regarding this scenario?

However, just because teachers think they "can" teach does not mean they "will." If many of a teacher's students are not learning, then that teacher is not competent. In the words of the late Madeline Hunter, "To say that I am an effective teacher, and acknowledge that my students may not be learning is the same as saying I am a great surgeon, but most of my patients die" (Villa & Thousands, 1995). Teachers who are intrinsically motivated and competent tend to assume full responsibility for instructional outcomes, regardless of whether or not the outcomes are as intended from the planning phase.

Of course every teacher realizes there are factors that the teacher cannot control, such as the negative effects on young people from poverty, lack of effective adult supervision, gangs, alcohol, and drug abuse, so they must do what they can within the confines of the classroom and resources of the school and district. *History brims with examples of how a relatively few, but positive, moments with a truly caring and knowledgeable adult can drastically change for the better the life of a young person whom until then had a history of mostly negative experiences.*

Now, as instructed by your course instructor, further your understanding of the responsibilities of a classroom teacher by completing Exercise 2.1, *The Teacher as Reflective Decision Maker,* found at end of this chapter.

SELECTED LEGAL GUIDELINES

Among teachers and teacher candidates, the topic of teacher and student rights generates discussions and concerns. You are, or will be, interested in teacher tenure laws, retirement laws, professional organizations, collective bargaining, legal requirements with respect to student discipline, teacher liability and insurance, and teacher negligence—topics this resource guide cannot pursue or discuss in depth.

Nevertheless, you must be knowledgeable about legal matters regarding teaching and supervising minors, as well as about copyright laws. Such knowledge can minimize the possibility of making errors that abuse the rights of students, that cause emotional or physical trauma to a student, or that could result in litigation or an abrupt and unpleasant end to your teaching career. The content in this chapter gives only some very basic, but important, information.

Student Rights

Students should be informed of their rights by their schools, and they should be encouraged to report any suspected violations of their rights to the school principal or other designated person. Many schools provide students with a publication of their rights.

RIGHT AGAINST DISCRIMINATION

Federal Law Title VI of the Civil Rights Act of 1964 prohibits any discrimination that is based on race, color, national origin, or gender. The Americans with Disabilities Act of 1990 prohibits discrimination against individuals with disabilities. Federal law Title IX of the Education Act Amendments of 1972 prohibits discrimination among students on the basis of their gender. In all aspects of school, students must be treated the same. This means, for example, that a teacher must not pit males against females in a subject-content quiz game—or for any other activity or reason. Further, no teacher, student, administrator, or other school employee should make sexual advances toward or sexually harass a student (i.e., speaking or touching in a sexual manner). *The school atmosphere must be one of trust, dignity, and respect among students and the adult staff.*

CELLULAR PHONES AND OTHER HANDHELD ELECTRONIC DEVICES

The right of students to possess and to use cellular phones and other mobile electronic devices while at school varies from state to state, from district to district, and from school to school. You will need to clearly understand and adhere to whatever policy is in force at the school where you teach.

Although in the recent past students were prohibited from possessing these devices on school property, for a variety of reasons, not the least of which are the shootings on school campuses such as at Columbine High School (Littleton, Colorado) in 1999 and the terrorist attack in September, 2001, on New York City, New Jersey, and Washington, DC, there is pressure from many parents and guardians for children to have access to cell phones while at school. More and more school districts are relaxing restrictions but are generally insisting that cell phones be off while students are in classes, unless, of course, the device is being used for instructional purposes as is increasingly the case. Many teachers, for example, are finding ways of helping students learn content via blogging (MacBride & Luehmann, 2008).

A problem some classroom teachers have experienced, besides the obvious distraction when a cell phone rings, is that of student inattentiveness to the lesson because the student was reading text messages, viewing photos, taking video camera photos, or playing games on the cell phone rather than attending to the instruction. Whatever the school and district policy, and unless they are being used for instructional purposes, as a classroom teacher you should have the policy common in most theaters and concerts; that is, students are expected upon entering your classroom to turn their electronic devices completely off and keep them off until students are dismissed from your classroom or instructed otherwise.

Because cell phones have become a common part of many students' existence, some teachers have been searching for and finding ways of using the technology to an educational advantage. For example, with the audio input feature of many of today's weblog sites, such as blogger.com, gabcast.com, and blogzy.com, students can use their cell phones to create blogs, collect and store data, and develop multimedia projects. An **audioblog** is similar to a podcast, in that it is a voice message from a phone that immediately posts to a blog site (Kolb, 2006).

A **podcast** is an audio or video file that is posted free on the web and can then be downloaded to a computer or mobile device, such as an iPod. Podcasting is becoming increasingly popular as teachers find new and creative ways and means of turning the relative new technology into valuable and useful learning experiences (Beilke, Stuve, & Williams-Hawkins, 2008; Hargardon, 2007; Rozema, 2007). Still, like with any other lesson format, creating lesson plans using podcasts and doing so with true educational value is anything but an easy task (Villano, 2007; Vincent & van't Hooft, 2007).

With the development of software and the advent of the **smartphone**, cell phones may eventually become the preferred classroom computer and are already being tested in some schools (Unmuth, 2009).

Teacher Liability and Insurance

Credentialed teachers and student teachers in public schools are usually protected by their school districts against personal injury litigation (i.e., a negligence suit filed as the result of a student being injured at school or at a school-sponsored activity). Although not all schools receive federal funding, Title II of the Elementary and Secondary Education Act of 1965 (ESEA), as reauthorized by the No Child Left Behind Act, ensures that teachers can undertake reasonable actions to maintain order and discipline in the classroom without the fear of litigation. Student teachers and credentialed teachers should investigate carefully the extent of their tort (i.e., any private or civil wrong for which a civil suit can be brought) liability coverage in districts where they work. If it is decided that the coverage provided is insufficient, a teacher may obtain additional liability coverage through private insurance agents and through affiliation with national teachers' organizations.

Teachers sometimes find themselves in situations where they are tempted to transport students in their own private automobiles, such as for field trips and other off-campus activities. Before ever transporting students in your automobile—or in private automobiles driven by others—you and other drivers should inquire from your insurance agents whether you have adequate automobile insurance liability coverage to do that and if any written permission or release from liability is needed. My advice is not to use your private vehicle for transporting students for school events; after all, if it is an important educational activity, then the school district should provide the necessary transportation support.

Inevitably, teachers take personal items to school, such as purses, cameras, cell phones, and various other electronic devices. It is unlikely that the school's insurance policy covers your personal items if stolen or damaged. A homeowner's or apartment renter's policy might. My advice: To the extent possible, avoid taking valuable personal items to school. Otherwise, keep the items in a secure location and out of sight so not to tempt thievery.

Student Safety Should Always Be on Your Mind

It is estimated that as many as 25 percent of injuries to young people happen while they are at school (Barrios, Jones, & Gallagher, 2007). As a responsible professional you need to make every effort to prevent accidents from happening to students while they are under your direct or even indirect (such as while you are walking in the hallways, across campus, in the parking lot or student drop-off area, and so forth) supervision requires your knowledge of potentially dangerous situations, your constant awareness and preparation, and knowledge of what to do if a situation arises. One of the things you can do is to become knowledgeable about any safe standards that have been developed either statewide or locally, especially as related to your curriculum area.

Teachers are responsible for preventing accidents and ensuring that the learning environment is as safe as possible. Nevertheless, accidents and resulting injuries do occur to students at school. During recess, a second-grade student falls and lands on a lawn sprinkler head that had not gone down when the system shut off, putting her eye out. During a language arts lesson, a student is injured by glass from a falling windowpane when the teacher attempts to open a jammed window. During shop class, a student is badly burned from the explosion of an acetylene gas tank. A student in biology is helicoptered to the hospital after, on a dare, he devoured a triple-latex-injected preserved bullfrog. So, you need to understand what you can do as a classroom teacher to prevent accidents from happening. And, you need to know what you should and should not do when an accident does happen. See the classroom safety rules and guidelines in Figure 2.2, and use the items as a basis for discussion with your classmates. The school in which you teach will, of course, have its own written rules and guidelines that may be more or less extensive than those presented here. Safety guidelines for a shop class, a gymnasium, or chemistry classroom and laboratory, for example, will be more extensive.

Figure 2.2 Safety procedures and guidelines for the classroom.

1. If an accident occurs, notify the school office immediately by telephoning or sending a pair of student runners to the office.

2. Give first aid *only* when necessary to save a minor's life or limb. When life or limb is not at risk, then follow school policy by referring the minor immediately to professional care. When immediate professional care is unavailable and you believe that immediate first aid is necessary, you can take prudent action, as if you were that child's parent or legal guardian. But you must be cautious and knowledgeable about what you are doing, so as to not cause further injury to the child.

3. Unless you are a licensed medical professional, you should *never* give medication to a minor, whether prescription or OTC. Refer to your school's policy on this. Be alert for students who have allergies or other medical problems, and be aware of what you can and must do if a particular student is having a medical problem while under your supervision.

4. For special situations such as in classrooms for teaching laboratory science, shop, home economics, and physical education, rules and procedures should be taught to the students, posted in a conspicuous place, and reviewed and rehearsed often.

5. When escorting students on a field trip, solicit adult volunteer help, even if the destination is only a short distance from the school. Unless otherwise specified in your school policies, a recommended guideline is one or more responsible adults for every 10 students.

6. Maintain a neatly organized classroom working environment, with aisles kept clear and books, coats, and backpacks in designated storage areas. In classrooms used for laboratory science and shop instruction in particular, students should not wear coats or any loose-fitting clothing that can easily knock over or become entangled in equipment.

7. Be aware of and enforce eye safety precautions and regulations regarding eye protection.

8. Avoid using flammable materials and alcohol burners. Use lighted candles and hot plates only with extreme care.

9. Maintain a well-supplied first aid kit in the classroom, even if you must supply it with your own funds.

10. With emergency procedures posted conspicuously in the classroom, be sure you know exactly what to do in emergency situations.

11. Every classroom should have an adequately charged ABC-type fire extinguisher readily available.

12. Use proper waste disposal procedures. Learn school district policies regarding disposal of various waste materials relevant to your classroom activities.

13. Maintain accurate labels on all drawers, cupboards, closets, and containers.

14. Students should never be encouraged and allowed to taste unknown substances.

15. Avoid having dangerous plants, animals, chemicals, and apparatus in the classroom.

16. Instruct students to *never* handle or bring dead animals into the classroom.

17. Handle pets with care and caution. For example, birds can carry psittacosis and salmonella bacteria. People should wash their hands thoroughly after handling bird feeders. Turtles and other animals also can carry salmonella bacteria. Dogs, rabbits, and other animals may harbor parasites. Some children are allergic to animal dander.

Figure 2.2   *continued*

18. Do not store heavy items on shelves above the heads of students.

19. Do not allow students to climb or to be in positions where they may fall.

20. Do not leave dangerously sharp objects, or those that may shatter, where students can obtain them without approval and supervision.

21. Avoid allowing students to overheat or to overexert themselves.

22. Never leave students unattended, for any reason, in the classroom, on the school campus, or while on a field trip.

23. Inspect electrical equipment for frayed cords and, if frayed, do not use until repaired.

24. Avoid overloading an electrical circuit. When in doubt, don't use it until it is checked and approved by maintenance personnel.

25. Disconnect electrical appliances, especially heating appliances, when they are not being used. Make sure to switch to off position before disconnecting or connecting any electrical appliance.

26. Avoid poking around the back of a computer, television monitor, projector equipment, or any electrical appliance when the appliance is plugged into an outlet.

27. Never touch an electrical cord with wet hands or when standing or leaning in water.

28. Avoid wrapping or coiling the cords of electrical appliances that are plugged in.

29. Keep magnets away from computers and other electronic devices.

30. Use extra caution when you or your students are using any mechanical equipment with moving parts.

31. Under no circumstances should human body fluids be used for science investigation or any other reason.

TEACHING STYLE

Teaching style is the way teachers teach, which includes their distinctive mannerisms complemented by their choices of teaching behaviors and strategies. A teacher's style affects the way that teacher presents information and interacts with the students. The manner and pattern of those interactions with students clearly determines a teacher's effectiveness—or lack thereof—in promoting student learning, positive attitudes about learning, and students' self-esteem.

A teacher's style is determined by the teacher's personal characteristics (especially the teacher's own preferred learning style), experiences, and knowledge of research findings about how people learn. Teaching style can be altered, intentionally or unintentionally, as a result of changes in any of those three areas.

The way teachers are taught to teach is a reflection of the expectations of U.S. culture. Teachers raised in a mainstream culture have elements of that culture embedded in their personal teaching approach. The selection of a particular teaching method reflects cultural values more than it argues for the superiority of the method. Some of these elements may need to be modified to meet the needs of students who have arrived from other cultures.

Díaz-Rico & Weed (2010), p. 287

Though there are other ways to label and to describe teaching styles, let's consider two contrasting styles—the **traditional style** (known also as the **conventional style**) and the **facilitating style** (see Table 2.1). Today's teacher must use aspects from each (i.e., be eclectic in style choice), but with a strong inclination toward the facilitating style. What I refer to as "traditional" and "facilitating" styles of teaching are often referred to in the literature as "didactic" and "constructivist" teaching, although constructivism (or "constructionism" as it is sometimes labeled) is a theory of learning rather than a precise method of teaching (Smerdon, Burkam, & Lee, 1999).

Multilevel Instruction, Individualized Instruction, and Differentiated Instruction: A Clarification of Terms

First of all, let's begin this section with clarification of what I, the author of this resource guide, mean by the terms *multilevel instruction, individualized instruction,* and *differentiated instruction.*

- **Multilevel instruction** refers to instruction that is targeted toward multiple levels of cognitive understanding and doing, and is the exact opposite of traditional, egalitarian based, "teaching to the middle."
- **Individualized instruction** is that designed specifically for a particular student learner (or sometimes for a small group of learners). It can also be referred to as **personalized instruction**.

The manner and pattern of a teacher's interactions with students clearly determines a teacher's effectiveness in promoting student learning, positive attitudes about learning, and students' self-esteem.

Table 2.1 A Contrast of Two Teaching Styles

Characteristic	Traditional Style	Facilitating Style
Teacher is:	Autocratic	Democratic
	Curriculum-centered	Student-centered
	Direct	Indirect
	Dominative	Interactive
	Formal	Informal
	Informative	Inquiry
	Prescriptive	Reflective
Classroom is:	Teacher-centered	Student-centered
	Linear (seats in rows and all facing front of room)	Grouped or circular with flexible arrangement
Instructional modes are:	Abstract learning	Concrete learning
	Teacher-centered discussion	Discussions
	Lectures	Peer and cross-age teaching
	Competitive learning	Collaborative and cooperative learning
	Some problem-solving	Problem solving
	Demonstrations by teacher from simple to complex	Student inquiries that begin with complex tasks and use instructional scaffolding and dialogue
	Transmission of information from teacher to students	Reciprocal teaching using a dialogue between the teacher and a small group of students, and then just among students

- **Differentiated instruction** is both multilevel and individualized; rather than fixed and targeted to a general recipient audience, it is flexible, variable, and adaptable in the processes used by and with students to reach desired ends.

Because, as discussed in Chapter 1, of increased student diversity in today's classrooms and because of pressure on schools and their teachers to connect learning experiences to educational standards and test preparation, to be most effective teachers today must use multilevel instruction, instruction that is individualized, personalized, and differentiated.

Students in your classroom have their own independent ways of knowing and learning. It is important

Table 2.2 Comparison of Three Theoretical Positions on Teaching Style

Theoretical Position	Philosophical Assumption About Learner's Mind	Main Focus in Teaching	Key Persons	Key Instructional Strategies
Romanticism-maturationism	neutral-passive to good-active	Additions of new ideas to a subconscious store of old ones	J. J. Rousseau S. Freud	Classic lecturing with rote memorization
Behaviorism	neutral-passive	Systematic changes to learner's environment to increase desired behaviors	J. Locke B. F. Skinner A. H. Thorndike R. Gagné J. Watson	Practice and reinforcement; workbook and drill exercises; programmed instruction
Cognitive-experimentalism, including constructivism	neutral-interactive	Facilitating learner's change in perceptions to become a more fully functioning self	J. Dewey L. Vygotsky J. Bruner J. Piaget A. W. Combs	Discovery, inquiry, project-centered teaching, cooperative learning, integrated curriculum

to attend to how each student best learns and where each student is developmentally—in other words, to *individualize both the content and the methods of learning.* And to do this effectively you must learn as much as you can about each of your students. In the words of Tomlinson (2005, p. 63), you must become "a student of your students."

In essence, although perhaps not as detailed as those prepared for special education students, at various times during the school year you will be developing personalized educational plans for each student. These may be prepared in collaboration with members of your teaching team. To accomplish this personalized instruction, you can use multilevel instruction. For example, while some students may be working independently of the teacher—that is, within the facilitating mode—others may be receiving direct instruction—that is, more within the traditional (or conventional) mode.

When personalizing and integrating student learning, multilevel instruction is an important and useful, perhaps even necessary, strategy. Project-centered teaching is an instructional method that easily allows for the provision of multilevel instruction.

The Theoretical Origins of Teaching Styles and Their Relation to Constructivism

Constructivism and the integration of curriculum are certainly not new concepts. The importance of constructivism and of curriculum integration approaches are found, for example, in the writings of Arthur W. Combs (1962) and Jean Piaget (1970), and a century or more ago in the writings of John Dewey (1902, 1910).

Instructional styles are deeply rooted in certain theoretical assumptions about learners and their development, and although it is beyond the scope of my intent for this resource guide to explore deeply those assumptions, three major theoretical positions with research findings, each of which is based on certain philosophical and psychological assumptions, suggest different ways of working with young people. The theoretical positions are described in the next three paragraphs. See Table 2.2.

Tied to the theoretical position of **romanticism-maturationism** is the assumption that the learner's mind is neutral-passive to good-active, and the main focus in teaching should be the addition of new ideas to a subconscious store of old ones. Key instructional strategies include classic lecturing with rote memorization.

Tied to the theoretical position of **behaviorism** is the assumption that the learner's mind is neutral-passive with innate reflexes and needs, and the main focus in teaching should be on the successive, systematic changes in the learner's environment to increase the possibilities of desired behavior responses. Key instructional strategies include practice and reinforcement as in workbook drill activities and programmed instruction.

Tied to the theoretical position of **cognitive-experimentalism** (including **constructivism** and **constructionism**) is the assumption that the learner is a neutral-interactive, purposive individual in simultaneous interaction with physical and biological environments. The main focus in teaching should be on facilitating the learner's gain and construction of new perceptions that lead to desired behavioral changes and ultimately to a more fully functioning individual. [Note: A person with a "fully functioning self" can be described only in terms of ideal behavior. As explained by Early C. Kelley, those characteristics are as follows: thinks well of himself and of others; sees his stake in others; sees himself as a part of a world in movement—in process of becoming; sees the value of mistakes; develops and holds human values and knows of no other way to live except in keeping with his values; sees himself as cast in a creative role (Combs, 1962, pp. 17–20).] Key instructional strategies include discovery, inquiry, project-centered teaching, cooperative and social-interactive learning, and integrated curriculum.

To be most effective with a diverse group of students, a teacher must be eclectic—but with a strong emphasis toward cognitive-experimentalism-constructivism-constructionism because of its divergence in learning and the importance given to learning as a change in perceptions—utilizing at appropriate times the best of strategies and knowledgeable instructor behaviors.

The eclectic teacher cannot be classified within any style dichotomy, such as "direct vs. indirect," "formal vs. informal," "traditional vs. progressive," or "didactic vs. facilitative."

Now, to further your understanding of teaching styles, and depending on course instructions, complete Exercises 2.2, *Using Observation of Classroom Interaction to Analyze One Teacher's Style* and 2.3, *Using a Questionnaire to Develop a Profile and a Statement About My Own Emerging Teaching Style,* found at the end of this chapter. After you finish those exercises, we proceed to the topic of commitment and professionalism.

COMMITMENT AND PROFESSIONALISM

The classroom teacher is expected to demonstrate commitment both to the school's stated mission and to the emotional, physical, social, and intellectual development of the students. Competent teachers not only expect and receive positive results in learning from their students while in the classroom, but also are interested and involved in the activities of the students outside the classroom and are willing to sacrifice personal time to give students attention and guidance.

Noninstructional Responsibilities

The aspects of the teacher as a decision maker with professional commitments take on a very real dimension when you consider specific noninstruction-related and instruction-related responsibilities of the classroom teacher. Shown in Figure 2.3 are 13 categories of items that should alert you to the many noninstructional matters with which you should become familiar, especially during your first year of teaching. Their importance and the amount of time they require are often underestimated by beginning teachers.

> There seems to be no end to the duties required of teachers. Is this the career that a 22-year-old English major envisions when he or she contemplates the joys of sharing his or her passion with new students?
>
> D. A. Heller (2004, p.4)

Figure 2.3 Noninstructional responsibilities of the classroom teacher.

1. Knowledgeable about activities of interest to students.
2. Familiarity with the school campus and community.
3. Acquainted with members of the faculty and the support staff.
4. Knowledgeable about school and district policies.
5. Familiar with the backgrounds of the students.
6. Knowledgeable about procedures for such routine matters as: planning and scheduling of before- and after-school activities; restroom regulations; distribution and collection of textbooks and other school materials; class dismissal; ordering of supplies; fire drills and severe weather; daily attendance records; school assemblies; sharing of instructional space with other teachers; arranging for and preparing displays for common areas of the school.
7. Your expected role in teaching common elements of the curriculum, such as reading, writing, thinking, social skills, and study skills.
8. Your expected role in the advisory or home base program.
9. Classroom duties such as: maintaining a cheerful, pleasant, and safe environment; obtaining materials needed for each lesson; keeping supplies orderly; supervising students who are helpers.
10. Your expected role in the parent–teacher organization and other community participation activities.
11. The many conferences that will be needed, such as those between teacher and teacher, teacher and student, teacher and parent or guardian, teacher, student, and parent/guardian, teacher and administrator, and teacher and community representative.
12. Professional meetings, such as those of the interdisciplinary team, other school and district committees, parent–teacher and community groups, and local, regional, state, and national professional organizations.
13. Time to relax and enjoy family, friends, and hobbies.

One item on the list in Figure 2.3 (item 9) includes the responsibility of providing a safe environment, both psychological and physical. The psychological aspect is discussed later in this chapter and continues in Chapter 3, and the physical safety aspect was discussed earlier.

Figure 2.4   Instructional responsibilities of the classroom teacher.

1. Becoming knowledgeable about the expected target learning outcomes.
2. Planning units and lessons.
3. Learning the needs and interests of the students so that lessons will reflect those needs and interests.
4. Incorporating relevant learning styles and learning modalities into the lessons.
5. Reading student papers.
6. Assessing and recording student progress.
7. Preparing the classroom.
8. Providing classroom instruction.
9. Thinking about professional growth and development, which may include attending university courses, attending workshops and other presentations offered by the school district or professional organizations, and reading professional literature.
10. Developing an effective classroom management system.
11. Becoming reacquainted with the developmental characteristics of students of the applicable age.
12. Learning the backgrounds of students with special problems who might cause concerns in the learning environment.
13. Developing strategies and plans for cross-age tutoring, peer coaching, cooperative learning, project-based learning, and other developmentally appropriate learning strategies.
14. Identifying resources and sources.
15. Devoting time to team planning.
16. Holding conferences with individual students and parents and guardians.

Instructional Responsibilities

The items illustrated in Figure 2.4 categorize the instructional responsibilities you will have as a classroom teacher. The 16 categories of instructional responsibilities are the primary focus of study of the remainder of this resource guide. After you have reviewed both the lists of instructional and noninstructional responsibilities of the classroom teacher, complete Exercise 2.4, *Reviewing the Professional Responsibilities of a First-Year Teacher* (end of this chapter), which is a model of a form of cooperative learning known as "jigsaw."

IDENTIFYING AND BUILDING YOUR INSTRUCTIONAL COMPETENCIES

The overall purpose of this resource guide is to assist you in building your instructional competencies so you can be a most effective professional. In order to do that, we need a starting place and this is it: the identification and presentation of 22 specific competencies. [Note: The following list of 22 competencies has evolved from its earliest inception as a simple (not annotated) listing of 20 "Characteristics of the Competent Teacher" (Kim & Kellough, 1983) to the current annotated list of 22 characteristics of the competent teacher (Kim & Kellough, 1991; Kellough, 1994; Kellough & Roberts, 1994; Kellough & Kellough, 1999). You are encouraged to compare the categories of responsibilities of this chapter and the 22 competencies listed next with the teacher competency standards used by your own state for teacher licensing.]

Characteristics of the Competent Classroom Teacher: An Annotated List

Please do not feel overwhelmed by the list; it may well be that no teacher expertly models all the characteristics that follow. The characteristics do, however, represent an ideal to strive for. You will continue to reflect on and build upon these competencies through your study of the remaining chapters of this book and, indeed, throughout your professional career.

1. *The teacher is knowledgeable about the subject matter.* You should have both historical understanding and current knowledge of the structure of the subject content you are expected to teach and of the facts, principles, concepts, and skills needed for that subject matter.

2. *The teacher is an "educational broker."* You will learn where and how to discover information about content you are expected to teach. You cannot know everything there is to know about each subject or topic—indeed, you will not always be able to predict all that is learned—but you should become knowledgeable about where and how to best research it and how to assist your students in developing those same skills.

3. *The teacher is an active member of professional organizations, reads professional journals, dialogues with colleagues, and maintains currency in methodology and about the students and the subject content the teacher is expected to teach.* Although this resource guide offers valuable information about teaching and learning, it is much closer to the start of your professional career than it is to the end. As a teacher, you are a learner among learners. Plan to spend your career in a perpetual mode of

reflection and learning through workshops, advanced course work, coaching and training, reading and study, and collaboration with and role modeling of significant and more experienced colleagues, much as is discussed in Chapter 11 of this resource guide.

4. *The teacher understands the processes of learning.* You will ensure that students understand classroom procedures, your expectations, and the lesson's target objectives. Students must feel welcome in your classroom and involved in learning activities, and they should have some control over the pacing of their own learning. Furthermore, when preparing your lessons, you will (a) consider the unique learning characteristics of each student; (b) see that content is presented in reasonably small doses—and in a logical and coherent sequence—while using visual, verbal, tactile, and kinesthetic learning activities with opportunities for coached practice and reinforcement; and (c) scaffold the learning (providing temporary support) by frequently checking for student comprehension to ensure that each student is getting it.

5. *The teacher uses effective modeling behaviors.* Your own behaviors must be consistent with those expected of your students. If, for example, you want your students to demonstrate regular and punctual attendance, to have their work done on time, to have their materials each day for learning, to demonstrate cooperative behavior and respect for others, to maintain an open and inquisitive mind and attitude, to demonstrate critical thinking, and to use proper communication skills, then you will do likewise, modeling those same behaviors and attitudes for the students. As a classroom teacher, you serve as a very important role model for your students. Whether you realize it or not, your behavior sends important messages to students that complement curriculum content. You serve your students well when you model inclusive and collaborative approaches to learning. The importance of effective modeling is one of several recurring themes in this resource guide.

6. *The teacher is open to change, willing to take risks, and willing to be held accountable.* If there were no difference between what is and what can be, then formal schooling would be of little value. A competent teacher knows not only of historical and traditional values and knowledge, but also of the value of change. The teacher thus is willing to carefully plan and experiment, to move between that which is known and that which is not. Realizing that little of value is ever achieved without a certain amount of risk and employment of personal strength of convictions, the competent teacher stands ready to be held accountable, as the teacher undoubtedly will be, for assuming such risks. As stated so clearly elsewhere, "no coward ever got the Great Teacher Award" (Wassermann, 1999).

7. *The teacher is nondiscriminatory toward gender, sexual preference, ethnicity, skin color, religion, physical disabilities,* *socioeconomic status, learning disabilities, national origin, or any other personal characteristic.* Among other things, this means no sexual innuendoes, religious or ethnic jokes, or racial slurs. It means being cognizant of how teachers, male or female, black or white, heterosexual or homosexual, U.S. born or not, Christian or other, knowingly or unknowingly, historically have mistreated certain students, and of how to avoid those same errors in your own behaviors. It means learning about and attending to the needs of individual students in your classroom. It means maintaining high, although not necessarily identical, expectations for all students.

8. *The teacher organizes the classroom and plans lessons carefully.* Long-range plans, no matter whether they include interdisciplinary thematic units or standard units, and daily lessons, no matter whether student centered or teacher centered, are prepared thoughtfully, reflected on, revised, and competently implemented with creative, motivating, and effective strategies and skill. Much of this resource guide is devoted specifically to assisting in your development of this competency.

9. *The teacher is a capable communicator.* The competent teacher uses thoughtfully selected words, carefully planned questions, expressive voice inflections, useful pauses, meaningful gestures, and productive and nonconfusing body language. Some of these expressions are carefully and thoughtfully planned during the preactive phase of instruction, and others, through practice and reflection, become second-nature skills. Throughout this book you will find useful suggestions for your development of this competency.

10. *The teacher functions effectively as a decision maker.* The exemplary classroom is a complex place, busy with fast-paced activities. In a single day you may engage in a thousand or more interpersonal exchanges with students, to say nothing about the numerous exchanges possible with the many adults with whom you will be in contact. The competent teacher is in control of classroom events rather than controlled by them. The teacher initiates, rather than merely reacts, is proactive, and is in control of interactions, having learned how to manage time to analyze and develop effective interpersonal behaviors.

11. *The teacher is in a perpetual learning mode, striving to further develop a repertoire of teaching strategies.* Competent teachers are good students, continuing their own learning by reflecting on and assessing their work, attending workshops, studying the work of others, and communicating with students, parents and guardians, and colleagues.

12. *The teacher demonstrates concern for the safety and health of the students.* The competent teacher consistently models safety procedures, ensuring precautions necessary to protect the health and emotional and physical safety of the students. The teacher strives to maintain a comfortable room temperature with adequate ventilation and to

prevent safety hazards in the classroom. Students who are ill are encouraged to stay home and to get well. If a teacher suspects a child is ill while at school, then school policy should be followed, which in all likelihood means notifying the school's office which in turn acts depending on the nature of the child's situation, or dialing 9-1-1 for immediate professional help.

If a teacher suspects a student may be suffering from neglect or abuse at home, the teacher appropriately and promptly acts upon that suspicion by following the school's written policy. If there is none, then telephone 1-800-4-1-CHILD (1-800-422-4453, the National Child Abuse Hotline) or use the hotline for your own state. Proof of abuse is not necessary. (See Figure 8.2, Chapter 8, for characteristics of children who may be abused or neglected).

13. *The teacher demonstrates optimism for the learning of every student, while providing a constructive and positive environment for learning.* Both common sense and research tell us clearly that students enjoy and learn better from a teacher who is positive and optimistic, encouraging, nurturing, and happy, rather than from a teacher who is negative and pessimistic, discouraging, uninterested, and grumpy.

14. *The teacher demonstrates confidence in each student's ability to learn.* For a student, nothing at school is more satisfying than a teacher who demonstrates confidence in that student's abilities. Unfortunately, for some students, a teacher's show of confidence may be the only positive indicator that student ever receives. Each of us can recall with admiration a teacher (or other significant person) who demonstrated confidence in our ability to accomplish seemingly formidable tasks. A competent teacher demonstrates this confidence with each and every student. This does not mean you must personally like every student with whom you will ever come into contact; it does mean that you accept each one as a person of dignity and who is worthy of receiving your respect and the benefits of your professional training and experiences.

15. *The teacher is skillful and fair in the employment of strategies for the assessment of student learning.* The competent teacher is knowledgeable about the importance of providing immediate, intensive intervention when learning problems become apparent, implementing appropriate learning assessment tools while avoiding the abuse of power afforded by the assessment process.

16. *The teacher is skillful in working with parents and guardians, colleagues, administrators, and the support staff and maintains and nurtures friendly and ethical professional relationships.* Teachers, parents and guardians, administrators, cooks, custodians, secretaries, school bus drivers, security personnel, and other adults of the school community all share a common purpose, and that is to serve the education of the students. It is done best when they do it knowledgeably and cooperatively.

17. *The teacher demonstrates continuing interest in professional responsibilities, challenges, and opportunities.* Knowing that ultimately each and every school activity has an effect upon the classroom, the competent teacher assumes an active interest in the school community. The purpose of the school is to serve the education of the students, and the classroom is the primary, but not only, place where this occurs. Every committee meeting, school event, advisory meeting, faculty meeting, school board meeting, office, program, and any other planned function related to school life shares in the ultimate purpose of better serving the education of the students who attend that school.

18. *The teacher exhibits a wide range of interests.* This includes interest in the activities of the students and the many aspects of the school and its surrounding community. The competent teacher is interesting because of his or her interests; a teacher with varied interests more often motivates and captures the attention of more students. A teacher with no interests outside his or her subject area and the classroom is likely to be viewed as an exceedingly dull person by students.

19. *The teacher shares a healthy sense of humor.* The positive effects of appropriate humor (i.e., humor that is not self-deprecating or disrespectful of others) on learning are well established: increase in immune system activity and decrease in stress-producing hormones; drop in the pulse rate; reduction of feelings of anxiety, tension, and stress; activation of T-cells for the immune system, antibodies that fight against harmful microorganisms, and gamma interferon, a hormone that fights viruses and regulates cell growth; and an increase in blood oxygen. Because of these effects, humor is a stimulant not only to healthy living, but to creativity and higher level thinking. As they should, students appreciate and learn more from a teacher who shares a sense of humor and laughs with them. Additionally, considerable evidence exists to show the importance of a healthy sense of humor to the development of a teacher's resilience and career longevity (Bobek, 2002).

20. *The teacher is quick to recognize a student who may be in need of special attention.* A competent teacher is alert to recognize any student who demonstrates behaviors indicating a need for special attention, guidance, or counseling. The teacher knows how and where to refer the student, doing so with minimal class disruption and without embarrassment to the student. For example, a pattern of increasingly poor attendance or of steady negative-attention-seeking behaviors are two of the more obvious early signals of the student who is potentially at risk of dropping out of school.

21. *The teacher makes specific and frequent efforts to demonstrate how the subject content may be related and relevant to the students' lives.* A potentially dry and dull topic is made significant and alive when taught by a competent teacher. Regardless of topic, somewhere competent

teachers are teaching that topic, and one of the significant characteristics of their effectiveness is they make the topic alive and relevant to themselves and to their students. Time and again studies point out what should be obvious: Students do not learn much from dull, meaningless "drill and kill" exercises and assignments. Such uninspired teaching may be at the root of the reason why too many young people are dropping out of formal schooling. Obtaining ideas from professional journals, attending workshops, communicating with colleagues either personally or via e-bulletin boards and web sites, and using project-based and interdisciplinary thematic instruction are ways of discovering how to make a potentially dry and boring topic interesting and alive for students (and for the teacher).

22. *The teacher is reliable.* The competent teacher can be relied on to fulfill professional responsibilities, promises, and commitments. A teacher who cannot be relied on is quick to lose credibility with the students and with colleagues and administrators. Regardless of a teacher's credential qualifications and potential for effectiveness, an unreliable teacher is an incompetent teacher.

Specific teacher behaviors are discussed in the following section; guidelines and resources to assist you in your development of these competencies permeate this resource guide.

TEACHER BEHAVIORS NECESSARY TO FACILITATE STUDENT LEARNING

Your ability to perform your instructional responsibilities effectively is directly dependent upon your knowledge of students and how they best learn and your knowledge of and the quality of your teaching skills. Directly related to teacher competencies discussed in the preceding section are specific teacher behaviors that are necessary to facilitate student learning. Development of your strategy repertoire along with your skills in using specific strategies should be ongoing throughout your teaching career. To be most effective, you need a large repertoire from which to select a specific strategy for a particular goal with a distinctive group of students. In addition, you need skill in using that strategy. Like intelligence, teaching style is neither absolutely inherited nor fixed, but continues to develop and emerge throughout one's professional career.

Three Basic Rules for Becoming a Competent Teacher

First, you must know why you have selected a particular strategy. An unknowing teacher is likely to use the teaching strategy most common in college classes—the lecture. However, as many beginning teachers have discovered

the hard way, the traditional lecture is seldom, if ever, an effective or appropriate way to instruct students in most K–12 grades. As a rule, unlike many college and university students, not many K–12 students are strong auditory learners by preference or by adeptness. For most of them, learning by sitting and listening is difficult. Instead, they learn best when physically (hands-on) and intellectually (minds-on) active—that is, when using tactile and kinesthetic experiences, touching objects, feeling shapes and textures, moving objects, and when together they are able to talk about and share what they are learning, that is, by learning collaboratively.

Second, basic teacher behaviors create the conditions needed to enable students to think and to learn, whether the learning is a further understanding of concepts, the internalization of attitudes and values, the development of cognitive processes, or the actuating of the most complex behaviors. The basic teacher behaviors are those that produce the following results: (a) students are physically and mentally engaged in the learning activities, (b) instructional time is efficiently used, and (c) classroom distractions and interruptions are minimal.

Third, the effectiveness with which a teacher carries out the basic behaviors can be measured by how well the students learn.

The basic teacher behaviors that facilitate student learning, discussed in detail next, are as follows: structuring the learning environment, accepting and sharing instructional accountability, demonstrating withitness and overlapping, providing a variety of motivating and challenging activities, modeling appropriate behaviors, facilitating student acquisition of data, creating a psychologically safe environment, clarifying whenever necessary, using periods of silence, and questioning thoughtfully.

Facilitating Behaviors and Instructional Strategies: A Clarification

Clearly at least some of the 10 basic behaviors are also instructional strategies. Questioning is one example. The difference is that whereas the behaviors must be in place for the most effective teaching to occur, strategies are more or less discretionary; that is, they are pedagogical techniques from which you may select but may not be obligated to use. For example, questioning and the use of silence are fundamental teaching behaviors whereas lecturing and showing videos are not. Thus, your task is twofold: (1) develop your awareness of and skills in using the fundamental teaching behaviors and (2) develop your repertoire and skills in selecting and using appropriate instructional strategies.

Starting now and continuing throughout your teaching career, you will want to evaluate your developing competency for each of the 10 fundamental facilitating behaviors and improve in areas where you need help. Consider the following descriptions and examples, and discuss them with your classmates. [Note: The meaning of key terms may be found in the glossary of this resource guide; additional discussion of key strategies may be found via its index.]

Structuring the Learning Environment

Structuring the learning environment means establishing an intellectual, psychological, and physical environment that enables all students to act and react productively. Specifically, you:

- Attend to the organization of the classroom as a learning laboratory to establish a positive, safe, and efficient environment for student learning.
- Establish and maintain clearly understood classroom procedures, definitions, instructions, and expectations. Help students to clarify the learning expectations and to establish clearly understood learning objectives.
- Help students assume tasks and responsibilities, thereby empowering them in their learning.
- Organize the students, helping them to organize their learning. Help students in the identification and understanding of time and resource constraints. Provide instructional scaffolds, helping students connect what is being learned with what the students already know or think they know and have experienced.
- Plan and implement techniques for schema building, such as providing content and process outlines, visual diagrams, and opportunities for thinking process mapping.
- Use techniques for students' metacognitive development, such as **think-pair-share**, in which students are asked to think about an idea, share thoughts about it with a partner, and then share the pair's thoughts with the entire class; **think-write-pair-share**, in which each student writes ideas about the new word and then shares in pairs before sharing with the entire class; and **jigsaw**, a cooperative learning strategy in which individuals or small groups of students are given responsibilities for separate tasks that lead to a bigger task or understanding, thereby putting together parts to make a whole (as done in this chapter with Exercise 2.4). [The jigsaw approach was originated by Aronson, Blaney, Stephan, Sikes, and Snapp (1978), followed by a modified version called Jigsaw II (Slavin, 1980).]
- Plan units and lessons that have clear and concise beginnings and endings with at least some of the planning done collaboratively with the students.
- Provide frequent summary reviews, often by using student self-assessment of what is being learned. Structure and facilitate ongoing formal and informal discussion based on a shared understanding of the rules of discourse.

Accepting and Sharing Instructional Accountability

While holding students accountable for their learning, the teacher is willing to be held accountable for the effectiveness of the learning process and outcomes (the "locus of control" as discussed at the start of this chapter). Specifically, you:

- Assume a responsibility for professional decision making and the risks associated with that responsibility. Share some responsibility for decision making and risk taking with the students. A primary goal in the students' education must be to see that students become accountable for themselves as learners and as citizens. Teachers are advised to work with their students as partners in their learning and development. One dimension of the partnership is shared accountability. One effective way of doing that is by using student portfolios.
- Communicate clearly to parents/guardians, administrators, and colleagues.
- Communicate to students that the accomplishment of learning goals and objectives is a responsibility they share with you.
- Plan exploratory activities that engage students in the learning.
- Provide continuous cues for desired learning behaviors and incentives contingent upon desired performance, such as grades, points, rewards, and privileges. Establish a clearly understood and continuous program of assessment that includes reflection and self-assessment.
- Provide opportunities for the students to demonstrate their learning, to refine and explore their questions, to inquire, and to share their thinking and results.

Demonstrating Withitness and Overlapping

First described by Jacob Kounin (1970), **withitness** and **overlapping** are separate but closely related behaviors. Withitness is the teacher's awareness of the whole group (i.e., the ability to remain alert in the classroom, to spot quickly and redirect potential student misbehavior, which is analogous to having "eyes in the back of your head"). Overlapping (or multitasking) is the ability to attend to several matters simultaneously. Specifically, you:

- Attend to the entire class while working with one student or with a small group of students, communicating this awareness with eye contact, hand gestures, body position and language, and clear but private verbal cues.
- Continually and simultaneously monitor all classroom activities to keep students at their tasks and to provide students with assistance and resources.
- Continue monitoring the class during any distraction, such as when a visitor enters the classroom or while the students are on a field trip.

- Demonstrate an understanding of when comprehension checks and instructional transitions are appropriate or needed.
- Dwell on one topic only as long as necessary for the students' understanding.
- Quickly intervene and redirect potential undesirable student behavior.
- Refocus or shift activities for a student when that student's attention begins to fade.

Consider the follow guidelines for developing classroom withitness.

- Avoid spending too much time with any one student or group; in classes of 20 or more students longer than 30 seconds may be approaching "too much time."
- Avoid turning your back to all or a portion of the students, such as when writing on the writing board.
- If two or more errant behaviors are occurring simultaneously in different locations, attend to the most serious first, while giving the other(s) a nonverbal gesture showing your awareness (e.g., by eye contact) and displeasure (e.g., with a frown).
- Involve all students in the act, not just one student or small group. Avoid concentrating on only those who appear most interested or responsive, sometimes referred to as the "chosen few."
- Keep students alert by calling on them randomly, asking questions and calling on an answerer, circulating from group to group during team learning activities, and frequently checking on the progress of individual students.
- Maintain constant visual surveillance of the entire class, even when talking to or working with an individual or small group of students and when meeting a classroom visitor at the door.
- Move around the classroom. Be on top of potential misbehavior and quietly redirect student attention before the misbehavior occurs or gets out of control.
- Try, during whole-class direct instruction, to establish eye contact with each student about once every minute. It initially may sound impossible to do, but it is not; it is a skill that can be developed with practice.

A prerequisite to being with it is the skill to attend to more than one matter at a time. This is referred to as overlapping ability, which today is called **multitasking**. The teacher with overlapping skills uses body language, body position, and hand gestures to communicate with students. Consider the following examples.

- Rather than bringing their papers and problems to her desk, the teacher expects students to remain seated and to raise their hands as the teacher circulates in the room monitoring and attending to individual students.

- The teacher takes care of attendance while visually or verbally monitoring the students during their warm-up activity.
- While attending to a messenger who has walked into the room, the teacher demonstrates verbally or by gestures that the teacher expects the students to continue their work.
- While working in a small group, a student raises a hand to get the teacher's attention. The teacher, while continuing to work with another group of students, signals with a hand gesture the awareness that the student wants attention and the intention to get to the student soon.
- Without missing a beat in her or his talk, the teacher aborts the potentially disruptive behavior of a student by gesturing, making eye contact, or moving closer to the student (using what is referred to as proximity control).

Providing a Variety of Motivating and Challenging Activities

The effective teacher uses a variety of activities that motivate and challenge all students to work to the utmost of their abilities and that engage and challenge the preferred learning styles and learning capacities of more of the students more of the time. Specifically, you:

- Demonstrate optimism toward each student's ability.
- Demonstrate an unwavering expectation that each student will work to the best of that student's ability.
- Show pride, optimism, and enthusiasm in learning, thinking, and teaching.
- View teaching and learning as an organic and reciprocal process that extends well beyond that which can be referred to as the traditional 2 by 4 by 6 curriculum—that is, a curriculum that is bound by the two covers of the textbook, the four walls of the classroom, and the six hours of the school day.
- Collaborate with the students to plan exciting and interesting learning activities, including those that engage the students' natural interest in the mysterious and the novel.

Modeling Appropriate Behaviors

Effective teachers model the very behaviors expected of their students. Specifically, you:

- Are prompt in returning student papers and offer comments that provide instructive and encouraging feedback.
- Arrive promptly in the classroom and demonstrate on-task behaviors for the entire class meeting, just as is expected of the students.
- Demonstrate respect for all students. For example, you do not interrupt when a student is showing

rational thinking, even though you may disagree with or frown upon the words used or the direction of the students' thinking.

- Demonstrate that making "errors" is a natural event while learning and during problem solving, and readily admit and correct mistakes you have made.
- Model and emphasize the skills, attitudes, and values of higher order intellectual processes. Demonstrate rational problem-solving skills and explain to the students the processes being engaged while problem solving.
- Model professionalism by spelling correctly, using proper grammar, and writing clearly and legibly.
- Practice communication that is clear, precise, and to the point. For example, use "I" when referring to yourself, and "we" when "we" is meant. Rather than responding to student contributions with simply "good" or "okay," tell specifically what about the response was good, or what made it okay.
- Practice moments of silence (see Using Periods of Silence that follows), thus modeling thoughtfulness, reflectiveness, and restraint of impulsiveness.
- Realize that students are also models for other students, reinforce appropriate student behaviors, and intervene when behaviors are inappropriate.

Facilitating Student Acquisition of Data

The teacher makes sure data are accessible to students as input they can process. Specifically, you:

- Create a responsive classroom environment with direct learning experiences.
- Ensure that major ideas receive proper attention and emphasis.

- Ensure that sources of information are readily available to students for their use.
- Select books, media, and materials that facilitate student learning.
- Ensure to the extent you can that equipment and materials are readily available for students to use.
- Identify and use resources beyond the walls of the classroom and the boundaries of the school campus.
- Provide clear and specific instructions.
- Provide feedback and feedback mechanisms about each student's performance and progress.
- Encourage students to organize and maintain devices to self-monitor their progress in learning and thinking.
- Select anchoring (also called model or benchmark) examples of student work that help students bridge what is being learned with what they already know and have experienced.
- Serve as a resource person and use collaborative and cooperative learning, thus regarding students as resources too.

Creating a Psychologically Safe Environment

To encourage the positive development of student self-esteem, to provide a psychologically safe learning environment, and to encourage the most creative thought and behavior, the teacher provides a positive, attractive, and stimulating classroom environment and appropriate nonjudgmental responses. (The next chapter, Chapter 3, is devoted to this theme.) Specifically, you:

- Avoid negative criticism. Criticism is often a negative value judgment, and "when a teacher responds to a student's ideas or actions with such negative words as

Serving as a resource person, the competent teacher plans within the lessons activities and behaviors that show respect for the experiences and ideas of individual students, thus regarding students as resources, too.

'poor,' 'incorrect,' or 'wrong,' the response tends to signal inadequacy or disapproval and ends the student's thinking about the task" (Costa, 1991, p. 54).

- Frequently use minimal reinforcement (i.e., nonjudgmental acceptance behaviors, such as nodding head, writing a student's response on the board, or saying "I understand"). Whereas elaborate or strong praise is generally unrelated to student achievement, minimal reinforcement, using words such as "right," "okay," "uh-huh," and "thank you," does correlate with achievement.

However, as implied in the discussion about modeling, be careful with a too frequent and thereby ineffective and even damaging use of the single word "good" following student contributions during a class discussion. Use the word only when the contribution was truly that—good—and better yet, say not only "good" but tell what specifically was good about the student's contribution. That provides a more powerful reinforcement by demonstrating that you truly heard the student's contribution and thus indeed thought it was good.

- Infrequently use elaborate or strong praise. Beyond the primary grades, teacher praise, a positive value judgment, has little or no value as a form of positive reinforcement. When praise is used for young and older adolescents it should be mild, private, and for student accomplishment, rather than for effort; for each child, the frequency in using praise should be gradually reduced. When praise is reduced, a more diffused sociometric pattern develops; that is, more of the children become directly and productively involved in the learning. Praise should be simple and direct, delivered in a natural voice without dramatizing (Good & Brophy, 2008).

Probably no statement in this resource guide raises more eyebrows than the statement that praise for most children beyond primary years has little or no value as a form of positive reinforcement. After all, praise may well motivate some people. However, at what cost? Praise and encouragement are often confused and considered to be the same (see Figure 2.5) but they are not, and they do not have the same long-term results. [Note:

Some researchers distinguish between praise that is "ineffective" and praise that is "effective," with the latter considered synonymous with the term "encouragement." For clarity, we prefer to use simply the terms praise (which is generally ineffective) versus encouragement (which is effective).] This is explained as follows:

> For many years there has been a great campaign for the virtues of praise in helping young people gain a positive self-concept and improve their behavior. This is another time when we must "beware of what works." Praise may inspire some students to improve their behavior. The problem is that they become pleasers and approval "junkies." These children (and later these adults) develop self-concepts that are totally dependent on the opinions of others. Other children resent and rebel against praise, either because they don't want to live up to the expectations of others or because they fear they can't compete with those who seem to get praise so easily. The alternative that considers long-range effects is encouragement. The long-range effect of encouragement is self-confidence. The long-range effect of praise is dependence on others. (Nelsen, 1987, p. 103)

Furthermore, some students (and perhaps some unknowing teachers, too) wrongly assume that intellectual ability is a fixed trait, and thus are more likely to seek and perform tasks that prove their intelligence and avoid ones that they might have difficulty with (Dweck, 2007). As teacher, your job is to assure students they can develop their intellectual ability through effort and education, thus encouraging them to assume challenges and learn from them. Praising students for effort encourages them.

In summary, be cautious with the use of praise, but *do* reinforce student efforts by recognizing specific personal accomplishments (Marzano, Pickering, & Pollock, 2001).

- Perceive your classroom as the place where you work and where students learn, and make that place of work and the tools available a place of pride—as positive, stimulating, and practical as possible.
- Plan within the lessons behaviors that show respect for the cultures, experiences, and ideas of individual students.
- Provide positive individual student attention as often as possible. Write sincere, reinforcing personalized

Figure 2.5 Examples of statements of praise versus encouragement.

Statement of Praise	*Statement of Encouragement*
1. Your painting is excellent.	1. It is obvious that you enjoy painting.
2. I am delighted that you behaved so well on our class field trip.	2. I am so delighted that we all enjoyed the field trip.
3. You did a good job on those word problems.	3. I can tell that you have been working and are enjoying it more.
4. Your oral report on your project was well done.	4. I can tell that you got really interested in your topic for the oral report on your project.
5. Great answer, Hannah!	5. Hannah, your answer shows that you gave a lot of thought to the question.

comments on student papers. Provide incentives and rewards for student accomplishments.

- Use nonverbal cues to show awareness, empathy, and acceptance of individual students. Use paraphrasing and reflective listening. Use empathic acceptance of a student's expression of feelings; demonstrate by words and gestures that you understand the student's position and that you truly care about how the student is doing. Perceiving the teacher as a truly caring adult can go a long way in supplying a young person with motivation to learn (Littky, 2004; Murdock & Miller, 2003).

Clarifying Whenever Necessary

Your responding behavior seeks further elaboration from a student about that student's idea or comprehension. Specifically, you:

- Help students to connect new content to that previously learned. Help students relate content of a lesson to students' other school and nonschool experiences. Help students make learning connections between disciplines.
- Politely invite a student to be more specific, to elaborate on or rephrase an idea, or to provide a concrete illustration of an idea.
- Provide frequent opportunity for summary reviews.
- Repeat or paraphrase a student's response, allowing the student to correct any other person's misinterpretation of what the student said or implied.
- Select instructional strategies that help students correct their prior notions about a topic.

Using Periods of Silence

Competent teachers use periods of silence in the classroom. Specifically, you:

- Actively listen when a student is talking.
- Allow sufficient think time, sometimes as long as 7 seconds (Rowe, 1974; Tobin, 1984, 1986, 1987), after asking a question or posing a problem.
- Keep silent when students are working quietly or attending to a visual display, and maintain classroom control with use of nonverbal signals and indirect intervention strategies.
- Pause while talking to allow for thinking and reflection.
- Use teacher silence, supported by body language and nonverbal gesturing (i.e., a nod of the head, a thumbs up), to stimulate group discussion.

Questioning Thoughtfully

Thoughtfully worded questions induce learning and stimulate thinking and the development of students' thinking skills. Specifically, you:

- Encourage student questioning without judging the quality or relevancy of a student's question. Attend to student questions, and respond and encourage other students to respond, often by building upon the content of a student's questions and student responses.
- Help students develop their own questioning skills and provide opportunities for students to explore their own ideas, obtain data, and find answers to their own questions and solutions to their problems.
- Plan questioning sequences that elicit a variety of thinking skills and that maneuver students to higher levels of thinking and doing.
- Use a variety of types of questions.
- Use questions to help students explore their knowledge, develop new understandings, and discover ways of applying their new understandings.

Questioning, an important instructional strategy as well as a basic facilitating behavior, is discussed in greater detail in Chapter 6.

TOOLS FOR INSTRUCTION

This final section of this chapter focuses on your responsibility for using the cognitive tools available for helping students construct their understandings. There is a large variety of useful and effective educational media, aids, and resources—electronic, print, and objects—from which to draw as you plan your instructional experiences, and the list of electronic tools seems to be growing faster and faster. You could easily become overwhelmed by the variety and sheer quantity of tools and materials available for classroom use. You could spend a lot of time reviewing, sorting, selecting, and practicing with these materials and tools. Although nobody can make the job easier for you, information in this section may expedite the process.

Long ago, when humankind was young and writing had not yet been invented, adults taught their children by means of very simple tools. Telling children what they should know was an important teaching technique, but there were other teaching and learning methods, too. Children learned to hunt by practicing with spears, by throwing sticks, and by simulating hunts of simulated animals. Parents taught geography by maps drawn in the sand and religion by pictures drawn on the walls of caves. Dance and drama portrayed the history, customs, and lore of a group. From the very earliest times, teachers have depended on diverse teaching tools to make their teaching interesting and effective. Today, teachers still depend on a variety of teaching tools. In some respects, modern teaching tools are much more sophisticated than those of older times. Yet we use our new tools for the same purposes and in much the same ways that our ancestors used theirs: to make things clear, to make instruction real, to spice up the learning process, and to

---

make it possible for students to teach themselves. Teaching would be impossible without some instructional aids.

As you peruse this final topic in this chapter, I remind you again, as I did in Chapter 1 (Figure 1.2), about starting your professional resources file.

The Internet

Originating from a Department of Defense project (called ARPAnet, named after the federal government's Advanced Research Projects Agency) at the University of California, Los Angeles, computer science department in 1969, to establish a computer network of military researchers, the federally funded Internet (also known as the "information superhighway," "cyberspace," or simply the "net") has become an enormous, steadily expanding, worldwide system of connected computer networks. As I am sure you are already aware, the Internet provides literally millions of resources to explore, with thousands more added every day. Today you can surf the Internet and find many sources about how to use it, and you can walk into most any bookstore and find hundreds of recent titles, most of which give their authors' favorite web sites. However, as you undoubtedly are well aware new technologies are steadily emerging and the Internet changes every day, with some

sites and resources disappearing or not kept current, others having changed their location and undergone reconstruction, and still other new ones appearing. Therefore, it would be superfluous for me, in this book, to get too enthused about sites that I personally have viewed and can recommend as teacher resources, although occasionally I do mention a site. But I am still recovering from just a few years ago when a site mentioned in one of my books and that had been one for teachers, became a porn site. Luckily a user let me know in time to have it removed from the book for the next printing.

CAUTIONS AND GUIDELINES FOR USING THE INTERNET

If you need more detailed information about the use of the Internet and other technology than can be provided in this resource guide, I refer you to *Teaching and Learning with Technology* (Lever-Duffy & McDonald, 2008) with its more than 50 pages alone devoted to the Internet and its use in teaching. In the remaining pages of this section I address the "how" of using the Internet from an academic perspective, beginning with the fictitious although feasible teaching scenario illustrated in the Classroom Vignette "Natural Disasters."

In this scenario, there is both a desirable aspect and a not-so-desirable aspect. It was good that the students used a worthy technological tool (the Internet) to research a variety of sources, including many primary ones. But when they published their document on the Internet and when they made copies of their guide to be sold, they did so without permission from original copyright holders and were thus infringing copyright law. Although it would take an attorney to say for sure, with this scenario it is probable that the students, teacher, school, and the school district would be liable. As is true for other documents (such as published photos, graphics, and text), unless there is an explicit statement that materials taken from the Internet are public domain, it is best to assume that they are copyrighted and should not be republished without permission from the original source.

There is such a proliferation of information today, from both printed materials and from information on the Internet, how can a person determine the validity and currency of a particular piece of information? When searching for useful and reliable information on a particular topic, as I am doing as I write this book, how can one be protected from wasting valuable time sifting through all the information? Students need to know that just because information is found on a printed page or is published on the Internet, it does not necessarily mean that the information is accurate or current.

Teaching all students how to access and assess web sites adds to their repertoire of skills for lifelong learning. Consider allowing each student or teams of students to become experts on specific sites during particular

CLASSROOM VIGNETTE

Natural Disasters

Let us suppose that the students from your "house" have been working nearly all year on an interdisciplinary thematic unit titled "Surviving Natural Disasters." As culmination to their study they published a document titled *Natural Disaster Preparation and Survival Guide for (name of their community)* and proudly distributed the guide to their parents and members of the community.

Long before preparing the guide, however, the students had to do research. To learn about the history of various kinds of natural disasters that had occurred or might occur locally and about the sorts of preparations a community should take for each kind of disaster, the students searched sources on the Internet, such as federal documents, scientific articles, and articles from newspapers around the world where natural disasters had occurred. They also searched in the local library and the local newspaper's archives to learn of floods, tornadoes, and fires that had occurred during the past 200 years. Much to their surprise, they also learned that their community is located very near the New Madrid Fault and did, in fact, experience a serious earthquake in 1811, although none since. As a result of that earthquake, two nearby towns completely disappeared; the Mississippi River reportedly flowed in reverse, and its course changed and even caused the formation of a new lake.

From published and copyrighted sources, including web sites, the students found many useful photographs, graphics, and articles, and they included those in whole or in part in their survival guide. They did so without obtaining permission from the original copyright holders or even citing those sources.

You and the other members of your teaching team and other people were so impressed with the students' work that students were encouraged to offer the document for publication on the school's web site. In addition, the document was received with so much acclaim that the students decided to place it for sale in the local library and retail outlets. This would help defray the original cost of duplication and enable them to continue the supply of guides.

The ability to work with information, whether in written, audio, or video form—to define a problem, understand the nature of the information available, use the best tools well to find the information needed, and then enlist the information effectively and ethically to address the issue at hand—may well be the most important skill of the 21st century.

William Badke (2009, p. 55)

---

units of study. It might be useful to start a chronicle of student-recorded log entries about particular web sites to provide comprehensive long-term data about those sites.

When students use information from the Internet, require that they print copies of sources of citations and materials so you can check for accuracy. These copies may be maintained in their portfolios.

Student work published on the Internet should be considered intellectual material and protected from plagiarism by others. Most school districts post a copyright notice on their home page. Someone at the school usually is assigned to supervise the school web site to see that district and school policy and legal requirements are observed.

Professional Journals and Periodicals

Figure 2.6 lists examples of the many professional periodicals and journals that can provide useful teaching ideas, web site information, and information about instructional materials and how to get them. Some of these may be in your university or college library and accessible through Internet sources.

The ERIC Information Network

The Educational Resources Information Center (ERIC) system (http://www.eric.ed.gov/), established by the United States Office of Education, is a widely used network providing access to information and research in education.

Copying Printed Materials

Remember that although on many web pages there is no notice, the material is still copyrighted. Copyright law protects original material; that is just as true for the intellectual property created by a minor as it is for that of an adult.

Although space here prohibits full inclusion of U.S. legal guidelines, your local school district should be able to provide a copy of current district policies for compliance with copyright laws. District policies should include guidelines for teachers and students in publishing materials on the Internet. If no district guidelines are available, adhere to the guidelines shown in Figure 2.6 when using printed materials.

When preparing to make a copy, you must find out whether the law under the category of "permitted use" permits the copying. If not allowed under "permitted use," then you must get written permission to reproduce the material from the holder of the copyright. If the address of the source is not given on the material, addresses may be obtained from various references, such as *Literary Market Place* (www.literarymarketplace.com) and *Ulrich's International Periodical's Directory* (www. ulrichsweb.com).

Figure 2.6   Selected professional journals and periodicals for teachers.

American Biology Teacher	*Mathematics Teacher, The*
American Educational Research Quarterly	*Middle School Journal*
American Music Teacher	*Modern Language Journal*
Childhood Education	*NEA Today*
Computing Teacher, The	*Negro Educational Review*
Educational Horizons	*New Advocate, The*
Educational Leadership	*OAH Magazine of History*
Edutopia	*Phi Delta Kappan*
English Journal	*Physical Education*
English Language Teaching Journal	*Reading Teacher*
Hispania	*Reading Today*
History Teacher	*School Arts*
Horn Book	*School Library Journal*
Instructor	*School Science and Mathematics*
Journal of Adolescent and Adult Literacy	*Science*
Journal of Chemical Education	*Science Activities*
Journal of Economic Education	*Science and Chidren*
Journal of Family and Consumer Sciences	*Science Scope*
Journal of Geography	*Science Teacher*
Journal of Learning Disabilities	*Social Education*
Journal of Physical Education and Recreation	*Social Studies*
Journal of Teaching in Physical Education	*Teacher Magazine*
Language Arts	*Teaching Pre K–8*
Language Learning	*TESOL Quarterly*
Learning and Instruction	*Young Children*

The Classroom Writing Board

As is true for an auto mechanic, a brain surgeon, or any other professional, a teacher has a professional responsibility to know when and how to use the tools of the trade. One of the tools available to almost every classroom teacher is the writing board. Can you imagine a classroom without a writing board?

They used to be, and in perhaps a few schools still are, slate blackboards (slate is a type of metamorphic rock). In today's classroom, however, the writing board is more likely to be either a board that is painted plywood (chalkboard), which, like the blackboard, is also becoming obsolete, to some extent because of the concern about the dust created from using chalk, or a white or colored (light green and light blue are common) **multipurpose dry-erase whiteboard** on which you write with special marking pens and erase with any soft cloth.

Some whiteboards include a metal backing allowing the board to support magnetic objects and displays. The multipurpose whiteboard can also be used as a projection screen and as a surface to which figures cut from colored transparency film will stick.

Extending the purposes of the multipurpose whiteboard and correlated with modern technology is an **interactive whiteboard** (IWB), a large interactive display that connects to a computer and projector. The projector projects the computer's desktop onto the board's surface, where users control the computer using a pen, finger, or other device. Whatever can be done and shown on a computer screen can be done at the IWB, with a group of students or the entire class. When connected to an LCD projector, images, including video clips, short films, and music, can be projected onto the whiteboard.

PERMITTED USES: YOU MAY MAKE

1. Single copies of:
   - A chapter of a book
   - An article from a periodical, magazine, or newspaper
   - A short story, short essay, or short poem whether or not from a collected work
   - A chart, graph, diagram, drawing, cartoon
   - An illustration from a book, magazine, or newspaper

2. Multiple copies for classroom use (not to exceed one copy per student in a course) of:
   - A complete poem if less than 250 words
   - An excerpt from a longer poem, but not to exceed 250 words
   - A complete article, story, or essay of less than 2,500 words
   - An excerpt from a larger printed work not to exceed 10 percent of the whole or 1,000 words
   - One chart, graph, diagram, cartoon, or picture per book or magazine issue

PROHIBITED USES: YOU MAY *NOT*

1. Copy more than one work or two excerpts from a single author during one class term (semester or year).
2. Copy more than three works from a collective work or periodical volume during one class term.
3. Reproduce more than nine sets of multiple copies for distribution to students in one class term.
4. Copy to create, replace, or substitute for anthologies or collective works.
5. Copy "consumable" works (e.g., workbooks, standardized tests, or answer sheets).
6. Copy the same work year after year.

Figure 2.7 Guidelines for copying printed materials that are copyrighted. (*Source:* Section 107 of the 1976 Federal Omnibus Copyright Revision Act.)

Information that is written on the board can then be transferred to the connected computer and monitor, where it can then be saved as a computer file, printed, cut and pasted into other applications, sent as email or fax message, or networked to other sites. School districts throughout United States, indeed globally, are rapidly outfitting their classrooms in every level of school with IWBs, of which there are many types and options.

In some systems such as Smart (www.smarttech.com) and Mimio (www.mimio.com), the finger is used in place of a mouse to open and run programs or move windows around. In the Numonics system, a multimedia pen is used directly on the board (www.numonics.com). The board may be annotated with notes and drawings saved onto the computer. A video recording can be made of the entire sequence of activities.

Becoming popular are *interactive writing pads*, wireless electronic pads that allow the teacher (and one or more students at a time using their own pads) to interact with their students from any place in the classroom, as well as with the IWB (see www.interwritelearning.com).

To gain the fullest potential from the use of electronically interactive boards, you will need more than brief technical training; you will need practice, experimentation, and reflection. Indeed, the IWB has introduced an entirely new factor into the culture of teaching by prompting changes in relationships, work patterns, and lesson preparation (Glover & Miller, 2007; Tanner & Jones, 2007). A useful education portal Education World provides information, links, and ideas for using an electronic whiteboard in the classroom (www.education-world.com/a_tech/tech/tech206 shtml). Additional discussion about media tools follows later in this chapter.

> Today's teachers are at the beginning of a revolution in technology that requires more than just technical training. It will require a great deal of experimentation and reflection on the part of dedicated teachers before they are able to realize the full potential of the technology to encourage interactive learning.
>
> Howard Tanner and Sonia Jones (2007)

Regardless of the type of writing board you have in your classroom, each day, each class, and even each new idea should begin with a clean board, except of course for announcements that have been placed there by you or another teacher. At the end of each class, clear the board, especially if another teacher follows you in using that room (professional courtesy).

Teaching in Practice

Creative Ideas in Using a SMART Board in a High School Mathematics Class

I teach with a SMART Board in my high school math classes every day. I don't use the chalkboard any more. In that way I can record all my class notes and examples on a file and at the end of the day, I download my class notes to my web page in pdf format. If a student is absent, the student can obtain the actual class notes at home, can even print them out, and in color. I also include my assignments on the web page. This turned out to be a huge, major reason to use a SMART Board.

Also by putting my notes on the web, parents/ guardians are able to see exactly what we do in my class each day, making unnecessary the age-old question, "What did you learn in school today?" So this is a great informational tool for the parents and a good public relations vehicle for me and our school.

Another thing I can do with the notes is that if we run out of time in class and I wanted to do another example, I will tell the students that I will do another example and it will be on my website if you need it.

This year I added something new: because of the upgraded features in SMART Notebook 10, I now record my actual class presentation every day as a video with sound. I then place these videos on my website, not only for the student who is absent, but also for the student who is there but needs to experience the class again, and at his/her pace. As a result my students can not only obtain the ACTUAL CLASS NOTES IN COLOR as pdf's, but they also get my actual explanations and see me teach them as I taught my students that day. These videos can be played using Windows Media Player (and can be played on iPods but I don't see that occurring often.:)) NOTE: the size of the videos has shrunk to about 30 MB per class period from about 500 MB per class period–very manageable.

If I have to miss school and I know ahead of time–for example, when I go to national conferences or teachers meetings–I can prerecord my class with sound and video of my presentation. The SMART Notebook software allows me to do this. My substitute teacher can just walk in, click on the video file, and it plays. The students see everything that I write on the white board–as I write it–and they hear my voice, but they do not see me. This has worked out very well.

Each year I assign about 50 practice problems (an entire actual AP exam) for my AP Calculus students to do over the Spring break. Using the recorder feature in Notebook, I created 50 mini-videos with the solutions to each of the problems. I burned a CD for each student with the mini-videos. So if a student had a question on number 7, he/she would "play" the video that explains problem 7. All in the comfort of the student's home! Instead of taking a week to "go over" the exam, I now can use that same week to do another complete exam. This has had immense measurable gains. Since I began doing this, my students' scores on the AP exam have increased by about 50%. I credit the SMART Notebook software for the increase in my students' scores.

Since my computer is always on during class to run the SMART Board, I am also connected to the Internet. So I can use the www in several ways:

- When we were doing mathematical modeling of a Ferris Wheel, a student asked me why it is called a Ferris Wheel. I didn't know so I clicked on Internet Explorer, went to google.com, and searched for Ferris Wheel.
- When we were doing a problem about the Gateway Arch in St. Louis, I was able to go to its website and let the students see a picture of what we were talking about. The website even had a PowerPoint presentation on how the Gateway Arch was constructed. By doing these things, it made the math problem we were doing much more real, more authentic.
- My plan next year is to find an Internet site each day as a class opener for what we are studying that day. I can start off the class by showing them an application of what we are going to study through the use of the Internet.
- When we were doing the Ohio Turnpike modeling problem, I was able to go to Ohioturnpike.com and find the toll fees by number of miles. I was able to capture the data using the software on the SMART Board as a picture and paste it into my class notes–it was very cool and very powerful.

I have integrated several other software programs using the SMART Board. My favorite software to use in conjunction with the SMART Board is TI-SmartView, a graphing calculator emulator. There are several versions of TI-SmartView: one for the 84 family and one for the Nspire (and Nspire CAS) family. The beauty of using graphing calculator emulators is that I can place an image of the handheld on the screen, press the buttons and the student sees the results of those actions immediately. And the best part is that I can just "pull" a screen shot of what is on the screen of the calculator into my SMART Board notes. This is EXTREMELY POWERFUL!

Also I am able to take screen shots of the calculator screen and paste those into my class notes using the capture feature in SMART Notebook. So that if a student is absent or not understanding, he/she can see what the calculator should be doing.

Source: Tom Reardon. (www.TomReardon.com) Used with permission.

Whatever the type of board, use color to highlight your board talk. This is especially helpful for students with learning difficulties. Beginning at the top left of the board, print or write neatly and clearly, with the writing intentionally positioned to indicate content relationships (e.g., causal, oppositional, numerical, comparative, categorical, and so on). Use the board to acknowledge acceptance and to record student contributions. Print instructions for an activity on the board, in addition to giving them orally.

Whatever type of board, use it without having to turn your back entirely on students and without blocking their view of the board. When you have a lot of material to put on a writing board, do it before class and then cover it, or better yet, put the material on transparencies and use the overhead projector or use a PowerPoint presentation rather than the board, or use both. Be careful not to write too much information.

The Classroom Bulletin Board and Other Nonprojected Visual Displays

Nonprojected visual displays of one type or another, such as bulletin boards, flip charts, magnetic boards, and felt boards, are found in nearly every classroom, and, although sometimes poorly used or not used at all, they can be relatively inexpensively transformed into attractive and valuable instructional tools. The bulletin board, for example, is a convenient location to post reminders, assignments and schedules, and commercially produced materials and to celebrate and display model student work and anchor papers. To create visual displays, some teachers use student assistants or committees, giving those students guidance and responsibility for planning, preparing, and maintaining displays. Additionally, there are many sites on the Web offering ideas and bulletin board displays.

When preparing a visual display, keep these guidelines in mind: The display should be simple, emphasizing one main idea, concept, topic, or theme, and captions should be short and concise; illustrations can accent learning topics; verbs can vitalize the captions; phrases can punctuate a student's thoughts; and alliteration can announce anything you wish on the board.

Finally, as in all other aspects of the classroom learning environment, remember to ensure that the display reflects gender and ethnic equity (discussed in Chapter 9).

The Community as a Resource

One of the richest resources for learning is the local community and the people and places in it. You will want to build your own file of community resources—speakers, sources for free materials, and field trip locations. Your school may already have a community resource file available for your use. However, it may need updating. A community resource file should contain information about (a) possible field trip locations; (b) community resource people who could serve as guest speakers, presenters, or mentors; and (c) local agencies that can provide information and instructional materials. See Figure 2.8.

There are many ways of using community resources, and quite a variety has been demonstrated by the schools specifically mentioned throughout this book (see "Schools" in the index). Here the discussion is limited to two often used, although sometimes abused, instructional tools: (a) guest speakers or presenters and (b) out-of-classroom and off-campus excursions, commonly called field trips.

Guest Speaker or Presenter

Bringing outside speakers or presenters into your classroom can be a valuable educational experience for students, but not automatically so. In essence, guest speakers can be classified within a spectrum of four

Bulletin boards can be designed as decorative, motivational, and instructional tools that invite student participation by establishing a theme and then asking questions and providing means by which students manipulate parts of the display to verify their answers, such as pockets or moveable parts. Students are often more interested in bulletin boards when they take an active part in deciding the purpose of the bulletin board and its design and construction.

Figure 2.8 Community resources for speakers, materials, and field trips.

Airport	Highway patrol station
Apiary	Historical sites and monuments
Aquarium	Industrial plant
Archeological site	Legislature session
Art gallery	Levee and water reservoir
Assembly plant	Library and archive
Bakery	Native American Indian reservation
Bird and wildlife sanctuary	Mass transit authority
Book publisher	Military installation
Bookstore	Mine
Broadcasting and TV station	Museum
Building being razed	Newspaper plant
Building under construction	Observatory
Canal lock	Oil refinery
Cemetery	Park
Chemical plant	Poetry reading
City or county planning commission	Post office and package delivery company
Courthouse	Police station
Dairy	Recycling center
Dam and flood plain	Retail store
Dock and harbor	Sanitation department
Factory	Sawmill or lumber company
Farm	Shopping mall
Fire department	Shoreline (stream, lake, wetland, ocean)
Fish hatchery	Telecommunications center
Flea market	Town meeting
Foreign embassy	Utility company
Forest and forest preserve	Universities and colleges
Freeway under construction	Warehouse
Gas company	Water reservoir and treatment plant
Geological site	Wildlife park and preserve
Health department and hospital	Weather bureau and storm center
Highway construction site	Zoo

types, two of which should not be considered. (a) Ideally, a speaker is both informative and inspiring. (b) A speaker may be inspiring but with nothing substantive to offer except for the possible diversion from the usual rigors of classroom work. (c) The speaker might be informative but boring to students. (d) At the worst end of this spectrum is the guest speaker who is both boring and uninformative. Just like any other instructional experience, making a guest speaking experience effective takes your careful planning. To make sure that the experience is beneficial to student learning, consider the following guidelines.

- If at all possible, meet and talk with the guest speaker in advance to discuss your students and your expectations for the presentation and to gauge how motivational and informative the speaker might be. If you believe the speaker might be informative but boring, then perhaps you can help structure the presentation in some way to make it a bit more inspiring. For example, stop the speaker every few minutes and involve the students in questions and discussions of points made.
- Prepare students in advance with key points of information that you expect them to obtain.
- Prepare students with questions to ask the speaker, things the students want to find out, and information you want them to inquire about.
- Follow up the presentation with a thank you letter to the guest speaker and perhaps further questions that developed during class discussions subsequent to the speaker's presentation.
- Be certain to have a backup lesson plan in the eventuality the guest is late or fails to show.
- Consider briefing the guest ahead of time about any dos and don'ts and any particular sensitivities among your students.

Field Trips

What is the most memorable field trip that you were ever on as a student? Do you recall what made it memorable?

Have you experienced a "virtual" field trip? You may want to discuss these questions and others like them and their responses with your classmates.

Today's schools typically have very limited funds for the transportation and liability costs for off-campus field trips. In some cases, there are no funds at all, in which case student field trips are electronic, online only. You may wish to begin now collecting ideas and resources for these "virtual" field trips. For example, for most teachers who would like their students to experience Yellowstone National Park, because of the distance, time, and cost, an actual field trip to the park is out of the question. They would benefit from knowing that the Division of Interpretation in Yellowstone National Park has prepared materials that take the park into the classroom via a virtual field trip (Fisher, 2008). For use in K–12 classrooms, Ball State University of Muncie, Indiana, has developed and provides more than 60 free or low-cost virtual field trips to museums, parks, and historic locations (http://www.bsu.edu/eft/home).

At times, parent–teacher groups and business and civic organizations help by providing financial resources so that children get valuable first-hand experiences that field trips so often afford.

To prepare for and implement a successful field trip, there are three important stages of planning—before, during, and after—and critical decisions to be made at each stage. Consider the following guidelines.

BEFORE THE FIELD TRIP

When the field trip is your idea (and not the students'), discuss the idea with your teaching team, principal, or department chair (especially when transportation will be needed) *before* mentioning the idea to your students. You may discover that the place you had in mind is in fact an overused sight for field trips and many or most of your students have already been there. Carefully consider the worth of the proposed field trip; do not use valuable resources for field trips for trivial learnings. The bottom line is that there is no cause served by getting students excited about a trip before you know if it is feasible.

Once you have obtained the necessary, but tentative, approval from school officials, take the trip yourself (or with team members), if possible. A previsit allows you to determine how to make the field trip most productive and what arrangements will be necessary. For this previsit you might consider taking a couple of your students along for their ideas and help. If a previsit is not possible, you still will need to arrange for travel directions, arrival and departure times, parking, briefing by the host, if there is one, storage of students' personal items, such as coats and lunches, provisions for eating and rest rooms, and fees, if any.

If there are fees, you need to talk with your school administration about who will pay the fees. If the trip is worth taking, the school should cover the costs. If that is

not possible, perhaps students can plan a fundraising activity, or financial assistance can be obtained from some other source. If this does not work, you might consider an alternative that does not involve costs.

Arrange for official permission from the school administration. This usually requires a form for requesting, planning, and reporting field trips. After permission has been obtained, you can discuss the field trip with your students and arrange for permissions from their parents or guardians. You need to realize that although parents or guardians sign official permission forms allowing their children to participate in the trip, these only show that the parents or guardians are aware of what will take place and give their permission for their child to participate. Although the permission form should include a statement that the parent or guardian absolves the teacher and the school from liability should an accident occur, it does not lessen the teacher's and the school's responsibilities should there be negligence by a teacher, driver, or chaperone.

Arrange for students to be excused from their other classes while on the field trip. Using an information form prepared and signed by you and perhaps by the principal, the students should then assume responsibility for notifying their other teachers of the planned absence from classes and for assuring them that whatever work is missed will be made up. In addition, you will need to make arrangements for your own teaching duties to be covered. In some schools, teachers cooperate by filling in for those who will be gone. In other schools, substitute teachers are hired. Sometimes teachers must hire their own substitute.

Arrange to have a cell phone available for your use during the trip. Some schools have a cell phone available for just that purpose. If not, and you do not have your own, perhaps one of the drivers or other adult chaperones does have one. Check it out.

Arrange for whatever transportation is needed. Your principal, or the principal's designee, will help you with the details. In many schools, someone else is responsible for arranging transportation. In any case, the use of private automobiles is ill advised, because you and the school could be liable for the acts of the drivers.

Arrange for the collection of money that is needed for fees. If there are out-of-pocket costs to be paid by students, this information needs to be included on the permission form. No students should ever be excluded from the field trip because of a lack of money. This can be a tricky issue, because there may be some students who would rather steal the money for a field trip than say they don't have it. Try to anticipate problems; hopefully the school or some organization can pay for the trip so that fees need not be collected from students and therefore potential problems of this sort are avoided.

Plan details for student safety and the monitoring of their safety from departure to return. Included should be a first-aid kit and a system of student control, such as a buddy system whereby students must remain paired throughout the trip. The pairs sometimes are given numbers that are recorded and kept by the teacher and the chaperones, and then checked at departure time, periodically during the trip, at the time of return, and again upon return. Use adult chaperones. As a very general rule, there should be one adult chaperone for every 10 students. Some districts have a policy regarding this. While on a field trip, at all times all students should be under the direct supervision of a dependable adult.

Plan the complete route and schedule, including any stops along the way. If transportation is being provided, you will need to discuss the plans with the provider.

Establish and discuss, to the extent you believe necessary, the rules of behavior your students should follow. Included in this might be details of the trip, its purpose, directions, what they should wear and bring, academic expectations of them (e.g., consider giving each student a study guide), and follow-up activities. Also included should be information about what to do if anything should go awry, for example, if a student is late for the departure or return, loses a personal possession along the way, gets lost, is injured, becomes sick, or misbehaves. For the latter, never send a misbehaving student back to school alone. Involve the adult chaperones in the previsit discussion. All of this information should also be included on the parental permission form.

If a field trip is supposed to promote some kind of learning, as undoubtedly will be the case unless the sole purpose is something like an end-of-term celebration, then to avoid leaving it to chance, the learning expectations need to be clearly defined and the students given an explanation of how and where they may encounter the learning experience. Before the field trip, students should be asked questions such as, What do we already know about _____? What do we want to find out about _____? How can we find out? Then, with their assistance, an appropriate guide can be prepared for the students to use during the field trip.

To further ensure learning and individual student responsibility for that learning, you may want to assign different roles and responsibilities to students, just as would be done in cooperative learning, ensuring that each student has a role with responsibility.

You may want to take recording equipment so the field trip experience can be relived and shared in class upon return. If so, roles and responsibilities for the equipment and its care and use can be assigned to students as well.

DURING THE FIELD TRIP

If your field trip has been carefully planned according to the preceding guidelines, it should be a valuable and safe experience for all. Enroute, while at the trip location, and on the return to school, you and the adult chaperones should monitor student behavior and learning just as you do in the classroom.

AFTER THE FIELD TRIP

Plan the follow-up activities. As with any other lesson plan, the field trip lesson is complete only when there is both a proper introduction and a well-planned closure. All sorts of follow-up activities can be planned as an educational wrap-up to this educational experience. For example, a bulletin board committee can plan and prepare an attractive display summarizing the trip. Students can write about their experiences in their journals or as papers. Small groups can give oral reports to the class about what they did and learned. Their reports can then serve as springboards for further class discussion and perhaps further investigations. Finally, for future planning, all who were involved should contribute to an assessment of the experience.

Media Tools

Media tools are instructional tools that depend on electricity to project light and sound and to focus images on screens. Included are projectors of various

---

Teaching in Practice

What Is Mr. Klutz's Problem and How Can It Be Remedied?

Although Mr. Klutz is considered to be a good beginning teacher, things rarely work well for him when he uses materials and media. Right in the middle of a lesson, he often discovers that he is missing some important piece of equipment or material he needs to complete the lesson, or a machine breaks down. Once, he was going to demonstrate how a candle extinguishes when covered with a glass jar. He had the candles and the jar, but he forgot to bring matches. Another time, he planned to use an overhead projector, only to find at the last minute that the electrical cord was not long enough to reach the wall outlet, and he did not have an extension cord. On another occasion when using slides, he found that he had placed them in the carousel upside down and backward. Yesterday, while he was demonstrating on the overhead screen with a computer, the computer froze. Such situations always seemed to happen at the worst unexpected time and surprise Mr. Klutz and spoil his plans and lesson presentations.

Questions for Discussion
1. Is it possible for Mr. Klutz's carelessness to result in other, more serious problems?
2. What action would you take to avoid such unexpected and unwanted outcomes?
3. Is it possible for a teacher considered "highly qualified" to be grossly incompetent in certain areas?

sorts, computers, CD-ROMs, DVDs, sound recorders, video recorders, in addition to the interactive electronic whiteboard discussed earlier. The aim here is not to provide instruction on how to operate equipment but to help you develop a philosophy for using it and to provide strategies for using media tools in your teaching. Except for the overhead projector, still used in many classrooms, I devote no attention here to other traditional if not archaic, perhaps even antediluvian, audiovisual equipment, such as film projectors, VCRs, and opaque and slide projectors. There are staff members on any school faculty who gladly will assist you in locating and using those tools if so desired.

It is important to remember that the role of media tools is to aid student learning, not to teach for you. You must still select the objectives, orchestrate the instructional plan, assess the results, and follow up the lessons, just as you do with various other instructional strategies. If you use media tools prudently, your teaching and students' learning will benefit.

WHEN EQUIPMENT MALFUNCTIONS

When using media equipment, it is nearly always best to set up the equipment and have it ready to go before students arrive. That helps avoid problems in classroom management that can occur when there is a delay because the equipment is not ready. Like any other competent professional, a competent teacher is ready when the work is to begin.

Of course, delays may be unavoidable when equipment breaks down or if a videotape breaks. Remember Murphy's law, which says if anything can go wrong, it will? It is particularly relevant when using audiovisual equipment. You want to be prepared for such emergencies. Effectively planning for and responding to this eventuality is an important element of your system of movement management and takes place during the planning phase of instruction. That preparation includes consideration of a number of factors.

When equipment malfunctions, three principles should be remembered:

1. Avoid dead time in the instruction.
2. Avoid causing permanent damage to equipment.
3. Avoid losing content continuity of a lesson.

So, what do you do when equipment breaks down? Again, the answer is: Be prepared for the eventuality. If a projector bulb expires, quickly insert another. That means you should have an extra bulb on hand. If the computer screen freezes during direct, whole-class instruction, you should probably quickly move to an alternate activity. If it is during multilevel instruction (discussed earlier in this chapter), then while maintaining your classroom withitness, you can probably take the time to treat this as a **teachable moment** and show the student who is working on the computer what to do,

which probably would be simply how to restart the computer. If it occurs during a PowerPoint presentation, then you might be able to continue simply by moving to an available overhead projector or to the writing board.

If, while teaching, a computer program freezes or aborts on the screen, or if a fuse blows, or for some other reason you lose power and you feel that there is going to be too much dead time before the equipment is working again, that is the time to go to an alternate lesson plan. You have probably heard the expression "go to Plan B." It is a useful phrase; what it means is that without missing a beat in the lesson, to accomplish the same instructional objective or another objective, you immediately and smoothly switch to an alternate learning activity. For you, the beginning teacher, it does *not* mean that you must plan two lessons for every one (although many experts believe it is a good idea for the teacher to always have an optional plan B at least in mind), but that when planning a lesson that uses media equipment, you should plan for an alternative activity, just in case. Then, you move your students into the planned alternative activity quickly and smoothly. Your state of preparedness and smoothness in your action will impress your students, with them seeing you as a competent and well-prepared professional.

THE OVERHEAD PROJECTOR

In addition to a writing board and a bulletin board, traditional classrooms were equipped with an overhead projector; although rather rapidly diminishing in number many still are. However, the overhead projector is rapidly being replaced by large computer monitors and computer projection systems (LCDs), the interactive whiteboard, and the document camera (discussed later in this section). Such systems allow the making of animated, interactive presentations with movement and video, typically using software such as Microsoft's PowerPoint.

For half a century, the overhead projector has been a versatile, effective, and reliable teaching tool. Except for the bulb burning out, not much else can go wrong with an overhead projector. There is no program to crash. Furthermore, the overhead projector is easier to learn to properly use and is less likely to crash during use. So, while knowing full well that our increasingly ingrained use of computing technology will result in the subsequent demise of the overhead projector in teaching, because the machine is still commonly found and frequently used, some time is spent in this resource guide discussing its use. Somewhat sadly I admit, this edition of the resource guide may well be the last time I mention the overhead projector.

The overhead projector projects light through objects that are transparent. A modern and properly functioning overhead projector usually works quite well in a fully lit room. Truly portable overhead projectors are available that can be carried easily from place to place in their compact cases.

Other types of overhead projectors include rear-projection systems that allow the teacher to stand off to the side rather than between students and the screen and overhead video projectors that use video cameras to send images that are projected by television monitors. Some schools use overhead video camera technology that focuses on an object, pages of a book, or a demonstration, while sending a clear image to a video monitor with a screen large enough for an entire class to clearly see.

In some respects, the overhead projector is more practical than the writing board, particularly for a teacher who is nervous. Using an overhead projector rather than the writing board can help avoid tension by decreasing the need to pace back and forth to the board. And by using an overhead projector rather than a writing board, a teacher can maintain both eye contact and physical proximity with students, both of which are important for maintaining classroom control.

GUIDELINES FOR USING THE OVERHEAD PROJECTOR

As with any projection equipment, find the best place in your classroom to position it. If there is no classroom projection screen, you can hang white paper or a sheet, use a white multipurpose board, or use a white or near-white wall.

Have you ever attended a presentation by someone who was not using an overhead projector properly? It can be frustrating to members of an audience when the image is too small, out of focus, partially off the screen, or partially blocked from view by the presenter. To use this proven teaching tool in a professional manner:

- Place the projector so the projected white light covers the entire screen and hits the screen at a 90-degree angle, and then focus the image to be projected.
- Face the students while using the projector. The fact that you do not lose eye contact with your students is a major advantage of using the overhead projector rather than the traditional writing board. (A PowerPoint presentation provides the same advantage.) What you write as you face your students will show up perfectly (unless out of focus or off the screen).
- Lay the pencil directly on the transparency with the tip of the pencil pointing to the detail being emphasized rather than using your finger to point to detail or pointing to the screen (thereby turning away from your students).
- To lessen distraction, you may find it advantageous to turn the projector off when you want student attention shifted back to you.

For writing on overhead projector transparencies, ordinary felt-tip pens are not satisfactory. Select a **transparency-marking pen** available at an office supply store. The ink of these pens is water soluble, so keep the palm of your hand from resting on the transparency or you will have ink smudges on your transparency and on your hand. Non-water-soluble pens—**permanent markers**—can be used, but the transparency must be cleaned with an alcohol solvent or a plastic eraser. When using a cleaning solvent, you can clean and dry with paper toweling or a soft rag. To highlight the writing on a transparency and to organize student learning, use pens in a variety of colors. Transparency pens tend to dry out quickly, and they are relatively expensive, so the caps must be taken on and off frequently, which is something of a nuisance when working with several colors. Practice writing on a transparency, and also practice making overlays. You can use an acetate transparency roll or single sheets of flat transparencies. Flat sheets of transparency come in different colors—clear, red, blue, yellow, and green—which can be useful in making overlays.

Some teachers prepare lesson outlines in advance on transparencies, which allows more careful preparation of the transparencies and means that they are ready for reuse at another time. Some teachers use an opaque material, such as a 3×5 note card, to block out prewritten material and then uncover it at the moment it is being discussed. For preparation of permanent transparencies, you will probably want to use permanent marker pens, rather than those that are water soluble and easily smudged. Heavy paper frames are available for permanent transparencies; marginal notes can be written on the frames. Personal computers with laser printers and thermal processing (copy) machines, probably located in the teacher's workroom or in the school's main office, can be used to make permanent transparencies.

Another function of the overhead projector is made possible by the fact that transparent objects can be placed on the platform and displayed on the screen, objects such as transparent rulers, protractors, and Petri dishes for science activities; even opaque objects can be used if you want simply to show silhouette, as you might in math and art activities. The overhead projector can also be used for tracing transparent charts or drawings into larger drawings on paper or on the writing board. The image projected onto the screen can be made smaller or larger by moving the projector closer or farther away, respectively, and then traced when you have the size you want. An overhead projector can be used also as a light source (spotlight) to highlight demonstrations (as also can an old but not yet discarded slide projector).

DIGITAL PROJECTOR AND THE DOCUMENT CAMERA

Digital projectors are devices that when connected to a computer, project images onto a screen or electronic whiteboard. They are useful for sharing computer images with the entire class. Another device for displaying images on a screen is the document camera, which is actually a camera-mounted video camera.

Although more expensive than overhead projectors, document cameras (also called digital visualizers, digital overheads, or docucams) are increasing in popularity in classrooms as a tool for displaying three-dimensional objects or writing on a nontransparent sheet of paper for the whole class to observe. When connected to a computer and projector, the document camera becomes a very versatile presentation tool. In addition to displaying text, you can project 3-D objects, slides, and other microscopic objects; you can zoom in on objects; and you can send video signals to a computer.

MULTIMEDIA PROGRAM

A *multimedia program is a collection of teaching and learning materials involving more than one type of medium and organized around a single theme or topic.* The types of media involved vary from rather simple kits—perhaps including CDs, games, activity cards, student worksheets, and manuals of instructions for the teacher—to sophisticated packages involving building-level site-licensed computer software, student handbooks, reproducible activity worksheets, classroom wall hangings, and online subscriptions to telecommunication networks. Some kits are designed for teacher use, others for individuals or small groups of students; yet many more are designed for the collaborative use of students and teachers. Teachers sometimes incorporate multimedia programs with learning activity centers.

TELEVISION, VIDEOS, AND DVDS

Everyone knows that television, videos, and DVDs represent a historically powerful medium. But we also know that for a student, watching TV, videos, and DVDs tends to be inactive experiences (video games are discussed in Chapter 7), and because students learn better when they are engaged beyond mere audio and visual senses, when using these devices the teacher must follow important guidelines, the most important of which are (1) to *always* review the material before using it with your students and (2) to involve the students beyond mere viewing and listening, perhaps by giving them a study guide with questions to be answered, to be used during or following the presentation.

The importance of your previewing the material cannot be overemphasized, as any teacher who has been in the profession for any length of time can share horror stories of the lazy and incompetent teacher who used a medium with students without first previewing it. For example, there is the high school history teacher who showed the movie *Defensing the Wishbone*, wrongly believing it was about World War II, and there was the tenured middle school teacher who showed movies literally every day, any movie that had arrived at school regardless of what it was about or who ordered it.

Combined with a television monitor, the DVD player is one of the more popular and frequently used tools in today's classroom. DVD programs can do nearly everything that the former 16-mm films and later the VCRs could do.

A TV camera and recorder makes it possible to record students during activities, practice, projects, and demonstrations as well as yourself when teaching. It gives students a marvelous opportunity to self-assess as they see and hear themselves in action.

Entire course packages, as well as supplements, are available on DVDs. The schools where you student teach and where you eventually are employed may have a collection of such programs. Some teachers make their own.

Carefully selected programs enhance student learning. For example, DVDs and CDs offer quick and efficient accessibility to thousands of visuals, thus providing an appreciated boost to teachers of students with limited language proficiency. With the use of frame control, students can observe phenomena, in detail, that previous students only read about.

Computers and Computer-Based Instructional Tools

As a teacher, the computer can be valuable to you in several ways. For example, the computer can help you manage the instruction by obtaining information, storing and preparing test materials, maintaining attendance and grade records, and preparing programs to aid in the academic development of individual students. This category of uses of the computer is referred to as **computer-managed instruction** (CMI).

The computer can also be used for instruction by employing various instructional software programs, and it can be used to teach about computers and to help students develop their metacognitive skills as well as their skills in computer use. When the computer is used to assist students in their learning, it is called **computer-assisted instruction** (CAI) or **computer-assisted learning** (CAL).

THE PLACEMENT AND USE OF COMPUTERS: THE ONLINE CLASSROOM

Teachers looking to make their classrooms more student centered, collaborative, and interactive increasingly turn to telecommunications networks. Webs of connected computers allow teachers and students from around the world to reach each other directly and gain access to quantities of information previously unimaginable. Students using networks learn new inquiry and analytical skills in a stimulating environment, and they can also gain an increased awareness of their role as world citizens. Just imagine, for example, students in a classroom in Kansas in direct online communication with scientists working at the North Pole, a reality today that was only dreamed of a mere generation ago.

As another example, many teachers of various subjects and all grade levels are discovering ways of using **Google Earth** to enhance student learning in fun and engaging ways (Adam & Mowers, 2007). Mapping the

Earth via the superimposition of images obtained from satellite imagery, aerial photography, and a geographic information system, Google Earth is a virtual globe, map, and geographic information program (see http://earth.google.com/userguide/v4/). Lucking, Christmann, and Whiting (2008) discuss how their students used Google Maps to combine data collected about local trees into a high-tech, interactive, multimedia map—a process of combining data and technology referred to as "mashup."

Some teachers have learned that teaching students how to use the computer software program's grammar checker can actually assist in helping meet the needs of the language arts curriculum (Potter & Fuller, 2008).

How you use the computer for instruction and learning is determined by several factors, including your knowledge of and skills in its use, the number of computers available for instructional use, where computers are placed in the school, the software and printers that are available, and the telecommunications capabilities (i.e., wiring and phone lines, modems, and servers). Some schools, such as The Denver School of Science and Technology (www.scienceandtech.org), a public charter grades 6–12 school where nearly half of the students come from low-income families) are fortunate enough to be able to provide each student with a laptop (see Zucker & Hug, 2008).

To the extent finances allow, schools continue to purchase or to lease computers and to upgrade their telecommunications capabilities. Perhaps with developing technology and the reduced cost factor, the near future will bring an increase classroom usage of **mobile handheld computers** (i.e., tablet PCs), one for each student.

As modern technologies have become more inventive and complicated, so too has the expense for schools. Whereas in the earlier days the so-called audiovisual and computer technology was overseen by a so-called tech coordinator, oftentimes a person who was a regular classroom teacher but who also possessed an additional and keen interest in computers and other high-tech gadgets, today that arrangement is inadequate. Because of the complicated high-tech systems used, today's school districts rely heavily on one or more full-time computer tech officers whose responsibilities extend far beyond individual classroom software and hardware technology to schoolwide and districtwide systems that include everything from applications software to networks, testing, and reporting systems upon which school funding is based (Villano, 2008).

Using Copyrighted Video, Computer, and Multimedia Programs

You have a responsibility to be knowledgeable about the laws on the use of copyrighted materials in teaching. The copyright and fair use laws seem to be ever-changing,

Figure 2.9 Copyright law for use of computer software. (*Source:* December, 1980, Congressional amendment to the 1976 Copyright Act.)

PERMITTED USES—YOU MAY:

1. Make a single back-up or archival copy of the computer program.
2. Adapt the computer program to another language if the program is unavailable in the target language.
3. Add features to make better use of the computer program.

PROHIBITED USES—YOU MAY *NOT*:

1. Make multiple copies.
2. Make replacement copies from an archival or back-up copy.
3. Make copies of copyrighted programs to be sold, leased, loaned, transmitted, or given away.

---

especially now due to new social networking tools, whether viewing a video on YouTube, adding a student writing blog on Blogger, or viewing a student-created video from Flickr. A working knowledge of copyright and privacy helps in understanding how to use these online collaborative tools in the classroom (Talab & Butler, 2007; Salpeter, 2008).

As with the use of printed materials that are copyrighted, when preparing to make any copy, you must find out whether the law under the category of "permitted use" permits the copying. If not allowed under "permitted use," then you must get written permission to reproduce the material from the holder of the copyright. Figure 2.9 presents guidelines for the copying of computer software.

Usually, when purchasing CD-ROMs, DVDs, and other multimedia software packages intended for school use, you are also paying for a license to modify and use its contents for instructional purposes. However, not all CD-ROMs and DVDs include copyright permission, so always check the copyright notice on any package you purchase and use. Whenever in doubt, do not use it until you have asked your district media specialists about copyrights or have obtained necessary permissions from the original source.

A general rule of thumb for use of any copyrighted material is to treat the work of others as you would want your own material treated were it protected by a copyright (see Figure 2.10.)

Although space in this resource guide prohibits full inclusion of U.S. legal guidelines, your local school district undoubtedly can provide you with a copy of current district policies to ensure your compliance with all copyright laws (Gold, 2006). See resources shown in Figure 2.11.

Figure 2.10 Fair use guidelines for using multimedia programs.

1. For portions of copyrighted works used in your own multimedia production for use in teaching, follow normal copyright guidelines (e.g., the limitations on the amount of material used, whether it be motion media, text, music, illustrations, photographs, or computer software).
2. You may display your own multimedia work using copyrighted works to other teachers, such as in workshops. However, you may *not* make and distribute copies to colleagues without obtaining permission from copyright holders.
3. You may use your own multimedia production for instruction over an electronic network (e.g., distance learning) provided there are limits to access and to the number of students enrolled. You may *not* distribute such work over any electronic network (local area or wide area) without expressed permission from copyright holders.
4. You must obtain permissions from copyright holders before using any copyrighted materials in educational multimedia productions for commercial reproduction and distribution or before replicating more than one copy, distributing copies to others, or for use beyond your own classroom.

Distance Learning

Distance learning (or **distance education**) is the term used when referring to any instructional situation in which the learner is separated in time or space from the point of instruction. With the technology of distance education, students in small rural schools can receive instruction in courses that, because of limited local resources, might otherwise have been unavailable to them (see, for example, Cunningham, Bradley, & Osborn, 2008); via the Internet all students can interact in real time with people from around the world. Indeed, one can now receive high school education solely via the Internet. If accredited, such schools are referred to as **virtual schools** or **cyberschools**.

It is predicted that learning and instruction over the Internet will be the driving force for educational changes in the 21st century, with an accompanying change in the role of the classroom teacher from less of a deliverer of instruction to more of a facilitator of learning both by providing individual tutoring and by helping students work together in groups (Schank, 2000). That prediction is likely made in part from the position that says today's young people are increasingly disengaged from traditional forms of instruction (which may be, in part at least, the cause of the recent increase in

Figure 2.11 Copyright information resources.

A Visit to Copyright Bay: http://www.stfrancis.edu/cid/copyrightbay/
American Society of Composers, Authors, and Publishers: http://www.ascap.com/index.html
Association for Information Media and Equipment (AIME), including Fair Use guidelines for multimedia: http://www.aime.org/links.php
Copyright and Fair Use information and resources: http://fairuse.stanford.edu/
Copyright Kids: http://www.copyrightkids.org/cbasicsframes.htm
Copyright Society of the USA: http://www.csusa.org/
Copyright Term and the Public Domain: http://www.copyright.cornell.edu/training/Hirtle_Public_Domain.htm
Copyright Website includes many useful tools for copyrighting your own work or researching copyright issues: http://www.benedict.com
Copyright.com provides access to copyright permission for millions of works in print and digital formats worldwide: http://www.copyright.com/
Copyright.Com: http://www.copyright.com/
Crash Course in Copyright from the University of Texas: www.utsystem.edu/ogc/Intellectualproperty/cprtindx.htm
Dance Heritage Coalition: A Copyright Primer for the Dance Community gives an overview of copyright issues including video production: http://www.danceheritage.org/publications/copyright.html
Internet Copyright Basics: http://server.remc12.k12.mi.us/lhslib/Copyright.htm
Internet Plagiarism: http://www.plagiarized.com
Internet Safety: What is covered by the Copyright?: http://www.wiredsafety.org/law/copyrights/covered.html
Library of Congress: http://www.copyright.gov/
Music Education, a site for helping to identify public domain songs and music: http://www.pdinfo.com/
Teachers Talking to Teachers: Video programs and series; Nine 2-hour video sessions—Session 6 is Technology and the Law, Copyright and Selection Policies: http://www.ncpublicschools.org/distancelearning/starschools/teacherstalking.html
United States Copyright Office: http://www.copyright.gov/
Visual Arts Educators Trademark and Copyright Law: http://www.artpoints.net/

school dropouts), but unless distance learning can offer an alternative model that meets their learning needs, the potential of distance learning will not reach fruition. And perhaps more importantly, distance learning alone may be insufficient to meet the needs of today's youth to be prepared with the skills needed to thrive in a global world (Hannum & McCombs, 2008).

> For motivated students led by online-savvy teachers, amazing learning outside of the brick and mortar school can take place and expand curricular possibilities. Unconstrained by place and time, students are learning and teachers are teaching, virtually and rigorously.
>
> Pamela Livingston (2008)

DISTANCE EDUCATION AND THE *TEACH ACT*

In 2002 the U.S. Congress passed the Technology, Education and Copyright Harmonization Act (TEACH) to better allow educators to copy documents and to use copyrighted materials in distance education, that is in non-face-to-face learning. As a result of that legislation, distance learning teachers are allowed to use a wider range of works; participants have greater latitude with respect to storing, copying, and digitizing materials; and students may participate in distance learning from virtually any location.

SUMMARY

You have reviewed the realities of the responsibilities of today's classroom teacher. Being a good teacher takes time, commitment, concentrated effort, and just plain hard work. Nobody truly knowledgeable about it ever said that good teaching was easy (or if they did they didn't know what they were talking about).

You have learned that your professional responsibilities as a classroom teacher will extend well beyond the four walls of the classroom, the 6 hours of the school day, the 5 days of the school week, and the 180 days of the school year. You learned of the many expectations. As you have read and discussed these responsibilities, you should have begun to fully comprehend the challenge and reality of being a competent classroom teacher.

Teaching style is the way teachers teach, their distinctive mannerisms complemented by their choices of teaching behaviors and strategies. Constantly open to change, one's teaching style develops from tradition, from one's beliefs and experiences, and from one's knowledge of research findings. You analyzed your own current beliefs, observed one teacher and that teacher's

style for that lesson, and began the development of your philosophy about teaching and learning—a philosophical statement that although perhaps altered over time should in some way be useful to you during future job interviews.

Exciting research findings continue to emerge from several related areas—about learning, conceptual development, and thinking styles—and from neurophysiology. The findings continue to support the hypothesis that a teacher's best teaching style choice is eclectic with a strong bent toward facilitating collaborative learning, at least until the day arrives when students of certain thinking styles can be practically matched to teachers with particular teaching styles. Future research will undoubtedly shed additional light on the relationships among pedagogy, pedagogical styles, and student thinking and learning.

Today, there seems to be much agreement that the essence of the learning process is a combination of self-awareness, self-monitoring, and active reflection. Students learn these skills best when exposed to teachers who themselves effectively model those same behaviors. The most effective teaching and learning is an interactive process, which involves not only learning, but also thinking about the process of learning.

You have learned of the variety of tools available to supplement your instruction and enhance student learning. When used wisely, these tools will help you reach more of your students more of the time. As you know, teachers must meet the needs of a diversity of students, many who are linguistically and culturally different. The material selected and presented in this chapter, as well as additional material in chapters to come, should be of help in doing that. The future will undoubtedly continue bringing technological innovations that will be even more helpful. New instructional delivery systems made possible by microcomputers and multimedia workstations may fundamentally alter what had become the traditional role of the classroom teacher. For example, Audience Response Systems (ARS), discussed in Chapter 6, known variously as personal response systems, interactive student response systems, and classroom performance systems, represent an exciting new tool for increasing student engagement (Barnes, 2008).

You should remain alert to developing technologies for your teaching. New instructional technologies are advancing at an increasingly rapid rate. You and your colleagues must maintain vigilance over new developments, constantly looking for those that will not only help make student learning meaningful and interesting, and your teaching effective, but are cost effective as well.

 Now go to Topics #4, 14, 14 and 16: **Motivation, Integrating Technology, Collaborating with Colleagues and Families**, and **Professional Responsibilities** in the MyEducationLab (www.myeducationlab.com) for your course, where you can:

- Find learning outcomes for these topics along with the national standards that connect to these outcomes.
- Complete Assignments and Activities that can help you more deeply understand the chapter content.
- Apply and practice your understanding of the core teaching skills identified in the chapter with the Building Teaching Skills and Dispositions learning units.

QUESTIONS FOR CLASS DISCUSSION

1. Explain how your effective use of a writing board can help students to understand relationships among verbal concepts or information.

2. Explain the difference between the teacher's use of praise and the use of reinforcement. Explain how you feel about that difference. Is it in your mind a significant difference? Explain why or why not.

3. Although some teachers promote the benefits of connecting with students via the social networking site Facebook, critics question whether teachers should even be communicating with students online. What do you see as the potential pros and cons? And, explain why or why not you will likely to do so with your students.

4. Has the purchase of new textbooks and library books become stagnated as schools use their available funds for technology? Have music and art programs suffered as a result of expenditures on technology (as well as the focus on standardized testing)? How are school districts finding funds necessary for the cost of technology, such as for the cost of wiring classrooms for networking, for updating computers, and for the planning, installation, and maintenance of complex computer networks? Or *are* districts finding the necessary funds? In this respect, is the "playing field" even or are some districts or individual schools worse off or better off than others? Is this an issue? In order to learn some answers, do some inquiring in the local schools where you are likely to do your student teaching or to become employed.

5. Bullying and harassment are and perhaps always have been a problem in many schools and communities. However, using the Internet as a medium in which to bully or harass is a new and seemingly growing phenomenon. The Internet has become a relatively unsupervised place where bullies can belittle, torment, and frighten others. Cyberstalking and cyberbullying, known also as online social cruelty or electronic bullying, is believed to peak during middle school years (Mustacchi, 2009). What, if anything, should the classroom teacher know and be prepared to do about this problem? (Hint: See Chapter 3.)

EXERCISE 2.1   THE TEACHER AS REFLECTIVE DECISION MAKER

INSTRUCTIONS: The purpose of this exercise is to learn more about the nature of the decisions and the decision-making process used by teachers. To accomplish this, you are to observe one teacher for 1 hour during that teacher's teaching. Tabulate as accurately as possible the number of decisions the teacher makes during that time period, and then share the results with your classmates. Obtain permission from a cooperating teacher by explaining the purpose of your observations. You will need to have a follow-up discussion with the cooperating teacher regarding your tabulations. A follow-up thank-you letter is appropriate.

School, teacher, and class observed: _____

1. Use the following format for your tabulations. You may first want to make your tabulations on a separate blank sheet of paper and then organize and transfer those tabulations to this page. Tabulate and identify each decision. To tabulate the decisions made before and after instruction, confer with the teacher after class.

DECISIONS MADE BEFORE INSTRUCTION

Examples:
- objectives of lesson
- amount of time to be devoted to particular activities
- classroom management procedures

DECISIONS MADE DURING INSTRUCTION

Examples:
- called on Roberta to answer a question
- teacher remained silent until students in back corner got quiet
- talked with tardy student

DECISIONS MADE AFTER INSTRUCTION

Examples:
- to review a particular concept tomorrow
- to arrange a conference with Sean to talk with him about his hostility in class
- to make a revision in Friday's homework assignment

2. What was the total number of decisions made by this teacher

   before instruction? _____   during instruction? _____   after instruction? _____

   Compare your results with those of others in your class.

3. Did you observe any evidence that this teacher assumed full responsibility for the learning outcomes of this class session? Describe the evidence.

4. What percentage of all decisions by this teacher

   were planned? _____   were spontaneous?_____

5. Did you share your results of this exercise with the cooperating teacher? His or her reaction?

6. Your conclusions from this exercise?

EXERCISE 2.2   USING OBSERVATION OF CLASSROOM INTERACTION TO ANALYZE ONE TEACHER'S STYLE

INSTRUCTIONS: The purpose of this exercise is to visit a classroom to observe and identify a teacher's instructional style. Be certain to obtain permission and to explain to the teacher that you are observing, not evaluating, teaching style. The host teacher may be interested in discussing with you the results of your observation. A follow-up thank-you letter is appropriate.

Observe the teacher's behavior at 1-minute intervals for a period of 10 minutes, and tabulate the appropriate item on the following chart. Continue this for the entire class meeting. You will need to make copies of the recording section of this form as each form is for one 10-minute interval.

Class, grade level, and school visited _____

_____

_____

Date of visit _____

	Minute										
	1	2	3	4	5	6	7	8	9	10	Total
Traditional Teacher Behaviors *Prescribing:* Giving advice or directions, being critical or evaluative, offering judgments											
Informing: Giving information, lecturing, interpreting											
Confronting: Directly challenging students											

Traditional behaviors total _____

Facilitating Teacher Behaviors *Relaxing:* Releasing tension, using humor											
Mediating: Asking for information, being reflective, encouraging self-directed problem solving											
Supporting: Approving, confirming, validating, listening											

Facilitating behaviors total _____

Total traditional behaviors divided by total facilitating behaviors (T/F ratio) _____

_____

Conclusions about the teacher's style _____

_____

_____

_____

_____

_____

_____

_____

Source: Adapted from J. Heron, *Six Category Intervention Analysis*, Guildford, England: Centre of Adult Education, University of Surrey, 1975.

_____

_____

_____

_____

_____

_____

_____

Did you discuss your observations with the teacher? _____

_____

_____

_____

_____

_____

_____

_____

EXERCISE 2.3   USING A QUESTIONNAIRE TO DEVELOP A PROFILE AND A STATEMENT ABOUT MY OWN EMERGING TEACHING STYLE

INSTRUCTIONS: The purpose of this exercise is to help you clarify and articulate your own assumptions about teaching and learning. You will develop a profile of your emerging teaching style and from that a statement representative of your current thinking and philosophy about teaching and learning. Proceed with the following five steps.

Step 1. Read each of the 50 statements and rate your feelings about each, giving a *1* if you strongly agree, a *2* if you are neutral, and a *3* if you strongly disagree.

Remember: 1 = strongly agree; 2 = neutral; 3 = strongly disagree

_____   1. Most of what children learn, they learn on their own.

_____   2. Children should be concerned about other students' reactions to their work in the classroom.

_____   3. An important part of schooling is learning to work with others.

_____   4. Children learn more by working on their own than by working with others.

_____   5. Children should be given opportunities to participate actively in class planning and implementation of lessons.

_____   6. In an effective learning environment, grades are inappropriate.

_____   7. Children enjoy working in a classroom that has clearly defined learning objectives and assessment criteria.

_____   8. I favor teaching methods and classroom procedures that maximize student independence to learn from their own experiences.

_____   9. Most of what children learn is learned from other children.

_____   10. Children should be concerned with getting good grades.

_____   11. An important part of teaching and learning is learning how to work independently.

_____   12. In the classroom, the teacher should not be contradicted or challenged by a student.

_____   13. Interchanges between children and a teacher can provide ideas about content better than those found in a textbook.

_____   14. For children to get the most out of a class, they must be aware of the primary concerns and biases of the teacher.

_____   15. Students should not be given high grades unless clearly earned.

_____   16. Learning should help the learner to become an independent thinker.

_____   17. Most of what children learn is learned from their teachers.

_____   18. A teacher who makes children do things they don't want to do is an ineffective teacher.

Source: Adapted from William H. Berquist and Steve R. Phillips, *A Handbook for Faculty Development*, June 1975, Washington, DC: The Council for Independent Colleges, June 1975, pp. 25–27.

_____ 19. Learning takes place most effectively under conditions in which children are in competition with one another.

_____ 20. A teacher should try to persuade students that particular ideas are valid and exciting.

_____ 21. To do well in school, children must be assertive.

_____ 22. Facts in textbooks are usually accurate.

_____ 23. I favor the use of teaching methods and classroom procedures that maximize student and teacher interaction.

_____ 24. Most of what children learn is learned from books.

_____ 25. A teacher who lets children do whatever they want is incompetent.

_____ 26. Students can learn more by working with an enthusiastic teacher than by working alone.

_____ 27. I favor the use of teaching methods and classroom procedures that maximize student learning of basic subject matter content.

_____ 28. Ideas of other students are useful for helping a student understand the content of lessons.

_____ 29. A student should study what the teacher says is important and not necessarily what is important to that student.

_____ 30. A teacher who does not motivate student interest in subject content is incompetent.

_____ 31. An important part of education is learning how to perform under testing and evaluation conditions.

_____ 32. Children can learn more by sharing their ideas than by keeping their ideas to themselves.

_____ 33. Teachers tend to give students too many assignments that are trivial.

_____ 34. Ideas contained in the textbook should be the primary source of the content taught.

_____ 35. Children should be given high grades as a means of motivating them and increasing their self-esteem.

_____ 36. The ideas a student brings into a class are useful for helping the child to understand subject content.

_____ 37. Students should study what is important to them and not necessarily what the teacher claims is important.

_____ 38. Learning takes place most effectively under conditions in which children are working independently of one another.

_____ 39. Teachers often give students too much freedom of choice in content, methods, and procedures.

_____ 40. Teachers should clearly explain what it is they expect from students.

_____ 41. Students' ideas about content are often better than ideas found in textbooks.

_____ 42. Classroom discussions are beneficial learning experiences.

_____ 43. A student's education should help the student to become a successful and contributing member of society.

EXERCISE 2.3 *(continued)*

____ 44. Learning takes place most effectively under conditions in which students are working cooperatively with one another.

____ 45. Teachers often are too personal with their students.

____ 46. A teacher should encourage children to disagree with or challenge that teacher in the classroom.

____ 47. Children have to be able to work effectively with other people to do well in school.

____ 48. For children to get the most out of school, they must assume at least part of the responsibility for their learning.

____ 49. Students seem to enjoy discussing their ideas about learning with the teacher and other students.

____ 50. A child's education should help the child to become a sensitive human being.

Step 2. From the list of 50 items, write the items (by their number) in two columns, those with which you strongly agreed and those with which you strongly disagreed. Ignore those items to which you gave a 2 (were neutral).

| *Strongly Agreed* | *Strongly Disagreed* |

Step 3. In groups of three or four, discuss your lists (in step 2) with your classmates. From the discussion, you may rerank any items you wish.

Step 4. You now have a finalized list of those items with which you were in agreement and those with which you disagreed. On the basis of those two lists, write a paragraph that summarizes your philosophy about teaching and learning. It should be no longer than one-half page in length. That statement is a theoretical representation of your present teaching philosophy.

Step 4. Compare your philosophical statement with the three theoretical positions as discussed prior to this exercise. Can you clearly identify your position? Name it:

Explain your rationale:

At the completion of this course, you may wish to revisit your philosophical statement, perhaps even make revisions to it. It will be useful to have your educational philosophy firmly implanted in your memory for teaching job interviews at a later date (see Chapter 10).

EXERCISE 2.4   REVIEWING THE PROFESSIONAL RESPONSIBILITIES OF A FIRST-YEAR TEACHER

INSTRUCTIONS: The purpose of this exercise is to review the responsibilities of a first-year teacher. Your class should divide into groups of four. Within each group, each member will play one of the following roles: (1) group facilitator, (2) recorder, (3) materials manager, and (4) reporter. The group is to select one of these six categories of responsibilities:

1. Audiovisual/media
2. Classroom environment
3. Clerical
4. Instructional
5. Professional activities
6. Supervision

The group will read the responsibilities for their selected category as they are listed on the card that relates to that responsibility. For example, the group discussing clerical responsibilities will be given the card labeled "Clerical Responsibilities." The group will prioritize those responsibilities, beginning with the most important. The group facilitator will lead this discussion. Under the guidance of the materials manager, the group may cut the cards apart so that they can be physically manipulated as priorities are discussed. The recorder should take notes on the group's work, which can then be discussed to develop the report that will be made to the class.

After a prearranged discussion time, the entire class will come together and each reporter will share the group's (1) prioritized order of responsibilities and (2) estimate of the amount of time that a beginning teacher might devote to these responsibilities each week.

As each group reports, all members of the class should enter its list of priorities and time estimate on the Recap Sheet.

After completion of this exercise, the class may wish to discuss the group dynamics of this model of cooperative learning. For discussion in either large or small groups, key questions might be:

1. Would you use this form of discussion in your own teaching?
2. How would you divide a class of students into groups of four?

Other questions may be generated by the group work.

CARD FOR EXERCISE 2.4
Audiovisual/Media Responsibilities

Selecting, ordering, and returning cassettes, films, DVDs, and other materials

Preparing and operating equipment	Reviewing selected materials
Planning class introduction to the audiovisual materials	Other audiovisual responsibilities as determined

Estimated hours a beginning teacher will devote to audiovisual/media responsibilities each week = _____

CARD FOR EXERCISE 2.4
Classroom Environment Responsibilities

Planning and constructing displays	Preparing bulletin boards
Reading, announcing, and posting class notices	Managing a classroom library
Opening and closing windows, arranging furniture, cleaning the writing board	Other classroom environment responsibilities as determined

Estimated hours a beginning teacher will devote to classroom environment responsibilities each week = _____

CARD FOR EXERCISE 2.4
Clerical Responsibilities

Maintaining attendance and tardy records	Entering grades, scores, or marks into a record book or onto the computer
Preparing progress and grade reports	Typing, drawing, and duplicating instructional materials
Locating resource ideas and materials to support lessons	Other clerical responsibilities as determined

Estimated hours a beginning teacher will devote to clerical responsibilities each week = _____

CARD FOR EXERCISE 2.4

Instructional Responsibilities

Giving additional instruction (e.g., to students who need one-to-one attention, those who have been absent, or small review groups)	Correcting student work
Preparing special learning materials	Preparing, reading, and scoring tests; helping students self-evaluate
Writing information on the board	Preparing long-range and daily lesson plans
Grouping for instruction	Other instructional responsibilities as determined

Estimated hours a beginning teacher will devote to instructional responsibilities each week = _____

CARD FOR EXERCISE 2.4

Professional Activites Responsibilities

Researching and writing teacher reports	Attending teachers' and school district meetings
Planning and attending parent–teacher meetings	Attending local teachers' organization meetings
Attending state, regional, and national professional organizations; taking university classes	Other professional activities responsibilities as determined

Estimated hours a beginning teacher will devote to professional activities each week = _____

CARD FOR EXERCISE 2.4

Supervision Responsibilities

Supervising before- or after-school activities	Supervising hallways, lunchrooms, and bathrooms
Supervising student assemblies	Supervising field trips
Supervising laboratory activities	Helping students settle disputes
Other supervision responsibilities as determined	

Estimated hours a beginning teacher will devote to supervision responsibilities each week = _____

EXERCISE 2.4   RECAP SHEET

Audiovisual/Media Responsibilities

1. _____

2. _____

3. _____

4. _____

5. _____

Estimated hours = _____

Classroom Environment Responsibilities

1. _____

2. _____

3. _____

4. _____

5. _____

6. _____

Estimated hours = _____

Clerical Responsibilities

1. _____

2. _____

3. _____

4. _____

5. _____

6. _____

Estimated Hours = _____

☞

EXERCISE 2.4 *(continued)*

Instructional Responsibilities

1. _____

2. _____

3. _____

4. _____

5. _____

6. _____

7. _____

8. _____

Estimated hours = _____

Professional Activities Responsibilities

1. _____

2. _____

3. _____

4. _____

5. _____

6. _____

Estimated hours = _____

Supervision Responsibilities

1. _____

2. _____

3. _____

4. _____

5. _____

6. _____

7. _____

Estimated Hours = _____

3 The Classroom Learning Environment

To become and to remain an effective teacher with a minimum of distractions in the classroom, you must (a) apply your knowledge of the characteristics and needs of the students with whom you work (knowledge gained from your prior coursework and reviewed in Chapter 1); (b) initiate, practice, develop, and model the behaviors that facilitate their learning (Chapter 2); and (c) do so in a conducive learning environment. The latter is the principal focus of this chapter.

Although competent teaching may be as much an intuitive art as it is a science, still it does not just happen. It begins with the deliberative planning and arranging of the learning environment and continues with selection of the curriculum and thoughtful planning of each phase of the learning process. This chapter deals with the planning, establishing, and managing of a classroom environment conducive to student learning.

To say that a learning environment is "conducive" means it is one that is caring and responsive, that has as its sole purpose aiding each learner in making the transitions necessary to succeed in school and in life. The planning, establishing, and managing of a conducive classroom learning environment derives from one's knowledge about children and how they learn, and from careful thought and planning, and should never be left for the beginning teacher to learn on the job in a sink-or-swim situation.

A conducive classroom learning environment is one that is emotionally safe, that helps students to perceive the importance of what is being taught, that helps them realize they can achieve, and that is instructive in the procedures for doing it. Students are willing to spend time on a learning task when they perceive value or reward in doing so, when they possess some ownership in

planning and carrying out the task, and when they feel they can, in fact, accomplish the task.

Thoughtful and thorough planning of your procedures for classroom management is as important an element of your preactive phase of instruction as is the planning of the curriculum with its units and lessons. Indeed, from an analysis of half a century of research studies, it is concluded that establishment and management of the classroom learning environment is the single most important factor influencing student learning (Want, Haertel, & Walberg, 1993).

This chapter presents guidelines and resources to help you establish and manage a classroom environment that is emotionally safe and conducive to the learning of each and every student. Specifically, upon completion of this chapter you should be able to:

1. As related to classroom management, distinguish between the concepts of consequences and punishment.
2. Describe a teacher's reasonable first reaction to students with various behaviors, such as one who is aggressively violent, one who is bullying another student, one who habitually lies, one who is defiant, one who tosses paper from across the room at the wastebasket, one who knowingly steals, and one who is just sitting and staring out the window.
3. Use examples to describe how each of the following contributes to effective classroom control: a positive approach, well-planned lessons, a productive start of the school term, classroom procedures and rules, consistency but with professional judgment in enforcing procedures and rules, correction of student misbehavior, and classroom management.

4. Describe ways you can help students establish and maintain self-control.
5. Describe important perceptions that must be in place.
6. Describe planning you would do for the first week of school.
7. Describe the importance of transitions and the characteristics of an effective instructional transition.
8. Describe the meaning and give an example of *sequenced consequences* as used in response to inappropriate student behavior.
9. Differentiate between direct and indirect intervention to refocus a student and describe situations where you would be most likely to use each.
10. Prepare an initial draft of your proposed classroom management system.

THE IMPORTANCE OF PERCEPTIONS

Unless you believe your students can learn, they will not. Unless you believe you can teach them, you will not. Unless your students believe they can learn and until they want to learn, they will not. Those facts were portrayed so well, for example, in the 1988 movie *Stand and Deliver* and the 2007 movie *Freedom Writers,* about the teaching lives of Jaime Escalante and Erin Gruwell, respectively.

We all know of or have heard of teachers, perhaps not as famous as Escalante and Gruwell, but nevertheless who obtain the very best from their students, even from those students many teachers find most challenging to teach. Regardless of individual circumstances, those teachers

- know, when given adequate support, all students can learn;
- expect the best from each student;
- establish a classroom environment that motivates students to do their best;
- manage their classrooms so class time is efficiently used, that is, with the least amount of distraction to the learning process.

Regardless of how well planned you are for the instruction, certain perceptions by students must be in place to support the successful implementation of those plans. Students must perceive

- the classroom environment as being supportive of their efforts;
- that you care about their learning, that you respect them as human beings, and that they are welcome in your classroom;
- the expected learning as being challenging but not impossible;
- the target learning outcomes as being worthy of their time and effort to try and achieve.

Those perceptions must be in place before productive learning can occur. It is about the establishment of those perceptions that this resource guide, especially this chapter, is centered.

CLASSROOM CONTROL—ITS MEANING— PAST AND PRESENT

Classroom control frequently is the greatest concern to beginning teachers—and they have cause to be concerned. Even experienced teachers sometimes find control difficult, particularly in schools where so many students come to school with so much psychological baggage and have already become alienated as a result of negative experiences in their lives.

In one respect, being a classroom teacher is analogous to being a truck driver who must remain alert while going down a steep and winding grade; otherwise, the truck most assuredly will get out of control, veer off the highway, and crash. This chapter has been thoughtfully designed to help you with your concerns about control—and to help you avoid a crash.

Historical Meaning of Classroom Control

To set the stage for your comprehension, consider what the term **classroom control** has meant historically and what it means today. In the 1800s, instead of classroom control, educators spoke of classroom discipline, and that meant punishment. Such an interpretation was consistent with the then-popular learning theory that assumed children were innately bad and that inappropriate behavior could be prevented by strictness or treated with punishment. Schools of the mid-1800s have been described as being "wild and unruly places," and "full of idleness and disorder" (Hyman & D'Allessandro, 1984, p. 24).

By the early 1900s, educators were asking, "Why are the children still misbehaving?" The accepted answer was that they were misbehaving because of the rigid punitive system. On this point, the era of progressive education began, providing students more freedom to decide what they would learn. The teacher's job, then, became one of providing a rich classroom of resources and materials to stimulate the student's natural curiosity. And because the system no longer would be causing misbehavior, punishment would no longer be necessary. Classes of the 1930s that were highly permissive, however, turned out to cause more anxiety than the restrictive classes of the 1800s.

Today's Meaning of Classroom Control and the Concept of Classroom Management

Today, rather than classroom "discipline," educators speak of classroom control, the process of controlling student behavior in the classroom. The most effective teacher is one who is in control of classroom events rather than controlled by them. Classroom control is an important aspect of the broader concept of classroom management. Classroom control is a component of a management plan designed to

- prevent inappropriate student behavior,
- help students develop self-control, and
- suggest procedures for dealing with inappropriate student behavior.

Effective teaching requires a well-organized, businesslike classroom in which motivated students work diligently at their learning tasks, free from distractions and interruptions. Providing such a setting for learning requires careful thought and preparation and is called **effective classroom management**. Effective classroom management is the process of organizing and conducting a classroom so that it maximizes student learning. As a new teacher, you should not underestimate how difficult this process can be.

> Today's teachers share a concern for selecting management techniques that enhance student self-esteem and that help students learn how to assume control of their behavior and ownership of their learning.

A teacher's procedures for classroom control reflect that teacher's philosophy about how young people learn and interpretation and commitment to the school's stated mission. In sum, those procedures represent the teacher's concept of classroom management. Although often eclectic in their approaches, today's teachers share a concern for selecting management techniques that enhance student self-esteem and that help students learn how to assume control of their behavior and ownership of their learning.

Although some schools subscribe heavily to one approach or another, many others are more eclectic, having evolved from the historical works of several leading authorities. Table 3.1 illustrates the main ideas of several authorities and provides a comparison of their recommended approaches. The guidelines and suggestions that are presented throughout this chapter represent an eclectic approach, borrowing from many of these authorities.

Classroom Management: Contributions of Some Leading Authorities

You are probably familiar with the term **behavior modification**, which describes several high-control techniques for changing behavior in an observable and predictable way; with **B. F. Skinner's** (Skinner, 1968, 1971) ideas about how students learn and how behavior can be modified by using reinforcers (rewards); and with how his principles of behavior shaping have been extended by others.

Behavior modification begins with four steps: (a) identify the behavior to be modified, (b) record how often and under what conditions that behavior occurs, (c) cause a change by reinforcing a desired behavior with a positive reinforcer, and (d) choose the type of positive reinforcers to award—**activity or privilege reinforcers**, such as playing a game, caring for a classroom pet, decorating the classroom, using a classroom learning center, being freed without penalty from doing an assignment or test, or running an errand for the teacher; **social reinforcers**, such as verbal attention or private praise, nonverbal attention, such as proximity to the teacher, facial expression of approval, such as a wink or smile, or bodily expression of approval, such as a thumbs up or high five; **graphic reinforcers**, such as numerals and symbols made by rubber stamps; **tangible reinforcers**, such as edibles, badges, certificates, stickers, or books; and **token reinforcers**, such as points, stars, or script or tickets that can be accumulated and cashed in later for a tangible reinforcer.

Using an approach that emphasizes both reinforcement for appropriate behaviors and punishment or consequences for inappropriate behaviors, **Lee Canter** and **Marlene Canter** developed their **assertive discipline** model that emphasizes four major points (Canter & Canter, 2002). First, as a teacher, you have professional rights in your classroom and should expect appropriate student behavior. Second, your students have rights to choose how to behave in your classroom, and you should plan limits for inappropriate behavior. Third, an assertive discipline approach means you clearly state your expectations in a firm voice and explain the boundaries for behavior. And fourth, you should plan a system of positive consequences (e.g., positive messages home, awards and rewards, special privileges) for appropriate behavior and establish consequences (e.g., time out, withdrawal of privileges, parent/guardian conference) for inappropriate student misbehavior, and you must follow through in a consistent way. In recent years, primarily because of its rather heavy emphasis on threat and punishment along with a lack of research to support its effectiveness, the assertive discipline model has lost favor (Good & Brophy, 2008).

In his **logical consequences** approach, **Rudolf Dreikurs** emphasized six points (Dreikurs & Cassel, 1972; Dreikurs, Grunwald, & Pepper, 1982). First, be fair, firm, and friendly and involve your students in developing and implementing class rules. Second, students need to clearly understand the rules and the logical consequences for misbehavior. For example, a logical consequence for a student who has painted graffiti on a school wall would be to either clean the wall or pay for a school custodian to do it. Third, allow the students to be responsible not only for their own actions but also for influencing others to maintain appropriate behavior in your classroom. Fourth, encourage students

Table 3.1   Comparing Approaches to Classroom Management

Authority	To Know What Is Going On	To Provide Smooth Transitions
Canter/Jones	Realize that the student has the right to choose how to behave in your class with the understanding of the consequences that will follow his or her choice.	Insist on decent, responsible behavior.
Dreikurs/Nelsen/Albert	Realize that the student wants status, recognition, and a feeling of belonging. Misbehavior is associated with mistaken goals of getting attention, seeking power, getting revenge, and wanting to be left alone.	Identify mistaken student goals; act in ways that do not reinforce these goals.
Ginott/Kohn	Communicate with the student to find out his or her feelings about a situation and about that student in general.	Invite student cooperation.
Glasser/Gordon/ Rogers/Gathercoal/ Freiberg/Marshall/ Sprick	Realize that the student is a rational being who can control his or her own behavior.	Help the student make good choices; good choices produce good behavior, and bad choices produce bad behavior.
Kounin	Develop withitness, a skill enabling you to see what is happening in all parts of the classroom at all times.	Avoid jerkiness, which consists of thrusts (giving directions before your group is ready), dangles (leaving one activity dangling in the verbal air, starting another one, and then returning to the first activity), and flip-flops (terminating one activity, beginning another one, and then returning to the first activity you terminated).
Skinner	Realize value of nonverbal interaction (i.e., smiles, pats, and handshakes) to communicate to students that you know what is going on.	Realize that smooth transitions may be part of your procedures for awarding reinforcers (i.e., points and tokens) to reward appropriate behavior.

To Maintain Group Alertness	To Involve Students	To Attend to Misbehavior
Set clear limits and consequences; follow through consistently; state what you expect; state the consequences and why the limits are needed.	Use firm tone of voice; keep eye contact; use nonverbal gestures and verbal statements; use hints, questions, and direct messages in requesting student behavior; give and receive compliments.	Follow through with your promises and the reasonable, previously stated consequences that have been established in your class.
Provide firm guidance and leadership.	Allow students to have a say in establishing rules and consequences in your class.	Make it clear that unpleasant consequences will follow inappropriate behavior.
Model the behavior you expect to see in your students.	Build student's self-esteem.	Give a message that addresses the situation and does not attack the student's character.
Understand that class rules are essential.	Realize that classroom meetings are effective means for attending to rules, behavior, and discipline.	Accept no excuses for inappropriate behavior; see that reasonable consequences always follow.
Avoid slowdowns (delays and time wasting) that can be caused by overdwelling (too much time spent on explanations) and by fragmentation (breaking down an activity into several unnecessary steps). Develop a group focus (active participation by all students in the group) through accountability (holding all students accountable for the concept of the lesson) and by attention (seeing all the students and using unison and individual responses).	Avoid boredom by providing a feeling of progress for the students, offering challenges, varying class activities, changing the level of intellectual challenge, varying lesson presentations, and using many different learning materials and aids.	Understand that teacher correction influences behavior of other nearby students (the ripple effect).
Set rules, rewards, and consequences; emphasize that responsibility for good behavior rests with each student.	Involve students in "token economies," in contracts, and in charting behavior performance.	Provide tangibles to students who follow the class rules; represent tangibles as "points" for the whole class to use to "purchase" a special activity.

to show respect for themselves and for others, and provide each student with a sense of belonging to the classroom. Fifth, recognize and encourage student goals of belonging, gaining status, and gaining recognition. And sixth, recognize but do not reinforce correlated student goals of getting attention, seeking power, and taking revenge.

Continuing the work of Dreikurs, **Linda Albert** (1989, rev. 1996) developed a **cooperative discipline** model. The cooperative discipline model makes use of Dreikurs' fundamental concepts, with emphasis added on the "three Cs": capable, connect, and contribute. Also building upon the work of Dreikurs, **Jane Nelsen** (Nelsen, 1987; Nelsen, Lott, & Glenn, 1993) provided guidelines for helping children develop positive feelings of self. Key points made by Nelsen and reflected throughout this resource guide are as follows: (a) use natural and logical consequences as a means to inspire a positive classroom atmosphere, (b) understand that children have goals that drive them toward misbehavior (attention, power, revenge, and assumed adequacy), (c) use kindness (student retains dignity) and firmness when administering consequences for a student's misbehavior, (d) establish a climate of mutual respect, (e) use class meetings to give students ownership in problem solving, and (f) offer encouragement as a means of inspiring self-evaluation and focusing on the student's behaviors.

William Glasser (1965, 1969, 1986, 1990, 1993) developed his concept of **reality therapy** (i.e., the condition of the present, rather than of the past, contributes to inappropriate behavior) for the classroom. Glasser emphasizes that students have a responsibility to learn at school and to maintain appropriate behavior while there. He emphasizes that with the teacher's help, students can make appropriate choices about their behavior in school—can, in fact, learn self-control. Finally, he suggests holding classroom meetings that are devoted to establishing class rules and identifying standards for student behavior, matters of misbehavior, and the consequences of misbehavior. Since the publication of his first book in 1965, Glasser has expanded his message to include the student needs of belonging and love, control, freedom, and fun, asserting that if these needs are ignored and unattended at school, students are bound to fail (Glasser, 1997).

Today's commitment to **quality education** is largely derived from the recent work of Glasser and the corresponding concept of the **personal-centered classrooms** as advanced by **Carl Rogers** and **H. Jerome Freiberg** in their 1994 book *Freedom to Learn* (Upper Saddle River, NJ: Prentice Hall). In schools committed to quality education and the person-centered classroom, students feel a sense of belonging, enjoy some degree of power of self-discipline, have fun learning, and experience a sense of freedom in the process (Freiberg, 1997, 1999; Jackson & Davis, 2000).

Paul Gathercoal built his **judicious discipline** model on a synthesis of professional ethics, good quality educational practice, and democratic principles and students' constitutional rights as outlined especially in the 1st, 4th, and 14th Amendments to the U.S. Constitution (Gathercoal, 1997). By allowing students the opportunity to experience individual freedoms and encouraging them to learn and practice the responsibilities emanating from their individual rights, students learn how to govern themselves. A number of schools report success in reducing student hostile behaviors by using a combination of judicious discipline and class meetings (Freiberg, 1999; McEwan & Gathercoal, 2000).

Haim G. Ginott emphasized ways for teacher and student to communicate in his communication model. He advised sending clear messages about situations rather than about the child. And he emphasized that teachers must model the behavior they expect from students. Ginott's suggested messages are those that express feelings appropriately, acknowledge students' feelings, give appropriate direction, and invite cooperation (Ginott, 1971; Manning & Bucher, 2001).

Thomas Gordon (1989) emphasized influence over control and decried use of reinforcement (i.e., rewards and punishment) as an ineffective tool for achieving a positive influence over a child's behavior. Rather than using reinforcements for appropriate behavior and punishment for inappropriate behaviors, Gordon advocated encouragement and development of student self-control and self-regulated behavior. To have a positive influence and to encourage self-control, the teacher (and school) should provide a rich and positive learning environment with rich and stimulating learning activities. Specific teacher behaviors include active listening (e.g., maintaining eye contact, rephrasing what the student has said, and asking relevant questions), sending I-messages (rather than you-messages), shifting from I-messages to listening when there is student resistance to an I-message, clearly identifying ownership of problems to the student when such is the case (i.e., not assuming ownership if it is a student's problem), and encouraging collaborative problem solving.

Fredric Jones (1987) also promoted the idea of helping students support their own self-control, by way of a negative reinforcement method—rewards follow wanted behavior. Preferred activity time (PAT) is an invention derived from the Jones Model. The Jones Model makes four recommendations. First, you properly structure your classroom so students understand the rules (the expectation standards for classroom behavior) and procedures (the means for accomplishing routine tasks). Second, you maintain control by selecting appropriate instructional strategies. Third, you build patterns of cooperative work. Finally, you develop appropriate backup methods for dealing with inappropriate student behavior.

Jacob Kounin (1970) is known for his identification of the **ripple effect** (i.e., the effect of a teacher's response to one student's misbehavior on students whose behavior was appropriate) and of withitness and overlapping ability (both of which are discussed in Chapter 2).

DEVELOPING YOUR OWN EFFECTIVE APPROACH TO CLASSROOM MANAGEMENT

As you review these contributions to today's approaches to effective classroom management, the expert opinions as well as the research evidence will remind you of the importance of

- concentrating your attention on desirable student behaviors;
- quickly and appropriately attending to inappropriate behavior, especially that which is lingering or likely to become disruptive;
- maintaining alertness to all that is happening in your classroom;
- providing smooth transitions, keeping the entire class on task, and preventing dead time (i.e., time when students have nothing to do); and
- involving students by providing challenges, class meetings, ways of establishing rules and consequences, opportunities to receive and return compliments, and chances to build self-control and self-esteem.

Using the criteria of your own perceptions, philosophy, feelings, values, and knowledge, you are encouraged to construct a classroom environment and management system that is positive and effective for you and your students, and then to consistently apply it while still being willing to modify it as time and circumstances dictate. Use the guidelines shown in Figure 3.1 to begin the thinking process for developing your personal plan for classroom management—the process that begins now, continues in Exercise 3.3 and throughout your professional career.

PROVIDING A SUPPORTIVE LEARNING ENVIRONMENT

It is probably no surprise to you to hear that teachers whose classrooms are pleasant, positive, and challenging but supportive places to be find that their students learn and behave better than do the students of teachers whose classroom atmospheres are harsh, negative, repressive, and unchallenging. What follows now are specific suggestions for making your classroom a pleasant, positive, and challenging place, that is, an environment that encourages and supports student learning.

Consider the Physical Layout

There is much in the arrangement of the classroom that can either contribute to or help prevent classroom management problems. Certainly, when talking about classrooms ranging grades 7–12, there is no one best way to arrange a classroom. To the extent allowed by the room, *the arrangement should be kept flexible so students may be deployed in the ways most suitable for accomplishing specific tasks.* The primary guideline, however, is simple. Just as is true with adults, when young people are seated side by side or facing one another, it is perfectly natural for them to talk to each other. Therefore, if your desire is to encourage social interaction, as when using small-group learning, seat students of groups close together; if you would rather they work interdependently, such as when taking independent achievement tests, separate them to the extent possible.

Some teachers; especially those of middle grades, have experienced success having students at the start of the school year design personal space dividers to provide privacy during testing and other independent activities. Attaching three approximately 8 × 10-inch rectangular sections of cardboard, can make space dividers. The divider is placed standing in front of the student making it impossible for neighboring students to see over or around. Dividers can be made from cardboard boxes or heavy folders of various sorts. It could be a project at the beginning of the year for each student to design and make an individual space divider that is then stored in the classroom for use on test days. Students enjoy being allowed to personalize their dividers.

It is unreasonable to place students in situations that encourage maximum interaction and then admonish or berate them for interacting, for whispering and talking. Sometimes, so not to disturb the learning going on in neighboring classrooms, you may need to remind

Figure 3.1   Developing a personal classroom management system.

MY EMERGING PLAN FOR CLASSROOM MANAGEMENT

Grade level (or range) _____   My name _____

Plans Before the First Day

1. Describe your classroom with respect to the physical room arrangement and organization and the positive and caring classroom community that you aim to create.
2. Describe communication you will initiate with your students and their families prior to the first day of school.
3. Describe characteristics of your classroom that will signal to the children that it is a friendly and safe place to be.
4. Describe how you will get to know the children and what you will do to help the children get to know you and each other.

The First Day

5. Describe how you will greet the children when they arrive for the first day.
6. Describe the rules or procedural expectations that you will have already in place and how they will be presented to the children.
7. Describe how you will have children contribute to these rules and expectations.
8. Describe your classroom procedures for
   - absences; making up missed work and instruction
   - assigning helpers for classroom jobs such as taking care of pets, plants, the calendar, bathroom monitor, and so forth
   - being in the classroom before and after school, and at recess and lunch time
   - bringing toys, plants, and pets into the classroom
   - collecting notes, money, and forms
   - distributing and collecting papers and materials
   - eating and drinking in the classroom
   - going to the bathroom
   - late arrival and early dismissal
   - movement in the halls
   - storing personal belongings
   - taking attendance
   - using the classroom sink, if there is one
   - using the pencil sharpener
   - using the teacher's desk
   - using the water fountain
   - using other materials and equipment
   - wearing hats and other articles of clothing in the classroom
   - what to do in an emergency situation
   - when a visitor comes into the classroom
9. Describe the class or morning opening; the class or day's closure.

Managing the Curriculum

10. Describe how you will help the children with their organization and assignments.
11. Describe your homework expectations. Will there be homework? How much and how often? Will parents and guardians be in-formed? If so, how? What is their involvement to be? Is there a school homework hotline?
12. Describe your procedure for incomplete, unacceptable, or incorrect student work. Is there a recovery option?
13. Do you plan to provide comments, feedback, or corrections on student work?
14. Will you use marks of some sort–grades, value words, figures, and so forth?
15. Will students be rewarded for their group work? How will you assess group learning? How will you assess individual learning from group work?
16. Describe the student portfolio expectation. Where will the portfolios be stored? When will students work on their portfolios?
17. Describe your plan for communication with parents/guardians.

Maintaining Classroom Relations and Personal Behavior

18. Describe how you will bring an off-task child back on task.
19. Describe how students will know what is and what is not an appropriate level of classroom noise.
20. Describe how you will signal a need for hands and when, if ever, it is okay to call out without using hands.
21. Describe how you will indicate your support for appropriate student behavior.
22. Describe how you will discourage inappropriate student behavior.
23. Describe your order of indirect and direct behavior intervention strategies.
24. Describe how you will signal your need for attention from the class and from a distracted student.
25. Describe how you will respond when two errant behaviors are happening simultaneously but at opposing locations in the classroom.

When the Going Gets Tough

26. Describe your pattern of escalating consequences.
27. Describe how you will deal with disrespectful, inappropriate comments from students.
28. Describe how you will respond to remarks that are sexist or racist or that stereotype people in inappropriate and cruel ways.
29. Describe how you will respond to serious and dangerous student behaviors.
30. Identify one person you can go to for support.

the students to keep their voices down. Some teachers even have a sign hung in the classroom where all can see that clearly designates the expected noise level on a given day or for a particular activity, such as *0* for *complete silence* (no talking), *1* for *whispering* or what some teachers refer to as "6-inch voice," and a *2* for *talking aloud in normal voice* (but within reason).

> Teachers who continually require students to sit still and stop talking apparently prefer to teach a grove of trees rather than a classroom full of students.
>
> Robert Sylwester, 2007 (permission via personal correspondence date 2/4/2009)

Create a Positive Ambiance

All students should feel welcome in your classroom and accepted by you as individuals of worth and dignity. Although these feelings and behaviors should be reciprocal, that is, expected of the students as well, they may have to begin with your frequent modeling of the behaviors expected of the students. You must help students know that any denial by you of a student's specific behavior is not a denial of that individual as a worthwhile person who is still welcomed into your classroom to learn as long as the student agrees to follow expected procedures.

Specific things you can do to create a positive classroom ambiance, some of which are repeated from preceding chapters and others that are addressed in later chapters, are as follows:

- Admonish behavior, not persons.
- Ensure that no discrimination is ever displayed against any individual student.
- Attend to the classroom's physical appearance and comfort—it is your place of work, show pride in that fact. Consider this: a study with eighth-grade students suggested that in a classroom atmosphere enhanced with a pleasant scented fragrance students required fewer redirections of their behavior from the teacher (Gabriel, 1999).
- In encouraging desirable student behavior, phrase directions in positive rather than negative language, using "dos" rather than "do nots."
- Be an interesting person and an optimistic and enthusiastic teacher.
- Encourage students to set high yet realistic goals for themselves, and then show them how to work in increments toward meeting their goal—letting each know that you are confident in the student's ability to achieve.
- Help students develop the skills necessary for collaborative and cooperative learning.
- Involve students in every aspect of their learning, including the planning of learning activities, thereby giving them partial ownership and responsibility in their learning.
- Make the learning enjoyable and even fun, at least to the extent possible and reasonable.
- Recognize and reward truly positive behaviors and individual successes, no matter how meager they might seem to be.
- Send positive and easily understood messages home to parents or guardians, even if you have to get help and write the message in the language of the student's home.
- Use varied, interesting, developmentally appropriate, and motivating learning activities.

Behaviors to Avoid When Using Encouragement to Motivate Students

Two items in the preceding list are statements about giving encouragement. When using encouragement to motivate student learning, there are a few important behaviors that you should *avoid* because they inhibit learning.

- Avoid comparing one student with another, or one class of students with another.
- Avoid encouraging competition among students except when all students have equal opportunity to win, when winning is determined primarily by degree of effort (and perhaps a degree of luck) rather than by ability level, and when reactions to the outcome emphasize the positive (i.e., winners are congratulated but losers are not criticized or ridiculed; the accomplishments of the class as a whole, not just of the winners, are acknowledged).
- Avoid ever giving up or appearing to give up on any student.

QUESTIONS FOR SELF-REFLECTION FOR ESTABLISHING A CONDUCIVE LEARNING ENVIRONMENT

Does Your Classroom Attractively Display . . .

- Agreed-upon classroom rules and procedures, a few major ones?
- Benchmark curriculum standards, the most important ones, with scoring rubrics?
- Helpful information about the expected mechanics for writing?
- Photographs of happy and proud students—current and past—in action?
- Reminders about procedures and deadlines for homework?
- Samples of exemplary student work, including writing and long-term projects? (with or without student names, depending on school policy)
- Student-created murals and collages that include all students, making each feel that he or she belongs?

- Avoid telling a student how much better he or she could be.
- Avoid using qualifying statements, such as "I like what you did, but . . ." or "It's about time."

Get to Know Your Students as People

For classes to move forward smoothly and efficiently, they should fit the students' learning styles, learning capacities, developmental needs, and interests. To make the learning meaningful and longest lasting, build the curriculum around student interests, capacities, perceptions, and perspectives. Therefore, you need to know your students well enough to be able to provide learning experiences that they will find interesting, valuable, intrinsically motivating, challenging, and rewarding. *Knowing your students is at least as important as knowing subject matter content* (Hoffman & Levak, 2003). Of course, looping and small learning communities help teachers get to know their students as people. Whether or not those opportunities immediately avail themselves, the following paragraphs describe a number of things you can do to get to know your students as people.

QUICKLY LEARN AND USE STUDENT NAMES

Like everyone else, young people appreciate being recognized and addressed by name. Quickly learning and using their names is an important motivating strategy. One technique for learning names quickly is to take snapshot photographs of each student on the first day. Later, students could use the photographs as a portion of the covers of their portfolios or space dividers. Another technique for learning names quickly is to use a seating chart. Laminate the seating chart onto an attractive, neon-colored clipboard that you can carry in class. Many teachers prefer to assign permanent seats and then make seating charts from which they can unobtrusively check the roll while students are doing seatwork. It is usually best to get your students into the lesson before taking roll and before doing other housekeeping chores. Ways of assigning student seating are discussed later in this chapter (see The First Day).

Addressing students by name every time you speak to them helps you to learn and remember their names. Be sure to quickly learn to pronounce their names correctly; that helps in making a positive impression. Another helpful way to learn student names is to return papers yourself by calling student names and then handing the papers to them, paying careful attention to look at each student and make mental notes that may help you associate names with faces.

CLASSROOM SHARING DURING THE FIRST WEEK OF SCHOOL

During the first week of school many teachers take time each day to have students present information about themselves or about the day's assignment. For instance, perhaps five or six students are selected each day to answer questions such as "What name would you like to be called by?" "Where did you attend school last year?" "Tell us about your hobbies and other interests, or about your summer or after-school job." "What interested you about last night's reading, or yesterday's lesson?"

> I once heard a student say, "At school, I need a pass to go to the bathroom, but at 3:00, I'm an assistant manager at McDonald's."
>
> Dennis Littky (2004, p. 44)

How the student answers such questions or participates in such activities can be as revealing as the information (or the lack thereof) that the student shares. From the sharing, you sometimes get clues about additional information you would like to know about the student.

OBSERVE STUDENTS IN THE CLASSROOM—DEVELOP AND PRACTICE YOUR WITHITNESS

During learning activities the wise teacher is constantly moving around the classroom and is alert to the individual behavior (nonverbal and verbal) of each student in the class, whether the student is on task or gazing off and perhaps thinking about other things. Be cautious, however; just because a student is gazing out the window does not mean the student is not thinking about the learning task. During group work is a particularly good time to observe students and get to know more about each one's skills and interests.

OBSERVATIONS OF AND CONVERSATIONS WITH STUDENTS OUTSIDE THE CLASSROOM

Another way to learn more about students is from observing them outside class, for example, at recess, athletic events, dances, performing arts presentations, lunch time (finding it an excellent time to get to know their students as well as to provide informal guidance/counseling, some high school teachers open their classrooms at noon for a brown-bag lunch with any students who wish to come), intramural activities, during advisory or homeroom, in the hallways, from home visits, and at club meetings. Observations made from outside the classroom can give information about student personalities, friendships, interests, and potentialities. For instance, you may find that a student who seems phlegmatic, lackadaisical, or uninterested in the learning activities in your classroom is a real fireball on the playground or on the playing field, or a major mover and shaker on the school's student council or at some other student gathering.

CONFERENCES AND INTERVIEWS WITH STUDENTS

Conferences with students, and sometimes with family members as well, afford yet another opportunity to show that you are genuinely interested in each student as a person as well as a student. Some teachers and teaching teams plan and conduct a series of conferences during the first few weeks in which, individually or in small groups of three or four, students are interviewed by the teacher or by members of the teaching team. Block scheduling is especially conducive to teacher–parent/guardian–student conferences. Such conferences and interviews are managed by using open-ended questions. The teacher indicates by the questions, by listening, and by nonjudgmental and empathic responses (i.e., being able to "step into the shoes" of the student, thereby understanding from where the student is coming), a genuine interest in the students.

Keep in mind, however, that older students in particular, although not necessarily, who feel they have been betrayed by prior adult associations may at first be distrustful of your sincerity. In such instances, do not force it. Be patient, but do not hesitate to take advantage of the opportunity afforded by talking with individual students outside of class time. Investing a few minutes of time in a positive conversation with a student, during which you indicate a genuine interest in that student, can pay real dividends (although it may not always be immediately obvious) when it comes to that student's interest and learning in your classroom.

When using interviews with students, consider having the students individually write one or two questions that they would like you to answer in the interview. This ensures that the student is an active participant in the interview.

STUDENT WRITING AND QUESTIONNAIRES

Much can be learned about students by what they write. It is important to encourage writing in your classroom, and (with varying degrees of intensity) to read everything that students write and submit to you, and to ask for clarification when needed. Useful for this are portfolios, blogs, and journals (see Index for locations).

Some teachers use open-ended, interest-discovering questionnaires. Student responses to questionnaires can provide ideas about how to tailor assignments for individual students. However, you must assure students that their answers are optional and that you are not invading their privacy.

In an interest-discovering questionnaire, students are asked to answer questions such as "When you read for fun or pleasure, what do you usually read?" "What are your favorite movies or TV shows?" "Who are your favorite performers?" "Athletes?" "Describe your favorite hobby or other non-school-related activity."

In an autobiographical questionnaire, the student is asked to answer questions such as "Where were you born?" Do you have siblings?" Do you have responsibilities at home; what are they?" How do you like to spend your leisure time?" Do you have a favorite hobby; what is it?" Many teachers model the process by beginning it with giving their own autobiographical responses to the students.

CUMULATIVE RECORD, DISCUSSIONS WITH COLLEAGUES, EXPERIENTIAL BACKGROUNDS, COMMUNITY AND HOME VISITS

The cumulative record for each student is maintained in the school office, and it contains information recorded from year to year by teachers and other school professionals. The information covers the student's academic background, standardized test scores, and extracurricular activities. However, the Family Educational Rights and Privacy Act (FERPA) of 1974, and revised in 1996, may forbid your viewing the record, except perhaps in collaboration with an administrator or counselor when you have a legitimate educational purpose for doing so. Although you must use discretion before arriving at any conclusion about information contained in the cumulative record, the record may afford information for getting to know a particular student better. Remember, though, a student's past is history and should not be held against that student, but used as a means for improved understanding of a student's experiences and current perceptions.

To better understand a student it is sometimes helpful to talk with the student's other teachers, advisor, or counselor, to learn of their perceptions and experiences with the student. Yet another way of getting to know students is to spend time in the neighborhoods in which they live, while, of course, keeping your personal safety utmost in mind. Observe and listen, finding and noting things that you can use as examples, connections, or as learning activities.

Visiting the student's home is yet another strategy that can enable the teacher to better know a student. When doing a home visit, it is a good idea to always be accompanied by another adult. Check with your school to see if the district offers guidelines and information for making home visits.

PREPARATION PROVIDES CONFIDENCE AND SUCCESS

For successful classroom management, beginning the school term well may make all the difference in the world. Remember that you have only one opportunity to make a first and lasting impression. Therefore, you should appear at the first session as well prepared and as confident as possible.

Perhaps in the beginning you will feel nervous and apprehensive, but being ready and well prepared will help you at least to appear confident. It is likely that every beginning teacher is nervous and apprehensive to some degree; the secret is not to appear nervous. Being well prepared provides the confidence necessary to cloud feelings of nervousness. A slow, under-the-breath counting to 10 at the start can be helpful, too. Then, if you proceed in a businesslike, matter-of-fact way, the impetus of your well-prepared beginning will, most likely, cause the day, week, and year to proceed pretty much as desired.

Effective Organization and Administration of Activities and Materials

In a well-managed classroom student movement about the classroom is routinized, controlled, and purposeful to the learning activities; students know what to do, have the materials needed to do it well, and remain on task while doing it. The classroom atmosphere is supportive, the assignments and procedures for doing them are clear, and the materials of instruction are current, interesting, and readily available. At all times, the teacher is in control of events, rather than controlled by them, ensuring that students are spending their time on appropriate tasks. For your work, your teaching, to be most effective, you must be skilled in managing that which occurs in your workplace—your classroom.

Natural Interruptions and Disruptions to Routine

As you devise and prepare to implement your management system (which will, by the way, be ever evolving), you must also be aware of your own moods and high-stress days and know that your own tolerance levels may vary some. Students, too, are susceptible to personal problems and events that can be the sources of high stress. As you come to know your students well, you will be able to ascertain when certain students are under an inordinate amount of stress and anxiety, come to school sleepy or hungry, or are emotionally distraught from unfortunate happenings at home or elsewhere.

You must understand that classroom routines may be interrupted occasionally, especially on certain days and at certain times during the school year. Students will not have the same motivation and energy level on each and every day. Energy level also varies throughout the school day. Your anticipation of—and thoughtful and careful planning for during the preactive phase of instruction—periods of high or low energy levels will help protect your own mental health. Depending on a number of factors, periods of high energy level might include:

- at the beginning of each school day
- before a field trip, a holiday, or a school event—such as a dance, picture day, athletic event, or a school assembly

- return to school from a field trip
- day of a holiday, such as Valentine's Day or Halloween
- day following a holiday
- day a substitute teacher is present
- state-mandated testing days
- grade report day
- immediately before or after lunch
- on a minimum day
- toward the end of each school day, toward the end of school each Friday afternoon, and toward the end of the school term or year

Although there may be no hard evidence, many experienced teachers will tell you that particularly troublesome days for classroom control are those days when there is a strong north wind or a full moon. One teacher jokingly (I suspect) said that on days when there is both a strong north wind and a full moon, she calls in sick.

How should you prepare for these so-called high-energy days? There are probably no specific guidelines that will work for all teachers, of all grade levels, and in all situations in each instance from the list. However, these are days to which you need to pay extra attention during your planning, days that students could possibly be restless and more difficult to manage, days when you might need to be especially forceful and consistent in your enforcement of procedures, or even compassionate and more tolerant than usual. Plan instructional activities that might be more readily accepted by the students. In no instance is it my intent to imply that learning ceases and playtime takes over. What little instructional time is available to a teacher during a school year is too precious for that ever to happen.

CLASSROOM PROCEDURES AND GUIDELINES FOR ACCEPTABLE BEHAVIOR

It is impossible to overemphasize the importance of getting the school term off to a positive and productive beginning, so this section begins with a presentation of how that is done.

Starting the School Term Well

There are but a few important key reminders to getting the school term off to an excellent beginning. Perhaps most important are for you to be *prepared* and to be *fair.* Preparation for the first day of school should include the determination of your classroom procedures and basic expectations for the behavior of the students while they are under your supervision. The procedures and expectations must be consistent with school policy and seem reasonable to your students, and in enforcing them you must be a fair and consistent professional. However, being coldly consistent is not the same as being fair and professional. As a teacher, you are a professional who deals in matters of human relations and who must exercise professional judgment. You are not a robot, nor are any of your students. Human beings differ from one another, and seemingly similar situations can vary substantially because the people involved are different. Consequently, your response, or lack of response, to each of two separate but quite similar situations may differ. To be most effective, learning must be enjoyable for students; it cannot be enjoyable when a teacher consistently acts like a marine drill sergeant. If a student infracts upon a rule, rather than assuming why, or seeming to not care why, or to overreact to the infraction, find out why before deciding your response. See, for example, Teaching in Practice: Late Homework Paper from an At-Risk Student.

In preparing your classroom management system, remember that too many rules and detailed procedures at the beginning can be a source of trouble. To avoid trouble, it is best at first to present only the minimum number of procedural expectations necessary for an orderly start to the school term. By the time students are beyond the primary grades, unless they are recent newcomers to the United States, they likely already know the expected procedures, that is, the general rules of expected behavior, although some of their prior teachers may not always have been consistent or even fair about applying these expectations. And, too, your general rules of expected behavior might just be in conflict with the rules or lack thereof in a student's home life. However, you have to start somewhere, and by establishing and sticking to a few explained general expectations (see discussion under The First Day) and to those that may be specific to your grade level or subject area, you can leave yourself some room for judgments and maneuvering.

Finally, consequences for not following established procedures must be reasonable, clearly understood, and fairly applied. The procedures should be quite specific so that students know exactly what is expected and what is not and what the consequences are when procedures are not followed.

Procedures Rather Than Rules; Consequences Rather Than Punishment

To encourage a constructive and supportive classroom environment, I encourage you (and your students) to practice thinking in terms of **procedures** (or *expectations*, or *standards* and *guidelines*) rather than of "rules," and of *consequences* rather than *punishment*. The rationale is this: to many people, the term **rules** has a more negative connotation than does the term *procedures* (Queen, Blackwelder, & Mallen, 1997). When working especially with a cohort of students, some rules are necessary, but some people feel that using the term *procedures* has a more positive ring to it. For example, a classroom rule might be that when one person is talking, we do not interrupt that person until he or she is finished. When that rule is broken, rather than reminding students of the rule, the emphasis can be changed to a procedure simply by reminding the students and asking, "What is our procedure (or expectation) when someone is talking?"

> After considering what experienced others have to say, the final decision is one of many that you as teacher must make and will be influenced by your own thinking and unique situation. That fact is what makes a teacher a professional.

I agree with those who believe that thinking in terms of and talking about *procedures* and *consequences* are more likely to contribute to a positive classroom ambiance than using the terms *rules* and *punishment*. Of course, some argue that by the time students are beyond the primary grades, you might as well tell it like it is. Especially if your group of students is linguistically and culturally mixed, you will need to be as direct and clear as possible to avoid sending confusing or mixed signals. It is important that expectations are communicated clearly to the students and followed consistently by you and other members of your teaching team.

Once you have decided on your initial expectations, you are ready to explain them to your students and to begin rehearsing a few of the procedures on the very first day of class. You will want to do this in a

---

Teaching in Practice

Late Homework Paper from an At-Risk Student

A high school junior turned in an English class assignment several days late, and the paper was accepted by the teacher without penalty although the teacher's policy was that late papers would be severely penalized. During the week that the assignment was due, the student had suffered a miscarriage. In this instance her teacher accepted the paper late sans penalty because the student carried a great deal of psychological baggage and the teacher felt that turning in the paper at all was a positive act; if the paper had not been accepted, or had been accepted only with severe penalty to her grade, then, in the teacher's opinion, the student would have simply quit trying and probably dropped out of school altogether.

Questions for Class Discussion
1. After reading the scenario, what were your immediate feelings or thoughts?
2. How did you feel about the teacher's action?
3. Did this scenario cause you to question how you will respond in similar situations? About whether you will or will not accept late papers from students?
4. Is it possible for a teacher to be both consistent and fair? Or is that even important?

positive way. Students work best in a positive atmosphere, when teacher expectations are clear to them, when procedures are stated in positive terms, when standards are clearly understood and agreed upon and have become routine, and when consequences for behaviors that are inappropriate are reasonable, clearly understood, and fairly applied.

The First Day

On the first day you will want to cover certain major points of common interest to you and the students. The following paragraphs offer guidelines and suggestions for meeting your students the first time.

GREETING THE STUDENTS AND THE FIRST ACTIVITY

While standing at the door, welcome your students with a smile as they arrive, and then greet the entire class with a friendly but businesslike demeanor. You should not be frowning or off in a corner of the room doing something else as students arrive. As you greet the students, tell them to take a seat and start on the first activity at their desk.

After your greeting, begin the first meeting immediately with some sort of assignment, perhaps with a written assignment already on each student desk. This ensures that students have something to do immediately upon arriving in your classroom. That first assignment might be a questionnaire each student completes. This is a good time to instruct students on the expected standard for heading their papers. After giving instructions on how papers are to be handed in, rehearse the procedure by collecting this first assignment.

STUDENT SEATING

One option for student seating is to have student names on the first assignment paper placed at student seats when students arrive for that first class session. Or, as an upper elementary or secondary school teacher you may prefer to have a seating chart displayed on the screen. Either way allows you to have a seating chart ready on the first day, from which you can quickly take attendance and begin learning student names. Another option, not exclusive of the first two, is to tell students that by the end of the week each should be in a permanent seat (either assigned by you or self-selected), from which you will make a seating chart that will help you to quickly learn their names and efficiently take attendance each day. Let them know, too, that from time to time you will redo the seating arrangement (if that is true).

INFORMATION ABOUT THE CLASS

After the first activity has been completed, discussed, and collected, explain to students about the class—what they will be learning and how they will learn it (covering work and study habits and your expectations regarding the quantity and quality of their work). This is a time you may choose to obtain student input into the course content (discussed in the next chapter), to give students a sense of empowerment or ownership. I advise you to put this information in a course syllabus, give each student a copy, and review it with them, specifically discussing your expectations about how books will be used; about student notebooks, journals, portfolios, and assignments; about what students need to furnish; and about the location of resources in the classroom and elsewhere.

CLASSROOM PROCEDURES AND ENDORSED BEHAVIOR

Now discuss in a positive way your expectations regarding classroom behavior, procedures, and routines. Students work best when teacher expectations are well understood with established routines. In the beginning it is important that there be no more procedures than necessary to get the class moving effectively for daily operation. Five or fewer expectations should be enough, such as those shown in Figure 3.2.

Too many procedural expectations at first can be restricting and even confusing to students. Most students beyond first grade already know these things, so you should not have to spend much time on the topic, except for those items specific to your classroom or course, such as dress and safety expectations for laboratory courses, shop and art classes, and physical education. Be patient with yourself on this, for finding and applying the proper level of control for a given group of students is one of the skills that you will develop with experience. And remember this: For even the most competent and experienced teachers, things in the classroom do not always run smoothly.

Although some schools traditionally have posted in the halls and in the classrooms a list of prohibited behaviors, exemplary schools and teachers tend to focus on the positive, on endorsed attitudes and behaviors. Displaying a list of "do nots" does not encourage a positive school or classroom atmosphere; a list of "dos" does.

Figure 3.2   Sample list of expectations for classroom behavior.

Our Classroom List of Dos

- Do arrive promptly and remain on task until excused by the teacher.
- Do listen attentively when others have the floor.
- Do show mutual respect.
- Do use appropriate language.
- Do demonstrate appreciation for the rights and property of others.

FIRST HOMEWORK ASSIGNMENT AND DISMISSAL

End the first class session with a positive statement about being delighted to be working with the students and then give the first homework assignment. The first homework assignment should perhaps be one that will not take too much student time and that each student can achieve full credit on with minimal effort. Be sure to allow yourself sufficient time to demonstrate where assignments will regularly be posted and to make assignment instructions clearly understood by every student, including a reminder of how you expect students to head their papers. This is also a good time to explain to your students your expectations regarding help from home, if any, on homework. (An identical explanation should be given to parents/guardians at the first meeting with them.)

When you are ready to dismiss students this first day and every day hereafter, my advice is to do so by moving to the classroom exit and then verbally excuse the students, giving each a smile as they leave the classroom.

Procedural Matters: What Students Need to Understand from Day One

When establishing classroom behavior expectations and procedures, remember this point: The learning time needs to run efficiently (i.e., with no "dead spots" when students have nothing to do), smoothly (i.e., routine procedures are established and transitions between activities are smooth), and with minimum distraction. As you prepare the guidelines, standards, and expectations for classroom behavior, you (and, if relevant, your teaching team) should consider some of the specifics about what students need to understand from the beginning. These specific points, then, should be reviewed and rehearsed with the students, sometimes several times, during the first week of school and then followed consistently throughout the school term. Important and specific things that students need to know from the start will vary considerably depending on your specific situation, but generally each of the following paragraphs describes things that all students need to understand from the beginning of the school term.

SIGNALING FOR YOUR ATTENTION AND HELP

At least at the start of the school term, most teachers who are effective classroom managers expect students to raise their hands until the teacher acknowledges (usually by a nonverbal gesture, such as eye contact or a nod or with a raised forefinger) that the student's hand has been seen. With that acknowledgment, the recommended procedure is that the student lowers his or her hand and returns to work. Whereas a teacher with fewer than 15 students may indeed relax this expectation—although in K–12 public schools a class of 15 or fewer

students is far from common—the expectation should not be ignored.

There are a number of important reasons for expecting students to raise their hands to be acknowledged before speaking. Two are that it allows you to (a) control the noise and confusion level and (b) be proactive in deciding who speaks. Even with a small group of students (15 or fewer), the latter is important if you are to be in control of classroom events, rather than controlled by them, and you are to manage a classroom with equality—that is, with equal attention to individuals regardless of their gender, ethnicity, proximity to the teacher, or another personal characteristic. I am not talking about students having to raise their hands before talking with their neighboring peers during group work; I am talking about disallowing students shouting across the room to get your attention and boisterously talking out freely and rudely interrupting others during whole-class discussions and instruction.

Another important reason for expecting students to raise their hands and be recognized before speaking is to discourage impulsive outbursts and to promote their emotional and intellectual maturity. An instructional responsibility shared by all teachers is to help students develop intelligent behaviors. Learning to control one's impulsivity is, as discussed later in Chapter 7, an intelligent behavior. Teaching youth to control their impulsivity is a highly important responsibility that, in my opinion, is too often neglected by too many teachers (and too many parents and guardians), the ramifications of which are frightening.

Some teachers employ the **three-before-me** (or similar) procedure to avoid dependence on the teacher and having too many students raising their hands for the teacher's attention and to encourage positive interaction among the students. The procedure is: When a student has a question or needs help, the student must quietly ask up to three peers before seeking help from the teacher. Again, as a beginning teacher, you need to try ideas and find what works best for you in your unique situation.

ENTERING AND LEAVING THE CLASSROOM

From the time that the class is scheduled to begin, teachers who are effective classroom managers expect students to be in their assigned seats or at their assigned learning stations and to be attentive to the teacher or to the learning activity until excused by the teacher. And remember, teachers, not bells or clocks, excuse students. For example, students should not be allowed to begin meandering toward the classroom exit in anticipation of the passing bell or the designated passing time; otherwise their meandering toward the door will begin earlier and earlier each day and the teacher will increasingly lose control. Besides, it is a waste of a very valuable and very limited resource—instructional time.

MAINTAINING, OBTAINING, AND USING MATERIALS FOR LEARNING AND ITEMS OF PERSONAL USE

Students need to know where, when, and how to store, retrieve, and care for items such as their outer garments, backpacks, books, pencils, and medicines, how to get papers and materials, and when to use the pencil sharpener and wastebasket. Classroom control is easiest to maintain when

- items that students need for class activities and for their personal use are neatly and safely arranged (e.g., backpacks stored under tables or chairs rather than in aisles) and located in places that require minimum foot traffic;

- there are established procedures that students clearly expect and understand;
- there is the least amount of student off-task time; and
- students do not have to line up to wait for anything.

Therefore, you will want to plan the room arrangement, equipment and materials storage, preparation of equipment and materials, and transitions between activities to avoid needless delays, confusion, and safety hazards. Remember this well: *For a beginning teacher in particular, problems in classroom control will most certainly occur whenever some or all students have nothing to do, even if only briefly.*

PROCEDURES, REWARDS, AND CONSEQUENCES OF ONE KINDERGARTEN CLASSROOM

Procedures	*Rewards*	*Consequences*
• Listen carefully	• Praise	• Verbal reminder
• Follow directions	• Smile	• Time out
• Raise hand to speak	• Preferred activity	• Notify principal and parent/guardian
• Respect self and others	• Self-respect	
	• Safe and productive classroom	

LEAVING CLASSROOM FOR A PERSONAL MATTER

Normally, students should be able to take care of the need for a drink of water or to go to the bathroom during recess or between classes; however, sometimes they do not, or for medical reasons or during long block classes cannot. Reinforce the notion that they should do those things before coming into your classroom or during the scheduled times, but be flexible enough for the occasional student who has an immediate need. I still vividly and shamefully remember the time during my first year of teaching that a seventh-grade student urinated while at her seat when I had refused to allow her to leave the classroom, thinking that she was faking the reason for which she had asked to leave. You may wonder what did I do next, so here it is. I declared a recess, evacuated the room, and after calling a custodian to come and clean the mess I went outside with the students, apologizing to the young lady student. So, although very embarrassing, we survived intact. Were it today, I would avoid the embarrassment that ensued by allowing the student to leave but accompanied by another student.

Whenever permitting a student to leave class for a personal reason, follow established school procedures, which may, for reasons of personal security, mean that students can leave the room only in pairs and with a hall pass or when accompanied by an adult.

REACTING TO A VISITOR OR AN INTERCOM ANNOUNCEMENT

Unfortunately, class interruptions do occur, and in some schools they occur far too often and for reasons that are not as important as interrupting the teaching

and learning process would imply. For an important reason, an administrator or some other person from the school's office may interrupt the learning to see the teacher or a student or to make an announcement to the entire class. Students need to understand what behavior is expected of them during those interruptions. When there is a visitor to the classroom, the expected procedure should be for students to continue their learning task unless directed otherwise by you. To learn more about class interruptions, now do Exercise 3.1 found at end of chapter.

WHEN LATE TO CLASS OR LEAVING EARLY

You must abide by school policies on early dismissals and late arrivals. Make your own procedures routine so students clearly understand what they are to do if they must leave your class early (e.g., for a medical appointment) or when they arrive late. Procedures in your classroom, and indeed throughout the school, should be such that late-arriving and early-dismissal students do not disturb you or other teachers or the learning in progress.

When students are allowed to interrupt the learning in progress because the teacher has not established such procedures, and these interruptions happen repeatedly and regularly, then the covert message conveyed, at least in that classroom if not by the hidden curriculum of the entire school, is that on the list of matters of importance academic instruction ranks relatively low.

CONSEQUENCES FOR INAPPROPRIATE BEHAVIOR

Most teachers who are effective classroom managers routinize their procedures for handling inappropriate

Figure 3.3   Sample model of consequences for inappropriate student behavior.

FIRST OFFENSE results in a direct, but unobtrusive (nonverbal) reminder to the student.

SECOND OFFENSE results in a private, but direct (verbal) reminder of expected behavior and the consequences of continued inappropriate behavior.

THIRD OFFENSE results in the student being given a time out in a supervised isolation area followed by a private teacher–student conference and the student's subsequent return to class. Parent/guardian notification may occur.

FOURTH OFFENSE results in a suspension from class until there is a student–parent/guardian–teacher (and perhaps the counselor or a school administrator) conference.

FIFTH OFFENSE results in the student being referred to the appropriate administrator or counselor (depending on the school's policy), sometimes followed by a limited or permanent suspension from that class or move to another school or an expulsion from school.

behavior and ensure that the students understand the consequences for inappropriate behavior. The consequences, which work best when they are consistent throughout the school, are posted in the classroom and may be similar to the five-step model shown in Figure 3.3.

EMERGENCY SITUATIONS, PRACTICE AND REAL

Students need to clearly understand what to do, where to go, and how to behave in emergency conditions, such as those that might occur because of a fire, storm, earthquake, or because of a disruptive campus intruder. Students (and teachers, too) must behave well during practice drills, as well as in real emergencies.

Time Out Procedure

When a time out is used to deal with a student's inappropriate behavior, the student should have something constructive to do during the time out. One suggestion is that, when instructed to take a time out, the student picks up a form (see Figure 3.4) from a known place near the classroom exit and completes the form while in the time-out area. When used in a consistent, calm, and nonpunitive manner, this procedure is productive for several reasons. While preserving the smooth flow of the classroom, the time out (a) gives the recipient student something constructive to do during the time out, (b) causes the student to reflect and assume ownership for his or her behavior that resulted in the time out, and (c) provides documentation that might be useful later in conferences with parents or guardians, team members, counselors, and school administrative personnel. A second time out for the same student during the same school day might be cause for a follow-up action, such as a conference between the student and members of that student's teaching team and school counselor. A third

time out during the same day may result in a trip to a school administrator, the school psychologist, and a parent or guardian conference before the student is allowed to return to the classroom.

To further your understanding of classroom management, and to begin the development of your own management system, now do Exercises 3.2 and 3.3 found at end of chapter.

USING POSITIVE REWARDS AS MOTIVATORS

Reinforcement theory contends that a person's gratification derived from receiving a reward strengthens the tendency for that person to continue to act in a certain way, whereas the lack of a reward (or the promise of a reward) weakens the tendency to act that way. For example, according to the theory, if a class of sixth-grade students are promised a reward of "preferred activity time (PAT) on Friday" if they work well all week long, then the students are likely to work toward that reward, thus improving their standards of learning. Some educators argue that (a) once the extrinsic reinforcement (i.e., the reward from outside the learner) has been removed, the desired behavior tends to diminish; and that (b) rather than extrinsic sources of reinforcement, focus should be on increasing the student's internal sense of accomplishment, an intrinsic reward. Further, rewarding students for complying with expected standard behavior sends the wrong message. It reinforces the mentality of, "What do I get (for doing what I am supposed to do)?" If common as a school practice, it carries over into home situations and eventually into adulthood. A principal does not reward a teacher for showing up on time, attending a faculty meeting, or having report cards prepared on time. Those are expected standard, professional behaviors. [Note: There are, however, persons who favor bestowing

Figure 3.4   Sample time out form.

TIME OUT

Your behavior failed to pass our classroom expectations and agreements. Those agreements are:

(1) attentive listening
(2) mutual respect of the rights and property of others
(3) right of each student to learn
(4) appreciation of others with no put-downs

Please reflect on your behavior today by answering the following questions.

1. Explain what you did in class that caused you to receive this time out.

2. What agreement(s) did you fail to honor by your behavior?

3. Did your behavior cause another person to feel embarrassed, angry, or hurt? _____

4. Did your behavior jeopardize the safety of yourself or others? _____

5. Did your behavior keep you or other students from their learning tasks? _____

6. Did your behavior keep another student from being heard by the teacher and class? _____

7. Did your behavior help or hinder the class work? _____ If yes, how?

8. Did your behavior break a school rule? _____ If yes, which one?

9. Explain in your own words what positive behaviors your teacher and classmates will observe from you when you return to class.

When you are ready to honor our class agreements, do the following:

1. Return to the classroom and place this completed and signed paper in the appropriate basket on my desk.
2. Return to your assigned seat without disturbing anyone.
3. Rejoin the classroom activity.

Student's signature _____ Date _____

financial rewards on schools, administrators, and teachers for successfully doing what they are supposed to do—teach children.] Perhaps, for the daily work of a teacher in a classroom of many diverse youngsters, the practical reality is somewhere between. After all, the reality of classroom teaching is less than ideal, and all activities cannot be intrinsically rewarding. Further, for many young people intrinsic rewards are often seemingly too remote to be effective.

The promise of extrinsic rewards is not always necessary or beneficial. Students generally will work harder to learn something because they want to learn it (i.e., it is intrinsically motivating) than they will merely to earn PAT, points, grades, candy, pizza party, sticker, or some other form of reward (called extrinsic motivator). In addition, regarding the promise of PAT on Friday, many students are so preoccupied with "the here and now" that for them the promise on Monday of preferred activity time on Friday probably will have little desired effect on their behavior on Monday. To them on Monday, Friday seems a long way off.

Activities that are interesting and intrinsically rewarding are not served by the addition of extrinsic rewards. This is especially true when working with those students who are already highly motivated to learn. Adding extrinsic incentives to learning activities that are already highly motivating tends to actually reduce student motivation. For most students, the use of extrinsic motivators should be minimal and is probably most useful in skills learning where there is likely to be a lot of repetition and the potential for boredom. If students are working diligently on a highly motivating student-initiated project of study, extrinsic rewards are not necessary and could even have negative effects (Kohn, 1993).

MANAGING CLASS SESSIONS

The guidelines for the first session with your students hold true for every session thereafter. When it is time for the class period to begin, you should start the learning activities at once. By beginning the class session without delay, you discourage the kind of fooling around and time wasting that might otherwise occur. To minimize problems with classroom control, you must practice this from the very first day of your teaching career. [Note: If student teaching is an element of the program you are in, then at the beginning of your student teaching you may need to follow the opening procedures already established by your cooperating teacher. If your cooperating teacher's procedures for classroom management are largely ineffective, or counter to what you believe they should be, then perhaps you should talk with your university supervisor about a different placement.]

Once class has begun, the pace of activities should be lively enough to keep students alert and productively

busy, without dead time, but not so fast as to discourage or lose some students. A good rule of thumb is this: The effective teacher manages a classroom where at no time does any student sit or stand around with nothing to do. Of course, there may well be variations to this rule when it comes to teachers with experience and who have earned their reputations as effective and highly respected teachers. But for now, at the beginning of your career it is a good rule to follow.

To maintain a smooth and brisk pace, and to lessen distractions and prevent dead time, consider the guidelines that follow.

Opening Activities

Although there are schools today that do not use a bell system to denote the beginning and ending of every class period, teachers still sometimes refer to the initial class activity as the *bell activity*. More frequently, perhaps, as well as more correctly, it is referred to as the *warm-up activity* or simply as the *opener*.

At the beginning of each class period, in order to take attendance and to attend to other routine administrative matters, most teachers expect the students to be in their assigned seats. You should greet the students warmly and start their learning quickly. Unless you really want responses, it is perhaps best to avoid greeting students with a rhetorical question such as "How was your weekend?" If you are teaching in a school where you must monitor attendance at the beginning of each class period and you are not yet comfortable with your overlapping skill, an effective management procedure is to have the overhead projector, or whatever projection system you have available, on when students arrive in class, with the day's agenda and immediate assignment or warm-up activity clearly displayed on the screen, which then is referred to after your greeting. Once administrative tasks are completed (usually in a matter of a minute or two, although I kid not when I say I once knew a tenured junior high school teacher—an entirely ineffective one I might add—who spent the entire class period doing attendance while students completed a worksheet), the day's lesson should begin, which could mean that students will move to other stations within the classroom.

When there are no announcements or other administrative matters to cover, you should try to begin the day's lesson immediately. Then, within a few minutes after the students have begun their lesson activities, take attendance. Perhaps the best routine, one that requires practice and overlapping skill, is to do both simultaneously—take attendance while starting the day's instructional activities. Whichever the case, once the class period has begun, routines and lesson activities should move forward briskly and steadily until the official end of the class period, or, in the event of extended class periods or blocks, until a scheduled break.

Many teachers vary the seating arrangement of their classrooms in ways that will accommodate specific types of learning activities and the varying learning modalities of the children.

Now turn to end of chapter and do Exercise 3.4 to learn further how experienced teachers open their class sessions.

Teaching in Practice

Beginning the Class Period with Mr. Scott

On the first day of schools, two students arrived a half-minute late to Mr. Scott's class. On the second day, three students were a minute late, and Mr. Scott waited to begin class until they were in their seats. On the third day, four students were 1 to 3 minutes late, and again Mr. Scott waited to begin class. By the end of the first week, Mr. Scott was delaying the start of the class for 7 minutes after the bell because students continued to amble in throughout this time period.

Questions for Class Discussion
1. What do you predict will be the situation by the end of the second week? Why?
2. What alternatives are open to Mr. Scott for Monday of the second week?
3. Which of the alternatives are likely to lead to a worse situation? Why?
4. Which of the alternatives promise to lead to improvement? Why?

Warm-up activities include any variety of things, such as a specific topic or question each student responds to by writing in his or her journal or the same topic or question that pairs (dyads) of students discuss and write about in their journals. Other activities include a problem to be solved by each student or student pair, the exchange and discussion of a homework assignment, the completion of the write-up of a laboratory activity, and the writing of individual or student dyad responses to worksheet or textbook questions.

Smooth Implementation of the Lesson

The lesson should move forward briskly and purposefully, with natural transitions from one lesson activity to the next and with each activity starting and ending conclusively, especially when using direct (teacher-centered) instruction. Transitions (discussed in the section that follows), in particular, are a most troublesome time for many novice teachers.

When giving verbal instructions to students, do so quickly and succinctly, without talking too long and giving so much detail that students begin to get restless and bored. Students can become bored with long-winded, verbal instructions from a teacher.

Once students are busy at their learning tasks, avoid interrupting them with additional verbal instructions, statements, or announcements that distract and get them off task, and that could as easily be written on the board or overhead transparency; interventions should be communicated to a student privately without disturbing the rest of the class. Most young people are easily distracted; do not be the cause of their distractions.

Helping students see and understand connections is a continuing responsibility for every classroom teacher.

With whole-class instruction, before starting a new activity, be sure that most students satisfactorily complete the present one. Students who finish early can work on an anchor or transitional activity (discussed in Chapter 5). End each activity conclusively before beginning a new activity, and with a relevant and carefully prepared transition, bridge the new activity with the previous one, so students understand the connection.

With skill in withitness, you will carefully and continuously monitor all students during the entire class period. If one or two students become inattentive and begin to behave inappropriately, quietly redirect their attention without distracting and interrupting the learning activities of the other students.

To help in the prevention of dead time and management problems, especially when using multiple learning tasks and indirect (student-centered) instruction, you will want to establish and rehearse the students in the use of anchor or transitional activities.

> It is probable that the greatest number of management problems occur during times of transitions.

Transitions Within Lessons

Transitions within lessons are the moments between activities or topics, times of change. It will probably take you a while to sharpen the skill of smooth transitions. Planning and consistency in execution are critical to mastering this important skill. With careful planning, a dependable schedule, and consistent routines, transitions usually occur efficiently and automatically, without disruption. Still, it is probable that for classroom teachers the greatest number of discipline problems occur during times of transitions, especially when students must wait for the next activity. To avoid problems during transitions, eliminate wait times by thinking and planning ahead. During your preactive phase of instruction plan your transitions and write them into your lesson plan.

Transitions in lessons are of two types, and at times, both are used. The first is achieved by the teacher's connecting one activity to the next so that students understand the relationship between the two activities. That is a **lesson transition**. The second type of transition occurs when some students have finished a learning activity but must wait for others to catch up before starting the next. This is an **anchor or transitional activity**. Anchor or transitional activities are ongoing, relevant tasks that students automatically move to whenever they have completed their individual or small-group learning activities, thus allowing no time where students have nothing to do but wait. A common example is when some students have finished a test while others have not. The wise and effective teacher plans a transitional activity and gives instructions or reminders for that activity or an ongoing activity before students begin the test.

During the planning (preactive phase) of instruction you should plan and rehearse nearly every move you

and the students will make, thinking ahead to anticipate and avoid problems in classroom control. Transitions are planned and students are prepared for them by clearly established transition routines. While in transition and waiting for the start of the next activity, students engage in these transitional activities. You can plan a variety of transitional activities relevant and appropriate to the topics being studied, although not necessarily related to the next activity of that particular day's lesson. Transitional activities may include any number of meaningful activities, such as journal writing, worksheet activity, lab reports, portfolio work, homework, project work, and even work for another teacher's class.

As a beginning teacher, it will take time to develop finesse in your application of these guidelines for effective lesson management; during your student teaching experience, your cooperating teacher and college or university supervisor will understand that it takes time and will help you develop and hone your skills.

INAPPROPRIATE STUDENT BEHAVIOR

Student behavior in the classroom that is inappropriate can range from minor acts to very serious ones. Sometimes student behaviors seen by the teacher as inappropriate are simply the demonstration of behaviors that are learned and even encouraged in the student's home. Sometimes the causes of student misbehavior are the result of problems that originated from outside the classroom and spilled over into it. Others are simply behaviors that result from the fact that whenever a group of young people are together for a period of time, mischief or fooling around will likely result. Still others are the result of something the teacher did or did not do. Described next, *in order of increasing seriousness*, are categories of student misbehavior that teachers sometimes experience and must deal with.

Transient Nondisruptive Behaviors

This least-serious category includes these common and usually nondisruptive behaviors: chatting with a neighbor; momentarily being off task; fooling around but not really bothering anyone; emotional outburst because the student is really "into the lesson"; brief whispering during a lesson; short periods of apparent inattentiveness, perhaps accompanied by visual wandering or daydreaming. Fortunately, in most instances, this type of behavior is transient, and sometimes it might even be best if you pretend for a moment or so to be unaware of it.

If the off-task behavior persists, all it may take to get the student back on task is an unobtrusive (private) redirection as means of keeping students focused. Examples of unobtrusive redirection, or what we refer to as **signal interference**, are eye contact, body language, gradual movement to a position closer in proximity to the student, smile or frown, quick use of the student's name without missing a beat in the lesson, and hand gestures. If this does not work, go to the next level intervention (one that is obtrusive) by calling on the student by name and reminding the student of the correct procedure or of what he or she is supposed to be doing.

Avoid asking an off-task student any question (such as, "John, what are the raw materials of photosynthesis?" when you know full well that John is not paying attention) or an inquiry ("John, why are you doing that?" John probably doesn't know why). Avoid also making a threat such as "John, if you don't turn around and attend to your work, I will send you to the office."

The bottom line is this: It is important that you not make "mountains out of molehills," or you could cause more problems than you would resolve. Make every effort to maintain students' focus on the lesson rather than on the off-task behavior.

Disruptions to Learning

This category includes incessant talking out of turn, walking about the classroom aimlessly and without permission, clowning, and throwing objects, all of which students know are behaviors that are unacceptable in the classroom. In responding to such misbehaviors, it is important that you have explained their consequences to students, and then, following your stated procedures, promptly and consistently deal with the violations. Too many beginning teachers (and veteran teachers as well) tend to ignore these misbehaviors (seemingly in the hope that, if not recognized, they will discontinue).

DEALING WITH TEMPORARY DISRUPTIVE BEHAVIOR CAUSED BY A SPECIAL EDUCATION STUDENT

Attention deficit and hyperactivity are characteristics often observed in students with learning and behavior disorders, and are manifested in fidgetiness, inability to engage in quiet activities, difficulty staying seated, and excessive talking (Vaughn & Bos, 2009). Temporary disruptive behavior caused by a special education student who is placed in your inclusive class might have to be occasionally ignored and accepted. For working with a special education student in the inclusive classroom there are special strategies you can learn and use, such as

- developing a special signaling system with that student, such as via eye contact, body language and proximity (moving closer to the student), or through
- nonverbal cueing or gesturing (teacher's finger to the lips, raised hand, pointing to both eyes to indicate "eyes on me"), or pointing to the screen or writing board to direct the student's focus, or by
- transitioning the student to another activity such as to the computer or the learning center.

Although it is important that you always think before you react to disruptive behavior, *totally not reacting to such misbehavior is, in fact, giving it your approval.* You must not ignore infractions of this type, for if you do, they most likely will escalate beyond your worst nightmare. Without displaying any anger (otherwise students are winning the battle for control), simply and quickly enforce understood consequences and keep the focus on the lesson, not the inappropriate behavior. In other words, strive to maintain your control of classroom events, rather than to become controlled by them.

There is sometimes a tendency among beginning teachers, especially when they have a problem with students goofing off and being disruptive, to assume that the entire group of students is being unruly, when, more often, it is only one, two, or maybe three students. You want to avoid saying to the entire group of students anything that implies you perceive them all as being unruly if, in fact, they are not. Such a false accusation will only serve to alienate the students who are being attentive to the learning task, and that is something you don't want to happen—ever!

Defiance, Cheating, Lying, and Stealing

When a student refuses to do what you say, the student's defiance may be worthy of temporary or permanent removal from the classroom. Depending upon your judgment of the seriousness of the act of defiance, you may simply give the student a time-out or you may suspend the student from class until there has been a conference about the situation, perhaps involving you, members of your teaching team, the student, the student's parent or guardian, and a school official.

An occurrence of cheating, lying, or stealing may be an isolated act, and the student may need only a one-on-one talk to find out what precipitated the behavior and what might be done to prevent it from occurring again. Indeed, whenever observing these behaviors and before responding, you must consider the personal characteristics and developmental level of the student. A kindergarten child who declares, for example, that he is Spiderman is not immoral and may from his viewpoint not even be lying. On the other hand, a high school student who claims that he is Spiderman may be in serious need of help. So, gauge your responses carefully.

A student who habitually exhibits any of these immoral behaviors may need to be referred to a specialist. My advice for when you suspect immoral behavior is that you discuss your concern with members of your teaching team and a school official.

Bullying, Fighting, Sexual Misconduct, and Violence

Acts in this category usually extend well beyond the purview and responsibility of one classroom teacher. For example, state law in California mandates five offenses for which a student must be immediately expelled: possessing a firearm, brandishing a knife, selling a controlled substance, committing sexual assault or battery, and possessing an explosive. Please do not think you must be capable of handling alone every act of student misbehavior, especially those of this category. To seek assistance is a sign of wisdom, not weakness.

In many ways, teaching is clearly different than it used to be. More and more often teachers are confronted with major problems of inappropriate behavior that have ramifications beyond the classroom or that began elsewhere and spill over into the classroom. If this happens, you may need to ask for help and should not hesitate to do so. Be certain that at your school you know where and how to obtain quick assistance when needed. As a student teacher or a newly employed teacher, one of the first things you will want to do is to find out what you should do in the event of such acting out. As a teacher, you must remain alert.

Today's schools are adopting a variety of types of schoolwide and classroom instructional programs designed to reduce or eliminate violent, aggressive student behaviors and to help all students succeed in school and to make the transitions necessary for success in adulthood. The most effective school programs for antiviolence use four strategies, which are to (1) teach social competence, (2) create a positive, calm environment, (3) establish behavior standards, and (4) establish rules and regulations for responding to violence (Schwartz, 1999).

Bullying, also known as punking, is the practice of verbal and physical violence, verbal teasing, shaming, humiliation, harassing, and exclusion from peers, done most frequently in public by males to males, for the purpose of affirming masculinity norms of toughness, strength, dominance, and control. Contrary to what many believe, the prevalence of bullying does not appear to be related to size of city, race/ethnicity, or geographical region, but happens in every school. It is not a natural condition of the young but rather a deliberate act that hurts its victims, both emotionally and physically, sometimes with long-lasting consequences (Phillips, 2007).

The fact that victims of bullying are unlikely to report it to adults means that teachers must keep bullying in mind when attempting to ascertain why a student seems hopeless, uncomfortable, withdrawn, on guard, and has problems eating and sleeping (Peterson & Ray, 2006). Teachers and other school personnel should learn to recognize the indicators of bullying (in both the victims and the bullies), and develop and practice schoolwide strategies that are designed to address and prevent bullying. When schools target and reduce bullying, there is a concomitant increase in academic performance (Scarpaci, 2006).

A form of bullying that every teachers needs to be aware of is that of **cyberbullying**, the sending of online

threatening messages, display of private messages, and posting of embarrassing video and photos online. Cyberbullying, and cyberstalking, are devastating forms of social cruelty among young people that have clearly become of major and serious concern within many schools (see, for example, Milson & Gallo, 2006; Li, 2006; and Prasad, 2007). You will want to become aware of efforts your school community is making to understand and reduce the deleterious effects of this form of social cruelty. Some useful websites are www.cyberbullying.us, www.stopcyberbullying.com, www.cyberbully.org, and www.challengeday.org.

TEACHER RESPONSE TO STUDENT MISBEHAVIOR

Rather than to punish, the goal in responding to student misbehavior should be to calmly intervene and redirect the student's focus and to do so successfully with the least amount of classroom disturbance. Typically, teachers respond to student classroom misbehaviors in one of three ways: hostile, assertive, or nonassertive. *The teacher's response should be assertive. Hostile and nonassertive responses should be avoided.* Unlike a hostile response, an assertive response is not abusive or derogatory to the student. Unlike a nonassertive response, an assertive response is a timely and clear communication to the student of what the teacher expects (Edwards, 1997).

Direct Versus Indirect Assertive Intervention Strategies: A Clarification

Appropriate assertive intervention strategies can be separated into two categories:

- direct, usually a verbal command from the teacher (in the past the direct intervention might have been more physical)
- indirect, such as eye contact, body language and proximity (moving closer to the student), nonverbal gesturing (teacher's finger to the lips, raised hand, pointing to both eyes to indicate "eyes on me"), or pointing to the screen or writing board to direct the student's focus

Too often, teachers intervene with direct intervention, when indirect intervention strategies are less obtrusive or disruptive and often more effective in redirecting a misbehaving student. Although the offense might be identical, the teacher's intervention for one student might have to be direct, whereas for another student indirect intervention is enough to put a stop to the student's inappropriate behavior.

Teaching in Practice

The Bully Project

"Cut ... CUT!!" ordered our director, Trevor. Silence filled the room. It was Tuesday morning and time for filmmaking.

I teach 8- to 11-year-olds with learning disabilities and ADHD in a resource room setting. Every year is a challenge to find a good fit between the nature of the students and the methods of teaching that bring out their best. This year most of my students had first-grade writing skills coupled with normal intelligence. That gap meant, for many, keen awareness of what they should be able to do, but could not, which led to above-average frustration with writing.

They are visual learners, seeing the world in images better than print; moviemaking was an appealing genre with which to encourage writing. It is a powerful real-world connection and highly motivating. Enter Jeni, the mother of one of my students, and her mom, Susan, our producers and professional filmmakers. They agreed to produce a movie written, directed, acted, and shot almost entirely by my students. The students worked on the project for 4 months. Every step of the way, the students were in charge of their movie. Throughout the week they would write, revise, and rehearse. Once a week they would shoot some of the scheduled 14 scenes along with documentary footage.

"A good movie is only as good as its story,'" advised Jeni. The class decided that it needed action, adventure, "kid power" (i.e., kids as the heroes), a dog, a horse, and an alien subplot. A common theme for the students was dealing with mean children, so the bully and the boy became the central focus of the story. In the end, the boy's friends came to his rescue, and to finish off the bully, the aliens sent him into deep space.

Along the way, we discovered many happy surprises:

- Sound mixing. Dalton, at 9 years old, was already aware that different characters have different musical themes. He used a text-to-speech program to dictate and revise a letter written to obtain approval for copyrighted space music. "I chose *Messenger* because it was dark and scary ... Please email us as fast as you can at Ms. Svegel's email address." The response, "I would be delighted to have you use this music," from the composer, who turned out to be a college professor in New York.
- Camera and sound people. Students operated handheld, point-and-shoot, and tripod cameras, as well as the boom mike. Under the watchful guidance of Susan, they learned to see with a third eye, making logical decisions for shooting each scene. As Alina, 8, informed me, "We should shoot the long shot over his [a character's] shoulder when he sees the principal down the hall."
- Green screen. They got to see how a green screen works firsthand. Krypto the Alien used fishing line to land the Lego spacecraft successfully onto the green screen. The bully flailed on a green cloth on the cafeteria floor, which became deep space in the movie.
- Teamwork. From the writing team to the credits team, to costumes, music and actors, all decisions were collaborative. Not once was there a meltdown or argument over decisions that had been made. The spirit of respect and cooperation stayed with us from start to finish. This from a group with many who wear weighted vests, chew gum, or play with fidget toys to calm themselves and focus.
- Flexibility. During the filming, we added five new students, so each needed to be written into the script. Krypto the Alien got a sidekick, Krypto Junior. The animals had to go. There was not enough time for students to do any film editing or to shoot on location. The day of the long shoot, one student forgot his costume. We called home to learn that it was still in the washer! His mom brought it in soaking wet. A couple of boys figured out that they could dry it somewhat using the dryer in the boys' bathroom. It went from soaked to damp. He wore it outside on a cold, chilly day and never complained.
- Connections. Our project connected to a real-life application of reading and writing, to each other, to our producers, to a music composer, to a newspaper journalist, and to people around the country when our story was picked up by the Associated Press and run in more than a dozen print and online publications.
- Perseverance. No one lost interest throughout the entire 4-month-long process. For young children—let alone those with sustained attention difficulties—this was extraordinary.
- Accomplishment. We made a movie! *The Bully and the Five Dollars*, a 13-minute short film produced by Closet Space Productions. We also shot the documentary footage. We did something that no one else in the school had done.
- Movie premiere. We had an opening night for our families. The cafeteria was packed with over 70 family members. As one student said, "This is the best night of my life!"

Source: Roberta Svegel. Used with permission.

Order of Behavior Intervention Strategies

To redirect a student's attention, your usual *first effort* should be indirect intervention. Your *second effort* could be the simplest (i.e., the most private, least obtrusive) direct intervention (e.g., simply saying the student's name in a normal voice, or if you believe necessary, "Jacob, please follow procedures" which is slightly more obtrusive than simply saying "Jacob"). Your *third effort,* one that in time interval closely follows the second (i.e., within the same class period), should follow your procedures as outlined in your management system, which might mean a time-out or detention and a phone call to the student's parent or guardian (in private, of course). Normally, such a third effort is not necessary. A *fourth effort,* still rarer, is to suspend the student from class (or school) for some period of time until decisions about the future of that student in this school are made by school officials in consultation with the student, the parents or guardians, and other professionals such as the school psychologist.

The use of direct intervention beyond that of mere name-dropping ("Jacob!") should be reserved for repetitive and serious misbehavior. When using direct intervention, you should give a direct statement ("Jacob, please follow procedures"), either reminding the student of what he or she is supposed to be doing or telling the student what to do. You should avoid asking rhetorical questions, such as "Jacob, why are you doing that?"

When giving students directions about what they are supposed to be doing, you may be asked by a student, "Why do we have to do this?" To that query, you may give a brief academic answer, but do not become defensive or make threats or be silly. As a matter of fact, because understanding reasons for doing something is so central to positive motivation, it may sometimes be beneficial to stop and truly explore with the students a satisfactory answer to the question (Vavilis & Vavilis, 2004).

One reason that direct intervention should be held in reserve is because by interrupting the lesson to verbally intervene, you are doing exactly what the student who is being reprimanded was doing—interrupting the lesson. Not only is that poor modeling but it can create a host of management problems. Another reason for holding direct intervention in reserve is that, when used too frequently, direct intervention loses it effectiveness.

TEACHER-CAUSED STUDENT MISBEHAVIOR

As a classroom teacher, one of your major responsibilities is to model appropriate behavior and not to contribute to or be the cause of problems in the classroom. Some student misbehaviors and problems in classroom control are caused or escalated by the teacher and could have been prevented or easily rectified had the teacher behaved or acted differently. Consider the information that follows, first in scenarios for case study review, followed by a presentation of mistakes to avoid.

Scenarios for Case Study Review

In addition to sometimes ignoring certain transient student behaviors, you should also avoid using negative methods of rule enforcement and ineffective forms of punishment, as exemplified in each of the following scenarios. You and your classmates can treat these scenarios as case studies for small groups to consider and then

discuss before the whole class. During your discussions, consider for each case (1) to what degree, if any, the teacher's action created a potential legal problem and (2) whether you consider the situation as relevant to the subject and grade level you intend to teach.

- *Capriciousness.* Because of her arbitrary and inconsistent enforcement of classroom expected procedures, Fran Fickle has lost the respect and trust of her students as well as control of her classes. Her students are constantly testing Fran to see how much they can get away with.
- *Extra assignments.* When students in Margaret Malopropros's seventh-grade reading class misbehave, she habitually assigns extra reading and written work as punishment, even for the most minor offenses. This behavior has simply reinforced the view of many of her students that school is drudgery, so they no longer look forward to her classes, and behavior problems in her class have steadily increased since the beginning of the school year.
- *Embarrassment.* When eighth-grade social studies teacher Denise Degradini was having difficulty controlling the behavior of one of her students, she got on the classroom phone and called the student's parent while the entire class of 33 students could overhear the conversation. She told the parent about the child's behavior in class and how she was going to have to give the student a referral if the student's behavior did not improve. From that one act, Denise lost all respect of her students. Class academic achievement grades plummeted for the rest of the year.
- *Group punishment.* Because Fred Flock has not developed his withitness and overlapping skills, he has the unfortunate habit of punishing the entire group for every instance of misbehavior. Yesterday, for example, because some students were noisy during a video presentation, he gave the entire class an unannounced quiz on the content of the film. He has lost the respect of the students, students are hostile toward him, and his problems with classroom control are steadily growing worse.
- *Harsh and humiliating punishment.* Vince Van Pelt has lost control of his classes and the respect of his students. His thrashing, whipping, tongue-lashing, and use of humiliation are ineffective and indicative of his loss of control. Parents have complained, and one is suing him. The district has given Mr. Van Pelt official notice of the nonrenewal of his contract.
- *Loud talk.* The noisiest person in Steve Shrill's class is Mr. Shrill himself. His constant and mistaken efforts to talk over the students have led to his own yelling and screaming, to complaints from neighboring teachers about the noise in his classes, and to a reprimand from the principal.

- *Lowered marks.* Eunice Erudite, a language arts/social studies teacher, has a policy of writing a student's name on the board each time the person is reprimanded for misbehavior. Then, when a student has accumulated five marks on the board, she lowers the student's academic grade by one letter. As a result of her not separating their academic and social behaviors, her students are not doing as well as they were at the start of the year. Parents and students have complained about this policy to the administration, arguing that the grades Ms. Erudite is giving do not reflect the students' academic progress or abilities.

- *Nagging.* Social studies teacher Paul Peck's continual and unnecessary scolding and criticizing of students upsets the recipient students and arouses resentment from their peers. His nagging resolves nothing, and, like a snowball building in size as it rolls down the hill, causes Mr. Peck more and more problems in the classroom.

- *Negative direct intervention.* In the humanities block class, Joshua swears more and more frequently and with graphic and startling language. Other students are beginning to behave similarly. Rather than giving Joshua alternative ways of expressing his feelings, Polly Premio, one team teacher, verbally reprimands Joshua each time this happens and threatens to notify his parents about it. Ms. Premio does not realize that by giving her attention to Joshua's swearing she is rewarding, reinforcing, and causing the increase in Joshua's unacceptable behavior.

- *Negative touch control.* When Ezzard, a fifth-grade bully, pushes and shoves other students out of his way for no apparent reason other than to physically manipulate them, his teacher, Tony Trenchant, grabs Ezzard and yanks him into his seat. What "roughneck" Tony the teacher does not realize is that he is using the very behavior (physical force) that he is trying to stop Ezzard from using. This simply confuses students and teaches them (especially Ezzard) that the use of physical force is okay if you are bigger or older than the recipient of that force. In this situation, unfortunately, hostility begets hostility.

- *Overreaction.* Randall, a 10th-grade student, was reading a magazine in class when his English teacher, Harriet Harshmore, grabbed it from Randall's hands, called it "pornographic," ripped out the offending pages, and tossed them into a waste basket. The magazine was *National Geographic,* and the "pornographic article" was on evolution and included drawings of unclothed humans. Harriet was later reprimanded by the school superintendent who said that, although he supported her right to put a stop to what she considered a class disruption, Ms. Harshmore had crossed the line when she damaged the magazine. The magazine, apparently a rare collector's issue, had been brought from Randall's home at his teacher's encouragement to bring reading material from home.

- *Physical punishment.* Mr. Fit, a middle school geography teacher, punishes students by sending them outside to run around the school track when they misbehave in his class. Last week, Sebastian, a student whom he told to go out and run four laps for "mouthing off in class," collapsed while running and died. Mr. Fit has been placed on paid leave and is being sued for negligence by Sebastian's parents.

- *Premature judgments and actions.* Because of Kathy Kwik's impulsiveness, she does not think clearly before acting, and more than once she has reprimanded the wrong student. Because of her hasty and faulty judgments, students have lost respect for her. For them, her French I class has become pure drudgery.

- *Taped mouths.* Miss Ductless taped the mouths of 20 of her fourth-grade students in order to keep them quiet. Later in the school day several of the students went to the school nurse complaining of allergic reactions caused by the duct tape. Until a full investigation is made, Miss Ductless has been relieved of her teaching duties.

- *Threats and ultimatums.* Threats and ultimatums from math teacher Bonnie Badger are known to be empty; because she does not follow through, her credibility with the students has been lost. Like wildfire, the word has spread around—"We can do whatever we want in old Badger's class."

- *Too hesitant.* Because Tim Timideo is too hesitant and slow to intervene when students get off task, his classes have increasingly gotten further and further out of his control, and it is still early in the school year. As a result, neighbor teachers are complaining about the noise from his classroom and Tim has been writing more and more referrals.

- *Writing as punishment.* Because they were "too noisy," science teacher Sam Scribe punished his class of 28 students by requiring each one to hand-copy 10 pages from encyclopedias. When the students submitted the completed assignment, he immediately tore up the pages in front of the students and said, "I hope you have learned your lesson and from now on will be quiet." Upon hearing about this, all six teachers of the school's English department signed and filed a complaint with the principal about Mr. Scribe's use of writing for punishment.

Preventing a Ship from Sinking Is Much Easier Than Is Saving a Sinking One: Mistakes to Avoid

During your beginning years of teaching, no one, including you, should expect you to be perfect. You should, however, be aware of common mistakes teachers make that often are the causes of student inattention and misbehavior. It is my estimation that as much as 95 percent of classroom control problems are teacher caused or teacher aggravated and are preventable. In this section, you will find descriptions of mistakes commonly made by teachers. To have a most successful beginning to your career, you will want to develop your skills to avoid these mistakes. To avoid making these mistakes requires both knowledge of the potential errors and a reflection upon one's own behaviors in relation to them.

The items are mostly grade-level and subject matter neutral, although clearly some may be more relevant to you than others, depending on your own particular teaching situation.

1. *Inadequately attending to long-range and daily planning.* A teacher who inadequately plans ahead is heading for trouble. Inadequate long-term and sketchy daily planning is a precursor to ineffective teaching and, eventually, to teaching failure. Students are motivated best by teachers who clearly are working intensely and intelligently for them.

Many beginning teachers plan their lessons carefully at first and their students respond well, and that is good. Then, sometimes after finding a few strategies that seem to work, their lesson planning becomes increasingly sketchy. They fall into a rut of doing pretty much the same thing day after day—lecture, discussion, videos, and worksheets seem all too common for these teachers. They fail to consider and plan for individual student differences. By midsemester they have stopped growing professionally and begin to experience increasing numbers of problems with students.

2. *Emphasizing the negative.* Too many warnings to students for their inappropriate behavior—and too little recognition for their positive behaviors—do not help to establish the positive classroom ambiance needed for the most effective learning to occur. Reminding students of procedures is more positive and will bring you quicker success than reprimanding students when they do not follow procedures.

Too often, teachers try to control students with negative language, such as "There should be no talking," and "No gum or candy in class or else you will receive detention," and "No getting out of your seats without my permission." Teachers sometimes allow students, too, to use negative and disrespectful language on each other, such as "Shut up!" Such language does not help instill a positive classroom climate. To encourage a positive atmosphere, use concise, positive, language. Tell students precisely what they are supposed to do rather than what they are not supposed to do. Disallow the use of disrespectful and negative language in your classroom.

3. *Not requiring students to raise hands and be acknowledged before responding, especially during large- and whole-group instruction.* While ineffective teachers often are ones who are controlled by class events, competent teachers are in control of class events. You cannot be in control of events and your interactions with students if you allow students to shout out their comments, responses, and questions the moment they feel like it. Successful teachers quickly establish their control of classroom events.

In addition, to reiterate a point made in Chapter 2, indulging their natural impulsivity is not helping students to grow intellectually or emotionally. When students develop the intelligent and mature behavior of impulse control, they think before acting. Students can and should be taught to think before acting or shouting out an answer. One of several reasons that teachers should insist on a show of student hands before a student is acknowledged to respond or question is to discourage students from the impulsive, disruptive, immature, disrespectful, and irritating behavior of shouting out in class.

4. *Allowing students' hands to be raised too long.* When students have their hands raised for long periods before you recognize them and attend to their questions or responses, you are providing them with dead time, which is time to fool around. Although you need not call on every student as soon as they raise a hand, you should acknowledge the student quickly, such as with a nod or a wave of your hand, so the student can lower the hand and return to work. Then you should get to the student as quickly as possible. Procedures for this should be clearly understood by the students and followed by you.

5. *Spending too much with one student or one group and not monitoring the entire group.* Spending too much time with any one student or small group of students is, in effect, ignoring the rest of the students. As a novice teacher you cannot afford to ignore the rest of the class, even for a moment. Wise teachers practice and develop their overlapping skill.

6. *Beginning a new activity before gaining the students' attention.* A teacher who consistently fails to insist that students follow procedures and who does not wait until all students are in compliance before starting a new activity is destined for major problems in classroom control. You must establish and maintain classroom procedures. Starting an activity before all students are in compliance is, in effect, telling the students that they do not have to follow expected procedures. You cannot afford to tell students one thing and then do another. (See number 51.)

My insistence on adhering to established procedures is not to imply that procedures came before human beings, they did not. Sometimes procedures need to be changed. If that notion becomes apparent, then do not fear talking about it with your students. But once procedures are agreed upon, everyone should comply.

7. *Pacing teacher talk and learning activities too fast (or, in some instances, too slow).* Pacing of the learning activities is one of the more difficult skills for beginning teachers. (It is also a skill that even skilled and experienced teachers sometimes fail to apply.) Students need time to disengage mentally and physically from one activity before engaging in the next. You must remember that this takes more time for a room of 25 or so students than it does for just one person, you. This is one reason I advise that transitions be planned and written into your lesson plan.

8. *Using a voice level that is always either too loud or too soft.* A teacher's voice that is too loud day after day can become irritating to some students, just as one that cannot be heard or understood can become frustrating.

9. *Assigning a journal entry without giving the topic prudent thought.* If the question or topic about which students are supposed to write is ambiguous or obviously hurriedly prepared—without your having given consideration to how students will interpret and respond to it—students will judge that the task is busywork (i.e., only something to keep them busy while you take attendance). If they do it at all, it will be with a great deal of commotion and much less enthusiasm than were they writing on a topic meaningful and interesting to them.

10. *Standing too long in one place.* Most of the time in the classroom, you should be gently mobile, schmoozing, "working the crowd."

11. *Sitting while teaching.* Unless you are physically unable to stand or to do so for long periods of time, in most situations as a beginning teacher there is no time to sit while teaching. It is difficult to monitor the class while seated. You cannot afford to appear that casual. (A tall stool might be a reasonable compromise and useful personal investment.)

12. *Being too serious and no fun.* No doubt, competent teaching is serious business. But students are motivated by and respond best to teachers who obviously enjoy working with them, helping them learn, and who are sentient of their interests and lives.

13. *Falling into a rut by using the same teaching strategy or combination of strategies day after day.* Because of their multitude of differences, students are motivated by and respond best to a variety of well-planned and meaningful learning activities.

14. *Inadequately using quiet wait time after asking a content question.* When expected to think deeply about a question, students need time to do it. A teacher who consistently gives insufficient time for students to think is teaching only superficially and at the lowest cognitive level and is destined for problems in student motivation and classroom control.

15. *Poorly or inefficiently using instructional tools.* The ineffective use of teaching tools such as books, writing board, and computer says to students that you are not a competent teacher. Would you want an auto mechanic who did not know how to use the tools of that trade when servicing your automobile? Would you want a brain surgeon who did not know how to use the tools of the trade to remove your tumor? Working with children in a classroom is no less important. Like a competent automobile mechanic or a competent surgeon, and as we emphasized in Chapter 2, a competent teacher selects and effectively uses the best tools available for the job to be done.

Some teachers have even been known to captivate their students by wheeling out and using for instruction an old tool, such as a filmstrip projector with old filmstrips, an opaque projector (great for showing real objects in color and three dimension), or tachistoscope, although the "wow" appeal benefit from using such old technology is usually short lived.

16. *Ineffectively using facial expressions and body language.* As said earlier, your gestures and body language communicate more to students than your words do. For example, one teacher did not understand why his class of seventh graders would not respond to his repeated expression of "I need your attention." In one 15-minute segment, he used that expression eight times. Studying video recording of that class period helped him understand the problem. His dress was very casual, and he stood most of the time with his right hand in his pocket. At 5 foot, 8 inches, with a slight build, a rather deadpan facial expression, and a nonexpressive voice, he was not a commanding presence in the classroom. After seeing himself on tape, he returned to the class wearing a tie, and he began using his hands and face more expressively. Rather than saying "I need your attention," he waited in silence for the students to become attentive. It worked, making him a more effective teacher.

17. *Relying too much on teacher talk.* Some have a tendency to rely too much on teacher talk. Too much teacher talk can be deadly. Unable to discern between the important and the unimportant verbiage, students will quickly tune a teacher out.

Some teachers rely too much on obtrusive verbal intervention and too little on nonverbal intervention techniques. For example, to verbally reprimand a student for the student's interruptions of class activities is to reinforce the very behavior you are trying to stop. In addition, verbally reprimanding a student in front of the student's peers can cause repercussions you do not want. Instead, develop your indirect, silent intervention techniques.

18. *Inefficiently using teacher time.* During the planning phase of instruction, think carefully about what you are going to be doing during every minute of instruction, and then plan for the most efficient and therefore the most productive use of your time in the classroom. Consider the following example. During a language arts brainstorming session a teacher is recording student contributions on a large sheet of butcher paper that has been taped to the wall. The teacher

solicits student responses, acknowledges those responses, holds and manipulates the writing pen, walks to the wall and records on the paper. Each of those actions requires decisions and movements that consume precious instructional time and that can distract the teacher from the students. An effective alternative should be to have a reliable student helper do the writing while the teacher handles the solicitation and acknowledgment of student contributions. That way the teacher has fewer decisions and fewer actions to distract, and the teacher does not lose eye contact and proximity with the classroom of students.

19. *Talking to and interacting with only half the class.* While leading a class discussion, some teachers tend to favor (by their eye contact and verbal interaction) only 40 to 65 percent of the students, sometimes completely ignoring the others for an entire class period. Knowing (consciously or not) that they are being ignored, those students will, in time, become uninterested, restless, and perhaps unruly. Remember to spread your interactions and eye contact throughout the entire class. If you are teaching in block or hour-long class periods, my advice to you is to establish eye contact with each student at least once each hour. And when I say to "establish" eye contact, I mean that the student knows that you are looking at her or him. Of course there are always exceptions to rules, such as, for example, you need to be sensitive to a student from a culture where extended eye contact may be unwanted or less common.

20. *Collecting and returning student papers before assigning students a task.* If, while turning in papers or waiting for their return, students have nothing else to do, they become restless and inattentive. It is best if students have something to do (for example, an anchor activity) while papers are being collected or returned.

21. *Interrupting students while they are on task.* It is not easy to get an entire classroom of 25 or so students on task. Once they are on task, you do not want to be a distraction. Try to give all instructions before students begin their work. The detailed instructions should be written in your lesson plan; that way you are less likely to forget anything. Once on task, if there is an important point you wish to make, write it on the board or screen. If you want to return papers while students are working, do so in a way and at a time that is least likely to interrupt students from their learning task.

22. *Using "shhh" to quiet students.* Using "shhh" makes the teacher sound unprofessional and something like a balloon with a slow leak, adding a distracting noise to the classroom. Do not use "shhh" in the classroom.

23. *Using poor body positioning.* Develop your skill of withitness by practice positioning your body so you can continue visually monitoring the entire class even while talking to and working with one student or a small group. Avoid turning your back for more than a second to even a portion of the class.

24. *Settling for less when you should be trying for more—not getting the most from student responses.* The most successful schools are those with teachers who expect and get the most from all students. Do not hurry a class discussion; "milk" student responses for all you can, especially when discussing a topic that students are obviously interested in. Ask a student for clarification or reasons for his or her response. Ask for verification of data. Have another student paraphrase what a student said. Seek deeper thought and meaning. Too often, the teacher will ask a question, get an abbreviated—often one word and low cognitive level—response from a student, and then move on to new content. Instead, follow up a student's response to your question with a sequence of questions, prompting and cueing to elevate the student's thinking to higher levels.

25. *Using threats.* Avoid making threats of any kind. One teacher, for example, told the students that if they continued with their inappropriate talking, they would lose their break time. The teacher should have had that consequence as an understood procedure and consequence and then taken away the break time for some students if warranted. A reminder of procedures and consequences is different than is the use of a threat. The difference between making a threat and reminding students of procedures and consequences is *not* minor.

26. *Punishing the entire class for the misbehavior of a few.* Although the rationale behind such action is clear (i.e., to get group pressure working for you), often the result is the opposite. Students who have been behaving well are alienated from the teacher because they feel they have been punished unfairly. Those students expect the teacher to be able to deal with the misbehaving students without punishing those who are not misbehaving, and of course they are right!

27. *Using global praise.* Global praise is nearly useless. An example is: "Class, your rough drafts were really wonderful." This is hollow and says nothing; it is useless verbalism. Instead, be informative by being specific—tell what it was about their drafts that made them so wonderful. As another example, after a student's oral response to the class, rather than simply saying "Very good," tell what about the student's response was so good.

28. *Using color meaninglessly.* The use of color on the writing board, transparencies, or a PowerPoint presentation is nice but will shortly lose its effectiveness unless the colors have meaning. If, for example, everything in the classroom is color-coded and students understand the meaning of the code, then use of color can serve a useful organizational function as well as an important mnemonic to student learning.

29. *Verbally reprimanding a student from across the classroom.* Not only is it a needless interruption of all students but by embarrassing the recipient student in the presence of the student's peers, it is likely to increase the "you versus them" syndrome, and that is something you

do not want. Reprimand if necessary, but do so quietly and privately.

30. *Interacting with only a "chosen few" students rather than spreading interactions around to all.* As a beginning teacher, especially, it is easy to fall into a habit of interacting with only a few students, especially those who are vocal and who seem to you to have significant contributions. Your job, however, is to teach every student assigned to your classroom. To do that, you must be proactive, not reactive, in your interactions.

31. *Not intervening quickly enough during inappropriate student behavior.* Except for those minor misbehaviors that are momentary and nondisruptive, inappropriate student behavior only gets worse, not better. It is best to nip it in the bud quickly and resolutely. A teacher who ignores inappropriate behavior, even briefly, is in effect approving it. In turn, that approval reinforces the continuation and escalation of inappropriate behaviors.

32. *Not learning and using student names.* A teacher who does not know or use names when addressing students is viewed by the students as impersonal and uncaring. To expedite your success, you should quickly learn their names and then refer to students by their names.

33. *Reading student papers only for correct (or incorrect) answers and not for process and thinking.* Reading student papers only for correct responses reinforces the false notion that the process of arriving at answers or solutions is unimportant and that alternative solutions or answers are impossible or unimportant. In effect, it negates the importance of the individual and the very nature and purpose of learning.

34. *Not putting time plans on the board for students.* Yelling out how much time is left for an activity interrupts student thinking; it implies that to you, at least, their thinking is unimportant. Avoid interrupting students once they are on task. Show respect for their on-task behavior. In this instance, write on the board before the activity begins how much time is allowed for it. Write the time it is to end. If during the activity a decision is made to change the end time, then write that changed time on the board.

35. *Asking global questions that nobody likely will answer.* Examples are "Does everyone understand?" and "Are there any questions?" and "How do you all feel about …?" It is a brave young soul who, in presence of peers, is willing to admit ignorance. And one I especially dislike is the one I have heard used on Monday mornings by too many teachers, which is "How was your weekend?" As if students were all expected to answer at the same time. It is a waste of precious instructional time to ask such questions. If you truly want to check for student understanding or opinions, then do a spot check by asking specific questions, allowing think time, and then calling on students. And train students in this process starting from the first of the school year. See Chapter 6, devoted entirely to the topic of "questioning."

36. *Failing to do frequent comprehension checks (every few minutes during most direct instruction situations) to see if students are understanding.* Too often, teachers simply plow through a big chunk of the lesson, or the entire lesson, assuming that students understand. Or, in the worst-case scenario, teachers hurry through a lesson without even seeming to care whether students are getting it. Students are quick to recognize teachers who do not care or who by their actions do not appear to care.

37. *Not monitoring for understanding during seatwork.* Frequent comprehension checks should be done, too, when students are doing seatwork. When assigning seatwork, be sure that your instructions include specifics about what is to be learned, how it is to be learned, and how the content is connected to previous material that students learned. Then during the seatwork monitor students not only to keep them on task but also to check for individual understandings.

38. *Using poorly worded, ambiguous questions.* Key questions you will ask during a lesson should be planned and written into your lesson plan. Refine and make precise the questions by asking them to yourself or a friend, and try to predict how students will respond to a particular question.

39. *Trying to talk over student noise.* This simply tells students that their making noise while you are talking is acceptable behavior. When this happens, everyone, teacher included, usually gets increasingly louder during the class period. About all you will accomplish when trying to talk over a high student noise level is a sore throat by the end of the school day and, over a longer period of time, an increasing potential for nodules on your vocal cords.

Incidentally, because teachers experience voice problems with far greater severity and frequency than do other workers, many school districts install either portable (system is worn by the teacher) or infrared wireless voice enhancement systems. Such systems help not only teachers' vocal health but also student academic achievement (McCarty, Ostrem, & Young, 2004).

40. *Wanting to be liked by students.* Forget about being liked! If you are a teacher, then teach! Respect is earned as a result of your effective teaching. Liking you, then, may evolve as a result. You are *not* your students' peer; you *are* their teacher—a professional and a very important adult role model.

41. *Permitting students to be inattentive to an educationally useful media presentation.* This usually happens because the teacher has failed to give the students a written handout of questions or guidelines for what they should acquire from the program. Sometimes students need an additional focus. Furthermore, a media presentation is usually audio and visual. To reinforce student learning, add the kinesthetic, such as the writing aspect when a handout of questions is supplied.

42. *Starting in stutters.* A stutter start is when the teacher begins an activity, is distracted, begins again, is distracted again, tries again to start, and so on. During stutter starts, students become increasingly restless and inattentive, and sometimes even amused by the teacher's futility, making the final start almost impossible for the teacher to achieve. Avoid stutter starts. Begin an activity clearly and decisively. This is most easily accomplished when lesson plans are prepared thoughtfully and in detail. Also important to the prevention of stutter starts is the teacher's overlapping ability. For example, a teacher who accepts the admit slip from an incoming tardy student without missing a beat in giving warm-up instructions or the lecture has developed overlapping skill. As another example, the teacher who can stop the ensuing inappropriate behavior of a student with the use of a nonverbal gesture (e.g., a stare, a quick pause in vocal delivery, or a change of proximity such as moving and standing adjacent to the student) without interrupting the content discussion or distracting the rest of the students has overlapping skill.

43. *Introducing too many topics simultaneously.* It is important that you not overload students' capacity to engage mentally by introducing different topics simultaneously.

44. *Failing to give students a pleasant greeting on the first day of the school year, or on each Monday, or the day back following a holiday, or to remind them to have a pleasant weekend or holiday.* Students are likely to perceive such a teacher as indifferent or unfriendly.

45. *Sounding egocentric.* Whether you are or are not egocentric, you want to avoid seeming so. Sometimes the distinction is subtle, although apparent, such as when a teacher says, "What I am going to do now is …" rather than "What we are going to do now is …" If you want to strive for group cohesiveness—a sense of "we-ness"—then teach not as if you are the leader and your students are the followers, but rather in a manner that empowers your students in their learning.

46. *Taking too much time to give verbal instructions for an activity.* Students become impatient and restless during long verbal instructions from the teacher. It is better to give brief instructions (a minute or two should do it) and get the students started on the task. For more complicated activities, teach three or four students the instructions and then have those students do miniworkshops with five or six students in each workshop group. This frees you to monitor the progress of each group.

47. *Taking too much time for an activity.* No matter what the activity, during your planning think carefully about how much time students can effectively attend to the activity. A general rule for most classes (age level and other factors dictate variation) is that when only one or two learning modalities are involved (e.g., auditory and visual), the activity should not extend beyond about 15 minutes; when more than two modalities are engaged

Teaching in Practice

Too Many Topics Introduced at Once

During the first 10 minutes of a high school history class the teacher started by introducing a warm-up activity, which was a journal write with instructions clearly presented on the overhead; the teacher also verbally explained the activity, although the teacher could have simply pointed to the screen, thereby nonverbally instructing students to begin work on the activity (without disturbing the thinking of those who had already begun). One minute later, the teacher was telling students about their quarter grades and how later in the class period they would learn more about those grades. Then the teacher returned to the warm-up activity, explaining it a second time (third time if one counts the detailed explanation already on the screen). Next the teacher reminded students of the school's new tardy rules (thereby introducing a third topic). At this time, however, most of the students were still thinking and talking about what the teacher had said about quarter grades, few were working on the warm-up activity, and hardly any were listening to the teacher talking about the new tardy rules. There was a lot of commotion among the students. The teacher had tried to focus student attention on too many topics at once, thus accomplishing little and losing control of the class in the process.

Questions for Class Discussion
1. What were your initial thoughts after reading this scenario?
2. What do you predict for the rest of the year for this teacher?
3. What specifically, if anything, should the teacher have done differently?
4. Do you believe this teacher would have benefited from viewing a videotaping of the entire class meeting?

(e.g., add tactile or kinesthetic), then the activity might extend longer, say for 20 to 30 minutes.

48. *Being uptight and anxious.* Consciously or subconsciously, students are quick to detect a teacher who worries that events will not go well. It is like a contagion; if you are uptight and anxious, your students will likely become the same. To prevent such corruption, at least to the extent it damages your teaching and your students' learning, you must prepare lessons carefully, thoughtfully, and thoroughly. Unless there is something personal going on in your life that is causing your anxiety, you are more likely to be in control and confident in the classroom when your lessons are well prepared. How do you know when a lesson is well prepared? You'll know! Usually, it is when you have developed a written lesson plan that you are truly excited about, proud of, and eager to implement.

If you do have a personal problem in your life that is distracting and making you anxious (and occasionally most of us do), you need to concentrate on ensuring that your anger, hostility, fear, or other negative emotions do not adversely affect your teaching and your interactions with students. Regardless of your personal problems your students will face you each day expecting to be taught whatever it is you are supposed to be helping them learn.

49. *Failing to apply the best of what is known about how young people learn.* Too many teachers unrealistically seem to expect success having all students in the classroom doing the same thing at the same time rather than having several alternative activities simultaneously occurring (called **multilevel instruction**) in the classroom. For example, a student who is not responding well, who is being inattentive and disruptive to a class discussion, might behave better if given the choice of moving to a quiet learning center to work alone. If, after trying this alternative activity, the student continues to be disruptive, then you may have to try still another alternative activity. You may have to send the student to another supervised (time-out) location out of the classroom, to a place previously arranged by you, until you have time after class or after school to talk with the student about the problem.

50. *Overusing punishment for classroom misbehavior—jumping to the final step without trying alternatives.* Teachers sometimes mistakenly either ignore inappropriate student behavior (see number 31) or they skip steps for intervention, resorting too quickly to punishment. They immediately send the misbehaving student outside to stand in the hall (not a wise choice if the student is not supervised) or too quickly assign detention (a usually ineffective consequence). Being quick to use punishment is not a lesson we should be teaching our youth. In-between steps to consider include (as discussed in number 49) the use of alternative activities in the classroom, or, if necessary, to a time-out location. It is useful to keep in mind that every young person is a work in progress.

When a child errs, it is very important that the child has the opportunity to recover and to learn from the error.

---

51. *Being vague and inconsistent.* Perhaps one of the most frequent causes of problems for beginning teachers derives from when they fail to say what is meant or to mean what they said. A teacher who gives only vague instructions or is inconsistent in his or her behaviors only confuses students (e.g., does not enforce that teacher's own classroom procedural expectations). If a teacher's verbal communication conflicts with his or her nonverbal messages, students can become not only confused but even resentful, and this too can affect their learning. When there is a discrepancy between what the teacher says and what that teacher does, the teacher's nonverbal signal will win every time. Actions do speak louder than

words! A teacher, for example, who emphasizes the importance of students getting their assignments in on time but then takes forever to read, evaluate, and return those same papers to the students is using inappropriate modeling. Or, as another example, a teacher who has just finished a lesson on the conservation of energy and does not turn off the room lights upon leaving the classroom for recess or lunch has, by inappropriate modeling behavior, created cognitive disequilibrium and sabotaged the real purpose for the lesson. And yet another example, a teacher who asks students not to interrupt others when they are on task but who repeatedly interrupts students when they are on task, is confusing students with that teacher's contradictory words and behavior. To avoid confusing students, think through what it is you really expect from your students and then ensure that your own verbal and nonverbal behaviors are consistent with those expectations.

Now do Exercise 3.5 (end of chapter) and then direct your attention to other specific instances of teacher behaviors, some of which reinforce or cause student misbehavior, by completing self-check Exercise 3.6 (end of chapter).

SITUATIONAL CASE STUDIES FOR ADDITIONAL REVIEW

To provide further insight into the day-by-day events that occur in teaching, as well as to stimulate your thinking about what you might do in similar situations, the following case studies are presented. Each is a situation that actually occurred. Analyze and discuss these in your class, using the accompanying questions to guide your thinking.

☐ Case 1. THE BOY WHO HANGS AROUND

Background

Bill is male, age 13, in life science. He is tall and awkward and has poor skin. His classmates consider him "crazy." He has minor police offenses and is apparently in conflict with his father. He has taken a liking to the life science teacher and spends many extra hours in the classroom. He is energetic and displays an inquisitive nature. He is quick to get interested in projects but almost as quick to lose interest. He likes to operate the DVD for the teacher, but he does not like to participate in discussions with the rest of the class. He likes personal chats with the teacher but feels that the other students laugh at him.

The Situation

Bill's IQ is 95. The teacher attempted to work with Bill in improving his feelings of inadequacy. The teacher had frank talks with Bill about his gangliness and his acne. What follows is actual material as written by Bill during the first semester of school:

September: "I want to make the best out of the time I am on earth, I want to be somebody, not just exist either. … The members of this class influence me and what I think of doing. … They also make me feel real low. Their teasing me has changed me. … The teacher of my science class has helped me very much. … My greatest problem is in holding my head up and fighting for myself. …"

October: "I have made a lot of headway in the past weeks. … I think I have done a good choice in the subject I am studying. … I also thank my teacher's actions toward me, that we may get to be very good friends, and learn a lot to know that teachers are human too, that they also have problems to solve and goals to head for."

November: "I don't have to fear anybody or anything on the idea of getting up and saying what I feel I have accomplished in this class and I have learned to make my own dississions on what I will study or maybe do when I get out of school."

December: "I have learned that I have confidence in others only when I have confidence in myself."

January: "I have my report on the effect of geabriilic acid on plants. … I told (the class) about all my failures and they were quite interested. I told them that I had failed four times … that my science teacher told me I should not give up at this point and that a seintice [scientist] does not give up. I had no longer stated that fact and they all seemed like they could help in some way. I think the report went over well."

The student developed courage to stand in front of his peers, holding his head high, and confidently reporting to the class how he kept at his plant experiment, even after four failures. He was proud of what he had learned about the work of the scientist. And he was even more proud that the students no longer teased and laughed at him.

Questions for Class Discussion

1. How did you feel after reading this case?
2. Did Bill learn anything that semester? What?
3. Did he learn science?
4. What did the teacher do to facilitate Bill's learning?
5. What is ahead for Bill in school?

☐ Case 2. THE BULLY

Background

Tony is considered by his peers to be one of the "tough guys." He is 14 and in the eighth grade at Green Middle School. Tony is prone to bullying, frequently quarrels with his fellow students and teachers, and is considered by his parents to be disobedient. He has a record of minor offenses that range from truancy to destruction of property to drunkenness and offensive behavior. In general, Tony gets his satisfaction in ways that are damaging and unfair to others.

It is obvious to school officials that Tony is beyond parental control. Tony's mother has no apparent ability to control Tony's behavior. His father frequently physically beats him.

Tony is not a member of any school organization of an extracurricular nature. His midterm progress shows that he is failing in three subjects.

At a school's football game Tony was arrested at halftime for riding around the track on a motorbike, while intoxicated.

The Situation

One of the subjects Tony is failing is English. Tony is a discipline problem in class, and although it makes the teacher feel guilty, she cannot help but be pleased when Tony is absent from class.

Questions for Class Discussion

1. Where is the problem?
2. Where is Tony heading?
3. What can and should be done, if anything? By whom? Is there anything positive that can be tried by Tony's English teacher?
4. What is the role for Tony? His teachers? His peers? The school administration? His parents? Society in general?
5. Is it too late for Tony?

☐ Case 3. THE PROBLEM OF MARY

Background

Mary has been characterized by her peers and by her teachers as being lonely, indifferent, and generally unhappy. She avoids both students and teachers. She will lie and cheat to avoid attention. Her "close" friends describe her as thoughtless and unkind. She often uses damaging remarks about members of her class, calling them conceited, teacher's pets. She considers members of her class to be thoughtless, unkind, and uninterested in her.

Mary will do what she has to do to achieve average success in her studies. Her association with adults, her parents, and her teachers would be described as one of "merely getting along," doing what "I have to do in order not to get too much attention."

The Situation

One of Mary's friends is another 14-year-old girl, Jane. Jane is an above-average student in school, seemingly well adjusted, and interested in people, and she has gotten to know Mary because they are neighbors and walk together to school. Because of Jane's interest in other people and her closeness to Mary, she has become interested in "trying to bring Mary out of her shell."

Mary has told Jane that she feels her teachers are unreasonably severe. Mary said, "The teachers are only interested in the popular kids." Jane disagreed. Mary said, "You only disagree because you are pretty and popular." At this point, the conversation was broken by a boy running up and saying, "Hey, Jane, you're late for the council meeting."

Questions for Class Discussion

1. Where is the problem?
2. What if you were Mary's teacher?
3. How did you feel after reading this case?
4. Have you known a Mary? If so, what was the outcome? What helped, what hindered?

☐ Case 4. FROM A DEADLY DARE

In an advanced biology class the students were just starting a lab involving the dissection of triple-latex-injected, formaldehyde-preserved bullfrogs. While the teacher was busy talking with a few students off to one side of the room—answering their questions and helping them get started on their work—she heard screaming and a commotion from the far side of the room. She looked up and immediately saw Robert, a junior, vomiting and convulsing. On a dare from other students, he had eaten his bullfrog, completely devouring it. Immediately the teacher sent a runner to the office (there was no phone in the classroom). Someone dialed 911, and an ambulance and paramedics soon arrived to take Robert to a nearby hospital, where his stomach was pumped and other treatment was administered. For the next 24 hours Robert was in very serious condition.

Questions for Class Discussion

1. What were your thoughts after reading this case?
2. Could the incident have been prevented?

☐ Case 5. STUDENT HAS A CRUSH ON TEACHER

During his first year of teaching it had become obvious that one of Mr. Kline's female sixth-grade students had developed a serious crush on him. One day, after class was over and all other students had left the room, she approached Mr. Kline and politely asked him if he had a photograph of himself that she could have.

Questions for Class Discussion

1. Is this a potentially serious situation?
2. How should Mr. Kline respond to the student's request?

☐ Case 6. DUCT TAPING A STUDENT'S MOUTH IS NOT AN ACCEPTABLE SOLUTION!

Carla, an eighth-grade teacher, was severely reprimanded for placing duct tape over the mouth of Michael, a special-needs student, in an effort to put a stop to Michael's incessant talking in class.

Questions for Class Discussion

1. After reading this, what were your thoughts?
2. Do you suppose sometimes out of desperation potentially good teachers do stupid things?
3. What if Carla ignored Michael's incessant talking? Do you suppose Carla and the class of students could have gotten used to it to the point where it was no longer a disturbing factor?
4. What, if anything, did you learn from this situation that might be helpful to you as you begin your own teaching career?

☐ Case 7. STUDENT COMPLAINS TO A STUDENT TEACHER ABOUT CONTINUED SEXUAL HARASSMENT BY A PEER

During the first week after John began his student teaching in eighth-grade history, one of his female students came to him after class and complained that a boy in the class has continued to sexually harass her even after she had reported it to the school vice-principal. She says that the harassment is beyond just verbal abuse, and she wants it stopped.

Questions for Class Discussion

1. After reading this case, what were your thoughts?
2. What, if anything, should John do?
3. What, if anything, did you learn from this situation that might be helpful to you during your own teaching career?

☐ Case 8. STUDENTS USE THE INTERNET FOR EXTRACURRICULAR ACTIVITY

During project work time in a language arts/social studies block, the teacher discovers a group of three students at a computer workstation viewing a graphic sex web site.

Questions for Class Discussion

1. After reading this, what were your immediate thoughts?
2. What should the teacher do?
3. How could the problem have been avoided?
4. What, if anything, did you learn from this case that might be helpful to you during your own teaching career?

☐ Case 9. REENACTMENT OF SLAVERY

Margaret, a white social studies teacher, attempted to enliven a fifth-grade study and discussion of slavery by binding the hands and feet of two African-American girls, one who volunteered while the other did not. The lesson prompted outrage from one girl's mother and the local chapter of the NAACP.

Questions for Class Discussion

1. After reading this scenario, what were your immediate thoughts?
2. Do you think Margaret had given careful thought about this action during her lesson planning, or was it the result of a spur of the moment thought?
3. What, if anything, should Margaret have done differently? What would you have done differently, were you the teacher?
4. What, if anything, did you learn from this case that might be helpful to you during your own teaching career?

☐ Case 10. USED THE "N-WORD" IN CLASS*

Janine teaches at an inner-city school. It is her first year of teaching and the first day of classes following the summer break. As students are arriving in her classroom, she overhears several students using the "n-word" as they call to and greet each other. Janine, a white teacher, does not react.

Questions for Class Discussion

1. After reading this scenario, what were your immediate thoughts?
2. What, if anything, should Janine have done differently? What would you have done differently, were you the teacher?
3. Do you believe there is anything a teacher should or should not do depending on whether the teacher hears the "n-word" used in each of these instances: without malice in the classroom, with malice in the classroom, in the hall, on the school campus?
4. What, if anything, did you learn from this case that might be helpful to you during your own teaching career?

SUMMARY

In this chapter, you learned ways to cope with the daily challenges of classroom teaching and of guidelines for effectively managing students in the classroom. Within that framework, your attention was then focused on specific approaches and additional guidelines for effective classroom management and control of the learning environment. You were offered advice for setting up and maintaining a classroom environment that is favorable to student learning, and for establishing procedures for efficiently controlling student behavior, helping them establish self-control, and encouraging student learning. To become an accomplished classroom manager takes thoughtful and thorough planning, consistent and confident application, and reflective experience. Be patient with yourself as you accumulate the prerequisite knowledge and practice and hone the necessary skills.

From this knowledge about establishing the most effective learning environment, in the next two chapters, the final two chapters on the preactive phase of instruction, you will be guided through important considerations for selecting the content for and planning units of instruction with lessons.

 Now go to Topic #3: **Classroom Management** in the MyEducationLab (www.myeducationlab.com) for your course, where you can:

- Find learning outcomes for this topic along with the national standards that connect to these outcomes.
- Complete Assignments and Activities that can help you more deeply understand the chapter content.
- Examine challenging situations and cases presented in the IRIS center resources.
- Apply and practice your understanding of the core teaching skills identified in the chapter with the Building Teaching Skills and Dispositions learning units.

QUESTIONS FOR CLASS DISCUSSION

1. Explain why you believe it is better to be strict with students at first and then relax once your control has been established, or to be relaxed at first and then tighten the reins later if students misbehave, or why you believe it doesn't really matter which method you use.

2. Explain what you would do if two errant behaviors occurred simultaneously in different locations in your classroom.

3. Explain what you would do if a student came to you and reported that fellow students were harassing him by throwing objects at him, slapping him, pulling his chair out from under him, and pretending to rape him.

4. Some educational psychologists dislike the teacher's use of tangible and token reinforcers, such as stickers and gold stars, considering their use disrespectful, manipulative, and only temporarily effective. Other psychologists and teachers disagree. What is your opinion? What recent research can you find to support or refute your opinion? Share your findings with your classmates.

5. One student hit a pregnant teacher, another exposed himself, and another stabbed a classmate with a pencil, all during the 2002–2003 school year. All were suspended from school for up to 2 weeks. Although not from the same school or even the same state, all were kindergartners. Some experts believe that the youngest school children are being suspended from school with greater frequency than ever. At schools in your geographic area, and for grade levels that you are interested in, investigate and share with others in your class what you can find about the use of home suspension versus on-campus suspension, and the frequency of each. Describe what information you can find about the advantages and disadvantages of each.

EXERCISE 3.1 OBSERVING A CLASSROOM FOR FREQUENCY OF EXTERNAL INTERRUPTIONS

INSTRUCTIONS: It is disconcerting how often teachers and student learning in classrooms of some schools are interrupted by announcements over the intercom, a phone call, or a visitor at the door. After all, no one would even consider interrupting a surgeon during the most climatic moments of an open-heart operation, nor a defense attorney at the climax of her summation, but far too often teachers are interrupted just at a critical point in a lesson. Once lost because of an interruption, student attention and that teachable moment is nearly impossible to recapture.

School administrators and office personnel must sometimes be reminded that the most important thing going on in the school is that which teachers have been hired to do—teach—and the act of teaching must not be frivolously interrupted. In my opinion, except for absolutely critical reasons, teachers should never be interrupted after the first 5 minutes of a class period and before the last 5 minutes. That policy should be established and rigidly adhered to. Otherwise, after many years of being a student, the lesson learned is that the least important thing going on at the school is that which is going on in the classroom. No wonder then it is so difficult for teachers in some schools to gain student attention and respect. That respect must be shown starting from the school's central office. Because the turnaround and refocus must somehow begin now, we have added this exercise to this book.

Arrange to visit a school classroom and observe for classroom interruptions created from outside the classroom.

1. School and class visited: _____

   _____

2. Time (start and end of class period): _____

3. Interruptions (tally for each interruption)

   3.1 intercom:

   3.2 phone:

   3.3 visitor at door:

   3.4 emergency drill:

   3.5 other (specify):

4. Total number of interruptions: _____

☞

EXERCISE 3.1 *(continued)*

5. My conclusion:

6. Share and compare your results and conclusion with your classmates.

7. My thoughts about how I, as a classroom teacher, will prevent, control, and deal with interruptions from outside the classroom.

 **EXERCISE 3.2   TEACHERS' CLASSROOM MANAGEMENT SYSTEMS**

INSTRUCTIONS: The purpose of this exercise is to interview two teachers, from two different grade levels, to discover how they manage their classrooms. Use the outline format that follows, conduct your interviews, and then share the results with your classmates, perhaps in small groups.

1. Teacher interviewed: _____

2. Date:_____

3. Grade level: _____

4. School: _____

5. Subject(s): _____

6. Please describe your classroom management system. Specifically, I would like to know your procedures for the following:

   a. How are students to signal that they want your attention and help?_____

   _____

   _____

   _____

   b. How do you call on students during question and discussion sessions? _____

   _____

   _____

   _____

   c. How and when are students to enter and exit the classroom? _____

   _____

   _____

   _____

   d. How are students to obtain the materials for instruction? _____

   _____

   _____

   _____

   e. How are students to store their personal items? _____

   _____

   _____

   f. What are the procedures for students going to the drinking fountain or rest room?

   _____

   _____

   _____

☞

EXERCISE 3.2 *(continued)*

g. What are your procedures during class interruptions? _____

_____

_____

_____

h. What are your procedures for tardies or early dismissals? _____

_____

_____

_____

i. What are your procedures for turning in homework? _____

_____

_____

_____

7. Describe your expectations for classroom behavior and the consequences for misbehavior.

_____

_____

_____

_____

_____

_____

In discussion with classmates following the interviews, consider the following. Many modern teachers advocate the use of a highly structured classroom; then, as appropriate over time during the school year, they share more of the responsibility with the students. Did you find this to be the case with the majority of teachers interviewed? Was it more or less the case in elementary schools, middle level schools, or high schools? Was it more or less the case with any particular subject area?

_____

_____

_____

_____

_____

_____

_____

_____

_____

_____

EXERCISE 3.3   BEGINNING THE DEVELOPMENT OF MY CLASSROOM MANAGEMENT SYSTEM

INSTRUCTIONS: The purpose of this exercise is to begin preparation of the management system that you will explain to your students during the first day or week of school. Answer the questions that follow, and share those answers with your peers for their feedback. Then make changes as appropriate. (Upon completion of this chapter, you may want to revisit this exercise to make adjustments to your management plan, as you will from time to time throughout your professional career.)

1. My teaching subject area and anticipated grade level: _____

   _____

2. Attention to procedures. Use a statement to explain my procedural expectation for each of the following:

   a. How are students to signal that they want my attention and help? _____

      _____

      _____

   b. How will I call on students during question and discussion sessions? _____

      _____

      _____

   c. How and when are students to enter and exit the classroom? _____

      _____

      _____

   d. How are students to obtain the materials for instruction? _____

      _____

      _____

   e. How are students to store their personal items? _____

      _____

      _____

   f. What are my procedures for students going to the drinking fountain or rest room?

      _____

      _____

   g. What are my procedures during class interruptions? _____

      _____

      _____

   h. What are my procedures for tardies or early dismissals? _____

      _____

      _____

EXERCISE 3.3 *(continued)*

    i. What are my procedures for turning in homework? _____

          _____

    j. What are my procedures for turning in late homework? _____

          _____

3. List of student behavior expectations that I will present to my class (no more than five):

    Rule 1 _____

    _____

    _____

    Rule 2 _____

    _____

    _____

    Rule 3 _____

    _____

    _____

    Rule 4 _____

    _____

    _____

    Rule 5 _____

    _____

    _____

4. Explanation of consequences for broken rules: _____

    _____

    _____

    _____

    _____

5. How my procedures, rules, or consequences may vary (if at all) according to the grade level taught, or according to any other criteria, such as in team teaching: _____

    _____

    _____

    _____

    _____

    _____

**EXERCISE 3.4   OBSERVATION AND ANALYSIS OF
HOW EXPERIENCED TEACHERS
OPEN CLASS MEETINGS**

INSTRUCTIONS: Select three experienced teachers, all of the same grade level and subject, to observe for how they begin their class meetings. Observe only the first 10 minutes of each period. After collecting these data, share, compile, and discuss the results as follows.

Grade level and subject discipline observed: _____

1. Make a check for each of the following observations that you make, and for each teacher place a number, 1, 2, 3, etc., for which of these things the teacher did first, second, third, etc., during that initial 10 minutes from the time students begin entering the classroom until after the official clock start of class (i.e., when class is supposed to begin).

	✔	Teacher 1	Teacher 2	Teacher 3
Greeting the students	___	___	___	___
Warm and friendly?	___	___	___	___
Giving an assignment (i.e., a warm-up activity)	___	___	___	___
Taking attendance	___	___	___	___
Talking with another adult	___	___	___	___
Talking with one or a few students	___	___	___	___
Readying teaching materials or equipment	___	___	___	___
Working at desk	___	___	___	___
Handing out student papers or materials	___	___	___	___
Other (specify)	___	___	___	___

2. For these three teachers, was there a common way in which they began class?

_____

_____

_____

_____

_____

_____

3. Compile your results with those of your classmates. Write the results here.

_____

_____

_____

_____

_____

_____

_____

_____

☞

EXERCISE 3.4 *(continued)*

4. Compare the results of observations for all similar subjects/grade level combinations. What are the similarities and differences?

_____

_____

_____

_____

_____

_____

_____

_____

_____

5. What are the conclusions you can reach as a class about teachers of particular grade levels and subject disciplines and how they spent the first 10 minutes of the class meeting?

_____

_____

_____

_____

_____

_____

_____

_____

EXERCISE 3.5 AVOIDING SENDING OPPOSING MESSAGES

INSTRUCTIONS: In the text preceding this exercise you read about the importance of a teacher's verbal and nonverbal messages being consistent or confluent and not confusing the students. Three examples are presented in that discussion. It is the purpose of this exercise to heighten your own awareness about the importance of consistency between what you say and what you do as a teacher to better ensure consistency.

1. Think of a recent real-life example where, in your opinion, a classroom teacher's nonverbal behavior and verbal message were inconsistent. Without being intrusive, describe in detail the situation (including grade level—elementary, secondary, or postsecondary) and the differing messages you believe that teacher conveyed to the students. _____

_____

_____

_____

_____

2. Describe the results of the inconsistency. In other words, how you could tell that the students were confused by the mixed signals sent by that teacher. _____

_____

_____

_____

_____

3. Did the teacher become aware that he or she sent contradictory messages? If so, was the situation clarified, and if so, how? Was the situation improved by the clarification? _____

_____

_____

_____

_____

4. Share this incident (steps 1–3) with your classmates.

5. Finally, after sharing incidents, describe what precautions you will take as a classroom teacher to avoid sending mixed messages and thus confusing your students.

   <u>Example: Instruct my students to inform me whenever they catch me being inconsistent in the messages I convey, and provide some sort of recognition or incentive for their alertness.</u> _____

_____

_____

_____

_____

EXERCISE 3.6 IDENTIFYING TEACHER BEHAVIORS THAT CAUSE STUDENT MISBEHAVIOR— A SELF-CHECK REVIEW EXERCISE

INSTRUCTIONS: The purpose of this exercise is to practice your awareness of the kinds of teacher behaviors to avoid—namely, those that tend to reinforce or cause student misbehavior. Place a check next to each of the following situations you believe illustrate teacher behaviors that cause or reinforce student misbehavior. Then identify what the teacher should do instead. Share your responses with your classmates. An answer key follows.

_____   1. Ms. Rodriquez is nearly always late in arriving to her senior English class that meets immediately after lunch and seldom begins class until at least 5 minutes past the time it is supposed to start.

_____

_____

_____

_____

_____

_____   2. Mr. Roohani ignores brief whispering between two students during a quiet activity in his sixth-grade social studies class.

_____

_____

_____

_____

_____

_____   3. While lecturing to her biology class, Ms. Whyte ignores brief talking between two students.

_____

_____

_____

_____

_____   4. During a class discussion in Mr. Stephen's social studies class, one student appears to be daydreaming and just staring out the window.

_____

_____

_____

_____

_____

_____ 5. During quiet study time in Mr. Orey's sixth-grade reading class, Mr. Orey asks for everyone's attention, verbally reprimands two students for horsing around, and then writes out a referral for each of the two students.

_____

_____

_____

_____

_____ 6. Ms. Fueyo advises her students to pay attention during the viewing of a film or else she will give them a quiz over the film's content.

_____

_____

_____

_____

_____ 7. Ms. Lee tells a student that because of his behavior in class today he must come in after school and be detained with her for 10 minutes, the same amount of time that he disturbed the class.

_____

_____

_____

_____

_____ 8. When Mr. Murai sees a seventh-grade student cheating on a science test, he walks over to the student, picks up the student's test paper, and tears it up in front of the student and the rest of the class.

_____

_____

_____

_____

_____ 9. While Ms. Wong is talking to her second-grade class, the school principal walks into the room. Ms. Wong stops her lecture and walks over to greet the principal and find out what the principal wants.

_____

_____

_____

_____

_____ 10. While a student learning team is giving its oral report to a third-grade class, Mr. O'Malley, the teacher, begins a conversation with several students in the back of the room.

_____

_____

_____

_____

_____

_____

Answer Key: You should have checked situations 1, 3, 5, 6, 7, 8, 9, and 10: these are teacher behaviors that reinforce or cause student misbehavior. For some situations, reasonable teachers will disagree. You should talk about these disagreements with your classmates and arrive at common understandings. Here are some thoughts on each of the 10 situations:

1. Ms. Rodriguez's behavior is poor modeling for her students. She must model what she expects—as well as what the school expects—of students. In this instance, she should model arriving and starting on time.

2. Minor infractions, such as this, are often best ignored, as long as the whispering is brief and not disturbing.

3. This should not be ignored. Students are expected to give their attention to the teacher or whoever has the floor at the moment—a show of common courtesy. By not attending to these students (perhaps by eye contact, proximity, name-dropping, or some other form of indirect intervention), Ms. Whyte is saying that it is okay for students to be discourteous and to talk during the teacher's lecture. In this instance, Ms. Whyte is not following through with classroom behavioral expectations. Her lack of follow-through will cause further and increasingly disturbing management problems.

4. Minor infractions are sometimes best ignored. Perhaps the student is really thinking about ideas presented in the discussion.

5. By his disruption of the class learning activity, Mr. Orey is reinforcing the very behavior he considers inappropriate from his students. This lack of consistency will cause continued problems in management for Mr. Orey.

6. Threats are unacceptable behaviors, from students or from teachers, and tests should never be administered as punishment. Ms. Fueyo could recommend that students take notes (mental or written) during the film and that these notes will serve as a focus for discussion after the film's showing. She also could advise them that there will be a follow-up quiz later.

7. By giving the student even more individual attention after school, Ms. Lee is reinforcing and rewarding the student's misbehavior that caused the student problem in the first place. Besides, this may not be safe for Ms. Lee to do. Detention, supervised by someone other than this teacher, is a better alternative.

8. Mr. Murai has taken no time to diagnose and to prescribe and thus is reacting too hastily and with hostility. This sort of teacher behavior reinforces the notion that the student is guilty until proven innocent and the notion that process is of greater importance than is the individual student. In addition, Mr. Murai violated this student's right to due process.

9. The error here is that by stopping her lesson, Ms. Wong and the principal are reinforcing the notion that classroom disruptions are acceptable—that the act of teaching is less important than other school business.

10. Mr. Edwards' behavior is both disrespectful and an example of poor modeling. Mr. Edwards and his class should be giving their full attention to the students' report. Mr. Edwards is not modeling the very behavior that he undoubtedly expects from his students when he is leading the class.

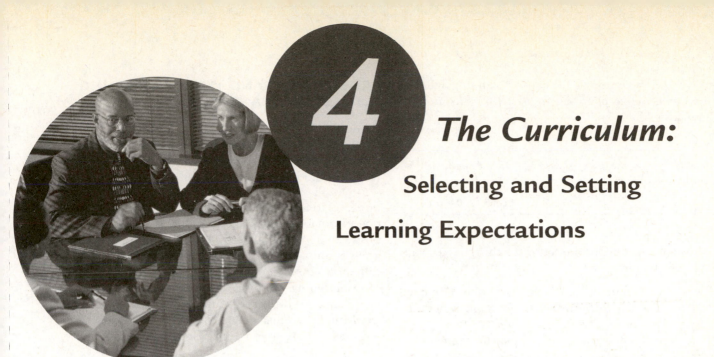

4

The Curriculum:

Selecting and Setting

Learning Expectations

Effective teaching does not just happen; it is produced through the thoughtful planning of each phase of the learning process. Most effective teachers begin their planning months before meeting their students for the first time. Daily lessons form parts of a larger scheme, which is designed to accomplish the teacher's long-range curriculum goals for the semester or year and to mesh with the school's mission and goals standards.

If learning is defined only as the accumulation of bits and pieces of information, then we already know everything about how to teach and how students learn. But the accumulation of pieces of information is at the lowest end of a spectrum of types of learning. Discoveries are still being made about the processes involved in higher forms of learning—that is, for meaningful understanding and the reflective use of that understanding. The results of recent research support the use of instructional strategies that help students make connections as they learn (Findley, 2002). These strategies include discovery learning, inquiry, collaborative and cooperative learning, interdisciplinary thematic instruction, and project-based learning, with a total curriculum that is integrated and connected to students' life experiences.

> As schools grow more diverse, so too must our understanding of what it means to be literate.
>
> Dana G. Thames & Kathleen C. York (2003)

The methodology uses what is referred to as **hands-on** and **minds-on learning**—that is, the learner is learning by doing and is thinking about what she or he is learning and doing. When thoughtfully coupled, these approaches help construct, and often reconstruct, the learner's perceptions. Hands-on learning engages the learner's mind, causing questioning and turning a learner's mind on. Hands-on/minds-on learning encourages students to question and then, with the teacher's guidance, devise ways of investigating satisfactory, although sometimes only tentative, answers to their questions.

As a classroom teacher, your instructional task then is twofold: (1) to plan hands-on experiences, providing the materials and the supportive environment necessary for students' meaningful exploration and discovery and (2) to facilitate the most meaningful and longest lasting learning possible once the learner's mind has been engaged by the hands-on learning, including although not necessarily limited to student learning of any curriculum which may be mandated by your state and local school district. To accomplish this requires your knowledge about curriculum and competence in the use of varied and developmentally appropriate methods of instruction. To assist you in the acquisition of that knowledge and competence is the primary purpose of this book.

Competent teaching is a kaleidoscopic, multifaceted, eclectic process. When preparing and writing a book to prepare one to teach, by necessity its authors must separate that kaleidoscopic process into separate topics, which is not always possible to do in a way that makes equal sense to all users of the book. So, here is the plan and my advice for you. This chapter and the next address the instructional planning aspect, first the necessary planning of the curriculum and then, following in Chapter 5, the detailed instructional planning necessary to bring the planned curriculum to fruition. As you proceed through these chapters and begin the development of your instructional plans, from time to time you will want to refer to particular topics in Chapters 7 through 10. The rationale for careful planning and the components of that planning are topics pursued now in this chapter.

> In a democracy, the last thing we need is a one-size-fits-all curriculum with one single set of goals for everyone.
>
> Elliot W. Eisner (2004, p. 8)

Specifically, upon completion of this chapter you should be able to:

1. Anticipate controversial topics and issues that may arise while teaching and what you might you do if and when they do arise.
2. Demonstrate ability to select and plan the sequence of content for instruction in a particular subject that is typically taught at a particular school and grade level.
3. Demonstrate an understanding of the rationale for planning for instruction, the levels of planning, and the components of a total instructional plan.
4. Demonstrate knowledge of the value of various types of documents that can be resources for curriculum and instructional planning.
5. Demonstrate understanding of how to help students to develop meaningful understandings while still scoring well on standardized achievement tests.
6. Demonstrate understanding of the concept of integrated curriculum and its relevance to curriculum and instruction.
7. Demonstrate an understanding of the distinction between curriculum content that is *essential* and that which is *supplemental.*
8. Demonstrate an understanding of the value and limitations of a syllabus, textbook, and other print resources for student learning.
9. Describe the relationship of instructional planning to the preactive and reflective thought-processing phases of instruction.
10. Differentiate among diagnostic assessment, formative assessment, and summative assessment and explain the place and use of each in instructional planning.
11. Explain both the value and the limitations afforded by using instructional objectives.
12. Explain the difference and the relationship between hands-on and minds-on learning.
13. Explain the connection among curriculum standards, instructional objectives, and assessment of student learning.
14. Explain the value of students being empowered with some decision making about course planning.
15. Prepare learning objectives for each of the three domains of learning and at various levels within each domain.

PROGRAM ORGANIZATION: PROVIDING SUCCESSFUL TRANSITIONS

Within the framework of school organization lie several components that form a comprehensive, albeit ever-changing, program. Central to the school's purpose and its organizational structure is the concerted effort to see that all students make successful transitions from one level to the next, from one grade to the next, from one school to the next, and from high school to work or postsecondary education. Every aspect of the school program is, in some way, designed to help students make those transitions.

Combining to form the program that students experience are two terms you will frequently encounter, **curriculum** and **instruction.** Let me next clarify those terms as they are used in this resource guide.

Curriculum and Instruction: Clarification of Terms

Originally derived from a Latin term referring to a race-course for the Roman chariots, among educators the term **curriculum** still has no singularly accepted definition. Some define it as the planned subject matter content and skills to be presented to students. Others say that the curriculum is only that which students actually learn. Still others hold the broad definition that the curriculum is all experiences students encounter, whether planned or unplanned, learned or unlearned.

Four programs are identified that contribute in different ways to student learning, that do, in fact, comprise the broadest definition of curriculum:

1. the program of studies (subjects studied; courses offered)
2. the program of student activities (e.g., sports, clubs, and organizations)
3. the program of services (e.g., transportation, meals, counseling, nurse station)
4. the hidden curriculum (i.e., the unplanned and subtle message systems within schools, as discussed in Chapter 1).

This working definition considers curriculum as being the *entire school program.* Accepting this broad definition of curriculum, the curriculum embraces every planned aspect of a school's educational program, including the classes that are designed specifically to advance skills and knowledge, and schoolwide services such as guidance, clubs and interest groups, visual and performing arts productions, student government, fundraising events, and athletic programs.

Instruction, too, has several definitions, some of which are not clearly distinguishable from curriculum. Whereas curriculum is usually associated with the content of the learning, instruction is associated with *methods* or *strategies*—that is, with ways of presenting content, conveying information, and facilitating student learning. Obviously, curriculum and instruction must be in tandem to positively affect student learning.

Core Curriculum

Core subjects of the curriculum as defined by the No Child Left Behind Act are English, reading or language arts, mathematics, science, foreign languages, civics and government, economics, arts, history, and geography. It is within these subjects, individually or in some combination, that **interdisciplinary thematic units (ITUs)** are taught. The purpose of teaching subject matter on a central theme is to avoid a departmentalized mentality that all too often communicates the wrong message to students—that learning is piecemeal and separate from one experience to another. To the contrary, the core curriculum facilitates the integration of subjects of the thematic units taught in tandem by the teaching team. Unfortunately, the decade long emphasis on high-stakes achievement testing, especially in reading and mathematics and now science, may be putting something of a damper on the inclusion of full integration of subjects and team memberships.

Curriculum Content: Essential Versus Supplemental

In today's schools curriculum content that is specified by mandated state curriculum standards is that which is required, that *must* be covered by instruction—it is *essential.* On the other hand, **supplemental content** is *not* mandated by the state standards, but rather is curriculum that is arbitrary and dependent upon the teacher's discretion.

Exploratory Opportunities

By middle school grades exploratory opportunities can be a substantial part of the school curriculum. The purpose of exploratory opportunities is to provide a variety of experiences to assist students in their discovery of areas of interest for future pursuit that will perhaps develop into a lifelong passion. Allowing students opportunities to discover and explore unusual and novel topics can spawn or rekindle interests in life and school. Exposing them to a range of academic, vocational, and recreational subjects for career options, community service, enrichment, and enjoyment, exploratories build on the inherent curiosity of the young adolescent.

Co-Curricular Versus Extracurricular

Traditionally, especially in secondary schools, student activities involving clubs and athletics have been commonly referred to as "extracurricular." That is because they are considered separate from the academic learning of the regular school day. However, in exemplary middle-level education many activities are significant components of the total educational program and are "co-curricular," rather than extracurricular. **Co-curricular** means that, regardless of whether they occur before, during, or after school or in some combination, the activities are vital to the total curriculum. They are integral to the total school experience and to the needs of the students, not simply add-ons or extras. Example co-curricular middle school program components are intramurals, study skills, and advisory/home base.

The sports program in the exemplary middle-level schools in particular emphasizes intramural participation rather than interscholastic competition (Wiles & Bondi, 2001). Some middle-level schools try to offer both, but most experts of middle-level curricula agree that emphasis on an intramural program is better suited to the needs of all students (McEwin, Jenkins, & Dickinson, 1996). Intramural sports programs are developed to promote participation by all students. The emphasis is on fun, teamwork, socialization, and peer relationships in an unthreatening and relaxed environment. Assessment is based on a student's willingness to cooperate with others and to participate, rather than on the student's skill or performance. Through intramurals, all students can recognize and feel that they are members of a cohesive group, that they are of value as individuals, and that more important than skilled performance is regular physical exercise.

Advisory/Home Base Program

The advisory (also called "home base") program in many middle-level schools, and found with increasing frequency in high schools as well (Champeau, 2006; Henriksen, Stichter, Stone, & Wagoner, 2008), is usually a separate class, ideally of 8 to 12 students (although, in reality, closer to 14 to 24) that meets daily for no less than 20 minutes, without interruptions, usually at the beginning of the school day. The primary purpose of the advisory is to ensure adult advocacy for each student, that each student is known well by at least one adult who can give positive and constructive individual attention to that student. In fact, in some schools the home base teacher remains with the same students throughout their years at that school.

Regardless of its housing and its label, the advisory program should promote a student's feeling of belonging to a group and is not intended to be used for mechanical tasks (although, in reality, it is often a time for announcements and other maintenance tasks). The program is for purposeful individual and small-group activities that deal with students' social relationships, transitioning, health education, and emotional/psychological development and well-being. The program should be a vehicle for dealing with students' affective needs and for teaching skills in organizing and studying, thinking, solving problems, making decisions, preventing violence, dealing with bullying, and for ensuring meaningful contacts with parents and guardians. In short, for the student, the advisory program, with its planned adult advocacy for each student, can be a very significant aspect of the total school curriculum.

PLANNING FOR INSTRUCTION: THREE LEVELS

As a classroom teacher, planning for instruction is a major professional responsibility. You will be responsible for planning at three levels—the school year, the units, and the lessons—with critical decisions to be made along the way and at each level.

You need not do all your instructional planning from scratch, and you need not do all your planning alone. As a matter of fact, much of the time you *should not* do all your planning alone. In many schools, teams of teachers develop the curricula. Teams of teachers collectively plan special programs for their specific cohorts of students. Team members either plan together or split the responsibilities and then share their individual plans. A final plan is then developed collaboratively.

Subscripted Scripted Programs

Some elementary and even middle-level schools subscribe to packaged curriculum programs, especially in reading and mathematics, which are preplanned and highly scripted for teacher use. The teacher's manual for the program includes an actual script and specifies the time to spend on a particular activity.

The writers of published scripted curriculum programs wrote for students of a particular developmental level in general; they did not know your students specifically. As a teacher using a scripted program, you still should tweak the program to address the needs of your particular group of students, making decisions about the content, instructional objectives, materials, teaching strategies, your responses to student behaviors, and assessments of the learning experiences. Without making such adjustments for a particular group of students, it would be impossible for any teacher to differentiate the instruction to adequately attend to the personal needs and differences of individual students.

> The most effective education of youngsters is the result of the combined efforts of a competent teacher using the best tools, not the result of tools alone.

Regardless of whether planning is done alone and from scratch, in collaboration with others, or from a commercially published, scripted program, the heart of productive planning is good decision making. To some degree or another, for every plan and at each of the three levels, you and your team must make decisions about educational standards to be addressed, goals and learning objectives to be set, the subject to be introduced, materials and equipment to be used, methods to be adopted, assessments to be made, and the tools to be used for those assessments. This decision-making process is complicated because so many options are available at each level. Decisions made at all three levels result in a total plan. *It is, in my opinion, this decision-making obligation and privilege that defines the teacher as an artist and classroom teaching as a profession.*

Although the planning process continues year after year, the task becomes somewhat easier after the first year as you learn to recycle plans. The process is also made easier via research and communication—by reviewing documents and sharing ideas and plans with other teachers.

Teacher–Student Collaborative Team Planning

At all levels of schooling, even with the current emphasis on standardized achievement testing, exemplary classrooms tend to be more project oriented and student and group centered than the common teacher- and subject-centered classroom of the past, in which the teacher served as the primary provider of information. Although most assuredly the teacher today is no less a determiner of what is ultimately learned by the students, today's students more actively participate in their learning in collaboration with the teacher. The teacher provides structure and assistance, but the collaborative approach requires that students inquire and interact, generate ideas, seriously listen and talk with one another, and recognize that their thoughts and experiences are valuable and essential to learning that is most meaningful and longest lasting.

Many teachers and teaching teams encourage their students to participate in the planning of some phase of their learning. Such participation tends to give students a proprietary interest in the activities, to satisfy the developmental need to explore knowledge, and to provide a sense of ownership to their learning, thereby increasing their motivation for learning. What students have contributed to the plan often seems more meaningful to them than what others have planned for them. And students like to see their own plans succeed. Thus, teacher–student collaboration in planning can be an effective motivational tool.

Reasons for Planning

Planning is done for a number of reasons, perhaps foremost of which is to ensure curriculum coherence, that is, to ensure that what is supposed to be learned is, in fact, learned. Periodic lesson plans are an integral component of a larger plan, represented by school-wide and districtwide mission statements and target standards, and by grade-level and course goals and objectives. Students' learning experiences are thoughtfully planned in sequence and then orchestrated by teachers who understand the rationale for their respective positions in the curriculum. Such plans do not preclude, of course, an occasional diversion from predetermined activities.

Another reason for planning is to ensure that the curriculum is developmentally appropriate for the intended students, that is, to give consideration to students' experiential backgrounds, developmental needs, learning capacities and styles, reading abilities, and exceptionalities. Without careful planning, teachers would not be able to differentiate the instruction and adequately attend to students' needs and differences.

Planning is necessary to ensure efficient and effective teaching with a minimum of classroom-control problems. After determining what to teach, you face the important task of deciding how to teach it. To efficiently use precious instructional time, planning should be accomplished with two goals in mind: not to waste anyone's time during the time allotted for instruction, and to select strategies that most effectively promote the anticipated student learning. As emphasized throughout this resource guide, a large portion of the instruction will be via student-centered, indirect instruction, although not exclusive of direct instruction.

Planning helps ensure program continuation. The program must continue even if you are absent and a substitute teacher is needed. Planning provides a criterion for reflective practice and self-assessment. After a learning activity and at the end of a school term, you can reflect on and assess what was done and how it affected student learning. Your plans represent a criterion recognized and evaluated by supervisors and administrators.

In addition to the many other reasons a teacher must plan and must do it carefully, good planning provides a boost to your own feelings of confidence and self-assuredness. Those who are experienced in such matters know that inadequate planning is usually a precursor to incompetent teaching. Put simply, failing to plan is planning to fail.

Like a good map, good unit and lesson planning facilitates reaching the destination with more confidence and fewer wrong turns.

Components of an Instructional Plan

A total instructional plan has several major components, described as follows.

Rationale component. This is a statement about why the content of the plan is important and how students will learn it. The statement should be consistent with the school's mission statement and the school district's benchmark curriculum standards.

Goals and objectives (standards) component. The goals and objectives represent the learning targets, that is, the specific knowledge, skills, and attitudes to be gained from the study. The plan's learning targets should be consistent with the rationale statement. This topic is discussed in the section titled Curriculum Standards that follows.

Articulation component. The articulation component shows the plan's relationship to the learning that preceded and the learning and experiences that will follow. This is referred to as **vertical articulation**. The plan should also indicate its **horizontal articulation**, which is its connectedness with other learning and activities occurring simultaneously across the grade level. Writing and literacy and thinking skills development are examples. Vertical and horizontal articulation representations are usually illustrated in curriculum documents and programs by scope and sequence charting.

Learning activities component. This is the presentation of organized and sequential units and lessons appropriate for the subject or grade level, and for the age and diversity of the learners.

Resources component. This is a listing of resources needed, such as print and electronic resources, artifacts (or realia), and community resource ideas, such as guest speakers or presenters, service learning projects, and field trip locations.

Assessment component. This is the appraisal of student learning and occurs as three parts: (a) before instruction begins, a **preassessment** (or diagnostic assessment) of what students already know or think they know about the topic; (b) during the instruction (**formative assessment**) to find out if students are learning that which is intended, that is, an assessment of learning as instruction is in process; and (c) at the end of the instruction (**summative assessment**) to determine the extent to which the students actually did learn.

Special considerations component. This is a place to make notes to remind yourself to consider special populations of students in your classroom, such as gifted learners, challenged learners (students with exceptionalities), and English language learners.

Curriculum Content Selection: Documents That Provide Guidance

Whether for a semester, a school year, or some other interval of time, when planning the content of the curriculum you should decide what specifically is to be

Figure 4.1   Web sites for national curriculum standards.

- American Indian Supplements
  http://www.doi.gov/bureau-indian-affairs.html
- Arts (visual and performing)
- AAHPERD
  http://www.aahperd.org
- MTNA
  http://www.mtna.org
- *Business*, NBEA
  http://www.nbea.org
- *Economics*, NCEE
  http://www.ncee.org
- *English/language arts/reading*
- IRA
  http://www.reading.org
- NCTE
  http://www.ncte.org
- *Foreign languages*, ACTFL
  http://www.actfl.org
- *Geography*, NCGE
  http://www.ncge.org

- *Health*, AAHPERD
  http://www.aahperd.org
- History/civics/social studies
- National Center for History in the Schools
  http://www.sscnet.ucla.edu/nchs
- NCSS
  http://www.ncss.org
- *Mathematics*, NCTM
  http://www.nctm.org
- *Physical education*, AAHPERD
  http://www.aahperd.org
- *Psychology*, APA
  http://www.apa.org
- *Science*, NSTA
  http://www.nsta.org
- NABT
  http://www.nabt.org
- *Technology*, ISTE
  http://www.iste.org

accomplished in that time interval. To help in setting goals, you will examine school and other resource documents for mandates and guidelines; communicate with colleagues to learn of common expectations; and probe, analyze, and translate your own convictions, knowledge, and skills into behaviors that foster the intellectual, psychological, and, in some instances, physical development of your students.

With the guidance provided by Exercises 4.1 through 4.4 (found at the end of this chapter), you will examine major documents that help guide you in selecting the content of your curriculum. These include national and state curriculum standards, school or district benchmark standards, curriculum frameworks and courses of study, and school-adopted materials. Sources for your examination of these documents include the Internet (see Figure 4.1), your college or university library, and personnel at local schools.

The following is the title of a news release article from ScienceDaily:

Students Benefit From Depth, Rather Than Breadth, In High School Science Courses

Retrieved from http://www.sciencedaily.com

A CONTINUING DILEMMA FOR THE CLASSROOM TEACHER

Breadth Versus Depth of Content Coverage

Many more things are worth teaching than we have time to teach in school, so breadth of topic coverage must be balanced against depth of development of each topic. This is an enduring dilemma that can only be managed in sensible ways, not a problem that can be solved once and for all. School curricula have drifted into addressing far too many topics and including too many trite or pointless details. Analyses in all of the subject areas suggest the need for teacher decision making about how to reduce breadth of coverage, structure the content around powerful ideas, and develop these ideas in depth.

Good & Brophy (2008, p. 283)

CURRICULUM STANDARDS

Curriculum standards are a definition of what students should know (content) and be able to do (process and performance). Although there is as yet no national curriculum in the United States, states, school districts, and national associations do require or recommend that certain standards be used to guide school instruction. In addition, federal law mandates that state standards be developed and improved in order for states to receive federal financial assistance.

At the national level, curriculum standards did not exist until those developed and released for mathematics education by the National Council of Teachers of Mathematics in 1989 (revised in 2000). Shortly after the release of the mathematics standards, support for national goals in education was endorsed by the National Governors Association, and the National Council on Education Standards and Testing recommended that in addition to those for mathematics, national standards for subject matter content in K–12 education be developed for the arts, civics/social studies, English/language arts/reading, geography, history, and science.

The U.S. Department of Education provided initial funding for the development of national standards. In 1994, the U.S. Congress passed the *Goals 2000: Educate America Act,* which was, in 1996, amended with an appropriations act that encouraged states to set curriculum standards. Long before, however, as was done for mathematics, national organizations devoted to various disciplines were already defining standards. The national standards that are available represent the best thinking by expert panels, including teachers from the field, about the essential elements of a basic core of subject knowledge that all K–12 students should acquire. They serve not as national mandates but rather as voluntary guidelines to encourage curriculum development to promote higher student achievement. To access these standards you can use the web sites shown in Figure 4.1.

Supplements to the national standards are available from the Bureau of Indian Affairs (BIA). The *American Indian Supplements* may be used by Indian nations as guides in their preparation of tribally specific local standards. They are also useful to school districts serving American Indian children in adapting state standards to be more culturally relevant to their communities.

Strongly influenced initially by the national standards, and then via federal requirements, individual states have developed their own standards for the various disciplines, which are accessible via your state department of education's web site.

Although many parents/guardians and educators object to what they see as already too much emphasis on assessment and school rankings, there is a something of a growing interest in the establishment of some sort of international benchmarking as a means of better preparing students for a competitive global economy (McNeil, 2008).

Curriculum Standards and High-Stakes Testing

Both national and state standards provide guidance to the developers of the standardized tests that are used in what is referred to as **high-stakes testing**, that is, the tests being given to determine student achievement, promotion, rewards to schools and even to individual teachers, and, in many states, as a requirement for graduation from high school.

The adoption of tougher learning standards throughout the United States, coupled with an emphasis on increased high-stakes testing to assess how schools and teachers are doing with respect to helping their students meet those standards, has provoked considerable debate, actions, and reactions among educators, parents, politicians, and from the world of business. Some argue that this emphasis on testing means too much "teaching to the test" at the expense of more meaningful learning, that it ignores the leverage that home, community, and larger societal influences have over the education of young people today. For example, in the words of Lauren Sosniak (2001),

> We need to find ways to ask what our communities, corporations, media, and all of our organizations and institutions are doing to promote the development of readers, writers, historians, scientists, artists, musicians, designers and crafts persons. Schools cannot do this work alone, in the 9% of [a child's K–12 lifetime in school] allotted to them. If this is only 'school work,' it is hard to imagine that our students will see it as a meaningful part of their lives and their futures. . . . For too long our schools have been held accountable for too much, with too little acknowledgement of the responsibilities of the rest of society.

Nevertheless, responding to the call for increased accountability, especially although not exclusively when state and federal funding may be withheld or jobs may be on the line for schools, teachers, and administrators where students do not score well, teachers in some schools put aside the regular curriculum for several weeks in advance of the testing date and concentrate on the direct preparation of their students for the test.

Although the interest has been rekindled in recent years, this oft-called "drill and kill" practice is certainly not new. For example, I can recall as a high school student in Ohio in the early 1950s being given what was called the *Every Pupil Test,* twice a year, one version in December, another version in April. For several weeks before the scheduled test, each of my teachers would set aside the regular curriculum to prepare we students directly for those tests by distributing and reviewing with us older versions of the tests. Today's interest in annual statewide testing caused this author to consider how it compares with past practices.

When comparing standardized testing of today with that of about half a century ago, it is probably safe to conclude that (a) the purpose for statewide standardized testing remains unchanged—it is to determine how well children are learning, at least to the extent determined by the particular test instrument; (b) test design is accomplished today with much greater precision and accuracy; but (c) today's focus on testing is taking precious time away from the most creative aspects of teaching and learning; and (d) the manner in which test results are being used today, and the long-term results of that use, may have ramifications considerably more serious than at any time before.

In schools with the necessary technology, that subscribe to software programs such as *eduTest.com* and *Homeroom.com*, and that have the appropriate number of computers necessary to provide access time to individual students, students can practice and prepare for the state-mandated tests online. Proponents of such online preparation argue that a major advantage is the immediate scoring of practice testing with feedback about each student's areas of weakness, thereby providing the teacher with information necessary for immediate remediation. If the arguments are accurate, then it would seem axiomatic that students of such technology-rich schools would clearly be at an advantage over those students who are in schools where this technology is not available. [Note: The disparity between those who have computer access and those who do not is sometimes referred to as *digital inequality* or the *digital divide*.] It would only follow that district and government agencies that mandate the standards and specific assessment practices should provide avenues and tools to ensure equity and success for all children toward reaching the expected learning outcomes within the designated learning time. Is in fact this so-called digital divide closing? It is closing but it is also a fact that the use of high tech information communication technology (ICT) for pedagogy, such as with podcasting and MP3 players, is not yet widely used in schools of low socioeconomic status, especially though not exclusively those of large inner cities (Beilke, Stuve, & Williams-Hawkins, 2008; Hohlfeld, Ritzhaupt, Barron, & Kemker, 2008).

Proceed now to Exercises 4.1, 4.2, 4.3, and 4.4 (found at the end of this chapter), through which you will explore a variety of types of curriculum documents.

STUDENT TEXTBOOKS

For several reasons—recognition of the diversity of learning styles, capacities, and modalities of students; changing concepts about literacy and habits of thought; enhanced graphics capabilities; economic pressures in the publishing industry; and the availability of electronic and other nonprinted materials—textbook appearance, content, and use have changed considerably in recent years and in all likelihood will continue to change.

Within the span of your teaching career, you will likely witness and even be a contributor to a revolution in the continuing redesign of school textbooks. Already some schools allow teachers in certain disciplines the option of choosing between traditional printed textbooks, textbook-loaded laptop computers and interactive computer programs, or some combination of these (Boon, Fore, & Spencer, 2007; McHale, 2008). As the first generation of computer-literate students work their way through the school systems, they are now more than ever likely to be learning from interactive programs, such as the online learning program called Odyssey (www.compasslearningodyssey.com/). These interactive programs not only allow the teacher to provide greater individualization of the learning, but also allow parents/guardians to go online and track the progress of their children.

With the continuing developments in technology, textbooks may take on a whole new appearance. With that will come dramatic changes in the importance and use of text as well as new problems for the teacher, some that are predictable and others we cannot even imagine. On the positive side, it is probable that the classroom teacher will have available a variety of "textbooks" to better address the reading levels, interests, abilities, and perhaps even the primary language of individual students. With these changes, the distribution and maintenance of reading materials could create a greater demand on the teacher's time. Regardless, dramatic and exciting events have begun to affect the teaching tool that had not changed much throughout the 20th century. The textbook of the not-so-distant future (see, for example, http://en.wikibooks.org/wiki) may become a handheld, multimedia, interactive, and personal tool that encompasses digitized text, multiple language use, sound, and video and allows for global communications.

Still, today, printed textbooks regulate a large percentage of the learning activity in the classroom. School districts periodically adopt new textbooks (usually every 4 to 8 years). If you are a student teacher or a first-year teacher, this will most likely mean that someone will say to you, "Here are the books you will be using."

Benefit of Textbooks to Student Learning

It is unlikely that anyone could rationally argue that textbooks are of no benefit to student learning. Textbooks can provide (a) an organization of basic or important content for the students that includes and is built around state curriculum standards, (b) a basis for deciding content emphasis, (c) previously tested activities and suggestions for learning, (d) information about other readings and resources to enhance student learning, and (e) a foundation for building higher order thinking activities (e.g., inquiry discussions and student research) that help develop critical thinking skills. The textbook, however, should not be the "be all and end all" of the instructional experiences.

Problems with Reliance on a Single Textbook

The student textbook is only one of many teaching tools, and not the ultimate word. Of the many ways in which you may use textbooks for student learning, the *least* acceptable is to show a complete dependence on a single book and require students simply to memorize material from it. This is the lowest level of textbook use and learning; furthermore, it implies that you are unaware of other significant resources and have nothing more to contribute to student learning.

Another potential problem brought about by reliance upon a single textbook is that because textbook publishers prepare books for use in a larger market—that is, for national or statewide use—a state- or district-adopted book may not adequately address issues of special interest and importance to the community in which you teach. That is one reason why some teachers and schools provide supplementary printed and electronic resources.

Still another problem brought about by reliance upon a single source is that the adopted textbook may not be at the appropriate reading level for many students. In today's heterogeneous classrooms, the level of student reading can easily vary by as much as two-thirds of the chronological age of the students. This means that if the chronological age is 12 years (typical for seventh-graders), then the reading-level range would be 8 years—that is, the class may have some students reading at only the preschool level, if at all, while others have college-level reading ability.

Examine student textbooks and teacher's editions of those books by doing end of chapter Exercise 4.5.

Guidelines for Textbook Use

Generally speaking, students benefit by having their own copies of a textbook in the current edition. However, because of budget constraints, this may not always be possible. The book may be outdated or quantities may be limited. When the latter is the case, students may not be allowed to take the books home or perhaps may only occasionally do so. In some high-poverty area schools students are not allowed to take textbooks from the classroom. In other classrooms, because of inadequate or misappropriated funding, there may be no textbook at all.

Encourage students to respect books by covering and protecting them and not marking in them. In many schools this is a rule; at the end of the term, students who have damaged or lost their books are charged a fee. As a matter of fact, this is why in some high-poverty area schools books are not issued at all. If their students lose or damage their books and are charged a fee, the fee goes unpaid because neither the students nor their parents/guardians can afford to pay it.

Yet, in classrooms of some school districts, there are two sets of the textbook, one set that remains for use in the classroom and another set that is assigned to students to use for studying at home. With that arrangement, students do not have to carry around in their backpacks the heavy books used for many subjects taught in today's schools.

Progressing through a textbook from the front cover to the back in one school term is not necessarily an indicator of good teaching. The textbook is one resource; to enhance their learning, students should be encouraged to use a variety of resources. Encourage students to search additional sources to update the content of the textbook. This is especially important in certain disciplines such as the sciences and social sciences, where the amount of new information is growing rapidly and students may have textbooks that are several years old. The library and sources on the Internet should be researched by students for the latest information on certain subjects, always keeping in mind, however, that just because something is found in print or on the Net does not mean that the information is accurate or even true. Maintain supplementary reading materials for student use in the classroom. School and community librarians and resource specialists usually are delighted to cooperate with teachers in the selection and provision of such resources.

Remember that in addition to whatever your credential, every teacher has responsibility to help students who have reading difficulties (Benjamin, 2007; Chehayl, 2008; McConachie et al., 2006; Taylor, 2006). Consequently you should do your best to individualize the learning for students of various reading abilities. Consider differentiated reading and workbook assignments in the textbook and several supplementary sources (see Multitext and Multireadings Approaches, a topic that follows). Except to make life simpler for the teacher, there is no advantage in all students working out of the same book and exercises. Some students benefit from the drill, practice, and reinforcement afforded by workbooks or software programs that accompany textbooks, but this is not true for all students, nor do all benefit from the same activity. In fact, the traditional printed workbook may eventually become extinct, as it is replaced by the modern technology afforded by electronic software. Computers and other interactive media provide students with a psychologically safer learning environment where they have greater control over the pace of the instruction, can repeat instruction if necessary, and can ask for clarification without the fear of having to do so publicly.

Teachers continue to invent methods to help students develop their higher level thinking skills and their comprehension of expository material. Some of these methods are shown in Figure 4.2.

Encourage students to be alert for errors in the textbook, both in content and printing—perhaps offering some sort of credit reward, such as credit points, when they bring an error to your attention. This can help students develop the skills of critical reading, critical thinking, and healthy skepticism.

What we read and how deeply we read shape both the brain and the thinker.

Maryanne Wolf and Mirit Barzillai (2009, p. 34)

Figure 4.2   Methods for helping students develop their higher-level thinking skills and their comprehension of expository materials.

- KQHL: Students ask what they want to know (K) about a topic, list the questions (Q) they need/want answered, ask how (H) they might find answers, and then later identify what they have learned (L) (Long, Drake & Halychyn, 2004).

- KWL: Students recall what they already know (K) about a topic, determine what they want to learn (W), and later assess what they have learned (L) (Ogle, 1986).

- KWLQ: Students record what they already know about a topic (K), formulate questions about what they want to learn about the topic (W), search for answers to their questions (L), and ask questions for further study (Q).

- KWHLS: Students identify what they already know about the topic of study (K), what they want to learn (W), how they plan to learn it (H), then what they learned (L), and finally how they will share that new knowledge with others (S).

- POSSE: *Predict* ideas, *organize* ideas, *search* for structure, *summarize* main ideas, and *evaluate* understanding (Englert & Mariage, 1991).

- PQRST: *Preview, question, read, state* the main idea, and *test* yourself by answering the questions you posed earlier (Kelly, 1994).

- QAR: Helping children understand *question* and *answer* relationships (Mesmer and Hutchins, 2002).

- RAP: *Read* paragraphs, *ask* questions about what was read, and *put* in your own words (Schumaker, Denton, & Deshler, 1984).

- Reciprocal teaching: Students are taught and practice the reading skills of summarizing, questioning, clarifying, and predicting (Palincsar & Brown, 1984).

- SQ3R: *Survey* the chapter, *ask* questions about what was read, *read, recite,* and *review* (Robinson, 1961).

- SQ4R: *Survey* the chapter, *ask* questions about what was read, *read* to answer the questions, *recite* the answers, *record* important items from the chapter into student notebooks, then *review* it all.

- SRQ2R: *Survey, read, question, recite,* and *review* (Walker, 1995.)

Multitext and Multireadings Approaches

Rather than a single textbook approach, consider using a strategy that incorporates many readings that vary in difficulty, detail, and vocabulary but have a common focus. Whatever the unit, teachers can include a wide range of materials: informational picture and chapter books; biographies and photographic essays; and Internet, newspaper, and magazine articles. Giving students a choice in what they read, the multiple reading source strategy helps all students become a part of the same community of readers (Robb, 2002). Especially useful for interdisciplinary thematic instruction, the strategy also allows for differences in reading ability and interest level and stimulates a sharing of what is read and being learned. By using a teacher's guide, such as the sample in Figure 4.3, all the students can be directed toward specific information and concepts, but they do not have to all read the same selections.

BEGINNING TO THINK ABOUT THE SEQUENCING OF CONTENT

As you have reviewed the rationale and components of instructional planning and examined curriculum standards, curriculum documents, and student reading materials, you have undoubtedly reflected on your own opinion regarding content that should be included in a subject at a particular grade level. Now it is time to obtain some practical experience in long-range planning.

Although some authors believe that after selecting the content the first step in preparing to teach is to prepare the objectives, others believe that a more logical starting point is to prepare a sequential topic outline—the next step in this chapter—from which you can then prepare the major target objectives (benchmark standards). With today's pressure on teachers to work from established and mandated benchmark standards, it may well be that many teachers today do, in fact, begin their curriculum development from those objectives.

Regardless of the approach used, the curriculum plan should satisfy three organizational requirements:

1. The plan should be organized around important ideas, concepts, and questions, all of which should correlate with mandated content standards.
2. The plan should reflect the interests and concerns of the recipient students.
3. The plan should be oriented toward the assessments and tasks that will be used for students in demonstrating what they have learned.

The curriculum plans, topic outlines, and instructional objectives may be presented to most beginning

Figure 4.3 Sample multiple readings guide and student's book bibliography.
(*Note:* the bibliography shown here is not intended to be inclusive, only to show how a multiple readings guide might appear.)

- Purpose: To engage students in multiple readings, critical thinking, and problem solving related to America's Revolutionary Times in 1776.

- Activities:

  1. By reading and browsing through several books and by carefully observing several illustrations of people in this particular time period and geographic area, the students can engage in critical thinking and problem solving by working in small groups. The bibliography that follows includes books suitable for a wide range of reading levels related to America in 1776. Students can respond to the following focus questions after multitext reading:
     a. What features of the land (features of government, society, etc.) seem to be important to the people in 1776?
     b. What occupations seem to be most important? What inventions (tools, machines) appear to be most useful?
     c. What do the answers to these questions tell us about the way of life of the people who lived in this time period (geographic area)?

  2. Back with the whole group, have the students from each group report on the responses to the questions. Engage students in dictating or writing a paragraph summarizing the responses to the questions.

  3. Students can meet with response partners to read their individually written paragraphs aloud to one another and provide suggestions to each other for rewriting the paragraphs.

- Bibliography

African American
Davis, B. *Black Heroes of the American Revolution.* (San Diego: Harcourt, 1976). Nonfictional account depicting contributions of African Americans during the revolutionary war. Includes drawings, etchings, bibliography, and an index.
Hansen, J. *The Captive.* (New York: Scholastic, 1994). Based on a journal written in the late 1700s, this is about Kofi, the 12-year-old son of an Ashanti chief. Kofi is sold and sent to America after a family slave murders his father. Kofi and others escape from the farm in Massachusetts and return to Africa. An epilogue relates his good life when he returned to Africa.
Millender, D. H. *Crispus Attucks: Black Leader of Colonial Patriots.* (New York: Macmillan, 1986). Biographical portrayal of the life of a Colonial African American and his contribution to the American Revolution.

European
Wade, M. D. *Benedict Arnold.* (New York: Franklin Watts, 1995). Biographical story of Arnold's life, his heroic deeds, in-cluding his leadership at the battle of Saratoga, his later traitorous actions, and his death in London. Includes infor-mation about his wife, Peggy Shippen.

Female Image
DePaul, L. G. *Founding Mothers: Women in America in the Revolutionary Era.* (Boston: Houghton Mifflin, 1975). Nonfictional account of the contributions of women during the revolution.
McGovern, A. *Secret Soldier: The Story of Deborah Sampson.* (New York: Scholastic, 1991). Story of a young woman who disguised herself as a boy and joined the army to serve in America's War for Independence.

Latino/Hispanic
Anderson, J. *Spanish Pioneers of the Southwest.* Illustrated by G. Ancona. (New York: Dutton, 1989). Nonfictional ac-count of the lives of the colonists on the east coast contrasted with the lives of the members of a pioneer family in a Spanish community in New Mexico in the 1700s and the family's hard work, harsh living conditions, and their traditions.

Native American
Hudson, J. *Dawn Rider.* (New York: Putnam, 1990). Fictional account of 16-year-old Kit Fox, a Blackfoot, forbidden to ride horses. She disobeys and her riding skills help her people when their camp is attacked.
Kinsey-Warock, N. *Wilderness Cat.* Illustrated by Mark Graham. (Minneapolis: Cobblehill, 1992). Lives of colonists are contrasted with the lives of Serena's family members when they moved to Canada in the 1700s. Even though the family trades with the Indians, they do not have enough to eat; Papa and Serena's brother leave to find work. Histori-cal fiction.

Religious Minority
Faber, D. *The Perfect Life: The Shakers in America.* (New York: Farrar, Straus, & Giroux, 1974). Escaping from England, Mother Ann with several followers voyages to America and set up the first settlement in New York in 1776. Nonfictional account detailing the Shaker influence on furniture construction, mechanical inventions, and their reli-gious beliefs.

teachers with the expectation that they will teach from them. For you this may be the case, but someone had to have written those outlines and objectives, and that someone was one or more present or former classroom teachers. As a new teacher, you must know how this is done, for someday it will be your task. To experience preparing a full semester content outline for a subject and grade level that you intend to teach, do Exercise 4.6 (end of chapter) now.

PREPARING FOR AND DEALING WITH CONTROVERSY

Controversial content and issues abound in teaching, in most disciplines. For example: in English/reading, over the use of certain books—see Exercise 4.7B at end of chapter; the continuing debate over sex education and to what extent, if at all, it should be approached in public schools; in social studies, over moral issues; and in science, over biological evolution. As a general rule, if you have concern that a particular topic or activity might create controversy, it probably will. During your teaching career, you undoubtedly will have to make decisions about how you will handle such matters.

Maintain a perspective with respect to your own goal, which is to obtain your teaching credential, and then a teaching job, and then tenure. Student teaching, in particular, is not a good time to become embroiled in controversy. If you communicate closely with your cooperating teacher and your college or university supervisor, you should be able to prevent major problems dealing with controversial issues.

Sometimes, during normal discussion in the classroom, a controversial subject will, however, emerge spontaneously, catching the teacher off guard. If this happens, think before saying anything. You may wish to postpone further discussion until you have a chance to talk over the issue with members of your teaching team or your supervisors. Controversial topics can seem to arise from nowhere for any teacher, and this is perfectly normal. Your students are in the process of developing their moral and value systems, and they need and want to know how adults feel about issues that are important to them, particularly those adults they hold in esteem—their teachers. Our youth need to discuss issues that are important to society, and there is absolutely nothing wrong with dealing with those issues as long as certain guidelines are followed.

First, students should learn about all sides of an issue. Controversial issues are open ended and should be treated as such. They do not have "right" answers or "correct" solutions. If they did, there would be no controversy. [Note: As used in this book, an "issue" differs from a "problem" in that a problem generally has a solution, whereas an issue has many opinions and several alternative solutions.] Therefore, the focus should be on process

as well as on content. A major goal is to show students how to deal with controversy and to mediate wise decisions on the basis of carefully considered information. Another goal is to help students learn how to disagree without being disagreeable—how to resolve conflict. To that end students need to learn the difference between conflicts that are destructive and those that can be constructive, in other words, to see that conflict (disagreement) can be healthy, that it can have value. A third goal, of course, is to help students learn about the content of an issue so, when necessary, they can make decisions based on knowledge, not on ignorance.

Second, as with all lesson plans, one dealing with a topic that could lead to controversy should be well thought out ahead of time. Potential problem areas and resources must be carefully considered and prepared for in advance. As emphasized by Walach (2008), when planning the content of instruction your vision must not be myopic nor your sensibilities naïve. Problems for the teacher are most likely to occur when the plan has not been well conceived.

Third, at some point all persons directly involved in an issue have a right to input: students, parents and guardians, community representatives, and other faculty. This does not mean, for example, that people outside of the school necessarily have the right to censor a teacher's plan, but it does mean that parents or guardians and students should have the right *sans penalty* not to participate and to select an alternate activity. Most school districts have written policies that deal with challenges to instructional materials. As a beginning teacher, you should become aware of policies of your school district. In addition, professional associations such as the NCTE, NCSS, NBTA, and NSTA publish guidelines for dealing with controversial topics, materials, and issues.

Fourth, there is nothing wrong with students knowing a teacher's opinion about an issue as long as it is clear that the students may disagree without reprisal or academic penalty. However, it is probably best for a teacher to wait and give an opinion only after the students have had full opportunity to study and report on facts and opinions from other sources. Sometimes it is helpful to assist students in separating facts from opinions on a particular issue being studied by setting up on the overhead or writing board a fact–opinion table, with the issue stated at the top and then two parallel columns, one for facts, the other for related opinions, as shown here.

Issue:_____	
Fact	Opinions

A characteristic that makes this nation so great is the freedom for all its citizens to speak out on issues. I agree with others in that this freedom proffered by the First Amendment of the Bill of Rights of the U.S. Constitution should not be excluded from public school classrooms. Teachers and students should be encouraged to express their opinions about the great issues of today, to study the issues, to suspend judgment while collecting data, and then to form and accept each other's reasoned opinions. We all must understand the difference between teaching truth, values, and morals and teaching *about* truth, values, and morals.

You must understand that as a public school teacher there are limits to your academic freedom, much greater than are the limits, for example, on a university professor. The primary difference is that the students with whom you will be working are not yet adults; because they are juveniles, they must be protected from dogma and allowed the freedom to learn and to develop their values and opinions, free of coercion from those who have power and control over their learning.

Now that you have read my opinion and suggested guidelines, what do you think about this topic, which should be important to you as a teacher? Use Exercises 4.7A and 4.7B (found at end of chapter) for the development and expression of your opinion.

AIMS, GOALS, AND OBJECTIVES: THE ANTICIPATED LEARNING OUTCOMES

Now that you have examined content typical of the curriculum, have experienced preparing a tentative content outline for a subject that you intend to teach, and understand some important guidelines for dealing with controversial topics, you are ready to write instructional objectives for that content learning.

Instructional objectives are statements describing what the student will be able to do upon completion of the planned learning experience. Whereas some authors distinguish between instructional objectives (hence referring to objectives that are not behavior specific) and **behavioral** or **performance objectives** (objectives that are behavior specific), the terms are used here as if they are synonymous to emphasize the importance of writing instructional objectives in terms that are measurable.

As a teacher, you frequently will encounter the compound structure that reads "goals and objectives," as you likely found in the curriculum documents that you reviewed (Exercises 4.1–4.4). A distinction needs to be understood. The easiest way to understand the difference between the two words, *goals* and *objectives,* is to look at your *intent.*

Goals are ideals that you intend to reach, that is, ideals that you would like to have accomplished. Goals may be stated as **teacher goals**, as **student goals**, or, collaboratively, as team goals. Ideally, in all three, the goal is the same. If,

for example, the goal is to improve students' reading skills, it could be stated as follows:

"To help students develop their reading skills"	*Teacher or course goal*
or	
"To improve my reading skills"	*Student goal*

Educational goals are general statements of intent and are prepared early in course planning. [Note: Some writers use the phrase "general goals and objectives," but that is incorrect usage. Goals *are* general; objectives are specific.] Goals are useful when planned cooperatively with students or when shared with students as advance mental organizers to establish a mind-set. The students then know what to expect and will begin to prepare mentally to learn it. From the goals, objectives are prepared. Objectives are *not* intentions. They are the actual behaviors that students are expected to display. In short, objectives are what students *do.*

The most general educational objectives are often called **aims**; the objectives of schools, curricula, and courses are called **goals**; the objectives of units and lessons are called **instructional** or **target objectives**. Aims are more general than goals and goals are more general than objectives. Instructional objectives are quite specific. Aims, goals, and objectives represent the targets, from general to specific statements of learning expectations, to which curriculum is designed and instruction is aimed.

Instructional Objectives and Their Relationship to Aligned Curriculum and Authentic Assessment

As implied in the preceding paragraphs, goals guide the instructional methods; objectives drive student performance. Assessment of student achievement in learning should be an assessment of that performance. When the assessment procedure matches the instructional objectives, it is sometimes referred to as assessment that is *aligned* or *authentic.* [Note: If the term **authentic assessment** sounds rather silly to you, I concur. After all, if the objectives and assessment do not match, then that particular assessment should be discarded or modified until it does match. In other words, assessment that is not authentic is "poor assessment" and should not be used.] When objectives, instruction, and assessment match the stated goals, we have what is referred to as an **aligned curriculum**. [Again, a curriculum that does not align is nonsensical and should be either corrected or discarded. You can even find in some literature the terms *authentic instruction* and *authentic teaching.* The rule still applies, and that is, instruction or teaching that is not authentic. . . . Need I say more?]

Goals are general statements, usually not even complete sentences, often beginning with the infinitive "to," which identify what the teacher intends the students to learn. Objectives, stated in performance terms, are

Figure 4.4   Examples of goals and objectives.

Goals

1. To acquire knowledge about the physical geography of North America.
2. To develop an appreciation for music.
3. To develop enjoyment for reading.

Objectives

1. On a map, the student will identify specific mountain ranges of North America.
2. The student will identify 10 different musical instruments by listening to an audio recording of the Boston Pops Symphony Orchestra and identify which instrument is being played at specified times as determined by the teacher.
3. The student will read two books, three short stories, and five newspaper articles at home within a 2-month period. The student will maintain a daily written log of these activities.

---

specific actions and should be written as complete sentences that include the verb "will" *to indicate what each student is expected to be able to do as a result of the instructional experience.* The last portion of the previous sentence is emphasized because, when writing instructional objectives for their unit and lesson plans, one of the most common errors made by teachers is to state what *they,* the teachers, intend to do rather than what the anticipated student performance is. The value of stating learning objectives in terms of student performance is well documented by research (Baker & Martin, 1998; Good & Brophy, 2008).

Though instructional goals may not always be quantifiable (i.e., readily measurable), instructional objectives should be measurable. Furthermore, those objectives then become the essence of what is measured in instruments designed to assess student learning; they are the learning targets. Consider the examples shown in Figure 4.4.

Learning Targets and Goal Indicators

One purpose for writing objectives in performance terms is to be able to assess with precision whether the instruction has resulted in the desired behavior. In many schools the educational goals are established as **learning targets**, competencies that the students are expected to achieve, and that were derived from the district and state curriculum standards. These learning targets are then divided into performance objectives, sometimes referred to as **goal indicators**. Instruction is designed to teach toward those objectives. When students perform the competencies called for by these objectives, their education is considered successful. This is known variously as **criterion-referenced, competency-based, performance-based, results-driven**, or **outcome-based education**. When the

objectives are aligned with specific curriculum standards, as they usually are or should be, then it can also be referred to as **standards-based education**. Expecting students to achieve one set of competencies before moving on to the next set is called **mastery (or quality) learning**. The success of the student achievement, teacher performance, and the school may each be assessed according to these criteria.

Overt and Covert Performance Outcomes

Assessment is not difficult to accomplish when the desired performance outcome is overt behavior, which can be observed directly. Each of the sample objectives of the preceding section is an example of an overt objective. Assessment is more difficult to accomplish when the desired behavior is covert, that is, when it is not directly observable. Although certainly no less important, behaviors that call for "appreciation," "discovery," or "understanding," for example, are not directly observable because they occur within a person, and so are covert behaviors. Covert behavior cannot be observed directly; therefore, the only way to tell whether the objective has been achieved is to observe behavior that may be indicative of that achievement. The objective, then, is written in overt language, and evaluators can only assume or trust that the observed behavior is, in fact, reasonably close to being indicative of the expected learning outcome.

Furthermore, when assessing whether an objective has been achieved—that learning has occurred—the assessment device must be consistent with the desired learning outcome. Otherwise, the assessment is not aligned; it is invalid. When the measuring device and the learning objective are compatible, we say that the assessment is authentic. For example, a person's competency to teach specific skills in mathematics to seventh-graders is best (i.e., with highest reliability) measured by directly observing that person *doing* that very thing—teaching specific skills in mathematics to seventh-graders. Using a standardized paper-and-pencil test of multiple-choice items to determine a person's ability to teach specific math skills to seventh-grade students is not authentic assessment. Or, as yet another example, a person's competency to teach a particular phonics lesson to first-graders is best measured (i.e., with highest reliability) by directly observing that person *doing* that very thing—teaching a particular phonics lesson to first-graders. Using a standardized paper-and-pencil test of multiple-choice items to determine a person's ability to teach a phonics lesson to first-graders is *not* authentic assessment. In either instance, although the particular multiple-choice item assessment device might be valid, it is *not* authentic.

Balance of Behaviorism and Constructivism

Whereas behaviorists assume a definition of learning that deals only with changes in overt behavior, constructivists hold that learning entails the construction or reshaping of mental schemata and that mental processes mediate learning. Thus, people who adhere to constructivism or cognitivism or constructionism are concerned with both overt and covert behaviors (DeLay, 1996; *Educational Leadership,* 1999; Geelan, 1997). Does this mean that you must be one or the other, a behaviorist or a constructivist? Probably not. For now, the point is that when writing instructional objectives, you should write most or all of your basic expectations (minimal competency expectations) in overt terms (the topic of the next section). On the other hand, you cannot be expected to foresee all learning that occurs nor to translate all that is learned into performance terms—most certainly not before it occurs.

Teaching Toward Multiple Objectives, Understandings, and Appreciations: The Reality of Classroom Instruction

Any effort to write all learning objectives in performance terms is, in effect, to neglect the individual learner for whom it purports to be concerned; such an approach does not allow for diversity among learners. Learning that is most meaningful to students is not so neatly or easily predicted or isolated. Rather than teaching one objective at a time, much of the time you should direct your teaching toward the simultaneous learning of multiple objectives, understandings, and appreciations. However, when you assess for learning, assessment is cleaner when objectives are assessed one at a time. More on this matter of objectives and their use in teaching and learning follows later in this chapter. Let's now consider how objectives are prepared.

PREPARING INSTRUCTIONAL OBJECTIVES

When preparing instructional objectives, you must ask yourself, "How is the student to demonstrate that the objective has been reached?" The objective must include an action that demonstrates that the objective has been achieved. Inherited from behaviorism, this portion of the objective is sometimes called the **anticipated measurable performance**.

Components of a Complete Objective

When completely written in performance terms, an instructional objective has four components, although in practice you are unlikely to use all four. To aid your understanding and as a mnemonic for remembering, you can refer to these components as the ABCDs of writing objectives.

One component is the *audience.* The *A* of the ABCDs refers to the student for whom the objective is intended. To address this, sometimes teachers begin their objectives

with the phrase "The student will be able to . . ." or, to personalize the objective, "You will be able to. . . ." [Note: To conserve space and to eliminate useless language, in examples that follow I delete the "be able to," and write simply "The student will. . . ." As a matter of fact I prefer use of "will" over "be able to." For brevity, writers of objectives sometimes use the abbreviation "TSWBAT . . ." for "The student will be able to . . ." or more simply "TSW . . ." for "The student will. . . ."]

The second component is the expected *behavior,* the *B* of the ABCDs. It is this second component that represents the learning target. The expected behavior (or performance) should be written with verbs that are measurable—that is, with action verbs—so that it is directly observable that the objective, or target, has been reached. Some verbs are too vague, ambiguous, and not clearly measurable. When writing overt objectives, you should avoid verbs that are not clearly measurable and covert verbs such as "appreciate," "comprehend," and "understand" (see Figure 4.5). For the three examples given in Figure 4.4, for Objectives 1 and 2, the behaviors (action or overt verbs) are "will *identify*," and, for Objective 3, the behaviors are "will *read* and *maintain.*"

Now do self-check Exercise 4.8 (end of chapter) to assess and to further your understanding.

Most of the time, when writing objectives for your unit and lesson plans, you will not bother yourself with including the next two components. However, as you will learn, they are important considerations for assessment.

The third component is the *conditions,* the *C* of the ABCDs—the setting in which the behavior will be demonstrated by the student and observed by the teacher. Conditions are forever changing; although the learning target should be clearly recognizable long before the actual instruction occurs, the conditions may not. Thus, in curriculum documents in particular, conditions are not often included in the objectives. However, when preparing to assess student learning toward specific objectives, you must consider the conditions within which the performance will be displayed. For the first sample objective, the conditions are "on a map." For the second sample objective, the conditions are "by listening to an audio recording of the Boston Pops Symphony Orchestra," and "specified times as determined by the teacher." For the third sample, for "the student will read . . . ," the conditions are "at home within a 2-month period."

The fourth component, again, that is not always included in objectives found in curriculum documents, is

Figure 4.5 Verbs to avoid when writing overt objectives.

appreciate	enjoy	indicate	like
believe	familiarize	know	realize
comprehend	grasp	learn	understand

the *degree* (or *level*) *of expected performance*—the *D* of the ABCDs. This is the ingredient that allows for the assessment of student learning. When mastery learning is expected, the level of expected performance is usually omitted (because it is understood). In teaching for mastery learning, the performance-level expectation is 100 percent. In reality, however, the performance level will most likely be 84 to 94 percent, particularly when working with a group of students, rather than with an individual student. The 4 to 14 percent difference allows for human error, as can occur when using written and oral communication. As with conditions, the level of performance will vary depending on the situation and purpose and thus is not normally included in the unit and lessons that teachers prepare. Now, to check your comprehension, do self-check Exercise 4.9 at the end of the chapter.

Performance level is used to assess student achievement, and sometimes it is used to evaluate the effectiveness of the teaching. Student grades might be based on performance levels; evaluation of teacher effectiveness might be based on the level of student performance. Indeed, with today's use of state-mandated, standardized testing, schools, administrators, and teachers are evaluated on the basis of student performance on those tests.

Now, with self-check Exercise 4.10 (at end of chapter), try your skill at recognizing student learning objectives that are measurable.

Classifying Instructional Objectives

When planning instructional objectives, it is useful to consider the three domains of learning objectives:

cognitive domain—involves intellectual operations from the lowest level of simple recall of information to complex, high-level thinking processes;
affective domain—involves feelings, emotions, attitudes, and values and ranges from the lower levels of acquisition to the highest level of internalization and action;
psychomotor domain—ranges from the simple manipulation of materials to the communication of ideas, and finally to the highest level of creative performance.

The Domains of Learning and the Developmental Needs of Students

Educators attempt to design learning experiences to meet the five areas of developmental needs of students: intellectual, physical, emotional/psychological, social, and moral/ethical. As a teacher, you must include objectives that address learning within each of these categories of needs. Whereas the intellectual needs are primarily within the cognitive domain and the physical are within the psychomotor, the other three categories of needs are mostly within the affective domain.

Too frequently, teachers focus on the cognitive domain and assume that the psychomotor and affective will take care of themselves. If the current nationwide focus on standardized achievement testing perseveres, this may become even more so. Many experts argue, however, that teachers should do just the opposite; that when the affective is directly attended to, the psychomotor and cognitive naturally develop. They argue that unless the social and emotional needs of students are adequately addressed, little happens cognitively (Hopping, 2000), and I agree. Whether the domains are attended to separately or simultaneously, you should plan your teaching so your students are guided from the lowest to highest levels of operation within each domain.

The three developmental hierarchies are discussed next to guide your understanding of each of the five areas of needs. Notice the illustrative verbs within each hierarchy. These verbs help you fashion objectives when you are developing unit plans and lesson plans. (To see how goals and objectives are fit into one lesson plan, see Figure 5.10 in Chapter 5, a multiple-day, project-centered, interdisciplinary, and transcultural lesson using worldwide communication via the Internet.) However, caution is urged, for there can be considerable overlap among the levels at which some action verbs may appropriately be used. For example, as shown in Figure 4.6, the verb *identifies* is appropriate in each of the objectives at different levels (given in parentheses) within the cognitive domain.

Cognitive Domain Hierarchy

In a widely accepted taxonomy of objectives, Bloom (1984) and his associates arranged cognitive objectives into classifications according to the complexity of the skills and abilities they embodied. The result was a ladder ranging from the simplest to the most complex intellectual processes. Within each domain, prerequisite to a student's ability to function at one particular level of the hierarchy is the ability to function at the preceding

Figure 4.6 Sometimes the same action verb may be used appropriately in objectives at different cognitive levels. For example, here the verb *identify* is used in objectives at four levels (identified in parentheses) within the cognitive domain.

The student will identify the correct definition of the term *osmosis.* (knowledge)
The student will identify examples of the principle of osmosis. (comprehension)
The student will identify the osmotic effect when a cell is immersed into a hypotonic solution. (application)
The student will identify the osmotic effect on turgor pressure when the cell is placed in a hypotonic solution. (analysis)

level or levels. In other words, when a student is functioning at the third level of the cognitive domain, that student is automatically also functioning at the first and second levels. Rather than an orderly progression from simple to complex mental operations, as illustrated by Bloom's taxonomy, other researchers prefer an organization of cognitive abilities that ranges from simple information storage and retrieval, through a higher level of discrimination and concept attainment, to the highest cognitive ability to recognize and solve problems (Gagné, Briggs, & Wager, 1994).

The six major categories (or levels) in Bloom's taxonomy of cognitive objectives are (a) *knowledge*—recognizing and recalling information; (b) *comprehension*—understanding the meaning of information; (c) *application*—using information; (d) *analysis*—dissecting information into its component parts to comprehend their relationships; (e) *synthesis*—putting components together to generate new ideas; and (f) *evaluation*—judging the worth of an idea, notion, theory, thesis, proposition, information, or opinion. In this taxonomy, the top four categories or levels—application, analysis, synthesis, and evaluation—represent what are called higher order cognitive thinking skills. [Note: Compare Bloom's higher order cognitive thinking skills with R. H. Ennis's, "A Taxonomy of Critical Thinking Dispositions and Abilities," and Qellmalz's "Developing Reasoning Skills," both in Barron and Sternberg (1987), and with Marzano's (1992) "complex thinking strategies."]

Space limitation prohibits elaboration here, but Bloom's taxonomy includes various subcategories within each of these six major categories. It is probably less important that an objective be absolutely classified than it is to be cognizant of hierarchies of thinking and doing and to understand the importance of attending to student intellectual behavior from lower to higher levels of operation in all three domains. Discussion of each of Bloom's six categories follows. [Note: Although beyond the scope of intent of this resource guide, you may wish to learn about efforts to update the original work of Bloom with what we know today about learning, cognition, and thinking, particularly as specific to your subject field, such as found for example in the writings of Anderson (2004); Amer (2006); Cochran and Conklin (2007); Crowe, Dirks, and Wenderoth (2008); Hanna (2007); Marzano and Kendall (2006); and Vosen (2008).]

KNOWLEDGE

The basic element in Bloom's taxonomy concerns the acquisition of knowledge—that is, the ability to recognize and recall information. (As discussed in Chapter 6, this is similar to the *input level* of thinking and questioning.) Although this is the lowest of the six categories, the information to be learned may not itself be of a low level. In fact, it may be of an extremely high level, and it is a serious error when children are taught to view facts

and substantive knowledge as being relatively unimportant (Booker, 2007).

Bloom (1984) included here knowledge of principles, generalizations, theories, structures, and methodology, as well as knowledge of facts and ways of dealing with facts.

Action verbs appropriate for this category include *choose, cite, complete, define, describe, identify, indicate, label, list, locate, match, name, outline, recall, recognize, select,* and *state*.

The following are examples of objectives at the knowledge level. Note especially the verb (in italics) used in each example:

- From memory, the student *will recall* the letters in the English alphabet that are vowels.
- The student *will list* the organelles found in animal cell cytoplasm.
- The student *will identify* the major parts of speech in the sentence.
- The student *will name* the positions of players on a soccer team.

The remaining five categories of Bloom's taxonomy of the cognitive domain deal with the *use* of knowledge. They encompass the educational objectives aimed at developing cognitive skills and abilities, including comprehension, application, analysis, synthesis, and evaluation of knowledge. The last four—application, analysis, synthesis, and evaluation—are referred to as *higher order thinking skills,* as are the higher categories of the affective and psychomotor domains.

COMPREHENSION

Comprehension includes the ability to translate, explain, or interpret knowledge and to extrapolate from it to address new situations. Action verbs appropriate for this category include *change, classify, convert, defend, describe, discuss, distinguish, estimate, expand, explain, generalize, give example, infer, interpret, paraphrase, predict, recognize, retell, summarize,* and *translate*.

Examples of objectives in this category include the following:

- From a sentence, the student *will recognize* the letters that are vowels in the English alphabet.
- The student *will describe* each of the organelles found in animal cell cytoplasm.
- The student *will give examples* of each of the major parts of speech from the paragraph.
- The student *will distinguish* the positions of players on a soccer team.

APPLICATION

Once learners understand information, they should be able to apply it. Action verbs in this category of operation include *apply, calculate, compute, demonstrate, develop, discover, exhibit, manipulate, modify, operate, participate, perform, plan, predict, relate, show, simulate, solve,* and *use.* Examples of objectives in this category include the following:

- The student *will use* in a sentence a word that contains at least two vowels.
- The student *will predict* the organelles found in plant cell cytoplasm.
- The student *will demonstrate* in a complete sentence each of the major parts of speech.
- The student *will relate* how the positions of players on a soccer team depend upon each other.

ANALYSIS

This category includes objectives that require learners to use the skills of analysis. Action verbs appropriate for this category include *analyze, arrange, break down, categorize, classify, compare, contrast, debate, deduce, diagram, differentiate, discover, discriminate, group, identify, illustrate, infer, inquire, organize, outline, relate, separate,* and *subdivide.* Examples of objectives in this category are as follows:

- From a list of words, the student *will differentiate* those that contain vowels from those that do not.
- Using the microscope, the student *will identify* the organelles found in animal cell cytoplasm.
- The student *will analyze* a paragraph for misuse of major parts of speech.
- At the writing board, the student *will illustrate* the different positions of players on a soccer team.

SYNTHESIS

This category includes objectives that involve such skills as designing a plan, proposing a set of operations, and deriving a series of abstract relations. Action verbs appropriate for this category include *arrange, assemble, categorize, classify, combine, compile, compose, constitute, create, design, develop, devise, document, explain, formulate, generate, hypothesize, imagine, invent, modify, organize, originate, plan, predict, produce, rearrange, reconstruct, revise, rewrite, summarize, synthesize, tell, transmit,* and *write.* Examples of objectives in this category include the following:

- From a list of words, the student *will rearrange* them into several lists according to the vowels contained in each.
- The student *will devise* a classification scheme of the organelles found in animal cell and plant cell cytoplasm according to their functions.
- The student *will write* a paragraph that correctly uses each of the major parts of speech.
- At the writing board, the student *will illustrate* an offensive plan that uses the different positions of players on a soccer team.

EVALUATION

This, the highest category of Bloom's cognitive taxonomy, includes offering opinions and making value judgments.

[Note: Some today consider "synthesis" as a higher level than "evaluation." However, as I said at the outset of this discussion, rather than an absolute classification it is in my opinion important that learners experience instruction designed to move their intellectual behavior from low to high levels of operation in all three domains.] Action verbs appropriate for this category of evaluation include *appraise, argue, assess, choose, compare, conclude, consider, contrast, criticize, decide, describe, discriminate, estimate, evaluate, explain, interpret, judge, justify, predict, rank, rate, recommend, relate, revise, standardize, summarize, support,* and *validate.* Examples of objectives in this category are as follows:

- The student *will listen to and evaluate* other students' identifications of vowels from sentences written on the board.
- While observing living cytoplasm under the microscope, the student *will justify* his or her interpretation that certain structures are specific organelles of a plant or animal cell.
- The student *will assess* a paragraph written by an anonymous student for the proper use of major parts of speech.
- The student *will interpret* the reasons for an opposing team's offensive use of the different positions of players on a soccer team.

Affective Domain Hierarchy

Krathwohl, Bloom, and Masia (1964) developed a useful taxonomy of the affective domain. The following are their major levels (or categories), from least internalized to most internalized: (a) *receiving*—being aware of the affective stimulus and beginning to have favorable feelings toward it; (b) *responding*—taking an interest in the stimulus and viewing it favorably; (c) *valuing*—showing a tentative belief in the value of the affective stimulus and becoming committed to it; (d) *organizing*—placing values into a system of dominant and supporting values; and (e) *internalizing*—demonstrating consistent beliefs and behavior that have become a way of life. Although there is considerable overlap from one category to another within the affective domain, these categories do give a basis by which to judge the quality of objectives and the nature of learning within this area. A discussion of each of the five categories follows.

RECEIVING

At this level, which is the least internalized, the learner exhibits willingness to give attention to particular phenomena or stimuli, and the teacher is able to arouse, sustain, and direct that attention. Action verbs appropriate for this category include *ask, choose, describe, differentiate, distinguish, give, hold, identify, locate, name, point to, recall, recognize, reply, select,* and *use.* Examples of objectives in this category are as follows:

- The student *listens attentively* to the instructions for the project assignment.
- The student *demonstrates sensitivity* to the property, beliefs, and concerns of others.

RESPONDING

At this level, learners respond to the stimulus they have received. They may do so because of some external pressure, because they find the stimulus interesting, or because responding gives them satisfaction. Action verbs appropriate for this category include *answer, applaud, approve, assist, command, comply, discuss, greet, help, label, perform, play, practice, present, read, recite, report, select, spend* (*leisure time in*), *tell,* and *write.* Examples of objectives at this level include the following:

- The student *completes* the project assignment.
- The student *cooperates* with others during group learning activities.

VALUING

Objectives at the valuing level deal with learner's beliefs, attitudes, and appreciations. The simplest objectives concern the acceptance of beliefs and values; the higher ones involve learning to prefer certain values and finally becoming committed to them. Action verbs appropriate for this level include *argue, assist, complete, describe, differentiate, explain, follow, form, initiate, invite, join, justify, propose, protest, read, report, select, share, study, support,* and *work.* Examples of objectives in this category are as follows:

- The student *protests* against reinstitution of the military draft.
- The student *argues* a position against abortion or pro-choice for women.

ORGANIZING

This fourth level in the affective domain concerns the building of a personal value system. Here the learner is conceptualizing and arranging values into a system that recognizes their relative importance. Action verbs appropriate for this level include *adhere, alter, arrange, balance, combine, compare, defend, define, discuss, explain, form, generalize, identify, integrate, modify, order, organize, prepare, relate,* and *synthesize.* Examples of objectives in this category are as follows:

- The student *recognizes* the value of serendipity when problem solving.
- The student *defends* the values of a particular subculture.

INTERNALIZING

This is the last and highest category within the affective domain, at which the learner's behaviors have become

consistent with his or her beliefs. Action verbs appropriate for this level include *act, complete, discriminate, display, influence, listen, modify, perform, practice, propose, qualify, question, revise, serve, solve,* and *verify.* Examples of objectives in this category include the following:

- The student's behavior *displays* self-assurance in working alone.
- The student *practices* cooperative behaviors in group activities.

Psychomotor Domain Hierarchy

Whereas identification and classification within the cognitive and affective domains are generally agreed upon, there is less agreement on the classification within the psychomotor domain. Originally, the goal of this domain was simply to develop and categorize proficiency in skills, particularly those dealing with gross and fine muscle control. The classification of the domain presented here follows this lead, but includes at its highest level the most creative and inventive behaviors, thus coordinating skills and knowledge from all three domains. Consequently, the objectives are in a hierarchy ranging from simple gross locomotor control to the most creative and complex, requiring originality and fine locomotor control—for example, from simply turning on a computer to designing a software program. From Harrow (1977) is the following taxonomy of the psychomotor domain: (a) *moving,* (b) *manipulating,* (c) *communicating,* and (d) *creating.* [Note: A similar taxonomy is that of Simpson (1972).]

MOVING

This level involves gross motor coordination. Action verbs appropriate for this level include *adjust, carry, clean, grasp, jump, locate, obtain,* and *walk.* Sample objectives for this category include the following:

- The student *will jump* a rope 10 times without missing.
- The student *will carry* the microscope to the desk correctly.

MANIPULATING

This level involves fine motor coordination. Action verbs appropriate for this level include *assemble, build, calibrate, connect, play, thread,* and *turn.* Sample objectives for this category are as follows:

- The student *will assemble* a kite.
- The student *will turn* the fine adjustment until the microscope is in focus.

COMMUNICATING

This level involves the communication of ideas and feelings. Action verbs appropriate for this level include *analyze, ask, describe, draw, explain,* and *write.* Sample objectives for this category are as follows:

- The student *will draw* what he or she observes on a slide through the microscope.
- The student *will describe* his or her feelings about cloning.

CREATING

Creating is the highest level of this domain, and of all domains, and represents the student's coordination of thinking, learning, and behaving in all three domains. Action verbs appropriate for this level include *create, design,* and *invent.* Sample objectives for this category include the following:

- The student will *create, choreograph,* and *perform* a dance pattern.
- The student *will design* and build a kite pattern.

Now, using self-check Exercise 4.11 (end of chapter), assess your recognition of performance objectives according to which domain they belong. Then, with Exercise 4.12 (end of chapter), begin writing your own objectives for use in your teaching.

USING THE TAXONOMIES

Theoretically, the taxonomies are constructed so that students achieve each lower level before being ready to move to the higher levels. However, because categories and behaviors overlap, as they should, this theory does not always hold in practice. Furthermore, *feelings and thoughts are inextricably interconnected; they cannot be neatly separated as might be implied by the taxonomies.*

The taxonomies are important in that they emphasize the various levels to which instruction and learning must aspire. For learning to be worthwhile, you must formulate and teach to objectives from the higher levels of the taxonomies as well as from the lower ones. Student thinking and behaving must be moved from the lowest to the highest levels. When all is said and done, it is, perhaps, the highest level of the psychomotor domain (creating) to which we aspire.

In using the taxonomies, remember that the point is to formulate the best objectives for the job to be done. In today's schools, using *results-driven* education models (known variously as *criterion-referenced, competency-based, performance-based,* and *outcome-based education*), those models describe levels of mastery standards (**rubrics**) for each outcome. The taxonomies provide the mechanism for ensuring that you do not spend a disproportionate amount of time on facts and other low-level learning and can be of tremendous help where teachers are expected to correlate learning activities to one of the school's or district's target outcome standards (see Figure 4.7).

Figure 4.7   Sample learning outcome standards.

Results-driven education helps produce people who are life-long learners, effective communicators, have high self-esteem, and:

PROBLEM SOLVERS

- are able to solve problems in their academic and personal lives
- demonstrate higher-level analytical thinking skills when they evaluate or make decisions
- are able to set personal and career goals
- can use knowledge, not just display it
- are innovative thinkers

SELF-DIRECTED LEARNERS

- are independent workers
- can read, comprehend, and interact with text
- have self-respect with an accurate view of themselves and their abilities

QUALITY PRODUCERS

- can communicate effectively in a variety of situations (oral, aesthetic/artistic, nonverbal)
- are able to use their knowledge to create intelligent, artistic products that reflect originality
- have high standards

COLLABORATIVE WORKERS

- are able to work interdependently
- show respect for others and their points of view
- have their own values and moral conduct
- have an appreciation of cultural diversity

COMMUNITY CONTRIBUTORS

- have an awareness of civic, individual, national, and international responsibilities
- have an understanding of basic health issues
- have an appreciation of diversity

Preparing objectives is essential to the preparation of good items for the assessment of student learning. Clearly communicating your performance expectations to students and then specifically assessing student learning against those expectations makes the teaching most efficient and effective, and it makes the assessment of the learning closer to being authentic. This does not mean to imply that you will write performance objectives for everything taught, nor will you always be able to accurately measure what students have learned. As said earlier, learning that is meaningful to students is not as easily compartmentalized as the taxonomies of educational objectives would seem to imply.

Observing for Connected (Meaningful) Learning: Logs, Portfolios, and Journals

In learning that is most important and that has the most meaning to students, the domains are inextricably interconnected. Consequently, when assessing for student learning, both during instruction (formative assessment) and at the conclusion of the instruction (summative assessment), you must look for those connections.

Ways of looking for connected learning include the following:

- Maintain a teacher's (or team's) log with daily or nearly daily entries about the progress of each student.
- Students maintain personal learning journals in which they reflect on and respond to their learning.
- Students assemble personal learning portfolios that document students' thinking, work, and learning experiences.

Dated and chronologically organized items that students place in their portfolios can include notes and communications; awards; brainstorming records; photos of bulletin board contributions and of charts; posters, displays, and models made by the student; records of peer coaching; visual maps; learning contract; record of debate contributions and demonstrations or presentations; mnemonics created by the student; peer evaluations; reading record; other contributions made to the class or to the team; record of service work; and test and grade records.

Students could maintain a response journal in which they reflect on and respond to their learning, using five categories described as follows (Fersh, 1993, pp. 22–24):

1. "I never knew that." In this category, student responses are primarily to factual information, responses to their new knowledge, to the bits and pieces of raw information often expected to be memorized regardless of how meaningful to students it might be. However, because this is only fragmented knowledge and merely scratches the surface of meaningful learning, it must not be the end-all of student learning. Learning that is truly meaningful goes beyond the "I never knew that" category, expands upon the bits and pieces, connects them, and allows the learner to make sense out of what is learned.
2. "I never thought of that." Here, student responses reveal an additional way of perceiving. Their responses may include elements of "I never knew that" but also contain higher level thinking as a result of their reflection on that knowledge.
3. "I never felt that." In this category, student responses are connected to the affective, eliciting more of an emotional response than a cognitive one. Learning what is truly meaningful is much more than intellectual understanding; it includes a "felt" meaning (Caine & Caine, 1997).
4. "I never appreciated that." Responses in this category reflect a sense of recognition that one's own life can be enriched by what others have created or done, or that something already known can be valued from an additional perspective.
5. "I never realized that." In this category, student responses indicate an awareness of overall patterns and dynamic ways in which behavior is holistic, establishing meaningful and potentially useful connections among knowledge, values, and purposes.

Still another type of journal is the **double entry journal** where the student records facts about things learned on the left side, and on the right side the student writes a personal response to the experience.

The use of portfolios and student journals is discussed further in Chapters 10 and 8, respectively.

Character Education and the Domains of Learning

Related especially to the affective domain, although not exclusive of the cognitive and psychomotor domains, is an interest in the development of students' values, especially those of honesty, kindness, respect, and responsibility, an interest in what is sometimes called character education. For example, Wynne and Ryan (1997, p. 1) said that "transmitting character, academics, and discipline—essentially, 'traditional' moral values—to pupils is a vital educational responsibility." Thus, if one agrees with that interpretation, then the teaching of moral values is the transmission of character, academics, and discipline and clearly implies learning that transcends the three domains of learning presented in this chapter. Stimulated by a perceived need to reduce student antisocial behaviors (such as drug abuse and violence) and to produce more respectful and responsible citizens, with a primary focus on the affective domain, many schools are developing curricula in character education and instruction in conflict resolution. Whether defined as ethics, citizenship, moral values, or personal development, character education has long been a component of public education in this country (Burrett & Rusnak, 1993; Otten, 2000).

As a teacher, you can contribute toward students' positive character development in two general ways, by

- providing a conducive classroom atmosphere, where students actively and positively share in the decision making and
- serving as a model students can proudly emulate.

Acquiring knowledge and developing understanding can enhance the learning of attitudes. Nevertheless, changing an attitude is often a long and tedious process, requiring the commitment of the teacher and the school, assistance from the community and parents/guardians, and the provision of numerous experiences that will guide students to new convictions. The following are some specific practices:

- Build a sense of community in the school and in the classroom, with shared goals, optimism, cooperative efforts, and clearly identified and practiced procedures for reaching those goals.
- Collaboratively plan with students action- and community-oriented projects that relate to curriculum themes; solicit student, family, and community members to assist in projects.
- Teach students to negotiate; practice and develop skills in conflict resolution, skills such as empathy, problem solving, impulse control, and anger management.
- Share and highlight examples of class and individual cooperation in serving the classroom, school, and community.
- Make student service projects visible in the school and community.
- Promote higher order thinking about value issues through the development of students' skills in questioning.
- Sensitize students to issues and teach skills of conflict resolution through debate, role play, simulations, and creative drama.

Online resources devoted to character education include www.character.org and www.charactercounts.org.

LEARNING THAT IS NOT IMMEDIATELY OBSERVABLE

Unlike behaviorists, constructivists do not limit the definition of learning to that which is observable behavior; nor should you. Bits and pieces of new information are stored in short-term memory, where the new information is "rehearsed" until ready to be stored in long-term memory. If the information is not rehearsed, it eventually fades from short-term memory. If it is rehearsed and made meaningful through connections with other stored knowledge, then this new knowledge is transferred to and stored in long-term memory, either by building existing schemata or by forming new schemata. As a teacher, your responsibility is to provide learning experiences that will result in the creation of new schemata as well as the modification of existing schemata.

> To be an effective teacher, the challenge is to use performance-based criteria simultaneously with a teaching style that encourages the development of intrinsic sources of student motivation and that allows, provides, and encourages coincidental learning—learning that goes beyond what might be considered predictable, immediately measurable, and representative of minimal expectations.

It has become clear to many teachers that to be most effective in helping students to develop meaningful understandings, much of the learning in each discipline can be made more effective and longer lasting when that learning is integrated with the whole curriculum and made meaningful to the lives of the students, rather than when simply taught as an unrelated and separate discipline at the same time each day.

As noted at the start of this chapter, if learning is defined only as the accumulation of bits and pieces of information, then we already know how that is learned and how to teach it. However, the accumulation of pieces of information is at the lowest end of a spectrum of types of learning. For higher levels of thinking and for learning that is most meaningful and longest lasting, the results of research support using (a) a curriculum where disciplines are integrated and (b) instructional techniques that involve the learners in social, interactive learning, such as project-centered learning, cooperative learning, peer tutoring, and cross-age teaching. When compared with traditional instruction, one characteristic of exemplary instruction today is the teacher's encouragement of dialogue among students in the classroom, to debate, discuss, and explore their own ideas.

INTEGRATED CURRICULUM

When learning about **integrated curriculum (IC)**, it is easy to be confused by the plethora of terms that are used, such as *integrated studies, thematic instruction, multidisciplinary teaching, interdisciplinary curriculum,* and *interdisciplinary thematic instruction.* In essence, regardless of which of these terms is being used, the reference is to the same thing.

Because the demarcation between the term *curriculum* and the term *instruction* is not always clear, let's assume that there is no difference between the two terms, that is, between what is curriculum and what is instruction. In other words, for the intent of this discussion, whether I use the term *integrated curriculum* or the term *integrated instruction*, I will be referring to the same thing.

The term *integrated curriculum* (or any of its synonyms mentioned previously) refers to both a way of teaching and a way of planning and organizing the instructional program so the discrete disciplines of subject matter are related to one another in a design that (a) matches the developmental needs of the learners and (b) helps to connect their learning in ways that are meaningful to their current and past experiences. In that respect, integrated curriculum is the antithesis of traditional, disparate, subject-matter-oriented teaching and curriculum designations.

The reason for the various terminology is, in part, because the concept of an integrated curriculum is not new. In fact, it has had a roller-coaster ride throughout the history of education in this country. Over time, those efforts to integrate student learning have had varying labels.

> People talk about how difficult it is to implement an integrated curriculum, which is taking the standard subject areas and combining them. That is ridiculous. The *world* is integrated! What is difficult is what schools do every day: unravel the world and all its vast knowledge and put it into boxes called subjects and separate things that are not separate in the real world.
>
> Dennis Littky (2004, p. 29)

Today's interest in curriculum integration has risen from several inextricably connected sources, especially the five that follow:

1. The success at curriculum integration enjoyed by middle-level schools since the 1960s
2. The literature-based, whole-language movement in reading and language arts that began in the 1980s [Note: Various movements and approaches have been used over the years to try to find the most successful approach to teaching English and the language arts—movements with names such as *whole language, integrated language arts, communication arts and skills, literature-based,* and so forth. Whatever the cognomen, certain common elements and goals prevail: student choice in materials to be read; student reading and writing across the curriculum; time for independent and sustained silent reading in the classroom; use of integrated language arts skills across the curriculum; and use of digital media.]

> The constructivist approach to literacy assumes that students are naturally motivated to read and write; the role of schooling is to provide them with the tools and guidance they need to acquire literacy skills in a developmentally appropriate, individually meaningful way. The new digital media can help to translate some of the goals of this student-driven approach into reality.
>
> Margaret Weigel and Howard Gardner (2009, p. 29)

3. The diversity of learners in the regular classroom coupled with growing acceptance of the philosophy that a certain percentage of school dropouts is not a viable assumption
4. The needs of the workplace, the advances in technology, and the concomitant trend of integrating vocational with academic education in secondary schools
5. The recent research in cognitive science and neuroscience demonstrating the necessity of helping students establish bridges between school and life, knowing and doing, content and context, with a parallel rekindled interest in constructivism as opposed to a strictly behaviorist philosophical approach to teaching and learning

An integrated curriculum approach may not necessarily be the best approach for every school, nor the best for all learning for every student, nor is it necessarily the manner by which every teacher should or must always plan and teach. As evidenced by practice, the truth of this statement becomes obvious. And, as by now you should be well aware, *it is my belief that a teacher's best choice as an approach to instruction—and to classroom management—is one that is eclectic.*

> Because there are various interpretations to curriculum integration, each teacher must make his or her own decisions about its use.

In attempts to connect students' learning with their experiences, efforts fall at various places on a spectrum or continuum, from the least integrated instruction (Level 1) to the most integrated (Level 4), as illustrated in Figure 4.8. It is not my intent that this illustration be interpreted as going from "worst-case scenario" (far left) to "best-case scenario" (far right), although some people may interpret it in exactly that

Figure 4.8 Levels of curriculum integration.

Least Integrated Level 1	Level 2	Level 3	Level 4	Most Integrated Level 5
Subject-specific topic outline	Subject-specific	Multidisciplinary	Interdisciplinary thematic	Integrated thematic
No student collaboration in planning	Minimal student input	Some student input	Considerable student input in selecting themes and in planning	Maximum student and teacher collaboration
Teacher solo	Solo or teams	Solo or teams	Solo or teams	Solo or teams
Student input into decision making is low.		Student input into decision making is high.		Student input into decision making is very high.

way. Figure 4.8 is meant solely to show how efforts to integrate fall on a continuum of sophistication and complexity. The following is a description of each level of the continuum.

Level 1 Curriculum Integration

Level 1 curriculum integration is the traditional organization of curriculum and classroom instruction, where teachers plan and arrange the subject-specific scope and sequence in the format of topic outlines, much as you did for Exercise 4.6. If there is an attempt to help students connect their experiences and their learning, then it is up to individual classroom teachers to do it. A student in a school and classroom that has subject-specific instruction at varying times of the day (e.g., language arts at 8:00, mathematics at 9:00, social studies at 10:30, and so on) from one or more teachers is likely learning at a Level 1 instructional environment, especially when what is being learned in one subject has little or no connection with content being learned in another. The same applies for a student, as found in many junior high schools, who moves during the school day from classroom to classroom, teacher to teacher, subject to subject, from one topic to another. A topic in science, for example, might be "earthquakes." A related topic in social studies might be "the social consequences of natural disasters." These two topics may or may not be studied by a student at the same time.

Level 2 Curriculum Integration

If the same students are learning English/language arts, social studies/history, mathematics, or science using a thematic approach rather than a topic outline, then they are learning at Level 2. At this level, themes for one discipline are not necessarily planned and coordinated to correspond or integrate with themes of another or to be taught simultaneously. At Level 2, the students may have some input into the decision making involved in planning themes and content from various disciplines. Before going further in this presentation of the levels of curriculum integration, let's stop and consider what is a topic and what is a theme.

For an integrated thematic unit (ITU) the difference between what is a topic and what is a theme is not always clear. For example, whereas "earthquakes" and "social consequences of natural disasters" are topics, "a survival guide to local natural disasters" could be the theme or umbrella under which these two topics could fall. In addition, themes are likely to be problem-based statements or questions; they often result in a product and are longer in duration than are topics. A theme is the point, the message, or the idea that underlies a study. When compared to a topic, a theme is more dynamic; the theme explains the significance of the study. It communicates to the

student what the experience means. Although organized around one theme, many topics make up an ITU. Often the theme of a study becomes more clear to students when an overall guiding question is presented and discussed, such as "What could we do to improve our living environment?" or "What happens in our community after natural disasters?"

Some educators predict the integrated curriculum of the future will be based on broad, unchanging, and unifying concepts (i.e., on conceptual themes). If so, it would be the recycling of an approach of a half century ago, as supported by the writings of Jerome Bruner (1960) and implemented in some of the National Science Foundation–sponsored curriculum projects of that era. In fact, there has already been action in that direction. For example, forming the basis for the national curriculum standards for social studies are 10 "thematic strands," including "people, places, and environments," and "power, authority, and governance." The national standards for science education are centered on unifying conceptual schemes, such as "systems, order, and organization," and "form and function." Many of the state curriculum documents are now centered on major concepts and central themes rather than on isolated facts.

Level 3 Curriculum Integration

When the same students are learning two or more of their core subjects around a common theme, such as the theme "natural disasters," from one or more teachers, they are then learning at Level 3 integration. At this level, teachers agree on a common theme, then they separately deal with that theme in their individual subject areas, usually at the same time during the school year. So what the student is learning from a teacher in one class is related to and coordinated with what the student is concurrently learning in another or several others. At Level 3, students may have some input into the decision making involved in selecting and planning themes and content. Some authors may refer to Levels 2 or 3 as **coordinated or parallel curriculum**.

Level 4 Curriculum Integration

When teachers and students collaborate on a common theme and its content, and when discipline boundaries begin to disappear as teachers teach about this common theme, either solo or as an interdisciplinary teaching team, Level 4 integration is achieved.

Level 5 Curriculum Integration

When teachers and their students have collaborated on a common theme and its content, discipline boundaries are truly blurred during instruction, and teachers of several grade levels and of various subjects teach toward student understanding of aspects of the common theme, then this is Level 5, an **integrated thematic approach**. [Note: For detailed accounts of teaching at this level of integration, see Stevenson and Carr (1993).]

Guidelines for integrating topics and for planning and developing an interdisciplinary thematic unit are presented in the next chapter.

Integrated Curriculum in a Standards-Based Environment

It should be reassuring to today's classroom teacher to know that students in any type of interdisciplinary or integrative curriculum do as well as, or oftentimes even better than, students in a conventional departmentalized program. Furthermore, this seems to hold true whether the program is taught by one teacher in a self-contained or block-time class or by an interdisciplinary teaching team (Vars & Beane, 2000).

PLANNING FOR INSTRUCTION: A SEVEN-STEP PROCESS

Earlier in the chapter it was noted that complete planning for instruction occurs at three levels: the year, the units, and the lessons. There are seven steps in the process:

1. *Course, grade-level, and school goals.* Consider and understand your curriculum goals and their relationship to the mission and goals of the school. Your course is not isolated on Mars but is an integral component of the total school curriculum.
2. *Expectations.* Consider topics, knowledge, and skills that you are expected to teach, such as those found in the districtwide standards and the course of study.
3. *Academic year, semester, trimester, or quarter plan.* Think about the goals you want the students to reach months from now. Working from your tentative content outline, and with the school calendar in hand, you begin by deciding the amount of time (e.g., the number of days) to be devoted to each topic (or unit), penciling those times onto the outline. You may need to work around mandatory, standardized achievement testing dates in such a way that the testing does not interrupt the flow of student learning.
4. *Course schedule.* This schedule becomes an element in the course syllabus that is presented to parents and students at the beginning of the term. However, the schedule must remain flexible to allow for the unexpected, such as the cancellation or interruption of a class meeting, a serendipitous discovery and inquiry by the students, or an extended study of a particular topic.
5. *Plans for each class meeting.* Working from the calendar plan or the course schedule, you are ready to prepare plans for each class meeting, keeping in

mind the abilities and interests of your students while making decisions about appropriate strategies and learning experiences. The preparation of daily plans takes considerable time and continues throughout the year as you arrange and prepare instructional notes, demonstrations, discussion topics and questions, classroom exercises, learning centers, guest speakers, materials and equipment, field trips, and tools for the assessment of student learning. Because the content of each class meeting is often determined by the accomplishments of and your reflections upon the preceding one, lessons are never "set in concrete" but need your continual revisiting, reflection, adjustments, and assessment.
6. *Instructional objectives.* Once you have the finalized schedule, and as you prepare the daily plans, you will complete your preparation of the instructional objectives. Those objectives are critical for proper development of the next and final step.
7. *Assessment.* The final step is that of deciding how to assess for student achievement. Included in this component are your decisions about how you will accomplish diagnostic or preassessment (i.e., the assessment of what students know or think they know at the start of a new unit or a new topic), formative assessment (the ongoing assessment on what the students are learning that takes place almost daily during a unit of study), and summative assessment (the assessment of students' learning at the conclusion of a unit of study). Also included in the assessment component are your decisions about assignments (discussed in Chapter 9) and the grading procedures (discussed in Chapter 10).

In Chapter 5, you proceed through these steps as you develop your first instructional plan. However, before starting that, let's consider one more topic relevant to the overall planning of the course—the syllabus.

THE SYLLABUS

A syllabus is a written statement of information about the workings of a particular class or course. As a student in postsecondary education, you have seen a variety of syllabi written by professors, each with their individual ideas and personal touches about what general and specific logistic information is most important for students to know about a course. Some instructors, however, err in thinking that a course outline constitutes a course syllabus; a course outline is just one component of a syllabus.

Not all K–12 school teachers use a course syllabus, at least as is described here, but for reasons that are explored in this discussion, I believe they should. Related to that belief are several questions that are answered next: "Why should teachers use a syllabus?" "What value is it?" "What use can be made of it?" "What purpose does it fulfill?" "How do I develop one?" "Can students have input into its content and participate in its development?" "Where do I start?" "What information should be included?" "When should it be distributed, especially if the children can not yet read?" "To whom should it be distributed?" and "How rigidly should it be followed?"

Use and Development of a Syllabus

The syllabus is printed information about the class or the course that is usually presented to the parents/guardians of primary grades children, and for grades 4 and up, to the students at the start of school. The syllabus may be developed completely by you or in collaboration with members of your teaching team. As you shall learn, it also can be developed collaboratively with students. As always, the final decision about its development is yours to make. However it is developed, the syllabus should be designed so that it helps establish a rapport between students, parents or guardians, and the teacher; helps students feel more at ease by providing an understanding of what is expected of them; and helps them to organize, conceptualize, and synthesize their learning experiences.

The syllabus should provide a reference, helping eliminate misunderstandings and misconceptions about the nature of the class—its rules, expectations, procedures, requirements, and other policies. It should provide students with a sense of connectedness (often by allowing students to work collaboratively in groups and actually participate in fashioning their own course syllabus).

The syllabus should also serve as a plan to be followed by the teacher and the students, and it should serve as a resource for substitute teachers and (when relevant) members of a teaching team. Each team member should have a copy of every other member's syllabus. In essence, the syllabus stands as documentation for what is taking place in the classroom for those outside the classroom (i.e., parents or guardians, school board members, administrators, other teachers, and students). For access by parents and other interested persons, some teachers include at least portions of their course syllabus, such as homework assignment specifications and due dates, with the school's web site on the Internet.

Some teachers give students a brief syllabus (see sample in Figure 4.9) on the first day and then, collaboratively with the students and other members of the teaching team, develop a more detailed syllabus during

Figure 4.9 Sample course syllabus. (*Courtesy of Angela Biletnikoff*)

English 8   **Room 23, Mrs. Biletnikoff**

Course Description

English 8 is a course designed to provide instruction in the areas of reading, analyzing, and writing about literature, while utilizing texts that support the coursework in History 8. Essay writing, especially descriptive writing, is emphasized. In addition to intensive vocabulary study, students will be writing on a daily basis. Also, the students will read one million words of outside texts, in addition to their assigned reading. The readings for English 8 are an eclectic mix (see the novels listed at the end of this syllabus).

Materials Required

Students are required to bring pen, pencil, and paper to class each day. Journal binder should be a two-pocket, three-prong paper binder. The school provides the vocabulary text and all literary texts.

Goals

- To understand and recognize the various aspects of literature: character, setting, plot, point of view, and theme.
- To increase vocabulary, preparing students for more advanced writing.
- To develop and enhance students' descriptive writing and organizational skills.
- To increase oral and listening skills.

Objectives

- Students will participate in projects, class discussions, journal writing, quizzes, essay writing, and tests that are designed to help them grasp the concepts of plot, setting, character, theme, and other literary devices. Through these activities, students will demonstrate improvement in their writing and oral/listening skills.
- Students will participate in class activities such as sustained silent reading (SSR), read aloud, and project development to help in their learning of the material.

Assignments

There are weekly vocabulary quizzes. There is also weekly vocabulary homework. Throughout the course, students will be writing journal entries, quickwrites, and essays. All completed and graded work is returned to the corresponding class file. Students are free to check the file before or after class.

Figure 4.9 *continued*

Assessment Components

- Students will complete weekly vocabulary quizzes.
- Quizzes are administered when the teacher needs to check the students' progress.
- Test dates will be announced in class and class time is used for test preparation.
- Class participation, including participation in group work, accounts for 15 percent of the student's grade; therefore, absences and tardiness can negatively effect this assessment component.

Method of Evaluation

Evaluation is done through oral and written quizzes and tests. Additionally, students are evaluated on class participation, assignments, projects, and class discussions. All grades are based on a point system.

Papers, quizzes, and tests	= 50% of total points
Homework	= 20% of total points
Journals	= 15% of total points
Group work and class participation	= 15% of total points

Grading Scale 90−100% of total points = A; 80 − 89% = B; 70−79% = C; 50−69% = D; < 50% < F; Grades are posted (by codes, not names) biweekly

Classroom Citizenship Behavior and Consequences for Inappropriate Behavior

Students are expected to demonstrate the 5Ps: be prompt, prepared, polite, productive, and positive. Students may earn 5 points per day by observing the 5Ps guidelines. Students may forfeit their citizenship points by excessive bathroom requests, tardiness, or leaving class without the teacher's approval.

Consequences for inappropriate behavior:

1st infraction = verbal warning
2nd infraction = 15 minutes at time out and a phone call to parent or guardian
3rd infraction = administrative referral and/or a call home
4th infraction = administrative referral and possible suspension

Note: Any step in the above process may be skipped at the teacher's discretion.

Attendance

Regular attendance is crucial for success. It enables the student to understand assignments and to take advantage of the guidance provided by the teacher and others. In addition, the students will receive immediate feedback regarding their progress. If a student needs to leave early or enter late, please make arrangements with the teacher beforehand, if possible.

Tardiness

Students are tardy when they are not in their seats when the tardy bell rings. Any student who elects to leave the classroom for any reason takes a tardy for that period. Tardiness affects citizenship as well as the privilege to participate in extracurricular activities before and after school.

Bathroom Privileges

Students are allowed two bathroom passes per quarter. Each pass is redeemed at the time of use. If the student does not use the two passes for the quarter, the student receives 5 extra points per pass, with a total of 10 points possible towards their citizenship grade. If a student chooses to use the bathroom beyond the two-pass limit, then that student forfeits the citizenship points (5) for the day.

Make-up

Students may make up assignments one day after returning from an excused absence. All other work is accepted at the teacher's discretion.

Extra Credit Work There is no "extra credit" work in this class.

Instructional Schedule for English 8, Fall Semester

Unit I   Introduction to the short story (2 weeks)
Vocabulary, journal, SSR, and outside readings begin
Unit II   *April Morning* (4–5 weeks)
Unit III *The Giver* (4–5 weeks)
Unit IV   *Diary of Anne Frank* (4–5 weeks)

the initial days of the start of school. Shown in Figure 4.10 are steps you can use as a collaborative learning experience where students spend time during the first (or an early) class meeting brainstorming content of their syllabus.

Content of a Syllabus

A syllabus should be concise, matter-of-fact, uncomplicated, and brief—perhaps no more than two pages—and, to be thorough and most informative, include the following information:

Descriptive information about the class or course. This includes the teacher's name, the course or class title, class period, days of class meetings, beginning and ending times, and room number.

Importance of the course. This information should describe the course, cite the ways students will profit from it, tell whether the course is a required course, and (if relevant) tell from which program it is in the curriculum (e.g., a core course, an elective, exploratory, or some other arrangement).

Learning targets. This should include major goals and a few objectives.

Materials required. Explain what materials are needed—such as a textbook, notebook, binder, calculator, supplementary readings, apron, safety goggles—and specify which are supplied by the school, which must be supplied by each student, and what materials must be available each day.

Types of assignments that will be given. These should be clearly explained in as much detail as possible this early in the school term. There should be a statement of your estimate of time required (if any) for homework each night. There should also be a statement about where daily assignments will be posted in the classroom (a regular place each day), and about the procedures for completing and turning in assignments and (if relevant) for making corrections to assignments once turned in. Include your policy regarding late work. Also, parents/guardians may need to know your expectations of them regarding helping with assignments. (Homework is discussed in Chapter 9.)

Attendance expectations. Explain how attendance is related to achievement grades and to promotion (if

Figure 4.10   Steps for involving students in the development of their course syllabus.

Step 1

Sometime during the first few days of the course, arrange students in heterogeneous groups (mixed abilities) of three or four members to brainstorm the development of their syllabus.

Step 2

Instruct each group to spend 5 minutes listing everything they can think of that they would like to know about the course. Tell students that a group *recorder* must be chosen to write their list of ideas on paper and then, when directed to do so, to transfer the list to the writing board or to sheets of butcher paper to be hung in the classroom for all to see (or on an overhead transparency—a transparency sheet and pen are made available to each group). Tell them to select a group *spokesperson* who will address the class, explaining the group's list. Each group could also appoint a *materials manager,* whose job is to see that the group has the necessary materials (e.g., pen, paper, transparency, chalk), and a *task master,* whose job is to keep the group on task and to report to the teacher when each task is completed.

Step 3

After 5 minutes, have the recorders prepare their lists. When a transparency or butcher paper is used, the lists can be prepared simultaneously while recorders remain with their groups. If using the writing board, then recorders, one at a time, write their lists on areas of the board that you have designated for each group's list.

Step 4

Have the spokesperson of each group explain the group's list. As this is being done, you should make a master list. If transparencies or butcher paper are being used rather than the writing board, you can ask for either as backup to the master list you have made.

Step 5

After all spokespersons have explained their lists, you ask the class collectively for additional input. "Can anyone think of anything else that should be added?"

Step 6

You now take the master list and design a course syllabus, being careful to address each question and to include items of importance that students may have omitted. However, your guidance during the preceding five steps should ensure that all bases have been covered.

Step 7

At the next class meeting, give each student a copy of the final syllabus. Discuss its content. (Duplicate copies to distribute to colleagues, especially those on your teaching team, interested administrators, and parents and guardians at back-to-school night.)

relevant) and the procedure for making up missed work. Typical school policy allows that, with an excused absence, missed work can be completed without penalty if done within a reasonable period of time after the student returns to school.

Assessment and marking/grading procedures. Explain the assessment procedures and the procedures for determining grades. Will there be quizzes (announced or not?), tests, homework, projects, and group work? What will be their formats, coverage, and weights in the procedure for determining grades? For group work, how will the contributions and learning of individual students be evaluated?

Other information specific to the class or course. Field trips? Special privileges? Computer work? Parental/guardian expectations? Homework hotline? Classroom procedures and expectations should be included here.

If you are a beginning teacher or are new to the school, to affirm that your policies as indicated in the first draft of your syllabus are not counter to any existing school policies, you probably should share your first draft of the syllabus with members of your team, your mentor, or the grade-level or department chairperson for their feedback.

SUMMARY

In your comparison and analysis of courses of study and teachers' editions of student textbooks, you discovered that many are accompanied by sequentially designed resource units from which the teacher can select and build specific teaching units. A resource unit usually consists of an extensive list of objectives, a large number and variety of activities, suggested materials, and extensive bibliographies for teacher and students.

Some courses of study contain actual teaching units that have been prepared by teachers of the school district. Beginning teachers and student teachers often ask, "How closely must I follow the school's curriculum guide or course of study?" To obtain an answer, you must talk with teachers and administrators of the school before you begin teaching.

Your final decisions about what content to teach are guided by (a) discussions with other teachers; (b) review of state curriculum documents, local courses of study, and articles in professional journals; (c) your personal convictions, knowledge, and skills; and (d) the unique characteristics of your students.

In this chapter you learned of the differences between the terms *aims, goals,* and *objectives.* Regardless of how these terms are defined, the important point is this:

Teachers must be clear about what it is they expect their students to learn, about the kind of evidence needed to verify their learning, and about communicating those things to the students so they are understood by the students.

Many teachers do not write specific objectives for all the learning activities in their teaching plans. However, when teachers do prepare specific objectives, teach toward them, and assess students' progress against them, student learning is enhanced; this is called performance-based teaching and criterion-referenced measurement. It is also known as an aligned curriculum. In schools using results-driven education mastery learning models, those models describe levels of mastery standards or rubrics for each outcome or learning target. The taxonomies are of tremendous help in schools where teachers are expected to correlate learning activities to the school's outcome standards.

As a teacher, you will be expected to (a) plan your lessons well, (b) convey specific expectations to your students, and (c) assess their learning against that specificity. However, because it tends toward high objectivity, there is the danger that such performance-based teaching could become too objective, which can have negative consequences. If students are treated as objects, then the relationship between teacher and student becomes impersonal and counterproductive to real learning. Highly specific and impersonal teaching can be discouraging to serendipity, creativity, and the excitement of discovery, to say nothing of its possibly negative impact on the development of students' self-esteem.

Performance-based instruction works well when teaching toward mastery of basic skills, but the concept of mastery learning is inclined to imply that there is some foreseeable end to learning, an assumption that is obviously erroneous. With performance-based instruction, the source of student motivation tends to be extrinsic. Teacher expectations, marks and grades, society, and peer pressures are examples of extrinsic sources that drive student performance. To be a most effective teacher, your challenge is to use performance-based criteria together with a teaching style that encourages the development of intrinsic sources of student motivation and that allows for, provides for, and encourages coincidental learning—learning that goes beyond what might be considered as predictable, immediately measurable, and representative of minimal expectations. In other words, although you must have clear goals and objectives and a routine that students can rely on from day to day, the most effective teachers consider and build upon the interests, experiences, and spontaneous nature of their students. Good teaching is *not* an inhuman experience.

QUESTIONS FOR CLASS DISCUSSION

1. Identify and describe various documents that influence the content of the curriculum for the grade level(s) you intend to teach.

2. More frequently in recent years we hear both beginning and experienced teachers complaining that there is not enough time to teach all curriculum content they are supposed to teach, with less to no time to teach topics they prefer to teach. We hear that they have less and less freedom to decide what is important for children to learn and do and to create learning activities for that learning. They are told they must spend more time on direct instruction and less on indirect instruction. There is not enough time for student-initiated exploratory learning. They have less time during the 180-day school year to teach because of the increased amount of time given to testing. There is less time for students to reflect on what is being learned. Interdisciplinary thematic instruction takes too much time, time they do not have because they must teach the prescribed curriculum to prepare the students for the state proficiency exams given in the spring. Once the spring testing is done, it is nearly impossible to refocus students on further learning—that once the testing is done, the students act as if the school year is over. Do any of these comments sound familiar to you? If so, what do you believe may be causing these concerns? Is there any danger to the profession if the act of teaching becomes so highly prescriptive? How will you plan to counter your own negative thinking as a teacher?

3. A teacher with 3 years of experience left teaching at age 24 to devote full time to family. Now, at the age of 40, with three children grown, the former teacher wants to return to the classroom as a school teacher. If this teacher were teaching in your areas (grade and subject) of interest, what will this person find has changed most and what the least? Why? How will the person's teaching schedule today likely be different from that of 24 years ago?

4. With today's emphasis on curriculum standards and high-stakes proficiency testing, the challenge is to design standards and tests that are not so high that many students cannot reach them nor so low they become meaningless and risk boring quicker learning children. The reality is, on any school campus there are students doing advanced mathematics and there are students who cannot do simple multiplication, and they are the same age. The question is this: For your subject field, is one set of standards sufficient or should there be multiple standards, such as a set of minimal standards and another set that will challenge the most capable students? Share your thoughts about this with your classmates.

5. It is sometimes said that teaching less can be better. Think back to your own K–12 schooling. What do you really remember? Do you remember lectures and drill sheets, or do you remember projects, your presentations, and your extra effort for artwork to accompany your presentation? Maybe you remember a compliment by a teacher or a compliment by peers. Most likely you do not recall the massive amount of content that was covered. Write a one-page essay expressing and defending your agreement or disagreement with the original statement of this paragraph. Share your essay with your classmates.

Now go to Topics #5 and 6: **Instructional Planning** and **Assessment** in the MyEducationLab (www.myeducationlab.com) for your course, where you can:

- Find learning outcomes for these topics along with the national standards that connect to these outcomes.
- Complete Assignments and Activities that can help you more deeply understand the chapter content.
- Examine challenging situations and cases presented in the IRIS center resources.
- Apply and practice your understanding of the core teaching skills identified in the chapter with the Building Teaching Skills and Dispositions learning units.

EXERCISE 4.1   EXAMINING NATIONAL CURRICULUM STANDARDS

INSTRUCTIONS: The purpose of this exercise is to become familiar with national curriculum standards for the subject(s) you intend to teach. Using the Internet addresses provided in Figure 4.1, review the standards that interest you. Use the following questions as a guideline for subject-area, small-group discussions. Following the small-group discussion, share the big ideas about the standards and perceptions of your group with the rest of your class.

Subject area (you may duplicate this form for each subject examined): _____

1. Title of the standards document reviewed, year of publication, and development agency.

2. Major educational goals as specified by the national standards.

3. Are the standards specific as to subject-matter content for each level of schooling, K–12? Explain.

4. Do the standards offer specific strategies for instruction? Describe.

5. Do the standards offer suggestions for teaching students who are culturally different, for students with special needs, for English language learners, and for students who are intellectually gifted and talented? Describe.

6. Do the standards offer suggestions or guidelines for dealing with controversial issues and topics? Give an example.

☞

EXERCISE 4.1 *(continued)*

7. Do the standards documents or their accompanying materials offer suggestions for specific resources? Describe.

8. Do the standards refer to assessment? Describe.

9. Do the standards promote or discourage inquiry, discovery learning, or critical thinking? If so, describe.

10. Is there anything else about the standards you would like to discuss and present?

EXERCISE 4.2   EXAMINING STATE CURRICULUM STANDARDS

INSTRUCTIONS: The purpose of this exercise is to become familiar with your state curriculum standards for the subject(s) you intend to teach. Using the Internet addresses provided in Figure 4.1, review the standards that interest you. Use the following questions as a guideline for subject-area, small-group discussions. Following the small-group discussion, share the big ideas about the standards and perceptions of your group with the rest of your class.

Subject area (you may duplicate this form for each subject examined): _____

1. Title of the standards document reviewed, year of publication, and development agency.

2. Major educational goals as specified by the state standards.

3. Are the standards specific as to subject-matter content for each level of schooling, K–12? Explain.

4. Do the standards offer specific strategies for instruction? Describe.

5. Do the standards offer suggestions for teaching students who are culturally different, for students with special needs, for English language learners, and for students who are intellectually gifted and talented? Describe.

6. Do the standards offer suggestions or guidelines for dealing with controversial issues and topics? Give an example.

EXERCISE 4.2 *(continued)*

7. Do the standards documents or their accompanying materials offer suggestions for specific resources? Describe.

8. Do the standards refer to assessment? Describe.

9. Do the standards promote or discourage inquiry, discovery learning, or critical thinking? If so, describe.

10. Is there anything else about the standards you would like to discuss and present?

EXERCISE 4.3 EXAMINING STATE CURRICULUM FRAMEWORKS

INSTRUCTIONS: The purpose of this exercise is to become familiar with curriculum documents published by your state department of education. You must determine whether that department publishes a curriculum framework for various subjects taught in schools. State frameworks provide valuable information about both content and process, and teachers need to be aware of these documents. You may want to duplicate this form so you can use it to evaluate several documents. After examining documents that interest you, use the following questions as a guideline for small- or large-group discussions.

1. Are there state curriculum documents available to teachers in your state? If so, describe them and explain how they can be obtained.

   Title of document: _____

   _____

   Source: _____

   _____

   Most recent year of publication: _____

   _____

   Other pertinent information: _____

   _____

2. Examine how closely the document follows the components presented in this chapter. Are any components omitted? Are there additional components? Specifically, check for these components:

	Yes	No
2.1. Statement of philosophy	____	____
2.2. Evidence of a needs assessment	____	____
2.3. Aims, goals, and objectives	____	____
2.4. Schemes for vertical articulation	____	____
2.5. Schemes for horizontal articulation	____	____
2.6. Recommended instructional procedures	____	____
2.7. Recommended resources	____	____
2.8. Assessment strategies	____	____

   Other: _____

3. Are the documents specific as to subject-matter content for each grade level? Describe evidence of both vertical and horizontal articulation schemes.

   _____

   _____

   _____

☞

EXERCISE 4.3 *(continued)*

4. Do the documents offer specific strategies for instruction? If yes, describe.

    _____

    _____

    _____

5. Do the documents offer suggestions and resources for working with students who are culturally different, for students with special needs, who are English language learners, and for students who are intellectually gifted and talented? Describe.

    _____

    _____

    _____

6. Do the documents offer suggestions or guidelines for dealing with controversial topics? If so, describe.

    _____

    _____

    _____

7. Do the documents distinguish between what shall be taught (mandated) and what can be taught (permissible)?

    _____

    _____

    _____

8. Do the documents offer suggestions for specific resources?

    _____

    _____

    _____

9. Do the documents refer to assessment strategies? Describe.

    _____

    _____

    _____

10. Is there anything else about the documents you would like to discuss in your group?

    _____

    _____

    _____

    _____

EXERCISE 4.4   EXAMINING LOCAL CURRICULUM DOCUMENTS

INSTRUCTIONS: The purpose of this exercise is to become familiar with curriculum documents prepared by local school districts. A primary resource for what to teach is referred to as a *curriculum guide* or *course of study*, which normally is developed by teachers of a school or district. Samples may be available in your university library or in a local school district resource center. Or perhaps you could borrow them from teachers you visit. Obtain samples from a variety of sources and then examine them using the format of this exercise. (You may duplicate this form for each document examined.) An analysis of several documents will give you a good picture of expectations. If possible, compare documents from several school districts and states.

Title of document: _____

District or school: _____

Date of document: _____

1. Examine how closely the documents follow the components presented in this chapter. Does the document contain the following components?

	Yes	*No*
1.1. Statement of philosophy	____	____
1.2. Evidence of a needs assessment	____	____
1.3. Aims, goals, and objectives	____	____
1.4. Schemes for vertical articulation	____	____
1.5. Schemes for horizontal articulation	____	____
1.6. Recommended instructional procedures	____	____
1.7. Recommended resources	____	____
1.8. Assessment strategies	____	____

2. Does the document list expected learning outcomes? If so, describe what they are.

_____

_____

_____

_____

3. Does the document contain detailed unit plans? If so, describe them by answering the following questions:

3.1 Do they contain initiating activities (how to begin a unit)? _____

3.2 Do they contain specific learning activities? _____

3.3 Do they contain suggested enrichment activities (as for gifted and talented students)? _____

3.4 Do they contain culminating activities (activities that bring a unit to a climax)? _____

3.5 Do they contain assessment procedures (for determining student achievement)? _____

3.6 Do they contain activities for learners with special needs, for English language learners, or for learners who are different in other respects? _____

3.7 Do they contain activities that address learning styles, multiple intelligences? _____

☞

EXERCISE 4.4 *(continued)*

4. Does it provide bibliographic entries for:

   • The teacher? _____

   • The students? _____

5. Does it list audiovisual, media, and other materials needed?

   _____
   _____
   _____
   _____
   _____

6. Does the document clearly help you understand what the teacher is expected to teach?

   _____
   _____
   _____
   _____
   _____

7. Are there questions not answered by your examination of this document? If so, list them for class discussion.

   _____
   _____
   _____
   _____
   _____

EXERCISE 4.5   EXAMINING STUDENT TEXTBOOKS AND TEACHER'S EDITIONS

INSTRUCTIONS: The purpose of this exercise is to become familiar with textbooks that you may be using in your teaching. Student textbooks are usually accompanied by a teacher's edition that contains specific objectives, teaching techniques, learning activities, assessment instruments, test items, and suggested resources. Your university library, local schools, and cooperating teachers are sources for locating and borrowing these enhanced textbooks. For your subject field of interest, select a textbook that is accompanied by a teacher's edition and examine the contents of both using the following format. If there are no standard textbooks available for your teaching field (such as might be the case for art, home economics, industrial arts, music, and physical education), then select a field in which there is a possibility you might teach. Beginning teachers are often assigned to teach in more than one field—sometimes, unfortunately, in fields for which they are untrained or have only minimal training. After completion of this exercise, share the book and your analysis of it with your colleagues.

Title of book: _____

Author(s): _____

Publisher: _____

Date of publication: _____

1. Analyze the teacher's edition for the following elements.

	Yes	No
a. Are its goals consistent with the goals of local and state curriculum documents?	____	____
b. Are there specific objectives for each lesson?	____	____
c. Does the book have scope and sequence charts for teacher reference?	____	____
d. Are the units and lessons sequentially developed, with suggested time allotments?	____	____
e. Are there any suggested provisions for individual differences?	____	____
for reading levels?	____	____
for students with special needs?	____	____
for students who are gifted and talented?	____	____
for students who have limited proficiency in English?	____	____
f. Does it recommend specific techniques and strategies?	____	____
g. Does it have listings of suggested aids, materials, and resources?	____	____
h. Are there suggestions for extension activities (to extend the lessons beyond the usual topic or time)?	____	____
i. Does the book have specific guidelines for assessment of student learning?	____	____

EXERCISE 4.5 *(continued)*

2. Analyze the student textbook for the following elements:

	Yes	No
a. Does it treat the content with adequate depth?	____	____
b. Does it treat ethnic minorities and women fairly?	____	____
c. Is the format attractive?	____	____
d. Does the book have good quality binding with suitable type size?	____	____
e. Are illustrations and visuals attractive and useful?	____	____
f. Is the reading clear and understandable for the students?	____	____
g. Is the content current and accurate?	____	____

3. Would you like to use this textbook? Give reasons why or why not.

_____

_____

_____

_____

_____

_____

_____

_____

_____

_____

_____

_____

_____

_____

_____

_____

_____

EXERCISE 4.6   PREPARING A FULL SEMESTER CONTENT OUTLINE

INSTRUCTIONS: The purpose of this exercise is for you to organize your ideas about subject content and the sequencing of content for one semester. Unless told otherwise by your instructor, you should select the subject (e.g., math, reading, science, history) and the grade level (K–12).

With *three levels of headings* (see example that follows), prepare a sequential topic outline (on a separate piece of paper as space is not provided here) for a subject and grade level you intend to teach. Identify the subject by title, and clearly state the grade level. This outline is of topic content only and does *not* need to include student activities associated with the learning of that content (i.e., do not include experiments, assignments, or assessment strategies).

For example, for the study of Earth science, three levels of headings might include:

I. The Earth's surface

    A. Violent changes in the Earth's surface

        1. Earthquakes

        2. Volcanoes

    B. Earth's land surface

        1. Rocks

If the study of Earth science was just one unit for a grade level's study of the broader area of "science," then three levels of headings for that study might include:

I. Earth science

    A. The Earth's surface

        1. Violent changes in the Earth's surface

Share your completed outline to obtain feedback from your colleagues and university instructor. Because content outlines are never to be "carved in stone," make adjustments to your outline when and as appropriate.

Content Outline Assessment Checklist

For the development of your own outline and for the assessment of outlines by others, here is a content outline assessment checklist:

- Does the outline address mandatory content standards?

    Yes _____ No _____ Comment: _____

_____

_____

_____

- Does the outline follow a logical sequence, with each topic logically leading to the next?

    Yes _____ No _____ Comment: _____

_____

_____

_____

☞

EXERCISE 4.5 *(continued)*

- Does the content assume prerequisite knowledge or skills that the students are likely to have?

    Yes _____ No _____ Comment:_____
    _____
    _____
    _____

- Is the content inclusive and to an appropriate depth?

    Yes _____ No _____ Comment: _____
    _____
    _____
    _____

- Does the content consider individual student differences?

    Yes _____ No _____ Comment: _____
    _____
    _____
    _____

- Does the content allow for interdisciplinary studies?

    Yes _____ No _____ Comment: _____
    _____
    _____
    _____

- Is the outline complete; are there no serious content omissions?

    Yes _____ No _____ Comment: _____
    _____
    _____
    _____

- Is any content of questionable value for this level of instruction?

    Yes _____ No _____ Comment: _____
    _____
    _____
    _____

EXERCISE 4.7A   DEALING WITH CONTROVERSIAL CONTENT AND ISSUES

INSTRUCTIONS: The purpose of this exercise is for you to discover controversial content and issues that you may face as a teacher and to consider what you can and will do about them. After completing this exercise, share it with members of your class.

1. After studying current periodicals and talking with colleagues in the school you visit, list two potentially controversial topics that you are likely to encounter as a teacher. (Two examples are given for you.)

Issue	*Source*
Rose Casement	*New Advocate 24(3): 204–213*
Breaking the Silence: The Stories of Gay and Lesbian	*(Summer 2002) People in children's Literature*
Racial profiling	*New York Times 9/21/01*

2. Take one of these issues and identify opposing arguments and current resources.

_____

_____

_____

_____

3. Identify your own positions on this issue.

_____

_____

_____

_____

4. How well can you accept students (and parents or guardians) who assume the opposite position?

_____

_____

_____

5. Share the preceding with other teacher candidates. Note comments that you find helpful or enlightening.

_____

_____

_____

_____

EXERCISE 4.7B   CENSORSHIP: BOOKS THAT ARE SOMETIMES CHALLENGED

INSTRUCTIONS: Continuing with the topic introduced in Exercise 4.7A, this exercise concentrates on certain books that, although frequently used in schools, are sometimes challenged by members of some communities. Book censorship becomes a concern when literature is the base for integrated teaching because there may be attempts to censor and ban books and curricular materials in the schools. Books that have been challenged include:

A Light in the Attic (Shel Silverstein)
And Tango Makes Three (Justin Richardson & Peter Parnell)
Annie on My Mind (Nancy Garden)
Are You There, God? It's Me, Margaret (Judy Blume)
Blubber (Judy Blume)
Bridge to Terabithia (Katherine Paterson)
Christine (Stephen King)
Fallen Angels (Walter Dean Myer)
Flowers for Algernon (Daniel Keyes)
Flowers in the Attic (V. C. Andrews)
Forever (Judy Blume)
Go Ask Alice (Anonymous)
I Know Why the Caged Bird Sings (Maya Angelou)
It's Perfectly Normal (Robie Harris)
Kaffir Boy: The True Story of a Black Youth's Coming of Age in Apartheid South Africa (Mark Mathabane)
Lord of the Flies (William Golding)
My Brother Sam Is Dead (James Lincoln Collier & Christopher Collier)

Of Mice and Men (John Steinbeck)
Olive's Ocean (Kevin Henkes)
Running Loose (Chris Crutcher)
Scary Stories to Tell in the Dark (Alvin Schwartz)
Slaughterhouse-Five (Kurt Vonnegut)
So Far From the Bamboo Grove (Yoko Kawashima Watkins)
The Adventures of Huckleberry Finn (Mark Twain)
The Arizona Kid (Ron Koertge)
The Catcher in the Rye (J. D. Salinger)
The Chocolate War (Robert Cormier)
The Color Purple (Alice Walker)
The Giver (Lois Lowry)
The Golden Compass (Philip Pullman)
The Handmaid's Tale (Margaret Atwood)
The Outsiders (S. E. Hinton)
The Perks of Being a Wallflower (Stephen Chbosky)
The Witches (Roald Dahl)
To Kill a Mockingbird (Harper Lee)
Ttyl (Lauren Myracle)

Review one of these books and explain how it might be challenged for censorship and how you would respond to the challenge. The organization of this exercise is left for your class to decide; I recommend that you assign small groups to review certain books, then report to the entire class so that all the books on the list have been addressed.

_____
_____
_____
_____
_____
_____
_____
_____
_____
_____
_____

EXERCISE 4.8   RECOGNIZING VERBS THAT ARE ACCEPTABLE FOR OVERT OBJECTIVES—A SELF-CHECK EXERCISE

INSTRUCTIONS: The purpose of this exercise is to check your recognition of verbs that are suitable for use in overt behavioral objectives. From the list of verbs below, circle those that *should not* be used in overt objectives—that is, those verbs that describe covert behaviors that are not directly observable and measurable. Check your answers against the answer key that follows. Discuss any problems with the exercise with your classmates and instructor.

1. apply	11. design	21. know
2. appreciate	12. diagram	22. learn
3. believe	13. enjoy	23. name
4. combine	14. explain	24. outline
5. comprehend	15. familiarize	25. predict
6. compute	16. grasp*	26. realize
7. create	17. identify	27. select
8. define	18. illustrate	28. solve
9. demonstrate	19. indicate	29. state
10. describe	20. infer	30. understand

Answer Key: The following verbs should be circled: 2, 3, 4, 13, 14, 16, 21, 22, 26, and 30. If you missed more than a couple, then you need to read the previous sections again and discuss your errors with your classmates and instructor. * Note: Words in English often have more than one meaning. For example, "grasp," as listed here could mean "to take hold," or it could mean "to comprehend." For the former it would be an acceptable verb for use in overt objectives; for the latter it would not.

EXERCISE 4.9   RECOGNIZING THE PARTS OF CRITERION-REFERENCED INSTRUCTIONAL OBJECTIVES—A SELF-CHECK EXERCISE

INSTRUCTIONS: The purpose of this exercise is to practice your skill in recognizing the four components of a behavioral objective. In the following two objectives, identify the parts of the objectives by underlining once the *audience,* twice the *behavior,* three times the *conditions,* and four times the *performance level* (that is, the degree or standard of performance).

Check your answers against the answer key that follows, and discuss any problems with this exercise with your classmates and instructor.

1. Given a metropolitan transit bus schedule, at the end of the lesson the student will be able to read the schedule well enough to determine at what times buses are scheduled to leave randomly selected locations with at least 90 percent accuracy.
2. Given five rectangular figures, you will correctly compute the area in square centimeters of at least four, by measuring the length and width with a ruler and computing the product using an appropriate calculation method.

Answer Key:

	Objective 1	*Objective 2*
Audience	the student	you
Behavior	will be able to read the schedule	will compute
Conditions	given a metropolitan transit bus schedule	given five rectangular figures
Performance level	well enough to determine (and) with at least 90 percent accuracy	correctly compute the area in square centimeters of at least four (80 percent accuracy)

EXERCISE 4.10   RECOGNIZING OBJECTIVES THAT ARE MEASURABLE—A SELF-CHECK EXERCISE

INSTRUCTIONS: The purpose of this exercise is to assess your ability to recognize objectives that are measurable. Place an *X* before each of the following that is an overt, student-centered instructional objective, that is, a learning objective that is clearly measurable. Although "audience," "conditions," or "performance levels" may be absent, ask yourself, "As stated, is this a student-centered and measurable objective?" A self-checking answer key follows. After checking your answers, discuss any problems with the exercise with your classmates and instructor.

_____   1. To develop an appreciation for literature.

_____   2. To identify those celestial bodies that are known planets.

_____   3. To provide meaningful experiences for the students.

_____   4. To recognize antonym pairs.

_____   5. To convert Celsius temperatures to Fahrenheit.

_____   6. To analyze and compare patterns of data on quartile maps.

_____   7. To develop skills in inquiry.

_____   8. To identify which of the four causes is most relevant to the major events leading up to the Civil War.

_____   9. To use maps and graphs to identify the major areas of world petroleum production and consumption.

_____   10. To know explanations for the changing concentration of atmospheric ozone.

Answer Key: You should have marked items 2, 4, 5, 6, 8, and 9.
Items 1, 3, 7, and 10 are inadequate because of their ambiguity. Item 3 is not even a student learning objective; it is a teacher goal. "To develop" and "to know" can have too many interpretations. Although the conditions are not given, items 2, 4, 5, 6, 8, and 9 are clearly measurable. The teacher would have no difficulty recognizing when a learner had reached those objectives.

EXERCISE 4.11   RECOGNITION OF COGNITIVE, AFFECTIVE, AND PSYCHOMOTOR OBJECTIVES—A SELF-CHECK EXERCISE

INSTRUCTIONS: The purpose of this exercise is to assess your ability to recognize objectives according to their domains. Classify each of the following instructional objectives by writing in the blank space the appropriate letter according to its domain: *C*—cognitive, *A*—affective, *P*—psychomotor. Check your answers with the key at the end; then discuss the results with your classmates and instructor.

_____ 1. The student will continue shooting free throws until the student can successfully complete 80 percent of the attempts.

_____ 2. The student will identify on a map the mountain ranges of eastern United States.

_____ 3. The student will summarize the historical development of the Democratic party of the United States.

_____ 4. The student will demonstrate a continuing desire to learn more about using the classroom computer for word processing by volunteering to work at it during free time.

_____ 5. The student will volunteer to tidy up the storage room.

_____ 6. After listening to several recordings, the student will identify the respective composers.

_____ 7. The student will translate a favorite Cambodian poem into English.

_____ 8. The student will accurately calculate the length of the hypotenuse.

_____ 9. The student will indicate an interest in the subject by voluntarily reading additional library books about earthquakes.

_____10. The student will write and perform a piano concerto.

Answer Key:

1. P   2. C   3. C   4. A   5. A   6. C   7. C   8. C   9. A   10. P

EXERCISE 4.12   PREPARING MY OWN INSTRUCTIONAL OBJECTIVES

INSTRUCTIONS: The purpose of this exercise is to begin writing your own behavioral objectives. For a subject and grade level of your choice, prepare 10 specific behavioral objectives. It is not necessary to include audience, conditions, and performance level unless requested by your course instructor. Exchange completed exercises with your classmates; discuss and make changes where necessary.

Subject: _____

Grade level: _____

1. Cognitive knowledge _____

   _____

   _____

   _____

   _____

   _____

   _____

2. Cognitive comprehension _____

   _____

   _____

   _____

   _____

   _____

   _____

3. Cognitive application _____

   _____

   _____

   _____

   _____

   _____

   _____

4. Cognitive analysis _____

   _____

   _____

   _____

   _____

   _____

☞

EXERCISE 4.5 *(continued)*

5. Cognitive synthesis _____

_____

_____

_____

_____

_____

_____

6. Cognitive evaluation _____

_____

_____

_____

_____

_____

_____

7. Psychomotor (low level) _____

_____

_____

_____

_____

_____

_____

8. Psychomotor (highest level) _____

_____

_____

_____

_____

_____

_____

9. Affective (low level) _____

_____

_____

_____

_____

_____

_____

10. Affective (high level) _____

_____

_____

_____

_____

_____

_____

5

Planning the Instruction

The teacher's edition of the student textbook and other resource materials may expedite your planning but should not substitute for it. You must understand how to create a good instructional plan. In this chapter you will learn how it is done.

Specifically, upon completion of this chapter you should be able to:

1. Complete a unit of instruction with sequential lesson plans.
2. Demonstrate understanding of the significance of the planned unit of instruction and the concept of planning curriculum and instruction as an organic process.
3. Distinguish between two types of instructional units—the standard unit and the integrated thematic unit.
4. Demonstrate understanding of the place and role of each of the four decision-making and thought-processing phases in unit planning and implementation.
5. Demonstrate understanding of self-reflection as a common thread important to the reciprocal process of teaching and learning.
6. Demonstrate an understanding of the differences between direct and indirect instruction and the advantages and limitations of each.
7. For a discipline and grade level, give examples of learning experiences from each of these categories, and when and why you would use each one: verbal, visual, vicarious, simulated, and direct; and examples of how, why, and when they could be combined.
8. Demonstrate your growing understanding of the meaning of *developmentally appropriate practice*.

9. Demonstrate growing awareness of various styles of teaching and learning and their implications for instructional design.
10. Demonstrate your growing understanding of the cyclical nature of instruction.
11. Demonstrate an understanding of the significance of the concepts of learning modalities and learning capacities and their implications for appropriate educational practice.

THE INSTRUCTIONAL UNIT

The instructional unit is a major subdivision of a course (for one course there are several to many units of instruction) and consists of learning activities that are planned around a central theme, topic, issue, or problem. Organizing the content of the semester or year into units makes the teaching process more manageable than when the teacher has no plan or makes only random choices.

The instructional unit is not unlike a chapter in a book, an act or scene in a play, or a phase of work when undertaking a project such as building a house. Breaking down information or actions into component parts and then grouping the related parts makes sense out of learning and doing. The unit brings a sense of cohesiveness and structure to student learning and avoids the piecemeal approach that might otherwise unfold. You can learn to articulate lessons within, between, and among unit plans and focus on important elements while not ignoring tangential information of importance. Students remember "chunks" of information, especially when those chunks are related to specific units.

Although the steps for developing any type of instructional unit are basically the same, units can be organized in a number of ways. We will consider two basic types of units—the standard unit and the integrated thematic unit (ITU).

A **standard unit** (known also as a **conventional** or **traditional unit**) consists of a series of lessons centered on a topic, theme, major concept, or block of subject matter. Each lesson builds on the previous lesson by contributing additional subject matter, providing further illustrations, and supplying more practice or other added instruction, all of which are aimed at bringing about mastery of the knowledge and skills on which the unit is centered.

When a standard unit is centered on a central theme, the unit may be referred to as a **thematic unit**. When, by design, the thematic unit integrates disciplines, such as combining the learning of science and mathematics, or combining social studies and English/language arts, or combining any number of disciplines, then it is called an **integrated (or interdisciplinary) thematic unit (ITU)**, or simply, an **integrated unit**.

Planning and Developing Any Unit of Instruction

Whether for a standard unit or an integrated thematic unit, steps in planning and developing the unit are the same and are described as follows.

1. *Select a suitable theme, topic, issue, or problem.* These may be already laid out in your course of study or textbook or already agreed to by members of the teaching team.
2. *Select the goals of the unit and prepare the overview.* The goals are written as an overview or rationale, covering what the unit is about and what the students are to learn. In planning the goals, you should (a) become as familiar as possible with the topic and materials used; (b) consult curriculum documents, as discussed in Chapter 4, for ideas; (c) decide the content and procedures (i.e., what the students should learn about the topic and how); (d) write the rationale or overview, where you summarize what you expect the students will learn about the topic; and (e) be sure your goals are congruent with the goals and standards of the course or grade-level program.
3. *Select instructional objectives.* In doing this, you should (a) include understandings, skills, attitudes, appreciations, and ideals; (b) be specific, avoiding vagueness and generalizations; (c) write the objectives in performance terms; and (d) be as certain as possible that the objectives will contribute to the major learning described in the overview.
4. *Detail the instructional procedures.* These procedures include the subject content and the learning activities, established as a series of lessons. Proceed with the following steps in your initial planning of the instructional procedures.
   a. By referring to curriculum documents, resource units, and colleagues as resources, gather ideas for learning activities that might be suitable for the unit.
   b. Check the learning activities to make sure they will actually contribute to the learning designated in your objectives, discarding ideas that do not.
   c. Make sure the learning activities are feasible. Can you afford the time, effort, or expense? Do you have the necessary materials and equipment? If not, can they be obtained? Are the activities suited to the intellectual and maturity levels of your students?
   d. Check resources available to be certain they support the content and learning activities.
   e. Decide how to introduce the unit. Provide **introductory activities** to arouse student interest; inform students of what the unit is about; help you learn about your students—their interests, their abilities, and their experiences and present knowledge of the topic; provide transitions that bridge this topic with that which students have already learned; and involve the students in the planning.
   f. Plan **developmental activities** that will sustain student interest, provide for individual student differences, promote the learning as cited in the specific objectives, and promote a project.
   g. Plan **culminating activities** that will summarize what has been learned, bring together loose ends, apply what has been learned to new situations, provide students with the opportunity to demonstrate their learning, and provide transfer to the unit that follows.
5. *Plan for preassessment and assessment of student learning.* Preassess what students already know or think they know. Assessment of student progress in achievement of the learning objectives should permeate the entire unit (i.e., as often as possible, assessment should be a daily component of lessons, that is, formative assessment, both formal and informal, is embedded in your teaching; assessment is the topic of Chapter 10). Plan to gather information in several ways, including informal observations, checklist observations of student performance and their portfolios, and paper-and-pencil tests. And remember that assessment must be congruent with the instructional objectives.
6. *Provide for the materials and tools needed to support the instruction.* The unit cannot function without materials. Therefore, you must plan long before the unit begins for media equipment and materials, references, reading materials, reproduced materials, and community resources. When given ample time to do so, librarians and media center personnel are usually more than willing to assist in finding appropriate materials to support your planned unit of instruction.

Unit Format, Inclusive Elements, and Time Duration

Follow the six preceding steps to develop any type of unit. In addition, two general points should be made. First, although there is no single best format for a teaching unit, there are minimum inclusions. Particular formats may be best for specific disciplines, topics, and types of activities. If you are in student teaching, your program for teacher preparation or your cooperating teacher(s) may provide the format you will be expected to follow. Regardless of the format, in any unit plan the following seven elements should be evident: (1) identification factors, including grade level, subject, topic, and time duration of the unit; (2) statement of rationale and general goals for the unit; (3) objectives of the unit; (4) materials and resources needed; (5) lesson plans; (6) assessment strategies; and (7) identification of how the unit will attend to student differences, such as variations in students' reading levels, experiential backgrounds, and special needs. For a

sample Standard Lesson Plan Assessment Rubric, see Figure 5.1.

Second, there is no set time duration for a unit plan, although, for specific units, curriculum guides will recommend certain time spans. Units may extend for a minimum of several days or, as in the case of some interdisciplinary thematic units, for several weeks, an entire semester, or even longer. However, be aware when standard units last more than 2 or 3 weeks, they tend to lose the character of clearly identifiable units. Sometimes, in the case of extended duration, units may even overlap. For any unit of instruction, the exact time duration will be dictated by several factors, including the topic, problem or theme, the interests and maturity of the students, intensity of the study, and the scope of the learning activities.

Figure 5.1 Standard unit plan assessment rubric.

For _____		Total Score _____ (possible 100)	
Points (number of points given to be written in appropriate box)	**10**	**7–9**	**0–6**
1. **Descriptive data** (grade level, subject, English proficiency and other student characteristics accounted for; time duration accounted for) Comment:	clear	acceptable	incomplete/absent
2. **Topic or theme Unit goals/rationale** Comment:	clear/appropriate well summarized	acceptable acceptable	ambiguous rambling/too brief
3. **Instructional (overt) objectives** (for ITU: all disciplines accounted for?) Comment:	good coverage well stated yes	acceptable activities/ objectives are partially mixed	incomplete/not overt no
4. **Lesson plans**: Comment	effective, well-planned and sequenced; format complete	acceptable partially	incomplete quite incomplete
5. **Ten lesson plans** (minimum) Comment:	well planned and complete	incomplete	none
6. **Learning activities** Comment:	excellent variety and developmentally appropriate; includes multicultural components	acceptable	incomplete not developmentally appropriate
7. **Materials** Comment:	complete listing; good variety	acceptable	incomplete
8. **Introductory activities** (for unit and each lesson) Comment:	well conceived	acceptable	inappropriate

(continued)

Figure 5.1   *(continued)*

9. **Culminating activity to unit** Comment:	well planned; ties it all together nicely	acceptable	inappropriate or absent
10. **Assessment procedures** Comment:	good variety; well planned; includes preassessment, formative and summative; matches the objectives	acceptable	inappropriate/ incomplete

THEORETICAL CONSIDERATIONS FOR THE SELECTION OF INSTRUCTIONAL STRATEGIES

As you prepare to detail your instructional plan, you will be narrowing in on selecting and planning the instructional activities. In Chapter 2, you learned about specific teacher behaviors that must be in place for students to learn. In the paragraphs that follow, you will learn more not only about how to implement some of those fundamental behaviors but also about the large repertoire of other strategies (see Figure 5.2), aids, media, and resources available to you. You will learn about how to select and implement from this repertoire.

Decision Making and Strategy Selection

You must make a myriad of decisions to select and effectively implement a particular teaching strategy. The selection of a strategy depends partially upon your decision whether to deliver information directly (direct, expository, or didactic instruction) or to provide students with access to information (indirect or facilitative instruction). Direct instruction tends to be teacher centered, whereas indirect instruction is more student centered. To assist in your selection of strategies it is important that you understand the terms and basic principles of learning summarized as follows.

Direct and Indirect Instruction: A Clarification of Terms

You are probably well aware that professional education is rampant with its own special jargon, which can be confusing to the neophyte. The use of the term **direct instruction** (or its synonym, **direct teaching**), and its antonym, **direct experience**, are examples of how confusing the jargon can be. The term *direct instruction* (or *direct teaching*, **expository teaching**, or **teacher-centered instruction**) can also have a variety of definitions, depending on who is doing the defining. For now, you should keep this distinction in mind—do not confuse the term *direct instruction* with the term *direct experience*. The two terms indicate two separate (though not incompatible) instructional modes. The dichotomy of pedagogical opposites shown in Figure 5.3 provides a useful visual distinction of the opposites. The terms in one column are similar if not synonymous, whereas they are near or exact opposites of those in the other column.

Figure 5.2   A list of instructional strategies.

Autotutorial	Guest presenter	Project
Brainstorming	Homework	Questioning
Coaching	Individualized instruction	Reading partner
Collaborative learning	Inquiry	Review and practice
Cooperative learning	Interactive media	Role-play
Debate	Instructional module	Investigation
Demonstration	Journal writing	Script writing
Diorama	Laboratory investigation	Silent reading
Discovery	Learning center	Simulation
Drama	Lecture	Study guide
Drill	Library/resource center	Symposium
Dyad learning	Metacognition	Telecommunications
Field trip	Mock-up	Term paper
Film	Multimedia	Textbook
Game	Panel discussion	Tutorial

Delivery mode of instruction	versus	Access mode of instruction
Didactic instruction	versus	Facilitative teaching
Direct instruction	versus	Indirect instruction
Direct teaching	versus	Direct experiencing
Expository teaching	versus	Discovery learning
Teacher-centered instruction	versus	Student-centered instruction

Figure 5.3 Pedagogical opposites.

DEGREES OF DIRECTNESS

Rather than thinking and behaving in terms of opposites as may be suggested by Figure 5.3, more likely your teaching will be distinguished by "degrees of directness," or "degrees of indirectness." For a unit of instruction, directions for a culminating project may be given by the teacher in a direct or expository minilecture, followed then by a student-designed inquiry that leads to the final project.

Rather than focus your attention on the selection of a particular model of teaching, I emphasize the importance of an eclectic model—selecting the best from various models or approaches. There will be times when you want to use a direct, teacher-centered approach, perhaps by a minilecture or a demonstration. And then there will be times when you will want to use an indirect, student-centered or social-interactive approach, such as the use of cooperative learning and investigative projects. And perhaps there will be times when you will be doing both at the same time, such as working with a teacher-centered approach with one small group of students, giving them direct instruction, while another group or several groups of students in areas of the classroom are working on their project studies (a student-centered approach). The information that follows and specific descriptions in Chapters 7, 8, and 9 will help you make decisions about when each approach is most appropriate and provide guidelines for their use.

Principles of Classroom Instruction and Learning: A Synopsis

A student does not learn to write by learning to recognize grammatical constructions of sentences. Neither does a person learn to play soccer solely by listening to a lecture about soccer. Learning is superficial unless the instructional methods and learning activities are developmentally and intellectually appropriate—that is, are (a) developmentally appropriate for the learners and (b) intellectually appropriate for the understanding, skills, and attitudes desired. Memorizing, for instance, is not the same as understanding. Yet far too often, memorization seems all that is expected of students in too many classrooms. The result is low-level learning, a mere verbalism or mouthing of poorly understood words and sentences. The orchestration of short-term memory exercises is not intellectually appropriate, and it is not teaching. A mental model of learning that assumes a brain is capable of doing only one thing at a time is invidiously incorrect (Jensen, 1998; Baker & Martin, 1998).

When selecting the mode of instruction, you should bear in mind fundamental principles of classroom instruction and learning, as shown in Figure 5.4.

Conceptual and Procedural Knowledge

Conceptual knowledge (also called **declarative knowledge**) refers to the understanding of relationships and abstractions, whereas **procedural knowledge** entails the recording in memory of the meanings of symbols and rules and procedures needed in order to accomplish tasks. (Motor skills, habits, and perceptual skills are examples of procedural knowledge.) Unless it is connected in meaningful ways for the formation of conceptual knowledge, the accumulation of memorized, procedural knowledge is fragmented and ill fated and will be maintained in the brain for only a brief time.

Figure 5.4 Fundamental principles of instruction and learning.

- Although students differ in their styles of learning and in their learning capacities, each can learn.
- Learning is most meaningful and longest lasting when it is connected to real-life experiences.
- No matter the grade level or what else you are prepared to teach, you are primarily a teacher of literacy and of thinking, social, and learning skills.
- Physical activity enhances learning. For elementary and middle school teaching, it is advisable that every lesson includes, to some degree, an activity involving the kinesthetic learning modality.
- Students must be actively involved in their own learning and in the assessment of their learning.
- Students need constant, understandable, positive, and reliable feedback about their learning.
- Students should be engaged in both independent study and cooperative learning and give and receive tutorial instruction.
- To a great degree, it is the mode of instruction that determines what is learned and how well it is learned.
- The teacher must hold high expectations for the learning of each student (but not necessarily identical expectations for every student) and not waiver from those expectations.

To help students establish conceptual knowledge, the learning for them must be meaningful. To help make learning meaningful for your students, you should use direct and real experiences as often as practical and possible. Vicarious experiences are sometimes necessary to provide students with otherwise unattainable knowledge; however, direct experiences that engage all the student's senses and all learning modalities are more powerful. Students learn to write by writing and by receiving coaching and feedback about their progress in writing. They learn to play soccer by playing soccer and by receiving coaching and feedback about their developing skills and knowledge in playing the game. They learn these things best when they are actively (hands-on) and mentally (minds-on) engaged in doing them. This is real learning, learning that is meaningful; it is **authentic learning**.

Direct Versus Indirect Instructional Modes: Strengths and Weaknesses of Each

When selecting an instructional strategy, there are two distinct choices (modes) from which you must make a decision: should you deliver information to students directly or should you provide students with access to information? (Refer to Figure 5.3.)

The **delivery mode** (known also as the **didactic, expository, or traditional style**) is to deliver information. Knowledge is passed on from those who know (the teachers, with the aid of textbooks) to those who do not (the students). Within the delivery mode, traditional and time-honored strategies are textbook reading, the lecture (formal teacher talk), questioning, and teacher-centered or teacher-planned discussions.

With the **access mode**, instead of direct delivery of information and direct control over what is learned, you provide students with access to information by working *with* the students. In collaboration with the students, experiences are designed that facilitate the building of their existing schemata and their obtaining new knowledge and skills. Within the access mode, important in-

structional strategies include cooperative learning, inquiry, and investigative, student-centered project learning, each of which most certainly will use questioning (although the questions more frequently will come from the students than from you or the textbook or some other source extrinsic to the student). Discussions and lectures on particular topics also may be involved. But when used in the access mode, discussions and lectures occur during or after (rather than precede) direct, hands-on learning by the students. In other words, rather than preceding student inquiry, discussions and lectures *result from* student inquiry, and then may be followed by further student investigation.

You are probably more experienced with the delivery mode. To be most effective as a classroom teacher, however, you must become knowledgeable and skillful in using access strategies. You should appropriately select and effectively use strategies from both modes, but with a strong favor toward access strategies. Strategies within the access mode clearly facilitate students' positive learning and acquisition of conceptual knowledge and help build their self-esteem, as well as contribute to positive social relationships. Thus, from your study of Chapters 7, 8, and Chapter 9, you will become knowledgeable about specific techniques so you can make intelligent decisions for choosing the best strategy for particular goals and objectives for your own discipline and the interests, needs, and maturity level of your own unique group of students.

Figures 5.5 and 5.6 provide an overview of the specific strengths and weaknesses of each mode. By comparing those figures, you can see that the strengths and weaknesses of one mode are nearly mirror opposites of the other. As noted earlier, although as a teacher you should be skillful in the use of strategies from both modes, for the most developmentally appropriate teaching you should concentrate more on using strategies from the access mode. Strategies within that mode are more student centered, hands-on, and concrete; students interact with one another and are actually or closer to doing what they are learning to do—that is, the learning is likely more authentic. Learning that occurs from the use of that mode is longer lasting (fixes into long-term memory). And, as the students interact with one another and with their learning, they develop a sense of "can do," which enhances their self-esteem.

SELECTING LEARNING ACTIVITIES THAT ARE DEVELOPMENTALLY APPROPRIATE

Returning to the soccer example, can you imagine a soccer coach teaching students the skills and knowledge needed to play soccer without ever letting them physically experience playing the game? Can you imagine a science teacher instructing students on how to read a thermometer without ever letting them actually read a real thermometer? Can you imagine a piano teacher teaching a student to play piano without ever

Figure 5.5 Delivery mode: Its strengths and weaknesses.

Delivery Mode

Strengths
- Much content can be covered within a short span of time, usually by formal teacher talk, which then may be followed by an experiential activity.
- The teacher is in control of what content is covered.
- The teacher is in control of time allotted to specific content coverage.
- Strategies within the delivery mode are consistent with competency-based instruction.
- Student achievement of specific content is predictable and manageable.

Potential Weaknesses
- The sources of student motivation are mostly extrinsic.
- Students have little control over the pacing of their learning.
- Students make few important decisions about their learning.
- There may be little opportunity for divergent or creative thinking.
- Student self-esteem may be inadequately served.

Figure 5.6 Access mode: Its strengths and weaknesses.

Access Mode

Strengths
- Students learn content in more depth.
- The sources of student motivation are more likely intrinsic.
- Students make important decisions about their own learning.
- Students have more control over the pacing of their learning.
- Students develop a sense of personal self-worth.

Potential Weaknesses
- Breadth of content coverage may be more limited.
- Strategies are time-consuming.
- The teacher has less control over content and time.
- The specific results of student learning are less predictable.
- The teacher may have less control over class procedures.

allowing the student to touch a real keyboard? Can you imagine a geography teacher teaching children how to find Afghanistan on a map without ever letting them put their eyes and hands on a real map? Unfortunately, still today, too many teachers do almost those exact things—they try to teach students to do something without letting the students actually practice doing it. Granted, for various legitimate reasons that we will get to later, sometimes a teacher must settle for a virtual reality activity rather than the real thing.

In planning and selecting developmentally appropriate learning activities, an important rule to remember is to select activities that are as close to the real thing as possible. That is learning through direct experiencing. When students are involved in direct experiences, they are using more of their sensory input channels, their learning modalities (i.e., auditory, visual, tactile, kinesthetic). And when all the senses are engaged, learning is more integrated and is most effective, meaningful, and longest lasting. This "learning by doing" is authentic learning—or hands-on/minds-on learning.

STYLES OF LEARNING AND IMPLICATIONS FOR TEACHING

Teachers who are most effective are those who adapt their teaching styles and methods to their students, using approaches that interest the students, that are neither too easy nor too difficult, that match the students' learning styles and learning capacities, and are relevant to the students' lives. This adaptation process is further complicated because each student is different from every other one. All do not have the same interests, abilities, backgrounds, or learning styles and capacities. As a matter of fact, not only do students differ from one another, but also each student's learning style can change to some extent from one day to the next (Harrison, Andrews, & Saklofske, 2003). What appeals to a student today may not have the same appeal tomorrow. Therefore, you need to consider both the nature of youth in general and each student in particular.

Learning Modalities

Learning modality refers to the **sensory portal** (or input channel) by which a student prefers to receive sensory reception (modality preference) or the actual way a student learns best (modality adeptness). Some students prefer learning by seeing, a **visual modality;** others prefer learning through instruction from others (through talk), an **auditory modality;** whereas many others prefer learning by doing and being physically involved, the **kinesthetic modality**, and by touching objects, the **tactile modality**. A student's modality preference is not always that student's modality strength.

Although primary modality strength can be determined by observing students, it can also be mixed and

At any age young people differ in many ways: Physical characteristics, interests, home life, intellectual ability, learning capacities, motor ability, social skills, aptitudes and talents, language skills, experience, ideals, attitudes, needs, ambitions, hopes, and dreams.

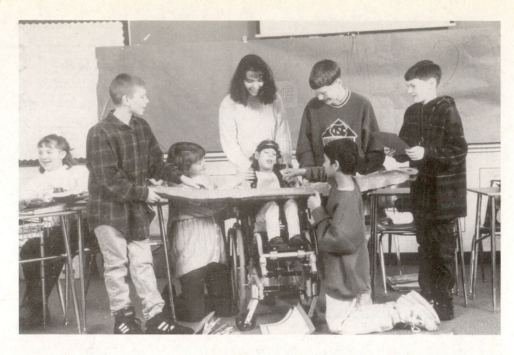

can change as the result of experience and intellectual maturity. As one might suspect, modality integration (i.e., engaging more of the sensory input channels, using several modalities at once or staggered) has been found to contribute to better achievement in student learning.

Because many students have neither a preference nor strength for auditory reception, teachers should severely limit their use of the lecture method of instruction, that is, of too much reliance on formal teacher talk. Furthermore, instructions using a singular approach, such as auditory (e.g., talking to the students), cheats students who learn better another way. This difference can affect student achievement. A teacher who only talks to the students or uses discussions day after day is shortchanging the education of learners who learn better another way, who are, for example, kinesthetic and visual learners.

As a general rule, many students prefer and learn best by touching objects, by feeling shapes and textures, by interacting with each other, and by moving things around. In contrast, learning by sitting and listening is difficult for many of them.

Some learning style traits significantly discriminate between students who are at risk of not finishing school and students who perform well. Students who are underachieving and at risk need (a) frequent opportunities for mobility; (b) options and choices; (c) a variety of instructional resources, environments, and sociological groupings, rather than routines and patterns; (d) to learn during late morning, afternoon, or evening hours, rather than in the early morning; (e) informal seating, rather than wooden, steel, or plastic chairs; (f) low illumination, because bright light contributes to hyperactivity; and (g) tactile/visual introductory resources

reinforced by kinesthetic (i.e., direct experiencing and whole-body activities)/visual resources, or introductory kinesthetic/visual resources reinforced by tactile/visual resources (Brand, Dunn, & Greb, 2002; Dunn, 1995; Rayneri, Gerber, & Wiley, 2003).

Regardless of the subjects you teach and regardless the grade level, an effective approach is to use strategies that integrate the modalities. When well designed, thematic units and project-based learning incorporate modality integration. *When teaching any group of students of mixed learning abilities, modality strengths, language proficiency, and cultural backgrounds, integrating learning modalities is a must for the most successful teaching.*

Learning Styles

Related to learning modality is **learning style**, which can be defined as independent forms of knowing and processing information. Learning style differences are also sometimes referred to as **learning style preferences** or **cognitive styles** (Parkay, Hass, & Anctil, 2010). Although some students may be comfortable with beginning their learning of a new idea in the abstract (e.g., visual or verbal symbolization), most need to begin with the concrete (e.g., learning by actually doing it). Many students prosper while working in groups, whereas others prefer working alone. Some are quick in their studies, whereas others are slow, methodical, cautious, and meticulous. Some can sustain attention on a single topic for a long time, becoming more absorbed in their study as time passes. Others are slower starters and more casual in their pursuits but are capable of shifting with ease from subject to subject. Some can study in the midst of music, noise, or movement, whereas others need quiet, solitude, and a desk or table. *The point is this: People vary in not only their skills and preferences in the way knowledge is received but also in how they mentally process information once it has been received.* This latter is a person's *style of learning.*

It is important to note learning style is *not* an indicator of intelligence, but rather an indicator of how a person learns. Although there are probably as many types of learning styles as there are individuals, David Kolb (1984) described two major differences in how people learn: how they perceive situations and how they process information. On the basis of perceiving and processing and earlier work by Carl Jung (1923) on psychological types, Bernice McCarthy (1997) described four major learning styles, presented in the following paragraphs.

The **imaginative learner** perceives information concretely and processes it reflectively. Imaginative learners learn well by listening and sharing with others, integrating the ideas of others with their own experiences. Imaginative learners often have difficulty adjusting to traditional teaching, which depends less on classroom interactions and students' sharing and connecting of their prior experiences. In a traditional classroom, the imaginative learner is likely an at-risk student.

The **analytic learner** perceives information abstractly and processes it reflectively. The analytic learner prefers sequential thinking, needs details, and values what experts have to offer. Analytic learners do well in traditional classrooms.

The **common sense learner** perceives information abstractly and processes it actively. The common sense learner is pragmatic and enjoys hands-on learning. Common sense learners sometimes find school frustrating unless they can see immediate use to what is being learned. In the traditional classroom the common sense learner is likely a learner who is at risk of not completing school, of dropping out.

The **dynamic learner** perceives information concretely and processes it actively. The dynamic learner also prefers hands-on learning and is excited by anything new. Dynamic learners are risk takers and are frustrated by learning if they see it as being tedious and sequential. In a traditional classroom the dynamic learner is likely an at-risk student.

Although the concept of learning styles and its usefulness to educators has in recent years been somewhat ignored and even challenged (Rayner, 2007; Good & Brophy, 2008), I, the author of this resource guide, continue my belief in the significance and importance of the concept of learning styles, perhaps more than ever because of inclusion and the diversity of learners in classrooms today. That said, I believe that what is most important for you to know is that (1) there are probably as many types of learning styles as there are individuals, that (2) not all students learn best in the same way, which means that (3) in order to reach more of the students more of the time, your instructional approaches must be varied.

The Three-Phase Learning Cycle

To understand conceptual development and change; researchers in the 1960s developed a Piaget-based theory of learning where students are guided from concrete, hands-on learning experiences to the abstract formulations of concepts and their formal applications. This theory became known as the **three-phase learning cycle** (Karplus, 1974). Long a popular strategy for teaching science, the learning cycle is showing to be useful in other disciplines as well (Barojas & Dehesa, 2001; Bevevino, Dengel, & Adams, 1999; Sowell, 1993). The three phases are (1) the **exploratory hands-on phase**, where students can explore ideas and experience assimilation and disequilibrium that lead to their own questions and tentative answers, (2) the **invention** or **concept development phase**, where, under the guidance of the teacher, students invent concepts and principles that help them answer their questions and reorganize their ideas (i.e., the students revise their thinking to allow the new information to fit), and (3) the **expansion or concept application phase**, another hands-on phase in which students try out their new ideas by applying them to situations that are relevant and meaningful to them. [Note: The three phases of the learning cycle are comparable to the three levels of thinking, described variously by others. For example, in Eisner (1979) the levels are referred to as "descriptive," "interpretive," and "evaluative."] During application of a concept, the learner may discover new information that causes a change in the learner's understanding of the concept being applied. *Thus, the process of learning is cyclical.*

VARIATIONS ON THE THEME
Interpretations or modifications of the three-phase cycle include McCarthy's 4MAT (McCarthy, 1997). With the 4MAT system, although no effort is made to label individual students according to learning style, teachers employ a learning cycle of instructional strategies to try and reach each student's learning style. The cycle takes the learners from feeling to reflecting to thinking and, finally, to acting. In this process they are likely using all four learning modalities.

The **constructivist learning theory** suggests learning is a process involving the active engagement of learners who adapt the educative event to fit and expand their individual world view (as opposed to the behaviorist pedagogical assumption that learning is something done to learners) and to accentuate the importance of student self-assessment (DeLay, 1996). In support of that theory, some variations of the learning cycle include a separate phase of assessment. *However, because I, the author of this resource guide, believe assessment of what students know or think they know should be a continual process, permeating all three phases of the learning cycle. I reject any treatment of assessment as a self-standing phase.*

Learning Capacities: The Theory of Multiple Intelligences

In contrast to learning styles, Gardner (1996) introduced what he calls learning capacities exhibited by individuals in differing ways. Originally and sometimes still referred to as multiple intelligences, or ways of knowing, capacities thus far identified are:

- *Bodily/kinesthetic:* ability to use the body skillfully and to handle objects skillfully
- *Existentialist:* ability to understand and pursue the ultimate philosophical questions, meanings, and mysteries of life
- *Interpersonal:* ability to understand people and relationships
- *Intrapersonal:* ability to assess one's emotional life as a means to understand oneself and others
- *Logical/mathematical:* ability to handle chains of reasoning and recognize patterns and orders
- *Musical/rhythmic:* sensitivity to pitch, melody, rhythm, and tone
- *Naturalist:* ability to draw on materials and features of the natural environment to solve problems or fashion products
- *Verbal/linguistic:* sensitivity to the meaning and order of words
- *Visual/spatial:* ability to perceive the world accurately and to manipulate the nature of space, such as through architecture, mime, or sculpture

Many educators believe that many of the students who are at risk of not completing school may be dominant in a cognitive learning style that is not in synch with traditional teaching methods. I wonder if that thought is or has been considered by users and supporters of various models of response to intervention (RtI) so popular now in elementary schools and some middle-level schools. It may be too early to tell. Although popular, educators are still learning about it, how it can improve teaching and learning, and what needs to be done to implement it effectively (Berkeley, Bender, Peaster, & Saunders, 2009; Canter, Klotz, & Cowan, 2008; Clark, 2009; Elliott, 2008a, 2008b; Fuchs & Deshler, 2007; Samuels, 2008; Sprick, 2009; Vaughn et al., 2008). It should be noted, however, that the essence of RtI, that is *the practice of providing high-quality instruction and intervention matched to student need, monitoring individual student progress frequently to make decisions about changes in instruction or goals, and applying student response data to important*

education decisions (Elliott, 2008b) is not entirely new. For example, several school districts in Minnesota are reported to have been using its major components for a couple of decades (Gibbons, 2008), and, as stated by Lauer (2008), "RtI is a natural evolution of what good middle level schools have focused on for years—creating responsive school systems that meet diverse learner needs in both the academic and affective realm." We return to the topic of RtI later in this chapter.

Traditional methods of instruction are largely of McCarthy's analytic style: information is presented in a logical, linear, and sequential fashion. Traditional methods also reflect three of the Gardner types: verbal/linguistic, logical/mathematical, and intrapersonal. Consequently, to better synchronize methods of instruction with learning styles, some teachers and schools have restructured the curriculum and instruction around Gardner's learning capacities (Campbell & Campbell, 1999; Delaney & Shafer, 2007) or around Sternberg's Triarchic Theory (English, 1998; Sternberg, 1998). Sternberg identified seven metaphors for the mind and intelligence (geographic, computational, biological, epistemological, anthropological, sociological, and systems) and proposed a theory of intelligence consisting of three elements: analytical, practical, and creative (Sternberg, Grigorenko, & Jarvin, 2001).

From the preceding information about learning, you must realize at least three important facts:

1. *Intelligence is not a fixed or static reality, but can be learned, taught, and developed.* This concept is important for students to understand, too. When students understand intelligence is incremental, that it is developed through use over time, they tend to be more motivated to work at learning than when they believe intelligence is a fixed entity (Brandt, 2000).
2. *Not all students learn and respond to learning situations in the same way.* A student may learn differently according to the situation or according to the student's ethnicity, cultural background, or socioeconomic status. A teacher who, for all students, uses only one style of teaching, or who teaches to only one or a few styles of learning, day after day is short-changing those students who learn better another way.
3. *Every student in your classroom has the potential for giftedness.* This fact has been proven time and again; don't forget it!

Regard each one of your students as a true genius—each in his or her own way—and create a classroom environment where that genius can be identified, nurtured, and made available to others.

Thomas Armstrong (1998, p. 69)

CLASSROOM VIGNETTE

Using the Theory of Learning Capacities (Multiple Intelligences) and Multilevel Instruction

In a fifth-grade classroom, during one week of a 6-week thematic unit on weather, students were concentrating on learning about the water cycle. For this study of the water cycle, with the students' help, the teacher divided the class into several groups of three to five students per group. While working on six projects simultaneously to learn about the water cycle: (1) one group of students designed, conducted, and repeated an experiment to discover the number of drops of water that can be held on one side of a new one-cent coin versus the number that can be held on the side of a worn one-cent coin; (2) working in part with the first group, a second group designed and prepared graphs to illustrate the results of the experiments of the first group; (3) a third group of students created and composed the words and music of a song about the water cycle; (4) a fourth group incorporated their combined interests in mathematics and art to design, collect the necessary materials, and create a colorful and interactive bulletin board about the water cycle; (5) a fifth group read about the water cycle in materials they researched from the Internet and various libraries; and (6) a sixth group created a puppet show about the water cycle. On Friday, after each group had finished, the groups shared their projects with the whole class.

Teaching in Practice

Joan Makes Significant Changes in Her Classroom Atmosphere

Joan is a fifth-grade teacher of a self-contained classroom. Her classroom consists of one wall in particular that is mostly windows. Until recently she kept the window curtains closed to keep students from being distracted by the outdoors. She heard teachers talking of reports of preliminary studies indicating that children learn mathematics in particular better with a background of soft classical music, and in natural lighting rather than in artificial lighting, so now she plays a background of soft classical music when children are learning mathematics, and keeps the curtains open and the ceiling lights turned off as often as possible. She also heard that some children learn certain subjects better at particular times of the day, so now rather than teaching each subject at the same time every day, she has established a new weekly schedule that varies the schedule from day to day. Although it is too early to say that student learning in any subject has significantly improved as a result of these changes, Joan has noticed a marked improvement in student behavior and motivation for learning.

Questions for Class Discussion

1. What were your thoughts upon reading about Joan and her teaching?
2. Can you find research evidence relevant to any of the changes made by Joan?
3. Have you ever heard of the Hawthorne effect? Do you suppose it might be a factor explaining the changes in student behavior noticed by Joan?
4. Has this vignette given you any ideas for use in your own teaching?

THE LEARNING EXPERIENCES LADDER

The Learning Experiences Ladder (Figure 5.7) is a visual depiction of a range of kinds of learning experiences from which a teacher may select. Hands-on/minds-on learning is at the bottom of the ladder. At the top are abstract experiences, where the learner is exposed only to symbolization (i.e., letters and numbers) and uses only one or two senses (auditory or visual). The teacher lectures while the students sit and watch and hear. Visual and verbal symbolic experiences, although impossible to avoid when teaching, are less effective in ensuring that planned and meaningful learning occurs. This is especially so with learners who have special needs, learners with ethnic and cultural differences, and English language learning (ELL) students. Thus, when planning learning experiences and selecting instructional materials, you are advised to select activities that engage the students in the most direct experiences possible and that are developmentally and intellectually appropriate for your specific group of students.

As can be inferred from the Learning Experiences Ladder, when teaching about tide pools (the first example for each step), the most effective mode is to take the students to a tide pool (direct experience), where students can see, hear, touch, smell, and perhaps even taste (if not polluted with toxins) the tide pool. The least effective mode is for the teacher to merely talk about the tide pool (verbal experience, the most abstract and symbolic experience), engaging only one sense—auditory.

Of course, for various reasons—such as time, matters of safety, lack of resources, or geographic location of your school—you may not be able to take your students to a tide pool. You cannot always use the most direct experience, so sometimes you must select an experience higher on the ladder. Self-discovery teaching is not always appropriate. Sometimes it is more appropriate to build upon what others have discovered and learned. Although learners do not need to "reinvent the wheel," the most effective and longest lasting learning is that which engages most or all of their senses. On the Learning Experiences Ladder, those are the experiences that fall within the bottom three categories—direct, simulated, and vicarious.

Figure 5.7   The Learning Experiences Ladder. (*Sources:* Earlier versions of this concept were Charles F. Hoban, Sr., et al., *Visualizing the Curriculum* [New York: Dryden, 1937], p. 39; Jerome S. Bruner, *Toward a Theory of Instruction* [Cambridge, MA: Harvard University Press, 1966], p. 49; Edgar Dale, *Audio-Visual Methods in Teaching* [New York: Holt, Rinehart & Winston, 1969], p. 108; and Eugene C. Kim and Richard D. Kellough, *A Resource Guide for Secondary School Teaching*, 2nd. ed. [Englewood Cliffs, NJ: Merrill/Prentice Hall, 1978], p. 136.)

A B S T R A C T

Verbal Experiences
Teacher talk, written words; engaging only one sense; using the most abstract symbolization; students physically inactive. *Examples:* (1) Listening to the teacher talk about tide pools. (2) Listening to a student report about the Grand Canyon. (3) Listening to a guest speaker talk about how the state legislature functions.

Visual Experiences
Still pictures, diagrams, charts; engaging only one sense; typically symbolic; students physically inactive. *Examples:* (1) Viewing slide photographs of tide pools. (2) Viewing drawings and photographs of the Grand Canyon. (3) Listening to a guest speaker talk about the state legislature and show slides of it in action.

Vicarious Experiences
Laser videodisc programs, computer programs, video programs; engaging more than one sense; learner indirectly "doing"; may be some limited physical activity. *Examples:* (1) Interacting with a computer program about wave action and life in tide pools. (2) Viewing and listening to a video program about the Grand Canyon. (3) Taking a field trip to observe the state legislature in action.

Simulated Experiences
Role-playing, experimenting, simulations, mock-up, working models; all or nearly all senses engaged; activity often integrating disciplines; closest to the real thing. *Examples:* (1) Building a classroom working model of a tide pool. (2) Building a classroom working model of the Grand Canyon. (3) Designing a classroom role-play simulation patterned after the operating procedure of the state legislature.

Direct Experiences
Learner actually doing what is being learned, true inquiry; all senses engaged; usually integrates disciplines; the real thing. *Examples:* (1) Visiting and experiencing a tide pool. (2) Visiting and experiencing the Grand Canyon. (3) Designing an elected representative body to oversee the operation of the school-within-the-school program and patterned after the state legislative assembly.

C O N C R E T E

Learning that is hands on and minds on is longer lasting because it engages more of the sensory input modalities.

Direct, Simulated, and Vicarious Experiences Help Connect Student Learning

Another value of direct, simulated, and vicarious experiences is that they tend to be interdisciplinary; that is, they blur or bridge subject-content boundaries. That makes those experiences especially useful for teachers who want to help students connect the learning of one discipline with that of others and to bridge what is being learned with their own life experiences. Direct, simulated, and vicarious experiences are more like real life. That means the learning resulting from those experiences is authentic.

Growing in popularity as educational tools, because of a variety of reasons, not the least of which is relative low cost, a rapidly increasing availability, and students' prior experiences with videogames, is the use of **multi-user virtual environments (MUVEs)**. Simulating real-world problems and realities, one program titled Virtual Enterprises International is designed to help students with their development of valuable job-readiness skills as well as academic skills by their establishing and running virtual businesses (Hughes & Golann, 2008); another titled The West Point Bridge Design (WPBD) engages science students in project-based learning (Bisogno & JeanPierre, 2008). It is your challenge to stay abreast of the development of and procedures for using MUVEs as they become available in your teaching field.

The most effective and longest-lasting learning is that which engages most or all of the learner's senses. This is true with adult learners, primary grade children, and students of any age group in between.

PLANNING AND DEVELOPING AN INTERDISCIPLINARY THEMATIC UNIT

The steps outlined earlier in this chapter are essential for planning any type of teaching unit, including the interdisciplinary thematic unit (ITU), which may consist of smaller subject-specific conventional units developed according to the immediately foregoing guidelines.

The primary responsibility for the development of ITUs can depend on a single teacher or upon the cooperation of several teachers who represent several disciplines. A teaching team may develop from one to several interdisciplinary thematic units a year. Over time, then, a team will have several units that are available for implementation. However, the most effective units are often those that are the most current or the most meaningful to students. This means that ever-changing global, national, and local topics provide a veritable smorgasbord from which to choose, and teaching teams must constantly update old units and develop new and exciting ones.

A caution is to see that one teaching team's unit does not conflict with others at the same or another grade level. If a school has two or more teams at the same grade level that involve the same disciplines, the teams may want to develop units on different themes and share their products. For example, a seventh-grade team must guard against developing a unit quite similar to one that the students had or will have at another grade level. Clear and open communication within, between, and among teams and schools within a school district are critical to the success of interdisciplinary thematic teaching.

Specific Guidelines for Developing an Interdisciplinary Thematic Unit

Specific guidelines for developing an ITU are presented in the following paragraphs.

Agree on the nature or source of the unit. Team members should view the interdisciplinary approach as a collaborative effort in which all members can participate if appropriate. Write what you want the students to receive from interdisciplinary instruction. Troubleshoot potential stumbling blocks.

Discuss subject-specific standards, goals and objectives, curriculum guidelines, textbooks and supplemental materials, and units already in place for the school year. Focus on what you are obligated or mandated to teach, and explain the scope and sequence of the teaching so all team members understand the constraints and limitations.

Choose a theme topic and develop a time line. From the information provided by each subject-specialist teacher in step 2, start listing possible theme topics that can be drawn from within the existing course outlines. Give-and-take is essential here, as some topics will fit certain subjects better than others. The chief goal is to find a topic that can be adapted to each subject without detracting from the educational plan already in place. This may require choosing and merging content from two or more other units previously planned. The theme is then drawn from the topic.

Sometimes themes are selected by the teacher or by a teaching team before meeting the students for the first time. Other times teachers in collaboration with students select them. Even when the theme is preselected, with guidance from the teacher, students still should be given major responsibility for deciding the final theme title (name), topics within the theme, and corresponding learning activities. Integrated thematic instruction works best when students have ownership in the study, that is, when they have been empowered with major decision-making responsibility.

The basis for theme selection should satisfy two criteria: The theme should (a) fit within the expected scope and sequence of mandated content and (b) be of interest to the students. Regarding the first criterion, many teachers have said that when they and their students embarked on an interdisciplinary thematic study, they did so without truly knowing where the study would go or what the learning outcomes would be—and they were somewhat frightened by that realization. But when the unit was completed, their students had learned everything (or nearly everything) that the teacher would have expected them to learn were the teacher to use a more traditional approach. And, it was more fun because the students were more intrinsically motivated! See Figure 5.8 for important questions to ask when selecting a theme.

Figure 5.8 Questions to ask when selecting a theme.

- Is the theme within the realm of understanding and experience of the teachers involved?
- Will the theme interest all members of the teaching team?
- Do we have sufficient materials and resources to supply information we might need?
- Does the theme lend itself to active learning experiences?
- Can this theme lead to a unit of the proper duration, that is, not too short and not too long?
- Is the theme helpful, worthwhile, and pertinent to the instructional objectives?
- Will the theme be of interest to students, and will it motivate them to do their best?
- Is the theme one with which teachers are not already so familiar that they cannot share in the excitement of the learning?
- Will this theme be of interest to students, and will it motivate them to do their best?

The second criterion is easy to satisfy, as it will most assuredly be when students are truly empowered with decision-making responsibility for what they learn and how they learn it. Once a general theme is selected (one that satisfies the first criterion), its final title, subtopics, and corresponding procedural activities should be finalized in collaboration with the students.

Establish two time lines. The first is for the team only and is to ensure that each member meets deadlines for specific work required in developing the unit. The second time line is for both students and teachers and shows the intended length of the unit, when it will start, and (if relevant) in which classes it will be taught.

Develop the scope and sequence for content and instruction. To develop the unit, follow the six steps for planning and developing a unit of instruction outlined earlier in this chapter. This should be done by each team member as well as by the group during common planning time so members can coordinate dates and activities in logical sequence and depth. This is an organic process and will generate both ideas and anxiety. Under the guidance of the team leader, members should strive to keep this anxiety at a level conducive to learning, experimenting, and arriving at group consensus.

Share goals and objectives. Each team member should have a copy of the goals and target objectives of every other team member. This helps to refine the unit and lesson plans and to prevent unnecessary overlap and confusion.

Give the unit a name. The unit has been fashioned and is held together by the theme that is chosen. Giving the theme a name and using that name communicates to the students that this unit of study is integrated, important, and meaningful to school and to life.

Share subject-specific units, lesson plans, and printed and nonprinted materials. Exchange the finalized unit to obtain one another's comments and suggestions. Keep a copy of each teacher's unit as a resource, and see if you could present a lesson using it as your basis (some modification may be necessary).

Field-test the unit. Beginning at the scheduled time and date, present the lessons. Team members may trade classes from time to time. Team teaching may take place.

Reflect, assess, and perhaps adjust and revise the unit. During planning time, team members should share and discuss their successes and failures and determine what needs to be changed and how and when that should be done to make the unit successful. Adjustments can be made along the way and revisions for future use can be made after completion of the unit.

The preceding are not absolutes and should be viewed only as guidelines. Differing teaching teams and levels of teacher experience and knowledge make the strict adherence to any plan less productive than would be the use of group-generated plans. In practice, the process that works well—one that results in meaningful learning for the students and in their positive feelings about themselves, about learning, and about school—is the appropriate process. For example, some teaching teams use what is sometimes called a **backward design** for their curriculum planning (Wiggins & McTighe, 1998). The popular procedure is generally as follows: (a) the involved teachers first study the state and district standards; (b) from the standards they select and establish target goals and objectives for their students; (c) they think of projects that will provide opportunities for their students to demonstrate that they have acquired the expected learning; and (d) they finalize their plan with supportive instructional activities. The model is called Understanding by Design (UbD), the title of the 1998 book by Wiggins and McTighe. For additional information see www.grantwiggins.org/ubd.html

Activities that engage the students in meaningful learning constitute the heart and spirit of the ITU: there are activities that start a unit into motion, that initiate the unit—*initiating activities;* there are the activities that comprise the heart of the unit—*ongoing developmental activities;* and, there are activities that bring the unit to a natural close—*culminating activities.*

The Common Thread

Central to the selection and development of all learning activities for interdisciplinary thematic instruction is a common thread of four tightly interwoven components: (a) The instruction is centered around a big and meaningful idea (theme) rather than on factitious subject areas; (b) the students and the teacher share in the decision making and responsibility for learning; (c) the

---

 CLASSROOM VIGNETTE

Interdisciplinary Thematic Instruction at West Salem Middle School

What began as an isolated, single-grade, telecommunications-dependent project for students at West Salem Middle School (Wisconsin) eventually developed into a longer-term, cross-grade interdisciplinary program of students and adults working together to design and develop a local nature preserve. Students began their adventure by interacting with explorer Will Steger as he led the International Arctic Project's first training expedition. Electronic online messages, via the Internet, allowed students to receive and send messages to Will and his team in real time. Students delved into the Arctic world, researching the physical environment and the intriguing wildlife, reading native stories and novels about survival, keeping their own imaginary expedition journals, learning about the impact of industrialized society on the Arctic, and conversing with students from around the world. But something very important was missing—a connection between the students' immediate environment and the faraway Arctic.

West Salem Middle School's focus became the local 700-acre Lake Neshonoc, an impoundment of the LaCrosse River, a tributary of the Mississippi. Although many students had enjoyed its recreational opportunities, they had never formally studied the lake. The Neshonoc Partners, a committee of parents, community leaders, teachers, students, and environmentalists, was established to assist in setting goals, brainstorming ideas, and developing the program for a year's study of the lake. Right from the start, students showed keen interest in active involvement in the project. A second committee, involving parents, students, and the classroom teacher, met during lunch time on a weekly basis to allow for more intensive discussions about the lake and the overall project.

The team of teachers brainstormed ideas to further develop an interdisciplinary approach to the study of Lake Neshonoc. Special activities, including an all-day "winter survival" adventure, gave students a sense of what the real explorers experience. Students learned about hypothermia,

winter trekking by cross-country skiing, and building their own snow caves.

For several weeks, students learned about the ecosystem of Lake Neshonoc through field experiences led by local environmentalists and community leaders. Guest speakers told their stories about life on the lake and their observations about the lake's health. Student sketchbooks provided a place to document personal observations about the shoreline, water testing, animal and plant life, and the value of the lake. From these sketchbooks, the best student creations were compiled to create books to share electronically with students with similar interests in schools from Russia, Canada, Missouri, South Carolina, Nevada, Wisconsin, and Washington, D.C. The opportunity to share findings about their local watershed sparked discussions about how students can make a difference in their own community. Comparative studies gave students a chance to consider how human's and nature impact other watersheds.

West Salem students worked with the local County Parks and Recreation Department to assist in developing a sign marking the new County Park where the nature sanctuary will reside. Students brainstormed design ideas and then constructed a beautiful redwood sign with the help of a local technical educational teacher. Today the sign is a symbol of the partnership that has been established between the students and the community. It is a concrete reminder that together we cam work for the common good of the community and the environment. Students celebrated the study of the lake with a closure. Will Steger, along with community leaders, parents, school board members, and staff, commended the students for what is sure to be the start of a long and enduring relationship—a partnership created out of common respect and appreciation for the value of our ecosystem.

Source: From "The Neshonoc Project: Profiles in Partnership," by J. Wee, Fall 1993, *World School for Adventure Learning Bulletin*, pp. 2–3. Adapted by permission.

CLASSROOM VIGNETTE

Learning from Dinosaurs

Once a theme is determined, instruction is planned around a sequence of activities that focus on that theme. Common to many elementary school teachers and to some middle school teachers as well is a theme that centers on the topic of dinosaurs. Whatever its selected title might be in a given situation, a thematic unit on dinosaurs can encompass any number of multidisciplinary activities related to the topic. For example,

- *History.* Students develop a graphic time line showing the long period of time that dinosaurs were dominant on this earth; they visit a museum that features dinosaur exhibits.
- *Mathematics.* Students categorize the types of dinosaurs and create graphs illustrating the variety and proportional sizes of dinosaurs.
- *Reading, writing, and art.* Students create and write illustrated stories about a favorite dinosaur.
- *Science.* Students speculate on both why the dinosaurs were so successful and on the events that led to their rather quick disappearance.

In her self-contained second-grade classroom, Kristie guided her students in a thematic unit on dinosaurs. Learning activities integrated science and math, drawing and crafts, music and reading, and publishing original books to support the study. Connecting reading to music, the students listened to a song about each dinosaur being studied. Students read sentence strips with the words of the song. They added sound effects, sang the song several times, and added a rhythmic beat with their own dinosaur-shape of books, wrote original pages, and created illustrations. To survey favorite dinosaurs, graphing was introduced. The students built their own graph in the classroom by drawing a favorite dinosaur and contributing it to a large graph. Students used individual copies of the graph to record what was added to the large graph and marked *Xs* with their pencils in the appropriate places. When the class graph was finished, the students read it and talked about the information they had gathered, guided by the teacher.

The culminating event took place at the school's spring Open House. Each student's assignment for Open House was to bring an adult and to explain to that person what he or she had been learning at school. Confidently, the students told their visitors about dinosaurs and proudly displayed their dinosaur books, dinosaur mobiles, dinosaur body shapes made from felt, and dinosaur clay models.

learning activities are selected so all students are actively engaged in their learning—that is, they are both physically active (hands-on learning) and mentally active (minds-on learning); and (d) there is steady reflection on and frequent sharing of what is being done and what is being learned.

Initiating Activities

An ITU can be initiated by a limitless variety of ways. You must decide which ways are appropriate for your educational goals and objectives, intended time duration, and your own unique group of students, considering the extent and diversity of their interests, abilities, and skills. You might start with a current event, a community problem, an artifact, a book, a media presentation, or something interesting found on the Internet. See Figure 5.9's description of *Katy and the Big Snow* to see how a kindergarten teacher helps students connect learning about mapping with the story they are about to hear the teacher read.

Developmental Activities

Once the ITU has been initiated, students become occupied with a variety of ongoing (developmental) activities. In working with students in selecting and planning the developmental activities, you will want to keep in mind the concept represented by the Learning Experiences Ladder (Figure 5.7) as well as the preselected goals and target objectives.

Culminating Activity

Just as with other types of unit plans, an ITU is brought to a close with a culminating activity. Such an activity often includes an exhibition or sharing of the product of the students' study. You could accept the students' suggestions for a culminating activity if it engages them in summarizing what they have learned with others. A culminating activity that brings closure to a unit can give the students an opportunity for synthesis (by assembling, constructing, creating, inventing, producing, or incorporating something) and even an opportunity to present that synthesis to an audience, such as by sharing their product on an existing school web site.

With a culminating activity, you can provide the opportunity for students to move from recording information to reporting on their learning. For example, one activity might be for students to take field trips to study something related to the theme, then synthesize their learning after the trip in a way that culminates the study. On field trips, students should be given notepads similar to the ones reporters use and asked to take notes and make sketches of what they learn. They can discuss what questions they have on the ride to the site. They can discuss what they liked and did not like on the ride back to school. After the trip, each student can choose something he or she saw and then build it to scale, so the students can have a scale model of something they saw on the trip that caught their interest. The students could then invite other classes in to examine the scale models and listen to student reports about why an object caught their interest. Students might also present an art show of drawings about the unit's theme, with a narration that informs others about their study. You might also schedule a culminating activity that asks students to report on individual projects—the aspect each student formerly reserved for individual study.

Culminating activities serve two purposes. They are opportunities for students to proudly demonstrate and share their learning and creativity in different and individual ways. And, it is from the culminating activity that you, the teacher, can do the summative assessment to determine how well target objectives were met. Examples of actual culminating activities and products of an ITU are endless. For example, the culminating activity of the kindergarten unit Katy and the Big Snow (see Figure 5.9) is a treasure hunt (the children are each given a treasure map to find "hidden" treasures); the culmination from the study by the students of West Salem Middle School (see the classroom vignette Interdisciplinary Thematic Instruction at West Salem Middle School) was the design and development of a community nature preserve.

Students at King Middle School (Portland, Maine) studied the shore life of Maine's Casco Bay for a year. The culminating activity of their study was the writing and publishing of a book that included their original illustrations and scientific descriptions of the flora and fauna found along the seashore. The book is now in the city's libraries where it can be borrowed for use by anyone taking a walk along the seashore.

For additional ideas for culminating projects, see A Collection of 130 Annotated Motivational Teaching Strategies with Ideas for Lessons, Interdisciplinary Teaching, Transcultural Studies, and Student Projects in Chapter 9.

PREPARING THE LESSON PLAN

As discussed in the previous chapter, step 5 of the seven steps of instructional planning is the preparation for class meetings. The process of designing a lesson is important in learning to provide the most efficient use of valuable and limited instructional time and the most effective learning for the students that meets the unit goals.

Notice the title of this section does not refer to the "*daily* lesson plan," but rather, "*the* lesson plan." The focus is on how to prepare a lesson plan, one that may, in fact, be a daily plan, or it may not. In some instances, a lesson plan may extend for more than one class period, perhaps 2 or 3 days (e.g., the lesson plan shown in Figure 5.10). In other instances, the lesson plan is in fact a daily plan and may run for an entire class period. In block scheduling, one lesson plan may run for part of, or for an entire 2-hour block of time.

Effective teachers are always planning for their classes. For the long range, they plan the scope and sequence and develop content. Within this long-range planning, they develop units, and within units, they design the activities to be used and the assessments of learning to be done. They familiarize themselves with books, materials, media, and innovations in their fields of interest. Yet, despite all this planning activity, the lesson plan remains pivotal to the planning process.

Rationale for Preparing Written Plans

Carefully prepared and written lesson plans show everyone—first and foremost your students, then your mentor, colleagues, your administrator, and, if you are a student teacher or teaching intern, your supervisor—that you are a committed professional. Sometimes, beginning teachers are concerned with being seen by their students using a written plan in class, thinking it may suggest that the teacher has not mastered the material. On the contrary, a lesson plan is tangible evidence that you are working at your job and demonstrates respect for the students, yourself, and for the profession. A written lesson plan shows that preactive thinking and planning have taken place. There is absolutely no excuse for appearing before a class without evidence of being prepared.

Written and detailed lesson plans provide an important sense of security, which is especially useful to a beginning teacher. Like a rudder on a ship, it helps keep you on course. Without it, you are likely to drift aimlessly. Sometimes a disturbance in the classroom can distract from the lesson, causing the teacher to get "off track" or forget an important element of the lesson. A written and detailed lesson plan provides a road map to guide you and help keep you on track.

Written lesson plans help you to be or become a reflective decision maker. Without a written plan, it is difficult or impossible to analyze how something might have been planned or implemented differently after the lesson has been taught. Written lesson plans serve as resources for the next time you teach the same or a similar lesson and are useful for teacher self-evaluation and for the evaluation of student learning and of the curriculum.

Written lesson plans help you organize material and search for "loopholes," "loose ends," or incomplete content. Careful and thorough planning during the preactive phase of instruction includes anticipation of how the lesson activities will develop as the lesson is being taught. During this anticipation you will actually visualize yourself in the classroom teaching your students. Use that visualization to anticipate possible problems.

Written plans help other members of the teaching team understand what you are doing and how you are doing it. This is especially important when implementing an interdisciplinary thematic unit. *Written lesson plans also provide substitute teachers with a guide to follow if you are absent.*

Figure 5.9   Sample partial ITU for kindergarten. *(Source: Courtesy of Tara Richardson.)*

KATY AND THE BIG SNOW, AN INTERDISCIPLINARY THEMATIC UNIT FOR KINDERGARTEN

Rationale: This unit is designed to teach children about maps. Over a unit duration of 10 days, a variety of disciplines and topics are addressed, such as reading, art, graphing, counting, writing, concept of community, science, music, and learning together. The unit is centered on the book *Katy and the Big Snow*, by Virginia Lee (Houghton Mifflin, 1976). Children compare and contrast the locations of people, places, and environments through studying the maps and being able to find a variety of places. By studying several maps and a world globe the students learn to distinguish between land and water and locate general areas referenced in historically based legends and stories. Students learn how to use map symbols and legend references to land, water, roads, and cities. Students will become able to use maps to determine the relative location of objects using near/far, left/right, and behind/in front. The students will construct maps of their neighborhood community.

Goals and objectives: The goal of this unit is for children to develop an understanding of the concept of maps, how to use maps, and to be able to create their own simple map. Specifically, the children will be able to [Framework Standard identified in parantheses but not included here]:

- Identify land versus water places on a map.
- Identify and name continents and oceans on a map.
- Demonstrate understanding that maps are drawings of places.
- Demonstrate understanding that a globe is a map of the world.
- Identify north, south, east, and west on a map.
- Identify the North and South Poles on a world map.
- Demonstrate understanding that countries are portions of larger continents.
- From a map or globe, identify each continent of the world.
- Demonstrate an understanding of how to read a map.
- Construct a map.
- Create a story map for *Katy and the Big Snow*.
- Grow crystals, and compare and contrast the crystals with snow.

Materials: [not included here]
Vocabulary: [not included here]
Content outline for unit: [not included here]

LESSON 1

- Display the local neighborhood/community map. Ask the children to name buildings and places that are in their community and show children where these places are on the map.
- Discuss briefly with the children what a community is.
- Ask for a volunteer to help you cover the map with the snow. This is the initiatory activity designed to help children connect with the coming story.
- Ask children to describe the qualities of snow.
- Ask children what would happen to a town if it is covered with a hard snowfall. How would they get around if the town is covered with snow?
- Explain to the children that they are going to hear a story that takes place in a town like theirs, that the story takes place where it is very cold and snowy.
- Display the book *Katy and the Big Snow*. Discuss the cover, title page, author, and illustrator. Discuss with the children what Katy is and what Katy might do. Instruct the children to listen to find out what Katy does when the big snowstorm hits town.
- Read the story and discuss it as you go along.
- End this lesson by teaching the children a winter song.

LESSONS 2–10 [NOT INCLUDED HERE]

ASSESSMENT

Formative assessment will be through observation of the children during discussions and activities and oral quizzing on their understanding of specifics about maps and mapping. [Checklists and rubrics are not included here.]
Materials and resources: [not included here]

Figure 5.10   Lesson plan sample: Multiple-day, project-centered, interdisciplinary, and transcultural lesson using worldwide communication via the Internet.

1. Descriptive Data

Teacher: _____   Class: <u>Integrated Language Arts/Science/Social Studies</u> Date: _____Grade level: <u>6–12</u>

Unit: <u>Investigative Research and Generative Writing</u>

Lesson Topic: <u>Writing Response and Peer Assessment via Internet</u>

Time duration: <u>Several days</u>

2. Goals and Objectives of Unit

Instructional Goals:

2.1. One goal for this lesson is for students to collaborate with and prepare response papers to peers from around the world who have shared the results of their own experimental research findings and research papers about ozone concentrations in the atmosphere.

2.2. The ultimate goal of this unit is for students around the world to prepare and publish for worldwide dissemination a final paper about global ozone levels in the atmosphere.

Objectives:

Cognitive:

a. Through cooperative group action, students will conduct experimental research to collect data about the ozone level of air in their environment. (application)
b. In cooperative groups, students will analyze the results of their experiments. (analyze)
c. Students will compile data and infer from their experimental data. (synthesis and evaluation)
d. Through collaborative writing groups, the students will prepare a final paper that summarizes their research study of local atmospheric ozone levels. (evaluation)
e. Through sharing via Internet, students will write response papers to their peers from other locations in the world. (evaluation)
f. From their own collaborative research and worldwide communication with their peers, the students will draw conclusions about global atmospheric ozone levels. (evaluation)

Affective:

a. Students will respond attentively to the response papers of their peers. (attending)
b. Students will willingly cooperate with others during the group activities. (responding)
c. The students will offer opinions about the atmospheric level of ozone. (valuing)
d. The students will form judgments about local, regional, and worldwide ozone levels. (organizing)
e. The students will communicate accurately their findings and attend diligently to the work of their worldwide peers. (internalizing)

Psychomotor:

a. The students will manipulate the computer so that their e-mail communications are transmitted accurately. (manipulating)
b. In a summary to the study, students will describe their feelings about atmospheric ozone concentrations. (communicating)
c. The students will ultimately create a proposal for worldwide dissemination. (creating)

3. Rationale

3.1. Important to improvement in one's writing and communication skills are the processes of selecting a topic, decision making, arranging, drafting, proofing, peer review, commenting, revising, editing, rewriting, and publishing the results—processes that are focused on in the writing aspect of this unit.

3.2. Student writers need many readers to respond to their work. Through worldwide communication with peers and dissemination of their final product, this need can be satisfied.

3.3. Students learn best when they are actively pursuing a topic of interest and meaning to them. Resulting from brainstorming potential problems and arriving at their own topic, this unit provides that experience.

3.4. Real-world problems are interdisciplinary and transcultural, involving writing (English), science, mathematics (data collecting, graphing, etc.), and intercultural communication. This unit is an interdisciplinary transcultural unit.

(continued)

Figure 5.10   *(continued)*

4. Procedure

Content:

At the start of this unit, collaborative groups were established via Intercultural E-mail Classroom Connections (IECC) with other classes from schools around the world. These groups of students from around the world conducted several scientific research experiments on the ozone level of their local atmospheric air. To obtain relative measurements of ozone concentrations in the air, students set up experiments that involved stretching rubber bands on a board, then observing the number of days until the bands broke. Students maintained daily journal logs of the temperature, barometric pressure, and wind speed/direction, and of the number of days that it took for bands to break. After compiling their data and preparing single-page summaries of their results, via the Internet, students exchanged data with other groups. From data collected worldwide, students wrote a one-page summary as to what conditions may account for the difference in levels of ozone. Following the exchange of students' written responses and their subsequent revisions based on feedback from the worldwide peers, students are now preparing a final summary report about the world's atmospheric ozone level. The intention is to disseminate this final report worldwide (to newspapers and via Internet).

Activity 1: Introduction (10 minutes)
Today, in think-share-pairs, you will prepare initial responses to the e-mail responses we have received from other groups from around the world. (Teacher shares the list of places from which e-mail has been received.) Any questions before we get started?

As we discussed earlier, here are the instructions: In your think-share-pairs (each pair is given one response received via e-mail), prepare written responses according to the following outline: (a) note points or information you would like to incorporate in the final paper to be forwarded via Internet; (b) comment on one aspect of the written response you like best; (c) provide questions to the sender to seek clarification or elaboration. I think you should be able to finish this in about 30 minutes, so let's try for that.

Activity 2: (30 minutes, if needed)
Preparation of dyad responses.

Activity 3: (open)
Let's now hear from each response pair.
Dyad responses are shared with whole class for discussion of inclusion in the response paper to be sent via Internet.

Activity 4: (open)
Discussion, conclusion, and preparation of final drafts to be sent to each e-mail correspondent to be done by cooperative groups (the number of groups needed to be decided by the number of e-mail correspondents at this time).

Activity 5: (open)
Later, as students receive e-mail responses from other groups the responses will be printed and reviewed. The class then responds to each using the same criteria as before and returns this response to the e-mail sender.

Closure:
The process continues until all groups (from around the world) have agreed upon and prepared the final report for dissemination.

5. Materials and Equipment Needed
School computers with Internet access; printers
Copies of e-mail responses

6. Assessment, Reflection, and Revision
Assessment of student learning for this lesson is formative:
   journals, daily checklist of student participation in groups, writing drafts

Reflective thoughts about lesson and suggestions for revision [to be filled in after lesson is completed]:

Those reasons clearly express the need to write detailed lesson plans. The list is not exhaustive, however, and you may discover additional reasons why written lesson plans are crucial to effective teaching. Two points must be made:

- Lesson planning is an important and ongoing process.
- Teachers must take time to plan, reflect, write, test, evaluate, and rewrite their plans to reach optimal performance.

In short, preparing written lesson plans is important work.

Assumptions About Lesson Planning

Not all teachers need elaborate written plans for every lesson. Sometimes effective and experienced teachers need only a sketchy outline. Sometimes they may not need written plans at all. Veteran teachers who have taught the topic many times in the past may need only the presence of a class of students to stimulate a pattern of presentation that has often been successful (though frequent use of old patterns may lead one into the rut of unimaginative and uninspiring teaching and most certainly does not take into full consideration the unique characteristics of the students in the present).

Considering the diversity among K-12 school teachers, their instructional styles, their students, and what research has shown, certain assumptions can be made about lesson planning.

- A plan is more likely to be carefully and thoughtfully plotted during the preactive phase of instruction when the plan is written out.
- Although not all teachers need elaborate written plans for all lessons, all effective teachers do have clearly defined goals and objectives in mind and a planned pattern of instruction for every lesson, whether that plan is written out or not.
- Beginning teachers need to prepare detailed, written lesson plans. In some schools teachers are required to post their plans on the school's electronic student information system, such as, for example, the program ProgressBook.
- The depth of knowledge a teacher has about a subject or topic influences the amount of planning necessary for the lessons.
- The diversity of students within today's classroom necessitates careful and thoughtful consideration about individualizing the instruction. These considerations are best implemented when they have been thoughtfully written into lesson plans.
- The skill a teacher has in remaining calm and in following a trend of thought in the presence of distraction will influence the amount of detail necessary when planning activities and writing the lesson plan.
- There is no particular pattern or format that all teachers need to follow when writing out plans. Some teacher preparation programs have agreed-on lesson plan formats for their teacher candidates; you need to know if this is the case for your program.

In summary, then, well-written lesson plans provide many advantages: They give a teacher an agenda or outline to follow in teaching a lesson; they give a substitute teacher a basis for presenting appropriate lessons to a class, thereby retaining lesson continuity in the regular teacher's absence; they are certainly very useful when a teacher is planning to use the same lesson again in the future; they provide the teacher with something to fall back on in case of a memory lapse, an interruption, or a distraction. Using a written plan demonstrates to students that you care and are working for them; and, above all, they provide beginners security because, with a carefully prepared plan, a beginning teacher can walk into a classroom with confidence and professional pride gained from having developed a sensible framework for that day's instruction. Naturally, this will require a great deal of work for at least the first year or two, but the reward of knowing that you have prepared and presented effective lessons will compensate for that effort. You can expect a busy first year of teaching.

A Continual Process

Lesson planning is a continual process even for experienced teachers, for there is always a need to keep materials and plans current and relevant. Because no two classes of students are ever identical, today's lesson plan will need to be tailored to the peculiar needs of each classroom of students. Moreover, because the content of instruction and learning will change as each distinct group of students and their needs and interests give input, and as new thematic units are developed, new developments occur, or new theories are introduced, your objectives and the objectives of the students, school, and teaching faculty will change.

For these reasons, lesson plans should be in a constant state of revision—never "set in concrete." Once the basic framework is developed, however, the task of updating and modifying becomes minimal. If your plans are maintained on a computer (now required by some schools), making changes from time to time is even easier.

Well Planned but Open to Last-Minute Change

The lesson plan should provide a tentative outline of the time period given for the lesson but should always remain flexible. A carefully worked plan may have to be set aside because of the unpredictable, serendipitous effect of a "teachable moment" (see the accompanying vignette) or because of unforeseen circumstances, such as a delayed school bus, an impromptu school assembly program, an emergency drill, or the cancellation of school due to inclement weather conditions. Student teachers often are appalled at the frequency of interruptions during a school day and of disruptions to their lesson planning that occur. A daily lesson planned to cover six aspects of a given topic may end with only three of the points having been considered. Although far more frequent than necessary in too many schools (recall Exercise 3.1), these occurrences are natural in a school setting and the teacher and the plans must be flexible enough to accommodate this reality.

Although you may have your lesson plans completed for several consecutive lessons, as can be inferred by the vignette involving Casey and her students, what actually transpires during the implementation of today's lesson may necessitate last-minute adjustments to the lesson you had planned for tomorrow. More than just occasionally, teachers have discontinued the rest of the week's planned lessons because the feedback received on Tuesday indicated that students did not comprehend Monday's lesson well enough to proceed to the next planned lesson.

Consequently, during student teaching in particular, it is neither uncommon nor unwanted to have last-minute changes penciled in your lesson plan. If, however, penciled-in modifications are substantial and might be confusing to you during implementation of the lesson, then you should rewrite the lesson plan.

> The greatest pedagogical error of our time is a simplistic insistence on clarity. To spell out every act of education for students so that they are never forced to look deep into themselves and come face to face with the primal "Huh?" is to deny them access to one of the most important parts of their humanity: the right to shape their own destiny.
>
> Andrew K. Davis (2001, p. 789)

The Problem of Time

A lesson plan should provide enough materials and activities to consume the entire class period or time allotted. In your planning for teaching you need to plan for every minute of every class period. *The lesson plan, then, is more than a plan for a lesson to be taught; it is a plan that accounts for the entire class period or time that you and your students are together in the classroom.* Planning is a skill that takes years of experience to master, especially when teaching a block of time that may extend for 90 or more minutes and that may involve more than one discipline and perhaps more than one teacher. As a beginning teacher, rather than run the risk of having too few activities to occupy the time the students are in your classroom, you should overplan. One way of ensuring that you overplan is to include "if time remains" activities in your lesson plan.

When a lesson plan does not provide sufficient activity to occupy the entire class period or time that the students are available for the lesson, that is when a beginning teacher often loses control of the class as behavior problems mount. Thus, it is best to prepare more than you likely can accomplish in a given period of time. This is not to imply that you should involve the students in meaningless busy work. Students can be very perceptive when it comes to a teacher who has finished the plan and is attempting to bluff through the minutes that remain before dismissal. And, they are not usually favorably responsive to meaningless busywork.

If you ever do get caught short—as most teachers do at one time or another—one way to avoid embarrassment is to have students work on what was described in Chapter 4 as an anchor activity (or transitional activity). This is an ongoing assignment, and students understand that whenever they have spare time in class they should be working on it. One decision a teacher must make is whether or not students are going to be mobile during anchor activity work. That is a decision that each teacher must make depending on the circumstances for that teacher.

Anchor activities can include any number of possibilities, and here are just a few common ones:

- journal writing
- lab work
- long-term project work

Teaching in Practice

A Teachable Moment

Casey was teaching an eighth-grade humanities block, a 2-hour block course that integrates student learning in social studies, reading, and language arts. On this particular day while Casey and her students were discussing the topic of Manifest Destiny, one of the students raised his hand and, when acknowledged by Casey, asked the question, "Why aren't we [referring to the United States] still adding states? [that is, adding territory to the United States]." Casey immediately replied with, "There aren't any more states to add." By responding too quickly, Casey missed one of those "teachable moments," moments when the teacher has the students right where she wants them, that is, where the students are the ones who are thinking and asking questions. What could Casey have done? When was Hawaii added as a state? Why hasn't Puerto Rico become a state? Guam? etc. Aren't those possibilities? Why aren't more states or territories being added? What are the political and social ramifications today and how do they differ from those of the 1800s?

- portfolio organization
- review material that has been covered that day or in recent days
- work at a learning center
- work on homework for this or another class

Regardless of how you handle time remaining, it works best when you plan for it and write that aspect into your lesson plan. Make sure students understand the purpose and procedures for these anchor assignments.

The Pressure of Standards-Based and High-Stakes Testing and the Felt Need To "Cover" the Prescribed Curriculum

As a result of today's heavy pressure on teachers to "teach to the standards" and to "cover the curriculum" so that their students do well on the mandated proficiency tests, and because for any given grade level or subject there is more content expected to be taught than there is time to teach it, fewer and fewer teachers will even recognize, let alone grasp and run with, the already too-few precious teachable moments that occur. Your challenge, of course, is to find a way of doing both—that is, to help students accomplish the required learning while not stifling the most meaningful and longest lasting learning that often is entirely unpredictable. There is the possibility that such prescriptive teaching could become so objective that it produces negative consequences. The danger is when the relationship between teacher and student becomes impersonal. Highly specific and impersonal teaching can be discouraging to serendipity, creativity, and the excitement of discovery, to say nothing of its possible negative impact on the development of students' self-esteem. Due to the emphasis on standardized testing, coupled with the fact that access mode strategies tend to consume more instructional time than do standard expository strategies, access strategies may indeed be too infrequently used in today's classroom (Jorgenson & Vanosdall, 2002).

Response to Intervention (RtI)

Today, specifically to identify students who are academically and/or behaviorally at risk, and to assist those students to be able to meet the required minimum competency standards, many elementary schools in particular, although not exclusive of secondary schools, are using the schoolwide strategy referred to as the response to intervention (RtI) program. Students so identified are given supplemental instruction during the school day in the regular classroom, along with weekly summative assessments of how they are doing. If after a period of time, usually about 8 weeks, inadequate progress is made the student is moved to Tier 2 (secondary intervention), which is comprised of a smaller number of students. Within the smaller group Tier 2 students are given intensive instruction, depending on their needs and abilities, with continued monitoring for progress. After a period of time, if the student has made satisfactory progress the student may be returned to the regular classroom. Or, if no progress is indicated, the student may be moved to Tier 3 (Tertiary Intervention). In Tier 3 the student receives a more individualized instruction that intensively targets the student's academic and behavioral deficits. After a period of time, the student may be returned to a Tier 2 or Tier 1 setting, or remain at Tier 3 or moved into a special services arrangement.

In an effort to eliminate the walls that have traditionally separated "general" from "special" education, the goal and task of the three-tiered RtI model is an early identification of students who are at risk, providing them with appropriate and more individualized instruction, so that the students can become successful learners and retain their class placement, rather than get discouraged and drop out of school altogether (Elliott, 2008b; Hawken, Vincent, & Schumann, 2008). For more information, see the RTI Action Network at http://www.rtinetwork.org/, the National Center on Response to Intervention at http://www.rti4success.org/, the Center for Comprehensive School Reform and Improvement at www.centerforcsri.org/, and Positive Behavior Intervention and Supports (PBIS) at http://www.pbisillinois.org/.

Caution about "The Weekly Planning Book"

A distinction needs to be made between actual lesson plans and the book for planning that some schools used to require teachers to maintain (and perhaps still do) and even submit to their supervisors a week in advance. Items that a teacher writes into the boxes in a weekly planning book most assuredly are *not* lesson plans; rather, the pages are a layout by which the teacher writes into the boxes to show what lessons will be taught during the day, week, month, or term. Usually the book, whether paper or electronic, provides only a small lined box for time periods for each day of the week. These books are useful for outlining the topics, activities, and assignments projected for the week or term, and still a few supervisors may use them to check the adequacy of teachers' course plans, but they are *not* lesson plans. Teachers and their supervisors who believe that the notations in the weekly planning book are actual lesson plans are fooling themselves. Student teachers and teaching interns should not use these in lieu of authentic lesson plans.

CONSTRUCTING A LESSON PLAN: FORMAT, ELEMENTS, AND SAMPLES

Although it is true that each teacher develops a personal system of lesson planning—the system that works best for that teacher in each unique situation—a beginning teacher needs a more substantial framework from which to work. For that, this section provides a "preferred" lesson plan format (see Figure 5.11). Nothing is hallowed about this format, however; your program of teacher preparation may have its own preferred format. Review the preferred format and samples, and unless your program of teacher preparation insists otherwise, use it with your own modifications until you find or develop a better model. All else being equal, you are encouraged, however, to begin your teaching following as closely as possible this "preferred" format.

For Guidance, Reflection, and Reference

While student teaching and during your first few years as a beginning teacher, your lesson plans should be printed from a computer or, if that is not possible, written out in an intelligible style. To ensure correct spelling, use a spell check and print your plans from the computer. Until you have considerable experience, you need to prepare and maintain detailed lesson plans for guidance, reflection, and reference.

> There is valid reason to suspect the effectiveness of teachers who say they have no need for a written plan because they have their lessons "in their heads." The hours and periods in a school day range from several to many, as do the number of students in each class. When multiplied by the number of school days in a week, a semester, or a year, the task of keeping so many things in one's head becomes mind-boggling. Few persons could effectively do that. The guidelines in this book are written for those teachers who want to be effective and exemplary, not mediocre or ineffective.

Basic Elements in a Lesson Plan

The preferred lesson plan format of this resource guide contains the following seven basic elements: (1) descriptive course data, (2) goals and objectives, (3) rationale, (4) procedure, (5) assignments and assignment reminders, (6) materials and equipment, and (7) a section for assessment of student learning, reflection on the lesson, and ideas for lesson revision. Compare those seven elements with those of whatever plan your program of teacher preparation expects you to use. These seven elements need not be present in every written lesson plan, nor must they be presented in any particular order. Nor are they inclusive or exclusive. You might choose to include additional components or subsections. For example, some model lesson plans include "rationale" or "purpose" as an additional element, probably found prior to "goals and objectives." In my thinking a statement of rationale or purpose is an important inclusion for the unit plan, but may be or maybe not for an individual lesson plan—your decision, although your teacher training program will likely have its preferred

model that you will be expected to follow. Figure 5.10, shown earlier, displays a completed multiple-day lesson that includes the seven elements and also incorporates many of the developmentally appropriate learning activities discussed in this resource guide.

Descriptive Data

A lesson plan's descriptive data is demographic and logistical information that identifies details about the class. Anyone reading this information should be able to identify when and where the class meets, who is teaching it, and what is being taught. Although as the teacher you know this information, someone else may not. Members of the teaching team, administrators, and substitute teachers (and, if you are the student teacher, your university supervisor and cooperating teacher) appreciate this information, especially when asked to fill in for you, even if only for a few minutes during a class session. Most teachers find out which items of descriptive data are most beneficial in their situation and then develop their own identifiers.

> The mark of a well-prepared, clearly written lesson plan is the ease with which someone else (such as another member of your teaching team or a substitute teacher) could implement it.

As shown in the sample plans of Figures 5.10 (language arts/science/social studies) and 5.12 (physical science), the descriptive data include:

1. *Name of course or class.* This serves as a heading for the plan and facilitates orderly filing of plans. For example:

   Language Arts/Science/Social Studies (integrated block class)/Physical Science

2. *Name of the unit.* Inclusion of this facilitates the orderly control of the hundreds of lesson plans a teacher constructs. For example:

Language Arts/ Science/ Social Studies	*Unit: Investigative Research and Generative Writing*
Physical Science	*Unit: What's the Matter*

3. *Topic to be considered within the unit.* This is also useful for control and identification. For example:

Language Arts/ Science/ Social Studies	Unit: Investigative Research and Generative Writing	*Topic: Writing Response and Peer Assessment via the Internet*
Physical Science	Unit: What's the Matter	*Topic: Density of Solids*

Figure 5.11 Preferred lesson plan format with seven components.*

---

1. Descriptive Data

Teacher: _____ Class: _____ Date: _____ Grade level: _____

Room number: _____ Period: _____ Unit: _____ Lesson Number: _____ Topic: _____

Anticipated noise level (high, moderate, low)

2. Goals and Objectives
Instructional goals:

Specific objectives:

[Note: all three domains not always present in every lesson]
Cognitive:

Affective:

Psychomotor:

3. Rationale [Note: rationale not always present in every lesson]

(continued)

Figure 5.11   *(continued)*

4. Procedure [Procedure with modeling examples, planned transitions, etc.; should usually take up most of the space of lesson plan, often a full page]
Content:
_____ minutes. Activity 1: Set (introduction)

_____ minutes. Activity 2:

_____ minutes. Activity 3: (the exact number of activities in the procedures will vary)

_____ minutes. Final Activity (Lesson Conclusion or Closure):

If time remains:

5. Special Considerations, Notes, and Reminders

6. Materials and Equipment Needed
    Media:
    Software:
    Other:

7. Assessment, Reflection, and Revision
    Assessment of student learning, how it will be done:

    Reflective thoughts about lesson after taught:

    Suggestions for revision if used again:

_____

*This blank lesson plan format is placed alone so, if you choose, you may remove it from the book and make copies for use in your teaching.

Although not included in the sample lesson plans in this resource guide, the teacher might include in the descriptive data the category of "anticipated classroom noise level," such as "high," "moderate," "low." Its inclusion, or at least considering the idea, is useful during the planning phase of instruction insofar as thinking about how active and noisy the students might become during the lesson, how you might prepare for that, and whether you should warn an administrator and teachers of neighboring classrooms.

Goals and Objectives

The instructional goals are general statements of intended accomplishments from that lesson. They usually are related to state- or district-mandated curriculum standards. This is where that information can be identified and shown.

Teachers and students need to know what the lesson is designed to accomplish. In clear, understandable language, the general goal statement provides that information. From the sample of Figure 5.12, the goals are as follows:

- To collaborate and prepare response papers to peers from around the world who have shared the results of their own experimental research findings and research papers about ozone concentrations in the atmosphere.
- For students worldwide to prepare and publish for worldwide dissemination a final paper about worldwide ozone levels in the atmosphere.

And, from the sample unit of Figure 5.12, goals are as follows:

- Understand that all matter is made of atoms.
- Develop a positive attitude about physical science.

Because the goals are also included in the unit plan, sometimes a teacher may include only the objectives in the daily lesson plan and not the goals. As a beginning teacher, it usually is a good idea to include both.

SETTING THE LEARNING OBJECTIVES

A crucial step in the development of any lesson plan is that of setting the objectives. It is at this point that many lessons go wrong and many beginning teachers have problems.

A Common Error and How to Avoid It

Teachers sometimes confuse "learning activity" (*how* the students will learn it) with the "learning objective" (*what* the student will learn as a result of the learning activity). For example, teachers sometimes mistakenly list what *they* intend to do—such as "lecture on photosynthesis" or "lead a discussion on the causes of the Civil War." They fail to focus on just what the learning objectives in these

activities truly are—that is, what the students will be able to do (performance) as a result of the instructional activity. Or, rather than specifying what the student will be able to do as a result of the learning activities, the teacher mistakenly writes what the students will do in class (the learning activity)—such as, "in pairs the students will do the 10 problems on page 72"—as if that were the learning objective. Although solving the problems correctly may well be the objective, "doing the 10 problems" is not. At the risk of sounding trite or belaboring the point, I emphasize the importance of the teacher being an accurate communicator. If the teacher's stated expectations are fuzzy, then the students may never get it.

When you approach this step in your lesson planning, to avoid error, ask yourself, "What should students be able to do as a result of the activities of this lesson?" Your answer to that question is your objective! Objectives of the lesson are included then as specific statements of performance expectations, detailing precisely what students will be able to do as a result of the instructional activities.

No Need to Include All Domains and Hierarchies in Every Lesson

I have known beginning teachers to worry needlessly over trying to include objectives from all three domains (cognitive, affective, and psychomotor) in every lesson they write. Please understand that not all three domains are necessarily represented in every lesson plan. As a matter of fact, any given lesson plan may be directed to only one or two, or a few, specific objectives. Over the course of a unit of instruction, however, all domains, and most if not all levels within each, should be addressed.

From the lesson shown in Figure 5.10, sample objectives, and the domain and level (in parentheses) within that domain, are as follows:

- Through cooperative group action, students will conduct experimental research to collect data about the ozone level of air in their environment. (cognitive, application)
- Through the Internet, students will write and share response papers to their peers from other locations in the world. (cognitive, evaluation)
- Students will form judgments about local, regional, and world ozone levels. (affective, organizing)
- Students will create a proposal for worldwide dissemination. (psychomotor, creating)

From the lesson illustrated in Figure 5.12, sample objectives include the following:

- Determine the density of a solid cube. (cognitive, application)
- Communicate the results of their experiments to others in the class. (psychomotor, communicating)

Figure 5.12   Sample of a unit plan with one daily lesson integrated. (*Source:* Courtesy of Will Hightower.)

UNIT PLAN SAMPLE WITH A DAILY LESSON

Course *Science*

Teacher _____   **Duration of Unit** *10 days*

Unit Title *What's the Matter?*   **Grade Level** *Grades 5–12*

Purpose of the Unit
This unit is designed to develop students' understanding of the concept of matter. At the completion of the unit, students should have a clearer understanding of matter and its properties, of the basic units of matter, and of the source of matter.

Rationale of the Unit
This unit topic is important for building a foundation of knowledge for subsequent courses in science. This can increase students' chances of success in those courses, and thereby improve their self-confidence and self-esteem. A basic understanding of matter and its properties is important because of daily decisions that affect the manipulation of matter. It is more likely that students will make correct and safe decisions when they understand what matter is, how it changes form, and how its properties determine its use.

Goals of the Unit
The goals of this unit are for students to

1. Understand that all matter is made of atoms.
2. Understand that matter stays constant and that it is neither created nor destroyed.
3. Develop certain basic physical science laboratory skills.
4. Develop a positive attitude about physical science.
5. Look forward to taking other science courses.
6. Understand how science is relevant to their daily lives.

Instructional Objectives of the Unit
Upon completion of this unit of study, students should be able to

1. List at least 10 examples of matter.
2. List the four states of matter, with one example of each.
3. Calculate the density of an object when given its mass and volume.
4. Describe the properties of solids, liquids, and gases.
5. Demonstrate an understanding that matter is made of elements and that elements are made of atoms.
6. Identify and explain one way the knowledge of matter is important to their daily lives.
7. Demonstrate increased self-confidence in pursuing laboratory investigations in physical science.
8. Demonstrate skill in communicating within the cooperative learning group.
9. Demonstrate skill in working with the triple-beam balance.

Unit Overview
Throughout this unit, students will be developing a visual learning map of matter. Information for the map will be derived from laboratory work, class discussions, lectures, student readings, and research. The overall instructional model is that of concept attainment. Important to this is an assessment of students' concepts about matter at the beginning of the unit. The preassessment and the continuing assessment of their concepts will center on the following:

1. What is matter and what are its properties? Students will develop the concept of matter by discovering the properties that all matter contains (that is, it has mass and takes up space).
2. Students will continue to build upon their understanding of the concept of matter by organizing matter into its four major states (that is, solid, liquid, gas, plasma). The concept development will be used to define the attributes of each state of matter, and students will gather information by participating in laboratory activities and class discussions.
3. What are some of the physical properties of matter that make certain kinds of matter unique? Students will experiment with properties of matter such as elasticity, brittleness, and density. Laboratory activities will allow students to contribute their observations and information to the further development of their concept of matter. Density activities enable students to practice their lab and math skills.
4. What are the basic units of matter, and where did matter come from? Students will continue to develop their concept of matter by working on this understanding of mixtures, compounds, elements, and atoms.

Figure 5.12   *(continued)*

Assessment of Student Achievement
For this unit, assessment of student achievement will be both formative and summative. Formative evaluation will be done daily by checklists of student behavior, knowledge, and skills. Summative evaluation will be based on the following criteria:

1.   Student participation as evidenced by completion of daily homework, classwork, laboratory activities, and class discussions, and by the information on the student behavior checklists.
2.   Weekly quizzes on content.
3.   Unit test.

Lesson Number _____   **Duration of Lesson** *1–2 hours* _____

Unit Title *What's the Matter?* _____   *Teacher* _____

Lesson Title *Mission Impossible* _____   **Lesson Topic** *Density of Solids* _____

Objectives of the Lesson
Upon completion of this lesson, students should be able to

1.   Determine the density of a solid cube.
2.   Based on data gathered in class, develop their own definition of density.
3.   Prepare and interpret graphs of data.
4.   Communicate the results of their experiments to others in the class.

Materials Needed

1.   Two large boxes of cereal and two snack-size boxes of the same cereal.
2.   Four brownies (two whole and two cut in halves).
3.   Four sandboxes (two large plastic boxes and two small boxes, each filled with sand).
4.   Two triple-beam balances.
5.   Several rulers.
6.   Six hand-held calculators.
7.   Eighteen colored pencils (six sets with three different colors per set).
8.   Copies of lab instructions (one copy for each statement).

Instructional Procedure with Approximate Time Line

ANTICIPATORY SET (10–15 MINUTES)
Begin class by brainstorming to find what students already know about density. Place the word on the board or overhead, and ask students if they have heard of it. Write down their definitions and examples. Hold up a large box of cereal in one hand and the snack-size box in the other. Ask students which is more dense. Allow them time to explain their responses. Then tell them that by the end of this lesson they will know the answer to the question and that they will develop their own definition of density.

LABORATORY INVESTIGATION (30–60 MINUTES)
Students are divided into teams of four students of mixed abilities. Each member has a role:

1.   *Measure master:* In charge of the group's ruler and ruler measurements.
2.   *Mass master:* In charge of the group's weighings.
3.   *Engineer:* In charge of the group's calculator and calculations.
4.   *Graph master:* In charge of plotting the group's data on the graph paper.

Each team has 8 minutes before switching stations. Each team completes three stations and then meets to make their graphs and to discuss results.

Station 1: **Cereal Box Density.** Students calculate the density of a large and a small box of cereal to determine if a larger and heavier object is more dense. The masses versus the volumes of the two boxes are plotted on graph paper using one of the pencil colors.

(continued)

Figure 5.12   *(continued)*

Volume (cm³)

Instructions

1. The density of any object is determined by dividing its mass by its volume. Density in grams is divided by volume in cubic centimeters. Example: 20 g/10 cm^3 ÷ 2 g/cm^3.

2. Measure the volume of the small cereal box (length × width × height), and use the balance to determine its mass in grams. The engineer can do the calculations on the calculator. The graph master should graph the results of each trial and connect two points with a straight line.

3. Repeat the procedure using the large box of cereal.

4. The engineer computes the density of both cereal boxes with the calculator and records the results on the proper blank below the graph.

Figure 5.12   *(continued)*

    a.   Density of large box of cereal _____

    b.   Density of small box of cereal _____

    c.   Density of large brownie _____

    d.   Density of small brownie _____

    e.   Density of large sandbox _____

    f.   Density of small sandbox _____

***Station 2:* Brownie Density.** Students calculate the density of a full-size brownie and a half-size brownie. Results are plotted on the same graph as in Station 1, but with the second color.
Instructions

1. The density of any object is determined by dividing its mass by its volume. Density in grams is divided by volume in cubic centimeters. Example: 20 g/10 cm^3 ÷ 2 g/cm^3.
2. Measure the volume of a small brownie (length × width × height), and use the balance to determine its mass in grams. The engineer can do the calculations on the calculator. The graph master should graph the results of each trial and connect two points with a straight line.
3. Repeat the procedure using the large brownie.
4. The engineer computes the density of both brownies and records the result on the proper blank.

***Station 3:* Sandbox Density.** Students calculate the density of a large and a small box filled with sand. Results are plotted on the graph, but with the third color.
Instructions

1. The density of any object is determined by dividing its mass by its volume. Density in grams is divided by volume in cubic centimeters. Example: 20 g/10 cm^3 ÷ 2 g/cm^3.
2. Measure the volume of the small sandbox (length × width × height), and use the balance to determine its mass in grams. The engineer can do the calculations on the calculator. The graph master should graph the results of each trial and connect two points with a straight line.
3. Repeat the procedure using the large sandbox.
4. The engineer computes the density of both boxes and records the result on the proper blank.

Lab Worksheet. Teams return to their seats to do the graphing, analyze the results, and answer the following questions from their lab sheets:

1. Is a larger, heavier object more dense than its smaller counterpart? Explain your evidence.
2. What is your definition of density?
3. Which is more dense, a pound of feathers or a pound of gold? Explain your answer.

LESSON CLOSURE (10 MINUTES OR MORE)
When all teams are finished, teams should display their graphs and share and discuss the results.

Concepts

1. Density is one of the properties of matter.
2. Mass and volume are related.
3. Density is determined by dividing mass by volume.

Extension Activities

1. Use a density graph to calculate the mass and volume of a smaller brownie.
2. Explore the story of Archimedes and the king's crown.

Evaluation, Reflection, and Revision of Lesson
Upon completion of this lesson and of the unit, revision in this lesson may be made on the basis of teacher observations and student achievement.

Rationale

The rationale is an explanation of why the lesson is important and why the instructional methods chosen will achieve the objectives. Parents, students, teachers, administrators, and others have the right to know why specific content is being taught and why the methods employed are being used. Prepare yourself well by setting a goal for yourself of always being prepared with intelligent answers to those two questions. This is a proper place to connect the lesson with the mandated benchmark standards.

Teachers become reflective decision makers when they challenge themselves to think about *what* (the content) students are learning, *how* (the learning activities) they are learning it, and *why* (the rationale) it must be learned. As illustrated in the sample unit of Figure 5.10, sometimes the rationale is included within the unit introduction and goals, but not in every lesson plan of the unit. Some lessons are carryovers or continuations of a lesson; I see no reason to repeat the rationale for a continuing lesson.

Procedure

The procedure consists of the instructional activities for a scheduled period of time. The substance of the lesson—the information to be presented, obtained, and learned—is the content. Appropriate information is selected to meet the learning objectives, the level of competence of the students, and the grade level or course requirements. To be sure your lesson actually covers what it should, you should write down exactly what minimum content you intend to cover. This material may be placed in a separate section or combined with the procedure section. The important thing is to be sure that your information is written so you can refer to it quickly and easily when you need to.

If you intend to conduct the lesson using discussion, you should write the key discussion questions. If you are going to introduce new material using a 10-minute lecture, then you need to outline the content of that lecture. The word *outline* is not used casually—you need not have pages of notes to sift through; nor should you ever read lengthy declarative statements to your students. You should be familiar enough with the content so that an outline (in as much detail as you believe necessary) will be sufficient to carry on the lesson, as in the following example of a content outline:

        Causes of Civil War
            A. Primary causes
                1. Economics
                2. Abolitionist pressure
                3. Slavery
                4. etc.
            B. Secondary causes
                1. North–South friction
                2. Southern economic dependence
                3. etc.

The procedure or procedures to be used, sometimes referred to as the **instructional components**, comprise the procedure element of the lesson plan. It is the section that outlines what you and your students will do during the lesson. Appropriate instructional activities are chosen to meet the objectives, to match the students' learning styles and special needs, and to ensure that all students have an equal opportunity to learn. Ordinarily, you should plan this section of your lesson as an organized entity having a beginning (an introduction or **set**), a middle, and an end (called the **closure**) to be completed during the lesson. This structure is not always needed, because some lessons are simply parts of units or long-term plans and merely carry on activities spelled out in those long-term plans. Still, most lessons need to include the following in the procedure: (a) an introduction, the process used to prepare the students mentally for the lesson, sometimes referred to as the set (establishes a mindset) or initiating activity (initiates the lesson); (b) **lesson development**, the detailing of activities that occur between the beginning and the end of the lesson, including the transitions that connect activities; (c) plans for **practice**, sometimes referred to as the follow-up—that is, ways that you intend to have students interacting in the classroom (such as individual practice, in dyads, or small groups)—receiving guidance or coaching from each other and from you; (d) the **lesson conclusion** (or closure), the planned process of bringing the lesson to an end, thereby providing students with a sense of completeness and, with effective teaching, accomplishment and comprehension by helping students to synthesize the information learned from the lesson; (e) a **timetable** that serves simply as a planning and implementation guide; (f) a **contingency plan** for what to do if you finish the lesson and time remains; and (g) **assignments**, that is, what students are instructed to do as follow-up to the lesson, either as homework or as in-class work, providing students an opportunity to practice and enhance what is being learned.

INTRODUCTION TO THE LESSON

Like any good performance, a lesson needs an effective beginning. In many respects the introduction sets the tone for the rest of the lesson by alerting the students that the business of learning is to begin. The introduction should be an attention getter. If it is exciting, interesting, or innovative, it can create a favorable mood for the lesson. In any case, a thoughtful introduction serves as a solid indicator that you are well prepared. Although it is difficult to develop an exciting introduction to every lesson taught each day, every day of the school week, there are always a variety of options available by which to spice up the launching of a lesson. You might, for instance, begin the lesson by briefly reviewing the previous lesson, thereby helping students connect the learning. Another possibility is to review vocabulary words from previous lessons and to introduce new ones.

Still another possibility is to use the key point of the day's lesson as an introduction and then again as the conclusion. Sometimes teachers begin a lesson by demonstrating a discrepant event (i.e., an event that is contrary to what one might expect), sometimes referred to as a "hook." Yet another possibility is to begin the lesson with a writing activity on some controversial aspect of the ensuing lesson. Sample introductions are:

For U.S. history, study of westward expansion:

- The teacher asks, "Who has lived somewhere other than (name of your state)?" After students show hands and answer, the teacher asks individuals why they moved to (name of your state). The teacher then asks students to recall why the first European settlers came to the United States, then moves into the next activity.

For science, study of the science process skill of predicting:

- The teacher takes a glass filled to the brim with colored water (colored so it is more visible) and asks students to discuss and predict (in dyads) how many pennies can be added to the glass before any water spills over the rim of the glass.

In short, you can use the introduction of the lesson to review past learning, tie the new lesson to the previous lesson, introduce new material, point out the objectives of the new lesson, help students connect their learning with other disciplines or with real life, or show what will be learned and why the learning is important, thereby inducing in students motivation and a mindset favorable to the new lesson.

LESSON DEVELOPMENT

The developmental activities that comprise the bulk of the plan are the specifics by which you intend to achieve the lesson objectives. They include activities that present information, demonstrate skills, provide reinforcement of previously learned material, and provide other opportunities to develop understanding and skill. Furthermore, by actions and words, during lesson development you should model the behaviors expected of the students. Students need such modeling. By effective modeling, you can exemplify the anticipated learning outcomes. Activities of this section of the lesson plan should be described in some detail so (a) you will know exactly what it is you plan to do, and (b) during the intensity of the class meeting, you do not forget important details and content. It is for this reason you should consider, for example, noting answers (if known) to questions you intend to ask and solutions (if known) to problems you intend to have students solve.

LESSON CONCLUSION

Having a concise closure to the lesson is as important as having a strong introduction. The concluding activity should summarize and bind together what has ensued

in the developmental stage and should reinforce the principal points of the lesson. One way to accomplish these ends is to restate the key points of the lesson. Another is to briefly outline the major points. Still another is to review the major concept. Sometimes the closure is not only a review of what was learned but also the summarizing of a question left unanswered that signals a change in your plan of activities for the next day. In other words, it becomes a **transitional closure**.

TIMETABLE

To estimate the time factors in any lesson can be very difficult, especially for the beginning teacher. A useful procedure is to gauge the amount of time needed for each learning activity and make a note of that alongside the activity and strategy in your plan, as shown in the preferred sample lesson plan format. Placing too much faith in your time estimate may be foolish—an estimate is more for your guidance during the preactive phase of instruction than for anything else. To avoid being embarrassed by running out of material, try to make sure you have planned enough meaningful work to consume the entire class period. If nothing else, this may include an anchor activity. Another important reason for including a time plan in your lesson is to give information to students about how much time they have for a particular activity, such as a quiz or a group activity.

Assignments

When an assignment is to be given, it should be noted in your lesson plan. When to present an assignment to the students is optional, but it should never be yelled as an afterthought as the students are exiting the classroom at the end of the class period. Whether they are to be begun and completed during class time or done outside of class, assignments should be written on the writing board, in a special place on the bulletin board, on the school's web site, in each student's assignment log maintained in a binder, or on a handout. Take extra care to be sure that assignment specifications are clear to the students. Many teachers give assignments to their students on a weekly or other periodic basis. When given on a periodic basis, rather than daily, assignments should still show in your daily lesson plans to remind yourself to remind students of them.

Once assignment specifications and due dates are given, it is a good idea *not* to make major modifications to them, and it is especially important not to change assignment specifications several days after an assignment has been given. Last-minute changes in assignment specifications can be very frustrating to students who have already begun or completed the assignment; it shows little respect to those students.

Understand the difference between assignments and procedures. An assignment tells students what is to be done, whereas procedures explain how to do it. Although an assignment may include procedures, spelling out procedures alone is not the same thing as giving an academic assignment. When students are given an assignment, they need to understand the reasons for doing it as well as have some notion of ways the assignment might be done.

Allowing time in class for students to begin work on homework assignments and long-term projects is highly recommended; it provides an opportunity for the teacher to provide individual attention to students. Being able to coach students is the reason for in-class time to begin assignments. The benefits of **coached practice** include being able to (a) monitor student work so a student does not go too far in a wrong direction, (b) help students to reflect on their thinking, (c) assess the progress of individual students, (d) provide for peer tutoring, and (e) discover or create a "teachable moment." For the latter, for example, while observing and monitoring student practice, the teacher might discover a commonly shared student misconception. The teacher then stops and discusses that and attempts to clarify the misconception or, collaboratively with students, plans a subsequent lesson centered on focusing on the common misconception.

Special Considerations, Notes, and Reminders

I recommend that in your lesson plan format you have a regular place for special notes and reminders, perhaps in the same location as assignments as illustrated in the preferred format. In that special section that can be referred to quickly, you can place reminders concerning such things as announcements to be made, school programs, assignment due dates, and makeup work or special tasks for certain students.

Materials and Equipment to Be Used

Materials of instruction include books, media, handouts, and other supplies necessary to accomplish the lesson's learning objectives. You must be *certain* that the proper and necessary materials and equipment are available for the lesson; to be certain requires planning. Teachers who, for one reason or another, have to busy themselves during class time looking for materials or equipment that should have been readied before class began are likely to experience classroom control problems. Plus, if it happens very often, it demonstrates incompetence" and the teacher loses credibility with the students. Teachers want students to be prepared; students expect competent teachers to be prepared. Competent teachers model preparedness and focus.

TEACHERTUBE: VIDEO SHARING FOR TEACHERS

In 2007 a video-sharing web site was launched to provide an online community for sharing videos useful in lesson plans. Called TeacherTube (www.teachertube.com), the free site was originated by Jason Smith, former classroom teacher, coach, school administrator, and presently superintendent of schools in Melissa, Texas. As stated by Smith (personal correspondence, 2009), "we, the founders of the site, seek to fill a need for a more educationally focused, safe venue for teachers, schools, and home learners. TeacherTube is a site to provide anytime, anywhere professional development with teachers teaching teachers. As well, it is a site where teachers can post videos designed for students to view in order to learn a concept or skill."

The teacher must assure that proper resources and materials are available for lessons. That takes planning. Students can't use what they don't have.

Assessment, Reflection, and Revision

Details of how you will assess how well students *are learning* (called **formative assessment**) and how well they *have learned* (called **summative assessment**) should be included in your lesson plan. This does not mean to imply that both types of assessment will be in every daily plan. Comprehension checks for formative assessment can be in the form of questions you ask and that the students ask during the lesson (in the procedural section), as well as various kinds of checklists.

For summative assessment, teachers typically use review questions at the end of a lesson (as a closure) or the beginning of the next lesson (as a review or transfer introduction), independent practice or summary activities at the completion of a lesson, and tests. The topic of assessment strategies is covered fully later in Chapter 10.

In most lesson plan formats, for the reflective phase of instruction there is a section reserved for the teacher to make notes or reflective comments about the lesson. Many student teachers seem to prefer to write their reflections at the end or on the reverse page of their lesson plans. As well as useful to yourself, reflections about the lesson are useful for those who are supervising you if you are a student teacher or a teacher being mentored or considered for tenure.

Writing and later reading your reflections can not only provide ideas that may be useful if you plan to use the lesson again at some later date, but also offer catharsis, easing the tension caused from teaching. To continue working effectively at a challenging task (i.e., to prevent intellectual downshifting or reverting to earlier learned, lower cognitive level behaviors) requires significant amounts of reflection.

If you have reviewed the sample lesson plan formats, proceed now to Exercise 5.1, where you will analyze a lesson that failed; then, as instructed by your course instructor, do Exercises 5.2 and 5.3.

SUMMARY

You have learned of the importance of learning modalities and instructional modes. You have learned about the importance of providing an accepting and supportive learning environment, as well as about teacher behaviors that are necessary to facilitate student learning beyond that of procedural knowledge.

With this chapter in particular you continued building your knowledge base about why planning is important and how units with lessons are useful pedagogical tools. Developing units of instruction that integrate student learning and provide a sense of meaning for the students requires coordination throughout the curriculum. Hence, for students, learning is a process of discovering how information, knowledge, and ideas are interrelated so they can make sense out of self, school, and life. Preparing chunks of information into units and units into lessons helps students to process and understand knowledge. You have developed your first unit of instruction and are well on your way to becoming a competent planner of instruction.

In these first five chapters of this resource guide, you have been guided through the pre-instructional processes necessary to prepare yourself to teach in a classroom. Later, after you have studied Chapter's 6 through 10 on specific strategies, aids, media, and resources to supplement your instruction, you may choose to revisit this chapter and to make revisions to your completed unit and lessons. Remember this always: Teaching plans, quite similar to this resource guide, should never be set in concrete, but subject to constant revision.

Now, in the next chapter, your attention is focused on the use of one of the most important strategies used in teaching—questioning.

QUESTIONS FOR CLASS DISCUSSION

1. In subject field discussion groups, list and describe specific considerations you should give to student safety (a topic that this resource guide cannot adequately otherwise address) when preparing instructional plans. Share your lists with other groups.

2. Give several reasons why both a student teacher and a first-year teacher need to prepare detailed lesson plans. Describe when, if ever, the teacher can or should divert from the written lesson plan.

3. Explain why, when taught by access strategies, students learn less content but learn it more effectively? For a teacher using access strategies extensively, could this cause a problem? Explain.

4. Recall one vivid learning experience from each level of your own schooling and reflect on those experiences with respect to their positions on the Learning Experiences Ladder. In small groups, share your reflections with members of your class. After sharing, discuss what, if anything, can be concluded.

5. From the content outline that you prepared in Chapter 4, select a topic that is typically taught by the use of symbolization (at or near the top of the Learning Experiences Ladder); then devise a technique by which, with limited resources, that same content could be taught more directly (at or close to the bottom of the ladder). Share your proposal with your classmates for their feedback.

myeducationlab
The Power of Classroom Practice

Now go to Topics #5 and 7: **Instructional Planning** and **Strategies for Teaching** in the MyEducationLab (www.myeducationlab.com) for your course, where you can:

- Find learning outcomes for these topics along with the national standards that connect to these outcomes.
- Complete Assignments and Activities that can help you more deeply understand the chapter content.
- Examine challenging situations and cases presented in the IRIS center resources.
- Apply and practice your understanding of the core teaching skills identified in the chapter with the Building Teaching Skills and Dispositions learning units.

EXERCISE 5.1   ANALYSIS OF A LESSON THAT FAILED

INSTRUCTIONS: The planning and structure of a lesson are often predictors of the success of its implementation. The purpose of this exercise is to read the following synopsis of the implementation of a lesson, answer the discussion questions individually, and use your responses as a basis for class discussion in small groups about the lesson.

The Setting: Junior high life science class; 1:12–2:07 P.M., spring semester.

SYNOPSIS OF EVENTS

1:12	Bell rings.
1:12–1:21	Teacher directs students to read from their text while he takes attendance.
1:21–1:31	Teacher distributes a ditto to each student; students are now to label the parts of a flower shown on the handout.
1:31–1:37	Silent reading and labeling of ditto.
1:37–1:39	Teacher verbally gives instructions for working on a real flower (e.g., by comparing it with the drawing on the handout). Students may use the microscopes if they want.
1:39–1:45	Teacher walks around room, giving each student a real flower.
1:45–2:05	Chaos erupts. There is much confusion with students wandering around, throwing flower parts at each other. Teacher begins writing referrals and sends two students to the office for their misbehavior. Teacher is flustered, directs students to spend remainder of period quietly reading from their texts. Two more referrals are written.
2:05–2:07	A few students begin meandering toward the exit.
2:07	End of period (much to the delight of the teacher).

QUESTIONS FOR CLASS DISCUSSION

1. Do you think the teacher had a lesson plan? If so, what (if any) were its good points? Its problems?

   _____

   _____

   _____

2. If you believed that the teacher had a lesson plan, do you believe the teacher had a written and detailed lesson plan? Explain. What is your evidence? _____

   _____

   _____

   _____

3. How might the lesson have been prepared and implemented to avoid the chaos?_____

   _____

   _____

   _____

4. Was the format of the lesson traditional? Explain. _____

   _____

   _____

   _____

☞

EXERCISE 5.1 *(continued)*

5. Have you experienced a class such as this? Explain. _____
   _____
   _____
   _____

6. Which teacher behaviors were probable causes of much of the chaos? (Hint: See Chapter 4.) _____
   _____
   _____
   _____

7. What teacher behaviors could have prevented the chaos and made the lesson more effective? _____
   _____
   _____
   _____

8. Within the 55-minute class period, students were expected to operate rather high on the Learning Experiences Ladder (see Figure 5.7). Consider this analysis: 9 minutes of silent reading; 10 minutes of listening; 6 minutes of silent reading and labeling; 2 minutes of listening; 6 minutes of action (the only direct experience); and an additional 22 minutes of silent reading. In all, there were approximately 49 minutes (89 percent of the class time) of abstract verbal and visual symbolization. Is that a problem? _____
   _____
   _____
   _____

9. What have you learned from this exercise? _____
   _____
   _____
   _____

EXERCISE 5.2A   PREPARING A LESSON PLAN

INSTRUCTIONS: Use the model lesson format or an alternative format that is approved by your instructor to prepare a _____-minute lesson plan (length to be decided in your class) for a grade and course of your choice. After completing your lesson plan, evaluate it yourself, modify it, and then have your modified version evaluated by at least three peers, using Exercise 5.2B for the evaluation, before turning it in for your instructor's evaluation. This exercise may be connected with Exercise 5.3.

EXERCISE 5.2B   SELF- AND PEER ASSESSMENT OF MY LESSON PLAN

INSTRUCTIONS: You may duplicate blank copies of this form for evaluation of the lesson you developed for Exercise 5.2A. Have your lesson plan evaluated by two of your peers and yourself. For each of the items below, evaluators should check either "yes" or "no," and write instructive comments. Compare the results of your self-evaluation with the other evaluations.

	No	Yes	Comments
1. Are descriptive data adequately provided?	____	____	_____
2. Are the goals clearly stated?	____	____	_____
3. Are the objectives specific and measurable?	____	____	_____
4. Are objectives correctly classified?	____	____	_____
5. Are objectives only low order or is higher order thinking expected?	____	____	_____
6. Is the rationale clear and justifiable?	____	____	_____
7. Is the plan's content appropriate?	____	____	_____
8. Is the content likely to contribute to achievement of the objectives?	____	____	_____
9. Given the time frame and other logistical considerations, is the plan workable?	____	____	_____
10. Will the opening (set) likely engage the students?	____	____	_____
11. Is there a preassessment strategy?	____	____	_____
12. Is there a proper mix of learning activities for the time frame of the lesson?	____	____	_____
13. Are the activities developmentally appropriate for the intended students?	____	____	_____

EXERCISE 5.2B *(continued)*

14. Are transitions planned?   ____ ____   _____

15. If relevant, are key questions written out   ____ ____   _____

    and key ideas noted in the plan?   _____

16. Does the plan indicate how coached   ____ ____   _____

    practice will be provided for each student?   _____

17. Is adequate closure provided in the plan?   ____ ____   _____

18. Are materials and equipment needed   ____ ____   _____

    identified, and are they appropriate?   _____

19. Is there a planned formative assessment,   ____ ____   _____

    formal or informal?   _____

20. Is there a planned summative assessment?   ____ ____   _____

21. Is the lesson coordinated in any way with   ____ ____   _____

    other aspects of the curriculum?   _____

22. Is the lesson likely to provide a sense of   ____ ____   _____

    meaning for the students by helping to   _____

    bridge their learning?   _____

23. Is an adequate amount of time allotted to   ____ ____   _____

    address the information presented?   _____

24. Is a thoughtfully prepared and relevant   ____ ____   _____

    student assignment planned?   _____

25. Could a substitute who is knowledgeable   ____ ____   _____

    follow the plan?   _____

Additional comments:

EXERCISE 5.3   PREPARING AN INSTRUCTIONAL UNIT: BRINGING IT ALL TOGETHER

INSTRUCTIONS: The purpose of this exercise is threefold: (1) to give you experience in preparing an instructional unit, (2) to assist you in preparing an instructional unit that you can use in your teaching, and (3) to start your collection of instructional units that you may be able to use later in your teaching. This assignment will take several hours to complete, and you will need to read ahead in this book. My advice, therefore, is to start the assignment early, with a due date much later in the course. Your course instructor may have specific guidelines for your completion of this exercise; what follows is the essence of what you are to do.

First, with help from your instructor divide your class into two teams, each with a different assignment pertaining to this exercise. The units completed by these teams are to be shared with all members of the class for feedback and possible use later.

TEAM 1

Members of this team, individually or in dyads, will develop standard teaching units, perhaps with different grade levels, grades K–12, in mind. (You will need to review the content of Chapters 6–10.) Using a format that is practical, *each member or pair of this team* will develop a minimum 2-week (10-day) unit for a particular grade level, subject, and topic. Regardless of format chosen, each unit plan should include the following elements:

1. Identification of (a) grade level, (b) subject, (c) topic, and (d) time duration.

2. Statement of rationale and general goals, including related standards.

3. Separate listing of instructional objectives for each daily lesson. Wherever possible, the unit should include objectives from all three domains—cognitive, affective, and psychomotor.

4. List of materials and resources needed and where they can be obtained (if you have that information). These should also be listed for each daily lesson.

5. Ten consecutive daily lesson plans (see Exercise 5.2A).

6. List of all items that will be used to assess student learning *during* and *at completion* of the unit of study.

7. Statement of how the unit will attend to the diversity of students one is likely to find; such as pertaining to students' reading levels, socioethnic backgrounds, and special needs.

TEAM 2

In collaboration, members of this team will develop interdisciplinary thematic units. Depending upon the number of students in your class, Team 2 may actually consist of several teams, with each team developing an ITU. Each team should consist of no less than two members (e.g., a math specialist and a science specialist) and no more than four (e.g., history/social studies, English/language arts/reading, mathematics, and science).

6 The Use of Questioning

A strategy of key importance to any mode of instruction is, as introduced in Chapter 2, questioning. Because you will use questioning for so many purposes, you must be skilled in its use to teach effectively. Because it is so important, and because it is so frequently used and abused, this first of four chapters specifically directed to the interactive phase of instruction focuses your attention on the development of your skills in using questioning to facilitate student learning. This chapter also introduces you to the first of three micro peer teaching exercises included in this resource guide.

Specifically, upon completion of this chapter you should be able to:

1. Contrast the levels of questioning and compare them with levels of thinking and doing.
2. Demonstrate developing skill in the use of questioning.
3. Demonstrate an understanding of the types of cognitive questions.
4. Describe ways of helping students to develop their metacognitive skills.
5. Explain the value and use of students' questions.
6. Identify categories of purposes for which questioning can be used as an instructional strategy.

PURPOSES FOR USING QUESTIONING

You will adapt the type and form of each question to the purpose for which it is asked. The purposes that questions serve can be separated into five categories, as follows:

1. *To politely give instructions.* An example is, "Mariya, would you please turn out the lights so we can better see what's on the screen?" Although they probably should

avoid doing so, teachers sometimes also use rhetorical questions for the purpose of regaining student attention and maintaining classroom control; for example, "Sam, would you please attend to your work?" Rhetorical questions can sometimes backfire on the teacher. In this case, for example, Sam might say "No"; then the teacher would have a problem that could have been avoided had the teacher been more direct and simply told Sam to attend to his work, rather than asking if he would.

2. *To review and remind students of classroom procedures.* For example, if students continue to talk when they shouldn't, you can stop the lesson and ask, "Class, I think we need to review the procedure we agreed on for when someone is talking. Who can tell me what the procedure is that we agreed upon?"

3. *To gather information.* Examples are "How many of you have finished the assignment?" or, to find out whether a student knows something, "Alge, can you please explain for us the difference between a synonym and antonym?"

4. *To discover student knowledge, interests, or experience.* Examples might be "How many of you think you know the process by which water in our city is made potable?" or "How many of you have visited the local water treatment plant?"

5. *To guide student thinking and learning.* It is this category of questioning that is the focus for your learning in this chapter. In teaching, questions in this category are used to

- *Build the curriculum.* It is the students' questions that provide the basis for the learning that occurs in an effective program that is inquiry based and project centered. More on this subject follows later in the section of this chapter titled Questions From Students: The Question-Driven Classroom and Curriculum.
- *Develop appreciation.* For example, "Do you now understand the ecological relationship between that particular root fungus, voles, and the survival of the large conifers of the forests of the Pacific Northwest?"
- *Develop student thinking.* For example, "What do you suppose the effects to the ecology are when standing water is sprayed with an insecticide that is designed to kill all mosquito larvae?"
- *Diagnose learning difficulty.* For example, "What part of the writer's argument don't you understand, Sarah?"
- *Emphasize major points.* For example, "If no one has ever been to the sun, how can we be confident that we know of what the sun is made of?"
- *Encourage students.* For example, "Okay, so you didn't remember the formula for glucose. What really impressed me in your essay is what you did understand about photosynthesis. Do you know specifically what part that was?"
- *Establish rapport.* For example, "We have a problem here, but I think we can solve it if we work together. What do you think ought to be our first step?"
- *Evaluate learning.* For example, "Siobhan, what is the effect when two rough surfaces are rubbed together?"
- *Give practice in expression.* For example, "Aggie, would you please share with us the examples of shadowing that you found?"
- *Help students in their metacognition.* For example, "Yes, something did go wrong. Do you still think your original hypothesis is correct? If not, then where was the error in your thinking? Or if you still think your hypothesis is correct, then where might the error have been? How might we verify?"
- *Help students interpret materials.* For example, "Something seems to be wrong with this compass. How do you suppose we can find out what is wrong with it? For example, if the needle is marked N and S in reverse, how can we find out if that is the problem?"
- *Help students organize materials.* For example, "If you really want to test your idea, then we are going to need certain materials. We are going to have to deal with some strategic questions here, such as, what do you think we will need, where can we find those things, who will be responsible for getting them, and how will we store and arrange them once we are ready to start the investigation?"
- *Provide drill and practice.* For example, "Team A has prepared some questions that they would like to use as practice questions for our upcoming exam, and they are suggesting that we use them to play the game of Jeopardy on Friday. Is everyone in agreement with their idea?"
- *Provide review.* For example, "Today, in your groups, you are going to study the unit review questions. After each group has studied and prepared its answers to these written questions, your group will pick another group and ask them your set of review questions. Each group has a different set of questions. Members of Team A are going to keep score, and the group that has the highest score from this review session will receive free pizza at tomorrow's lunch. Ready?"
- *Show agreement or disagreement.* For example, "Some of you believe that United States should not have invaded Iraq. Explain why you agree or disagree with that conclusion."
- *Show relationships, such as cause and effect.* For example, "What do you suppose would be the global effect if just one inch of the total Antarctic ice shelf were to melt rather suddenly?"

QUESTIONS TO AVOID ASKING

Although it is important to avoid asking rhetorical questions, questions for which you do not want a response, you should also avoid asking questions that call for little or no student thinking, such as those that can be answered with a simple yes or no or some other sort of alternative answer response. Unless followed up with questions calling for clarification, questions that call for simple responses have little or no learning and diagnostic value; they encourage guessing and inappropriate student responses that can cause classroom control problems for the teacher.

> Never deliberately ask questions for the purpose of embarrassing or punishing a student or that in any way deny the student's dignity.

Questions that embarrass or punish tend to damage the student's developing self-esteem and serve no meaningful academic or instructional purpose. Questioning is an important instructional tool that should be used by the teacher only for academic reasons. Although it is not always possible to predict when a student might be embarrassed by a question, a teacher should never deliberately ask questions for the purpose of embarrassment or punishment. For example, avoid asking a student a content question when you sense the student was not paying attention or does not know the answer. When done deliberately to punish or embarrass, that teacher's action borders on abuse!

TYPES OF COGNITIVE QUESTIONS: A GLOSSARY

Let us now define, describe, and provide examples for each of the types of cognitive (or mental) questions that you will use in teaching. Please note that although we refer to these in the traditional fashion as cognitive questions, any question type could relate to any of the three domains of learning (cognitive, affective, or psychomotor).

Analytic Question

The analytic question is used to encourage students to analyze and even critique information before them. For example, "In what way was that news headline misleading?" "How might we solve this problem?" and "How could we improve the beginning paragraph?"

Clarifying Question

The clarifying question is used to gain more information from a student to help the teacher better understand a student's ideas, feelings, and thought processes. Often, asking a student to elaborate on an initial response will lead the student to think more deeply, restructure his or her thinking, and while doing so, discover a fallacy in the original response. Examples of clarifying questions are "What I hear you saying is that you would rather work alone than in your group. Is that correct?" "So, Denise, you think the poem is a sad one, is that right?" There is a strong positive correlation between student learning, the development of metacognitive skills (i.e., their thinking about thinking), and the teacher's use of questions that ask for clarification (Costa, 1991). In addition, by seeking clarification, you are likely to be demonstrating an interest in the student and in the student's thinking, and that is good.

Convergent-Thinking Question

Convergent-thinking questions, also called **narrow questions**, are low-order thinking questions that have a single correct answer (such as recall questions). Examples of convergent-thinking questions are "If the circumference of a circle is 31 meters, what is its radius?" "What engineering feat allowed Xerxes to invade Greece in 481 B.C.E.?" When using questions of this type, try to come back with follow-up questions so the student answering can demonstrate thinking beyond rote memory.

Cueing Question

If you ask a question to which, after sufficient **wait time**, which is longer than 2 seconds and as long as 7 seconds (Rowe, 1974; Tobin, 1984, 1986, 1987), no students respond or to which their responses indicate they need more information, then you can ask a question that cues the answer or response you are seeking. In essence, you are going backward in your questioning sequence, to cue the students. For example, as an introduction to a lesson on the study of prefixes, a teacher asks students, "How many legs each do crayfish, lobsters, and shrimp have?" and there is no accurate response. The teacher might then cue the answer with the following information and question, "Those animals belong to the class Decapoda. Does that give you a clue about the number of legs they have?" If that clue is not enough, and after allowing sufficient time for students to think (2–7 seconds), then the teacher might ask, "What is a decathlon?" or "What is the decimal system?" or "What is a decimeter?"

When questioning students over reading material, you can use the **question–answer relationship** (QAR) strategy (McIntosh & Draper, 1996). QAR involves asking a question and, if a student is unable to respond, providing one of three types of cues. "Right there" is used for questions for which the answer can be found explicitly stated in the sentence or paragraph. "Search and think" means the answer is not directly stated and therefore must be inferred. "On your own" is used for critical thinking questions for which the answers are neither explicit nor inferred in the text (Choate & Rakes, 1998).

Divergent-Thinking Question

Divergent-thinking questions (also known as *broad, reflective,* or *thought questions*) are open-ended (i.e., usually having no singularly correct answer), high-order thinking questions (requiring analysis, synthesis, or evaluation), which require students to think creatively and to leave the comfortable confines of the known and reach out into the unknown. Examples of questions that require divergent thinking are "Do you believe Mark Twain was racist?" "What measures could be taken to reduce crime in our neighborhood?" and "What measures could be taken that would improve the post-lunchtime trash problem on our school's campus?"

Evaluative Question

Whether convergent or divergent, some questions require students to place a value on something or to take a stance on some issue; these are referred to as evaluative questions. If the teacher and the students agree on certain premises, then the evaluative question would also be a convergent question. If original assumptions differ, then the response to the evaluative question would be more subjective, and therefore divergent. Examples of evaluative questions are "Should the United States allow clear-cutting in its national forests?" and "Should the Electoral College be abolished?" and "Is it environmentally sound for the military to intentionally sink old warships into the bottom of the oceans?"

Focus Question

A focus question is any question that focuses student thinking. For example, the first question of the preceding paragraph can be a focus question when the teacher asking it is attempting to focus student attention on the issues—environmental, economic, political—involved with clear-cutting.

Probing Question

Similar to a clarifying question, the probing question requires student thinking to go beyond superficial first-answer or single-word responses. Examples of probing questions are "Why, Eloy, do you think every citizen has the right to have a gun?"

Probing questions are effective for encouraging and engaging student thinking *before* a particular learning experience, that is, for establishing a mindset. For example, "How many consecutive drops of water do you predict we could place on this one-cent coin before any water would run off the edge?"

SOCRATIC QUESTIONING

In the fifth century B.C.E., Socrates, the famous Athenian teacher, used the art of questioning so successfully that to this day we still hear of the Socratic method (Paul & Edler, 2006; Phillips, 2000; Schneider, 2000). Much of what we know of Socrates comes from Aristotle and the writings of Plato, both of whom were his students. What, exactly, is the Socratic method? Socrates' strategy was to ask his students a series of leading questions that gradually snarled them up to the point where they had to look carefully at their own ideas and think rigorously for themselves. Today that strategy is referred to as the Socratic approach or method.

Socratic discussions were informal dialogues taking place in a natural, pleasant environment. Although Socrates sometimes had to go to considerable lengths to ignite his students' intrinsic interest, their response was natural and spontaneous. In his dialogues, Socrates tried to aid students in developing ideas. He did not impose his own notions on the students. Rather, he encouraged

them to develop their own conclusions and draw their own inferences. Of course, Socrates may have had preconceived notions about what the final learning should be and carefully aimed his questions so that the students would arrive at the desired conclusions. Still, his questions were open-ended, causing divergent rather than convergent thinking. The students were free to go mentally wherever the facts and their thinking led them.

Throughout history teachers have tried to adapt that which they believe to be the methods of Socrates to the classroom. In some situations, these methods have been quite successful and are a major mode of instruction. However, it is important to understand that Socrates used this method in the context of a one-to-one relationship between the student and himself. Some teachers have adapted it for whole-class, direct instruction by asking questions first of one student and then of another, moving slowly about the class. This technique may work, but it is difficult because the essence of the Socratic technique is to build question on question in a logical fashion so that each question leads the student a step further toward the understanding sought. When you distribute the questions around the classroom, you may find it difficult to build up the desired sequence and to keep all the students involved in the discussion. Sometimes you may be able to use the Socratic method by directing all the questions at one student—at least for several minutes—while the other students look on and listen in. That is how Socrates did it. When the topic is interesting enough, this technique can be quite successful and even exciting, but in the long run, the Socratic method works best when the teacher is working in one-on-one coaching situations or with small groups of students, rather than in whole-class, direct instruction.

In Socratic questioning the focus is on the questions, not answers, and thinking is valued as the quintessential activity (Brogan & Brogan, 1995). In essence, to conduct Socratic questioning, with the student or class, identify a problem (either student or teacher posed) and then ask the students a series of probing questions designed to cause them to examine critically the problem and potential solutions to it. The main thrust of the questioning and the key questions must be planned in advance so that the questioning will proceed logically. To think of quality probing questions on the spur of the moment is too difficult. You will be using the Socratic method in a micro peer teaching exercise later in this chapter (Exercise 6.7).

LEVELS OF COGNITIVE QUESTIONS AND STUDENT THINKING

Questions posed by you are cues to your students to the level of thinking expected of them, ranging from the lowest level of mental operation, requiring simple recall of knowledge (convergent thinking), to the highest, requiring divergent thought and application of that thought. It is important that you are aware of the levels of thinking, that you understand the importance of attending to student thinking from low to higher levels of operation, and that you understand that what for one student may be a matter of simple recall of information, may for another require a higher-order mental activity, such as figuring something out by deduction.

You should structure and sequence your questions (and assist students in developing their own skill in structuring and sequencing their questions) in a way that is designed to guide students to higher levels of thinking. For example, when students respond to questions in complete sentences that provide supportive evidence for their ideas, it is fairly safe to assume that their thinking is at a higher level than were the response an imprecise and nondescriptive single-word answer.

To help your understanding, three levels of questioning and thinking are described. [Note: Others have described this three-tiered model of thinking variously. For example, in Eisner's *The Educational Imagination* (1979), the levels are "descriptive," "interpretive," and "evaluative."] There is a similarity between these three levels of questions and the six levels of thinking and doing from Bloom's (1984) taxonomy of cognitive objectives (Chapter 4). For your daily use of questioning it is just as useful but more practical to think and behave in terms of the following three levels, rather than six.

1. *Lowest level: Gathering and recalling information.* At this level questions are designed to solicit from students concepts, information, feelings, or experiences that were gained in the past and stored in memory. Sample key words and desired behaviors include the following:

complete, count, define, describe, identify, list, match, name, observe, recall, recite, select

Thinking involves receiving data through the senses, followed by the processing of those data. Inputting without processing is brain dysfunctional. Information that has not been processed is stored only in short-term memory.

2. *Intermediate level: Processing information.* At this level questions are designed to draw relationships of cause and effect, to synthesize, analyze, summarize, compare, contrast, or classify data. Sample key words and desired behaviors are

analyze, classify, compare, contrast, distinguish, explain, group, infer, make an analogy, organize, plan, synthesize

Thinking and questioning that involve processing of information can be conscious or unconscious. When students observe the teacher thinking aloud, and when they are urged to think aloud, to think about their thinking, and to analyze it as it occurs, they are in the process of developing their intellectual skills.

At the processing level, this internal analysis of new data may challenge a learner's preconceptions (and misconceptions or what are sometimes referred to as **naïve theories**) about a phenomenon. The learner's brain will naturally resist this challenge to existing beliefs. The greater the mental challenge, the greater will be the brain's effort to draw upon data already in storage. With increasing data, the mind will gradually examine existing concepts and ultimately, as necessary, develop new mental concepts.

If there is a match between new input and existing mental concepts, no problem exists. Piaget (1977) called this process **assimilation**. If, however, in processing new data there is no match with existing mental concepts, then the situation has created what Piaget called **cognitive disequilibrium**. The brain does not "like" this disequilibrium and will drive the learner to search for an explanation for the discrepancy. Piaget called this process **accommodation**. However, although learning is enhanced by challenge, in situations that are threatening, the brain is less flexible in accommodating new ideas. As discussed in Chapter 3, that is why each student must feel welcomed in the classroom, and learners must perceive the classroom environment as challenging but nonthreatening, what is referred to as an environment of **relaxed alertness** (Caine, 2000).

Questions and experiences must be designed to elicit more than merely recall memory responses (assimilation). Many teachers find it useful to use discrepant events to introduce concepts. **Discrepant events** are phenomena that cause cognitive disequilibrium, thus stimulating higher-level mental functioning. However, merely exposing students to a discrepant event will not in itself cause them to develop new conceptual understandings. It simply stirs the mind into processing, without which mental development does not occur (see Figure 6.1).

3. *Highest level: Applying and evaluating in new situations.* Questions at the highest level encourage learners to think intuitively, creatively, and hypothetically, to use their imagination, to expose a value system, or to make

Figure 6.1 Example of a discrepant event demonstration.

Combustible Won't Burn

Practice this first. Wrap a dollar bill (or a $20 if you are confident) around a drinking glass. While holding the bill tightly around the glass, try to ignite the bill with a match or lighter. The paper bill will not ignite because the glass conducts the heat away too rapidly, maintaining the paper below its kindling point. After removing the bill from the glass you may (if you wish and are wealthy) ignite the bill for a moment to prove to the students that it will indeed burn.

a judgment. Sample key words and desired behaviors are as follows:

apply, build, evaluate, extrapolate, forecast, generalize, hypothesize, imagine, judge, predict, speculate

You must use questions at the level best suited for the purpose, use questions of a variety of different levels, and structure questions in a way intended to move student thinking to higher levels.

> When teachers use higher-level questions, their students tend to score higher on tests of critical thinking and on standardized tests of achievement (Newton, 1978; Redfield & Rousseau, 1981).

With the use of questions as a strategy to move student thinking to higher levels, the teacher is facilitating the students' intellectual development. Developing your skill in using questioning requires attention to detail and practice. The following guidelines will provide that detail and some practice, but first, do self-check Exercise 6.1 (located at end of this chapter) to check your understanding of the levels of questions.

GUIDELINES FOR USING QUESTIONING

Rather than simply to fill students' minds with bits and pieces of information that will likely last only a brief time in their short-term memory, your goal should be to help your students learn how to solve problems, make decisions and value judgments, think creatively and critically, and feel positive about themselves, their schools, and their learning. Important to the realization of these goals are how you construe your questions and how you implement your questioning strategy.

Preparing Questions

When preparing questions, consider the guidelines presented in the following paragraphs.

Make sure that key cognitive questions are planned, thoughtfully worded, and written into your lesson plan. Thoughtful preparation of questions helps to ensure that they are clear and specific, not ambiguous, that the vocabulary is appropriate, and that each question matches its purpose. Incorporate questions into your lessons as

instructional devices, welcomed pauses, attention grabbers, and checks for student comprehension. Thoughtful teachers even plan questions that they intend to ask specific students, targeting questions to the readiness level, interest, or learning profile of a student.

Match questions with their target purposes. Carefully planned questions are sequenced and worded to match the levels of cognitive thinking expected of students. To help students in developing their thinking skills, you need to demonstrate how to do this. To demonstrate, you must use terminology that is specific and that provides students with examples of experiences consonant with the meanings of the cognitive words. You should demonstrate this every day so students learn the cognitive terminology. As stated by Brooks and Brooks (1993, p. 105), "framing tasks around cognitive activities such as analysis, interpretation, and prediction—and explicitly using those terms with students—fosters the construction of new understandings." See the three examples in Figure 6.2.

Implementing Questioning

Careful preparation of questions is half the skill in questioning. Implementation is the other half. Here are guidelines for effective implementation.

Ask your well-worded question before calling on a student for a response. A common error is calling on a student and then asking the question, such as, "Sean, would you please tell us what you believe the author meant by the title 'We Are One'?" Although probably not intended by the teacher, as soon as the teacher called on Sean, that signaled to the rest of the students in the classroom that they were released from having to pay further attention and from having to think about the question. The preferred strategy is to phrase the question, allow time for all students to think, and then call on Sean and other students for their interpretations of the author's meaning of the title.

Avoid bombarding students with too much teacher talk. Sometimes teachers talk too much. This could be especially true for teachers who are nervous, as might be the case for many during the initial weeks of their student teaching. Knowing the guidelines presented here will help you avoid that syndrome. Remind yourself to be quiet after you ask a question that you have carefully

Figure 6.2   Examples of questions that use appropriate cognitive terminology.

Instead of	*Say*
"How else might it be done?"	"How could you apply ...?"
"Are you going to get quiet?"	"If we are going to hear what Joan has to say, what do you need to do?"
"How do you know that is so?"	"What evidence do you have?"

formulated. Some teachers even put a reminder per se in their lesson plans. Sometimes, due to lack of confidence, and especially when a question has not been carefully planned, the teacher asks the question and then, with a slight change in wording, asks it again, or asks several questions, one after another. That is too much verbiage. It is called "machine gun questioning" and only confuses students, allowing too little time for them to think.

After asking a question, provide students with adequate time to think. The pause after asking a question is called **wait time** (or **think time**). Knowing the subject better than the students know it and having given prior thought to the subject, too many teachers fail to allow students sufficient time to think after asking a question. In addition, by the time they have reached the intermediate grades, students have learned pretty well how to play the "game"—that is, they know that if they remain silent long enough, the teacher will probably answer his or her own question. After asking a well-worded question, you should remain silent for a while, allowing students time to think and to respond. If you wait long enough, they usually will. You may need to rehearse your students on this procedure.

After asking a question, how long should you wait before you do something? You should wait at least 2 seconds, and perhaps as long as 7 seconds or sometimes even longer (when it appears it is needed because students are still thinking). Stop reading now and look at your watch or a clock to get a feeling for how long 2 seconds is. Then, observe how long 7 seconds is. Did 7 seconds seem a long time? Because most of us are not used to silence in the classroom, 2 seconds of silence can seem quite long, and 7 seconds may seem eternal. If, for some reason, students have not responded after a period of 2 to 7 seconds of wait time, then you can ask the question again (but do not reword an already carefully worded question or students are likely to be confused, thinking perhaps it is a new question). Pause for several seconds; then if you still have not received a response, you can call on a student, then another, if necessary, after sufficient wait time. Soon you will get a response that can be built upon. Avoid answering your own question!

Now, to better understand the art of questioning, the importance of well-worded questions and well-prepared and clear instructions, and of allowing students time to think, do Exercise 6.2, *Think Time and the Art of Questioning: An In-Class Exercise,* found at the end of this chapter.

Practice gender equity. To practice gender equity, follow these four rules when using questioning: (a) Avoid going to a boy to bail out a girl who fails to answer a question; (b) avoid going to a boy to improve upon a girl's answer (For the first, without seeming to badger, try to give the student clues until she can answer with success. For the second, hold and demonstrate high expectations for all students.); (c) allow equal wait time regardless of student gender; and (d) call on boys and girls equally.

Practice calling on all students. You must call on not just the quick or the slow, not just the boys or the girls, not only those in the front or middle of the room, but all of them. To do these things is important and may take your concentrated effort. To ensure that students are called on equally, some teachers have in hand laminated copies of their seating charts, perhaps on bright, neon-colored clipboards (gives students a visual focus), and, with a wax pencil or water-soluble marker, make a mark next to the name of the student each time he or she is called on. With the seating chart laminated, and using erasable markers, the marks can be erased at the end of the day and the seating chart used over and over.

Give the same minimum amount of wait time (think time) to all students. This, too, will require concentrated effort on your part, but is important to do. A teacher who waits for less time when calling on a slow student or students of one gender or students with limited English language skills is showing a prejudice or a lack of confidence in certain students, both of which are detrimental when a teacher is striving to establish for all students a positive, equal, and safe environment for classroom learning. Show confidence in all students, and never discriminate by expecting less or more from some than from others. Although some students may take longer to respond, it is not necessarily because they are not thinking or they have less ability. There may be cultural differences to think about, in that some cultures simply allow more wait time than others do. There may also be learning disabilities to consider. But the important point here is to individualize to allow students who need more time to have it. Variation in wait time allowed should not be used to single out some students and to lead to lower expectations but rather to allow for higher expectations.

Require students to raise their hands and be called on. Of course, there are always possible and reasonable exceptions to most any rule, including this one, but as a general and important procedure for when you ask questions, instead of allowing students to randomly shout out their answers, expect them to raise their hands and to be called on before they respond. Establish that procedure and stick with it. If you do relax the rule (such as you might in small-group instruction), let the students know. Using the rule, however, helps to ensure both that you call on all students equally, fairly distributing your interactions with the students, and that girls are not interacted with less because boys tend to be more obstreperous. Even in college classrooms, when allowed by the instructor, male students tend to outtalk and to interrupt their female peers. Even in same-gender classrooms, some students tend to be more vocal while others are less so and, when allowed by the instructor, tend to monopolize and control the flow of the verbal interactions. At all levels of education, and regardless of subject, every teacher has the responsibility to guarantee a nonbiased classroom and an equal distribution of interaction time in the classroom. That is impossible to do when students are allowed to speak out at will.

Another important reason for this advice is to aid students in learning to control their impulsivity. Controlling one's impulsivity is one of the characteristics of intelligent behavior, as discussed in Chapter 7. One of your many instructional responsibilities is to help students develop and cherish this intelligent behavior.

Actively involve as many students as possible in the questioning–answering discussion session. The traditional method of the teacher asking a question and then calling on a student to respond is essentially a one-on-one interaction. Students not called on are likely to view that as their opportunity to disengage in the lesson at hand. Even though you call on one student, you want the other students not to mentally disengage. There are many effective ways to keep all engaged.

To keep all students mentally engaged, you will want to call on students who are sitting quietly and have not raised their hands as well as those who have, but avoid badgering or humiliating an unwilling participant. When a student has no response, you might suggest he or she think about it and even write down some thoughts, and you will come back to the student to ensure he or she eventually understands or has an answer to the original question.

By dividing a single question into several parts, the number of students involved can be increased. For example, "What are the causes of the Civil War? Who can give one reason?" followed then by "Who can give another?" Or, you can involve several students in answering a single question. For example, ask one student for an answer, such as to the question "What was the first battle of the Civil War?", ask a second to read the text aloud to verify the student's answer, then ask a third to explore the reason or thinking that makes it the accepted answer.

Carefully gauge your responses to students' answers to your questions. The way you respond to students' answers influences students' subsequent participation. Responses by the teacher that encourage students' participation include probing for elaboration, discussing students' answers, requesting justification, asking how answers were arrived at, and providing positive reinforcement.

In gauging your responses to students' answers to your questions, you must be cognizant of cultural characteristics and differences of your students. How students respond to questioning is in part culturally dependent, and understanding these differences can be very helpful toward your effectiveness in using questioning. For example, among many Native American groups, once one student gives an incorrect answer, no other student will give the correct answer; not because they do not know it, but because it would be culturally inappropriate to "upstage" the shamed student. Also, for many cultures, giving a "guess" answer when one is not 100 percent sure is disrespectful. This can have an impact on how a student responds in class. Having relevant knowledge about the cultural heritage of students in your particular classroom will help you become more reflective and responsive in using questioning.

Use strong praise sparingly. Although a teacher's use of strong praise is sometimes okay, when you want students to think divergently and creatively, you should be stingy with the use of strong praise to student responses. Strong praise from a teacher tends to terminate divergent and creative thinking. Strong praise can also cause children to become dependent on external sources of praise—to become "praise junkies." (Refer to discussion in Chapter 2 about praise versus encouragement.)

One of your goals is to help students realize intrinsic sources for motivation, that is, an inner drive of intent or desire that causes them to want to learn. Use of strong praise tends to build conformity, causing students to depend on outside forces—that is, the giver of praise—for their worth rather than upon themselves. An example of a strong praise response is "That's right! Very good." On the other hand, passive acceptance responses, such as, "Okay, that seems to be one possibility," keep the door open for further thinking, particularly for higher-level, divergent thinking.

Another example of a passive acceptance response is one used in brainstorming sessions, when the teacher says, "After asking the question and giving you time to think about it, I will hear your ideas and record them on the board." Only after all student responses have been heard and recorded does the class begin its consideration of each. That kind of nonjudgmental acceptance of all ideas in the classroom will generate from the students a great deal of expression of high-level thought.

Using an Audience Response Student Clicker System

When available at their school, teachers are finding advantageous the use of a wireless electronic instant-response system where when asked a question by the teacher (or anyone else), students can individually and anonymously respond with their little keypads, often called clickers, with a yes or no or, depending on the question, a multiple-choice response. Some clickers now allow for open-ended responses. Two obvious advantages of using the device are (1) the privacy afforded to individual students along with the feeling of freedom to respond and to do so honestly, and (2) the teachers being able to know immediately which students are having difficulty and which topics need additional coverage time. At least one maker now has an application usable on the iPhone and the Blackberry. To learn more about the devices and their availability, see www. audiencerespose. com, www. optiontechnologies. com, www. qomo. com, and www. turningtechnologies. com.

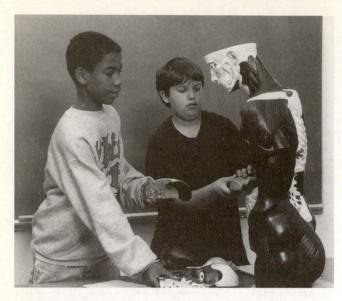

Students can be taught the skills in the use of questioning and can practice those skills while peer coaching.

QUESTIONS FROM STUDENTS: THE QUESTION-DRIVEN CLASSROOM AND CURRICULUM

Student questions can and should be used as springboards for further questioning, discussions, and investigations. Students should be encouraged to ask questions that challenge the textbook, the process, or other persons' statements, and they should be encouraged to seek the supporting evidence behind a statement.

> The most intellectually demanding tasks lie not so much in solving problems as imposing questions. The kind of schools we need would be staffed by teachers who are as interested in questions students ask after a unit of study as they are in the answers students give.
>
> Elliot W. Eisner (2002, p. 579)

Being able to ask questions may be more important than having right answers. Knowledge is derived from asking questions. Being able to recognize problems and to formulate questions is a skill and the key to problem-solving and critical-thinking skill development (Ciardiello, 2000). You have a responsibility to encourage students to formulate questions and to help them word their questions in such a way that tentative answers can be sought. That is the process necessary to build a base of knowledge that can be drawn upon whenever necessary to link, interpret, and explain new information in new situations.

Questioning: The Cornerstone of Critical Thinking, Real-World Problem Solving, and Meaningful Learning

With real-world problem solving, there are usually no absolute right answers. Rather than "correct" answers, some are simply better than others. The student with a problem needs to learn how to

1. recognize the problem;
2. formulate a question about that problem (e.g., Should I argue with Mom about this or not? Should I date this person or not? Should I take this late after-school job or not?);
3. collect data; and
4. arrive at a temporarily acceptable answer to the problem, while realizing that at some later time new data may dictate a review of the former conclusion.

For example, if an astronomer believes she has discovered a new planetary system, there is no textbook or teacher or any other outside authoritative source to which she may refer to inquire if she is correct. Rather, on the basis of her self-confidence in identifying problems, asking questions, collecting data, and arriving at a tentative conclusion based on those data, she assumes that, for now, her conclusion is safe.

Help students learn the difference between asking questions that are descriptive and those that are comparative. An example descriptive question is "How many people live in lower-altitude deserts of the world?" Changing that to a comparative question, we could have "Are low-desert populations of people fewer in number than populations living in high deserts?" From the first question the asker would likely get a simple number, whereas changing the question to a comparative one opens new avenues for further learning. A simple comparative question might lead to a unit of study lasting weeks and that overlaps many disciplines.

Encourage students to ask questions about content and process. As emphasized in *Tried and True* (United States Department of Education, 1997), question asking often indicates that the inquirer is curious, puzzled, and uncertain; it is a sign of being engaged in thinking. And, yet, in too many classrooms too few students ask questions. Students should be encouraged to ask questions. From students, there is no such thing as a "dumb" question. Sometimes students, like everyone else, ask questions that could just as easily have been looked up, are truly irrelevant, or show lack of thought or sensitivity. Those questions can consume precious class time. For a teacher, they can be frustrating. A teacher's initial reaction may be to quickly and mistakenly brush off that type of question with sarcasm, while assuming that the student is too lazy to look up an answer. In such instances, you are advised to think before responding and to respond kindly and professionally, although in the busy life of a classroom teacher, that may not always be so easy to remember to do. However, be assured, there is a reason for a student's question. Perhaps the student is signaling a need for recognition or simply demanding attention.

In large schools, it is sometimes easy for a student to feel alone and insignificant (although this seems less the case with schools that use a school-within-a-school plan and where teachers and students work together in interdisciplinary teams, or, as in looping, where one cadre of teachers remains with the same cohort of students for two or more years). When a student makes an effort to interact with you, that can be a positive sign, so gauge carefully your responses to those efforts. If a student's question is really off track, off the wall, out of order, and out of context with the content of the lesson, consider this as a possible response: "That is an interesting question (or comment) and I would very much like to talk with you more about it. Could we meet at freeze time, or at some other time that is mutually convenient?"

Avoid bluffing an answer to a question for which you do not have an answer. Nothing will cause you to lose credibility with students any faster than faking an answer. There is nothing wrong with admitting that you do not know. It helps students realize that you are human. It helps them maintain an adequate self-esteem, realizing that they are okay. What is important is that you know where and how to find possible or tentative answers and that you help students develop that same knowledge and those same process skills.

> Children who have been provoked to reach beyond themselves, to wonder, to imagine, to pose their own questions are the ones most likely to learn.
>
> Maxine Greene (1988)

Now, to reinforce your understanding, do Exercises 6.3 through 6.7, found at the end of this chapter.

SUMMARY

Central to helping students in their learning and in their learning to learn is helping them to understand and develop their intelligent behaviors. This chapter presented a great deal of information about one teaching strategy in particular, which will be perhaps the most important one in your instructional repertoire. Questioning is the cornerstone to meaningful thinking, communication, learning, and real-world problem solving. The art of its use in instruction is something you will continue to develop throughout your teaching career.

QUESTIONS FOR CLASS DISCUSSION

1. Have you ever noticed that some teachers seem to anticipate a lower-level response to their questions from particular students? Discuss your answer and the reasons for such teacher behavior with your classmates.

2. Do you believe a teacher should verbally respond to every student's comment or question? Explain why or why not. If not, on what basis does the teacher decide when and how to respond?

3. Explain the meaning of this statement: Rather than looking for what students can reiterate, we should look for what they can demonstrate and produce. Explain why you agree or disagree with the concept.

4. It is claimed that questions stimulate certain kinds of thought responses. What mental operations must students engage in to answer this question: What is the most important reason that sea level deserts have a relatively small population of humans? (That is, what would the student need to know and in what sequence would they have to process information in order to answer the question?)

5. Explain why you believe it is or is not a good idea to assign reflective questions (i.e., open-ended, "thought" questions) for homework. What research evidence can you find to support or refute your opinion?

 Now go to Topic #7: **Strategies for Teaching** in the MyEducationLab (www.myeducationlab.com) for your course, where you can:

- Find learning outcomes for this topic along with the national standards that connect to these outcomes.
- Complete Assignments and Activities that can help you more deeply understand the chapter content.
- Examine challenging situations and cases presented in the IRIS center resources.
- Apply and practice your understanding of the core teaching skills identified in the chapter with the Building Teaching Skills and Dispositions learning units.

EXERCISE 6.1   IDENTIFYING THE COGNITIVE LEVELS OF QUESTIONS—A SELF-CHECK EXERCISE

INSTRUCTIONS: The purpose of this exercise is to test your understanding and recognition of the levels of questions. Mark each of the following questions with a

   1, if it is at the lowest level of mental operation, gathering and recalling data.
   2, if it is at the middle level, processing data.
   3, if it is at the highest level, applying or evaluating data in a new situation.

Check your answers against the key that follows. Resolve problems by discussing them with your classmates and instructor.

_____   1. What are the differences between an Asian elephant and an African elephant?

_____   2. How are the natural habitats of the Asian and African elephants similar? How are they different?

_____   3. Which of the elephants do you think is the more interesting?

_____   4. For what does the elephant use its tusks?

_____   5. Do all elephants have tusks?

_____   6. Did the trick ending make the story more interesting for you?

_____   7. How might these evergreen needles be grouped?

_____   8. How do these two types of pine needles differ?

_____   9. For how many years was the Soviet Union a communist-dominated nation?

_____   10. How many republics do you believe will be in the new Commonwealth of Independent States (the former Soviet Union) by the year 2020?

_____   11. Why do you think the city decided to move the zoo?

_____   12. How would the park be different today had the zoo been left there?

_____   13. How do zoos today differ from those of the mid-nineteenth century?

_____   14. Should a teacher be entitled to unemployment benefits during the summer or when school is not in session?

_____   15. If $4X + 40 = 44$; what is X?

_____   16. What happens when I spin this egg?

_____   17. How does this poem make you feel?

_____   18. What will happen when we mix equal amounts of the red and yellow solutions?

_____   19. What is the capital of West Virginia?

_____   20. What will be the long-term global effects if the rain forests continue to be removed at the present rate?

Answer Keys 1. = 1 (recall); 2. = 2 (compare); 3. = 3 (judge); 4. = 3 (imagine); 5. = 3 (extrapolate); 6. = 3 (evaluate); 7. = 2 (classify); 8. = 2 (contrast); 9. = 1 (recall); 10. = 3 (predict); 11. = 2 (explain cause and effect); 12. = 3 (speculate); 13. = 2 (contrast); 14. = 3 (judge); 15. = 1 (recall of how to work the problem) 16. = 1 (observe); 17. = 1 (describe); 18. = 3 (hypothesize); 19. = 1 (recall); 20. = 3 (speculate or generalize)

 ## EXERCISE 6.2 THINK TIME AND THE ART OF QUESTIONING: AN IN-CLASS EXERCISE

INSTRUCTIONS: The purpose of this exercise is to further your understanding of the art and power of questioning, the importance of well-worded questions with well-prepared and clear instructions, and the need to give students time to think. A secondary purpose is to experience and discuss the use of role-play simulations in learning.

1. Role-play simulation: From your class ask for three volunteers. One volunteer will read the lines of the teacher, Angel, a second will read the one line of the student, while the third volunteer uses a stop watch to direct Angel and the student to speak their lines at the designated times. The rest of your class can pretend to be students in Angel's high school English class.

1:00 *Angel:* "Think of a man whom you admire, perhaps a father figure, and write a three-sentence paragraph describing that person." Students begin their writing.

1:00:05 *Angel:* "Only three sentences about someone you admire. It might be your father, uncle, anyone."

1:00:07 *Student:* "Does it have to be about a man?"

Angel: "No, it can be a man or a woman, but someone you truly look up to."

1:01 Angel works the rows, seeing that students are on task.

1:01:10 *Angel:* "Three sentences are all you need to write."

1:01:15 *Angel:* "Think of someone you really admire, and write three sentences in a paragraph that describes that person."

1:01:30 *Angel:* "Someone you would like to be like."

1:02 Angel continues walking around helping students who are having difficulty. All students are on task.

1:04 *Angel:* "Now I want you to exchange papers with the person behind or beside you, read that person's description of the person they admire, and describe a setting that you see their person in. Write a paragraph that describes that setting."

1:04-1:05 Students exchange papers; teacher walks around seeing that everyone has received another student's paper.

1:05 *Angel:* "Where do you see that person being? Below the paragraph, I want you to write a new paragraph describing where you see this person, perhaps in an easy chair watching a ball game, on a porch, in a car, or in the kitchen cooking."

1:05:10 *Angel:* "Describe a scene you see this person in."

☞

EXERCISE 6.2 *(continued)*

    1:05:15   *Angel:* "After you read the description, I want you to create a setting for the person described."

    1:05:18   Students seem confused either about what they are reading (e.g., asking the writer what a word is or means) or what they are supposed to do.

    1:05:19   *Angel:* "Anything is fine. Use your imagination to describe the setting."

    1:05:22   *Angel:* "Describe a setting for this person."

    1:09   *Angel:* "Now I want you to exchange papers with yet another person and after reading the previous two paragraphs written by two other students, write a third paragraph describing a problem you think this admired person has."

2. After the role-play simulation, hold a whole-class discussion or small-group discussions and use the following as a springboard for your discussion: Describe what you believe are the good points and weak points of this portion of Angel's lesson and her implementation of it.

3. Lastly, hold a discussion sharing opinions and experiences about role-play simulations as a strategy for teaching and learning.

EXERCISE 6.3 EXAMINING COURSE MATERIALS FOR LEVEL OF QUESTIONING

INSTRUCTIONS: It is the purpose of this exercise for you to examine course materials for the levels of questions presented to students. For a subject and grade level you intend to teach, examine a textbook (or other instructional material) for the questions posed to the students, perhaps at the ends of the chapters. Also examine workbooks, examinations, instructional packages, and any other printed or electronic material used by students. Complete the exercise that follows; then share your findings with your classmates.

1. Materials examined (include date of publication and target students): _____

_____

2. Questions at the recall (lowest) level: _____

_____

_____

_____

_____

3. Questions at the processing (intermediate) level: _____

_____

_____

_____

_____

4. Questions at the application (highest) level: _____

_____

_____

_____

_____

5. Approximate percentages of questions at each level: _____

  a. Recall = _____%

  b. Processing = _____%

  c. Application = _____%

6. Did you find evidence of question-level sequencing? If so, describe it.

_____

_____

_____

_____

☞

EXERCISE 6.3 *(continued)*

7. After sharing and discussing your results with your classmates, what do you conclude from this exercise?

_____

_____

_____

_____

8. When using instructional materials that you believe have a disproportionately high percentage of questions at the input (or recall) level; in addition to the two examples provided, what should or could you do?

Example 1: Have students scan chapter subheadings and develop higher-level cognitive questions based on the subheadings, which they would then answer through their reading.

Example 2: Require students to defend their answers to low-level cognitive chapter review and end-of-chapter questions with textual information and experience.

_____

_____

_____

_____

_____

_____

EXERCISE 6.4   THE COGNITIVE LEVELS OF CLASSROOM VERBAL INTERACTION

INSTRUCTIONS: The purpose of this exercise is to develop your skill in recognizing the levels of classroom questions. Arrange to visit an elementary or secondary school classroom. On the lines provided here, tally each time you hear a question (or statement) from the teacher that causes students to gather or recall information, to process information, or to apply or evaluate data. In the left column, you may want to write additional key words to assist your memory. After your observation, compare and discuss the results of this exercise with your colleagues.

School and class visited: _____

Date of observation: _____

QUESTION OR STATEMENT

Level

Tallies of Level of Question or Statement

Recall level
(key words: complete, count, define, describe, and so on)

1. _____

_____

_____

_____

_____

Processing level
(key words: analyze, classify, compare, and so on)

2. _____

_____

_____

_____

_____

Application level
(key words: apply, build, evaluate, and so on)

3. _____

_____

_____

_____

_____

EXERCISE 6.5   PRACTICE IN RAISING QUESTIONS TO HIGHER LEVELS

INSTRUCTIONS: The purpose of this exercise is to further develop your skill in raising questions from one level to the next higher level. Complete the blank lines with questions at the appropriate levels (for the last series, create your own recall question and then vary it for the higher levels). Share and discuss your responses with your classmates.

Recall Level	Processing Level	Application Level
1. How many of you read a newspaper today?	1. Why did you read a newspaper today?	1. What do you think would happen if nobody ever read a newspaper again?
2. What was today's newspaper headline?	2. Why was that important enough to be a headline?	2. What news items do you think will be in tomorrow's paper?
3. Who is the vice-president of the United States today?	3. How does the work done by this vice-president compare with that done by the previous vice-president?	3.
4. How many presidents has the United States had?	4.	4.
5.	5.	5.

EXERCISE 6.6   CREATING COGNITIVE QUESTIONS

INSTRUCTIONS: The purpose of this exercise is to provide practice in writing cognitive questions. Read the following example of verse. Then, from that verse, compose three questions about it that would cause students to identify, list, and recall; three that would cause students to analyze, compare, and explain; and three that would cause students to predict, apply, and hypothesize. Share and check questions with your peers.

WE ARE ONE

Truth, love, peace, and beauty,
We have sought apart
    but will find within, as our
Moods—explored, shared,
    questioned, and accepted—
Together become one and all.

Through life my friends
We can travel together,
for we now know
each could go it alone.

To assimilate our efforts into one,
While growing in accepting,
and trusting, and sharing the
    individuality of the other,
Is truly to enjoy our greatest gift—
Feeling—knowing love and compassion.

Through life my friends
We are together,
for we must know
we are one.

—R. D. Kellough

RECALL QUESTIONS

1. (to *identify*) _____

_____

_____

_____

2. (to *list*) _____

_____

_____

_____

3. (to *recall*) _____

_____

_____

_____

EXERCISE 6.6 *(continued)*

PROCESSING QUESTIONS

1. (to *analyze*) _____

_____

_____

_____

2. (to *compare*) _____

_____

_____

_____

3. (to *explain*) _____

_____

_____

_____

APPLICATION QUESTIONS

1. (to *predict*) _____

_____

_____

_____

2. (to *apply*) _____

_____

_____

_____

3. (to *hypothesize*) _____

_____

_____

_____

EXERCISE 6.7   A COOPERATIVE LEARNING AND MICRO PEER TEACHING EXERCISE IN THE USE OF QUESTIONING—MICRO PEER TEACHING I

INSTRUCTIONS: The purpose of this exercise is to practice preparing and asking questions that are designed to lead student thinking from the lowest level to the highest. Before class, prepare a 5-minute lesson for posing questions that will guide the learner from lowest to highest levels of thinking. Teaching will be one-on-one, in groups of four, with each member of the group assuming a particular role—teacher, student, judge, or recorder. Each of the four members of your group will assume each of those roles once for 5 minutes. (If there are only three members in a group, the roles of judge and recorder can be combined during each 5-minute lesson; or, if there are five members in the group, one member can sit out each round, or two can work together as judge.) Each member of the group should have a tally sheet.

SOME SUGGESTED LESSON TOPICS ARE AS FOLLOWS:

- Teaching styles
- Characteristics of youngsters of a particular age
- Learning styles of students
- Assessment of learning achievement
- A skill or hobby
- Teaching competencies
- A particular teaching strategy
- Student teaching and what it will really be like

EACH GROUP MEMBER SHOULD KEEP THE FOLLOWING ROLE DESCRIPTIONS IN MIND:

- *Teacher (sender).* Pose recall (input), processing, and application (output) questions related to the topic chosen.
- *Student (receiver).* Respond to the questions of the teacher.
- *Judge.* Identify the level of each question or statement used by the teacher and the level of the student's response.
- *Recorder.* Tally the number of each level of question or statement used by the teacher (S = sender) as indicated by the judge; also tally the level of student responses (R = receiver). Record any problems encountered by your group.

TALLY SHEET

		Minute	Input	Processing	Output
Sender _____		1 S			
Receiver _____		R			
		2 S			
		R			
		3 S			
		R			
		4 S			
		R			
		5 S			
		R			

TALLY SHEET

	Minute	Input	Processing	Output
Sender _____	1 S			
Receiver _____	R			
	2 S			
	R			
	3 S			
	R			
	4 S			
	R			
	5 S			
	R			

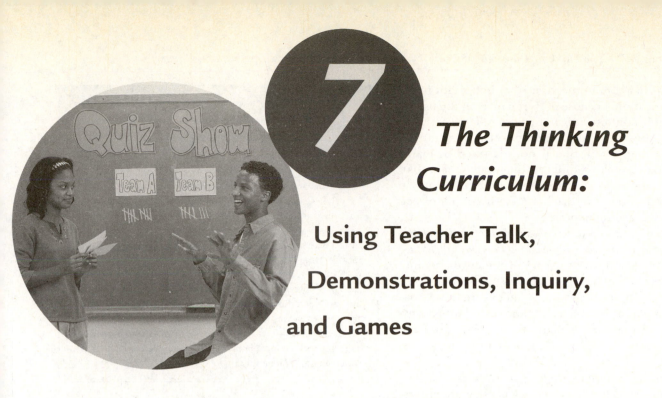

The Thinking Curriculum:

Using Teacher Talk,

Demonstrations, Inquiry,

and Games

Perhaps no other strategy is used more often by teachers than teacher talk, so this chapter begins with a presentation of guidelines for using that vital and significant instructional strategy.

A strategy related to teacher talk is the demonstration, which is addressed later in the chapter, followed by guidelines for other important strategies, namely, inquiry and discovery, and games.

Specifically, upon completion of this chapter you should be able to:

1. Make an effective demonstration performed either by yourself, by some students, or collaboratively between you and students.
2. Demonstrate an understanding of the relationship between problem solving, discovery, and inquiry.
3. Explain ways of integrating strategies for integrated learning.
4. Describe when and demonstrate how to use inquiry for student learning.
5. Describe when and how to use teacher talk for instruction.
6. Demonstrate your knowledge of advantages and disadvantages of each of seven categories of games for learning.

TEACHER TALK: FORMAL AND INFORMAL

Teacher talk encompasses both lecturing to students and talking with students. For our purposes here, a lecture is considered formal teacher talk, whereas a discussion with students is considered informal teacher talk.

Cautions in Using Teacher Talk

Whether your talk is formal or informal, there are certain cautions that you need to be mindful of. Perhaps the most important is that of *talking too much*. If a teacher talks too much, the significance of the teacher's words may be lost because some students will tune the teacher out.

Another caution is to avoid *talking too fast*. Students can hear faster than they can understand what they hear. It is a good idea to remind yourself to talk at a reasonable pace and to check frequently for student comprehension of what you are talking about. And, when working with ELL students, you will want to talk even more slowly and do more frequent checks for comprehension. It is also important to remember that your one brain is communicating with many student brains, each of which responds to sensory input (auditory in this instance) at different rates. Because of this, you will need to pause to let words sink in and you will need to pause during transitions from one point or activity to the next.

A third caution is to be sure you are being *heard and understood*. Sometimes teachers talk in too low a pitch or use words that are not understood by many of the students, or both. You should vary the pitch of your voice, and you should stop and help students with their understanding of vocabulary that may be new to them.

A fourth caution is to remember that *just because students have heard something before does not necessarily mean that they understand it or learned it*. From the earlier discussions of learning experiences (such as The Learning Experiences Ladder in Chapter 5), remember that although verbal communication is an important form of communication, because of its reliance on the use of abstract symbolization, it is not a very reliable form of communication. Teacher talk relies on words and on skill in listening, a skill that is not mastered by many young people (or many adults for that matter). For that and other reasons, to ensure student understanding, it is good to reinforce your teacher talk with either direct or simulated learning experiences.

A related caution is to *resist believing that students have attained a skill or have learned something that was taught previously by you or by another teacher.* During any discussion (formal or informal), rather than assuming that your students know something, you should ensure they know it. For example, if the discussion and a student activity involve a particular math skill or thinking skill, then you will want to make sure that students know how to use that skill.

Still another problem is *talking in a humdrum monotone.* Students need teachers whose voices exude enthusiasm and excitement (although not to be overdone) about the subject and about teaching and learning. Such enthusiasm and excitement for learning are contagious. A voice that demonstrates genuine enthusiasm for teaching and learning is more likely to motivate students to learn.

A final caution is *just because your speaking (auditory output) channel is engaged does not mean that you should disengage your sensory input channels.* This is another time when the competent teachers' skills of withitness and overlapping are apparent. While a competent teacher is talking, that teacher is still seeing and listening and capable of changing physical location in the classroom.

Keep those cautions in mind as you study the general principles and specific guidelines for the productive and effective use of teacher talk.

Teacher Talk: General Guidelines

Certain general guidelines should be followed whether your talk is formal or informal. First, *begin the talk with an advance organizer.* **Advance organizers** are introductions that mentally prepare students for a study by helping them make connections with material already learned or experienced—a **comparative organizer**—or by providing students with a conceptual arrangement of what is to be learned—an **expository organizer** (Ausubel, 1963). The value of using advance organizers is well documented by research (Good & Brophy, 2008). An advance organizer can be a brief introduction or statement about the main idea you intend to convey and how it is related to other aspects of the students' learning (an expository organizer), or it can be a presentation of a discrepancy to arouse curiosity (a comparative organizer, in this instance causing students to compare what they have observed with what they already knew or thought they

CLASSROOM VIGNETTE

A Precious Moment in Teaching with Advice to Beginning Teachers

I share with you this teaching vignette that I find both humorous and indicative of creative thinking.

While teaching a history lesson, the teacher began the lesson with the question, "What comes to mind when you hear the words 'Puritan' and 'Pilgrim'?" Without hesitation, a rather quiet student voice replied, "Cooking oil and John Wayne." Although this particular incident happened perhaps too long ago now to ring a bell with college-age students of today, to me it represented one of those rare and precious moments in teaching, reaffirming my belief that every teacher is well advised to maintain throughout his or her teaching career a journal in which such intrinsically rewarding moments can be recorded so as to be reviewed and enjoyed again years later.

knew). Preparing an organizer helps you plan and organize the sequence of ideas, and its presentation helps students organize their own learning and become motivated about it. An advance organizer can also make their learning meaningful by providing important connections between what they already know and what is being learned.

Second, *your talk should be planned so that it has a beginning and an end, with a logical order between.* During your talk, you should reinforce your words with visuals. These visuals may include writing unfamiliar terms on the board (helping students learn new vocabulary), visual organizers, and prepared graphs, charts, photographs, and various audiovisuals.

Third, *pacing is important.* Your talk must move briskly, although not too fast. For many beginning teachers the ability to pace the instruction is a difficult skill (the tendency among many is to talk too fast and too much), but one that improves with experience. Until you have developed skill in pacing lessons, you may need to remind yourself during lessons to slow down and provide silent pauses (allowing for think time) and frequent checks for student comprehension. Specifically, your talk should

- Be brisk, though not too fast, but with occasional slowdowns to change the pace and to check for student comprehension. Allow students time to think, to ask questions, and to make notes (Marzano, Pickering, & Pollock, 2001).
- Have a time plan. A talk planned for 10 minutes, if interesting to students, will probably take longer. If not interesting to them, it will probably take less time.
- Always be planned with careful consideration given for the characteristics of the students. For example, if you have a fairly high percentage of ELL students or

of students with special needs, then your teacher talk may be less brisk, sprinkled with even more visuals, repeated statements and simpler word use, and frequent checks for student comprehension.

Fourth, *encourage student participation.* Their active participation enhances their learning. This encouragement can be planned as questions that you ask or as time allowed for students to comment and ask questions or as some sort of a visual and conceptual outline that students complete during the talk.

Fifth, *plan a clear ending (closure).* Be sure your talk has a clear ending, followed by another activity (during the same or next class period) that will help secure the learning. As for all lessons, you want to strive for planning a clear and mesmerizing beginning, an involving lesson body, and a firm and meaningful closure.

Teacher Talk: Specific Guidelines

Specific guidelines for using teacher talk are presented in the following paragraphs.

Understand the various reasons for using teacher talk. Teacher talk, formal or informal, can be useful to discuss the progress of a unit of study, explain an inquiry, introduce a unit of study, present a problem, promote student inquiry or critical thinking, provide a transition from one unit of study to the next, provide information otherwise unobtainable to students, share the teacher's experiences, share the teacher's thinking, summarize a problem, summarize a unit of study, and teach a thinking skill by modeling that skill.

Clarify the objectives of the talk. Your talk should center around one idea. The learning objectives, which should not be too numerous for one talk, should be clearly understood by the students.

Choose between informal and formal talk. Although an occasional formal "cutting edge" lecture may be appropriate for some classes, spontaneous, interactive informal talks of 5 to 12 minutes are preferred. Very rarely, if ever, should a teacher give long lectures with no teacher–student interaction. Remember, though, a formal period-long noninteractive lecture, common in some college teaching, is developmentally inappropriate when teaching most groups of students of grades K–12. However, to arouse student interest and to provide new information in relatively small and intellectually digestible chunks, the lecture may be appropriate. If, during your student teaching, you have doubt or questions about your selection and use of a particular instructional strategy, discuss it with your cooperating teacher or your university supervisor, or both. When you have doubt about the appropriateness of a particular strategy, trust your intuition—without some modification, the strategy probably is inappropriate.

Teaching in Practice

When Student Attention Begins to Drift

Today's youth are used to electronic interactions as well as "commercial breaks," and the capacity to surf channels to find something of personal interest—for many lessons, especially those that are teacher-centered, after about 8 minutes student attention is quite likely to begin to waft. For that eventuality you need lesson elements planned to recapture student attention. These planned elements can include any number of things, such as

- analogies to help connect the topic to students' experiences
- humor
- pauses for emphasis and to allow information to register
- sensory cues, such as eye contact and proximity (as in your moving around the room)
- verbal cues, such as voice inflections and name dropping
- visual cues, such as the use of overhead displays, charts, board drawings, excerpts from CDs, realia, and body gestures

Question for Class Discussion

1. Can you think of other elements that could be used to recapture waning student attention, perhaps specific to your grade level or subject field? Discuss your ideas with your classmates.

Vary strategies and activities frequently. Perhaps most useful as a strategy for recapturing student attention is to change to an entirely different strategy or learning modality. For example, from teacher talk (a teacher-centered strategy) you would change to a student activity (a student-centered strategy). Notice that changing from a lecture (mostly teacher talk) to a teacher-led discussion (mostly more teacher talk) would not be changing to an entirely different modality. Figure 7.1 provides a comparison of different changes.

As a generalization, when using teacher-centered direct instruction, with most classes you will want to change the learning activities about every 8 to 15 minutes. (That is one reason that in the preferred lesson plan format presented in Chapter 5, you find space for at least four activities, including the introduction and closure.) This means that in a 50- or 60-minute time block, you should probably plan three or four *sequenced* learning activities, with some that are teacher centered and many others that are more student centered. In a 90-minute block, plan five or six learning activities.

In exemplary classrooms, rather than using teacher-centered direct instruction, teachers often have several activities *concurrently* being performed by individuals, dyads, and small groups of students (i.e., the teachers use multitasking or multilevel instruction).

Figure 7.1   Recapturing student attention by changing the instructional strategy.

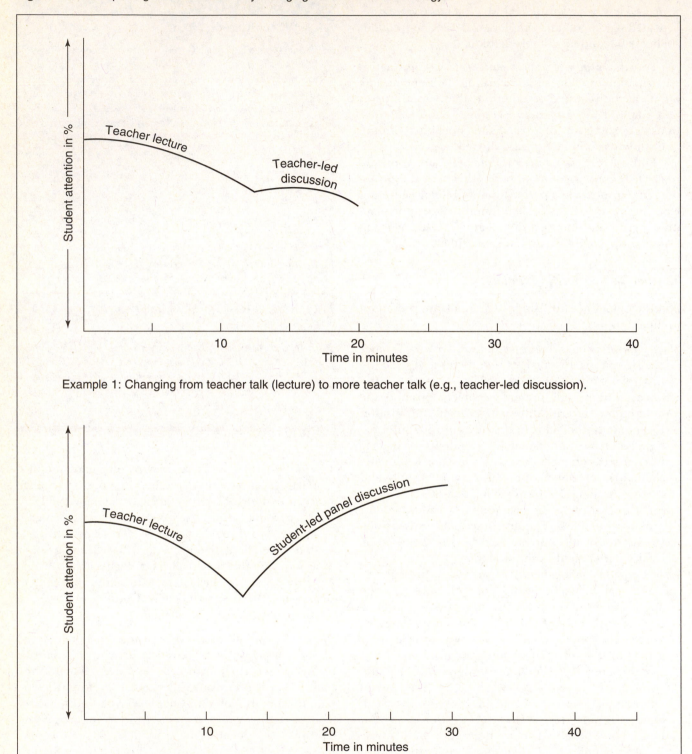

Example 1: Changing from teacher talk (lecture) to more teacher talk (e.g., teacher-led discussion).

Example 2: Changing from teacher talk (teacher-centered activity) to student-led panel discussion (student-centered activity).

Figure 7.1   *(continued)*

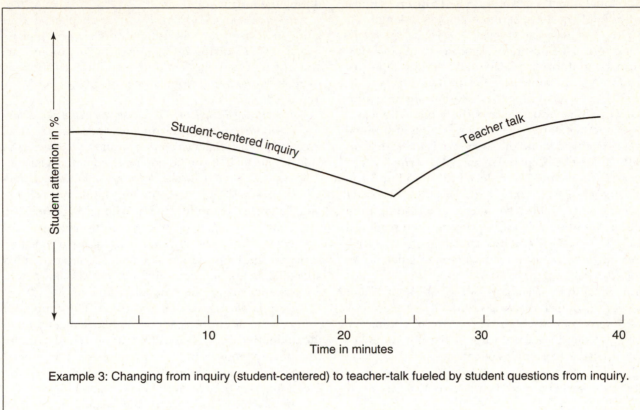

Example 3: Changing from inquiry (student-centered) to teacher-talk fueled by student questions from inquiry.

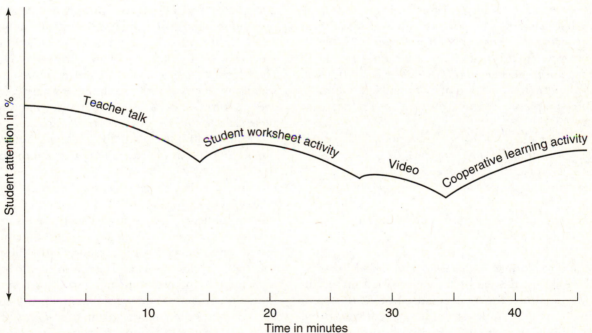

Example 4: Changing from teacher talk (teacher-centered activity) to cooperative learning activity (student-centered activity).

Multilevel instruction is particularly important for use during long block periods, called **macroperiods**, typically double periods, or about 2 hours in length.

Prepare and use notes as a guide to yourself for your talk. Planning your talk and preparing notes to be used during formal and informal teacher talk is important—just as important as is implementing the talk with visuals. There is absolutely nothing wrong with using notes during your teaching. You can carry them on a clipboard, perhaps a neon colored one that gives students a visual focus as you move around the room. Your notes for a formal talk can first be prepared in narrative form; for class use though, they should be reduced to an outline form. *Talks to students should always be from an outline, never read from prose.* The only time that a teacher's reading from prose aloud to students is appropriate is when reading a brief, published article (such as in science or social studies) or portions of a story or a poem (such as in reading/English/language arts).

In your outline, use color coding with abbreviated visual cues to yourself. You will eventually develop your own coding system—though keep whatever coding system you use simple lest you forget what the codes are for. Consider these examples of coding:

- Where *media* will be used, mark *M,* or *V* for *visual,* or *PP* for *PowerPoint.*
- Where transition of ideas occurs and you want to allow silent moments for ideas to sink in, mark *P* for *pause, T* for a *transition,* or *S* for moments of *silence.*
- Where you intend to stop and ask a question, mark *TQ* for *teacher question* or *TQ (student name)* when you intend to ask the question of a particular student.
- Where you plan *reviews* and *comprehension checks,* mark *R* and *CS.*
- Where you plan *small-group work,* mark *SG,* or for *cooperative learning group work,* mark *CLG.*
- Where you plan to have a *discussion,* mark *D.*
- Where you plan to switch to an *investigatory* activity, mark *I.*
- Where you want to stop and allow time for *student questions,* mark *SQ* or *?.*

Share your note organization with your students. Sharing with them how you organize for your work is important modeling for them for their organization of their own learning. Teach the students how to take notes and what kinds of things they should write down, including how to summarize. Teaching students note taking and summarizing skills is to help them with what researchers refer to as "two of the most useful academic skills students can have" (Marzano et al., 2001, p. 29). Use various colors to outline and highlight your talk; encourage your students to use colored pencils for note taking, so their notes can be color coded to match your writing board notes. This not only enhances their learning, but also keeps them productively and kinesthetically occupied during the instruction.

Rehearse your talk. Using your lesson plan as your guide, rehearse your talk using a video recorder, or rehearse it while talking into a mirror or to a roommate. You may want to include a time plan for each subtopic to allow you to gauge your timing during implementation of the talk.

Avoid racing through the talk solely to complete it by a certain time. It is more important that students understand some of what you say than that you cover it all and they understand little or none of it. If you do not finish, continue it later.

Augment your talk with multisensory stimulation and allow for think time. Your presentation should not rely too much on verbal communication. When using visuals, do not think that you must be constantly talking; after clearly explaining the reason for using a particular visual, give students sufficient time to look at it, think about it, and ask questions about it. The visual is new to the students, so give them time to take it in.

Carefully plan the content of your talk. The content of your talk should supplement and enhance that found in the student textbook rather than simply rehash content from the textbook. Students may never read their book if you tell them in an interesting and condensed fashion everything that they need to know from it.

Monitor your delivery. Your voice should be pleasant and interesting to listen to rather than a steady, boring monotone or a constantly shrieking, irritating, high pitch. On the other hand, it is good to show enthusiasm for what you are talking about, for teaching and learning. Occasionally use dramatic voice inflections to emphasize important points and meaningful body language to give students a visual focus. So not to appear phony, practice these skills so they become second nature.

Additionally, to maintain students' focus on the important content of your talk try to avoid too frequent use of *verbal fill-ins,* such as "you know" and "ah,ah." Overuse of verbal fill-ins probably derives from the subconscious thought that "If I don't continue talking I will lose my audience," when in fact such useless injections into the talk are more likely to cause just the opposite—loss of the audiences' concentration on the substance of your talk. In the worse case scenario members of the audience find themselves focusing solely on counting the times the speaker uses a verbal fill-in such as "you know."

When teaching a large group of students (by "large group," I mean more than 8 students), *avoid standing in the same spot for long periods of time.* (I consider 10 minutes in the same spot to be a long time.) Be mobile! Even during direct instruction, you need to monitor student behavior and to engage occasional signal interference (as discussed in Chapter 3). It is especially during extended periods of direct instruction that a beginning teacher's skills in withitness and overlapping behaviors are likely to be put to the test.

View the vocabulary of the talk as an opportunity to help students with their word morphology. Words you use should be easily understood by the students, though you should still model professionalism and help students develop their vocabulary—both the vocabulary of your special discipline and the more general vocabulary of the English language. During your lesson planning, predict when you are likely to use a word that is new to most students, and plan to stop to ask a student to explain its meaning and perhaps demonstrate its derivation. Help students with word meaning. This assists students with their remembering. Regardless of subject or grade level, *every teacher is a teacher of literacy and of language arts.* Knowledge of word morphology is an important component of skilled reading and includes the ability to generate new words from prefixes, roots, and suffixes. For some students, nearly every subject in the curriculum is basically a foreign language. That is certainly true for some English language learners, for whom teacher talk, especially formal teacher talk, should be used sparingly, if at all. As repeated often throughout this resource guide, every teacher has the responsibility of helping students learn how to learn, and that includes helping students develop their word comprehension skills, reading skills, thinking and memory skills, and their motivation for, as well as confidence in, learning.

For example, when introducing to students the word *hermaphrodite*, the science teacher is afforded an opportunity to teach a bit of Greek mythology in the process of helping the students with the meaning of that important term in biology, through showing students the origin of the word's two roots (Hermes, or Mercury, the messenger of the gods, and Aphrodite, or Venus, goddess of love and beauty). Taking time to teach a bit of Greek mythology provides the science teacher a chance to cross disciplines and in doing so perhaps capture the interest of a few more students.

Words formed from parts of two words are called *blends*—for example, *smog* from *smoke + fog, brunch* from *breakfast + lunch,* and *blog* from *web + log.* The prefixes *e-* and *i-* have combined to form many new words and concepts over recent decades (e.g., *e-commerce* and *iTunes*). Students can become word detectives and discover new blends through shopping (Wal-Mart?) or advertisements, or add to their enjoyment of learning English by finding new words and creating their own. The study of word morphology adds fun to learning English as well as word power.

Díaz-Rico & Weed (2010, p. 37)

Give thoughtful and intelligent consideration to student diversity. While preparing your talk (during the preactive phase of your instruction), consider students in your classroom who are culturally and linguistically different and those who have special needs. Personalize the talk for them by choosing your vocabulary carefully and appropriately, speaking slowly and methodically,

repeating often, and by planning meaningful analogies and examples and relevant audio and visual displays.

Use familiar examples and analogies to help students make relevant connections (bridges). Although this sometimes takes a great deal of creative thinking as well as action during the planning phase of instruction, it is important that you do your best to connect the talk with ideas and events with which the students are already familiar. The most effective talk is one that makes frequent and meaningful connections between what students already know and what they are learning, that bridges what they are learning with what they have experienced in their lives. Of course, to do this well means you need to "know" your students (see "Get to Know Your Students as People" in Chapter 3).

Establish eye contact frequently. Your primary eye contact should be with your students—always! That important point cannot be overemphasized. Only momentarily should you look at your notes, your visuals, the projection screen, media equipment, the writing board, and other adults or objects in the classroom. Although you may raise your eyebrows in doubt when you read this, it is true and it is important that with practice you can learn to scan a classroom of 30 students, establishing eye contact with each student about once every 60 seconds. To "establish" eye contact means that the student is aware that you are looking at him or her. Frequent eye contact can have two major benefits. First, as you "read" a student's body posture and facial expressions, you obtain clues about that student's attentiveness and comprehension. Second, eye contact helps to establish rapport between you and a student. A look with a smile or a wink from the teacher to a student can say so much! Be alert, though, for students who are from cultures where eye contact is infrequent or unwanted and could have negative consequences. In other words, don't push it!

Frequent eye contact is easier when using a screen display (such as with the overhead projector or a PowerPoint presentation) than when using the writing board. When using a writing board, you have to turn at least partially away from your audience; you may also have to pace back and forth from the board to the students in order to retain that important proximity to them.

While lecturing on a topic, you must remain aware and attentive to everything that is happening in the classroom (i.e., to student behavior as well as to the content of your lecture). No one truly knowledgeable about it ever said that good teaching is easy. But don't dismay; with the knowledge of the preceding guidelines and with practice, experience, and intelligent reflection, you will in time develop the skills.

Now do Exercise 7.1 (at end of this chapter).

DEMONSTRATION

Most students like demonstrations. They like demonstrations because the person doing the demonstration is actively engaged in a learning activity rather than merely verbalizing about it. Demonstrations can be used at any grade level in teaching any subject and for a variety of reasons. The teacher demonstrates role-playing in preparation for a social studies simulation. Select students demonstrate how they solved a problem. A language arts/English teacher demonstrates clustering to students ready for a creative writing assignment. A science teacher demonstrates the effect of combining an acid and a base to form saltwater. The physical education teacher or student volunteer demonstrates the proper way to serve in volleyball.

Reasons for Using Demonstrations

A demonstration can be designed to serve any of the following functions, and the reasons for using a particular demonstration should be communicated to the students.

- assist in recognizing a solution to an existing problem; to bring an unusual closure to a lesson or unit of study
- conserve time and resources (as opposed to the entire class doing that which is being demonstrated)
- establish discrepancy recognition
- establish problem recognition
- give students an opportunity for vicarious participation in active learning
- illustrate a particular point of content
- introduce a lesson or unit of study in a way that grabs the students' attention
- model or demonstrate a skill, such as a skill in sports, inquiry, thinking, note taking, summarizing, social behavior, library use, or a skill useful in conflict resolution
- reduce potential safety hazards (where the teacher demonstrates with materials that are too dangerous for students to handle)
- review or summarize a topic or unit of study
- test a hypothesis

Guidelines for Using Demonstrations

When planning a demonstration, consider the following guidelines.

Decide the most effective way to conduct the demonstration. It might be a verbal or a silent demonstration by a student or the teacher, by the teacher with a student helper, by a student with the teacher as helper, to the entire class or to small groups, or by some combination of these, such as first by the teacher followed by a repeat of the demonstration by a student or succession of students.

Be sure that the demonstration is visible to all students. To accomplish this, some classrooms use overhead mirrors or video cameras connected to large-screen television monitors.

Practice with the materials and procedure before demonstrating to the students. During your practice, try to prepare for anything that could go wrong during the real demonstration; if you don't, as Murphy's Law states, if anything can go wrong, it probably will. Then, if something does go wrong during the live demonstration, use that as an opportunity for a teachable moment; engage the students in working with you to try to learn what went wrong, or if that is not feasible, then go to Plan B (an emergency alternate plan that you prepared during lesson planning).

Consider your pacing of the demonstration, allowing for enough student wait-see-and-think time. At the start of the demonstration, explain the learning objectives. Remember this familiar adage: Tell them what you are going to do, show them, and then help them understand what they saw. As with any lesson, plan your closure and allow time for questions and discussion. During the demonstration, as in other types of teacher talk, use frequent stops to check for student understanding.

Consider using special lighting to highlight the demonstration. (One teacher uses an old "recycled" slide projector as a spotlight source.) And finally, be sure the demonstration table and area are free of unnecessary objects that could distract, be in the way, or pose a safety hazard.

With potentially hazardous demonstrations, such as might occur in physical education, science, or shop classes, you must model proper safety precautions. Wear safety goggles, have fire-safety equipment at hand, and position a protective, transparent shield between the demonstration table and nearby students.

Students teaching other students principally through group work and demonstrations is common practice in schools today using what is referred to as a **focused-learning approach**, where students perform a major hands-on role in classroom instruction.

TEACHING THINKING FOR INTELLIGENT BEHAVIOR

Pulling together what has been learned about learning and brain functioning, teachers are encouraged to integrate explicit thinking instruction into daily lessons. In other words, teachers should help students develop their thinking skills. As their thinking skills develop, students develop a sense of "I can," with an accompanying feeling of "I enjoy." Art Costa (1991, p. 19) expresses it this way:

> In teaching for thinking, we are interested not only in what students know but also in how students behave when they don't know. ... Gathering evidence of the performance and growth of intelligent behavior ... requires "kid-watching": observing students as they try to solve the day-to-day academic and real-life problems they encounter. ... By collecting anecdotes and examples of written, oral, and visual expressions, we can see students' increasingly voluntary and spontaneous performance of these intelligent behaviors.

Characteristics of Intelligent Behavior

Characteristics of intelligent behavior that you should model, teach for, and observe developing in your students, as identified by Costa and Kallick (2000), are described in the following paragraphs. (Note: See also Armstrong's [1998] 12 qualities of genius—curiosity, playfulness, imagination, creativity, wonderment, wisdom, inventiveness, vitality, sensitivity, flexibility, humor, and joy.)

Drawing on knowledge and applying it to new situations. A major goal of formal education is for students to apply school-learned knowledge to real-life situations. To develop skills in drawing on past knowledge and applying that knowledge to new situations, students must be given opportunities to practice doing that very thing. Problem recognition, problem solving, and project-based learning are significantly important ways of providing that opportunity to students.

Finding humor. The positive effects of humor on the body's physiological functions are well established (see Chapter 2). Humor liberates creativity and provides high-level thinking skills, such as anticipation, finding novel relationships, and visual imagery. The acquisition of a sense of humor follows a developmental sequence similar to that described by Piaget (1972) and Kohlberg (1981). Initially, young children and immature adolescents (and some immature adults) may find humor in all the wrong things—human frailty, ethnic humor, sacrilegious riddles, and ribald profanities. Later, creative young people thrive on finding incongruity and will demonstrate a whimsical frame of mind during problem solving.

Creating, imagining, innovating. All students must be encouraged to do and must be discouraged from saying "I can't." Students must be taught in such a way as to encourage intrinsic motivation rather than reliance on extrinsic sources. Teachers must be able to offer criticism constructively so that the student understands that criticism is not a criticism of self. In exemplary educational programs, students learn the value of feedback. They learn the value of their own intuition, of guessing—they learn "I can."

Listening with understanding and empathy. Some psychologists believe that the ability to listen to others, to empathize with and to understand their point of view, is one of the highest forms of intelligent behavior. Empathic behavior, nearly the exact opposite of egoism, is an important skill for conflict resolution. In class meetings, brainstorming sessions, think tanks, town meetings, advisory councils, board meetings, and in legislative bodies, people from various walks of life convene to share their thinking, to explore their ideas, and to broaden their perspectives by listening to the ideas and reactions of others.

Managing impulsivity. When students develop impulse control they think before acting. Impulsive behavior can worsen conflict and inhibit effective problem solving (Goos & Galbraith, 1996). Students can be taught to think before shouting out an answer, to wait their turn, to raise their hand to be called on before answering, and to think before beginning a project or task and before arriving at conclusions with insufficient data. One of several reasons that teachers should routinely expect a show of student hands before a student is acknowledged to respond or question is to help students develop control over the impulsive behavior of shouting out in class (Brandt, 2000; Goleman, 1995; Harrington-Lueker, 1997). Indeed, research clearly indicates that the quality of one's emotional intelligence—that is, to exercise self-control, to empathize with others, to work collaboratively and cooperatively—is a much more significant predictor of success in the workplace than is any analytical measure of intelligence (Goleman, 1998; Goleman, Boyatzis, & McKee, 2002).

Persisting. Persistence is staying with a task until it is completed. People with an internal locus of control (discussed in Chapter 2) tend to show more persistence. Consider the following examples.

- *Clara Barton.* Nearly single-handedly and against formidable odds, Clara Barton persevered to form the American Red Cross in 1882.
- *Amelia Earhart.* Born in 1898, Earhart demonstrated from the time that she was a young girl that she was creative, curious, and persistent. After learning to fly in 1920, in just 8 more years she became the first woman to fly the Atlantic Ocean, thereby paving the way for other women to become active in aviation.
- *Lewis H. Latimer.* Born in 1848, the son of escaped slaves, Latimer served in the U.S. Navy during the Civil War. After the war he studied drafting, eventually becoming chief draftsman for both General Electric and Westinghouse. Among his career achievements were his patent drawings for Alexander Graham Bell's first telephone, his invention of a method to make a carbon filament for a light bulb that was made by one of Thomas Edison's competitors, and his supervision of the installation of the first electric lights in New York City, Philadelphia, Montreal, and London. Later, in 1884, he went to work for Edison.

- *Wilma Rudolf.* As the result of childhood diseases, Wilma Rudolf, at the age of 10, could not walk without the aid of leg braces. Just 10 years later, at the age of 20, she was declared to be the fastest running woman in the world, having won three gold medals in the 1960 World Olympics.

Questioning and posing problems. Young people are usually full of questions, and, unless discouraged, they do ask them. As educators, we want students to be alert to, and recognize, discrepancies and phenomena in their environment and to freely inquire about their causes. In exemplary programs, students are encouraged to ask questions and then from those questions to develop a problem-solving strategy to investigate their questions.

Remaining open to continuous learning. Intelligent people are in a continuous learning mode, always eager to learn and find new ways of learning.

Responding with wonderment and awe. Young children express wonderment, an expression that should never be stifled. Through effective teaching, students can recapture that sense of wonderment as an effective teacher guides them into a sense of "I can" and an expression of the feeling of "I enjoy."

Striving for accuracy. Growth in this behavior is demonstrated when students take time to check their work, review the procedures, and hesitate to draw conclusions with only limited data.

Taking responsible risks: venture forth and explore ideas beyond the usual zone of comfort. Such exploration, of course, must be done with thoughtfulness; it must not be done in ways that could put the student at risk psychologically or physically. Using the analogy of a turtle going nowhere until it sticks its neck out, classroom teachers should model this behavior and provide opportunities for students to develop this intelligent behavior by using techniques such as brainstorming strategies, divergent-thinking questioning, think-pair-share, cooperative learning, inquiry, and project-based learning.

Thinking and communicating with clarity and precision. Strive for clarity and accurate communication in both written and oral form. Shown in Figure 7.2 are humorous

sample sentences (taken from newspapers) that lack clarity and precision in written expression. A useful academic exercise is to have students, perhaps in dyads, read and then rewrite each sentence, and then share and compare their rewrites.

Thinking about thinking (metacognition). Learning to plan, monitor, assess, and reflect on one's own thinking is another characteristic of intelligent behavior. Small-group learning, journals, student-led portfolio conferences, self-assessment, and thinking aloud in dyads are strategies that can be used to help students develop this intelligent behavior (Stright & Supplee, 2002). Thinking aloud is good modeling for your students, helping them to develop their own cognitive skills of thinking, learning, and reasoning (Astington, 1998).

Thinking flexibly. Sometimes referred to as **lateral thinking** (De Bono, 1970), flexibility in thinking is the ability to approach a problem from "the side," or from a new angle, using a novel approach. With modeling by the teacher, students can develop this behavior as they learn to consider alternative points of view and to deal with several sources of information simultaneously.

Thinking interdependently. Real-world problem solving has become so complex that seldom can any person go it alone. As stated by Elias (2001, p. 2), "We live in an interdependent world; there is no such thing, in any practical sense, as independence and autonomy. We live lives of synergy and linkage." Not all students come to school knowing how to work effectively in groups. They may exhibit competitiveness, narrow-mindedness, egocentrism, ethnocentrism, or criticism of others' values, emotions, and beliefs. Listening, consensus seeking, giving up an idea to work on someone else's, empathy, compassion, group leadership, cooperative learning, knowing how to support group efforts, and altruism are all behaviors indicative of intelligent human beings, and they can be learned by students at school and in the classroom.

Using all the senses. As discussed in previous chapters, as often as is appropriate and feasible, to best learn students should be encouraged to use and develop all their sensory input channels (i.e., verbal, visual, tactile, and kinesthetic).

Figure 7.2   Sample sentences that lack clarity and precision.

1. The burglar was about 30 years old, white, 5′ 10″, with wavy hair weighing about 150 pounds.
2. The family lawyer will read the will tomorrow at the residence of Mr. Carlson, who died June 19 to accommodate his relatives.
3. Mrs. Maureen Doolittle, who went deer hunting with her husband, is very proud that she was able to shoot a fine buck as well as her husband.
4. Organ donations from the living reached a record high last year, outnumbering donors who are dead for the first time.
5. The dog was hungry and made the mistake of nipping a 2-year-old that was trying to force feed it in his ear.
6. We spent most of our time sitting on the back porch watching the cows playing Scrabble and reading.
7. Hunting can also be dangerous, as in the case of pygmies hunting elephants armed only with spears.

We should strive to help our own students develop these characteristics of intelligent behavior. In Chapter 2 you learned of specific teacher behaviors that facilitate this development. Now, let's review additional research findings that offer important considerations in the facilitation of student learning and intelligent behavior.

Direct Teaching for Thinking and Intelligent Behavior

The curriculum of any school includes the development of skills that are used in thinking, skills such as *classifying*, *comparing* and *contrasting*, *concluding*, *generalizing*, *inferring*, and others (see Figure 7.4). Because the academic achievement of students increases when they are taught thinking skills directly, many researchers and educators concur that direct instruction should be given to all students on how to think and behave intelligently.

Several research perspectives have influenced today's interest in the direct teaching of thinking. The *cognitive view of intelligence* asserts that intellectual ability is not fixed but can be developed. The *constructivist approach to learning* maintains that learners actively and independently construct knowledge by creating and coordinating relationships in their mental repertoire. The *social psychology view of classroom experience* focuses on the learner as an individual who is a member of various peer groups and a society. The *perspective of information processing* deals with the acquisition, elaboration, and management of information.

Rather than assuming students have developed thinking skills, teachers should devote classroom time to teaching them directly. When teaching a thinking skill directly, the subject content becomes the vehicle for thinking. For example, a social studies lesson can teach students how to distinguish fact and opinion; a language arts lesson instructs students how to compare and analyze; and a science lesson can teach students how to set up a problem for their inquiry. Inquiry teaching and discovery learning are both useful tools for learning and for teaching thinking skills.

INQUIRY TEACHING AND DISCOVERY LEARNING

Intrinsic to the effectiveness of both inquiry and discovery is the assumption that students would rather actively seek knowledge than receive it through traditional direct instruction (i.e., information delivery) methods such as lectures, demonstrations, worksheets, and textbook reading. Although inquiry and discovery are important teaching tools, there is sometimes confusion about exactly what inquiry teaching is and how it differs from discovery learning. The distinction should become clear as you study the section discussing these two important tools for teaching and learning.

Although inquiry and discovery are well recognized as valuable teaching tools, they do tend to consume more instructional time than do traditional methods of information delivery (direct instruction). Coupled with that and the current emphasis on standardized testing, classroom use of inquiry and discovery methods may be in jeopardy (Jorgenson & Vanosdall, 2002).

> Experiences afforded by inquiry help students understand the importance of suspending judgment and also the tentativeness of answers and solutions to problems. With those intelligent understandings, students eventually are better able to deal with life's ambiguities.

Problem Solving

Perhaps a major reason why inquiry and discovery are sometimes confused is that, in both, students are actively engaged in problem solving. **Problem solving** can be thought of as the ability to recognize, identify, define, or describe a problem, determine the preferred resolution, identify potential solutions, select strategies, test solutions, evaluate outcomes, and revise any of these steps as necessary (Costa, 1985). For example, a problem-solving model for teaching history involves posing the problem, determining what is known and what information must be obtained, developing tentative models or solutions, conducting research to test them, then evaluating the collected data to draw conclusions (Thornton, 2001).

Inquiry versus Discovery

Problem solving is *not* a teaching strategy but a high-order intellectual behavior that facilitates learning. What a teacher can and should do is provide opportunities for students to identify and tentatively solve problems. Experiences in inquiry and discovery can provide those opportunities. With the processes involved in inquiry and discovery, teachers can help students develop the skills necessary for effective problem solving. Two major differences between discovery and inquiry are (a) who identifies the problem and (b) the percentage of decisions that are made by the students. Table 7.1 shows three levels of inquiry, each level defined according to what the student does and decides.

It should be evident from Table 7.1 that what is called *Level I inquiry* is actually traditional, didactic, workbook, and "cookbook" teaching, where both the problem and the process for resolving it are identified and defined for the student. The student then works through the process to its inevitable resolution. If the process is well designed, the result is inevitable, because the student "discovers" what was intended by the writers of the program. This level is also called *guided inquiry* or *discovery*, because the

Table 7.1   Levels of Inquiry*

	Level I (not true inquiry)	Level II	Level III
Problem Identification	By teacher or textbook	By teacher or textbook	By student
Process of Solving the Problem	Decided by teacher or text	Decided by student	Decided by student
Identification of Tentative Solution	Resolved by student	Resolved by student	Resolved by student

*The levels of inquiry are adapted from "the three different levels of openness and permissiveness ... for laboratory enquiry" by Joseph J. Schwab, *The Teaching of Science as Enquiry* (Cambridge, MA: Harvard University Press, 1962), p. 55.

Children need to learn the skills of problem solving, and how to do it in groups as well as alone. Real-world problem solving has become so complex that seldom can any person do it alone.

students are carefully guided through the investigation to (the predictable) "discovery."

Level I is, in reality, a strategy within the delivery mode, the advantages of which were described in Chapter 5. Because Level I "inquiry" is highly manageable and the learning outcome is predictable it is probably best for teaching basic concepts and principles. Students who never experience learning beyond Level I are missing an opportunity to engage their highest mental operations, and they seldom (or never) get to experience more motivating, real-life problem solving. Furthermore, those students may come away with the false notion that problem solving is a linear process, which it is not. As illustrated in Figure 7.3, true inquiry is cyclical rather than linear. For that reason, Level I is not true inquiry because it is a linear process. Real-world problem solving is a cyclical rather than linear process. One enters the cycle whenever a discrepancy or problem is observed and recognized, and that can occur at any point in the cycle.

True Inquiry

By the time students are in middle school years, they should be provided experiences for true inquiry, which begins with *Level II inquiry*, where students actually decide and design processes for their inquiry. In true inquiry there is an emphasis on the tentative nature of conclusions, which makes the activity more like real-life problem solving, where decisions are always subject to revision if and when new data so prescribe.

At *Level III inquiry* students recognize and identify the problem as well as decide the processes and reach a conclusion. In project-centered teaching students are usually engaged at this level of inquiry. By the time students are in high school, Level III inquiry should be a major strategy for instruction, which is often the case in schools that use cross-age teaching and interdisciplinary thematic instruction. But, it is not easy; like most good teaching practices, it is a lot of work. But also like good teaching, the intrinsic rewards concomitant with the

Figure 7.3   The inquiry cycle.

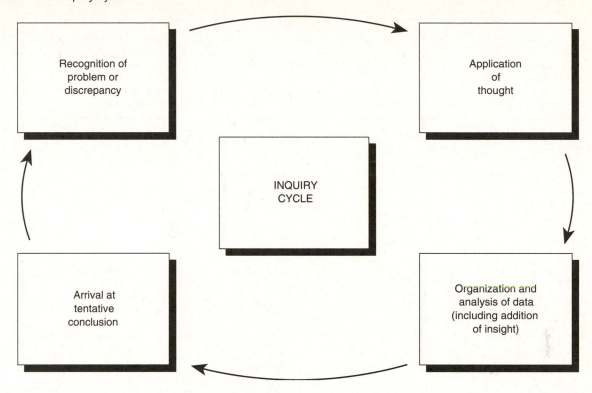

CLASSROOM VIGNETTE

Problem Solving and Decision Making in the Real World Is an Integrated and Interdisciplinary Inquiry Activity

On any given day or specified time period, teachers and students can look at a problem or subject of study from the point of view of many separate disciplines. Such an interdisciplinary approach to some matter of concern has been adopted not only by educators but by other professionals as well. It is the mode of meaningful learning and real-life problem solving.

For example, consider the fact-finding and decision-making approach of public officials in the state of Colorado when confronted with the task of making decisions about projects proposed for watersheds in their state. While gathering information, the officials brought in Dave Rosgen, a state hydrologist. Rosgen led the officials into the field to demonstrate specific ways by which he helped control erosion and rehabilitate damaged streams. He took the officials to Wolf Creek, where they donned high waders. Rosgen led the group down the creek to examine various features of that complex natural stream. He pointed out evidence of the creek's past meanders, patterns that he had incorporated into his rehabilitation projects. In addition to listening to this scientist's point of view, the public officials listened to other experts to consider related economic and political issues before making final decisions about projects that had been proposed for watersheds in that state.

During interdisciplinary thematic units, students study a topic and its underlying ideas as well as related knowledge from various disciplines on an ongoing basis. The teacher, sometimes with the help of students and other teachers and adults, introduces experiences designed to foster ideas and skills from various disciplines, just as Rosgen introduced information from hydrology, to develop literacy skills through the unit. For instance, the teacher might stimulate communication skills through creative writing and other projects. Throughout the unit, the students are guided in exploring ideas related to different disciplines to integrate their knowledge.

fact that students achieve meaningful learning make the effort worthwhile. As exclaimed by one teacher using interdisciplinary thematic instruction with student-centered inquiry, "I've never worked harder in my life, but I've never had this much fun, either."

The Critical Thinking Skills of Discovery and Inquiry

In true inquiry, students generate ideas and then design ways to test those ideas. The various processes used represent the many critical thinking skills. Some of those

Figure 7.4   Inquiry cycle processes.

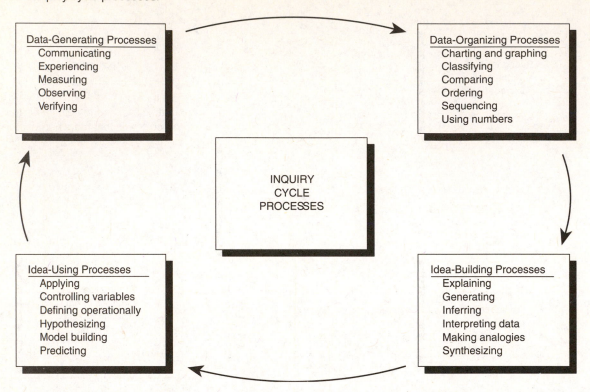

skills are concerned with generating and organizing data; others are concerned with building and using ideas. Figure 7.4 provides four main categories of these thinking processes and illustrates the place of each within the inquiry cycle.

Some processes in the cycle are discovery processes, and others are inquiry processes. Inquiry processes include the more complex mental operations (including all of those in the idea-using category). Project-centered teaching provides an avenue for doing that, as does problem-centered teaching.

Inquiry learning is a higher-level mental operation that introduces the concept of the discrepant event, something that establishes cognitive disequilibrium (using the element of surprise to challenge their prior notions, sometimes called naïve theories) to help students develop skills in observing and being alert for discrepancies (Echevarria, 2003). Such a strategy provides opportunities for students to investigate their own ideas about explanations. Inquiry, like discovery, depends upon skill in problem solving; the difference between the two is in the amount of decision-making responsibility given to students. Experiences afforded by inquiry help students understand the importance of suspending judgment and also the tentativeness of answers and solutions. With those intelligent understandings, students eventually are better able to deal with life's ambiguities. When students are not provided these important educational experiences, their education is incomplete.

One of the most effective ways of stimulating inquiry is to use materials that provoke students' interest. These materials should be presented in a nonthreatening, noncompetitive context, so students think and hypothesize freely. The teacher's role is to encourage students to form as many hypotheses as possible and then support their hypotheses with reasons. After the students suggest several ideas, the teacher should begin to move on to higher order, more abstract questions that involve the development of generalizations and evaluations. True inquiry problems have a special advantage in that they can be used with almost any group of students. Members of a group approach the problem as an adventure in thinking and apply it to whatever background they can muster. Background experience may enrich a student's approach to the problem, but is not crucial to the use or understanding of the evidence presented to that student. Locating a Colony, Figure 7.5, is a Level II inquiry. As a class, do the inquiry now.

INTEGRATING STRATEGIES FOR INTEGRATED LEARNING

In today's exemplary K–12 classrooms, instructional strategies are combined to establish the most effective teaching–learning experience. For example, in an integrated language arts program, teachers are interested in their students' speaking, reading, listening, thinking, study, and writing skills. These skills (and not

Figure 7.5   Locating a colony: a Level II inquiry. (*Source:* Adapted by permission from unpublished material provided by Jennifer Devine and Dennis Devine.)

Presentation of the Problem. In groups of three or four, students receive the following information.

Background. You (your group is considered as one person) are one of 120 passengers on the ship *Prince Charles.* You left England 12 weeks ago. You have experienced many hardships, including a stormy passage, limited rations, sickness, cold and damp weather, and hot, foul air below deck. Ten of your fellow immigrants to the New World, including three children, have died and been buried at sea. You are now anchored at an uncertain place, off the coast of the New World, which your captain believes to be somewhere north of the Virginia Grants. Seas are so rough and food so scarce that you and your fellow passengers have decided to settle here. A landing party has returned with a map they made of the area. You, as one of the elders, must decide at once where the settlement is to be located. The tradesmen want to settle along the river, which is deep, even though this seems to be the season of low water levels. Within 10 months they expect deep-water ships from England with more colonists and merchants. Those within your group who are farmers say they must have fertile, workable land. The officer in charge of the landing party reported seeing a group of armed natives who fled when approached. He feels the settlement must be located so that it can be defended from the natives and from the sea.

Directions, step one: You (your group) are to select a site on the attached map that you feel is best suited for a colony. Your site must satisfy the different factions aboard the ship. A number of possible sites are already marked on the map (letters *A–G*). You may select one of these locations or use them as reference points to show the location of your colony. When your group has selected its site, list and explain the reasons for your choice. When each group has arrived at its tentative decision, these will be shared with the whole class.

Directions, step two: After each group has made its presentation and argument, a class debate is held about where the colony should be located.

Notes to teacher: For the debate, have a large map drawn on the writing board or on an overhead transparency, where each group's mark can be made for all to see and discuss. After each group has presented its argument for its location and against the others, we suggest that you then mark on the large map the two, three, or more hypothetical locations (assuming that, as a class, there is no single favorite

location yet). Then take a straw vote of the students, allowing each to vote independently rather than as members of groups. At this time you can terminate the activity by saying that if the majority of students favor one location, then that, in fact, is the solution to the problem—that is, the colony is located wherever the majority of class members believe it should be. No sooner will that statement be made by you than someone will ask, "Are we correct?" or "What is the right answer?" They will ask such questions because, as students in school, they are used to solving problems that have right answers (Level I inquiry teaching). In real-world problems, however, there are no "right" answers, though some answers may seem better than others. It is the process of problem solving that is important. You want your students to develop confidence in their ability to solve problems and understand the tentativeness of "answers" to real-life problems.

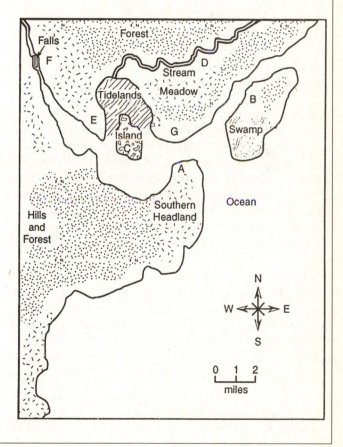

Problem solving and decision making in the real world is an integrated and interdisciplinary inquiry activity. To effectively learn the skills necessary to identify and solve problems and to make intelligent decisions, children need coached practice in an integrated and interdisciplinary learning environment.

textbooks) form a holistic process that is the primary aspect of integrated language arts.

In the area of speaking skills, oral discourse (discussion) in the classroom has a growing research base that promotes methods of teaching and learning through oral language. These methods include cooperative learning, instructional scaffolding, and inquiry teaching.

In cooperative learning groups, students discuss and use language for learning that benefits both their content learning and skills in social interaction. Working in heterogeneous groups, students participate in their own learning and can extend their knowledge base and cultural awareness with students of different backgrounds. When students share information and ideas, they are completing difficult learning tasks, using divergent thinking and decision making, and developing their understanding of concepts. As issues are presented and responses are challenged, student thinking is clarified. Students assume the responsibility for planning within the group and for carrying out their assignments. When needed, the teacher models an activity with one group in front of the class, and when integrated with student questions, the modeling can become inquiry teaching. Activities can include any from a variety of heuristics, such as the following:

Brainstorming. Members generate ideas related to a key word and record them. Clustering or chunking, mapping, and the Venn diagram are variations of brainstorming.

Chunking or clustering. Groups of students apply mental organizers by clustering information into chunks for easier manipulation and remembering.

Comparing and contrasting. Similarities and differences between items are found and recorded.

Inferring. For instance, students assume the roles of different people (real or fictional) and infer their motives, personalities, and thoughts.

Memory strategies. The teacher and students model the use of acronyms, mnemonics, rhymes, or clustering of information into categories to promote learning. Sometimes, such as in memorizing the social security number, one must learn by rote information that is not connected to any prior knowledge. To do that, it is helpful to break the information to be learned into smaller chunks, such as dividing the eight-digit social security number into smaller chunks of information (with, in this instance, each chunk separated by a hyphen). Learning by rote is also easier if one can connect that which is to be memorized to some prior knowledge. Strategies such as these are used to bridge the gap between rote learning and meaningful learning and are known as **mnemonics** (Mastropieri & Scruggs, 1998; Raschke, Alper, & Eggers, 1999; van Hell & Mahn, 1997). Sample mnemonics are as follows:

- The notes on a treble staff are *FACE* for the space notes and *Empty Garbage Before Dad Flips (EGBDF)* for the line notes. The notes on the bass staff are *All Cows Eat Granola Bars (ACEGB)* for space notes and *Grizzly Bears Don't Fly Airplanes (GBDFA)* for line notes.
- The order of the planets from the Sun is *My Very Educated Mother Just Served Us Nine Pizzas*—Mercury, Venus, Earth, Mars, Jupiter, Saturn, Uranus, and Neptune.
- The names of the Great Lakes are *HOMES* for *H*uron, *O*ntario, *M*ichigan, *E*rie, and *S*uperior.

- To remember when to use "affect" versus "effect," remember *RAVEN* for *R*emember *a*ffect (is a) *v*erb, *e*ffect (is a) *n*oun.
- To remember when a vowel is not pronounced, use "When vowels go walking, the first one does the talking."
- To remember when to use "principle" versus "principal," remember "The principal is your pal."
- Visual mnemonics are useful too, such as remembering that Italy is shaped in the form of a boot.

Outlining. Each group completes an outline that contains some of the main ideas but with subtopics omitted.

Paraphrasing. In a brief summary, each student restates a short selection of what was read or heard.

Reciprocal teaching. In classroom dialogue, students take turns at summarizing, questioning, clarifying, and predicting (Carter, 1997; Marzano et al., 2001; Palincsar & Brown, 1984).

Review. Frequent review of material being learned is essential, but it is most effective when the students are actively involved in planning and implementing the review as opposed to their being passive respondents to a review conducted by the teacher (Wolfe, 2001).

Study strategies. Important strategies that should be taught explicitly include vocabulary expansion, reading and interpreting graphic information, locating resources, using advance organizers, adjusting one's reading rate, and skimming, scanning, and study reading (Choate & Rakes, 1998).

Visual tools. A variety of terms for visual tools useful for learning have been invented (some of which are synonymous), such as brainstorming web, cluster, cognitive map, conflict map, graphic organizer, mind-mapping web, semantic map, spider map, thinking process map, Venn diagram, and visual scaffold. Visual tools are separated into three categories according to purpose: (a) *brainstorming tools* (such as mind mapping, webbing, and clustering) for the purpose of developing one's knowledge and creativity; (b) *task-specific organizers* (such as life cycle diagrams used in biology, decision trees used in mathematics, and text structures in reading); and (c) *thinking process maps* for encouraging cognitive development across disciplines (Hyerle, 1996). It is the latter about which we are interested here.

Based on Ausubel's (1963) theory of meaningful learning, thinking process mapping has been found useful in helping students change prior notions (i.e., their misconceptions or *naïve views*). It can help students in their ability to organize and to represent their thoughts, as well as to help them connect new knowledge to their past experiences and precepts (Brown, 2003; Novak, 1990, 1998; Plotnick, 1997; van Boxtel, van der Linden, Roelofs, & Erkens, 2002). Simply put, concepts can be understood as classifications that attempt to organize the world of objects and events into a smaller number of categories. In everyday usage, the term *concept* means idea, as when someone says, "My concept of love is not the same as yours." Concepts embody a meaning that develops in complexity with experience and learning over time. For example, the concept of love that is held by a 2nd-grader is unlikely to be as complex as that held by an 11th-grader. Thinking process mapping is a graphical way of demonstrating the relationship between and among concepts.

Typically, a thinking process map refers to a visual or graphic representation of concepts with bridges (connections) that show relationships. Figure 7.6 shows a partially complete thinking process map in social studies, where students have made connections of concept relationships related to fruit farming and marketing. The general procedure for thinking process mapping is to have the students (1) identify important concepts in materials being studied, often by circling those concepts; (2) rank the concepts from the most general to the most specific; and (3) arrange the concepts on a sheet of paper, connect related ideas with lines, and define the connections between the related ideas.

One specific type of thinking process map is the **vee map**. This is a V-shaped road map completed by students, as they learn, showing the route they follow from prior knowledge to new and future knowledge.

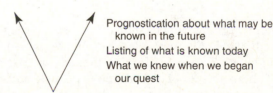

Prognostication about what may be known in the future
Listing of what is known today
What we knew when we began our quest

Venn diagramming is a thinking process mapping tool for comparing concepts or, for example, two stories, to show similarities and differences. Using stories as an example, a student is asked to draw two circles that intersect and to mark the circles one and two and the area where they intersect three. In circle one, the student lists characteristics of one story, and in circle two lists the characteristics of the second story. In the area of the intersection, marked three, the student lists characteristics common to both stories.

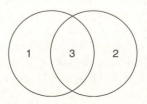

Figure 7.6   Sample partially completed thinking process map.

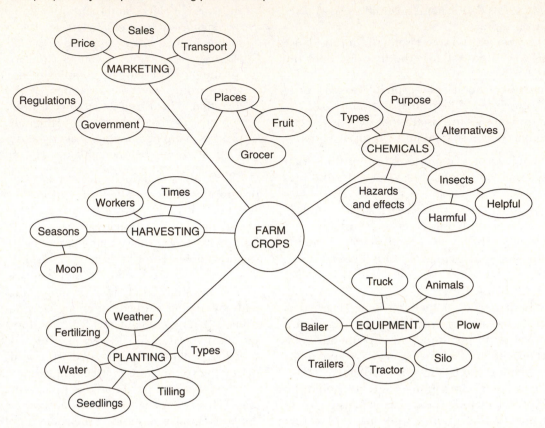

Venn diagrams can be useful for assessing for higher order thinking. For example, the sample assessment item in Figure 7.7 assesses for the student's understanding of the concepts of the universe, planets, and the Earth's moon. For scoring or marking the student's response, each possible response has a maximum score of 3, one point for three distinct responses that are obvious elements of the item.

The **visual learning log** (VLL) is another kind of road map completed by students showing the route they follow from prior knowledge to new and future knowledge, except that the VLL consists of pictograms (free-form drawings) that each student makes and that are maintained in a journal.

The value of these representations is believed to be that they engage what psychologists refer to as the "dual-coding" theory of information storage (Pavio, 1971, 1990), that knowledge is stored in the brain in two forms, a linguistic form and a nonlinguistic form, the latter of which is stored as mental pictures and as sensory sensations (Marzano et al., 2001). Again, the oft-repeated message of this resource guide is that the most effective and longest lasting learning is not that of verbiage alone but that which engages most or all of the senses.

> We live in the age of "Pro-Ams." Pro-Ams—professional amateurs—become experts at whatever they have developed a passion for. Young people are using the Internet, communication media, digital tools, and membership in virtual communities of practice to develop technical expertise in such areas as digital video, digital storytelling, machinima, fan fiction, history and civilization simulations, music, graphic art, political commentary, robotics, anime, fashion design, and nearly every other endeavor the human mind can think of.
>
> J. P. Gee & M. H. Levine (2009, p. 49)

EDUCATIONAL GAMES

The use of games for teaching is currently undergoing a rejuvenation in interest and use. The reasons for this renewed interest are varied, not the least of which includes the fact that we have reached an age in which multimedia, such as video games and computer-generated games, are commonplace in the lives of youth; students today grew up with the media, which means that they are comfortable with it. Another reason is likely that of the rapidly increasing diversity of our society. It has long been known that because they are experiences that tend

Figure 7.7   Sample assessment item using Venn diagramming.

Instructions: From the diagram write down all you can tell from the diagram about planet Earth.

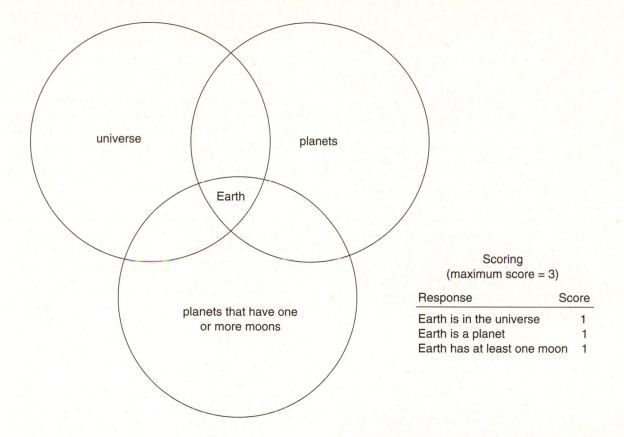

Scoring
(maximum score = 3)

Response	Score
Earth is in the universe	1
Earth is a planet	1
Earth has at least one moon	1

to involve several senses, involve several learning modalities, and tend to engage higher order thinking skills, games can be quite effective as learning tools.

Devices classified as educational games include a wide variety of learning activities, such as simulations, role-play and sociodrama activities, mind games, board games, computer games, video games, and sporting games—all of which provide valuable learning experiences for participants.

Of all the arts, drama involves the learner-participant most fully—intellectually, emotionally, physically, verbally, and socially. Interactive drama, which is role-playing, a simplified form of drama, is a method by which students can become involved with literature. Studies show that students' comprehension increases and they are more highly motivated to read if they are involved in analyzing and actively responding to the characters, plot, and setting of the story being read (Coney & Kanel, 1997).

Simulations, a more complex form of drama, serve many of the developmental needs of young people. They provide for interaction with peers and allow students of differences to work together on a common project. They engage students in physical activity and provide them the opportunity to try out different roles, which help them

CLASSROOM VIGNETTE

*Chemistry Students Write
and Stage a One-Act Play*

For the purpose of motivating more of his students to enjoy and learn chemistry, and perhaps also to find regeneration in his interest in teaching, Robert, a high school chemistry teacher with 11 years of experience, decided that this year he would try some teaching strategies that were new to his teaching of chemistry. Early in the year, in preparation for a unit on the study of oxygen and other gases, he told the 28 students in one of his chemistry classes that, if they were interested, he would like for them to plan, write, and stage a one-act play about the life of Joseph Priestley, the theologian and scientist, who in 1774, discovered what he called "dephlogisticated air," later named *oxygen* by Lavoisier. Furthermore the students would be given 1 week to plan. The play would be presented and videotaped in class. The students accepted Robert's idea with enthusiasm and immediately went about the task of organizing and putting their ideas into motion. They took on the challenging task with such vigor and seriousness that they asked Robert for an additional 3 days to prepare. Sean, a bright 11th-grade student, who

(continued)

was really more interested in theater than science, was selected by the students to play the role of Priestley and also to be the producer. Other students played lesser rolls. Students with special interest in writing wrote the play. Others with interest in art and stagecraft assumed the task of designing and preparing the set, and another assumed the role of sound stage manager. The resulting 60-minute presentation was more successful than Robert, and perhaps the students, could ever have anticipated, so much so that the school principal requested that the students put on the play two more times, once for the entire student body, a second time for the school's parent–teacher–student organization, both times resulting in standing ovations.

During the performance before the PTO, the student production was simultaneously recorded by the local cable television network and later played several times over the community cable channel. Robert later said that during this experience the students learned far more content than they ever would have via his traditional approach to the topic, plus these students were highly motivated in chemistry for the entire rest of the year. Sean went on to attend the University of California where he graduated with honors with a degree in theater and a minor in chemistry.

GAMES IN THE CLASSROOM AND THE UNDERPERFORMING STUDENT

High-stakes state assessments have recently spotlighted the underperforming student. Faced with the probability of barring a large number of students from graduation, one high school teacher found a unique way to get students excited about studying the language arts and math skills required for the state tests.

The teacher, while at Camelback High School (Phoenix, Arizona), was assigned to teach a special class for those students who were likely to fail the state graduation test. The students, including a good number of students with special needs and students still learning English, were generally apathetic toward trying again to learn what they had failed to learn in math and English class.

They were apathetic, that is, until their teacher told them, "Put away your pencils and notebooks. Today we're going to play a video game!" After a demonstration by the teacher of how the game worked, the students, every single one of them, were concentrating hard on achieving the best score in the class . . . on a video game. In a few minutes Jacinto, one of the more competitive students, exclaimed, "I beat the game." The teacher recorded Jacinto's score and encouraged Jacinto to try to beat the game in fewer than 100 seconds. Jacinto accepted the challenge.

Did the students know that they were learning math? Certainly. The goal of the game was to state the range and domain (e.g., $22 < y < 97$ and $65 < x < 144$) of 10 randomly displayed functions. Once students earned an A for "beating the game," they were encouraged to earn another A by turning in a time of under 100 seconds. Toward the end of the period, Jacinto and four other students were vying for the lowest time. When the dismissal bell rang, Ana had beaten Jacinto by 1 second, but the real reward was when they were asked to express the range and domain of a function on the state math assessment test.

Source: Mark Greenberg, by permission.

to better understand themselves. Role-play simulations can provide concrete experiences that help students to understand complex concepts and issues, and they provide opportunities for exploring values and develop skill in decision making. Indeed, in the not so distant future, because it involves a learning that is powerfully effective, that young people are familiar with, and that is based on the best of what we know about how people learn, we are likely to see greater use of technology-based simulation games in teaching with far less teacher-centered direct instruction (Foreman, 2004).

Educational games can play an integral role in interdisciplinary teaching and, as indicated in the scenario that follows, serve as valuable resources for enriching the effectiveness of students' learning. As with any other instructional strategy, the use of games should follow a clear educational purpose, have a careful plan, and be congruent with the instructional objectives.

Classification of Educational Games

What are educational games? Seven types of games fall under the general heading of "educational games." Table 7.2 shows the seven types, with characteristics and examples of each.

Functions of Educational Games

As said above, games can be powerful tools for teaching and learning. A game can serve several of the following functions, and the functions of a particular game being used should be communicated to the students.

- add variety and change of pace, providing a break from the usual rigors of learning
- assess student learning
- encourage lateral thinking
- encourage learning through peer interaction
- enhance student self-esteem
- enhance student social relationships
- motivate students
- offer learning about real-life issues through simulation and role-playing
- provide learning through tactile and kinesthetic modalities, as well as through linguistics
- provide problem-solving situations and experiences
- provide skill development and motivation through computer usage
- provide skill development in inductive thinking
- provide skill development in verbal communication and debate
- reinforce convergent thinking

Table 7.2 Classification of Educational Games

Type	Characteristics	Examples
1. Pure game*	Fun	*Ungame, New Games*
2. Pure contest	Stimulates competition; built-in inefficiency‡	Political contests (e.g., U.S. presidential race)
3. Pure simulation*	Models reality	Toddler play
4. Contest/game	Stimulates competition; fun; built-in inefficiency	Golf; bowling; *Trivial Pursuit*
5. Simulation/game*	Models reality; fun	*SIMCITY*; *Our Town's Planning Commission Meeting*§
6. Contest/simulation	Stimulates competition; models reality; built-in inefficiency	Boxcar Derby of Akron, Ohio
7. Simulation/game/contest	Models reality; fun; stimulates competition; built-in inefficiency	*Monopoly, Life, Careers*

*These game types do not emphasize competition and thus are particularly recommended for use in the classroom as learning tools.
‡This means that rules for accomplishing the game objective make accomplishment of that objective less than efficient. For example, in golf the objective is to get the ball into the hole with the least amount of effort, but to do that, one has to take a peculiarly shaped stick (the club) and hit the ball, find it, and hit it again, continuing that sequence until the ball is in the hole. Yet, common sense tells us that the best way to get the ball into the hole with the least amount of effort would be to simply pick up the ball and place it by hand into the hole.
§See J. V. Vort, "Our Town's Planning Commission Meeting," *Journal of Geography* 96(4), 183–190 (July–August 1997).

- review and reinforce subject-matter learning
- stimulate critical thinking
- stimulate deductive thinking
- teach both content and process

Sources for useful educational games include professional journals (see box that follows) and the Internet.

Now, as instructed by your course instructor, do Exercise 7.2 (end of chapter), the second micro peer teaching exercise of this resource guide.

RECENT TEACHER-MADE GAMES WITH SOURCES

Board Games

Interdisciplinary game for teaching molecular biology in high school (Cardoso et al., 2008); "Journey to Egypt," for learning about Egypt (Selvidge, 2006); "Journey to Freedom: The Power to Read and Write," for all grade levels, created by Karanja Crews—designed to reinforce basic literacy concepts, increase reading comprehension, and discover what it was like living as a slave and trying to earn freedom as they traveled the Underground Railroad—for information, see www.readers2leaders.net; "Metric Madness," for learning about the metric system (Kroon, 2007).

Card Games

For teaching proper grammar, all grade levels (Erwin, 2009)—for information, see www.hammerthegrammar.com

For teaching about plant ecology (Lehnhoff, Woolbaugh, & Rew, 2008).

Drama: For English Language Development classrooms (Bernal, 2007).

Puzzle: Using the Monty Hall Paradox, a game designed to develop students' understanding of the scientific method (Overway, 2007).

Reading Game for Music: "Note Twister," a game that engages students in using duct tape to form musical notes (McHenry, 2008).

Role play: To teach glycolysis and the Krebs cycle (Ross, Tronson, & Ritchie, 2008).

Sudoku Puzzles

Teaching the chemistry of art and color (Welsh, 2007); Teaching mathematics (de Mestre, 2007).

Using handheld computers and global positioning systems (Villano, 2008).

Video Games

Understanding thermoregulation (Dibley & Parish, 2007).

Using commercial off-the-shelf (COTS) games (Charsky & Mims, 2008); Why and how of using video games (Annetta, 2008); Virtual online game: "Medical Mysteries," incorporates online virtual experiments using episodes from television's "CSI" designed to address National Science Education Content Standards (Miller, 2007).

Word Games

Differentiated vocabulary unit games (Culter & Groenke, 2008; Smith, 2008).

SUMMARY

Central to your selection of instructional strategies should be those that encourage students to become independent thinkers and skilled learners who can help in the planning, structuring, regulating, and assessing of their own learning and learning activities. This chapter has presented guidelines for some of the most frequently used and useful ways of helping students become independent thinkers and skilled learners.

The use of games in education will undoubtedly continue and develop, especially from the emerging digital technology, such as massively multiplayer online games (MMOGs) (Steinkuehler, 2008). You will want to stay alert to that and other emerging technologies.

QUESTIONS FOR CLASS DISCUSSION

1. Many cognitive researchers agree that students should spend more time actively using knowledge to solve problems and less time reading introductory material and listening to teachers. Describe the meaning of this statement and how you now feel about it with respect to your decision to become a classroom teacher. Do you expect to act on their suggestion? Explain why not, or how you will do it.

2. Explain the meaning of *integrating strategies for integrated learning*.

3. Are there any cautions that as a teacher you need to be aware of when using games for teaching? If there are, describe them.

4. Test scores typically do not measure skills and intelligent behaviors such as critical thinking, persistence, cooperation, ingenuity, patience, creativity, originality, and flexibility in thinking. How should students who demonstrate achievement in intelligent behaviors be recognized?

5. Return to your response to question number 4 of Questions for Discussion at the end of Chapter 1. Modify it if necessary. Share your modifications with those of your classmates.

Now go to Topics #10 and 11: **Inductive Models** and **Inquiry Models** in the MyEducationLab (www.myeducationlab.com) for your course, where you can:

- Find learning outcomes for these topics along with the national standards that connect to these outcomes.
- Complete Assignments and Activities that can help you more deeply understand the chapter content.
- Apply and practice your understanding of the core teaching skills identified in the chapter with the Building Teaching Skills and Dispositions learning units.

EXERCISE 7.1   THE LECTURE—SUMMARY REVIEW AND PRACTICE

INSTRUCTIONS: The purpose of this exercise is to provide a summary review to check your comprehension of this important, often used, and sometimes abused teaching strategy. Answer each of the following questions, and then share your responses with your classmates.

1. Describe how the lecture differs from informal teacher talk. _____

_____

_____

_____

2. Although sometimes a useful strategy, lecturing should be used sparingly in high school teaching, even more sparingly in middle school teaching, and perhaps not at all in lower grades. Why is it less useful than some other teaching strategies? _____

_____

_____

_____

3. Specifically, when might you use a lecture? _____

_____

_____

_____

4. What can a lecturer do to arouse and maintain student interest in the lecture? _____

_____

_____

_____

5. Identify principles that should be kept in mind when a teacher is planning a lecture. _____

_____

_____

_____

6. Identify at least five things you can do to ensure that your lecture is successful. _____

_____

_____

_____

7. Thinking back to classes given by the best lecturers in your college experience, what did that professor do that made his or her lectures better than average? _____

_____

_____

_____

EXERCISE 7.1 *(continued)*

8. Thinking of a lecture or informal talk given by one of your current professors or colleagues, what aids did the lecturer use to spice up the lecture? What devices might have been used that were not? If you were the lecturer, would you have performed differently? If so, explain how.

_____

_____

_____

_____

9. For a specific topic at a grade level and in your subject field, prepare a major instructional objective. Identify the major points that you would try to make and how you would try to get those points across in a lecture designed to support that objective.

Field: _____   Grade level: _____

Topic: _____   Major objective: _____

Major points: _____

_____

_____

Methods of achieving: _____

_____

_____

Estimate of amount of time needed to present this lecture: _____

10. Now implement the lecture of the previous item (number 9) to a group of peers and obtain their feedback, using the criteria of item 8 for that feedback. If the equipment is available, you may wish to video record your lecture so you can watch it and evaluate it yourself. After implementing the lecture and obtaining evaluative feedback from your peers, prepare a self-evaluation of this experience, again using the criteria of item 8. Share this self-evaluation with your course instructor. Use separate paper for the self-evaluation.

EXERCISE 7.2   DEVELOPING A LESSON USING LEVEL II INQUIRY, THINKING SKILL DEVELOPMENT, A DEMONSTRATION, OR AN INTERACTIVE LECTURE—MICRO PEER TEACHING II

INSTRUCTIONS: The purpose of this exercise is to provide the opportunity for you to create a brief lesson (about 20 minutes of instructional time but to be specified by your instructor) designed for a specific grade level and subject and to try it out on your peers for their feedback in an informal (i.e., nongraded) micro peer teaching demonstration.

Divide your class into four groups. The task of members of each group is to prepare lessons (individually) that fall into one of the four categories: Level II inquiry; thinking level; demonstration; interactive lecture. Schedule class presentations so that each class member has the opportunity to present her or his lesson and to obtain feedback from class members about it. For feedback, class members who are the "teacher's" audience can complete the assessment rubric shown after this exercise (by circling one of the three choices for each of the 10 categories) and give their completed form to the teacher for use in analysis and self-assessment. Before your class starts this exercise you may want to review the scoring rubric and make modifications to it that the class agrees on.

To structure your lesson plan, use one of the sample lesson plan formats presented in Chapter 6; however, each lesson should be centered around one major theme or concept and be planned for about 20 minutes of instructional time.

Group 1: Develop a Level II inquiry lesson.

Group 2: Develop a lesson designed to raise the level of student thinking.

Group 3: Develop a lesson that involves a demonstration.

Group 4: Develop a lesson that is an interactive lecture.

EXERCISE 7.2 *(continued)*

PEER AND SELF-ASSESSMENT RUBRIC FOR USE WITH EXERCISE 7.2

For: _____   *Group:* _____

	1	0.5	0
1. Lesson beginning Comment:	effective	less effective	not effective
2. Sequencing Comment:	effective	less effective	rambling
3. Pacing of lesson Comment:	effective	less effective	too slow or too fast
4. Audience involvement Comment:	effective	less effective	none
5. Motivators (e.g., analogies, verbal cues, humor, visual cues, sensory cues) Comment:	effective	less effective	not apparent
6. Content of lesson Comment:	well chosen	interesting	boring or inappropriate
7. Voice of teacher Comment:	stimulating	minor problem	major problems
8. Vocabulary used Comment:	well chosen	appropriate	inappropriate
9. Eye contact Comment:	excellent	average	problems
10. Closure Comment:	effective	less effective	unclear or none

OTHER COMMENTS:

_____

_____

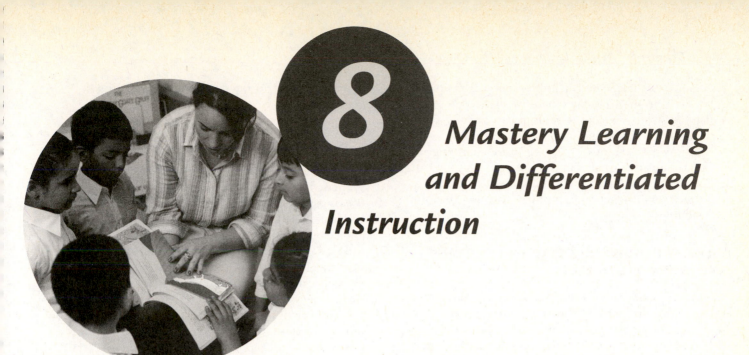

8

Mastery Learning and Differentiated Instruction

Learning is an individual or personal experience. Yet as a classroom teacher you will be expected to work effectively with students on other than an individual basis—perhaps 30 or more at a time. Much has been written on the importance of differentiated instruction for learners. Virtually all the research concerning effective instructional practice emphasizes greater individualization of instruction (Carroll, 1994), and today it is done primarily via what is known as **differentiated instruction**, which is varying the methods and content of instruction according to individual student differences and needs in order to attain the most from the learning experiences.

> In a differentiated classroom, the teacher proactively plans and carries out varied approaches to content, process, and product in anticipation of and response to student differences in readiness, interest, and learning needs.
>
> Carol Ann Tomlinson (2005, p. 7)

We know of the individuality of the learning experience, and we know that although some students are primarily verbal learners, many more are primarily visual, tactile, or kinesthetic learners. As the classroom teacher, you find yourself in the difficult position of simultaneously ministering to many separate and individual learners with individual learning capacities, styles, and preferences. How is it best done? Not by having every student learn the same thing at the same time by doing the same activity, but rather by allowing all students to access the same curriculum but via varying entry points, learning activities, and outcomes that are personalized to individual student's needs. Differentiated

instruction is not a single instructional strategy but a variety of strategies.

To differentiate the instruction, exemplary schools and teachers use a variety of strategies—small learning communities, exploratory programs, cooperative learning groups, project-based learning, personalized learning plans, self-instructional modules, and independent study—to respond to individual student competencies, interests, needs, and abilities. They also use nonconventional scheduling so that teaching teams can vary the length of time in periods and also vary the size of instructional groups and the learning strategies within a given time period.

Common sense tells us that student achievement in learning is related to both the quality of attention and the length of time given to learning tasks. Building upon a model developed earlier by John Carroll (1963), Benjamin Bloom (1987) developed the concept of individualized instruction called mastery learning, saying that students need sufficient time on task (i.e., engaged time) to master content before moving on to new content.

Differentiating the learning to provide quality learning for each student is the focus of this chapter, whereas in the chapter that follows our focus is on how to personalize the learning in groups.

Specifically, upon completion of this chapter you should be able to:

1. Describe the meaning of *mastery (quality) learning* and its implications for teaching.
2. Explain how the teacher can differentiate the instruction to ensure success for each student.
3. Demonstrate an awareness of appropriate curriculum options and instructional practices for specific

groups of learners, including the diversity of students found in today's inclusive classroom.

4. Demonstrate developing skills in recognizing, celebrating, and building upon student diversity.

5. Demonstrate your developing understanding of how to ensure equality in the classroom.

6. Demonstrate skill in the development of a personalized self-instructional module for use in your teaching.

TODAY'S EMPHASIS: QUALITY LEARNING FOR EVERY STUDENT

Emphasis today is on mastery of content, or quality learning, for every student. By *mastery of content*, I mean that the student demonstrates use of what has been learned. Because of that emphasis and research that indicates that quality learning programs positively affect achievement, the importance of the concept of mastery learning has resurfaced and is becoming firmly entrenched. For example, the nationwide approach of standards-based instruction relies on a goal-driven curriculum model with instruction that focuses on the construction of individual knowledge through mastery and assessment of student learning against the anticipated outcomes. In some instances, unfortunately, attention may be on the mastery of only minimum competencies; thus, in those instances students may not always be encouraged to work and learn to the maximum of their talents and abilities.

Assumptions About Mastery, or Quality, Learning

Although the original model of mastery, or quality, learning emphasized individualized tutoring, it has been successfully modified for use within the context of group instruction (Gentile & Lalley, 2003; Good & Brophy, 2008). The concept of mastery learning is based on certain assumptions (Battistini, 1995; Horton, 1981):

1. Mastery learning can ensure that students experience success at each level of the instructional process—experiencing success at each level provides incentive and motivation for further learning.

2. Mastery of content, or quality learning, is possible for each learner.

3. Most learning is sequential and logical.

4. Most desired learning outcomes can be specified in terms of observable and measurable performance.

5. Although all students can achieve mastery, to master a particular content some students may require more time than others—the teacher and the school must provide for this difference in time needed to complete a task successfully.

6. For quality learning to occur, it is the instruction that must be modified and adapted, not the students—traditional tracking or ability grouping do not fit.

Elements of any Mastery Learning Model: The Cycle of Teaching

The essence of mastery (quality) learning is the *cycle of teaching* and contains the following elements:

1. Clearly defined target learning objectives with preset mastery performance expectations

2. Preassessment of the learner's present knowledge

3. Instructional component, with a rich variety of choices and options for students

4. Frequent practice, reinforcement, and comprehension checks (a form of formative assessment), with corrective instruction at each step of the way to keep the learner on track

5. Postassessment (summative assessment) to determine the extent of student mastery of the learning objectives

Strategies for Personalizing (Individualizing) the Instruction Now

You can immediately provide personalized instruction by

• starting study of a topic from where the students are in terms of what they know (or think they know) and

To a great degree, student achievement in learning is determined by two factors: (1) how well students understand and follow procedures, and (2) the mode of instruction. Both of these factors are under the control of the teacher.

what they want to know about the topic (as in think-pair-share, discussed in Chapter 2); see also KWL and similar strategies in Figure 4.2 of Chapter 4);

- providing students with choices from a rich variety of learning pathways, resources, and hands-on experiences to learn more about the topic;
- providing multiple instructional approaches (i.e., using multilevel instruction in a variety of settings, from learning alone to whole-class instruction);
- using self-instructional modules (as in Exercise 8.1), computers, and other electronic devices to provide programmed instruction and practice for individual students without your immediate or steady involvement; and
- empowering students with responsibility for decision making, reflection, and self-assessment.

WORKING WITH AND INDIVIDUALIZING THE LEARNING EXPERIENCES FOR SPECIFIC LEARNERS

For working with specific learners, consider the guidelines that follow and refer back to these guidelines often during your preactive (planning) phase of instruction during the first few years of your teaching. Additionally, many teachers have told us they find it valuable to refer to the guidelines during the instruction phase.

Recognizing and Working with Students with Special Needs

Students with disabilities (referred to also as students with **special needs** or students with **exceptionalities**) include those with disabling conditions or impairments in any one or more of the following categories: mental retardation, hearing, speech or language, visual, emotional, orthopedic, autism, traumatic brain injury, other health impairment, or specific learning disabilities. To receive special education services, a child must have a disability in one or more of the categories, and by reason thereof, the child needs special education and related services. In other words, not all children who have a disability need services available via special education. For example, a child with a hearing impairment would be entitled to special services when the impairment is so severe that the child cannot understand what is being said even when the child is equipped with a hearing aid.

To the extent possible, students with special needs must be educated with their peers in the regular classroom. Public Law 94-142, the Education for All Handicapped Children Act (EAHCA) of 1975 (now known as the Individuals with Disabilities Education Act, IDEA), and all its amendments that followed, including its 2004 revision and reauthorization, mandate that all children have the right to a free and appropriate education, as well as to nondiscriminatory assessment. Emphasizing normalizing the educational environment for students with disabilities, legislation requires provision of the least restrictive environment (LRE) for these students. An LRE is an environment that is as normal as possible.

Today's popularity with response to intervention (RtI), as discussed in Chapter 5, is an outgrowth of the changes made in 2004 to the Individuals with Disabilities Act. Although many states and school districts use RtI practices to help identify students with specific learning disabilities, RtI is more than just a special education initiative. It is part of the total effort to help every child succeed in learning. For example, Long Beach Unified School District is California's third largest urban school district with more than 90,000 students, 84 percent of whom are minority and 68 percent of whom qualify for free and reduced price lunch, and where over 46 languages are spoken. The district universally screens every entering eighth-grader for skills on various measures, and then tiers students into the levels of instruction they need (Elliott, 2008).

A CONTINUUM OF DIFFERENCES

Students with disabilities fall along a continuum of learner differences rather than as a separate category of student (Meyer & Rose, 2000). Because of their wide differences, some students identified as having special needs may be placed in the regular classroom for the entire school day, called **full inclusion**. Some students may be in a regular classroom the greater portion of the school day, called **partial inclusion**, or only for designated periods. Although there is no single, universally accepted definition of the term **inclusion**, Good and Brophy (2008, p. 221) describe it as "the concept that classrooms should be designed and operated as inclusive learning environments flexible enough to meet the needs of all students, whether or not they carry special educational labels." (The term *inclusion* has largely replaced use of an earlier and similar term, **mainstreaming**.) As a classroom teacher you will need information and skills specific to teaching learners with special needs who are included in your classes.

Generally speaking, teaching students who have special needs requires more care, better diagnosis, greater skill, more attention to individual needs, and an even greater understanding of the students. The challenges of teaching students with special needs in the regular classroom are great enough that to do it well you need specialized training beyond the general guidelines presented here. At some point in your teacher preparation you may be required to take one or more courses in working with learners with special needs in the regular classroom. If not, you may find useful the book by Vaughn and Bos (2009) titled *Strategies for Teaching Students with Learning and Behavior Problems*.

When a student with special needs is placed in your classroom, your task is to deal directly with the differences between this student and other students in your classroom. To do this, you need to understand the general characteristics of different types of learners with special needs, to identify the student's unique needs relative to your classroom, and to design lessons that teach to different needs at the same time, called multilevel teaching, a strategy that has been discussed throughout this resource guide.

Just because a student has been identified as having one or more special needs does not preclude that person from being gifted or talented. Gifted students with disabling conditions remain a major group of poorly recognized and underattended to youth, perhaps because focus on accommodations for their disabilities precludes adequate recognition and development of their gifts and talents (Willard-Holt, 1999).

Congress stipulated in P.L. 94-142 that an individualized education program (IEP) be devised annually for each child with special needs. According to that law, an IEP is developed for each student each year by a team that includes special education teachers, the child's parents or guardians, and the classroom teachers. The IEP contains a statement of the student's present educational levels, the educational goals and measurable objectives or benchmarks for the year, specifications for the services to be provided and the extent to which the student should be expected to participate in the regular education program, and the evaluative criteria for the services to be provided (for specific guidance, see Pierangelo & Giuliani, 2007). Consultation by special and skilled support personnel is essential in all IEP models. A consultant works directly with teachers or with students and parents. As a classroom teacher, you may play an active role in preparing the specifications for the students with special needs assigned to your classroom and assume a major responsibility for implementing the program.

As found by Newmann (1992) and emphasized by Good and Brophy (2008), the most important factor contributing to success in working with students in general and at-risk students in particular is the development of a *culture of inclusion* characterized by the teacher's

(a) acceptance and welcoming attitude toward all students,
(b) communication of positive expectations,
(c) support for their learning efforts, with
(d) instruction that features thoughtful classroom discourse and work on authentic learning activities, that is, real or simulated learning activities that provide the student with useful life skills and knowledge.

GUIDELINES FOR WORKING WITH STUDENTS WITH SPECIAL NEEDS IN THE INCLUSIVE CLASSROOM

Although the guidelines represented by the paragraphs that follow are important for teaching all students, they are especially important for working with students with special needs.

- Familiarize yourself with exactly what the special needs of each learner are. Privately ask the student with special needs whether there is anything he or she would like for you to know and that you specifically can do to facilitate his or her learning.

- Adapt and modify materials and procedures to the special needs of each student. For example, a student who has extreme difficulty sitting still for more than a few minutes will need planned changes in learning activities. When establishing student seating arrangements in the classroom, give preference to students according to their special needs. Try to incorporate into lessons activities that engage all learning modalities—visual, auditory, tactile, and kinesthetic. Be flexible in your classroom procedures. For example, allow the use of audio recorders for note taking and test taking when students have trouble with the written language. As another example, although children with ADHD (attention-deficit/hyperactivity disorder) can often be quite restless, it may be best for their learning to allow them to move all they want so long as they don't harm themselves, or others, or cause classroom damage.

- Provide high structure and clear expectations by defining the learning objectives in behavioral terms. Teach students the correct procedures for everything. Break complex learning into simpler components, moving from the most concrete to the abstract, rather than the other way around. Check frequently for student understanding of instructions and procedures and for comprehension of content. Use computers and other self-correcting materials for drill and practice and for provision of immediate, constructive, and private feedback to the student.

- Exercise your withitness, monitoring students for signs of restlessness, frustration, anxiety, and off-task behaviors. Be ready to reassign individual learners to different activities as the situation warrants. Established classroom learning centers (discussed in Chapter 9) can be a big help.

- Have all students maintain assignments for the week or some other period of time in an assignment book or in a folder kept in their notebooks. Post assignments in a special place in the classroom (and perhaps on the school's Web site) and frequently remind students of assignments and deadlines.

- Maintain consistency in your expectations and in your responses. Learners with special needs, particularly, can become frustrated when they do not understand a teacher's expectations and when they cannot depend on a teacher's reactions.

- Plan interesting activities to bridge learning, activities that help students connect what is being learned with their real world. Making that connection helps motivate students and keep them on task.

- Plan questions and questioning sequences, and write them into your lesson plans. Plan questions you ask learners with special needs so they are apt to answer them with confidence. Use signals to let students know you are likely to call on them in class (e.g., prolonged eye contact or mentioning your intention to the student before class begins). After asking a question, give the student adequate time to think and respond. Then, after the student responds, build upon the student's response to indicate the student's contribution was accepted as being important.

- Provide for and teach toward student success. Offer students activities and experiences that ensure each student's success and mastery at some level. Use of student portfolios can give evidence of progress and help in building student confidence and self-esteem.
- Provide scaffolded instruction, that is, give each student as much guided or coached practice as time allows. Provide time in class for students to work on assignments and projects. During this time, you can monitor the work of each student while looking for misconceptions, thus ensuring students get started on the right track.
- Provide help in the organization of students' learning. For example, give instruction in the organization of notes and notebooks. Have a three-hole punch available in the classroom so students can place their papers into their notebooks immediately, thus avoiding disorganization and the loss of papers. During class presentations use an overhead projector with transparencies; students who need more time can then copy material from the transparencies. Ask students to read their notes aloud to each other in small groups, thereby aiding their recall and understanding, and encouraging them to take notes for meaning rather than for rote learning. Encourage and provide for peer support, peer tutoring or coaching, and cross-age teaching (discussed in the 9 chapter). Ensure the learner with special needs is included in all class activities to the fullest extent possible.

Recognizing and Working with Students of Cultural and Linguistic Differences

Practicing the concept of being a student of your students, you must quickly determine the language and ethnic groups represented by the students in your classroom.

Teaching in Practice

Help! No Aide Today

Hannah is a kindergarten teacher. Of the 22 students in Hannah's class, one, Aliya, is a child with special needs with multiple disabilities including Down syndrome and severe hearing loss. On this day, Aliya's aide failed to come to school. The aide also failed to notify the school that she would be absent. Hannah is the only adult in class today. Aliya needs to go to the bathroom now. What would you do were you Hannah?

A major problem for recent newcomers, as well as some ethnic groups, is learning a second (or third or fourth) language. Although in many schools it is not uncommon for more than half the students to come from homes where the spoken language is not English, standard English is a necessity in most communities of this country if a person is to become vocationally successful and enjoy a full life. Learning to communicate reasonably well in English can take an immigrant student at least a year and probably longer, and from 3 to 7 years to catch up academically in English. By default, then, an increasing percentage of public school teachers in the United States are teachers of English language learners (ELLs). Helpful to the success of teaching ELLs are the demonstration of respect for students' cultural backgrounds, long-term teacher–student cohorts (such as in looping), and the use of active and cooperative learning. There are numerous programs specially designed for English language learners. Most use the acronym LEP (limited English proficiency) with five number levels, from Level 1 that designates non-English-speaking, although the student may understand single sentences and speak simple words or phrases in English, to Level 5, sometimes designated FEP (fluent English proficiency), for the student who is fully fluent in English, although the student's overall academic achievement may still be less than desired because of language or cultural differences. Generally, students who are identified as being at Level 3 and higher are capable of successfully participating in lessons that include reading and writing instruction in the content areas.

Some schools use a "pullout" approach, where a portion of the student's school time is spent in special bilingual classes and the rest of the time the student is placed in regular classrooms. In some schools, LEP students are placed in academic classrooms that use a simplified or "sheltered" English approach.

Used in many secondary schools in particular are "newcomer" programs (Echevarria & Graves, 2007). Although varied in their methods, their purpose is to acculturate new immigrant student arrivals to life in the United States, assisting them in acquiring beginning English language skills while developing skills and knowledge in academic areas.

For schools that participate in NCLB legislation (they accept federal funding), ELLs as a subgroup must meet Adequate Yearly Progress (AYP) targets for reading and mathematics proficiency and they must meet Annual Measurable Achievement Objectives (AMAOs) for English-language proficiency.

Regardless of the program and its source of funding, specific techniques recommended for teaching ELL students include the following:

- Allowing more time for learning activities than one normally would.

- Allowing time for translation by a classroom aide or by a classmate and allowing time for dialogue to clarify meaning, encouraging the students to transfer into English what they already know in their native language.
- Avoiding jargon or idioms that might be misunderstood. (See the classroom vignette that follows.)
- Dividing complex or extended language discourse into smaller, more manageable units.
- Giving directions in a variety of ways.
- Giving special attention to key words that convey meaning and writing them on the board.
- Repeating instructions, using the same words.
- Maintaining high expectations of each learner.
- Reading written directions aloud, and then writing the directions on the board.
- Speaking clearly and naturally but at a slower than normal pace, while placing emphasis on key words, phrases, and concepts by varying intonation and incorporating pauses.
- Using a variety of examples and observable models.
- Using briefer and simpler sentences than usual.
- Using simplified vocabulary without talking down to students.

ADDITIONAL GUIDELINES FOR WORKING WITH LANGUAGE-MINORITY STUDENTS

While they are becoming more competent in English-language usage, LEP students can learn the same curriculum in the various disciplines as native English-speaking students. Although the guidelines presented in the following paragraphs are important for teaching all students, they are especially important when working with language-minority students.

Present instruction that is concrete and that includes the most direct learning experiences possible. Use the most concrete (least abstract) forms of instruction.

Build upon (or connect with) what the students already have experienced and know. Building upon what students

already know, or think they know, helps them connect their knowledge and construct their understandings.

Encourage student writing. One way is by using student journals (discussed later in Chapter 10). Two kinds of journals that are appropriate when working with LEP students are dialogue journals and response journals. **Dialogue journals** are used for students to write anything that is on their minds, usually on the right page. Teachers, parents, and classmates then respond on the left page, thereby "talking with" the journal writers (Werderich, 2002). **Response journals** are used for students to write (record) their responses to what they are reading or studying.

Help students learn the vocabulary. Assist ELLs in learning two vocabulary sets: the regular English vocabulary needed for learning and the new vocabulary introduced by the subject content. For example, while learning science, a student is dealing with both the regular English language vocabulary and the special vocabulary of science.

To the extent possible, *involve parents or guardians or siblings.* Students whose primary language is not English may have other differences about which you will also need to become knowledgeable. These differences are related to culture, customs, family life, and expectations. To be most successful in working with language-minority students, you should learn as much as possible about each student. Parents (or guardians) of new immigrant children are usually truly concerned about the education of their children and may be very interested in cooperating with you in any way possible. In a study of schools recognized for their exemplary practices with language-minority students, the schools were recognized for their friendliness to parents, that is, for welcoming parents in a variety of innovative ways (Minicucci et al., 1995).

Plan for and use all learning modalities. As with teaching young people in general, in working with language-minority students you need to use multisensory approaches—learning activities that involve students in auditory, visual, tactile, and kinesthetic learning activities.

Use visual aids. In particular, those that are student made—e.g., bulletin boards, pictures, cartoons, maps, charts, graphs, posters, diagrams and drawings, games, videos, and other multimedia sources—can be especially helpful when teaching students whose first language is not English (Allison & Rehm, 2007; Carrier, 2005).

Provide scaffolded reading experiences, that is, a framework of activities for use in prereading (such as preteaching vocabulary and predicting outcomes), during reading (such as guided reading and silent reading activities), and postreading (such as playacting and writing) of any genre of text (Fitzgerald & Graves, 2005).

When bringing in names of experts—such as artists, authors, historians, scientists, mathematicians—use examples of non-Western sources rather than solely those from the United States.

 CLASSROOM VIGNETTE

A Teachable Moment

While Elina was reading aloud in her English class, she had a little difficulty with her throat (due to a cold) and stumbled over some words. The teacher jokingly commented, "That's okay Elina, you must have a horse in your throat." Quickly, Mariya, a recent immigrant from the Ukraine, asked, "How could Elina have a horse in her throat?" The teacher ignored Mariya's question. Missing this teachable moment, the teacher, continuing with the planned lesson, gave Elina the option of continuing the reading or choosing someone else to continue the reading.

Use peer tutoring, pairing native English-language-speaking students with ELLs, whereby they become teachers and resources for each other, encouraging not just the learning of content but also the establishment of friendships between students of varying backgrounds (Allison & Rehm, 2007).

Use small-group cooperative and collaborative learning. Cooperative and collaborative learning strategies are particularly effective with language-minority students because they provide opportunities for students to produce language in a setting less threatening than is speaking before the entire class.

Use the benefits afforded by modern technology. For example, computer networking allows students to write and communicate with peers from around the world as well as participate in "publishing" their classroom work.

ADDITIONAL GUIDELINES FOR WORKING WITH STUDENTS OF DIVERSE BACKGROUNDS

To be compatible with, and be able to teach, students who come from backgrounds different from yours, you need to believe that, given adequate support, all students *can* learn—regardless of gender, social class, physical characteristics, language, religion, and ethnic or cultural backgrounds. You also need to develop special skills that include those in the following guidelines, each of which has been discussed in detail in prior chapters. To work successfully and most effectively with students of diverse backgrounds, you should

- Build the learning around students' individual learning styles, such as is done at Gateway High School (San Francisco, California). Personalize learning for each student, much like what is done by using the IEP with learners with special needs. For example, at Frances W. Parker Charter Essential School (Devens, Massachusetts), parents, students, and teachers meet in the fall to identify goals that become the foundation of a personalized learning plan for each student. Involve students in understanding and in making important decisions about their own learning, so they feel ownership (i.e., a sense of empowerment and connectedness) of that learning.

> If we aspire to meet the challenge of leaving no child behind, we must provide diverse learners with diverging pathways that lead to their success. I look forward to the day when our schools offer every student the opportunity to become a leading expert on a chosen topic.
>
> Dr. Mel Levine (2003)

- Communicate positively with every student and with the student's parents or guardians, learning as much as you can about the student and the student's culture, and encouraging family members to participate in the student's learning. Involve parents, guardians, and other members of the community in the educational program so all have a sense of ownership and responsibility and feel positive about the school program.

- Establish and maintain high expectations, although not necessarily the same expectations, for each student. Both you and your students must understand that intelligence is not a fixed entity, but a set of characteristics that—through a feeling of "I can" and with proper coaching—can be developed.

- Teach individuals by using a variety of strategies to achieve an objective or by using a number of different objectives at the same time (multilevel teaching).

- Use techniques that emphasize collaborative and cooperative learning—that deemphasize competitive learning.

- Use alternative and multiple means of assessing student learning rather than relying solely on the student's use of English language.

> To reinforce her ELLs' learning of important concepts in life science, their English language skills, and to develop a sense of community membership, high school teacher Miriam Westervelt uses a variety of scaffolded activities, including outdoor inquiries, nature journaling, and multicultural gardening (Westervelt, 2007).

Recognizing and Working with Students Who Are Gifted

Historically, educators have used the term **gifted** when referring to a person with identified exceptional ability in one or more academic subjects, and **talented** when referring to a person with exceptional ability in one or more of the visual or performing arts (Clark & Zimmerman, 1998). Today, however, the terms more often are used interchangeably, which is how they are used for this resource guide, that is, as if they are synonymous (Callahan, 2001).

Sometimes, unfortunately, in the regular classroom gifted students are neglected (Feldhusen, 1998; Gross, 2000). At least some of the time, it is probably because there is no singularly accepted method for identification of these students. In other words, students who are gifted in some way or another may go unidentified as such. For placement in special classes or programs for the gifted, school districts traditionally have used grade point averages and standard intelligence quotient (IQ) scores. On the other hand, because IQ testing measures linguistic and logical/mathematical aspects of giftedness, it does not account for others, and thus gifted students sometimes are unrecognized. They also are sometimes among the students most at risk of dropping out of school (Saunders, 2003).

To work most effectively with gifted learners, you must first identify their talents. This can be done not only by using tests, rating scales, and auditions, but also by observations in the classroom, out of the classroom, and from knowledge about the student's life away from school. With those information sources in mind, indicators of superior intelligence are (Schwartz, 1997)

- a strong sense of self, pride, and worth;
- an ability to assume adult roles and responsibilities at home or at work;
- an ability to cope with school while living in poverty;
- an ability to cope with school while living with dysfunctional families;
- an ability to extrapolate knowledge to different circumstances;
- an ability to lead others;
- an ability to manipulate a symbol system;
- an ability to reason by analogy;
- an ability to retrieve and use stored knowledge to solve problems;
- an ability to think and act independently;
- an ability to think logically;
- an understanding of one's cultural heritage; and
- creativity and artistic ability.

Curriculum Tracking

Every student, not only those identified as being gifted, needs a challenging academic environment. Although grouping and tracking students into classes based on interest and demonstrated ability is still practiced (such as reading groups, grade-level retention, accelerated groups, and special education placement), an overwhelming abundance of sources in the literature adamantly opposes the homogeneous grouping of students according to ability, or **curriculum tracking**, as it has long been known. Grouping and tracking do not seem to increase overall achievement of learning, but they do promote inequity (Schwartz, 2000). Tracking is acceptable when it is based upon grouping students according to their interests or vocational aspirations, but tracking students on the basis of race, intelligence, or social class is *not* acceptable and should not be practiced.

Meaningful Curriculum Options: Multiple Pathways to Success

Because of what is now known about learning and intelligence, the trend today is to assume that every student, to some degree and in some area of learning and doing, has the potential for giftedness and to provide sufficient curriculum options, or multiple pathways, so each student can reach those potentials. Clearly, achievement in school increases and students learn more, enjoy learning, and remember more of what they have learned when the instruction is developmentally appropriate for

the needs of the particular students and when individual learning capacities, styles, and modalities are identified and accommodated.

To provide relevant curriculum options, a trend in exemplary schools is to eliminate from the school curriculum what have traditionally been the lower and general curriculum tracks and instead provide curriculum options to ensure a positive environment with success for each student. While attempting to diminish the discriminatory and damaging effects on students believed caused by tracking and homogeneous ability grouping, educators have devised and are refining numerous other seemingly more productive ways of attending to student differences, of providing a more challenging but supportive learning environment, and of stimulating the talents and motivation of each and every student. Because the advantage gained from utilizing a combination of responsive practices concurrently is generally greater than is the gain from using any singular practice by itself, in many instances in a given school the practices overlap and are used simultaneously. These practices are shown in Figure 8.1.

When working in the regular classroom with a student who has special gifts and talents, you are advised to

- Collaborate with students in some planning of their personal objectives and activities for learning.
- Emphasize skills in critical thinking, problem solving, and inquiry.
- Identify and showcase the student's special gift or talent.
- Involve the student in selecting and planning activities, encouraging the development of the student's leadership skills.
- Plan assignments and activities that challenge the students to the fullest of their abilities. This does not mean overloading them with homework or giving identical assignments to all students. Rather, carefully plan so students' time spent on assignments and activities is quality time on meaningful learning.
- Provide in-class seminars for students to discuss topics and problems they are pursuing individually or as members of a learning team.
- Provide independent and self-paced learning and dyad learning opportunities. Gifted and talented students often prefer working alone or with another gifted student.
- Use curriculum compacting, a process that allows a student who already knows the material to pursue enriched or accelerated study (Willard-Holt, 2003). Plan and provide optional and voluntary enrichment activities. Learning centers, special projects, learning contracts, and computer and multimedia activities are excellent tools for provision of enriched learning activities.
- Use diagnostic assessments for reading level and subject-content achievement so you are better able to prescribe objectives and activities for each student.

Figure 8.1   Multiple pathways to success: productive ways of attending to student differences, of providing a positive and challenging learning environment, and of stimulating the talents, interests, and motivation of each and every student.

- Adult advocacy relationships for each student
- Assuring bilingual programs are intellectually stimulating and designed for integration with mainstream education
- Collaborative and cooperative learning opportunities in the classroom
- Community service learning that is connected in some way to the academic program
- Curriculum compacting (opportunity for accelerated study)
- Flexible block scheduling
- High expectations for each student
- Integration of appropriate technology into the curriculum
- Interdisciplinary learning and teaming
- Looping
- Mastery learning with instructional scaffolding
- Opportunity and encouragement for accelerated college entrance
- Opportunity for academic help for every student
- Opportunity to attend a high school class while still in the middle grade, or college while still in high school
- Opportunity to skip a traditional grade level
- Options for high school graduation, such as in 3 years, 4 years, or 5 years, without prejudice or penalty
- Peer and cross-age instruction
- Personal problems assistance
- Personalized education planning and instruction
- Recovery opportunities
- Thematic instruction
- Theme schools and smaller learning communities
- Ungraded or multiage grouping
- Within-class and across discipline student-centered projects

Recognizing and Working with Students Who Take More Time but Are Willing to Try

Students who are slower to learn typically fall into one of two categories: (1) those who try to learn but simply need more time to do it, and (2) those who do not try, referred to variously as underachievers, recalcitrant, or reluctant learners. Practices that work well with students of one category are often not those that work well with those of the second—making life difficult for a teacher of 30 students, half who try and half who do not (Kellough, 1970). It is worse still for a teacher of a group of 30 or so students, some who try but need time, one or two who are academically talented, two or three who have special needs but not the same special needs, a few LEP students, and several who not only seem unwilling to try but who are also disruptive in the classroom. And, by the way, this last example is probably closer to reality for the vast majority of teachers.

Remember this well: Just because a student is slow to learn does not mean the student is less intelligent; some students just plain take longer, for any number of reasons. As just one example, from brain research it is known that the front of the brain, the neo-cortex, the part that controls goal setting, planning, and choice making, is the last part of the brain to develop (Sylwester, 2003). It is also known that the neo-cortex develops earlier in females, usually between ages 11 and 15, whereas in males it develops from late teens into the early 20s. Consequently, expecting the same behavioral

maturity from middle school females and males may be unreasonable (Vawter, 2009).

The following guidelines may be helpful when working with a student who is slow but willing to try:

- Adjust the instruction to the student's preferred learning style, which may be different from yours and from other students in the group.
- Be less concerned with the amount of content coverage than with the student's successful understanding of content that is covered. Teach toward mastery (although this may be antagonistic to modern emphasis on improved student scores on high-stakes assessment tests).
- Discover something the student does exceptionally well, or a special interest, and try to connect the student's learning with that.
- Emphasize basic communication skills, such as speaking, listening, reading, and writing, to ensure that the student's skills in these areas are sufficient for learning the intended content.
- Get to know each student, at least well enough that you have empathy for where the person is coming from. For example, as many as half of adolescents from high-poverty inner-city neighborhoods feel hopeless that they will be able to improve their lives (Bolland, 2003). Commit yourself to helping them understand the power of education in finding their way out of such feelings of hopelessness.

- Help the student learn content in small sequential steps with frequent checks for comprehension. Use instructional scaffolding.
- If necessary, help the student to improve his or her reading skills, such as pronunciation and word meanings.
- If using a single textbook, be certain the reading level is adequate for the student; if it is not, then for that student use other more appropriate reading materials. Many exemplary teachers maintain a variety of optional texts in their classroom just for this purpose.
- Maximize the use of in-class, on-task work and cooperative learning, with close monitoring of the student's progress. Avoid relying much on successful completion of traditional out-of-class assignments unless you can supply coaching to the student in the classroom.
- Vary the instructional strategies, using a variety of activities to engage the visual, verbal, tactile, and kinesthetic modalities.
- When appropriate, use frequent positive reinforcement, with the intention of building the student's confidence and self-esteem.

Recognizing and Working with Recalcitrant Learners

For working with recalcitrant learners, you can use many of the same guidelines from the preceding list, except you should understand that the reasons for these students' behaviors may be quite different from those for the other category of slow learners. Slower learning students who are willing to try may be slow because of their learning style, because of genetic factors, or a combination of those and any number of other reasons. They are simply slower at learning. But they can and will learn. Recalcitrant learners, on the other hand, may be generally quick and bright thinkers but reluctant even to try because of a history of failure, a history of boredom with school, low confidence level for academic work, a poor self-concept, severe personal problems that distract from school, or any variety and combination of reasons, many of which are emotional/psychological in nature.

Whatever the case, a student identified as being a slow or recalcitrant learner might, in fact, be quite gifted or talented in some way, but because of personal problems, have a history of increasingly poor school attendance, poor attention to schoolwork, poor self-confidence, and an attitude problem. With those factors in mind, consider the following guidelines when working with recalcitrant learners:

- As the school year begins, learn as much about each student as you can. Be cautious in how you do it, though, because many of these students will be suspicious of any interest you show in them. Be businesslike, trusting, genuinely interested, and patient. A second caution: Although you learn as much as possible about each student, what has happened in the past is history. Use the information not as ammunition, something to be held against the student, but as insight to help you work more productively with the student.
- While you will want to be cautious about lecturing to these students, a well-chosen, well-implemented, and engaging teacher presentation is usually well received and can turn them on to learning.
- Early in the school term, preferably with the help of adult volunteers (e.g., using professional community members as mentors has worked well at helping change the student's attitude from rebellion to one of hope, challenge, and success), work out a personalized education program with each student.
- Engage the students in learning by using interactive media, such as the Internet.
- Engage the students in active learning with real-world problem solving and perhaps community service projects.
- Forget about trying to "cover the subject matter," concentrating instead on student learning of some things well. Practice mastery (although this may go against the grain of modern emphasis on improved student scores on high-stakes achievement tests). A good procedure is to use thematic teaching and divide the theme into short segments. Because school attendance for these students is sometimes sporadic, try personalizing their assignments so they can pick up where they left off and move through the course in an orderly fashion even when they have been absent excessively. Try ensuring some degree of success for each student.
- Help students develop their studying and learning skills, such as concentrating, remembering, and comprehending. Mnemonics, for example, is a device these students respond to positively, and they are often quick and creative in inventing their own.
- If using a single textbook, determine whether the reading level is appropriate; if it is not, then for that student discard the book and select other more appropriate reading materials.
- Make sure your classroom procedures and rules are understood at the beginning of the school term and be consistent about following them.
- Maximize the use of in-class, on-task work and cooperative learning, with close monitoring of the student's progress. Do not rely on successful completion of traditional out-of-class assignments unless the student receives coached guidance from you before leaving your classroom.
- Use simple language in the classroom. Be concerned less about the words the students use and the way they use them and more about the ideas they are expressing. Let the students use their own idioms without carping too much on grammar and syntax. Always take care, though, to use proper and professional English yourself.

• When appropriate, use frequent positive reinforcement, with the intention of increasing the student's sense of personal worth. When using praise for reinforcement, however, try to direct your praise to the deed rather than the student.

Recognizing and Working with Abused Children

Child abuse is a grave matter of pressing national concern. Teachers in all states are now legally mandated to report any suspicion of child abuse. It is a serious moral issue not to report such suspicion, and lawsuits for negligence have been brought against educators for not doing so. To report suspicion of child abuse, follow your school's written policy. If there is none, you can telephone 1-800-4-A-CHILD or use the hotline for your state. Proof of abuse is not necessary.

Although physical abuse and certain kinds of neglect, such as improper clothing and inadequate dental care, may be the easiest to spot, other types of abuse such as incest, emotional abuse, and malnutrition are just as serious. Characteristics of children who are abused or neglected are shown in Figure 8.2. An abused or neglected child in your classroom needs to feel welcome and secure while in the classroom. For additional guidance in working with such a student, contact experts from your local school district (e.g., the school psychologist) and obtain guidelines from your state department of education or from the local Children's Protective Services (CPS) agency.

LEARNING ALONE

Although some students learn well in pairs (dyads), and others learn well with their peers in groups—collaboratively, cooperatively, or competitively—or collaboratively with adults, and others learn well in combinations of these patterns, researchers tell us that more than 10 percent of K–12 students learn best alone (Dunn, 1995). Learning-alone students often are gifted, nonconforming, able to work at their own pace successfully, comfortable using media, or seemingly underachieving but potentially able students.

Some learning-alone students do well with unconventional instructional strategies, such as **contract learning packages**—that is, agreements between the teacher and individual students to proceed with tasks appropriate to their readiness, interests, or learning profiles in a sequence and at a pace each student selects. Learning contracts motivate students to learn while providing the teacher with more instructional flexibility and control.

Perhaps equally if not more important is that learning by contract can (1) formalize and ensure the gradual release of responsibility for learning that is often talked about but infrequently practiced; (2) harness

Figure 8.2 Characteristics of children who may be abused or neglected.

• Apathy, short attention span, and lack of interest in school

• Apparent lack of supervision

• Bruised or swollen lip; mouth, lip, or tongue lacerations

• Difficulty walking or sitting

• Evidence of drug or alcohol abuse

• Expression of little to no emotion when hurt

• Fear of everyone and everything

• Fear of going home after school

• Fear of parent/guardian and other adults

• Frequent absence from school

• Frequent depression, sudden crying, evidence of poor self-image, extreme withdrawal

• Frequent expression of an extreme hunger

• Frequently tired and often falls asleep in class

• Inappropriate interest in or knowledge of sexual acts

• Strong and unpleasant body odor

• Sudden and dramatic changes in behavior

• Undue craving for attention or affection

• Unexplained bites, fractures, lacerations, burns, welts, bruises, and/or scars in various stages of healing and capitalize upon student motivation to read and to learn the standards-driven content that they are expected to acquire; (3) encourage and require students to apply transportable and useful skills, traits, and dispositions (e.g., time management, task prioritization); and (4) allow the willing and able students to move forward with efficiency, without delay (Greenwood & McCabe, 2008). For a learning-alone student, instructional packages utilizing a multisensory approach are most apt to encourage and ensure academic success.

One technique that can be used to ensure mastery of learning is the self-instructional module (SIM), which is a learning package (written, on audio- or video recording, or on computer) specifically designed with an individual student in mind, and that can be used as part of a learning contract.

The SIM uses small sequential steps, with frequent practice and immediate learning feedback to the student. It is designed to teach a relatively small amount of material, at the mastery level, requiring a brief amount of learning time (about 30 minutes for middlegrades students). *The SIM can be designed to teach any topic, at any grade level, in any subject, for any domain or combination of domains of learning.* Exercise 8.1 is a self-instructional module designed to guide you through the completion of your first SIM.

SUMMARY

This chapter has continued the development of your repertoire of instructional strategies, specifically with techniques for addressing the individual needs and characteristics of students. And, with the completion of Exercise 8.1 you have undoubtedly created what might be called a "perfect lesson plan." Although you may or may not continue writing and using SIMs in your teaching, you have learned a technique of teaching that ensures learning takes place, and from that experience ways of tweaking all your planning so to best meet the needs of each and every student in your classes.

The next chapter will continue the development of your repertoire of teaching strategies.

QUESTIONS FOR CLASS DISCUSSION

1. Describe today's meaning of the term *mastery learning*. Explain why you believe mastery learning is or is not possible for every student.
2. Describe the meaning of *the cycle of teaching* and how you would use it as a teacher.
3. Explain the significance of *personalizing the instruction* and how with a classroom of 30 students you would do it.
4. What concerns you most about teaching the diversity of students you are likely to have in a classroom? Share those concerns with others in your class. Categorize your group's concerns. By accessing an Internet teacher bulletin board, see what kinds of problems classroom teachers are currently concerned about. Are assessment practices, curriculum expectations, scheduling, grading, group learning, and classroom management high in frequency of concern? Are the concerns of teachers as expressed on the Internet similar to yours? As a class, devise a plan and time line for attempting to ameliorate your concerns.
5. Using modern software to enhance their project presentations, students are learning to put their presentations on computerized video shows that they fill with colorful animation, bold topic headings and neat rows of points they wish to make, each introduced with a highlight mark. Some educators are concerned that too many young people become fixated on fonts and formats and other aspects of the technology without actually giving much deep thought to the content of their presentations. Share your opinions about this.

Outside school, many students are accomplished authors, filmmakers, animators, and recording artists.

Michele Knobel & Dana Wilber (2009, p. 21)

Now go to Topics #7, 12 and 13: **Strategies for Teaching, Diversity: Cultural and Linguistic** and **Inclusion and Special Needs** in the MyEducationLab (www.myeducationlab.com) for your course, where you can:

- Find learning outcomes for these topics along with the national standards that connect to these outcomes.
- Complete Assignments and Activities that can help you more deeply understand the chapter content.
- Examine challenging situations and cases presented in the IRIS center resources.
- Apply and practice your understanding of the core teaching skills identified in the chapter with the Building Teaching Skills and Dispositions learning units.

EXERCISE 8.1   PREPARING A SELF-INSTRUCTIONAL MODULE*

INSTRUCTIONS: The purpose of this exercise is to guide you through the process of preparing a self-instructional module for use in your own teaching. The exercise continues for several pages; it is important that you follow it step by step, beginning with the following boxed-in "cover page."

SELF-INSTRUCTIONAL MODULE NUMBER: 1

Instructor's Name: Professor Richard D. Kellough
School: California State University, Sacramento
Course: Methods of Teaching K–12
Intended Students: Students in teacher preparation
Topic: How to Write a Self-Instructional Module
Estimated Working Time: 10 hours

For the challenge of today's classroom . . .

THE SELF-INSTRUCTIONAL MODULE

You are about to embark upon creating and writing a perfect lesson plan. The result of your hard work will be an instructional module in which you will take a lot of pride. More important, you will have learned a technique of teaching that ensures learning takes place. For what more could you ask?

Let us get to the essence of what this self-instructional module (SIM) is: This SIM is about how to write a SIM. The general objective is to guide you gently through the process of preparing and writing your first SIM. Let's begin the experience with background about the history of the SIM.

A History

Research evidence indicates that student achievement in learning is related to time and to the *quality of attention* being given to the learning task. You knew that already! In 1968, Benjamin Bloom developed a concept of individualized instruction called mastery learning, based on the idea that students need sufficient time on task to master content before moving on to new content. Did you know that? _____. (Please read along with a pencil, and fill in the blanks as you go.)

EXERCISE 8.1 *(continued)*

Although Bloom is usually given credit for the concept of mastery learning, the idea did not originate with him. He reinforced and made popular a model developed earlier by John Carroll. In 1968, Fred Keller developed a similar model called the Keller Plan, or the Personalized System of Instruction (PSI). The PSI quickly became a popular teaching technique in the community and four-year colleges. In about 1972, enter Johnson and Johnson (not of the Band-Aid family, but Rita and Stuart Johnson), who developed their model of mastery learning and called it the Self-Instructional Package (SIP). Since 1972, I (Richard D. Kellough) have been developing my version, the Self-Instructional Module, which you are now experiencing. As you will learn, *frequent comprehension checks and corrective instructions* are important to the effectiveness of the SIM.

One other thing. There are several devices available to individualize instruction, but the SIM has the flexibility to be adaptable for use at all grade levels, from kindergarten through college. I believe the following to be the reasons for the popularity of this strategy:

- The SIM allows the teacher to *create an experience that ensures learning*. Creating makes you feel good; when your students learn, you feel good—two reasons for the SIM's popularity.
- The SIM is truly *individualized*, because it is a module written for an individual student, with that student in mind as it is being written.
- Although it takes time to prepare, the SIM *requires little financial expenditure*, a fact important to today's teacher.
- Once you have prepared your first SIM, you might see that you have begun a series. Subsequent modules are easier to do, and you may see the value in having a series available.
- With today's emphasis on the *basics*, the SIM is particularly helpful for use in remediation.
- When you finish your SIM, you will have collected the content that could be used for a computer program.
- With today's *large and mixed-ability classes*, teachers need help! Here is time and cost-effective help!
- With emphasis today on competency-based instruction, the SIM makes sense.

How are we doing so far? _____ Are your interests and curiosity aroused? _____ Do you have questions? _____ If so, write them down, then continue.

Questions: _____

_____

_____

_____

What Is the Self-Instructional Module and Why Use It?

The SIM is a learning module designed for an individual student; it is self-instructional (i.e., if you, the teacher, drop dead—heaven forbid—the student can continue to learn), and *it requires about 30 minutes of learning time*. The final module can be recorded on tape, video, or computer disk; it can be written in booklet form; or it can exist in any combination of these.

Here are ways that teachers have found the SIM to be useful:

- As an *enrichment* activity for an accelerated student.
- As a strategy for makeup for a student who has been absent.
- As a strategy for a student in need of *remediation*.
- As a strategy for introducing basic information to an entire class, freeing the teacher to work with individual students, making the act of teaching more *time-efficient*, a particularly significant value of the SIM.
- As a learning experience especially coordinated with manipulatives, perhaps in connection with a science experiment, library work, a computer, a tape recording, a videotape, a DVD, hands-on materials for an activity, or any combination of these.

One other point before we stop and check your comprehension: *The single most important characteristic of the SIM is that it uses small sequential steps followed by immediate and corrective feedback to the learner.* In that respect, the SIM resembles programmed instruction.

 Stop the action!

Let's check your learning with the review questions and instructions that follow.

COMPREHENSION CHECK 1

Answer the following three questions, then check your responses by reviewing Feedback Check 1. If you answer all three questions correctly, continue the package; otherwise, back up and review.

1. How would you define a SIM? _____

_____

2. What is the single most important characteristic of the SIM? _____

_____

3. What is one way that the SIM could be used in your own teaching, a way that currently stands out in your thinking?

_____

_____

FEEDBACK CHECK 1

1. Although we will continue development of the definition, at this point it should resemble this: The SIM is an individualization of learning—teaching strategy that teaches toward mastery learning of one relatively small bit of content by building upon small, sequential steps and providing corrective feedback throughout.
2. Referring to the small, sequential steps, followed by immediate and corrective feedback.
3. Your answer is probably related to one of those listed earlier but it could differ.

How Does the SIM Differ from Other Kinds of Learning Packages?

Another characteristic of the SIM is the *amount of learning contained in one module.* Each SIM is designed to teach a relatively small amount of material, but to do it well. *This is a major difference in the SIM from other types of learning activity packages.*

And, in case you have been wondering about what the SIM can be designed to teach, I want to emphasize that it *can be designed*

- For any topic,
  - At any grade level,
    - In any discipline,
      - For cognitive understanding,
        - For psychomotor development, and
          - For affective learning.

That probably brings to your mind all sorts of thoughts and questions. Hold them for a moment, and let's do another comprehension check.

EXERCISE 8.1 *(continued)*

Stop the action and check your learning.

COMPREHENSION CHECK 2

Answer the following two questions, then check your responses in the feedback box that follows.

---

1. How does the SIM differ from other self-contained learning packages?

   _____

   _____

   _____

2. Although teachers frequently emphasize learning that falls within the cognitive domain, is it possible for the SIM to be written to include learning in the psychomotor and affective domains? Yes or no? _____

FEEDBACK CHECK 2

1. Length of learning time is shorter for the SIM, and it is written with an individual student in mind. It is written to teach one thing well, to one student.
2. The SIM can be written for any domain, although evaluation is trickier for the affective and for the highest-level psychomotor.

Perhaps we should now say a word about what we mean when we use the expression *teach one thing well*—that is, to explain what is meant by mastery learning. Theoretically, if the package is being used by an individual student, performance level expectation is 100 percent. In reality, performance level will most likely be between 85 and 95 percent, particularly if you are using the SIM for a group of students rather than an individual. That 5 to 15 percent difference allows for human errors that can occur in writing and in reading.

Now that you have learned what the SIM is—and how this learning strategy differs from other learning activity packages—it is time to concentrate on developing your SIM. Please continue.

SIM DEVELOPMENT

How Do I Develop a SIM?

As with any good lesson plan, it takes time to develop an effective SIM. Indeed, preparation of your first SIM will test your imagination and writing skills! Nevertheless, it will be time well spent; you will be proud of your product. *It is important that you continue following this module, step by step; do not skip parts, or I will assume no responsibility for your final product! Understand?* _____ Development of your SIM emphasizes the importance of

- Writing the learning objectives clearly, precisely, and in behavioral terms.
- Planning the learning activities in small, sequential steps.
- Providing frequent practice and learning comprehension checks.
- Providing immediate feedback, corrective instruction, and assurance to the learner.
- Preparing evaluative questions that measure against the learning objectives.

As you embark on preparing what may be the perfect lesson plan, keep in mind the following two points:

1. Prepare your first SIM so it will take no more than

---

30 minutes for young adolescents.

2. Use a *conversational tone* in your writing. Write in the first person, as though you are talking directly to the student for whom it is intended. For example, when speaking of the learning objectives, use *You will be able to* rather than *The student will be able to.* Keep in mind that you are communicating with one person rather than with an entire class (even though you may be preparing your package for entire class use). It helps to pretend that you are in a one-on-one situation tutoring the student at the writing board.

 Stop the action, and again check your learning.

COMPREHENSION CHECK 3

Answer the following two questions; then check your responses in Feedback Check 3.

1. What maximum learning-time duration is recommended? _____

2. What major item of importance has been recommended for you to keep in mind as you write your SIM?

_____

_____

FEEDBACK CHECK 3

1. Approximately 30 minutes.
2. Write in the first person, as if you are speaking directly to the student.

Now that I have emphasized the *length of learning time* and *the personalization of your writing,* here are other important reminders.

1. Make your SIM attractive and stimulating. Consider using cartoons, puns, graphics, scratch-and-sniff stickers, and interesting manipulatives. Use your creative imagination! Use both cerebral hemispheres!

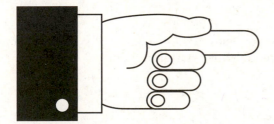

Add sketches, diagrams, modules, pictures, magazine clippings, humor, and a conversational tone, as students appreciate a departure from the usual textbooks and worksheets.

2. Use colleagues as resource persons, brainstorming ideas as you proceed through each step of module production.

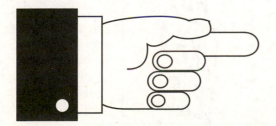

During production, use your best cooperative learning skills.

☞

EXERCISE 8.1 *(continued)*

3. The module should not be read (or heard) like a lecture. It *must* involve small sequential steps with frequent practice and corrective feedback instruction (as modeled in this module).

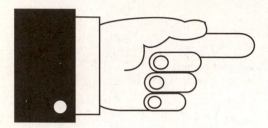

". . . *and with the course material broken down into small, self-instructional units, students can move through at individual rates.*"

4. The module should contain a variety of activities, preferably involving all four learning modalities—*visual, auditory, tactile,* and *kinesthetic.*

5. Vary margins, indentations, and fonts so the final module does not have the usual textbook or worksheet appearance with which students are so familiar. Build into your module the "Hawthorne Effect."

Note about the cosmetics of your SIM: My own prejudice about the SIM is that it should be spread out more than the usual textbook page or worksheet. Use double-spaced lines, varied margins, and so on. Make cosmetic improvements after finishing your final draft. Write, review, sleep on it, write more, revise, add that final touch. This modular packet that you are using has been "toned down" and modified for practical inclusion in this textbook.

6. Your SIM does not have to fit the common 8 ½ × 11-inch size. You are encouraged to be creative in the design of your SIM's shape, size, and format.
7. Like all lesson plans, the SIM is subject to revision and improvement after use. Use your best creative writing skills. *Write, review, sleep on it, write more, revise, test, revise.* . . .

Perhaps before proceeding, it would be useful to review the preceding points. Remember, too, the well-written module *will ensure learning.* Your first SIM will take several hours to produce, but it will be worth it!

Proceed with the steps that follow.

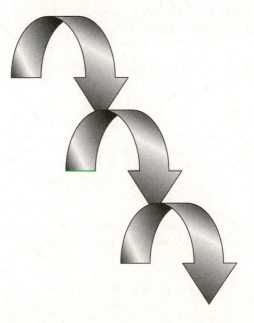

☞

EXERCISE 8.1 *(continued)*

STEPS FOR DEVELOPING YOUR SIM

Instructions: It is important that you proceed through the following module development step by step.

One thing you will notice is that immediately after writing your learning objectives, you will prepare the evaluative test items; both steps precede the preparation of the learning activities. That is not the usual order followed by a teacher when preparing lessons, but it does help to ensure that test items match objectives. Now, here we go! *Step by step,* please.

Note: From here on, write on separate paper for draft planning.

Step 1. Prepare the cover page. It should include the following items:

- Instructor's name (that is you)
  - School (yours)
    - Class or intended students (whom it's for)
      - Topic (specific but not wordy)
        - Estimated working time

For a sample, refer to the beginning of this module. You can vary the design of the cover page according to your needs.

Step 2. Prepare the instructional objectives. For now, these should be written in specific behavioral terms. Later, when writing these into your module introduction, you can phrase them in more general terms.

Recommended is the inclusion of at least one attitudinal (affective) objective, such as "Upon completion of this module, you will tell me your feelings about this kind of learning."

STEP 3. COMPREHENSION CHECK 4

Share with your colleagues what you have accomplished (with steps 1 and 2) to solicit their valuable feedback and input.

Step 4. Depending on feedback (from step 3), modify items 1 and 2, if necessary. For example, after listing the learning instructions, you may find that you really have more than one module in preparation, and within the list of objectives you may find a natural cut-off between modules 1 and 2. You may discover that you have a *series* of modules begun.

Step 5. Prepare the pretest. If the learner does well on the pretest, there may be no need for the student to continue the module. Some modules (like this one) may not include a pretest, though most will. And if this is your first SIM writing experience, I think you *should* include a pretest.

Suggestion: The pretest need not be as long as the posttest but should include a limited sample of questions to determine whether the student already knows the material and need not continue with the module. A pretest also serves to set the student mentally for the SIM.

Step 6. Prepare the posttest. The pretest and posttest could be identical, but usually the pretest is shorter. It is important that both pretest and posttest items actually test against the objectives (of step 2). Try to keep the items objective (e.g., multiple-choice type), avoiding as much as possible the use of subjective test items (e.g., essay type), but do include at least one item measuring an affective objective (see boxed item in step 2).

Important reminder: If your module is well written, the student should achieve 85 to 100 percent on the posttest.

STEP 7. COMPREHENSION CHECK 5

Share with colleagues your pretest and posttest items (providing a copy of your objectives) for suggested improvement changes before continuing to the next step.

Use the following space to write notes to yourself about ideas you are having and regarding any materials you may need to complete your module.

Dear Self—

_____

_____

_____

_____

_____

Good work so far! Before continuing, take a break.

It is time to stop working for a while . . .   . . . and go play!

Step 8. Okay, enough play; it is time to prepare the text of your SIM. This is the "meat" of your module—what goes between the pretest and the posttest. It is the INSTRUCTION. *Reminder:* For the SIM to be self-instructional, the learner should be able to work through the module with little or no help from you.

An important ingredient in your module is the *directions*. The module should be self-directed and self-paced. Therefore, each step of the module should be clear to the learner, making you, the instructor, literally unnecessary. *Everything needed by the learner to complete the module should be provided with the module.*

EXERCISE 8.1 *(continued)*

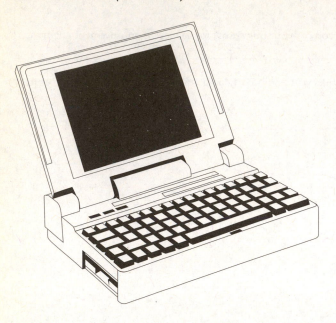

Use small, sequential steps with frequent practice cycles, followed by comprehension checks and corrective feedback. Make it fun and interesting with a variety of activities for the student, activities that provide for learning in several ways, from writing to reading, from viewing a videotape to drawing, from listening to a tape recording to doing a hands-on activity. And be certain the activities correlate with the learning objectives. The learning cycles should lead to satisfaction of the stated objectives, and the posttest items *must* measure against those objectives.

STEP 9. COMPREHENSION CHECK 6

Test your package. Try it out on your colleagues as they look for content errors, spelling and grammar errors, and clarity, as well as offer suggestions for improvement. Duplicate and use the SIM Assessment Form provided at the end of this exercise.

Stop the action! Congratulations on the development of your first SIM! However, two additional steps need your consideration.

Step 10. Revise, if necessary. Make appropriate changes to your SIM as a result of the feedback from your colleagues. Then you are ready to give your SIM its first real test—try it out on the student for whom it is intended.

Step 11. Further revisions. This comes later, after you have used it with the student for whom it was originally intended. Like any other well-prepared lesson or unit plan, it should always be subject to revision and to improvement, never "set in concrete."

SIM ASSESSMENT FORM

1. Module identification
   Author: _____
   _____
   _____

   Title of SIM: _____
   _____
   _____

2. Module Objectives: Do they tell the student
   a. What the student will be able to do? _____
   _____
   _____
   _____
   _____

   b. How the student will demonstrate this new knowledge or skill? _____
   _____
   _____
   _____
   _____

   Is there a clear statement (overview or introduction) of the importance, telling the learner what will be learned by completing the module?
   _____
   _____
   _____

3. Pretest _____
   _____
   _____
   _____
   _____
   _____
   _____

4. Activities (practice cycles)
   Are small, sequential steps used? _____
   _____
   _____
   _____
   _____

Are there frequent practice cycles, with comprehension checks and corrective feedback to the learner?

_____

_____

_____

_____

5. Posttest: Does it test against the objectives? _____

_____

_____

_____

_____

6. Clarity and continuity of expression: _____

_____

_____

_____

_____

7. Is the module informative, attractive, and enjoyable? _____

_____

_____

_____

_____

8. Additional comments useful to the author of this module: _____

_____

_____

_____

_____

_____

9 Organizing and Guiding Student Learning in Groups

Rather than diluting standards and expectations, believing in the learning potential of every student, exemplary schools and teachers are those able to effectively modify the key variables of time, methodology, and grouping to help each individual student achieve mastery of the curriculum. These variables can be attuned or modified to better accommodate each learner's needs. Ways in which time is modified were discussed in Chapter 1. Ways of varying the methodology are addressed throughout the book. In this final chapter on strategies, the focus is on ways of grouping students to enhance positive interaction and quality learning for each student.

In the most effective instructional environments, during any given week or even day of school, as well as when possibly working alone, a student will likely experience a succession of group settings. Ways of grouping students for quality instruction is the general topic of both this and the previous chapter, from personalized and individualized instruction to working with dyads, small groups, and large groups. You also will learn how to use assignments and homework and how to coordinate various forms of independent and small-group, project-based study. The chapter ends with the presentation of a collection of 130 motivational teaching strategies with ideas for lessons, interdisciplinary teaching, transcultural studies, and student projects, what many past users of this resource guide have reported as itself well worth the price of the book.

Specifically, upon completion of this chapter, you should be able to:

1. Explain the advantages and disadvantages of various ways of grouping students for quality learning.
2. Explain further (beyond the content of the previous chapter) how the teacher can personalize the instruction to ensure success for each student.

3. Demonstrate an understanding of the meaning and importance of equity in the classroom and how it can be achieved and maintained.
4. Demonstrate a theoretical and practical understanding of how to effectively use each of these instructional strategies: assignments, homework, written and oral reports, large-group learning, cooperative and small-group learning, learning centers, paired learning, problem-based learning, and projects.
5. Demonstrate your developing understanding of the meaning of *developmentally appropriate practice*.

LEARNING IN PAIRS

It is sometimes advantageous to pair students (dyads) for learning. Four types of dyads are described as follows.

Peer tutoring or mentoring. Peer mentoring, tutoring, or peer-assisted learning (PAL) is a strategy whereby one classmate tutors another. It is useful, for example, when one student helps another who has limited proficiency in English or when a student skilled in math helps another who is less skilled. For many years, it has been demonstrated repeatedly that peer teaching is a significant strategy for promoting active learning (Fuchs et al., 2001; McLauchlan, 2002; Thrope & Wood, 2000). The use of classwide peer tutoring (CWPT) is especially beneficial in elementary schools for learning basic academic skills (Bowman-Perrott, Greenwood, & Tapia, 2007). However, like with any other instructional strategy, peer tutoring is not without its potential problems. For example, the tutor may not be prepared to handle the tutee's wrong answer or poor logic (Chi, Siler, & Jeong, 2004), which might mean you will want to record the tutoring session or in some way prepare the tutor for the eventuality (Good & Brophy, 2008).

Cross-age coaching. Cross-age coaching is a strategy whereby one student coaches another from a different, and sometimes lower, grade level (Jacobson et al., 2001; Potenza, 2003; Rutherford, Rostine, Bell, & Beugin, 2003). This is similar to peer tutoring, except that the coach is from a different age/grade level than the student being coached. Cross-age coaching seems more effective when used to provide supervised practice rather than for stand-alone instruction (Good & Brophy, 2008).

Paired team learning. Paired team learning is a strategy whereby students study and learn in teams of two. Students identified as gifted work and learn especially well when paired. Specific uses for paired team learning include drill partners, science buddies, reading buddies, book report pairs, summary pairs, homework partners, project assignment pairs, and elaborating and relating pairs.

Think-pair-share. Think-pair-share is where students are asked to think about an idea, share thoughts about it with a partner, and then share the pair's thoughts with the entire class; *think-write-pair-share* and *jigsaw* are additional strategies (all three of which are discussed in Chapter 2, and jigsaw you experienced in Exercise 2.4).

The Learning Center

Another significantly beneficial way of pairing students for instruction (as well as of individualizing the instruction and learning alone and integrating the learning) is by using the learning center (LC) or learning station. [Note: Whereas each **learning center** is distinct and unrelated to others, **learning stations** are sequenced or in some way linked to one another, as in the TEAMS approach.] The LC is a special area located in the classroom where one student (or two, if student interaction is necessary or preferred at the center; or as many as four or five students in the case of learning stations) can quietly work and learn at the student's own pace more about a special topic or to improve specific skills. All materials needed are provided at that center, including clear instructions for operation of the center.

Whereas the LC used to be thought of as belonging to the domain of elementary school teachers with self-contained classrooms, now, with block scheduling and longer class periods in many secondary schools, the LC has special relevance and usefulness for all teachers, regardless of grade level or subject. [See, for example, Movitz and Holmes (2007) for how two high school English teachers designed and used learning centers, and specifically a center for a unit they called "Mostly Medieval."]

The value of learning centers as instructional devices undoubtedly lies in the following facts. LCs can provide instructional diversity. While working at a center, the student is giving time and quality attention to the learning task (learning toward mastery) and is likely to be engaging his or her most effective learning modality or integrating several modalities or all of them.

Learning centers are of three types. In the **direct-learning center**, performance expectations for cognitive learning are quite specific, and the focus is on mastery of content. In the **open-learning center**, the goal is to provide opportunity for exploration, enrichment, motivation, and creative discovery. In the **skill center**, as in a direct-learning center, performance expectations are quite specific, but the focus is on development of a particular skill or process.

In all instances, the primary reason for using a learning center is to individualize—that is, to provide collections of materials and activities adjusted to the various readiness levels, interests, and learning profiles of students. Other reasons to use an LC are to provide (a) a mechanism for learning that crosses discipline boundaries; (b) a special place for a student with exceptional needs; (c) opportunities for creative work, enrichment experiences, and multisensory experiences; and (d) the opportunity to learn from learning packages that utilize special equipment or media of which only one or a limited supply may be available for use in your classroom (e.g., science materials, a microscope, a computer, a DVD player, or some combination of these). Learning centers should always be used for educational purposes, *never* for punishment.

The learning center is a special station located in the classroom where an individual student (or a pair of students, if student interaction is necessary for the center) can quietly work and learn at his or her own pace.

To adapt instruction to the curriculum and to students' individual needs and preferences, teachers can design a learning environment that includes several learning stations, each of which uses a different medium and modality or focuses on a special aspect of the curriculum. Students then rotate through the various stations according to their needs and preferences (Reiser & Butzin, 2000).

To construct an LC, you can be as elaborate and as creative as your time, imagination, and resources allow. Students can even help you plan and set up learning centers, which will relieve some of the burden from your busy schedule. The following paragraphs present guidelines for setting up and using this valuable instructional tool.

The center should be designed with a theme in mind, preferably one that integrates the students' learning by providing activities that cross discipline boundaries. Decide the purpose of the center, and give the center a name such as "the center for the study of wetlands," "walking tour of Jerusalem," "patterns in nature," "the United Nations," "sound editing," "our state capitol," "the center for worldwide communication," or "history of the overseas highway," and so on. The purpose of the center should be clearly understood by the students.

The center should be designed so as to be attractive, purposeful, and uncluttered and should be identified with an attractive sign. Learning centers should be activity oriented (i.e., dependent on the student's manipulation of materials, not just paper-and-pencil tasks).

Topics for the center should be related to the instructional program—for review and reinforcement, remediation, or enrichment. The center should be self-directing (i.e., specific instructional objectives and procedures for using the center should be clearly posted and understandable to the student user). An audio- or videocassette or a computer program is sometimes used for this purpose. The center should also be self-correcting (i.e., student users should be able to tell the ways by which they have completed the task, whether or not they have done it correctly and have learned).

The center should contain a variety of activities geared to the varying abilities and interest levels of the students. A choice of two or more activities at a center is one way to provide for this.

Materials to be used at the center should be maintained at the center, with descriptions for use provided to the students. Materials should be safe for student use, and you or another adult should easily supervise the center. Some centers may become more or less permanent centers, that is, remain for the school term or longer, whereas others may change according to what is being studied at the time. Finally, to ensure equal access to all students and to monitor student activity in the center, it is advisable to establish a system for doing so, such as a log-in journal, a sign-up sheet, or a system of rotation.

Teaching in Practice

A Guided Mathematics Instructional Model as Developed and Used by a Primary Grade Teacher

Nine years ago I stepped out of my comfort zone and looked "outside the box" to try an unconventional approach to teaching math. Today, I feel I am a much better teacher as a result. Not only do I have a greater understanding of how students learn mathematics and, therefore, how they should be taught, but also, more significantly, the academic success of my students has improved dramatically.

Like countless other teachers, my mathematics instruction was done whole group. Students were forced to follow along and try to grasp the concepts and/or skills being taught whether they were ready for them or not. Teacher proximity was key. When I was near a student, he/she looked engaged and seemed to understand what was being taught. Unfortunately, those students who were not near me often lost interest if the skill was too challenging, and others appeared bored because it was something they already knew. Test days were true days of reckoning when scores reflected just how much the students actually understood.

I had seen fabulous results when teaching Guided Reading with small groups of students who were all on the same ability level. Why couldn't math be taught in the same fashion? The students were already used to rotating through center-based activities. For my sake as well as the students, I knew I needed to try.

A diagnostic benchmark assessment that our school uses at the beginning of each year helped me to place my students into ability groups. These four homogeneously leveled groups of students, each comprised of about six students, would see me every day for about 12 to 15 minutes of "individualized" instruction. Depending on the skill or concept being taught to the whole class and each group's level of expertise with that skill or concept, student groups would receive differentiated instruction, either challenging students or providing more in-depth learning to help the students develop the necessary foundation for true understanding to occur. I felt it was crucial to establish a safe, nonthreatening atmosphere that provided students with an opportunity to interact with a variety of manipulatives to encourage hands-on exploration. A fun activity where learning was simply a by-product was also necessary. Although every good teacher has a goal in sight, the best mathematics instruction should be about self-discovery. Students need to be lead on a journey to develop their own "ah hah" moments. Only then can children gain a stronger, more internalized connection between skills and concepts and ultimately, a deeper level of conceptual knowledge and understanding.

(continued)

But, what about the students who were not receiving direct instruction? Because there are five strands in math—Number Sense, Measurement, Geometry and Spatial Sense, Algebraic Thinking, and Data Analysis and Probability—I decided to create five math centers, each center focusing on a different strand in math. Students would be grouped heterogeneously, so that when a student was pulled from a center to participate in small-group instruction, there would still be other stronger students remaining at the center. The maximum number of students at a center would be four, not too big, not too small.

I began Guided Math at the beginning of the school year. Therefore, centers had to be introduced before I could even begin seeing my first Guided Math group. I spent the next 4 to 6 weeks introducing one center at a time. This was done whole group and I made sure that each center activity was entertaining and engaging enough that students would enjoy, their time spent there.

After the first center was taught and truly understood, it was time to introduce the second. Once I was certain the students understood this second center, then our 60-minute math block was spent with half of the students engaged in center one, while the other half of the students participated in center two. After about 20 minutes, students rotated, engaging in the other center. Every few days a new center was introduced whole group and students were given the opportunity to rotate through each of the centers. After each day spent at math centers, students engaged in a classroom meeting where we discussed what went well, what difficulties were experienced, and how they were resolved. The students were not only gaining knowledge regarding the math concept, but also learning other life-long skills such as responsibility, cooperation, and problem solving.

Once all five centers had been introduced and students were actively engaged in them, I had the opportunity to travel from center to center to watch the students at work. This provided me with a chance to ensure that students truly did know what was expected of them at each center. It was very exciting to hear the conversations that were transpiring at the centers and to hear the math jargon that the students used so comfortably and expertly.

After the introduction period, I was able to begin pulling homogeneous groups for math instruction. I am still amazed by how well I know what each student is capable of in math. This is extremely beneficial not only for parent conferences but also for report card comments and grades. No longer am I under the misguided conception that just because one student responds with the correct answer, everyone in the class knows the answer! Students cannot "hide" when working in a teacher-guided group. Everyone participates, students and teacher alike. We have one another's undivided attention for 12 to 15 minutes, which gives me the opportunity to discern which students understand and which need further clarification.

The activities at the math centers are an extension of what the students have worked on during Guided Math groups. Their familiarity with the game or activity allows them to take it to a new level of complexity. I believe in open-ended centers where the results are different each and every time a student participates. Center activities should also be differentiated so that while everyone participating is working on the same skill or concept, entry points, learning tasks, and outcomes are tailored to meet each individual student's needs. Centers are changed approximately every 6 weeks, thus providing students with ample opportunity to explore and develop a deeper understanding. The materials used at the centers are simple inexpensive items that include decks of cards, dominoes, dice, and spinners.

I believe in building a mathematics program that engages and empowers the students. Although there is a place for drill and practice, today's math students need to be challenged to think and problem solve. Although the correct answer is important, the process by which students gain the answer is even more so. Students must be prepared to explain and show how they determined their solution. Therefore, oral and written communication as well as the use of pictures, diagrams, and models emphasize students' ability to reason mathematically and problem solve. My Guided Math block allows students to do this while learning concepts and skills that provide them with the opportunity to become successful mathematicians.

Source: Elizabeth A. Valentine. Used with permission.

LEARNING IN SMALL GROUPS

Small groups are those involving three to five students, in either a teacher- or a student-directed setting. Using small groups for instruction, including the cooperative learning group (CLG), enhances the opportunities for students to assume greater control over their own learning, sometimes referred to as **empowerment**.

Purposes for Using Small Groups

Small groups can be formed to serve a number of purposes. They might be useful for a specific learning activity (e.g., **literature circles**, where students who have read the same self-selected story or novel discuss their reading [Martin, 1998; Scott, 1994], or **reciprocal reading groups**, where students take turns asking questions, summarizing, making predictions about, and clarifying a story [Slater & Horstman, 2002]). Or, they might be formed to complete an activity that requires materials that are of short supply or to complete a science experiment or a project, lasting only as long as the project does. Teachers have various rationales for assigning students to groups. Groups can be formed by grouping students according to (a) personality type (e.g., sometimes a teacher may want to team less assertive students together in order to give them the opportunity for greater management of their own learning), (b) social pattern (e.g., sometimes it may be necessary to break up a group of rowdy friends, or it may be desirable to broaden the association among students), (c) common interest, (d) learning styles (e.g., forming groups of either mixed styles or of styles in common), or (e) according to their abilities in a particular skill or their knowledge in a particular area. One specific type of small-group instruction is the cooperative learning group.

COOPERATIVE LEARNING

Lev Vygotsky (1962, 1978) studied the importance of a learner's social interactions in learning situations. Vygotsky argued that learning is most effective when learners cooperate with one another in a supportive learning environment under the careful guidance of a teacher. In a recent study, Willis (2007) found that when she allowed her middle school students to collaborate interactively with one another to achieve common instructional goals, her students became more invested and engaged in their learning than when taught by more traditional autocratic methods. Cooperative learning, group problem solving, problem-based learning, and cross-age tutoring are instructional strategies that have grown in popularity as a result of research evolving from the work of Vygotsky and others.

> When students participate in engaging learning activities in well-designed, supportive cooperative groups, . . . their brain scans show facilitated passage of information from the intake areas into the memory storage regions of the brain.
>
> Dr. Judy Willis (2007)

The Cooperative Learning Group (CLG)

The **cooperative learning** group is a heterogeneous group (i.e., mixed according to one or more criteria, such as ability or skill level, ethnicity, learning style, learning capacity, gender, and language proficiency) of usually three to five students (although the largest recommended is six and the smallest is two) who work together in a teacher- or student-directed setting, emphasizing support for one another. Oftentimes, a CLG consists of four students of mixed ability, learning styles, gender, and ethnicity, with each member of the group assuming a particular role. When using CLGs, not all groups need be of same number of students, such as with four; for example, while four might be the number for most groups, some groups might work best with just three members whereas for another group the number might be five.

Over the course of a school year, not only the number of members but the actual membership within a group can and often should be changed from several to many times. Groups that remain together for longer periods of time, up to 6 weeks, tend to form stronger bonds, develop more complex collaborative skills, and can tackle more complex tasks. Generally, groups should remain together long enough to feel successful but not so long that bonds formed become counterproductive.

The Theory and Use of Cooperative Learning

The theory of cooperative learning is that when small groups of students of mixed backgrounds and capabilities work together toward a common goal, members of the group increase their friendship and respect for one another. As a consequence, each individual's self-esteem is enhanced, students are more motivated to participate in higher-order thinking, and academic achievement is accomplished. In short, the effective use of heterogeneous cooperative learning helps students grow academically, socially, and emotionally, and they enjoy doing it (Acar & Tarhan, 2008; Slavin, 1996; Willis, 2007).

There are several techniques for using cooperative learning (Coelho, 1994; Johnson, Johnson, & Holubec, 1998; Sharan & Sharan, 1992). Yet the primary purpose of each is for the groups to learn—which means, of course, that individuals within a group must learn. Group achievement in learning, then, is dependent upon the learning of individuals within the group. Rather than competing for rewards for achievement, members of the group cooperate with one another by helping one another learn so that the group reward will be a good one. Normally, the group is rewarded on the basis of group achievement, though individual members within the group can later be rewarded for individual contributions. Because of peer pressure, when using CLGs, you must be cautious about using group grading. For grading purposes, bonus points can be given to all members of a group; individuals can add to their own scores when everyone in the group has reached preset standards. The preset standards must be appropriate for all members of a group. Lower standards or improvement criteria could be set for students with lower ability so that everyone feels rewarded and successful. To determine each student's term grades, individual student achievement is measured later through individual students' results on tests and other criteria, as well as through each student's performance in the group work.

Roles Within the Cooperative Learning Group

It is advisable to assign roles (specific functions) to each member of the CLG. (The lesson plan shown in the unit plan of Figure 5.12, Chapter 5, shows the use of a CLG activity using assigned roles for a lesson in science.) These roles should be rotated, either during the activity or from one time to the next. Although titles may vary, typical roles are as follows:

- Group facilitator—role is to keep the group on task, to ensure participation by each member of the group, and to keep track of the time as allowed for the task.
- Materials manager—role is to obtain, maintain, and return materials needed for the group to function.
- Recorder—role is to record all group activities and processes, and perhaps to periodically assess how the group is doing.
- Reporter—role is to report group processes and accomplishments to the teacher or to the entire class. When using groups of four members, the roles of recorder and reporter can easily be combined.
- Thinking monitor—role is to identify and record the sequence and processes of the group's thinking. This role encourages metacognition and the development of thinking skills.

It is important that students understand and perform their individual roles and that each member of the CLG performs the tasks as expected. No student should be allowed to ride on the coattails of the group. Furthermore, the use of CLG seems to work best when structured for the group rather than when unstructured (Gillies, 2007, 2008). So, how can it be structured? Read on.

What Students and the Teacher Do When Using Cooperative Learning Groups

Actually, for learning by CLGs to work, each member of the CLG must understand and assume two roles or responsibilities—the role he or she is assigned as a member of the group and that of seeing that all others in the group are performing their roles. Sometimes this requires interpersonal skills that students have yet to learn or to learn well. This is where the teacher must assume some responsibility too. Simply placing students into CLGs and expecting each member and each group to function and to learn the expected outcomes may not work. In other words, skills of cooperation must be taught, and if all your students have not yet learned the skills of cooperation, then you will have to teach them. This does not mean that if a group is not functioning, you immediately break up the group and reassign members to new groups. Important to group learning is learning the process of how to work out conflict. For a group to work out a conflict may require your assistance. With your guidance the group should be able to discover the problem that is causing the conflict, then identify some options and mediate at least a temporary solution. If a particular skill is needed, then, with your guidance, students identify and learn that skill.

When to Use Cooperative Learning Groups

CLGs can be used for problem solving, investigations, opinion surveys, experiments, review, project work, test making, or almost any other instructional purpose. Just as you would for small-group work in general, you can use CLGs for most or any purposes at any time, but as with any other type of instructional strategy, it should not be overused.

Cooperative Group Learning, Assessment, and Grading

Normally, the CLG is rewarded on the basis of group achievement, though individual members within the group can later be rewarded for individual contributions (see Figure 9.1). Because of peer pressure, when using CLGs, you must be cautious about using group grading (Guskey, 1996; Kagan, 1995). Some teachers give bonus points to all members of a group to add to their individual scores when everyone in the group has reached preset criteria. In establishing preset standards, the standards can be different for individuals within a group, depending on each member's ability and past performance. It is important that each member of a group feels rewarded and successful. For determination of students' report card grades, individual student achievement is measured later through individual results on tests and other sources of data.

Why Some Teachers Experience Difficulty Using CLGs

Sometimes, when they think they are using CLGs, teachers have difficulty and either give up trying to use the strategy or simply tell students to divide into groups for an activity and call it cooperative learning. As emphasized earlier, for the strategy to work, each student must be given training in and have acquired basic skills in interaction and group processing and must realize that individual achievement rests with that of their group. And, as true for any other strategy, the use of CLGs must not be overused—teachers must vary their strategies.

For the use of CLGs to work well, advanced planning and effective management are a must. Students must be instructed in the necessary skills for group learning. Each student must be assigned a responsible role within the group and be held accountable for fulfilling that responsibility. And, when a CLG activity is in process, groups must be continually monitored by the teacher for possible breakdown of this process within a group. In other words, while students are working in groups, the teacher must exercise skills of withitness (discussed in Chapter 2). When a potential breakdown is noticed, the teacher quickly intervenes to help the group get back on track. Oftentimes, the teacher will

Figure 9.1   Sample scoring rubric for assessing individual students in cooperative learning group project. Possible score = 50. Scorer marks a relevant square in each of the five categories (horizontal rows), and the student's score for that category is the small number in the top right corner within that square. (*Source:* Courtesy of Susan Abbott and Pam Benedetti, Elk Grove School District, Elk Grove, CA.)

	9–10	8	7	1–6
Goals	Consistently and actively helps identify group goals; works effectively to meet goals.	Consistently communicates commitment to group goals; carries out assigned roles.	Sporadically communicates commitment to group goals; carries out assigned role.	Rarely, if ever, works toward group goals or may work against them.
Interpersonal Skills	Cooperates with group members by encouraging, compromising, and/or taking a leadership role without dominating; shows sensitivity to feelings and knowledge of others.	Cooperates with group members by encouraging, compromising, and/or taking a leadership role.	Participates with group, but has own agenda; may not be willing to compromise or to make significant contributions.	May discourage others, harass group members, or encourage off-task behavior. Makes significant changes to others' work without their knowledge or permission.
Quality Producer	Contributes significant information, ideas, time, and/or talent to produce a quality product.	Contributes information, ideas, time, and/or talent to produce a quality product.	Contributes some ideas, though not significant; may be more supportive than contributive; shows willingness to complete assignment but has no desire to go beyond average expectations.	Does little or no work toward the completion of group product; shows little or no interest in contributing to the task; produces work that fails to meet minimum standards for quality.
Participation	Attends daily; consistently and actively utilizes class time by working on the task.	Attends consistently; sends in work to group if absent; utilizes class time by working on the task.	Attends sporadically; absences/tardies may hinder group involvement; may send in work when absent; utilizes some time; may be off task by talking to others, interrupting other groups, or watching others do the majority of the work.	Frequent absences or tardies hinder group involvement; fails to send in work when absent; wastes class time by talking, doing other work, or avoiding tasks; group has asked that member be reproved by teacher or removed from the group.
Commitment	Consistently contributes time out of class to produce a quality product; attends all group meetings as evidenced by the group meeting log.	Contributes time out of class to produce a quality product; attends a majority of group meetings as evidenced by the group meeting log.	Willing to work toward completion of task during class time; attends some of the group meetings; may arrive late or leave early; may keep inconsistent meeting log.	Rarely, if ever, attends group meetings outside of class or may attend but hinders progress by the group; fails to keep meeting log.

carry a clipboard or other handheld recording device with students' names and lesson tasks and objectives in order to record student progress as she/he monitors the group at work.

During CLG work you are advised to only answer questions that derive from a group, not from individual students. Questions from individuals should be dealt with in that group.

Finally, at the completion of the activity, like with any other lesson, you should reflect on the activity and note changes for future lessons. Did the lesson go as well as you would have liked? Did the students achieve the desired outcomes? Why or why not? If repeated, what changes would you make?

LEARNING IN LARGE GROUPS

As defined for purposes of this resource guide, large groups are those that involve more than five students, usually the entire class. Most often, they are teacher directed. Student presentations and whole-class discussions are two techniques that involve the use of large groups.

Student Presentations

Students should be encouraged to be presenters for discussion of the ideas, opinions, and knowledge obtained from their own independent and small-group study. Several techniques encourage the development of certain skills such as studying and organizing material, discovery, discussion, rebuttal, listening, analysis, suspending judgment, and critical thinking. Possible forms of discussions involving student presentations are described in the following paragraphs.

- *Debate.* The debate is an arrangement in which oral presentations are made by members of two opposing teams on topics preassigned and researched. The speeches are followed by rebuttals from each team (Koenig, 2001).
- *Jury trial.* The jury trial is a discussion approach in which the class simulates a courtroom, with class members playing the various roles of judge, attorneys, jury members, bailiff, and court recorder.
- *Panel.* The panel is a setting in which four to six students, with one designated as the chairperson or moderator, discuss a topic about which they have studied, followed by a question-and-answer period involving the entire class. The panel usually begins with each panel member giving a brief opening statement.
- *Research report.* One or two students or a small group of students gives a report on a topic that they investigated, followed by questions and discussion by the entire class.
- *Roundtable.* The roundtable is a small group of three to five students who sit around a table and discuss among themselves (perhaps with the rest of the class listening and later asking questions) a problem or issue that they have studied. One member of the panel may serve as moderator.
- *Symposium.* Similar to a roundtable discussion but more formal, the symposium is an arrangement in which each student participant presents an explanation of his or her position on a preassigned topic researched by the student. Again, one student should serve as moderator. After the presentations, questions are accepted from the rest of the class.

To use these techniques effectively, students may need to be coached by you—individually, in small groups, or in whole-class sessions—on how and where to gather information; how to listen, take notes (Marzano, Pickering, & Pollock, 2001), select major points, organize material, and present a position succinctly and convincingly (see Figure 9.2); how to play roles; and how to engage in dialogue and debate with one another.

Whole-Class Discussion

Direct, whole-class discussion is a teaching technique used frequently by most or all teachers. On this topic, you should consider yourself an expert. Having been a student in formal learning for at least 15 years, you are undoubtedly knowledgeable about the advantages and disadvantages of whole-class discussions, at least from your personal vantage point. So, as instructed by your course instructor, explore your knowledge and share your experiences by responding to Exercise 9.1A (at the end of chapter). Then do Exercise 9.1B, where guidelines for using whole-class discussion will be generated.

EQUALITY IN THE CLASSROOM

Especially when conducting direct, whole-group discussions, it is easy for a teacher to fall into the trap of interacting with only "the stars" or only those in the front of the room or on one side or only the most vocal and assertive. You must exercise caution and avoid falling into that trap. To ensure a psychologically safe and effective environment for learning for every person in your classroom, you must attend to all students and try to involve all students equally in all class activities. You must avoid any biased expectations about certain students, and you must avoid discriminating against students according to their gender or some other personal characteristic.

You must avoid the unintentional tendency of teachers of *both sexes* to discriminate on the basis of gender. For example, teachers, along with the rest of society, historically have had lower expectations for girls than for boys in mathematics and science. They tend to call on and encourage boys more than girls. They often

Figure 9.2   Sample scoring rubric for small-group or individual presentation.

GROUP PRESENTATION SCORING RUBRIC

5. Presentation was excellent. Clear understanding of their project and organized in delivery.

- Made eye contact throughout presentation
- Spoke loud enough for all to hear
- Spoke clearly
- Spoke for time allotted
- Stood straight and confidently
- Covered at least five pieces of important information
- Introduced project
- All members spoke

4. Presentation was well thought out and planned.

- Made eye contact throughout most of presentation
- Spoke loud enough and clearly most of the time
- Spoke for almost all of the time allotted
- Covered at least four pieces of important information
- Introduced project
- All members spoke

3. Adequate presentation. Mostly organized.

- Made eye contact at times
- Some of the audience could hear the presentation
- Audience could understand most of what was said
- Spoke for about half the time allotted
- At least half of the team spoke
- Covered at least three pieces of important information
- Project was vaguely introduced

2–1. Underprepared presentation. Disorganized and incomplete information.

- No eye contact during presentation
- Most of the audience was unable to hear presentation
- Information presented was unclear
- Spoke for only a brief time
- Covered less than three pieces of information
- Project was not introduced or only vaguely introduced

---

let boys interrupt girls but praise girls for being polite and waiting their turn. To avoid such discrimination you may take special effort, no matter how aware of the problem you might be.

To guarantee equity in interaction with students, many teachers have found it helpful to ask someone secretly to tally classroom interactions between the teacher and students during a class discussion. After an analysis of the results, the teacher arrives at decisions about his or her own attending and facilitating behaviors. Such an analysis is the purpose of Exercise 9.2. You are welcome to make blank copies and share them with your teaching colleagues.

In addition to the variables mentioned at the beginning of Exercise 9.2, the exercise can be modified to include responses and their frequencies according to other teacher–student interactions, such as your calling on all students equally for responses to your questions or to assist you with classroom helping jobs, your chastising students for their inappropriate behavior, or your asking questions to assume classroom leadership roles.

Ensuring Equity

In addition to the advice given in Chapter 6 about using questioning, there are many other ways of ensuring that students are treated fairly in the classroom, including the following:

- During whole-class instruction, insist that students raise their hands and be called on by you before they speak.

- Encourage students to demonstrate an appreciation for one another by applauding all individual and group presentations.
- Have and maintain high expectations, although not necessarily identical expectations, for all students.
- Insist on politeness in the classroom. For example, a student can be shown appreciation—such as with a sincere "thank you" or "I appreciate your contribution," with whole-class applause, or with a handshake or a genuine smile—for her or his contribution to the learning process.
- Insist students are allowed to finish what they are saying without being interrupted by others. Be certain that you model this behavior yourself.
- Keep a stopwatch handy to unobtrusively control the wait time given for each student. Although at first this idea may sound impractical, it works.
- Use a seating chart attached to a clipboard, and next to each student's name, make a tally for each interaction you have with a student. This also is a useful way to maintain records to reward students for their contributions to class discussion. Again, it is workable at any grade level. The seating chart can be laminated so it can be used day after day simply by erasing the marks of the previous day.

Now, according to your instructor's directions, do Exercise 9.2, through which you will examine a teacher's behavior with students according to gender.

Cultural equity calls for teachers to

- accept students' personalization of instruction
- use multicultural examples to illustrate points of instruction
- listen carefully to the stories and voices of the students from various cultures
- tie together home and school for the benefit of the students

Díaz-Rico & Weed (2010, pp. 309–310)

LEARNING FROM ASSIGNMENTS AND HOMEWORK

An assignment is a statement of what the student is to accomplish and is tied to a specific instructional objective. Assignments, whether completed at home or at school, can ease student learning in many ways, but when poorly planned they can discourage the student and upset an entire family. Homework can be defined as any out-of-class task that a student is assigned as an extension of classroom learning. Like all else that you do as a teacher, it is your professional responsibility to think about and plan carefully any and all homework assignments you give to students.

Before giving students any assignment, consider how you would feel were you given the assignment, how you would feel were your own child given the assignment, about how much out-of-class time you expect the assignment to take, and to what extent, if any, parents and guardians and other family members should or could be involved in assisting the child with the assignment.

The time a student needs to complete assignments beyond school time will vary according to grade level and school policy. For elementary grades in particular, there seems always to be ongoing debate about the value of homework. Perhaps the issue is or should be not with the value of homework per se but with the quality of the homework assigned. Having said that, very generally, children in grades K–3 may be expected to spend from none to about 15 minutes each school night on homework, whereas children in middle grades may spend an hour or more, and high school students may need to spend several hours a night doing homework. Some school districts recommend the 10-minute guideline, that is 10 minutes of homework to each child for the grade the child is in: 10 minutes for first graders, 20 minutes for second graders, 80 minutes for eighth graders, and so on (Fairbanks, Clark, & Barry, 2005).

Purposes for Assignments

Purposes for giving homework assignments can be any of the following: to constructively extend the time that students are engaged in learning, to help students to develop personal learning, to help students develop their research skills, to help students develop their study skills, to help students organize their learning, to individualize the learning, to involve parents and guardians in their children's learning, to provide a mechanism by which students receive constructive feedback, to provide students with the opportunity to review and practice what has been learned, to reinforce classroom experiences, and to teach new content.

Guidelines for Using Assignments

To use assignments, consider the guidelines in the following paragraphs. Whereas an assignment is a statement of what the student is to accomplish, procedures are statements of how to do something. Although students may need some procedural guidelines, especially with respect to your expectations on an assignment, generally, you will want to avoid supplying too much detail on how to accomplish an assignment.

Plan early and thoughtfully the types of assignments you will give (e.g., daily and long range; minor and major; in class, at home, or both; individual, paired, or group), and prepare assignment specifications. Assignments must correlate with specific instructional objectives and should never be given as busy work or as punishment. For each assignment, let students know what the purposes are; for example, whether the assignment is to prepare the student for what is to come in class, to practice what has been learned in class, or to extend the learning of class activities.

Use caution in giving assignments that could be controversial or could pose a hazard to the safety of students. In such cases (especially if you are new to the community), before giving the assignment it is probably a good idea to talk it over with members of your teaching team, the departmental chair, or an administrator. Also, for a particular assignment, you may need to have parental or guardian permission or support for students to do it, or be prepared to give an alternate assignment for some students.

Provide *differentiated, tiered,* or *optional assignments*—assignment variations given to students or selected by them on the basis of their interests and learning capacities (Willard-Holt, 2003; Tomlinson & Strickland, 2005). Students can select or be assigned different activities to accomplish the same objective, such as read and discuss, or they can participate with others in a more direct learning experience. After their study, as a portion of the assignment, students share what they have learned. This is another example of using multilevel teaching.

Teachers have found it beneficial to prepare personalized study guides, while reading textbook chapters, with questions to be answered and activities to be completed by the student as homework. One advantage of a study guide is that it can make the reading more than a visual experience. A study guide can help to organize student learning by accenting instructional objectives, emphasizing important points to be learned, providing a guide for studying for tests, and encouraging the student to read the homework assignment.

Teachers need to understand that homework can not only help students learn factual information, develop study skills, and involve parents or guardians as facilitators in their child's education but also overwhelm students and cause them to dislike learning, encourage them to take shortcuts (such as copying others' work), and prevent them from participating in extracurricular activities. Teachers sometimes underestimate just how long it will take a student to complete a homework assignment or how a particular assignment can disrupt the relationships in the child's home. With these considerations in mind, think carefully about all homework assignments before you make them.

Some students find homework and assignments very difficult, especially those students who have limited English proficiency or special needs and those who have little to no support from home. As an aide to these students in particular and to any student in general, many teachers use student volunteers to serve as homework helpers to assist other students both during class and after school, perhaps by exchanging telephone numbers or email addresses. In some schools, teachers also use older students and even paid college students and adults as mentors. By using students' eagerness for online discussion, some teachers have discovered some success through their creation of engaging electronic homework assignments where students share their ideas and give feedback to one another about the content of the assignment (Kitsis, 2008).

As a general rule, homework assignments should stimulate thinking by arousing a student's curiosity, raising questions for further study, and encouraging and supporting the self-discipline required for independent study.

Determine the resources that students will need to complete assignments, and check the availability of these resources. This is important; students cannot be expected to use that which is unavailable to them. Many will not use that which is not readily available. Do not forget that the digital divide is still a reality.

Avoid yelling out assignments as students are leaving your classroom. When giving assignments in class, you should write them on a special place on the writing board, give a copy to each student, require that each student write the assignment into an assignment folder (an expectation in many schools), or include them in the course syllabus, taking extra care to be sure that assignment specifications are clear to students and to allow time for students to ask questions about an assignment. It is important that your procedure for giving and collecting assignments be consistent throughout the school year.

Students should be given sufficient time to complete their assignments. In other words, avoid announcing a new assignment that is due the very next day. As a general rule, assignments should be given much earlier than the day before they are due.

Although not always possible, try to avoid changing assignment specifications after they are given. Especially avoid changing them at the last minute. Changing specifications at the last minute can be very frustrating to students who have already completed the assignment, and it shows little respect for those students.

It is my opinion that time in class should be provided for students to begin work on homework assignments so that the teacher can give them individual attention (called **guided or coached practice**). And, of course, it is of absolute importance that you DO give the in-class homework time your undivided attention so the time is not a dead-air waste of time for anyone. Your ability to coach students is the reason for in-class time to begin work on assignments, and that means giving students your attention during that time. The benefits of this coached practice include being able to (a) monitor student work so that a student does not go off too far in a wrong direction, (b) help students reflect on their thinking, (c) assess the progress of individual students, and (d) discover or create a "teachable moment." For example, regarding the latter, while monitoring students doing their work, you might discover a commonly shared student misconception. Then, taking advantage of this teachable moment, you stop and talk about that and attempt to clarify the misconception.

If the assignment is important for students to do, then you must give your full and immediate attention to the product of their efforts. Read almost everything that students write. Students are more willing to do homework when they believe it is useful, when it is treated as an integral component of instruction, when it is read and evaluated by the teacher, and when it counts in the grading.

Provide feedback about each student's work, and be positive and constructive in your comments. Always think about the written comments that you make to be relatively certain they will convey your intended message to the student. When writing comments on student papers, consider using a color other than red, such as green or blue. Although to you this may sound trite, to many people red brings with it a host of negative connotations (e.g., blood, hurt, danger, stop), and young people often perceive it as punitive.

Most routine homework assignments should *not* be graded for accuracy, only for completion. Rather than giving a percentage or numerical grade, with its negative connotations, consider marking assignment papers with constructive and reinforcing comments and symbols you have created for this purpose.

Regardless of grade level and subject taught, you must give attention to the development of students' reading, listening, speaking, and writing skills. Attention to these skills must also be obvious in your assignment specifications and your assignment grading policy. Reading is crucial to the development of a person's ability to write. For example, to foster higher-order thinking, students in any subject can and should be encouraged to write (in their journals), or draw representations of, their thoughts and feelings about the material they have read.

Opportunities for Recovery

Using the concept of mastery (quality), learning would seem to me to dictate the need for a policy whereby students are able to revise and resubmit assignments for reassessment and grading. Although it is important to encourage positive initial efforts by students, sometimes, for a multitude of reasons, a student's first effort is inadequate or is lacking entirely. Perhaps the student is absent from school without legitimate excuse, or the student does poorly on an assignment or fails to turn in an assignment on time, or at all. Although accepting late work from students is extra work for the teacher, and although allowing the resubmission of a marked or tentatively graded paper increases the amount of paperwork, many teachers report that it is worthwhile to give students the opportunity for recovery and a day or so to make corrections and resubmit an assignment for an improved score. However, out of regard for students who do well initially and to encourage a best first effort, you are advised against allowing a resubmitted paper to receive an *A* grade (unless, of course, it was an *A* paper initially). Some teachers and schools provide recovery methods that encourage students by recognizing both achievement and improvement on report cards and by providing students with second opportunities for success on assignments, although at some cost to encourage a strong first effort.

Students sometimes have legitimate reasons for not completing an assignment by the due date. It is my opinion that the teacher should listen and exercise professional judgment in *each* instance. As someone once said, there is nothing democratic about treating unequals as equals. The provision of recovery options seems a sensible and scholastic tactic. After all, eventual success is much better than no success.

How to Avoid Having So Many Papers to Grade That Time for Effective Planning Is Restricted

A waterloo for some beginning teachers is that of being buried beneath mounds of homework to be read and marked, leaving less and less time for effective planning. To keep this from happening to you, consider the following suggestions. Although, in my opinion, the teacher should read almost everything that students write, papers can be read with varying degrees of intensity and scrutiny, depending on the purpose of the assignment. For assignments that are designed for learning, understanding, and practice, you can allow students to check them themselves using either self-checking or peer checking. During the self- or peer checking, you can walk around the room, monitor the activity, and record whether a student did the assignment or not, or, after the checking, you can collect the papers and do your recording. Besides reducing the amount of paperwork for you, student self- or peer checking provides other advantages: (a) It allows students to see and understand their errors, (b) it encourages productive peer dialogue, and (c) it helps them develop self-assessment techniques and standards. If the purpose of the assignment is to assess mastery competence, then the papers should be read, marked, and graded only by you.

CAUTION ABOUT USING PEER CHECKING
Peer checking can, however, be a problem. Sometimes during peer checking of student work, students may spend more time watching the person checking their paper than they do accurately checking the one given to them. And use of peer checking does not necessarily allow a student to see or understand his or her mistakes.

Of even greater concern is the matter of privacy. When Student A becomes knowledgeable of the academic success or failure of Student B, Student A, the "checker," could cause emotional or social embarrassment to Student B. Peer checking of papers should perhaps be done only for the editing of classmates' drafts of stories or research projects, making suggestions about content and grammar, but not assigning a grade or marking answers right or wrong. To protect students' privacy rights, like the public posting of grades, the use of peers grading each other's papers also should be avoided. Harassment and embarrassment have no place in a classroom; they prohibit a safe learning environment.

PROJECT-CENTERED LEARNING: GUIDING LEARNING FROM INDEPENDENT AND GROUP INVESTIGATIONS, PAPERS, AND ORAL REPORTS

For the most meaningful student learning to occur, independent study, individual writing, student-centered projects, and oral reports should be major features of your instruction. There will be times when the students are interested in an in-depth inquiry of a topic and will want to pursue a particular topic for study. This undertaking of a learning project can be flexible—an individual student, a team of two, a small group, or the entire class can do the investigation. The **project** is a relatively long-term investigative study from which students produce something called the culminating presentation.

Figure 9.3   Sample choices for culminating presentation.

After reading <u>(name of novel),</u> students make a culminating presentation that is focused on representing various themes and events as depicted in the novel. Students may choose from the following:

1. Story in a shoebox — A representation of major events in the novel through the presentation of various symbolic objects.
2. Poster board presentation — A poster board designed with at least five different events depicted and titled appropriately. May use miniature drawings or graphics.
3. Sketching/drawing — A collection of detailed drawings depicting at least five major events in the novel.
4. Model — A model depicting the geography that serves as the setting of the novel.
5. Play or skit — A 5–8 minute play or skit performed by the student(s) in class, with a script for the teacher to follow. Must involve at least one major event in the novel.

It is a way for students to apply what they are learning. The **culminating presentation** is a final presentation that usually includes an oral and written presentation accompanied by a hands-on item of some kind (e.g., a display, play or skit, book, song or poem, multimedia presentation, diorama, poster, maps, charts, and so on). See culminating presentations in Figure 9.3.

Values and Purposes of Project-Centered Learning

The values and purposes of encouraging project-centered learning are to

- develop individual skills in cooperation and social interaction;
- develop student skills in writing, communication, and in higher-level thinking and doing;
- foster student engagement, independent learning, and thinking skills;
- optimize personal meaning of the learning to each student by considering, valuing, and accommodating individual interests, learning styles, learning capacities, and life experiences;
- provide an opportunity for each student to become especially knowledgeable and experienced in one area of subject content or in one process skill, thus

adding to the student's knowledge and experience base and sense of importance and self-worth;
- provide an opportunity for students to become intrinsically motivated to learn because they are working on topics of personal meaning, with outcomes and time lines that are relatively open ended;
- provide an opportunity for students to make decisions about their own learning and to develop their skills in managing time and materials; and
- provide an opportunity for students to make an important contribution.

As has been demonstrated time and again, when students choose their own projects, integrating knowledge as the need arises, motivation and learning follow naturally (McCullen, 2000; Tassinari, 1996). The use of senior projects is reported to be particularly valuable as a means of sustaining students' interest in school during their final year of high school (see Figure 9.4).

Guidelines for Guiding Students in Project-Centered Learning

In collaboration with the teacher, students select a topic for the project. Some experts suggest planning projects backward, that is by first identifying the desired results

Figure 9.4   Sample senior project overview. (*Source*: Sheldon High School, Elk Grove, CA. Used with permission.)

At Sheldon High School (Elk Grove, CA), Senior Project is a four-part endeavor on which our seniors work all year. The four parts are:

1. The project—a stretch or challenge for each student that will take the student a minimum of 15 hours beyond the school day to complete.

2. The paper—an MLA style research paper on a topic related to the project.

3. The portfolio—a collection of documentation that shows the process used and time spent completing the project.

4. The culminating presentation to a board that is comprised of teachers, parents, district office officials, and

    community leaders—a 10-minute oral presentation followed by a 5-minute question-and-answer period.

(the objectives), then determining acceptable evidence, followed lastly by planning the learning experience (Fagan & Sherman, 2002). Regardless, what you can do is to stimulate ideas and provide anchor studies (also called model or benchmark examples). You can stimulate ideas by providing lists of things students might do, by mentioning each time an idea comes up in class that this would be a good idea for an independent, small-group or class project, by having former students tell about their projects, by showing the results of other students' projects, by suggesting Internet resources and readings that are likely to give students ideas, and by using class discussions to brainstorm ideas.

Sometimes a teacher will write the general problem or topic in the center of a graphic web and ask the students to brainstorm some questions. The questions will lead to ways for students to investigate, draw sketches, construct models, record findings, predict items, compare and contrast, and discuss understandings. In essence, this kind of brainstorming is the technique often used by teachers in collaboration with students for the selection of an interdisciplinary thematic unit of study.

Allow students to individually choose whether they will work alone, in pairs, or in small groups. If they choose to work in groups, then help them delineate job descriptions for each member of the group. For project work, groups of four or fewer students usually work better than groups of more than four. Even if the project is one the whole class is pursuing, the project should be broken down into parts with individuals or small groups of students undertaking independent study of these parts.

You can keep track of the students' progress by reviewing weekly updates of their work. Set deadlines with the groups. Meet with groups daily to discuss any questions or problems they have. Based on their investigations, the students will prepare and present their findings in culminating presentations.

Provide coaching and guidance. Work with each student or student team in topic selection as well as in the processes of written and oral reporting. Allow students to develop their own procedures, but guide their preparation of work outlines and preliminary drafts, giving them constructive feedback and encouragement along the way. Aid students in their identification of potential resources and in the techniques of research. Assist the students, for example, in their understanding of the concepts of accuracy and reliability (Fisher, 2002).

Your coordination with the school library and other resource centers is central to the success of project-centered teaching. Frequent drafts and progress reports from the students are a must. With each of these stages, provide students with constructive feedback and encouragement. Provide written guidelines, and negotiate time lines for the outlines, drafts, and the completed project.

Promote sharing. Insist that students share both the progress and the results of their study with the rest of the class. The amount of time allowed for this sharing will, of course, depend upon many variables. The value of this type of instructional strategy comes not only from individual contributions but also from the learning that results from the experience and the communication of that experience with others. For project work and student sharing of the outcomes of their study, some teachers have their students use the KWHLS strategy, where the students identify what they already *K*now about the topic of study, *W*hat they want to learn, *H*ow they plan to learn it, then what they *L*earned, and how they will *S*hare with others what was learned from the study.

Without careful planning, and unless students are given steady guidance, project-based teaching can be a frustrating experience for both the teacher and the students, and especially for a beginning teacher who is inexperienced in such an undertaking. Students should do projects because they want to and because the project seems meaningful. Therefore, students with your guidance should decide what project to do and how to do it. Your role is to advise and guide students so they experience success. If the teacher or teaching team lays out a project in too much detail, that then is a procedure rather than a student-centered project. There must be a balance between structure and opportunities for student choices and decision making. Without frequent progress reporting by the student and guidance and reinforcement from the teacher, a student can get frustrated and quickly lose interest in the project. What do I mean by "frequent"? In my opinion, as a general rule progress reports from students should be weekly or even more often than weekly.

Writing as a Required Component of Project-Centered Learning

Provide options but insist that writing be a component of each student's work. Research examining the links among writing, thinking, and learning has helped emphasize the importance of writing. Writing is a complex intellectual behavior and process that helps the learner create and record understanding—that is, to construct meaning.

> The more we write and talk, the more we have to write and say.
>
> Peter Elbow (2004, p. 13)

When teachers use project-centered teaching, a paper and an oral presentation are usually automatically required of all students. It is recommended that you use the **I-search paper** instead of the traditional research paper. Under your careful guidance, the student (a) lists things that she or he would like to know, and from the list selects one, which becomes the research topic; (b) conducts the study while maintaining a log of activities and findings, which becomes a process journal; (c) prepares a booklet that presents the student's findings, and that consists of paragraphs and visual representations; (d) prepares a summary of the findings, including the significance of the study and the student's personal feelings; and (e) shares the project as a final oral report with the teacher and classmates.

Assessing the Final Product

The final product of the project, including papers, oral reports, and presentations, should be graded. The method of determining the grade should be clear to students from the beginning, as well as the weight of the project grade toward each student's term grade. Provide students with clear descriptions (rubrics) of how evaluation and grading will be done. Evaluation should include meeting deadlines for drafts and progress reports. The final grade for the study should be based on four criteria: (a) how well it was organized, including meeting draft deadlines; (b) the quality and quantity of both content and procedural knowledge gained from the experience; (c) the quality of the student's sharing of that learning experience with the rest of the class; and (d) the quality of the student's final written or oral report. For oral presentations, a sample scoring rubric and a checklist are shown in Figures 9.1 and 9.2, respectively, and for scoring rubrics for other aspects of project study, see Figures 5.1 (Chapter 5), 10.10 and 10.11 (Chapter 10).

> Exhibitions are public demonstrations of mastery that occur at culminating moments, such as at the conclusion of a unit of study, the transition from one level of schooling to the next, and graduation, and that require students to speak publicly, use evidence, present engaging visual displays, and otherwise demonstrate mastery to the audience.
>
> Jill Davidson (2009)

WRITING ACROSS THE CURRICULUM

Because writing is a discrete representation of thinking, every teacher should consider himself or herself to be a teacher of writing. In exemplary schools, using multiple technologies to teach writing—paper and pencil, email, electronic mailing lists, and software packages (Yancey, 2004)—student writing is encouraged in all subjects, at all grade levels, across the curriculum (Peterson, 2007). For example, Burns (2004) suggested that a teacher of mathematics give writing assignments that fall into these four categories:

- maintaining journals or logs
- solving problems

- explaining mathematical ideas
- writing about learning processes

Oftentimes, and especially with a prominence of standardized writing assessments (Baldwin, 2004), all teachers of a particular school, and even district, are expected to assess students' papers using the same scoring rubric.

Kinds of Writing

A student should experience a variety of kinds of writing rather than the same form, class after class, year after year. Perhaps most important is that writing should be emphasized as a process that illustrates one's thinking, rather than solely as a product completed as an assignment. Writing and thinking develop best when students experience, during any school day, various forms of writing to express their ideas, such as the following.

Autobiographical incident. The writer narrates a specific event in his or her life and states or implies the significance of the event.

Evaluation. The writer presents a judgment on the worth of an item—book, movie, artwork, consumer product—and supports this with reasons and evidence.

Eyewitness account. The writer tells about a person, group, or event that was objectively observed from the outside.

Firsthand biographical sketch. Through incident and description, the writer characterizes a person he or she knows well.

Interpretation. The writer conjectures about the causes and effects of a specific event.

Problem solving. The writer describes and analyzes a specific problem and then proposes and argues for a solution.

Report of information. The writer collects data from observation and research and chooses material that best represents a phenomenon or concept.

Story. Using dialogue and description, the writer shows conflict between characters or between a character and the environment.

Preventing Plagiarism

Students need to be taught the skills of writing from sources, how to summarize and credit that which was found in their research. Beginning in the early grades, children should be taught the meaning of intellectual property, skills needed for online research, and techniques for evaluating the credibility of both online and print-based sources (Howard & Davies, 2009).

Journals and Blogs

Many teachers across the curriculum have their students maintain journals, paper or electronic, in which

Teaching in Practice

Students Who Supposedly Can't Write, Can—and They Do! Mr. Mayo Uses Blogs to Encourage Student Writing

Last year, I set up blogs for eight students in a remediation class I teach. The students in this class had failed one or more parts of the fifth grade Standards of Learning state test here in Virginia. They lose an elective in sixth grade and have to take this remediation class to work on their reading and writing skills. These are the students who supposedly can't write. Well, they can, and they did. They wrote a lot once they had their own blogs.

Each student assumed a nickname for an online blog identity. My first assignment: Write about your favorite hobby. It ended up being the most productive writing day of the entire semester.

Here's Shiloh, aka Kangaroo, on her favorite hobby, canoeing:

> Whin I cone whith my dad in his cone he sters and I have to whouch for rocks. He gets rilly mad if we hit one. You may not think it is easy to brake a cone, but this one man hit a rock on one of the tuffest rivers and the cone got raped aroun a ruck. It was cool looking. My dad jumd on it and poped the dint rit out.

Here's another sample from Cody, aka Fox. He's writing about his favorite hobby, BMX biking:

> My favorite thing to do is bikeing. I like to bike that I have a biking club. My biking clubs name is The Ghost Rider Kings. We are very good. We can do some good tricks. We can do indos, ghost riders, skids, Biddle caps, snakes. I can do the Biddle cap very good.

When asked to write about something they love to do, the students wrote enthusiastically. The writing was fun and purposeful. Blogs make student writing more accessible. With blogs, students know that what they write is going to be immediately published. They take their writing more seriously.

Here's a quote from, Todd, aka Giraffe, about writing on his blog:

> I used to hate writing but now I like it the day I came I was angry that I was in remediation and knew it

would be boring but I was wrong and waited until we actually started the class. Now I know that if I am here for the rest of the year I will just learn more and more.

My remediation students were amazed at the amount of writing they did in their blogs. They regularly scrolled up and down the screen reading and marveling at everything they had written. They talked to each other about what they had written and compared entries.

As students begin to accumulate a large amount of writing, they begin to feel more confident. They also begin to see themselves as writers. Not only were they interested in their own blogs, they became curious about what others were up to. The clean and accessible format of the writing naturally builds curiosity. Students talk spontaneously to each other about their writing and their ideas. They actually start to point out sentence-level errors to each other as they discuss their writing.

Student blogs help create a sense of community by making student writing accessible to anyone who has Internet access. With blogs, a student's peers, relatives, teachers, and administrators are invited to watch a student's growth. The more people who read a student's work, the more likely they are to talk to that student about their writing. This helps create a sense of community that is otherwise hard to imagine. Parents can check in whenever they feel like it to see what their kids are doing in school. Interested parties get a candid sense of student writing in their true voices. This helps establish a dialogue between parent and child and draws parents into the classroom in a new way. With blogs, students are more likely to care about what they write because they have a built-in audience.

This experience has convinced me that blogs can be a powerful motivator to get students to write and to take their writing more seriously. For the next school year, I am setting up blogs for all 120 of my students and will ask my students to write in their blogs as much as possible. They only restriction that might exist would be caused by the limited availability of laptop computer carts.

Source: George Mayo. Used with permission.

---

the students keep a log of their activities, findings, and thoughts (i.e., **process journal**) and write their thoughts about what it is they are studying (response journal). Actually, commonly used are two types of response journals: dialogue journals and reading-response journals. **Dialogue journals** are used for students to write anything that is on their minds, usually on the right side of a page, while peers, teachers, and parents or guardians respond on the left side, thereby "talking with" the journal writer. **Response journals** are used by students to write (and perhaps draw— a "visual learning log") their reactions to whatever is being studied.

Normally, academic journals are *not* the personal diaries of the writer's recollection of daily events and the writer's thoughts about the events. Rather, the purpose of journal writing is to encourage students to write, to think about their writing, to record their creative thoughts about *what they are learning*, and to share their written thoughts with an audience—all of which help in the development of their thinking skills, in their learning, and in their development as writers. Students are encouraged to write about experiences, both in school and out of school, that are related to the topics being studied. They should be encouraged to record their feelings about what and how they are learning.

> When their audience is the whole world, students are motivated to be the best writers they can.
>
> Davis & McGrail (2009)

Journal writing provides practice in expression and should *not* be graded by the teacher. Negative comments and evaluations from the teacher will discourage creative and spontaneous expression by students. Teachers should read the journals and then offer constructive and positive feedback, but teachers should avoid negative comments or grading the journals. For grading purposes, most teachers simply record whether or not a student does, in fact, maintain the required journal.

The National Council of Teachers of English (NCTE) has developed guidelines for journal writing.

A COLLECTION OF 130 ANNOTATED MOTIVATIONAL TEACHING STRATEGIES WITH IDEAS FOR LESSONS, INTERDISCIPLINARY TEACHING, TRANSCULTURAL STUDIES, AND STUDENT PROJECTS

Today's young people are used to multimillion-dollar productions on television, stage, CDs and DVDs, arcade and online games, and the movie screen. When they come to school, into a classroom, and are subjected

STUDENTS WRITING NOVELS

Many teachers today, at all grade levels, are experiencing success with encouraging writing by having their students write novels. Much of the popularity for this has grown from participation in NaNoWriMo (National Novel Writing Month; http://www.nanowrimo.org), which encourages quantity writing, rather than quality, and is open to adults as well as to children of all ages. Because of its encouragement of quantity without assessment of quality, the program is not without its critics. However, teachers whose students have participated seem amazed at the resulting benefits; even students they never expected would write are now writing and as a result have become less afraid of words and more comfortable with the writing process (Pogash, 2009).

each day to something short of a high-budget production, it is little wonder that they sometimes react in a less than highly motivated fashion. No doubt, today's youth are growing up in a highly stimulating instant action society, a society that has learned to expect instant electronic communication, instant information retrieval, instant headache relief, instant meals, instant gratification, instant replays, and perhaps, in the minds of many youth, instant high-paying employment with signing bonuses for jobs that entail more fun than hard work. In the light of this cultural phenomenon, I am on your side: the classroom teacher is on the firing line each day and is expected to perform—perhaps instantly and entertainingly, but most certainly in a highly competent and professional manner—in situations that are far from ideal. In any case, you must gain your students' attention before you can teach them.

In this, the final section of this chapter, you will find the presentation of an annotated list of ideas, many of which have been offered over recent years by classroom teachers. (See also Web site listings at the conclusion of this chapter.) Although the ideas are organized according to discipline, and some may be more appropriate for one group of students or grade level than another, you may profit from reading all entries for each field. Although a particular entry might be identified as specific to one discipline, it might also be useful in others (many of them can be used in interdisciplinary teaching—for example, number 1 can clearly be combined with mathematics and science, as well as art), or it might stimulate a creative thought for your own stock of motivational techniques, such as an idea for a way to utilize the theory of multiple-learning capacities, to incorporate technology, or to emphasize the multicultural aspect of a lesson in math, social studies, or whatever the central discipline or theme of a lesson or unit of instruction.

The Visual and Performing Arts

1. As part of a unit combining design or creativity with science, have students construct, design, and decorate their own kites. Designate a launch date and time.
2. Use lyrics from popular music to influence student work in class, such as putting the lyrics into pictures.
3. Utilize the outdoors or another environment, such as a shopping mall, for a free drawing experience.
4. Invite a local artist who has created a community mural to speak to the class about the mural. Plan and create a class mural, perhaps, on a large sheet of plywood or some other location approved by the school administration. For example, at Chartiers Valley Intermediate School (Pittsburgh, Pennsylvania), for more than a decade, as a culminating project in the school's visual arts program, each fifth-grade class has contributed its own section to

a growing mural in the school cafeteria. In another example, students in a rural Missouri high school collaborated online with students in an urban New York high school to create a mural in real space that celebrates the strengths of their two communities (Stein, 2001).

5. Create a mandala to demonstrate the importance of individual experience, as in interpreting paintings and interpreting poetry.

6. Study masks. Collect books, magazines, posters, films, videos, computer software programs, and so forth that show different kinds of masks people around the world wear. Ask students to identify the similarities and differences in the masks. Have them research the meanings that mask characters have in various cultures. Have students design and create their own masks to illustrate their own personalities, cultures, and so forth.

7. As a portion of a unit on the creative process, have each student draw or sketch on a piece of paper, then pass it on to the next person, and that person will make additions to the drawing. Instructions could include "improve the drawing," "make the drawing ugly," "make the drawing 17th century," and "add what you think would be necessary to complete the composition."

8. Instructions for students: Imagine that you're a bird flying over the largest city you have visited. What do you see, hear, smell, feel, and taste? Draw a "sensory" map.

9. Assign a different color to each student. Have the students arrange themselves into warm and cool colors and explain their decisions (why blue is cool, etc.). Discuss people's emotional responses to each of the colors.

10. Watch video of dances from various countries and cultures. Invite students to identify similarities and differences. Ask them to research the meanings and occasions of particular dances.

11. Challenge students to discover ways that music, art, and dance are used in their community.

12. Find a popular song that students like. Transpose the melody into unfamiliar keys for each instrument. This makes the student want to learn the song, but in the process the student will have to become more familiar with his or her instrument.

13. Set aside one weekend morning a month and hold small, informal recitals (workshops) allowing students to participate/observe the performance situations among their peers and themselves. (Students might be told previously about these "special days" and encouraged to prepare a selection of their own choosing.)

14. Play a group-activity rhythm game, one such as the "Dutch Shoe Game," to get students to cooperate, work together, and enjoy themselves using rhythm. Participants sit in a circle, and as the song is sung, each person passes one of his or her shoes to the person on the right in rhythm to the music. Shoes continue to be passed as long as verses are sung.

15. Choose a rhythmical, humorous poem or verse to conduct as if it were a musical work. The students read the poem in chorus while you stand before them and conduct. Students must be sensitive to the intonation, speed, inflection, mood, and dynamics that you expect them to convey in their reading.

16. Organize a Retired Senior Citizens Volunteer Program (RSCVP) with senior citizens presenting folk art workshops with students, and where the students and seniors work together to create artwork for the school and community.

17. Students from Elkhorn Area Middle School (Elkhorn, Wisconsin) organized an Improv Troupe, which creates and performs unscripted, improvisational skits about social issues relevant to today's youth.

18. If your school and/or community has a relatively large population of Hispanics, offer a mariachi music class, or something similar for and if another ethnic population is prevalent. Doing so may help keep students in school and make immigrant parents/ guardians feel more involved with the school.

19. In 2005, four teachers in Pennsylvania began writing songs and performing as a rock band as a way of teaching grammar and writing. Perhaps from their site at www.thegrammarheads.com, you can get some ideas for your own teaching.

Family and Consumer Economics, Foods, and Textiles

20. Often the foods we like originated from another area of our country or another place in the world. Have the students identify such foods and where they originated—foods such as spaghetti, enchiladas, fajitas, wontons, tacos, quiches, croissants, teriyaki, fried rice, pizza, hot dogs, hamburgers, noodles, tomatoes, chocolate, potatoes, hoagies, chop suey, ice cream cones, submarines, and poor boys. Have them list the names and origins, and place pictures of the food in place on a large world map.

21. Take photos of class members at special events such as dinners, fashion shows, field trips, and projects. Build a scrapbook or bulletin board with these, and display these on campus or on the school Web site and at spring open house or in a display case at school or in a shopping mall store window.

22. Plan thematic units on cultural foods, using the traditions, costumes, and music of a particular culture. Have the students decorate the room. Invite guests such as the principal, school board president, and city mayor for a visit and perhaps tasting treat.

23. Have a committee of students plan and create a school display of pictures of 100-calorie portions of basic nutritional foods and popular fad foods that contain only empty calories. Do the same with pictures of foods and their specific carbohydrate contents.

24. Pin the names of different garments on the backs of students. The students are then to sort themselves into different wash loads.

25. For a clothing unit, hold a "new look day." Ask each student to bring in an idea of something that can be done to give clothes a new look, a fun touch, or an extended wearing life. Their ideas may include appliqués, embroidery, tie-dye, batik, colorful patches, and restyling old clothes into current or creative fashions.

26. Have the students research, create, write, practice, and present skits on topics such as consumer fraud and identify theft.

27. Periodically have students plan a menu, prepare the food, and serve it to invited senior citizens from the community.

28. Organize a program with senior citizens and students working together on a community garden.

29. Plan a program at a senior citizens' center whereby students and seniors work together on planning and decorating the center for special occasions and holidays.

30. With your students, plan a community service program. For example, at Discovery Middle School (Vancouver, Washington), students provide child-care, cross-age tutoring, and companionship to preschool, elementary school, and elderly clients at off-campus locations.

31. Have students work on a project about culture and how culture affects our lives, such as the way we dress, eat, worship, celebrate, and communicate.

32. Challenge students to plan ways to educate the school and surrounding community about general nutrition and exercise.

> When we encourage young children to think of themselves as writers, their achievement soars.
>
> Katie Wood Ray (2004, p. 15)

English, Languages, and the Language Arts

33. Organize a paper or electronic letter-writing activity between senior citizens and your students.

34. For a unit on the Renaissance, have students create a wall-to-wall mural depicting a village of the times. Teams of students can research customs, costumes, and architecture. Others may paint or draw.

35. On a U.S. road map, have students find the names of places that sound "foreign" and categorize the names according to nationality or culture. Students could research when and how places got their names.

36. Set up this problem to enhance understanding of parts of speech. Provide several boxes (shoe boxes work fine) containing different parts of speech. Each student is to form one sentence from the fragments chosen from each box, being allowed to discard only at a penalty. The students then nonverbally make trades with other students to make coherent and perhaps meaningfully amusing sentences. A student may trade a noun for a verb but will have to keep in mind what parts of speech are essential for a sentence. Results may be read aloud as a culmination to this activity.

37. Students can match American English and British English words (or any other combination of languages), such as cookies and biscuits, hood and bonnet, canned meat and tinned meat, elevator and lift, flashlight and torch, subway and tube, garbage collector and dustman, undershirt and vest, sweater and jumper, and gasoline and petrol. Have students compare pronunciations and spellings.

38. English words derive from many other languages. Have students research and list some, such as ketchup (Malay), alcohol (Arabic), kindergarten (German), menu (French), shampoo (Hindi), bonanza (Spanish), piano (Italian), kosher (Yiddish), and smorgasbord (Swedish).

39. For an exercise in objective versus subjective writing, after a lesson on descriptive writing, bring to class a nondescript object, such as a potato, and place it before the class. Ask them to write a paragraph either describing the potato in detail, that is, its color, size, markings, and other characteristics, or describing how the potato feels about them.

40. Read a story to the class but without its ending. Then ask the students (as individuals or in think-write-share pairs) to invent and write their own endings or conclusions.

41. Challenge students to create an advertisement (decide for radio, TV, the Internet, or print medium) using a propaganda device of their choice.

42. Invite students (individually or in pairs) to create and design an invention and then to write a "patent description" for the invention.

43. Using think-write-share pairs, invite students to write a physical description of some well-known public figure, such as a movie star, politician, athlete, or musician. Other class members may enjoy trying to identify the "mystery" personality from the written description.

44. A bulletin board may be designated for current events and news in the world of writers. New books and recordings as well as reviews may be included.

News of poets and authors (student authors and poets too) may also be displayed.

45. Everyone has heard of or experienced stereotyping. For example: Girls are not as athletic as boys, boys are insensitive, women are better cooks than men, and men are more mechanical than women. Ask students to list stereotypes they have heard and examples they find in media. Have students discuss these questions: Have you ever felt stereotyped? How do you suppose these stereotypes came to be? Does stereotyping have any useful value? Can it be harmful?

46. Remove the text from a newspaper comic strip, and have the students work in pairs to create the story line; or, give each pair a picture from a magazine, and have the pair create a story about the picture.

47. Use newspaper and Internet want ads to locate jobs as a base for completing job application forms and creating letters of inquiry.

48. To develop language and listening skills, use video recording equipment to record student-written employer–employee role-play situations, interviews for jobs, or child–parent situations.

49. Invite students to choose a short story from a text, and write it into a play and perform the play for their parents and guardians and other family members.

50. To begin a poetry unit, ask students to bring in the lyrics to their favorite songs. Show how these fit into the genre of poetry.

51. Invite students to analyze commercial advertisements that might be classed as "ecopornographic," that is, ads for a product that is potentially damaging to our environment.

52. Have students analyze commercial advertisements for the emotions to which they appeal, for the techniques used, and for their integrity. Try the same thing with radio, youth magazines, theater advertisements, Web sites, and other media.

53. Change the learning environment by moving to an outdoor location, and ask students to write poetry to see if the change in surroundings stimulates or discourages their creativeness. Discuss the results. For example, take your class to a large supermarket to write, or to a mall, or to a lake, or into a forest, or to an athletic stadium.

54. Use your state's seal to initiate the study of the concept of interpretations. Have students analyze the seal for its history and the meaning of its various symbols.

55. Provide puppets in native costume for students to use in practicing dialogue when learning a language or in development of language skills.

56. Have students use the Internet to establish communication with students from another place in the world.

57. As a class or small-group project, design a page on your school Web site.

58. Use drama to build language arts and thinking skills. Have students write dialogue, set scenes, and communicate emotions through expressive language and mime.

59. Establish a community-service learning literacy project. For example: Students from Greenville High School (Greenville, Tennessee) serve as mentors to local elementary school children to help the children develop their reading and comprehension skills.

60. A teacher uses a digital camera to take pictures of her students acting out scenes from a book being read in class. She puts the photos on slides and asks the students to describe their actions in words. From this activity, the students then create their own books.

61. Invite your students to create and write a movie script by viewing any 5- to 10-minute scene taken from a film and then writing a script for that scene.

62. Students from a school in Arizona became pen pals with inner-city students from Toledo, Ohio. The experience not only proved beneficial for their lessons in language arts but also promoted their knowledge about their city and state, resulting in cross-curricular learning (Lemkuhl, 2002).

63. Challenge your students to look for, create, and collect *palindromes,* a series of words or sentences or numbers, that read the same backward or forward. Examples are the names *Ava* and *Otto,* the words *race car* and *solos,* the date *4.04.04,* and the year *2002.*

64. An English as a second language teacher at Falling Creek Middle School (Richmond, Virginia) gave her ELL students the task of designing a three-dimensional model of a city of the future to help them learn English and to interact with other students. They used an interactive computer game, SimCity (http://simcitysocieties.ea.com), to design their cities and then created their three-dimensional models, which were ultimately presented to their classmates and visitors, describing how they chose the name of their city and made decisions about it.

Writing and drawing graphic novels is an authentic composing activity.

J. B. Carter (2009, p. 72)

Mathematics

65. Collaboratively plan with students a role-play unit where members role-play the solar system. Students calculate their weights, set up a proportion system, find a large field, and as a culmination to the project actually simulate the solar system, using their own

bodies to represent the sun, planets, and moons. Notify local media of the culminating event.

66. Encourage students to look for evidence of the Fibonacci number series (e.g., 1, 1, 2, 3, 5, 8, 13, 21, 43, etc.), both within and outside of mathematics, such as in nature and in manufactured objects. Here are examples of where evidence may be found: piano keyboard, petals of flowers, spermatogenesis, and oogenesis. Perhaps your students might like to organize a Fibonacci Club and through the Internet establish communication with similar clubs around the world.

67. After students research the history of the cost of a first-class, U.S. postage stamp, ask them to devise ways of predicting its cost by the year they graduate, the year they become grandparents or retire or some other target year.

68. Provide students a list of the frequencies of each of the 88 keys and strings on a piano (a local music store can provide the information). Challenge students to derive an equation to express the relation between key position and frequency. After they have done this, research and tell them about the Bösendorfer piano (Germany) with its nine extra keys at the lower end of the keyboard. See if students can predict the frequencies of those extra keys.

69. Using a light sensor to measure the intensity of a light source from various distances, have students graph the data points and then, with their scientific calculators, find the relevant equation.

70. Students can participate in a parachute creation contest. Using plastic from trash bags, string, and a bobby pin as the skydiver, the challenge is to design a parachute with the least surface area and longest hang time.

71. Establish a service-learning project, mentoring children of lower grades.

72. With students you already know as peer coaches, teach your students how to play chess. Invite the students to plan chess moves for homework, using combination theory and probability. In collaboration with an art or shop teacher, some students may wish to extend the study by creating their own chessboards and pieces.

73. Invite your students to survey and map the school grounds.

Some teachers, especially of mathematics and science, have learned to use magic in their teaching not only to grab students' attention but as a means of enhancing their conceptual understandings. See for example "Selecting and Using Mathemagic Tricks in the Classroom (Matthews, 2008).

Physical Education

74. Ask your students to choose individually (or in dyads) a famous athlete they most (or least) admire. A short report will be written about the athlete. The student will then discuss the attributes and/or characteristics that they admire (or dislike) in the athlete and how they feel they can emulate (or avoid) those qualities. After all pairs of students have made their presentations, as a class devise two lists, one of common attributes admired, the other of qualities to avoid.

75. Challenge students, in small learning groups, to create an exercise routine to their favorite music recording and share it with the class. Then, have them discuss how they arrived at decisions along the way.

76. Divide your class into groups. Given the basic non-locomotor skills, have each group come up with a "people machine." Each student within the group is hooked up to another demonstrating a nonlocomotor skill and adding some sort of noise to it. Have a contest for the most creative people machine.

77. Give students a chance to design a balance-beam routine that has two passes on the beam and that must include front support mount, forward roll, leap, low or high turn, visit, chassé, and cross-support dismount. These routines will be posted to show the variety of ways the different maneuvers can be put together.

78. Divide the class into groups. Challenge each group to create a new game or activity for the class, using only the equipment they are given. Let the class play their newly created games.

Science

79. Challenge students to create and test their own science tools and materials, such as microscopes, using stems of bamboo with a drop of water in each end or litmus indicators using the petals of flowers.

80. Record sounds of the environment. Compare and write about day versus night sounds, fall versus spring sounds, foggy day versus sunny day sounds, busy mall versus residential back yard sounds, single residential dwelling versus multiple residential dwelling sounds.

81. With appropriate permissions and adult supervision, plan an overnight campout in which students must "live off the land" with only sleeping bags, clothing, and other essentials (water), and no electronics. (Take a cell phone for security purposes.)

82. Plan a year-long project where each student, or small group of students, must develop knowledge and understanding of some specific piece of technology. Each project culmination presentation must have five components: visual, oral, written, artistic, and creative.

83. Invite students to identify and use a social relationship, such as landlord–tenant relationships, to create a role-play simulation of predator–prey relationships.

84. For a life science class, on the first day of class give each student one live guppy in a test tube and one live cactus plant in a 3-inch pot. Tell the students that the minimum they each need to pass the course is to bring their pet plant and fish back to you during the final week of school, alive.

85. If you are a life science teacher, make sure your classroom looks like a place for studying life rather than a place of death.

86. With each student playing the role of a cell part, have students set up and perform a role-play simulation of cells.

87. Divide your class into groups, and ask each group to create an environment for an imaginary organism using discarded items from the environment. By asking questions, each group will try and learn about other groups' "mystery" organism.

88. Have each student, or student pair, "adopt" a chemical element. The student then researches that element and becomes the class expert whenever that particular substance comes up in discussion. There could be a special bulletin board for putting up questions on interesting or little-known facts about the elements.

89. Milk can be precipitated, separated, and the solid product dried to form a very hard substance that was, in the days before plastic, used to make buttons. Challenge your students to make their own buttons from milk.

90. As a class or interdisciplinary team project, obtain permission and "adopt" a wetland area or some other environmental project that is located near the school.

91. Invite students to research the composition and development of familiar objects. For example, the ordinary pencil is made of cedar wood from the forests of the Pacific Northwest. The graphite is often from Montana or Mexico and is reinforced with clays from Georgia and Kentucky. The eraser is made from soybean oil, latex from trees in South America, reinforced with pumice from California or New Mexico, and sulfur, calcium, and barium. The metal band is aluminum or brass, made from copper and zinc, and mined in several states of the United States and in several provinces of Canada. The paint to color the wood and the lacquer to make it shine are made from a variety of different minerals and metals, as is the glue that holds the wood together.

92. Invite students to locate and design large posters to hang on the classroom walls that show the meaning of words used in science that are not typical of their meaning in everyday language usage—the words *theory* and *Spanish moss* are examples.

93. To bridge cultural differences, allow students to design large posters to hang on the classroom walls showing potential differences in perceptions or views according to ethnoscience and formal science.

94. With your students, plan a community service project. For example, students of the Powder River County School District (Broadus, Montana) adopt community flower gardens and conduct an annual food drive for the needy. At Great Falls Middle School (Montague, Massachusetts), students research and produce television documentaries on subjects related to energy. The documentaries are broadcast on the local cable channel to promote energy literacy in the school and community. Students at Baldwyn Middle School (Baldwyn, Mississippi) plan and care for the landscaping of the local battlefield/museum, and students from Hollidaysburg Area Senior High School (Hollidaysburg, Pennsylvania) cleaned up and restored a local cemetery.

95. Sometimes projects become ongoing, permanent endeavors with many spin-off projects of shorter duration. For example, what began as a science classroom project at W. H. English Middle School (Scottsburg, Indiana) has become what is perhaps the largest animal refuge shelter in the Midwest. As another example, located near the estuary at the mouth of the Columbia River in Wahkiakum County Washington, students at Wahkiakum High School participate in interdisciplinary projects that have included habitat restoration, a salmon hatchery, stream restoration, tree planting, and recreating the final leg of the historic Lewis and Clark expedition.

96. Invite students to research and produce TV documentaries on subjects related to energy or on a health-related topic. To promote energy or health-related literacy in the school and surrounding community, a local TV channel might be willing to broadcast the documentaries.

97. During their study of atomic theory, have students read and discuss. J.R. Hersey's *Hiroshima* (Random House, 1989).

98. Ask students to inquire as to whether a nearby zoo/SPCA or botanical garden/commercial nursery has an animal or plant loan program.

99. Have a group of students research from the Internet and library the literature and report on the plant *Morinda citrifolia*. Have them share their findings with the rest of the class.

100. Have students use bobble head toys to explore force and motion (Foster, 2003).

Social Studies/History

101. Invite the students to organize an improvisation troupe to create and perform skits about social issues relevant to today's youth. Perform the skits at school events, at parent–teacher organization meetings, and for community groups.

102. In collaboration with your students, develop a yearlong, three-phase project. During the first phase, students individually research the question, "Who am I?"; during the second phase, "Who are they?"; during the third phase, "Who are we?" Multimedia presentations should be included in the students' culminating presentation.

103. Organize an Intergenerational Advocacy program, in which students and senior citizens work together to make a better society for both groups (MacBain, 1996).

104. Initiate a service-learning project where, for an extended period of time, students work directly with community organizations and agencies. For example, at John Ford Middle School (St. Matthews, South Carolina) students incorporate The Constitutional Right Foundation "City Youth" program into the curriculum, helping to make decisions about areas of the community that need improvement.

105. During their study of Ancient Egypt, invite students to create and build their own model pyramids; in science, students could study simple machines that will help in their pyramid building.

106. Invite students to plan how they would improve their living environment, beginning with the classroom, moving out to the school, home, community, state, country, and finally global.

107. Start a pictorial essay on the development and/or changes of a given area in your community, such as a major corner or block adjacent to the school. This is a study project that could continue for years and that has many social, political, and economic implications.

108. Invite your students in small groups or as a class project to build a model that represents their community.

109. Start a folk hero study. Each year ask, "Which prominent human being, who has lived during a particular period of time, do you most (or least) admire?" Collect individual responses to the question, tally results, and discuss. After you have done this for several years, you may wish to share with your class for discussion purposes the results of your surveys of previous years.

110. Start a sister class program. Establish a class relationship with another similar class from another school around the country or the world, perhaps by using the Internet.

111. During their study of westward expansion, challenge students to organize a role play of a simulated family movement to the West in the 1800s. What items would they take? What would they toss out of the wagon to lighten the load? Where would they stop and settle? Or would they stop, turn around, and return to their point of origin? What issues would enter into their decision making?

112. Invite students to collect music, art, or athletic records from a particular period of history. Have them compare their collections with the music, art, or recordings of today and predict the music, art, or recordings of the future.

113. Using play money, and establish a capitalistic economic system within your classroom. Salaries may be paid for attendance and bonus income for work well done, taxes may be collected for poor work, and a welfare section established somewhere in the room.

114. Divide your class into small groups, and ask each group to make predictions as to what world governments, world geography, world social issues, world health, world energy, or some other related topic will be like some time in the future. Let each group give its report, followed by debate and discussion. With guidance from the school administration, plant the predictions in some secret location on the school grounds for a future discovery.

115. As an opener to a unit on the U.S. Constitution, have students design their own classroom (or school) "bill of rights."

116. On one day, behave toward your students in class as if your class were a socialist society; the next day as if they were a fascist society; on another day as a communist society; etc. At the end of the simulation, have students discuss and compare their feelings and thoughts about each day's experience.

117. Using Legos or sugar cubes as construction blocks, and with assigned roles, challenge students to simulate the building of the Great Wall of China.

118. At Indian Trail Junior High School (Addison, Illinois), all eighth-graders and teachers from not only social studies but various other content areas, including English, mathematics, physical education, and science, work together on a "real-world," problem-based project titled the Inspector Red Ribbon Unit. The unit focuses on a social problem that has truly occurred too many times—the prom night automobile accident.

119. Establish a caring and antiviolence program. For example, high school students in Lynn Haven, Florida, work as tutors/mentors with elementary school children to help boost confidence and self-esteem among both groups of students.

120. During an interdisciplinary thematic unit of study (the history and literature of the medieval period of Europe), have students study and build model castles.

121. With guidance from three teachers using a common philosophical approach based on Glasser's Choice Theory, Reality Therapy, and ideas from his book *The Quality School,* students of eighth-grade history at Longfellow Middle School (La Crosse, Wisconsin) designed and built their own middle school nation (Frost, Olson, & Valiquette, 2000).

122. At Davis Senior High School (Davis, California), students in U.S. history are given this assignment for an activity titled "Creating a Candidate." The assignment is done in student dyads. "Research electronic and print media about the progressive movement in early California history. Determine relevant issues a candidate for governor of the state in 1910 would need to address. Create a fictitious candidate. Your exhibition must include (a) an election poster, (b) a slogan, (c) a theme song that you must sing, and (d) a 5-minute platform speech addressing the issues, your proposed solutions, and the position of your opponents."

123. During their study of the U. S. Constitution, invite students to organize debates on current issues, such as gun control and civil rights.

124. In collaboration with other classes, invite your students to design and implement a schoolwide conflict resolution program.

125. Plan time each week for students to comment on the week's classroom activities or to compliment a peer.

126. Organize a study to determine how well students, who have arrived in the United States, from other countries are integrated into your community and school's culture.

127. Invite students to research, identify, and discuss current plagiarism and copyright issues.

Vocational Career Dual Education

128. At North Penn High School (Lansdale, Pennsylvania), students designed and built equipment for the school's child development playground.

129. Blue Hills Regional Technical School (Canton, Massachusetts) attracts students from grades 9 through 12 by giving them a dual education, where upon graduation the students receive not only a high school diploma but also competency recognition for technical achievement.

130. Dual enrollment programs are collaborative efforts between high schools and colleges, in which high school students are permitted to take college courses, thus providing students not only with a challenging academic experience but also with the opportunity to earn college credit prior to high school graduation. In some instances, the college might be a career technical college in which case the student earns technical skills training and accreditation while completing high school. Dual enrollment is a promising strategy in guiding students through completion of the high school diploma while simultaneously giving them career training or postsecondary education credits or both.

SUMMARY

This chapter has continued the development of your repertoire of teaching strategies. As you know, young people can be quite peer conscious, can have relatively short attention spans for experiences in which they are uninterested, and can prefer active, multisensory experiences. Most are intensely curious about things of interest to them. Cooperative learning, student-centered projects, and teaching strategies that emphasize shared discovery and inquiry within a psychologically safe environment encourage the most positive aspects of thinking and learning. Central to your strategy selection should be those strategies that encourage students to become independent thinkers and skilled learners who can help in the planning, structuring, regulating, and assessing of their own learning and learning activities. For additional ideas and information about working with heterogeneous groups of students, see the Special Connections Web site (www.specialconnections.ku.edu).

QUESTIONS FOR CLASS DISCUSSION

1. Do you have concerns about using project-based teaching and not being able to cover all the content you believe should be covered? Think back to your own schooling. What do you really remember? Most likely you remember projects, yours and other students' presentations, the lengthy research you did, and your extra effort for the artwork to accompany your presentation. Maybe you remember a compliment by a teacher or a pat on the back by peers. Most likely you do not remember the massive amount of content that was covered. Discuss your feelings about this with your classmates. Share common experiences and common concerns.

2. Divide into teams of four, and have each team develop one learning center for a specified use at a particular subject and grade level. Set up and share the LCs in your classroom.

3. Explain how a teacher can tell when he or she is truly using cooperative learning groups for instruction as opposed to traditional, small-group learning.

4. When a student is said to be on task, does that necessarily imply that the student is mentally engaged?

Is it possible for a student to be mentally engaged although not on task? Explain your answers.

5. Describe three things you will do to help students develop their writing skills.

CONTENT AREA WEBSITES

Arts

- American Alliance for Theatre & Education http://www.aate.com
- Crayola Creativity Center http://www.crayola.com
- World Wide Arts Resources http://wwar.com

History/Social Studies

- Best of History Web Sites http://www.besthistorysites.net
- Choices Program http://www.choices.edu/index.cfm
- Civics Online http://civics-online.org
- Facing History and Ourselves http://facinghistory.org
- FedWorld http://www.fedworld.gov
- Historical Text Archive http://historicaltextarchive.com
- History Net http://www.thehistorynet.com
- Houghton Mifflin Social Studies Center http://www.eduplace.com/ss
- Mexico Online http://www.mexonline.com
- National Council for the Social Studies http://www.socialstudies.org

Language and Literacy

- National Clearinghouse for English Language Acquisition & Language Instruction Education Programs http://www.ncela.gwu.edu
- Second language learning http://www.sdkrashen.com

Mathematics

- Math Archives http://archives.math.utk.edu
- Math Forum http://forum.swarthmore.edu
- Mega Mathematics http://www.c3.lanl.gov/mega-math

- PlaneMath http://www.planemath.com
- Show-Me Project http://www.showmecenter.missouri.edu

Mathematics and Science

- National Science Digital Library Middle School Portal http://msteacher.org

Science and Health

- Centers for Disease Control and Prevention; National Center on Birth Defects and Developmental Disabilities http://www.cdc.gov/ncbddd
- Columbia Education Center lesson plan collection http://www.col-ed.org/cur/science.html#scil
- Dive and Discover http://www.divediscover.whoi.edu
- Electronic Zoo http://netvet.wustl.edu/e-zoo.htm
- EXCITE (Excellence in Curriculum Integration through Teaching Epidemiology) http://www.cdc.gov/excite
- LifeQuest Expedition http://www.questnetwork.com
- National Institutes of Health http://science.education.nih.gov
- National Institute on Alcohol Abuse and Alcoholism http://www.niaaa.nih.gov
- Stanford Solar Center http://solar-center.stanford.edu
- Technology Enhanced Learning in science http://www.telscenter.org
- Windows to the Universe http://www.windows.umich.edu

Publishers of Student Writing

- *New Moon* (for girls ages 8–14) http://www.newmoon.org
- Potato Hill Poetry http://www.potatohill.com
- Stone Soup http://www.stonesoup.com/index.html
- *What If* (for Canadians) http://www.whatifmagazine.com

Service Learning

- National Service-Learning Clearinghouse http://www.servicelearning.org
- National Service-Learning Exchange http://www.nslexchange.org

---

 Now go to Topic #9: **Group Interaction Models** in the MyEducationLab (www.myeducationlab.com) for your course, where you can:

- Find learning outcomes for this topic along with the national standards that connect to these outcomes.
- Complete Assignments and Activities that can help you more deeply understand the chapter content.
- Apply and practice your understanding of the core teaching skills identified in the chapter with the Building Teaching Skills and Dispositions learning units.

EXERCISE 9.1A   WHOLE-CLASS DISCUSSION AS A TEACHING STRATEGY: WHAT DO I ALREADY KNOW?

INSTRUCTIONS: The purpose of this exercise is to explore your knowledge and share your experiences about whole-class discussion. Answer the following questions, and then share your responses with your class, perhaps in discussion groups organized by subject field or grade level.

1. Your grade-level interest or subject field: _____

2. For what reasons would you hold a whole-class discussion? _____

_____

_____

_____

_____

3. Assuming that your classroom has movable seats, how would you arrange them? _____

_____

_____

_____

_____

4. What would you do if the seats were not movable? _____

_____

_____

_____

_____

5. What rules would you establish before starting the discussion? _____

_____

_____

_____

_____

6. Should student participation be forced? Why or why not? If so, how? _____

_____

_____

_____

7. How would you discourage a few students from dominating the discussion? _____

_____

_____

_____

_____

8. What preparation should be expected of the students and teacher before beginning the discussion?

_____

_____

_____

_____

9. How would you handle digression from the topic? _____

_____

_____

_____

_____

10. Should students be discussion leaders? Why or why not? If so, what training, if any, should they receive, and how? _____

_____

_____

_____

_____

11. What teacher roles are options during a class discussion? _____

_____

_____

_____

_____

12. When is each of these roles most appropriate? _____

_____

_____

_____

_____

13. When, if ever, is it appropriate to hold a class meeting for discussing class procedures, not subject matter?

_____

_____

_____

_____

_____

_____

14. Can brainstorming be a form of whole-class discussion? Why or why not? _____

_____

_____

_____

_____

EXERCISE 9.1A *(continued)*

15. What follow-up activities would be appropriate after a whole-class discussion? On what basis would you decide to use each? _____

_____

_____

_____

_____

_____

16. What sorts of activities should precede a class discussion? _____

_____

_____

_____

_____

_____

_____

_____

17. Should a discussion be given a set length? Why or why not? If so, how long? How is the length to be decided?

_____

_____

_____

_____

_____

_____

18. Should students be graded for their participation in class discussion? Why or why not? If so, how? On what basis? By whom? _____

_____

_____

_____

_____

_____

19. For effective discussions, 10 to 12 feet is the maximum recommended distance between participants. During a teacher-led discussion, what can a teacher do to keep within this limit? _____

_____

_____

_____

_____

_____

20. Are there any pitfalls or other points of importance that a teacher should be aware of when planning and implementing a whole-class discussion? If so, explain them and how to guard against them. _____

_____

_____

_____

_____

_____

_____

EXERCISE 9.1B   WHOLE-CLASS DISCUSSION AS A TEACHING STRATEGY: BUILDING UPON WHAT I ALREADY KNOW

INSTRUCTIONS: The purpose of this exercise is to generate guidelines for using whole-class discussion as an instructional strategy. Share your responses to Exercise 9.1A with your colleagues. Then individually answer the first two questions below. Next, as a group, use all three questions to guide you as you generate a list of five general guidelines for the use of whole-class discussion as a strategy in teaching. Share your group's guidelines with the entire class. Then, as a class, derive a final list of general guidelines.

1. How effective was your small-group discussion in sharing Exercise 9.1A? _____

_____

_____

_____

_____

_____

2. What allowed for or inhibited the effectiveness of that small-group discussion? _____

_____

_____

_____

_____

_____

_____

3. How effective is this small-group discussion? Why? _____

_____

_____

_____

_____

_____

_____

_____

GENERAL GUIDELINES GENERATED FROM SMALL-GROUP DISCUSSION

1. _____

_____

2. _____
   _____

3. _____
   _____

4. _____
   _____

5. _____
   _____

GENERAL GUIDELINES: FINAL LIST DERIVED FROM WHOLE CLASS

_____
_____
_____
_____
_____
_____
_____
_____
_____
_____
_____
_____
_____
_____
_____
_____
_____
_____
_____
_____
_____
_____
_____
_____
_____
_____

EXERCISE 9.2   TEACHER INTERACTION WITH STUDENTS ACCORDING TO STUDENT GENDER

INSTRUCTIONS: The purpose of this exercise is to provide a tool for the analysis of your own interactions with students according to gender.

This activity can be used to check for teacher interaction with many kinds of student differences. For example, you can use the activity to check teacher interaction between students of different language or cultural backgrounds, students from different economic backgrounds, or students with different academic ability levels. To become accustomed to the exercise, you should do a trial run in one of your university classes, then use it during your student teaching, and again during your first years of teaching. The exercise can be modified to include (1) the amount of time given for each interaction, (2) the response time given by the teacher according to student gender, and (3) other student characteristics, such as ethnicity.

Prior to class, select a student (this will be you during the trial run recommended above) or an outside observer, such as a colleague, to do the tallying and calculations as follows. Ask the person to tally secretly the interactions between you and the students by placing a mark after the name of each student (or on the student's position on a seating chart) with whom you have verbal interaction. If a student does the tallying, that student should not be counted in any of the calculations.

Exact time at start: _____

Exact time at end: _____

Total time in minutes: _____

| Total in class today = _____ | Girls = _____ | Boys = _____ |
| | % Girls = _____ | % Boys = _____ |

Tally of Interactions	
With girls	*With boys*

Total Interactions = _____

% with girls = _____   % with boys = _____

Teacher Reflections and Conclusions: _____

_____

_____

_____

_____

_____

10 Assessing and Reporting Student Achievement

As you know by now, for the sake of clarity and sensible organization, this resource guide is centered on the three phases of effective instruction. Preceding chapters addressed the *preactive* or *planning* phase of instruction (Chapters 1–5) and the *interactive* or *teaching* phase of instruction (Chapters 6–9); the focus in the two remaining chapters (Chapters 10–11) is on the *analyzing and reflecting* phase, or, as I prefer to call it, the *assessment and projection* component of effective instruction. Together, these are the three thought-processing and decision-making phases of effective instruction. It is neither likely nor advisable that one should or could effectively learn about one phase entirely exclusive of the others. The phases are inextricably intertwined, with each affected by and dependent upon the others. Indeed, teaching and learning are reciprocal processes that depend on and affect one another. Thus, the assessment component of instruction deals with both how well the students are learning and how well the teacher is teaching. This chapter addresses the former.

Rather than a separate phase, assessment is really an integral and ongoing process in the total educational arena. Curricula, buildings, materials, specific courses, teachers, supervisors, administrators, equipment, and yes, even school board members and politicians at all levels of government—all must be periodically assessed in relation to student learning, the purpose of the school. When gaps between anticipated results and student achievement exist, efforts are made (or should be) to eliminate those factors that seem to be limiting the educational output or to improve the situation in some other way. Thus, educational progress occurs.

Much concern today is expressed over the use of what is often referred to as **high-stakes assessment**. An assessment is called high stakes if use of the assessment's results carry serious consequences, such as a student's grade promotion or graduation from high school rests on the student's performance on a single test. I agree with the many educators who argue that important decisions that affect a student's educational career should not rest on a single test score alone but on multiple sources of data that accumulate over a period of time. In the previous edition of this resource guide, I stated that I share in the concern that placing high reliance on a single source of data would likely result in an increase, rather than an improvement, in the school dropout rate. In a joint announcement made in 2001, executive directors of the National Association of Elementary School Principals (NAESP) and the National Association of Secondary School Principals (NASSP) stated, "Test results should not be used to reward or punish a school, a system, or a state, but instead should be used as diagnostic tools to improve teaching and learning. Tests should not be used for high-stakes purposes or as exit exams" (Ferrandino & Tirozzi, 2001). Warnings went unheeded, and today it is clear that high-stakes testing continues and as discussed in Chapter 1, the nation now has a dropout crisis, with more than one million students dropping out of school every year, and even among those who do graduate from high school and go on to college a significant number of them require remedial coursework (Wise, 2008).

> Because they are so unrealistic and counterproductive, the NCLB legislation and other mandates sustaining the current high-stakes testing overkill are likely to disappear before long, or at least to be reshaped into something more sensible.
>
> Good & Brophy (2008, p. 297)

However, it is true that to learn effectively, students need to know how they are doing and how they can improve. Similarly, to be an effective teacher, you must be informed about what the student knows, feels, and can do so that you can help the student build skills, knowledge, and attitudes. Therefore, you and your students need continuous feedback on their progress and problems in order to plan appropriate learning activities and to make adjustments to those already planned. If this feedback says that progress is slow, you can provide alternative activities; if it indicates that some or all of the students have already mastered the desired learning, you can eliminate unnecessary activities and practice for some or all of the students. In short, assessment provides a key for competent teaching, differentiated instruction, and effective learning.

The importance of continuous assessment mandates that you are knowledgeable about various principles and techniques of assessment. This chapter explains some of those and shows you how to construct and use assessment instruments. It clarifies terms related to assessment, suggests procedures to use in the construction of assessment items, and identifies the advantages and disadvantages of a variety of types of assessment items and procedures.

It is neither my purpose nor does space in this resource guide allow a consideration of standardized achievement testing. Rather, the focus is on **nonstandardized, criterion-referenced tests**, tests that you design (or collaboratively design) for your own unique group of students for determination of their level of learning on particular instructional objectives. In no way do I intend to devalue the concern that you as a classroom teacher will have for high-stakes, standardized, norm-referenced, achievement testing. It simply means that my purpose and space in this resource guide do not allow for in-depth attention to that particular topic. If relevant to you and your teaching, your school and district will provide special instructions for preparing students and for administering the mandated standardized achievement tests.

In addition, this chapter discusses grading and, to a limited extent, the reporting of student achievement, two responsibilities that can consume much of a teacher's time. Grading can be both time consuming and frustrating for teachers. What should be graded? Should grades (or marks) represent student growth, level of achievement in a group, effort, attitude, general behavior, or a combination of these? What should determine grades—homework, tests, projects, class participation and group work, or some combination of these? What should be their relative weights? And in what way should the records be recorded and maintained? These are just a few of the questions that have plagued teachers, parents/guardians, and the profession for a century or more of education in this nation.

In many schools today, electronic programs, such as ProgressBook (www.progressbook.com), are used by teachers to post homework assignments, grades, and email communication to parents as well as to students, both of whom can have accounts with the school that allow them to access the program. Such electronic programs as ProgressBook are designed to provide a classroom management system to support current standards-based practices.

Relatively new on the assessment scene, and directly correlated with the concept of **mastery learning** (as discussed in Chapter 8), is the program of assessment referred to as **curriculum-based measurement** (CBM), a process of identifying and then tracking a student's development in basic skills, particularly in reading, spelling, and mathematics (Zimmerman & Dibenedetto, 2008). Rather than traditional content-specific testing of learning for specific instructional units or modules, when using curriculum-based measurement basic skills and content are identified for which the student should be competent by the end of the school year. From that a number of as many as 30 tests are developed and administered over the course of that school year, each test using alternate questions while all are designed to cover that same basic curriculum material. The tests are administered periodically, such as weekly, with the results graphed and analyzed to track the progress of individual students, identifying those who may prosper from special help. Research shows that the use of CBM not only provides an effective and efficient way to fulfill the Adequate Yearly Progress (AYP) accountability requirements of No Child Left Behind (Fuchs & Fuchs, 2004) but also helps teachers significantly improve the learning achievement of struggling students (Fuchs, Fuchs, & Courey, 2005; Fuchs, Fuchs, & Zumeta, 2008; Stecker, Fuchs, & Fuchs, 2005; Good & Brophy, 2008).

The development of the student encompasses growth in the cognitive, affective, and psychomotor domains. Traditional, objective, paper-and-pencil tests provide only a portion of the data needed to indicate student progress in those domains. Many experts today, as indeed they have in the past, question traditional sources of data and encourage the search for, development of, and use of

---

A HIGH SCHOOL ENGLISH TEACHER'S USE OF COMPETENCY-BASED MEASUREMENT

Students study vocabulary gradually over a period of time. They begin by collecting words from readings, listing them on a designated whiteboard. From those lists they then prepare practice quizzes to exchange with one another and engage in frequent vocabulary discussions that emphasize recognition of context clues and other language decoding strategies.

Deanna L. Nelson (2008)

alternative means to assess more authentically the students' development of thinking and higher level learning. Although many things are not yet clear, one thing that is clear is that various techniques of assessment with the resultant multiple kinds of data must be used to determine how the student works, what the student is learning, and what the student can produce as a result of that learning. As a teacher, you must develop a repertoire of means of assessing learner behavior and academic progress. Be patient and kind to yourself, for to become truly skilled in the practices of assessment will take time, practice, and reflection.

Just as in the rest of the teaching field, practices in assessment are subject to change, which means that as a teacher you must stay abreast of those changes (the major topic of the next and final chapter of this resource guide). For example, we are only now becoming aware of how online and offline reading engage different skills and how because of that techniques used in the assessment of reading must take those differences into account (Coiro, 2009).

Although marks and grades have been a part of school for more than a century, and although it is clear to many experts that the conventional report card with marks or grades falls short of being a developmentally appropriate procedure for reporting the academic performance or progress of learners, and although some schools are experimenting with other ways of reporting student achievement in learning, letter grades, especially for secondary schooling, still seem firmly entrenched—parents, students, colleges, and employers have come to expect grades as evaluations. However, a variety of systems of assessment and reporting have evolved, are still evolving, and will likely continue to evolve throughout your professional career. Most school systems today use real-time Internet information systems to manage student data, a procedure that is beyond the scope of this resource guide, that you will learn about at your teaching assignment.

When teachers are aware of alternative systems, they may be able to develop assessment and reporting practices that are fair and effective for particular situations. So, after beginning with assessment, the final focus in this chapter considers briefly today's principles and practices in grading and reporting the achievement of students.

Specifically, upon completion of this chapter you should be able to:

1. Demonstrate an understanding of the importance of the assessment component of teaching and learning.
2. Demonstrate an understanding of the concept of authentic assessment.
3. Explain the value of and give an example of a performance assessment that could be used at a particular grade level and discipline.
4. Explain why criterion-referenced grading is preferred over norm-referenced grading.
5. Explain how rubrics, checklists, portfolios, and journals are used in the assessment of student learning.
6. Describe the importance of self-assessment and reflection in teaching and learning.
7. Describe means a teacher can use to help students reduce and manage their test anxiety.
8. Recall guidelines for meeting with parents and guardians.
9. Describe the meaning and importance of the concept of assessment as being *embedded* in daily instruction.
10. Create valid, reliable, and unambiguous test items, both traditional and "authentic."

PURPOSES AND PRINCIPLES OF ASSESSMENT

Assessment of achievement in student learning is designed to serve several purposes. These are as follows:

To assist in student learning. This is the purpose usually first thought of when speaking of assessment, and it is the principal topic of this chapter. For the classroom teacher, it is (or should be) the most important purpose.

To identify students' strengths and weaknesses. Identification and assessment of students' strengths and weaknesses are necessary for two reasons: to structure and restructure the learning activities and to restructure the curriculum. Concerning the first, for example, data on student strengths and weaknesses in content and process skills are important in planning activities appropriate for both skill development and intellectual development. This is **diagnostic assessment** (known also as **preassessment**). For the second, data on student strengths and weaknesses in content and skills are useful for making appropriate ongoing modifications to the curriculum. Diagnosing and adjusting the instruction on the basis of the diagnostic results is sometimes referred to as **adaptive assessment**, which is a standard procedure when differentiating the instruction.

To assess the effectiveness of a particular instructional strategy. It is important you understand how well a particular strategy helped accomplish a particular goal or objective. Exemplary teachers continually reflect on and evaluate their strategy choices, using a number of sources—student achievement as measured by assessment instruments, their own intuition, informal feedback given by the students, and, sometimes, informal feedback given by colleagues, such as members of a teaching team, or mentor teachers.

To assess and improve the effectiveness of curriculum programs. Committees composed of teachers and administrators and sometimes parents/guardians and students and other members of the school and community continually assess components of the curriculum. The assessment is done while students are learning (i.e., adaptive and formative assessments) and afterward (summative assessment).

To assess and improve teaching effectiveness. To improve student learning, teachers are periodically evaluated on the basis of (a) their commitment to working with students; (b) their ability to cope with students at a particular age, developmental, or grade level; (c) the achievement of subject matter knowledge by the students they teach; and (d) their ability to show mastery of appropriate instructional techniques.

To provide data that assist in decision making about a student's future. Assessment of student achievement is important in guiding decision making about course and program placement, promotion, school transfer, class standing, eligibility for honors and scholarships, and career planning.

To provide data in order to communicate with and involve parents/guardians in their children's learning. Parents/guardians, communities, and school boards all share in an accountability for the effectiveness of the learning of the children's learning. Today's schools are reaching out more than ever before and engaging parents, guardians, and the community in their children's education. All teachers play an important role in the process of communicating with, reaching out to, and involving parents/guardians and the community.

Because the welfare and, indeed, the future of so many people depend on the outcomes of assessment, it is impossible to overemphasize its importance. For a learning endeavor to be successful, the learner must have answers to basic questions: Where am I going? Where am I now? How do I get where I am going? How will I know when I get there? Am I on the right track for getting there? These questions are integral to a good program of assessment. Of course, in the process of teaching and learning, the answers may be ever changing, and the teacher and students continue to assess and adjust plans as appropriate and necessary. As you are reminded many times in this resource guide, the exemplary school is in a mode of continuous change and progress.

Based on the questions in the preceding paragraph, the following are principles that guide the assessment program and that are reflected in the discussions in this chapter.

- A teacher's responsibility is to facilitate student learning and to assess student progress in that learning, and for that, the teacher is, or should be, held accountable.
- Assessment is a continuous process, imbedded in the teacher's daily instruction. The selection and implementation of plans and activities require

continuing monitoring and assessment to check on progress and to change or adopt strategies to promote desired behavior.

- Assessment is a reciprocal process that includes assessment of teacher performance as well as student achievement.
- Evidence and input data for knowing how well the teacher and students are doing should come from a variety of sources and types of data-collecting devices.
- Reflection and self-assessment are important components of any successful assessment program. Reflection and self-assessment are important if students are to develop the skills necessary for them to assume increasingly greater ownership of their own learning. Reflection and self-assessment are important for the continued and increasing effectiveness of a teacher.
- Students need to know how well they are doing.
- Teachers need to know how well they are doing.
- Parents/guardians need to know how well their children and schools are doing.
- The program of assessment should aid teaching effectiveness and contribute to the intellectual, social, and psychological growth of students.

THE LANGUAGE OF ASSESSMENT

When discussing the assessment component of teaching and learning, it is easy to be confused by the terminology used. The following clarification of terms is offered to aid your reading and comprehension.

Assessment and Evaluation

Assessment is the relative neutral process of finding out what students are learning. **Evaluation** is the more subjective process of making sense of what was found out. For the purposes of this resource guide, I consider the difference between the two terms too slight to matter.

Measurement and Assessment

Measurement refers to quantifiable data about specific behaviors. Tests and the statistical procedures used to analyze the results are examples. Measurement is a descriptive and objective process; that is, it is relatively free from human value judgments.

Assessment includes objective data from measurement but also other types of information, some of which are more subjective, such as information from anecdotal records and teacher observations and ratings of student performance. In addition to the use of objective data (data from measurement), assessment also includes arriving at value judgments made on the basis of subjective information.

An example of the use of these terms is as follows. A teacher may share the information that Maggie Applebee received a score in the 90th percentile on the eighth-grade statewide achievement test in reading (a statement of measurement) but may add that "according to my assessment of her work in my language arts class, she has not been an outstanding student" (a statement of assessment).

Validity and Reliability

The degree to which a measuring instrument actually measures that which it is intended to measure is the instrument's **validity**. For example, when we ask if an instrument (such as a performance assessment instrument) has validity, the following would be key questions concerning that instrument:

- Does the instrument adequately sample the intended content?
- Does it measure the cognitive, affective, and psychomotor knowledge and skills that are important to the unit of content being tested?
- Does it sample all the instructional objectives of that unit?

The accuracy with which a technique consistently measures that which it is meant to gauge is its **reliability**. If, for example, you know that you weigh 125 pounds, and a scale consistently records 125 pounds when you stand on it, then that scale has reliability. However, if the same scale consistently records 117 pounds when you stand on it, we can still say the scale has reliability. By this example, then, it should be clear to you that an instrument could be reliable (it produces similar results when used again and again) although not necessarily valid. In this second instance, the scale is not measuring what it is supposed to measure, so although it is reliable, it is not valid. Although a technique might be reliable but not valid, a technique must have reliability before it can have validity. The greater the number of test items or situations on a particular content objective, the higher the reliability. The higher the reliability, the more consistency there will be in students' scores measuring their understanding of that particular objective.

Authentic Assessment: Advantages and Disadvantages

When assessing for student achievement, you must use procedures that are compatible with the instructional objectives that in turn coincide or align with the curriculum standards. This is referred to as **authentic assessment**. Other terms used for authentic assessment are *accurate, active, aligned, alternative,* and *direct.* Although **performance assessment** is sometimes used, performance assessment refers to the type of student response being assessed, whereas authentic assessment refers to the assessment situation. Although not all performance assessments are authentic, assessments that are authentic are most assuredly performance assessments (Oosterhof, 2001).

In English/language arts, for example, although it may seem fairly easy to develop a criterion-referenced test, administer it, and grade it, tests often measure language *skills* rather than language use. It is extremely difficult to measure students' communicative competence with a test. Tests do not measure listening and talking very well, and a test on punctuation marks, for example, does not indicate students' ability to use punctuation marks correctly in their own writing. Instead, tests typically evaluate students' ability to add punctuation marks to a set of sentences created by someone else or to proofread and spot punctuation errors in someone else's writing. An alternative and a far better approach is to examine how students use punctuation marks in their own writing (Tompkins & Hoskisson, 1991). An authentic assessment of punctuation, then, would be an assessment of a performance item that involves students in writing and punctuating their own writing. For the authentic assessment of the student's understanding of that which the student has been learning, you would use a performance-based assessment procedure (Berman, 2007).

Consider another example: "If students have been actively involved in classifying objects using multiple characteristics, it sends them a confusing message if they are then required to take a paper-and-pencil test that asks them to 'define classification' or recite a memorized list of characteristics of good classifications schemes" (Rakow, 1992, p. 3). An authentic assessment technique would be a performance item that actually involves the students in classifying objects. In other words, to obtain an accurate assessment of a student's learning, the teacher uses a performance-based assessment procedure, that is, a procedure that requires students to produce rather than to select a response.

Advantages claimed for the use of authentic assessment include (a) the direct (also known as performance-based, criterion-referenced, outcome-based, or standard-based) measurement of what students should know and can do and (b) an emphasis on higher-order thinking. On the other hand, disadvantages of authentic assessment include a higher cost, difficulty in making results consistent and usable, and problems with validity, reliability, and comparability. Unfortunately, a teacher may never see a particular student again after conclusion of a given school semester or academic year, and the effects that teacher had on a student's values and attitudes may never be observed by that teacher at all. In schools where groups or teams of teachers remain with the same cohort of students—as in the increasing popular small learning community concept and looping programs (discussed in Chapter 1)—those teachers often do have opportunity to observe the positive changes in their students' values and attitudes.

Diagnostic, Formative, and Summative Assessment

Assessing a student's achievement is a three-stage process, involving (as described in the preceding chapter)

1. **Diagnostic assessment** (also called **preassessment**)—the assessment of the student's knowledge and skills *before* the new instruction.
2. **Formative assessment**—the assessment of learning *during* the instruction (also called **adaptive assessment** if/when the assessment instruments are modified to fit individual students' skill and knowledge levels). Unlike summative assessments, which rely mostly on end-of-term test scores to gauge student achievement, formative assessments help shape instruction through repeated measures and feedback as students are in the process of learning. The quality and manner of feedback to students is an important component of formative assessment (Brookhart, 2008).
3. **Summative assessment**—the assessment of learning *after* the instruction, ultimately represented by the student's final term, semester, or year achievement grade.

Grades (or marks) shown on unit tests, progress reports, and interim reports are examples of formative evaluation reports. However, an end-of-chapter test or a unit test is summative when the test represents the absolute end of the student's learning of material for that instructional unit.

ASSESSING STUDENT LEARNING: THREE AVENUES

Three general avenues are available for assessing a student's achievement in learning. You can assess

1. What the student *says*—the quantity and quality of a student's contributions to class discussions.
2. What the student *does*—a student's performance (e.g., the amount and quality of a student's participation in the learning activities).
3. What the student *writes*—as shown by items in the student's portfolio (e.g., homework assignments, checklists, project work, and written tests).

Although your own situation and personal philosophy will influence the levels of importance and weight you give to each avenue of assessment, you should have a strong rationale if you value and weigh the three avenues for assessment differently than one-third each.

Assessing What a Student Says and Does

When evaluating what a student says, you should listen to the student's oral reports, questions, responses, and interactions with others and observe the student's attentiveness, involvement in class activities, creativeness, and responses to challenges. Notice that we say, you should listen and observe. While listening to what the student is saying, you should also be observing the student's nonverbal behaviors. For this you can use narrative observation forms (see Figure 10.1), and you can use observations with checklists and scoring rubrics (see sample checklists in Figures 10.2, 10.4, and 10.5 and sample scoring rubrics in Figures 5.1 (of Chapter 5), 10.3, 10.10, and 10.11) and periodic conferences with the student.

With each technique used, you must proceed from your awareness of anticipated learning outcomes (the instructional objectives), and you must assess a student's progress toward meeting those objectives. That is referred to as a **criterion-referenced assessment**.

OBSERVATION FORM
Figure 10.1 illustrates a sample generic form for recording and evaluating teacher observations of a student's verbal and nonverbal behaviors. With modern

Figure 10.1 Sample form for evaluating and recording student verbal and nonverbal behaviors.

Student _____ Course _____ School _____		
Observer _____ Date _____		Period _____
Objective	Desired behavior	What student did, said, or wrote
Teacher's (observer's) comments:		

technology, such as is afforded, for example, by the software program *Learner Profile* (www.learnerprofile.com), teachers can record student's grades, track assignments, organize student information, and develop reports. Teachers can use Learner Profile on their computer and Learner Profile to Go on their Palm or Palm-compatible PDA.

CHECKLIST VERSUS SCORING RUBRIC

As you can see from the sample rubric and sample checklist shown in Figure 10.2, there is little difference between what is a checklist and what is a rubric: the difference is that rubrics show the degrees for the desired characteristics, whereas checklists usually show only the desired characteristics. The checklist could easily be made into a scoring rubric, and the rubric could easily be made into a checklist.

Rubrics provide an excellent method of informing learners about learning expectations; many teachers have students participate in the construction of a specific rubric to be used during the learning process. Although not difficult to prepare, like any instrument used for assessment, a rubric must accurately assess the expected learning outcomes. In addition to samples provided in this resource guide, there are many sources available to guide you in the specifics of rubric prepara-

tion and use, such as Boston (2002), Brookhart (2008), Danielson (1997, 1998), and Moskal (2003).

GUIDELINES FOR ASSESSING WHAT A STUDENT SAYS AND DOES

When assessing a student's verbal and nonverbal behaviors in the classroom, you should

- Maintain an anecdotal record (teacher's log) book or folder with a separate section in it for your records of each student.
- For a specific activity, list the desirable behaviors.
- Check the list against the specific instructional objectives.
- Record your observations as quickly as possible following your observation. Audio or video recordings, and, of course, computer software programs can help you maintain records and check the accuracy of your memory, but if this is inconvenient, you should spend time during school, immediately after school, or later that evening recording your observations while they are still fresh in your memory.
- Record your professional judgment about the student's progress toward the desired behavior, but think it through before transferring it to a permanent record.

Figure 10.2 Checklist and rubric compared.

Sample rubric for assessing a student's skill in listening.

Score Point 3—Strong listener:
Responds immediately to oral directions
Focuses on speaker
Maintains appropriate attention span
Listens to what others are saying
Is interactive
Score Point 2—Capable listener:
Follows oral directions
Usually attentive to speaker and to discussions
Listens to others without interrupting
Score Point 1—Developing listener:
Has difficulty following directions ·
Relies on repetition
Often inattentive
Has short attention span
Often interrupts the speaker

Sample checklist for assessing a student's skill in map work:

Check each item if the map comes up to standard in this particular category.

_____ 1. Accuracy

_____ 2. Neatness

_____ 3. Attention to details

- Write comments that are reminders to yourself, such as "Discuss observation with the student," "Check validity of observation by further testing," "Discuss observations with student's mentor" (e.g., an adult representative from the community), and "Discuss observations with other teachers on the teaching team."

Assessing What a Student Writes

When assessing what a student writes, you can use worksheets, written homework and papers, student journal writing, student writing projects, student portfolios, and tests (all discussed later in this chapter). In many schools, portfolios, worksheets, and homework assignments are the tools usually used for the formative evaluation of each student's achievement. Tests, too, should be a part of this evaluation, but tests are also used for summative evaluation at the end of a unit and for diagnostic purposes such as the response to intervention (RtI) program.

Your summative evaluation of a student's achievement and any other final judgment made by you about a student can have an impact upon the psychological and intellectual development of that student. Special attention is given to this later in the section titled Recording Teacher Observations and Judgments.

Use the following guidelines when assessing what a student writes.

Student writing assignments, test items, and scoring rubrics (see Figure 10.3) should be criterion referenced. They should correlate with and be compatible with specific instructional objectives. Regardless of the avenue chosen and their relative weights given by you, you must evaluate against the instructional objectives. Any given objective may be checked by using more than one method and by using more than one instrument. Subjectivity, inherent in the assessment process, may be reduced as you check for validity, comparing results of one measuring strategy against those of another.

Read nearly everything a student writes. [Note: We are not referring here to student diaries and private journals, which are just that—private—and which should be left at home, not brought to school.] Regarding schoolwork, if it is important for the student to do the work, then it is equally important that you give your professional attention to the product of the student's efforts. Of course, in deference to the teacher's productive and efficient use of valuable time, student papers can be read with varying degrees of intensity and scrutiny depending on the purpose of the assignment.

Provide written or verbal comments about the student's work, and be positive in those comments. Rather than just writing "good" on a student's paper, briefly state what made it good in your opinion. Rather than simply saying or pointing out that the student did not do it right, tell or show the student what is acceptable and how to achieve it. For reinforcement, use positive comments and encouragement as frequently as possible.

Think before writing a comment on a student's paper, asking yourself how you think the student (or a parent or guardian) will interpret and react to the comment and if that is a correct interpretation or reaction to your intended meaning.

Avoid writing evaluative comments or grades in student journals. Student journals are for encouraging students to write, to think about their thinking, and to record their creative thoughts. In journal writing, students should be encouraged to write about their experiences in school and out of school and especially about their experiences related to what is being learned. They should be encouraged to write their feelings about what is being learned and about how they are learning it. Writing in journals gives them practice in expressing themselves in written form and in connecting their learning and should provide nonthreatening freedom to do it. Comments and evaluations from teachers might discourage creative and spontaneous expression. You can write simple, empathic comments such as "Thank you for sharing your thoughts" or "I think I understand what makes you feel that way."

Figure 10.3   Sample scoring rubric for assessing student writing. (*Source: Writing Inservice Guide for English Language Arts and* TAAS, Texas Education Agency, 1993, TX.)

Score Point 4—correct purpose, mode, audience; effective elaboration; consistent organization; clear sense of order and completeness; fluent

Score Point 3—correct purpose, mode, audience; moderately well elaborated; organized but possible brief digressions; clear, effective language

Score Point 2—correct purpose, mode, audience; some elaboration; some specific details; gaps in organization; limited language control

Score Point 1—attempts to address audience; brief, vague, unelaborated; wanders off topic; lack of language control; little or no organization; wrong purpose and mode

When reading student learning journals, talk individually with students to seek clarification about their expressions. Student learning journals are useful to the teacher (of any subject) in understanding the student's thought processes and writing skills (diagnostic assessment) and should *not* be graded. For grading purposes, teachers may simply record whether the student is maintaining a journal and, perhaps, an assessment regarding the quantity of writing in it, but no judgment should be made about the quality.

When reviewing student portfolios, discuss with students individually the progress in their learning as shown by the materials in their portfolios. As with student learning journals, the portfolio should *not* be graded or compared in any way with those of other students. I return to this point later in the chapter. Its purpose is for student self-assessment and to show progress in learning. In order to self-assess, to show progress in learning, students should keep in their portfolios all or major samples of papers related to the course.

Assessment for Affective and Psychomotor Domain Learning

Whereas assessment of cognitive domain learning lends itself to traditional written tests of achievement, the assessment of learning within the affective and psychomotor domains is best suited by the use of performance checklists where student behaviors can be observed in action. However, many educators today are encouraging the use of alternative assessment procedures (i.e., alternatives to traditional paper-and-pencil written testing). After all, in learning that is most important and that has the most meaning to students: the domains are inextricably interconnected. As I have said previously, learning that is meaningful to students is not as easily compartmentalized as the taxonomies of educational objectives would imply. Alternative assessment strategies include the use of projects, portfolios, skits, papers, oral presentations, and performance tests.

STUDENT INVOLVEMENT IN ASSESSMENT

Students' continuous self-assessment should be planned as an important component of the assessment program. If students are to progress in their understanding of their own thinking (**metacognition**) and in their intellectual development, as discussed in Chapter 7, then they must receive instruction and guidance on how to become more responsible for their own learning. During that empowerment process, they learn to think better of themselves and their individual capabilities. Achieving this self-understanding and improved self-esteem requires the experiences afforded by successes, along with guidance in self-understanding and self-assessment.

To meet these goals, teachers provide opportunities for students to think about

- what they are learning,
- how they are learning it, and
- how far they have progressed.

Specifically, to engage students in the assessment process, you can provide opportunities for the students to

- identify learning targets that are especially valued by the students,
- help in the design of assessment devices for the units of study,
- evaluate the tests (if any) that are furnished by the textbook publisher in terms of how well they match learning targets identified by you and your students, and
- help interpret assessment results.

To aid in the interpretation of results, students can maintain portfolios of their work, using rating scales or checklists periodically to self-assess their progress, and discuss their self-assessments with their parents/guardians and teacher.

Using Portfolios

Portfolios are used by teachers as a means of instruction and by teachers and students as one means of assessing student learning. Although there is scant research evidence to support or refute the claim, educators believe that the instructional value comes from the process of the student's assembling and maintaining a personal portfolio. During that creative process, the student is expected to self-reflect, to think critically about what has and is being learned, and to assume some responsibility for his or her own learning. Increasingly, teachers and their students are using electronic portfolios (**e-portfolio**) (Acker & Halasek, 2008; Barrett, 2007; Fahey, Lawrence, & Paratore, 2007; Feldman & Matjasko, 2007; Fitzgerald, 2007; Lambert, DePaepe, Lambert, & Anderson, 2007; Maxwell & Lassak, 2008; Waters, 2007).

Student portfolios, including electronic portfolios, fall into three general categories, and the purpose in a given situation may transcend some combination of all the three. The categories are

- **selected works portfolio**, in which students maintain samples of their work as prompted by the teacher;
- **longitudinal or growth portfolio**, which is oriented toward outcome-driven goals and includes samples of student work from the beginning to the end of the school term (or thematic unit of study) to exemplify achievement toward the goals; and
- **passport or career portfolio**, which contains samples of student work that will enable the student to transition, such as from one grade level to the next or from school to work.

Student portfolios should be well organized and, depending on the purpose (or category), should contain assignment sheets, class worksheets, the results of home-work, project binders, forms for student self-assessment and reflection on their work, and other class materials thought important by the students and teacher. Software packages, such as *Grady Profile* (www.aurbach.com), are available for the development of student electronic portfolios.

PORTFOLIO ASSESSMENT: KNOWING AND DEALING WITH ITS LIMITATIONS

Although portfolio assessment as an alternative to tradi-tional methods of evaluating student progress has evi-denced some popularity in recent years, establishing standards has been difficult. Research on the use of portfolios for assessment indicates that validity and reli-ability of teacher evaluation are often quite low. In ad-dition, portfolio assessment is not always practical for use by every teacher. For example, if you are the sole art teacher for a school and are responsible for teaching art to every one of the 400 students in the school, you are unlikely to have the time or storage capacity for 400 portfolios. For your assessment of student learning, the use of checklists, rubrics, and student self-assess-ment may be more practical.

Before using portfolios as an alternative to tradi-tional testing, you are advised to carefully consider and clearly understand the reasons for doing it and its prac-ticality in your situation. Then carefully choose portfo-lio content, establish rubrics or expectation standards, anticipate grading problems, and consider and prepare for reactions from parents and guardians.

While emphasizing the criteria for assessment, rat-ing scales and checklists provide students with means of expressing their feelings and give the teacher still an-other source of input data for use in assessment. to pro-vide students with reinforcement and guidance to improve their learning and development, and teachers can meet with individual students to discuss their self-assessments. Such conferences should provide students with understandable and achievable short-term goals as well as help them develop and maintain adequate self-esteem.

Although almost any instrument used for assessing student work can be used for student self-assessment, in some cases it might be better to construct specific instru-ments with the student's understanding of the instrument in mind. Student self-assessment and self-reflection should be done on a regular and continuing basis so the student can make comparisons periodically. You will need to help students learn how to analyze these comparisons. Comparisons should provide a student with information previously not recognized about the student's progress and growth.

Using Checklists

One of the items that can be maintained by students in their portfolios is a series of checklists. Checklist items can be used easily by a student to compare with previous self-assessments. Items on the checklist will vary depending on your purpose, subject, and grade level. (See sample forms, Figures 10.4 and 10.5.) Open-ended questions allow the student to provide additional infor-mation as well as to do some expressive writing. After a student has demonstrated each of the skills satisfacto-rily, a check is made next to the student's name by the teacher, either alone or in conference with the student.

GUIDELINES FOR USING PORTFOLIOS FOR ASSESSMENT

Following are general guidelines for using student port-folios in the assessment of learning:

- Contents of the portfolio should reflect course goals, learning standards, and target objectives.
- Determine what materials should be kept in the port-folio and announce clearly when (post schedule in room), how, and by what criteria portfolios (post list-ing of required contents) will be reviewed.
- Portfolio maintenance should be the students' responsibility.
- Portfolios should remain in the classroom.
- Students should be encouraged to personalize their portfolios (e.g., with brightly decorated and tasteful exteriors with the student's photo).
- Students should date all items in their portfolios.
- The portfolio should not be graded or compared in any way with those of other students. Its purpose is for student self-assessment and for showing progress in learning. For this to happen, students should keep in their portfolio all papers, or major sample papers, re-lated to the course. For grading purposes, you can simply record whether or not the portfolio was main-tained and, by checklist, whether all items required are in the portfolio.

MAINTAINING RECORDS OF STUDENT ACHIEVEMENT

You must maintain well-organized and complete records of student achievement. You may do this in a written record book or most likely in an electronic record book. At the very least, the record should include attendance records and all records of scores on tests, homework, projects, and other assignments.

Daily interactions and events occur in the classroom that may provide informative data about a student's intellectual, emotional, social, and physical develop-ment. Maintaining a dated log of your observations of these interactions and events can provide important

Figure 10.4   Sample checklist: Assessing a student's oral report.

Checklist: Oral Report Assessment

Student _____   Date _____

Teacher _____   Time _____

Did the student:	Yes	No	Comments
1. Speak so that everyone could hear?	_____	_____	_____
2. Finish sentences?	_____	_____	_____
3. Seem comfortable in front of the group?	_____	_____	_____
4. Give a good introduction?	_____	_____	_____
5. Seem well informed about the topic?	_____	_____	_____
6. Explain ideas clearly?	_____	_____	_____
7. Stay on the topic?	_____	_____	_____
8. Give a good conclusion?	_____	_____	_____
9. Use effective visuals to make the presentation interesting?	_____	_____	_____
10. Give good answers to questions from the audience?	_____	_____	_____

Figure 10.5   Sample checklist: Student learning assessment for use with interdisciplinary thematic instruction.

Checklist: Interdisciplinary Thematic Unit Learning

Student _____   Date _____

Teacher _____   Time _____

Can the student:	Yes	No	Comments/Evidence
1. Identify theme, topic, main idea of the unit?	_____	_____	_____
2. Identify contributions of others to the theme?	_____	_____	_____
3. Identify problems related to the unit study?	_____	_____	_____
4. Has the student developed skills in:	_____	_____	_____
Applying knowledge	_____	_____	_____
Assuming responsibility	_____	_____	_____
Classifying	_____	_____	_____
Categorizing	_____	_____	_____
Decision making	_____	_____	_____
Discussing	_____	_____	_____
Gathering resources	_____	_____	_____
Impulse control	_____	_____	_____
Inquiry	_____	_____	_____
Justifying choices	_____	_____	_____
Listening to others	_____	_____	_____
Locating information	_____	_____	_____
Metacognition	_____	_____	_____

(continued)

Figure 10.5 *(continued)*

Has the student developed skills in (cont.):	Yes	No	Comments/Evidence
Ordering	_____	_____	_____
Organizing information	_____	_____	_____
Problem recognition/identification	_____	_____	_____
Problem solving	_____	_____	_____
Reading text	_____	_____	_____
Reading maps and globes	_____	_____	_____
Reasoning	_____	_____	_____
Reflecting	_____	_____	_____
Reporting to others	_____	_____	_____
Self-assessing	_____	_____	_____
Sharing	_____	_____	_____
Studying	_____	_____	_____
Summarizing	_____	_____	_____
Thinking	_____	_____	_____
Using resources	_____	_____	_____
Working with others	_____	_____	_____
Working independently	_____	_____	_____
(Others unique to the unit)	_____	_____	_____

Additional teacher and student comments:

information that might otherwise be forgotten. At the end of a unit and again at the conclusion of a grading term, you will want to review your records. During the course of the school year, your anecdotal records (and those of other members of your teaching team) will provide important information about the progress of each student and ideas for attention to be given to individual students.

Recording Teacher Observations and Judgments

You must think carefully about any written comments that you intend to make about a student. Adolescents can be quite sensitive to what others say about them and most particularly to comments about them made by a teacher.

Additionally, we have seen anecdotal comments in students' permanent records that said more about their teachers who made the comments than about the recipient students. Comments that have been carelessly, hurriedly, and thoughtlessly made can be detrimental to a student's welfare and progress in school. A teacher's comments must be professional; that is, they must be diagnostically useful to the continued intellectual and psychological development of the student. This is true for any comment you make or write, whether on a student's paper, on the student's permanent school record, electronically, or on a message sent to the student's home.

As an example, consider the following unprofessional comment observed in one student's permanent record. A teacher wrote, "John is lazy." Describing John as "lazy" could be done by anyone; it is nonproductive, and it is certainly not a professional diagnosis. How many times do you suppose John needs to receive such negative descriptions of his behavior before he begins to believe that he is lazy and as a result acts that way even more often? Written comments like that can also be damaging because they may be read by the teacher who next has John in class and lead that teacher to perpetuate the same expectation of John. To say that John is lazy merely describes behavior as judged by the teacher who wrote the comment. More important, and more professional, would be for the teacher to try to analyze why John is behaving that way, then to prescribe activities that are likely to motivate John to assume more constructive charge of his own learning behavior.

For students' continued intellectual and emotional development, your comments should be useful, productive, analytical, diagnostic, criterion referenced, and prescriptive. The professional teacher makes diagnoses and prepares prescriptions; a professional teacher does not label students as "lazy," "vulgar," "slow," "stupid," "difficult," or "dumb." The professional teacher sees the behavior of a student as being goal directed. Perhaps "lazy" John found that particular behavioral pattern won him attention. John's goal, then, was attention (don't we all need attention?), and John assumed negative, perhaps even self-destructive, behavioral patterns to reach that goal. The professional task of any teacher is to facilitate the learner's understanding (perception) of a goal and help the student identify acceptable behaviors positively designed to reach that goal.

That which separates the professional teacher from "anyone off the street" is the teacher's ability to go beyond mere description of behavior. Keep that in mind when you write comments that will be read by students, by their parents or guardians, and by other teachers.

GRADING AND MARKING STUDENT ACHIEVEMENT

If conditions were ideal (which they are not), and if teachers did their job perfectly (which many of us do not), then all students would receive top marks (the ultimate in mastery or quality learning), and there would be less of a need to talk about grading and marking. Mastery learning implies that some end point of learning is attainable, but there probably is no end point. In any case, because conditions for teaching are never ideal and we teachers are mere humans, let us continue with this topic of grading that is undoubtedly of special interest to you, to your students, to their parents or guardians, and to school counselors, administrators and school boards, potential employers, providers of scholarships, and college admissions officers.

> A teacher's concern should not be with deciding which students are better than others but in helping all of them succeed.

The term *achievement* is used frequently throughout this resource guide. What is the meaning of the term? Achievement means accomplishment, but is it accomplishment of the instructional objectives against preset standards, or is it simply accomplishment? Most teachers probably choose the former, where the teacher subjectively establishes a standard that must be met in order for a student to receive a certain grade for an assignment,

project, test, quarter, semester, or course. Achievement, then, is decided by degrees of accomplishment.

Preset standards are usually expressed in percentages (degrees of accomplishment) needed for marks or ABC grades. If no student achieves the standard required for an A grade, for example, then no student receives an A. On the other hand, if all students meet the preset standard for the A grade, then all receive A's. Determining student grades on the basis of preset standards is referred to as **criterion-referenced grading**.

Criterion-Referenced Versus Norm-Referenced Grading

Whereas criterion-referenced (or competency-based) grading is based on preset standards, **norm-referenced** grading measures the relative accomplishment of individuals in the group (e.g., one classroom of 4th graders or one classroom of 10th-grade English students) or in a larger group (e.g., all 4th graders or all students enrolled in 10th-grade English) by comparing and ranking students and is commonly known as "grading on a [normal] curve." Because it encourages competition and discourages cooperative learning, for the determination of student grades *norm-referenced grading is not recommended.* Norm-referenced grading is educationally dysfunctional. For your personal interest, after several years of teaching, you can produce frequency-distribution studies of grades you have given over a period of time, but *do not* give students grades that are based on a curve. Grades for student achievement should be tied to performance levels and determined on the basis of each student's achievement toward preset standards. As stated elsewhere, "Teachers who develop success-oriented partnerships with students have no use for grading on a curve. They know they are not the best teacher they can be until every student attains an A—demonstrating the highest possible achievement on rigorous high-quality assessments" (Stiggins, 2001, p. 444).

In criterion-referenced grading, the aim is to communicate information about an individual student's progress in knowledge and work skills in comparison to that student's previous attainment or in the pursuit of an absolute, such as content mastery. Criterion-referenced grading is featured in continuous-progress curricula, competency-based curricula, and other programs that focus on quality learning and differentiated education.

Criterion-referenced grading is based on the level at which each student meets the specified objectives (standards) for the course or grade level. The objectives must be clearly stated to represent important student learning outcomes. This approach implies that effective teaching and learning result in high grades (A's) or marks for most students. In fact, when a mastery concept is used, the student must accomplish the objectives before being allowed to proceed to the next learning task. The philosophy of teachers who favor criterion-referenced procedures recognizes individual potential. Such teachers accept the challenge of finding teaching strategies to help students progress from where they are to the next designated level. Instead of wondering how Sally compares with Juanita, the comparison is between what Sally could do yesterday and what she can do today and how well these performances compare to the preset standard.

Most school systems use some sort of combination of both norm-referenced and criterion-referenced data usage. Sometimes both kinds of information are useful. For example, a report for a student in the eighth grade might indicate how that student is meeting certain criteria such as an A grade for addition of fractions. Another entry might show that this mastery is expected, however, in the sixth grade. Both criterion- and norm-referenced data may be communicated to the parents or guardians and the student. Appropriate procedures should be used: a criterion-referenced approach to show whether or not the student can accomplish the task, and if so, to what degree, and a norm-referenced approach to show how well that student performs compared to the larger group to which the student belongs. The latter is important data for achievement testing on state standardized testing, some of which is related to NCLB legislation, for college admissions officers, and for committees that appropriate academic scholarships.

Determining Grades

Once entered onto school transcripts, grades have significant impact upon the futures of students. When determining achievement grades for student performance, you must make several important and professional decisions. Although in a few schools, and for certain classes or assignments, only marks such as E, S, and I or "pass/no pass" are used, percentages of accomplishment and letter grades are used for most high schools, while many middle and elementary schools now use numbers 1–4 rather than letters, especially for end-of-year reporting of a student's meeting of the academic standards for English and mathematics, but not exclusive of other academic areas. For example, a report card for a second-grader might show scores, for say 40 separate skills, such as 10 in mathematics, 10 in language arts, 2 in science, 2 in social studies, and 16 in assorted areas such as art, music, physical education, technology, and learning behaviors such as respect and responsibility. Although the report card itself may consist of just one page, it may be accompanied by an explanatory guide consisting of multiple pages. The lowest mark of 1 indicates a student has not met the state's academic standards in the particular skill, whereas the top mark of 4 indicates the student has met the standards with distinction. Such reporting is referred to as *standards-based reporting*.

DETERMINING LETTER GRADES

For determining student grades, consider the guidelines presented in the following paragraphs.

At the start of the school term, explain your marking and grading policies first to yourself, then to your students and to their parents or guardians at "back-to-school night," or by a written explanation that is sent home, put on your web site, or all three. Share with students and parents/guardians sample scoring and grading rubrics. In addition, include your grading policy in the syllabus.

When converting your interpretation of a student's accomplishments to a letter grade, be as objective as possible. For the selection of criteria for ABC grades, select a percentage standard, such as 92 percent for an A, 85 percent for a *B*, 75 percent for a *C*, and 65 percent for a *D*. The cutoff percentages used are your decision, although the district, school, program area, team, or department may have established guidelines that you are expected to follow.

For the determination of students' final grades, many teachers use a point system, in which things that students write, say, and do are given points (but not for journals or portfolios, except, perhaps, for whether the student does one or not); then the possible point total is the factor for grade determination. For example, if 92 percent is the cutoff for an *A* and 500 points are possible, then any student with 460 points or more (500 × .92) has achieved an *A*. Likewise, for a test or any other assignment, if the value is 100 points, the cutoff for an *A* is 92 (100 × .92). With a point system and preset standards, the teacher and students, at any time during the grading period, always know the current points possible and can easily calculate a student's current grade standing. Then, as far as a current grade is concerned, students always know where they stand in the course.

Build your grading policy around degrees of accomplishment rather than failure and where students proceed from one accomplishment to the next. This is *continuous promotion*, not necessarily the promotion of the student from one grade level to the next, but within the classroom. (However, rather than grade-level designations, some schools use the concept of continuous promotion from the time of student entry into the school through the student's graduation or exit from it.)

Remember that *assessment* and *grading* are not synonymous. Assessment implies the collection of information from a variety of sources, including measurement techniques and subjective observations. These data, then, become the basis for arriving at a final grade, which in effect is a final value judgment. Grades are one aspect of evaluation and are intended to communicate educational progress to students and to their parents or guardians; for the grade to be valid as an indicator of that progress, you *must* use a variety of sources of data for determination of a student's final grade.

ABOUT MAKEUP WORK

Decide beforehand your policy about makeup work, ensuring that it is consistent with any schoolwide policy standards on the issue that might exist. Students will be absent and will miss assignments and tests, so it is best that your policies about late assignments and missed tests be clearly communicated to students and to their parents or guardians. For makeup work, please consider the following.

Homework Assignments. I recommend that after due dates have been negotiated or set for assignments, no credit or reduced credit be given for work that is turned in late. Sometimes, however, a student has legitimate reasons for not being able to complete the assignment by the due date, and the teacher must exercise a professional judgment in each instance. (Consider the Teaching in Practice feature "Late Homework Paper from an At-Risk Student" in Chapter 3.) *Although it is important that teachers have rules and procedures—and that they consistently apply those—the teacher is a professional who must consider all aspects of a student's situation and, after doing so, show compassion, caring, and regard for the human situation.*

Tests If students are absent when tests are given, you have several options. Some teachers allow students to miss or discount one test per grading period. Another technique is to allow each student to substitute a written homework assignment or project for one missed test. Still another option is to give the absent student the choice of either taking a makeup test or having the next test count double. When makeup tests are given, the makeup test should be taken within a week of the regular test unless there is a compelling reason (e.g., medical or family problem) why this cannot happen. Once more than a week has passed, then I recommend an automatic option of one of the choices other than the makeup test. Whatever your policy, be sure it is well stated and understood by students.

Sometimes students miss a testing period, not because of being absent from school but because of involvement in other school activities. In those instances, the student may come in on makeup day or may be able to arrange to come in and take the test during another of your class periods, or your prep period, on that day or the next. If a student is absent during performance testing, the logistics and possible diminished reliability of having to re-administer the test for one student may necessitate giving the student an alternate paper-and-pencil test or some other option.

Makeup Day. Some high school teachers set aside an afternoon each week after school, or perhaps during "freeze time" (see Chapter 1), at which time students can come to the classroom and make up quizzes, tests, laboratories, or other in-class assignments. Sometimes these arrangements are done by department with teachers taking turns sharing the after-school supervision. Students are responsible for checking with their teacher about what they must make up and for arranging their schedules so that they can remain after school on a makeup day to complete their assignments.

Quizzes. Many teachers give frequent and brief quizzes, as often as every day. As opposed to tests, quizzes are usually brief (perhaps taking only 5 minutes of class time) and intended to reinforce the importance of frequent study and review. (However, quizzes should be prepared using the same care and precision as presented in the guidelines that follow in the sections for testing and preparation of assessment items.) When quizzes are given at frequent intervals, no single quiz should count very much toward the student's final grade; therefore, you will probably want to avoid having to schedule and give makeup quizzes for students who were absent when a quiz was given. The following are reasonable options to administering makeup quizzes.

- Give a certain number of quizzes during a grading period, say 10, but allow a student to discount a few quiz scores, say 2 of the 10, thereby allowing the student to discount a low score or a missed quiz.
- Count the next quiz double for a student who missed one due to absence. The only problem with this option is when a student misses several quizzes. If a student misses several quizzes, then for that student count the unit test a certain and relative percentage greater.

I see absolutely no positive educational value in using "pop" or unannounced quizzes when determining student grades.

Policies such as a teacher's refusing to accept late work, giving grades of zero, and refusing to allow students to redo their work may be intended as punishment for poor performance, but such policies do not really teach students to be accountable, and they provide little useful information about students' mastery of content material.

Rick Wormeli (2006)

Caution About Assigning Zero Credit. Be cautious before ever assigning a score of zero to a student for a missed or incomplete assignment, test, quiz, or for cheating, especially when using a point system for grading. Depending on the weight of the assignment in relation to the total points possible for the grading period, the assigning of a zero grade can have an extreme negative effect on the student's total grade, thus becoming an act of punishment by the teacher rather than a fair representation of the grade earned (or, in this instance, not earned) by the student. [Note: See the persuasive argument for using a 4-point rather than 100-point grading system as put forward in an article by Douglas Reeves (2004).] This is another example where you, the teacher, must exercise professional judgment. In addition to those mentioned, alternatives to using a zero grade include ignoring the missing grade and calculating the student's final (quarter or semester) percentage grade using, for that student, a lesser total points possible or, if not counter to school policy, assigning a grade of "incomplete" that gives the student some additional time to complete the work.

TESTING FOR ACHIEVEMENT

One source of information used for determining grades is data obtained from testing for student achievement. There are two kinds of tests, those that are standardized and those that are not.

Standardized (Formal) Versus Nonstandardized (Informal) Tests

Whereas *informal tests* are constructed by classroom teachers, *standardized (formal) tests* are those that have been designed by specialists, usually by specialists within commercial testing bureaus, and that are then administered, scored, and interpreted under standard conditions (Linn & Gronlund, 2000). Standardized tests are used by states and districts to determine and compare student achievement, principally in the subjects of reading and mathematics. On usually a state or national level, norms for particular age groups of children are established for its administration to large groups of children. Standardized tests are also used in college entrance requirements. Standardized, norm-referenced tests are best for diagnostic purposes and should not be used for determining student grades.

The administration of standardized achievement tests and the use of their results are major concerns to classroom teachers and school administrators in particular. In some locales, their salaries and indeed their jobs are contingent on the results of student scores on standardized achievement tests. It is neither my purpose nor does space in this book allow a consideration of standardized achievement testing. Rather, the focus is on nonstandardized, criterion-referenced tests, ones that you design (or collaboratively design) for your own unique group of students for determination of their level of learning on particular instructional objectives.

Competent planning, preparing, administering, and scoring of tests is an important professional skill. You may want to refer to the guidelines that follow while you are student teaching, then again during your initial years as an employed teacher.

Purposes for Informal Testing

Informal tests can be designed for several purposes, and a variety of kinds of tests and alternate test items will keep your testing program interesting, useful, and reliable. As a college student, you are probably most experienced with testing for measuring achievement, but as a classroom teacher you will use tests for other reasons as well. Additional purposes for testing are to

- assess and aid in curriculum development;
- determine teaching effectiveness;
- help students develop positive attitudes, appreciations, and values;
- help students increase their understanding and retention of facts, principles, skills, and concepts;
- motivate students;
- provide diagnostic information for planning for individualization of the instruction;
- provide review and drill to enhance teaching and learning; and
- provide informational data for students and their parents/guardians.

Frequency for Informal Testing

Assessment for student learning should be continual; that is, it should be going on every minute of every class day. For grading or marking purposes, it is difficult to generalize about how often to formally test for student achievement, but I believe that testing should be cumulative and frequent. By "cumulative," I mean that each assessment should assess the student's understanding of previously learned material as well as the current unit of study; that is, it should assess connected learning. By "frequent," I mean as often as once a week for classes that meet daily. Advantages of assessment that is cumulative include the review, reinforcement, and articulation of old material with the most recent. *Advantages of frequent and imbedded assessment include a reduction in student anxiety over tests and an increase in the validity of the summative assessment.*

Anxiety: Symptom Recognition and Helping Students (and Yourself) Deal With It

Test taking is becoming an increasingly complex and important facet in the educational lives of young people and begins at an increasingly younger age. For example, as early as grade 3 children in many states must pass tests in reading and mathematics to be promoted to the next grade level. Children who are still preteens are now taking the Scholastic Aptitude Test (SAT), an entrance examination requirement for many colleges and universities, usually taken in the junior year of high school. Some young adolescent children take the SAT for the

Teacher stress is higher than any time we can remember. High-stakes testing, pressure to finish the curriculum, inflexible scripted teaching programs that leave no room for creative innovation, highly structured and labor-intensive behavior programs, along with many other factors, all contribute to stress.

Curwin, Mendler, & Mendler (2008, p. 125)

If as a teacher you believe you may be experiencing a degree of anxiety, not from having to take tests per se but from pressure of having to administer state-mandated tests, then you may profit from practicing the following techniques for stress management:

1. Doing breathing exercise: inhale and hold breath while counting to 10, then exhale slowly. Repeat 10 times.
2. Changing your environment for a few minutes, either actually by taking a walk or by closing your eyes and imagining yourself in a relaxing place.
3. Doing stretching exercises for 5 to 10 minutes, stretching legs, arms, back, shoulders, and neck.

Test Construction

After determining the reasons for which you are designing and administering a test, you need to identify the specific instructional objectives the test is being designed to measure. As you learned earlier, your written instructional objectives are specific so that you can write assessment items designed to measure against those objectives, and that is referred to as criterion-referenced assessment. When the objectives are aligned with specific curriculum standards, as they usually are or should be, then it can also be referred to as **standards-based assessment**.

The first step in test construction is identification of the purposes for the test. The second step is to identify the objectives to be measured, and the third step is to prepare the test items, ensuring you have a balance of question types and not solely low-order recall questions. The best time to prepare draft items is after you have prepared your instructional objectives—while the objectives are fresh in your mind, which means before the lessons are taught. After a lesson is taught, you will want to rework your first draft of the test items related to that lesson to make any modifications to the draft items resulting from your reflection on the instruction that occurred.

Administering Tests

For many students, test taking can be a time of high anxiety. Children demonstrate test anxiety in various ways. Just before and during the test, some are quiet and

practice, and others take it to qualify for talent search programs such as the California State University at Sacramento Talent Search Program or the program at Johns Hopkins University Center for Talented Youth. Because of increased pressures on young people, you may have learners in your classroom who knowingly or unknowingly experience and indicate symptoms of test anxiety, symptoms such as sleeplessness, nausea, and headaches. As can be expected from the increased amount of standardized testing nationwide, overall test anxiety in youth of all levels is reported to be on the increase (Casbarro, 2004; Fulk, 2003). Today, test anxiety can be a major factor contributing to a variety of negative outcomes (Harris & Coy, 2003). You can help alleviate students' test-related stress by learning and teaching both test-taking strategies and techniques that your students can use to manage their anxiety.

Potential causes of test anxiety in young people include (a) expectations of the adults in their lives, and the child's fear of not meeting those expectations, (b) peer pressures, and (c) the feeling of lack of control or the inability to change one's current life situation.

When working with an anxious student, you can help by (a) establishing a rapport with the student whereby the student has confidence in your suggestions and (b) giving specific suggestions to the student, such as to be positive about the outcomes, to use test time efficiently and wisely, to be prepared, to read directions carefully, to make an outline before answering a performance or essay-type question, and to use practice testing.

To further assist in the learner's control of anxiety, help the child learn relaxation techniques such as deep breathing while counting to 10, stretching out and then contracting body muscles and then relaxing, and thinking of a happy memory. School counselors may know of intervention services for referral of the most serious cases of test anxiety.

thoughtful, whereas others are noisy and disruptive. To more accurately measure student achievement, you will want to take steps to reduce their anxiety. To control or reduce student anxieties, consider the following discussion as guidelines for administering tests.

Because many people respond best to familiar routine, plan your assessment program so tests are given at regular intervals and administered at the same time and in the same way. In some secondary schools in particular, days of the week are assigned to departments for administering major tests. For example, Tuesdays might be for English/language arts and mathematics testing, and Wednesday is the day for social studies and science testing.

Avoid tests that are too long and that will take too much time. Sometimes new teachers have unreasonable expectations of children about their attention spans during testing. Frequent testing with frequent sampling of student knowledge is preferred over infrequent and long tests that attempt to cover everything.

Attend to creature comforts. Try to arrange the classroom so it is well ventilated, the temperature is comfortable, and, when giving paper-and-pencil tests individually, the seats are well spaced. If spacing is a problem, then consider using individual privacy protectors (see Consider the Physical Layout in Chapter 3, group testing, or alternate forms of the test, where students seated adjacent to one another have different forms of the same test (e.g., multiple-choice answer alternatives are arranged in different order).

Before distributing the test, explain to students what they are to do when finished, such as quietly begin an anchor activity, because not all of the students will finish at the same time. For many young people it is unreasonable to expect them to just sit quietly after finishing a test; they need something to do. However, as a former teacher, I personally had no problem with my students who upon finishing a test wished simply to put their heads down on their desks and rest.

When ready to test, do not drag it out. Distribute tests quickly and efficiently. Once testing has begun, avoid interrupting the students. (It is amazing how often teachers interrupt students once the students are at a task, while those same teachers resent being interrupted themselves.) Items or announcements of important information can be written on the board or, if unrelated to the test, held until all are finished with the test. Stay in the room and visually monitor the students. If the test is not going to take an entire class period (and most shouldn't), and it is a major test, then administer it at the start of the class period, if possible, unless you are planning a test review just prior to it (although that seems rather late to conduct a meaningful review; a review just prior to giving the test is likely to upset those who discover they don't know the material like they thought they did). It is improbable that any teacher can

effectively teach a lesson with a reasonable degree of student interest in it just prior to or immediately following a major test.

Controlling Cheating

Whatever the causes, some students will try to cheat on tests. There are steps you can take to discourage cheating or to reduce the opportunity and pressure that cause students to cheat.

PREVENTING CHEATING
Space students, use alternate forms of the test, or use privacy protectors. Frequent testing and not allowing a single test to count too much toward a term grade reduce test anxiety and the pressure that can cause cheating. Prepare test questions that are clear and unambiguous, thereby reducing student frustration caused by a question or instructions that students do not understand. Avoid tests that are too long and that will take too much time. During long tests, some students become discouraged and restless, and that is a time when classroom management problems can occur.

By their sheer nature, performance tests can cause even greater pressure on students and can also provide greater opportunity for cheating. When administering performance tests to an entire class, it is best to have several monitors, such as members of your teaching team. If that is not possible, consider testing groups of students rather than individuals. Evaluation of test performance, then, would be based on group rather than individual achievement. However, I tend to agree with those who argue against the use of any kind of assessment of an individual that is based to any degree on group process and functioning. It is very difficult, if not impossible, to rationalize giving an individual student a grade based on a group task.

Consider using open-text and open-notebook tests or allowing each student to prepare a page of notes to use during the test. When students can use their books and notes, it not only reduces anxiety but also helps with their organization of information and the retention of what has been learned. The use of open-notes and open-book testing is an adaptation that is appreciated by many students (Eilertsen & Valdermo, 2000; Nelson, Jayanthi, Epstein, & Bursuck, 2000).

STOPPING CHEATING
The preceding paragraphs provide hints to prevent students from cheating. If you suspect cheating is occurring, move and stand in the area of the suspected student. Usually that will stop it.

DEALING WITH CHEATING
When you suspect cheating has occurred, you are faced with a dilemma. Unless your suspicion is backed by solid

proof, you are advised to ignore it, but keep a close watch on the student the next time to prevent cheating from happening. Think not of your job as *catching* students being dishonest but as *discouraging* dishonesty. If you have absolute proof that a student has cheated, then you are obligated to proceed with school policy on student cheating, and that may call for a session with the counselor or the student and the student's parent or guardian, perhaps an automatic *F* grade on the test.

Determining the Time Needed to Take a Test

Again, avoid giving tests that are too long and that will take too much time. As a general rule (and I am speaking of teacher-made tests, not about standardized achievement tests, tests given to high school students for college entrance requirements, or other tests given to students that are out of the teacher's control), testing duration should be limited to

- 10–20 minutes for most K–3 situations,
- 30–40 minutes maximum for grades 4–8, and
- 60 minutes maximum for high school testing.

Preparing and administering effective tests is a skill that you will develop over time. In the meantime, it is

Table 10.1 Approximate Time to Allow for Testing as Determined by the Types of Items*

Type of Test Item	Time Needed Per Item
Matching	30 seconds per matching item
Completion	30 seconds
Multiple-choice	30–60 seconds
Completion drawing	2–3 minutes
Arrangement	2–3 minutes
Identification	2–3 minutes
Short explanation	2–3 minutes
Essay and performance	10 or more minutes

*Students with special needs or ELL students, of course, may need more time per item, or may need to have the test administered in briefer sessions or some other accommodation depending on the individual's special-needs situation.

best to test frequently and to use tests that sample student achievement rather than try for a comprehensive measure of that achievement.

Some students take more time on a test than do others. You need to avoid giving too much time, or classroom management problems will result. On the other hand, you do not want to cut short the time needed by students who can do well but need more time to think and to write. As a very general guide, use the table of time needed for different types of test items (Table 10.1). This is only a guide for determining the approximate amount of time to allow students to complete a test. For example, for a test made up of 10 multiple-choice items, 5 arrangement items, and 2 short-explanation items, you would want to plan for about 30 minutes for students to complete the test.

PREPARING ASSESSMENT ITEMS

Preparing and writing the best assessment items is yet another professional skill, and to become proficient at it takes study, time, practice, feedback, and reflection. Because of the importance of an assessment program, please assume this professional charge seriously and responsibly. Although poorly prepared items take no time at all to construct, they will cause you more trouble than you can ever imagine. As a professional you should take time to study different types of assessment items that can be used and how best to write them, and then practice writing them. Remember, when preparing assessment items, ensure that they match and sufficiently cover the instructional objectives. In addition, you should prepare

---

Teaching in Practice:
Teachers Caught Cheating

Trying to Gain an Advantage for Their Students (or Trying to Make Themselves Look Good)

- A teacher was placed on leave, and more than a dozen eighth-graders were retested after they allegedly were prepped with questions that showed up on their state social studies exam.
- In another state, students reported that adult tutors guided their pencils to the correct answers while they took the mandatory state math test.
- In yet another state it was reported that some teachers read answers to students during the test, finished sentences for students in essays, allowed students to correct wrong answers, and photocopied secure tests to review in class.

Questions for Class Discussion
1. After reading this, how did you feel? What were you thinking?
2. What do you suppose causes teachers to commit such behaviors? Have you as a student ever experienced similar behavior from a teacher?
3. What lessons are learned by the students of teachers who commit such acts as these?
4. How, as a teacher, will you handle pressures caused by mandatory achievement testing?

each item carefully enough to be reasonably confident that each item will be understood by the student in the manner that you anticipate its being understood. With the diversity of students in today's public school classroom, especially with respect to their proficiency in oral and written English language and the inclusion of students with exceptionalities, this is an especially important point. For your most important tests, such as unit tests and semester exams, ask a trusted colleague or friend to read your test for clarity and errors and to check the test's key for accuracy. Finally, after administering a test you must take time to analyze the results and reflect on the value of each item before ever using that item again.

Classification of Assessment Items

Assessment items can be classified into verbal (oral or written words), visual (pictures and diagrams), and manipulative or performance (handling of materials and equipment, performing). Written verbal items have traditionally been the items most frequently used in testing. However, visual items and visual tests are useful; for example, when working with students who lack fluency with the written word or when testing ELL students.

Performance items and tests are useful when measuring for psychomotor skill development. Common examples are performance testing of a student's ability to carry a microscope or hold a jumping rope in place (gross motor skill) or to focus a microscope or to jump rope (fine motor skill). Performance testing also can and should be part of a wider testing program that includes testing for higher level thinking skills and knowledge, as, for example, when a student or small group of students are given the problem of creating from discarded materials a habitat for an imaginary animal and then display, write about, and orally present their product to the rest of the class.

As previously noted, educators have an interest in this last described form of performance testing as a means of assessing learning that is closer to measuring for the real thing—that is authentic. In a program for teacher preparation, micro peer teaching and student teaching are examples of performance assessment; that is, assessment practices used to assess the teacher candidate's ability to teach (to perform). It seems axiomatic that assessment of student teaching is a more authentic assessment of a candidate's ability to teach than would be a written (paper-and-pencil test) or verbal (oral test) form of assessment. Although less direct and perhaps less reliable than a checklist observation and analysis of a student teacher actually teaching, an observation of a student teacher's analysis of a video-recorded episode of another teacher's performance would be another way of more authentically assessing a teacher's ability to teach than would be a simple paper-and-pencil test without the visuals provided by the video recording.

Performance Testing

Performance testing is usually more expensive and time consuming than is verbal testing, which in turn is more time demanding and expensive than is written testing. However, a good program of assessment will use alternate forms of assessment and not rely solely on one form (such as written) and one type of written item (such as multiple choice).

The type of test and items that you use depend upon your purpose and objectives. Carefully consider the alternatives within that framework. To provide validity checks and to account for the individual differences of students, an assessment program should include items from all three types. That is what writers of articles in professional journals are referring to when they talk about *alternative assessment*. They are encouraging the use of multiple assessment items, as opposed to the traditional heavy reliance on objective items, such as multiple-choice questions.

General Guidelines for Preparing for Informal Assessment of Student Learning

Every test that you create and administer to your students should represent your best professional effort. It should be clean and sans spelling and grammar errors. As already mentioned, a quickly and poorly prepared test can cause you more grief than you can imagine. One that is obviously hurriedly prepared and wrought with spelling and grammar errors will quickly be frowned upon by discerning parents or guardians. If you are a student teacher, such sloppiness and unprofessional output will certainly bring about an admonishment from your university supervisor and, if it continues, your speedy release from the teacher preparation program. Consider the following general guidelines when preparing to assess student learning:

- Ensure that all objectives or relevant standards are being measured.
- Ensure that each item is clear and unambiguous to all students.
- Ensure that each item is reliable; that it measures the intended objective. It is usually a good idea to have more than one item measuring for the same objective.
- Because it is time consuming to write the most effective assessment items, you are advised to maintain a bank of items, with each item coded according to its matching instructional objective and according to its domain of learning (cognitive, affective, or psychomotor), and perhaps according to its level within

the hierarchy of a particular domain. Another code could indicate whether the item requires thinking that is recall, processing, or application. Computer software programs are available for this. Ready-made test item banks are available and accompany many programs or textbooks. If you use them, be certain that the items match your course objectives and that they are well written. It does not follow that because they were published they are well written or match what students were supposed to have learned. When preparing items for your test bank, use your creative thinking and best writing skills. Prepare items that match your objectives, put them aside, think about them, and then work them over again.

- Include several kinds of items and assessment instruments.
- Plan each item to be difficult enough for the poorly prepared student but easy enough for the student who is well prepared.

Attaining Content Validity

To ensure that your test measures what is supposed to be measured, you can construct a table of specifications. A two-way grid indicates behavior in one dimension and content in the other (see Figures 10.6 and 10.7).

In this grid, behavior relates to the three domains: cognitive, affective, and psychomotor. In Figure 10.6, the cognitive domain is divided, according to Bloom's (1984) taxonomy, into six categories: knowledge or simple recall, comprehension, application, analysis, synthesis (often involving an original product in oral or written form), and evaluation. [Note: I tend to agree with those today who place "synthesis" last, that is,

higher than "evaluation."] The specifications table in Figure 10.6 does not specify levels within the affective and psychomotor domains.

To use a table of specifications, the teacher examining objectives for the unit decides what emphasis should be given to the behavior and to the content. For example, if vocabulary development is a concern for this sixth-grade study of matter and energy, then probably 20 percent of the test on vocabulary would be appropriate, but 50 percent would be unsuitable. This planning enables the teacher to design a test that fits the situation rather than a haphazard test that does not correspond to the objectives either in content or behavior emphasis. Because this is to be an objective test and it is so difficult to write objective items to test affective and psychomotor behaviors, this table of specifications calls for no test items in these areas. If these areas are included in the unit objectives, some other assessment devices must be used to test learning in these domains. The teacher could also show the objectives tested, as indicated within parentheses in Figure 10.6. Then, a check later on inclusion of all objectives is easy.

Preferred by some teachers is the alternative table shown in Figure 10.7. Rather than differentiating among all six of Bloom's cognitive levels, this table separates cognitive objectives into just three levels: those that require simple low-level recall of knowledge, those that require information processing, and those that require application of new knowledge. In addition, the affective and psychomotor domains each are divided into low- and high-level behaviors. A third alternative, not illustrated here, is a table of specifications that shows all levels of each of the three domains.

Figure 10.6 Table of specifications I.

CONTENT	BEHAVIORS								TOTAL
Social Studies Grade 6	*Cognitive*						Affec-tive	Psycho-motor	
Ancient Greece	**Knowledge**	**Comprehension**	**Application**	**Analysis**	**Synthesis**	**Evaluation**			
I. Vocabulary Development		2 (1, 2)	1 (2)						3
II. Concepts		2 (3, 4)	2 (4)						4
III. Applications	1 (5)	1 (5)	1 (5)	1 (5)	1 (5)	1 (5)			6
IV. Problem solving		1 (6)		1 (6)					2
TOTAL	1	6	4	2	1	1			15

Figure 10.7   Table of specifications II.

CONTENT	BEHAVIORS							TOTAL
	Cognitive			*Affective*		*Psychomotor*		
	Input	Processing	Application	Low	High	Low	High	
I.								
II.								
III.								
IV.								
TOTAL								

ASSESSMENT ITEMS: DESCRIPTIONS, EXAMPLES, AND GUIDELINES FOR PREPARING AND USING 12 TYPES

This section presents descriptions, advantages and disadvantages, and guidelines for preparing and using 12 types of assessment items. When reading about the advantages and disadvantages of each, you will notice that some types are appropriate for use in direct or performance assessment, whereas others are not.

Arrangement

Description: Terms or real objects are to be arranged in a specified order.

Example 1: Arrange the following list of events on a timeline in order of their occurrence: Maximilian I elected King of Germany; Maximilian I becomes Holy Roman Emperor; Diet of Augsburg establishes Council of Regency, divides Germany into six regions; Charles I of Spain becomes Holy Roman Emperor; Ferdinand I assumes the title of Holy Roman Emperor.

Example 2: The assortment of balls on the table represents the planets in our solar system. [Note: The balls are of various sizes, such as marbles, golf balls, tennis balls, basketballs, and so on, each labeled with a planetary name, with a large beach ball that is labeled *Sun*.] Arrange the balls in their proper order around the sun.

Advantages: This type of item tests for knowledge of sequence and order and is good for review and for starting discussions and for performance assessment. Example 2 is also an example of a performance test item.

Disadvantages: Scoring could be difficult, so be cautious, meticulous, and open to lateral thinking when using this type for grading purposes.

Guidelines for use: To enhance reliability, you may need to include instructions to students to include the rationale for their arrangement, making it a combined arrangement and short-explanation type of assessment, allowing space for explanations on an answer sheet.

Useful for small, heterogeneous group assessment to allow students to share and learn from their collaborative thinking and reasoning.

Completion Drawing

Description: An incomplete drawing is presented, and the student is to complete it.

Example 1: Connect the following items with arrow lines to show the stages from introduction of a new bill until it becomes law (items not included here).

Example 2: In the following food web (not included here), draw arrow lines indicating which organisms are consumers and which are producers.

Advantages: This type requires less time than would a complete drawing that might be required in an essay item. Scoring is relatively easy although be advised to be alert and allow for lateral thinking.

Disadvantages: Care needs to be exercised in the instructions so students do not misinterpret the expectation.

Guidelines for use: Use occasionally for diversion, but take care in preparing. This type can be instructive when assessing for student thinking and reasoning as it can measure conceptual knowledge. Consider making the item a combined completion-drawing, short-explanation type by having students include their rationales for their drawing completion. Be sure to allow space for their explanations. Useful for small, heterogeneous group assessment to allow students to share and learn from their collaborative thinking and reasoning.

Completion Statement

Description: Sometimes called a "fill-in" item, an incomplete sentence is presented and the student is to complete it by filling in the blank space(s).

Example 1: A group of words that have a special meaning, such as "a skeleton in the closet," is called a(n).
_____.

Example 2: To test their hypotheses, scientists and social scientists conduct _____.

Advantages: This type is easy to devise, take, and score.

Disadvantages: When using this type, there is a tendency to emphasize rote memory and measure procedural knowledge only. Provision of a word bank of possible answers is sometimes useful to reduce dependency on rote memory. It is difficult to write this type of item to measure conceptual knowledge and higher levels of cognition. You must be alert for a correct response different from the expected. For example, in Example 2, although the teacher's key has "experiments"as the correct answer, a student might answer the question with "investigations"or "tests"or "research"or "trials,"or some other response that is equally valid.

Guidelines for use: Use occasionally for review or for preassessment of student knowledge. Avoid using this type for grading unless you can write quality items that extend student thinking beyond mere recall. In all instances, avoid copying items verbatim from the student book. As with all types, be sure to provide adequate space for students' answers and large spaces for students with motor control difficulties. Try to use one only one blank per item. Try also to keep the blanks equal in length. Useful for small, heterogeneous group assessment to allow students to share and learn from their collaborative thinking and reasoning.

Correction

Description: This is similar to the completion type except that sentences or paragraphs are complete but with italicized or underlined words that can be changed to make the sentences correct.

Example 1: The work of the TVA was started by building sand castles. A sand castle is a wall built across a kid to stop its flow. The sand castle holds back the football so the *kids* do not overflow their backpacks and cause tears.

Example 2: 1, 1, 2, 3, 5, 8, *12*, 21, 34, *87*, 89

Advantages: Writing this type can be fun for the teacher for the purpose of preassessment of student knowledge or for review. Students may enjoy this type, especially when used only occasionally, for the tension relief afforded by the incorrect absurdities. This type is useful for introducing words with multiple meanings.

Disadvantages: As with the completion type, the correction type tends to measure for low-level recall and rote memory (although this is not necessarily the case in Example 2; if a student is unfamiliar with the Fibonacci number series in mathematics, it would be a relatively high-level question). The underlined incorrect items could be so whimsical that they might cause more class-room disturbance than you want.

Guidelines for use: Use occasionally for diversion and discussion. Try to write items that measure higher level cognition. Consider making it a combined correction, short-explanation type. Be sure to allow space for student explanations.

Essay

Description: A question or problem is presented, and the student is to compose a response in the form of sustained prose, using the student's own words, phrases, and ideas, within the limits of the question or problem.

Example 1: In the story just read, does the author elaborate the setting in great detail or barely sketch it? Explain your response.

Example 2: A healthy, green coleus plant sitting in front of you has been planted in fertile soil and sealed in a glass jar. If we place the jar on the windowsill where it will receive strong sunlight and the temperature inside the jar is maintained between 60 and 80 degrees Fahrenheit, how long do you predict the plant will live? Justify your prediction.

Advantages: This type measures conceptual knowledge and higher mental processes, such as the ability to synthesize material and express ideas in clear and precise written language. It is especially useful in integrated thematic teaching. It provides practice in written expression and can be used in performance assessment, as is the case for Example 2.

Disadvantages: Essay items require a good deal of time to read and to score. They tend to provide an unreliable sampling of achievement and are vulnerable to teacher subjectivity and unreliable scoring. Furthermore, they tend to punish the student who writes slowly and laboriously, who has limited proficiency in the written language but who may have achieved as well as a student who writes faster and is more proficient in the language. Essay items tend to favor students who have fluency with words but whose achievement may not necessarily be better. In addition, unless the students have been given instructions on the meaning of key directive verbs and how to respond to them, the teacher should not assume that all students understand such verbs (such as *explain* in the first example and *justify* in the second).

Guidelines for use:

1. When preparing an essay-only test, many questions, each requiring a relatively short prose response (see the short-explanation type, page 342), are preferable to a smaller number of questions requiring long prose responses. Briefer answers tend to be more precise, and the use of many items provides a more reliable sampling of student achievement. When preparing a short prose response, be sure to avoid using words verbatim from the student textbook.

2. Allow students adequate test time for a full response.

3. Different qualities of achievement are more likely comparable when all students must answer the same questions, as opposed to providing a list of essay items from which students may select those they answer.

4. After preparing essay items, make a tentative scoring key, deciding the key ideas you expect students to identify and how many points will be allotted to each.

5. Students should be informed about the relative test value for each item. Point values, if different for each item, can be listed in the margin of the test next to each item.

6. Inform students of the role of spelling, grammar, and sentence structure in your scoring of their essay items.

7. When reading student essay responses, read all student papers for one item at a time in one sitting, and, while doing that, make notes to yourself; then repeat and while reading that item again, score each student's paper for that item. Repeat the process for the next item, but modify the order of the pile of papers so you are not reading them in the same order read by the student. While scoring essay responses, keep in mind the nature of the objective being measured, which may or may not include the qualities of handwriting, grammar, spelling, punctuation, and neatness.

8. To nullify the "halo effect" that can occur when you know whose paper you are reading, have students put their name on the back of the paper or use a number code rather than having students put their names on essay papers, so while reading the papers, you are unaware of whose paper is being read.

9. Although having some understanding of a concept, many students are not yet facile with written expression, so you must remember to be patient, tolerant, positive, and prescriptive. Mark papers with positive and constructive comments, showing students how they could have explained or responded better.

10. Prior to using this type of test item, give instruction and practice to students in responding to key directive verbs that will be used (see Figure 10.8).

Grouping

Description: Several items are presented, and the student is to select and group those that are in some way related.

Example 1: Separate the following words into two groups (words are not included here); those that are homonyms, place in group A, and those that are not homonyms, place in group B.

Example 2: Circle the figure that is least like the others (showing a wrench, screwdriver, saw, and swing).

Advantages: This type of item tests knowledge of grouping and can be used to measure conceptual knowledge, for higher levels of cognition, and to stimulate discussion. As Example 2 shows, it can be similar to a multiple-choice type item.

Disadvantage: Remain alert for the student who has an alternative but valid rationale for her or his grouping.

Guideline for use: To allow for an alternative correct response, consider making the item a combination grouping, short-explanation type, being certain to allow adequate space to encourage student explanations.

Identification

Description: Unknown "specimens" are to be identified by name or some other criterion.

Example 1: Identify each of the plant specimens on the table by their common names.

Example 2: Identify by style each of the three poems shown on the screen.

Advantages: Verbalization (i.e., the use of abstract symbolization) is less significant, as the student is working with real materials; should be measuring for higher level learning than simple recall. The item can also be written to measure procedural understanding, such as for identification of steps in booting up a computer program. This is another useful type for authentic and performance assessments.

Disadvantages: Because of a special familiarity with the material, some students may have an advantage over others; to be fair, "specimens" used should be equally familiar or unfamiliar to all students. This type takes more time than many of the other items types, both for the teacher to prepare and for students to do.

Guidelines for use: Whatever "specimens" are used, they must be familiar to all or to none of the students, and they must be clear, not confusing (e.g., fuzzy photographs or unclear photocopies, dried and incomplete plant specimens, and garbled music recordings can be confusing and frustrating to try and discern). Consider using dyad or team rather than individual testing.

Matching

Description: Students are to match related items from a list of numbered items to a list of lettered choices or in some way connect those items that are the same or related. Or, to eliminate the paper-and-pencil aspect and make the item more direct, use an item such as "Of the materials on the table, pair up those that are most alike."

Example 1: In the blank space next to each description in Column A (stem or premises column), put the letter of the correct answer from Column B (answer or response column).

Figure 10.8   Meaning of key directive verbs for essay item responses.

Compare asks for an analysis of similarity and difference, but with a greater emphasis on similarities or likenesses.

Contrast asks more for differences than for similarities.

Criticize asks for the good and bad of an idea or situation.

Define means to express clearly and concisely the meaning of a term, as from a dictionary or in the student's own words.

Diagram means to put quantities or numerical values into the form of a chart, graph, or drawing.

Discuss means to explain or argue, presenting various sides of events, ideas, or situations.

Enumerate means to name or list one after another, which is different from "explain briefly" or "tell in a few words."

Evaluate means to express worth, value, and judgment.

Explain means to describe, with emphasis on cause and effect.

Generalize means to arrive at a valid generalization from provided specific information.

Identify means to state recognizable or identifiable characteristics.

Infer means to forecast what is likely to happen as a result of information provided.

Illustrate means to describe by means of examples, figures, pictures, or diagrams.

Interpret means to describe or explain a given fact, theory, principle, or doctrine within a specific context.

Justify means to show reasons, with an emphasis on correct, positive, and advantageous.

List means just that, to simply name items in a category or to include them in a list, without much description.

Outline means to give a short summary with headings and subheadings.

Prove means to present materials as witnesses, proof, and evidence.

Relate means to tell how specified things are connected or brought into some kind of relationship.

Summarize means to recapitulate the main points without examples or illustrations.

Trace means to follow a history or series of events, step by step, by going backward over the evidence.

A (Stem Column)	B (Answer Column)
____ 1. Current president of the United States	A. George W. Bush
____ 2. Most recent past president of the United States	B. Barack Obama
____ 3. U.S. president at the conclusion of WW II	C. Thomas Jefferson
____ 4. First president of the United States	D. Harry S. Truman
	E. George Washington

Column A	Column B
ann/enn	conquer
auto	large
min	self
vic/vinc	small
	year

Advantages: Matching items can measure ability to judge relationships and to differentiate between similar facts, ideas, definitions, and concepts. They are easy to score and can test a broad range of content. They reduce guessing, especially if one group (e.g., answer column) contains more items than the other, are interesting to students, and are adaptable for performance assessment.

Example 2: Match items in Column A (stem column) to those of Column B (answer column) by drawing lines connecting the matched pairs.

Disadvantages: Although the matching item is adaptable for performance assessment, items are not easily adapted to measure higher cognition. Because all parts must be homogeneous, it is possible that clues will be given, thus reducing item validity.

Guidelines for use: The number of items in the response or answer column should exceed the number in the stem or premises column. The number of items in the stem column to be matched should not exceed 10. Less is better. Matching sets should have high homogeneity (i.e., items in both columns or groups should be of the same general category; avoid, for example, mixing dates, events, and names). Answers in the response column should be kept short, one or two words each, and ordered logically, such as alphabetically. If answers from the response column can be used more than once, and that is advised to avoid guessing by elimination, the directions should so state. Be prepared for the laterally thinking student who can legitimately defend an "incorrect" response. To eliminate the paper-and-pencil aspect and make the item more direct, use an item such as "of the materials on the table, pair up those that are most alike."

Multiple Choice

Description: This type is similar to the completion item in that statements are presented (the stem), sometimes in incomplete form, but with several options or alternatives, requiring recognition or even higher cognitive processes rather than mere recall.

Example 1: Of four cylinders with the following dimensions, the one that would cause the highest pitched sound would be

a. 4 inches long and 3 inches in diameter
b. 8 inches long and 3 inches in diameter
c. 4 inches long and 1 inch in diameter
d. 8 inches long and 1 inch in diameter

Example 2: Which one of the following is a pair of antonyms?

a. loud–soft
b. halt–finish
c. absolve–vindicate
d. procure–purchase

Advantages: Items can be answered and scored quickly. A wide range of content and higher levels of cognition can be tested in a relatively short time. This type is excellent for all testing purposes—motivation, review, and assessment of learning.

Disadvantages: Unfortunately, because multiple-choice items are relatively easy to write, there is a tendency to write items measuring only for low levels of cognition. Multiple-choice items are excellent for major testing, but it takes care and time to write quality questions that measure higher levels of thinking and learning.

Guidelines for use:

1. If the item is in the form of an incomplete statement, it should be meaningful in itself and imply a direct question rather than merely lead into a collection of unrelated true and false statements.

2. Use a level of language that is easy enough for even the poorest readers and those with limited proficiency in English to understand; avoid unnecessary wordiness.

3. If there is much variation in the length of alternatives, arrange the alternatives in order from the shortest to the longest (i.e., first alternative is the shortest, last alternative is the longest). For single-word alternatives, consistent use of arrangement of alternatives is recommended, such as by length of answer or alphabetically.

4. Arrangement of alternatives should be uniform throughout the test and listed in vertical (column) form rather than in horizontal (paragraph) form.

5. If there is more than one correct response, then students should be instructed to identify all responses they believe are correct. Questions that have more than a single correct response should be worth more than one point each, such as a point for each correct response.

6. Incorrect responses (distracters) should be plausible and related to the same concept as the correct alternative. Although an occasional humorous distracter, may help relieve test anxiety, along with absurd distracters they should generally be avoided. They offer no measuring value and increase the likelihood of the student guessing the correct response.

7. It is not necessary to maintain a fixed number of alternatives for every item, but the use of less than three is not recommended. Although it is not always possible to come up with four or five plausible responses, the use of four or five reduces chance responses and guessing, thereby increasing reliability for the item. If you cannot think of enough plausible distracters, include the item on a test the first time as a completion item. As students respond, wrong answers will provide you with a number of plausible distracters that you can use the next time to make the item a multiple-choice type item.

8. Some students may work better when allowed to circle their selected response rather than writing its letter or number in a blank space.

9. Responses such as "all of these" or "none of these" should be used only when they will contribute

more than another plausible distracter. Care must be taken that such responses answer or complete the item. "All of the above" is a poorer alternative than "none of the above" because items that use it as a correct response need to have four or five correct answers; also, if it is the right answer, knowledge of any two of the distracters will cue it.

10. Every item should be grammatically consistent. For example, if the stem is in the form of an incomplete sentence, it should be possible to complete the sentence by attaching any of the alternatives to it.

11. The stem should state a single and specific point.

12. The stem must mean the same thing to every student.

13. The item should be expressed in positive form. A negative form can present a psychological disadvantage to students. Negative items are those that ask what is *not* characteristic of something or what is the *least* useful. Discard the item if you cannot express it in positive terminology.

14. The stem must not include clues that would clue the correct alternative. For example,
    A four-sided figure whose opposite sides are parallel is called _____
    a. a triangle
    b. an octagon
    c. a trapezoid
    d. a parallelogram
    Use of the word *parallel* clues the answer.

15. There must be only one correct or best response. However, this is easier said than done (refer to guideline 20).

16. Measuring for understanding of definitions is better tested by furnishing the name or word and requiring choice between alternative definitions than by presenting the definition and requiring choice between alternative words.

17. Avoid using alternatives that include absolute terms such as *never* and *always*.

18. Multiple-choice items need not be entirely verbal. Consider the use of realia, charts, diagrams, videos, and other visuals. They will make the test more interesting, especially to students with low verbal abilities or to those who have limited proficiency in English, and, consequently, they will make the assessment more direct.

19. Once you have composed a series of multiple-choice items or a test comprised completely of this item type, tally the position of answers to be sure they are evenly distributed, to avoid the common psychological habit (when there are four alternatives) of having the correct alternative in the third position. In other words, when alternative choices are A, B, C, and D, or 1, 2, 3, and 4, unless the test designer is aware and avoids it, more correct answers will be in the "C" or "3" position than in any other.

20. Consider providing space between test items for students to include their rationales for their response selections, thus making the test a combination multiple-choice and short-explanation item type. This provides for the measurement of higher levels of cognition and encourages writing. It provides for the student who can rationalize an alternative that you had not considered plausible, especially possible today with the diversity of cultural experiences represented by students. For example, I recall the story of the math question on a test that asked if a farmer saw eight crows sitting on a fence and shot three of them, how many would be left. Of course, the "correct" response on the answer key was five. However, one critical thinking student chose "none" as his response, an answer that was marked "wrong" by the teacher. However, the student was thinking that those crows that weren't shot would be frightened and would all fly away, thus he selected "none" as his answer.

21. While scoring, on a blank copy of the test, for each item tally the incorrect responses. Analyze incorrect responses for each item to discover potential errors in your scoring key. If, for example, many students select B for an item for which your key says the correct answer is A, you may have made a mistake on your scoring key or in teaching the lesson.

22. Sometimes teachers attempt to discourage cheating by preparing several versions of the multiple-choice exam with the questions in different order. This could be giving one group of students an unfair advantage if the order of their questions are in the same sequence in which the information was originally presented and learned and for another group of students the questions are in a random order. To avoid this, questions should be in random order on every version of the exam.

Performance

Description: Provided with certain conditions or materials, the student solves a problem or accomplishes some other action.

Example 1: Write a retelling of your favorite fable and create a diorama to accompany it.

Example 2: (As a culminating project for a unit on sound, groups of students were challenged to design and make their own musical instruments.) The performance assessment included the following:

1. Play your instrument for the class.
2. Show us the part of the instrument that makes the sound.

3. Describe the function of other parts of your instrument.
4. Demonstrate how you change the pitch of the sound.
5. Share with us how you made your instrument.

Example 3: Demonstrate your understanding of diffusion by designing and completing an experiment using only those chemicals and materials located at this learning station.

Example 4: Measure and calculate to the nearest centimeter the "within bounds only"square footage of our football playing field.

Advantages: Performance test item types come closer to direct measurement (authentic assessment) of certain expected outcomes than do most other types. As has been indicated in discussions of the preceding question types, other types of questions can actually be prepared as performance-type items, that is, where the student actually does what he or she is being tested for.

Disadvantages: This type can be difficult and time consuming to administer to a group of students. Adequate supply of materials could be a problem. Scoring may tend to be subjective. It could be difficult to give makeup tests to students who were absent.

Guidelines for use: Use your creativity to design and use performance tests, as they tend to measure well the important objectives. To set up a performance assessment situation, see the instructions in Figure 10.9. To reduce subjectivity in scoring, prepare distinct scoring guidelines (rubrics), as was discussed in scoring essay-type items and as shown in Figures 10.10 and 10.11.

Short Explanation

Description: The short explanation question is like the essay type but requires a shorter answer.

Example 1: Briefly explain in a paragraph how you would end the story.

Example 2: Briefly explain why organ pipes are made to vary in length.

Figure 10.9   Procedure for setting up a performance assessment situation.

1. Specify the performance objective.
2. Specify the test conditions.
3. Establish the standards or criteria (scoring rubric) for judging the quality of the process and/or product.
4. Prepare directions in writing, outlining the situation, with instructions that the students are to follow.
5. Share the procedure with a colleague for feedback before using it with students.

Advantages: As with the essay type, student understanding is assessed, but this type takes less time for the teacher to read and to score. By using several questions of this type, a greater amount of content can be covered than with a lesser number of essay questions. This type of question is good practice for students to learn to express themselves succinctly in writing.

Disadvantages: Some students will have difficulty expressing themselves in a limited fashion or in writing. They need practice, coaching, and time.

Guidelines for use: This type is useful for occasional reviews and quizzes and as an alternative to other types of questions. For scoring, establish a scoring rubric and follow the same guidelines as for the essay-type item.

True–False

Description: A statement is presented that students are to judge as being accurate or not.

Example 1: A suffix is any bound morpheme added to the end of a root word. T or F?

Example 2: Christopher Columbus discovered America in 1492. T or F?

Advantages: Many items can be answered in a relatively short time, making broad content coverage possible. Scoring is quick and simple. True–false items are good as discussion starters, for review, and for diagnostic evaluation (preassessment) of what students already know or think they know.

Disadvantages: It is sometimes difficult to write true–false items that are purely true or false or without qualifying them in such a way that clues the answer. In the second sample question, for example, the student may question whether Columbus really did discover America or misunderstand the meaning of "discovering America."Weren't there people already there when he landed? Where, in fact, did he land? What is meant by "America"? Example 2 is poor also because it tests for more than one idea—Columbus, America, and 1492.

Much of the content that most easily lends itself to the true–false type of test item is trivial. Students have a 50 percent chance of guessing the correct answer, thus giving this item type both *poor validity* and *poor reliability*. Scoring and grading give no clue about why the student missed an item. Consequently, the disadvantages of true–false items far outweigh the advantages; *pure true–false items should not be used for arriving at grades.* For grading purposes, you may use modified true–false items (see guideline 11 that follows), where space is provided between items for students to write in their explanations, thus making the item a combined true–false, short-explanation type.

Guidelines for use:

1. For preparing a false statement, first write the statement as a true statement, then make it false by changing a word or phrase.

Figure 10.10 Sample scoring rubric for student project presentation. Possible score = 100. Scorer marks a relevant square in each of the six categories (the horizontal rows), and the student's score for that category is the number within that square. (*Source*: Elk Grove School District, Elk grove, California.)

Professional Presentation	**14–15** Well organized; smooth transitions between sections; all enthusiastically participate and share responsibility.	**12–13** Well organized with transitions, students confer/present ideas; group shows ability to interact; attentive discussion of research.	**11** Shows basic organization; lacks transitions; some interaction; discussion focuses mostly on research.	**1–10** Unorganized, lacks planning; no transitions; reliance on spokesperson; little interaction; disinterest; too brief.
Engagement of Audience	**14–15** Successfully and actively engages audience in more than one pertinent activity; maintains interest throughout.	**12–13** Engages audience in at least one related activity; maintains attention through most of presentation.	**11** Attempts to engage audience in at least one activity; no attempt to involve entire audience. May not relate in significant way.	**1–10** Fails to involve audience; does not maintain audience's attention; no connection with audience. No relationship between activity and topic.
Use of Literature	**18–20** Strong connection between literature and topic; significant, perceptive explanation of literature; pertinent to topic. At least two pieces used.	**16–17** Clear connection between literature and topic; clear explanation; appropriate to topic. Two pieces used.	**14–15** Weak connection to topic; unclear explanation; one genre; one piece used.	**1–13** No connection to topic; no explanation; inappropriate literature; no literature.
Knowledge of Subject	**18–20** Strong understanding of topic; knowledge factually relevant, accurate, and consistent; solution shows analysis of evidence.	**16–17** Good understanding of topic; uses main points of information researched; builds solution or examination of major evidence.	**14–15** Shows general understanding; focuses on one aspect, discusses at least one other idea; uses research, attempts to add to it; solution refers to evidence.	**1–13** Little understanding or comprehension of topic; uses little basic information researched; forms minimal solution; relies on solely own opinions without support.
Use of Media	**18–20** Effectively combines and integrates three distinct forms with one original piece; enhances understanding; offers insight into topic.	**16–17** Combines two forms with one original piece; relates to topic; connection between media and topic is explained.	**14–15** Includes two or three forms but no original piece; media relates to topic. Explanation may be vague or missing.	**1–13** On form; no original piece; connection between media and topic is unclear.
Speaking Skills	**9–10** Clear enunciation; strong projection; vocal variety; eye contact with entire audience; presentation posture; solid focus with no interruptions.	**8** Good enunciation; adequate projection; partial audience eye contact; appropriate posture.	**7** Inconsistent enunciation; low projection with little vocal variety; inconsistent posture.	**1–6** Difficult to understand; inaudible; monotonous; no eye contact; inappropriate posture; interruptions and distractions.

Figure 10.11   Sample scoring rubric for student research paper. Possible score = 100. Scorer marks a relevant square in each of the six categories (the horizontal rows), and the student's score for that category is the number within that square. (*Source*: Elk Grove School District, Elk grove, California.)

	14–15	12–13	11	1–10
Parenthetical References	All documented correctly. Paper's references document a wide variety of sources cited—at least five from bibliography.	Most documented correctly. Few minor errors. At least three sources from bibliography are cited.	Some documented correctly. Some show no documentation at all. May not correlate to the bibliography.	Few to none are documented. Does not correlate to the bibliography. May be totally absent.
	14–15	**12–13**	**11**	**1–10**
Bibliography and Sources	Strong use of library research. Exceeds minimum of five sources. Bibliography is correctly formatted.	Good use of library research. Exceeds minimum of five sources. Bibliography has few or no errors in format.	Some use of library research. Meets minimum of five sources. Bibliography is present but may be problematic.	Fails to meet minimum standards for library research. Bibliography has major flaws or may be missing.
	14–15	**12–13**	**11**	**1–10**
Mechanics/Format	Correct format and pagination. Neat title page, near-perfect spelling, punctuation, and grammar.	Mostly correct format and pagination. Neat. Few errors in title page, spellings, punctuation, and grammar.	Errors in format and pagination. Flawed title page. Distracting errors in spelling, punctuation, and grammar.	Incorrect format. Title page is flawed or missing. Many errors in spelling, punctuation, and grammar. Lack of planning is obvious. Paper is difficult to read.
	9–10	**8**	**7**	**1–6**
Thesis	An original and comprehensive thesis that is clear and well thought out. All sections work to support it.	Comprehensive and well-focused thesis, which is clearly stated. All sections work to support it.	Adequate thesis that is understandable but may be neither clear nor focused. It covers the majority of the issues found in the sections.	Inadequate thesis that is disconnected from the research or may be too broad to support. May be convoluted, confusing, or absent.
	18–20	**16–17**	**14–15**	**1–13**
Completeness/ Coherence	Paper reads as a unified whole. There is no repetition of information. All sections are in place, and transitions between them are clearly developed.	Paper reads as a unified whole with no repetition. All sections are in place, but transitions between them are not as smooth.	Paper has required sections. Repetitions may be evident. The paper does not present a unified whole. Transitions are missing or inadequate.	Paper lacks one or more sections and makes no attempt to connect sections as a whole unit. Sections may be grossly repetitive or contradictory.
	23–25	**20–22**	**18–19**	**1–16**
Thinking/Analyzing	Strong understanding of the topic. Knowledge is factually relevant, accurate, and consistent. Solutions show analysis of research discussed in paper.	Good understanding of the topic. Uses main points of information researched. Solutions build on examination of research discussed in paper.	General understanding of topic. Uses research and attempts to add to it; solutions refer to some of the research discussed.	Little understanding of topic. Uses little basic information researched. Minimal examination of the topic. Solutions may be based solely on own opinions, without support.

2. Try to avoid using negative statements, because they tend to confuse students.

3. A true–false statement should include only one idea.

4. Use close to an equal number of true and false items.

5. Try to avoid using specific determiners (e.g., "always," "all,"or "none"), because they usually clue that the statement is false. Also avoid words that may clue that the statement is true (e.g., "often," "probably,"and "sometimes").

6. Avoid words that may have different meanings for different students.

7. Avoid using verbatim language from the student textbook.

8. Avoid trick items, such as a slight reversal of numbers in a date.

9. Rather than using symbols for the words *true* and *false* (sometimes teachers use symbols such as + and –) which might be confusing, or having students write the letters *T* and *F* (sometimes a student does not write the letters clearly enough for the teacher to be able to distinguish which it is), have students either write out the words true and false or, better yet, have them simply circle T and F in the left margin of each item as indicated by the two examples provided.

10. Proofread your items (or have a friend do it) to be sure that the sentences are well constructed and are free from typographical errors.

11. To avoid "wrong"answers, caused by variations in thinking, and to make the item more valid and reliable, students should be encouraged to write in their rationale for selecting true or false, making the item a *modified true–false* item. For example,

    When a farmer saw eight crows sitting on the fence surrounding his cornfield, he shot three of them. Five were left on the fence. T or F? _____

    Explanation: _____

    _____

    _____

As stated earlier, for grading purposes, you may use modified true–false items, thus making the item a combined true–false, short-explanation type and allowing for divergent and critical thinking. Another form of modified true–false item is the "sometimes-always-never"item, where a third alternative, "sometimes,"is introduced to reduce the chance for guessing.

Now, depending on course instructions, do Exercise 10.1 (at end of this chapter) to start the development of your skill in writing assessment items. As you work on Exercise 10.1, you may want to correlate it with your previous work on Exercises 4.12, 5.2A, and 5.3.

TIME FOR A FUN BREAK—SPEAKING OF LATERAL THINKING

The following are reported to be children's answers to a teacher's questions.

1. Q: Name the four seasons. A: Salt, pepper, mustard, and vinegar.

2. Q: How is dew formed? A: The sun shines down on the leaves and makes them sweat.

3. Q: How can you delay milk turning sour? A: Keep it in the cow.

4. Q: Name a major disease associated with cigarette smoking. A: Premature death.

5. Q: What is the meaning of "varicose"? A: Nearby.

6. Q: What is the meaning of "benign"? A: It is what you will be after you be eight.

7. Teacher: Maria, go to the map and find North America.

   Maria: Here it is.
   Teacher: Correct. Now, Mark, who discovered America?
   Mark: Maria.

8. Teacher: John, why are you doing your math on the floor?

   John: You told me to do it without using tables.

9. Teacher: Donald, what is the chemical formula for water?

   Donald: H I J K L M N O
   Teacher: No that's wrong.
   Donald: But yesterday you said it's H to O.

10. Teacher: Andrew, what do you call a person who keeps on talking when no one is listening.

    Andrew: A teacher.

REPORTING STUDENT ACHIEVEMENT

One of your responsibilities as a classroom teacher is to report student progress in achievement to parents or guardians as well as to the school administration for record keeping. In some schools, the reporting is of student progress and effort as well as of achievement. As described in the discussions that follow, reporting is done in at least two, and sometimes more, ways. However, for secondary schools, letter grades on electronic reports are the usual method for reporting student learning.

The Grade Report

Periodically, a grade report is issued (generally from four to six times a year, depending upon the school, its purpose, and its type of scheduling). Grade reports may be recorded and distributed electronically via a classroom management system such as provided by ProgressBook, (www.progressbook.com), or paper reports are distributed to students during an advisory period or they may be mailed to the student's home. Whichever means of distribution is used, this grade report represents an achievement grade (formative assessment). The final report of the semester is also the semester grade, and for courses that are only one semester long it is the final grade (summative assessment). In essence, the first and sometimes second reports are progress notices; the semester grade is the one that is transferred to the student's transcript of records.

In addition to the student's academic achievement, you must report the student's social behaviors (classroom conduct) while in your classroom. Whichever reporting form is used, you must separate your assessments of a student's social behaviors from the student's academic achievement. Academic achievement (or accomplishment) is represented by a letter (sometimes a number) grade (A through E or F, or E, S, and U, or 1 to 5, and sometimes with minuses and pluses) and the social behavior by a "satisfactory"or an "unsatisfactory"(or by more specific items) or supplemented by teacher-written or computer-generated comments. There may also be a place on the reporting form for teachers to check whether basic grade-level standards have been met, especially in reading and mathematics. [Note: In some states, reporting to parents/guardians of a child's standardized achievement testing results is done by a centralized reporting agency and is outside the individual teacher's or school's responsibility.]

TEACHER–PARENTAL/GUARDIAN CONNECTIONS

Study after study shows that when parents or guardians are involved in their child's school and school work, students learn better and earn better grades, and teachers experience more positive feelings about teaching. As a result, schools constantly are searching for improved ways to communicate with and to involve parents/guardians.

Contacting Parents/Guardians

Whenever preparing to establish contact with parents and guardians, try to discover before the contact is made any pertinent information you might need about the home situation, such as, for example, whether there are language barriers or cultural differences you should be aware of, something you can learn about from that first assignment you give students (see Chapter 3).

Although it is not always obligatory, some teachers purposefully contact parents or guardians over telephone or by email, especially when a student has shown a sudden turn for either the worse or the better in academic achievement or in classroom behavior. That initiative and contact by the teacher are usually welcomed by parents/guardians and can lead to productive conferences with the teacher. An electronic conference (telephone or email) can save valuable time for both the teacher and the parent/guardian.

Another way of contacting parents/guardians is by letter. Contacting a child's parent/guardian by letter gives time to think and to make clear your thoughts and concerns to that parent/guardian and to invite them to respond at their convenience by letter, over phone, or by arranging to have a conference with you.

In absence of a computer-link assignment/progress report hotline, or in addition to that, most schools have a progress report form that, upon request by a parent/guardian, can be sent home as often as agreed upon by the teacher and the parent/guardian.

Meeting Parents/Guardians

You will meet some of the parents/guardians early in the school year during "back-to-school"night (or "Meet the Teacher"or "Curriculum"night as it is variously called) and throughout the year in individual conferences and later in the year during spring open house. For the beginning teacher, these meetings with parents/guardians can be anxious times. The following paragraphs provide guidelines to help you with those experiences.

Back-to-school (or Meet the Teacher or Curriculum) night is the evening early in the school year when parents and guardians come to the school and meet their children's teachers. The parents and guardians arrive either at the student's home base or in the auditorium for a greeting and a few words from various school officials and then proceed through a simulation of their child's school day; as a group, they meet each class and each teacher for a few minutes. Later, in the spring, many schools host an "open house"where parents and guardians may have more time to talk individually with teachers, although the major purpose of the open house is for the school and teachers to celebrate and display the work and progress of the students.

At back-to-school night, parents/guardians are eager to learn as much as they can about their children's teachers. You will meet each group of parents/guardians for a brief time, usually about 10 minutes. During that meeting, you will provide them with a copy of the course syllabus, make some straightforward remarks about yourself, and talk about the course, its requirements, your expectations of the students, and how they, the parents and guardians, might help.

Although there will be precious little time for questions from the parents/guardians, during your introduction the adults will be delighted to learn that you have your program well planned, are a "task master,"appreciate their interest, and welcome their participation. They will be happy to hear your willingness to communicate with them. Parents/guardians will be pleased to know that you are "from the school of the three Fs"—that is, that you are firm, friendly, and fair. For any parent/guardian who indicates an urgent need to talk with you as soon as possible, try to schedule a mutually convenient private conference time in person or via telephone for later that evening or during the next few days.

Specifically, parents/guardians will expect to learn about your curriculum—goals and objectives, any long-term projects, class size, schedules for tests, and grading procedures. They will want to know what you expect of them: Will there be homework, and if so, to what extent, if any, should they help their child with it? [Note: The answer to the preceding question is in the nature of the help given; parents and other family members should encourage and help facilitate their children doing homework, but they should be careful, however, not to actually do the homework for their child (Marzano, Pickering, & Pollock, 2001).] How can parents/guardians contact you? Try to anticipate other questions. Your principal, department chair, or colleagues can be of aid in helping you anticipate and prepare for these questions. Of course, you can never prepare for the question or comment that comes from left field. Just remain calm and avoid being flustered (or at least appear so). Ten minutes will fly by quickly, and parents and guardians will be reassured to know you have things under control.

Parent/Guardian Conference

When meeting parents or guardians for conferences, you should be as specific as possible when explaining to a parent/guardian the progress of that adult's child in your class. And, again, express your appreciation for their interest. Be helpful to his or her understanding, and do not saturate the parent/guardian with more information than needed. Resist any tendency to talk too much. Allow time for the parent or guardian to ask questions. Keep your answers succinct. Never compare one student with another or with the rest of the class. If the parent or guardian asks a question for which you do not have an answer, tell the person you will try to find an answer and will phone him or her as quickly as you can, and do it. Have the student's portfolio and other work with you during the parent/guardian conference so you can show the parent/guardian examples of what is being discussed. Also, have your grade book on hand, or a computer printout of it, but be prepared to protect from the person the names and records of the other students.

Sometimes it is helpful to have a three-way conference, a conference with the parent or guardian, the student, and you, or a conference with the parent/guardian, the principal or counselor, and several or all of the student's teachers. If, especially as a beginning teacher, you would like the presence of an administrator or school counselor at a parent/guardian–teacher conference as backup, do not be hesitant to arrange that.

Some educators prefer a *student-led conference,* arguing the advantages resulting from increased student involvement, student goal setting, student reflection, and student responsibility (Conderman, Ikan, & Hatcher, 2000). Another school reports that when students were put in charge of the conferences, parent/guardian attendance at conferences more than doubled (Farber, 1999). Typically, with student-led conferences, students also prepare and share their individual portfolios (Roberts, 2000).

When a parent/guardian asks how she or he may help in the student's learning, the paragraphs that follow offer suggestions for your consideration. Many schools have made special and successful efforts to link home and school. At some schools, through homework hotlines, parents/guardians have phone access to their children's assignment specifications and to their progress in their schoolwork, and parents and guardians with a personal computer and a modem have access to tutorial services to assist students with assignments.

Helping students become critical thinkers is one of the aims of education and one that parents and guardians can help with by reinforcing the strategies being used in the classroom. Ways to do this are to ask "what if"questions; think aloud as a model for the student's thinking development; encourage the student's own metacognition by asking questions such as "How did you arrive at that conclusion?"or "How do you feel about your conclusion now?"and asking these questions about the student's everyday social interactions, topics that are important to the student. Ask the student to elaborate on his or her ideas, accepting that fact that the student may make mistakes, but encourage the student to learn from them.

Dealing with an Angry Parent or Guardian

If a parent or guardian is angry or hostile toward you and the school, the paragraphs that follow offer guidelines for dealing with that hostility.

Remain calm and positive in your discussion with the adult, allowing the parent or guardian to talk out his or her hostility while you say very little; usually, the less you say, the better off you will be. What you do say must be objective and to the point of the student's work in your classroom. The parent or guardian may just need to vent frustrations that might have very little to do with you, the school, or even the student.

Do *not* allow yourself to be intimidated, put on the defensive, or backed into a verbal corner. If the parent/guardian tries to do so by attacking you personally, do not press your defense at this point. Perhaps the parent/guardian has made a point that you should take time to consider, and now is a good time to arrange for another conference with the parent/guardian for about a week later. In a follow-up conference, if the parent/guardian agrees, you may want to consider bringing in a mediator, such as another member of your teaching team, an administrator, or a school counselor.

Just as with your students, put up with no foul language from the adult, letting the parent/guardian know that if it continues, the conversation is over. Always know where the nearest adult is, so if help is needed, you know how to quickly get it. If at all you feel physically threatened, cut the conversation off, reminding the person that it is a felony, misdemeanor to cause a disruption at school, and that if the feeling of being threatened continues, you will call security.

You must *not* talk about other students; keep the conversation focused on the progress of this parent or guardian's child. The adult is not your rival, or should not be. You both share a concern for the academic and emotional well-being of the child. Use your best skills in critical thinking and problem solving, trying to focus the discussion by identifying the problem, defining it, and then arriving at some decision about how mutually to go about solving it. To this end, you may need to ask for help from a third party, such as the student's school counselor. If agreed to by the parent, please take that step.

Parents and guardians do *not* need to hear about how busy you are, about your personal problems, or about how many other students you are dealing with on a daily basis, unless, of course, a parent or guardian asks. Parents and guardians expect you to be a capable professional who knows what to do and is doing it.

SUMMARY

Assessment is an integral and ongoing factor in the teaching–learning process; consequently, this chapter has emphasized the importance of your including the following in your teaching performance:

- Using a variety of instruments to collect a body of evidence to most reliably assess the learning of students that focus on their individual development.
- Basing assessments on the target objectives and material that has been taught.
- Considering your assessment and grading procedures carefully, planning them, and explaining your policies to the students and, when relevant, to parents/guardians.

- Involving students in the assessment process; keeping students informed of their progress.
- Maintaining accurate and clear records of assessment results so that you will have ample data on which to base your judgmental decisions about achievement.
- Returning tests and other papers promptly, reviewing answers to all questions, and responding to inquiries about marks given.
- Striving for objective and impartial assessment.
- Trying to minimize confusion about grades, cheating, and teacher subjectivity by involving students in the planning, reinforcing individual student development, and providing an accepting and stimulating learning environment.

QUESTIONS FOR CLASS DISCUSSION

1. Investigate various ways that schools in your geographic area are experimenting with assessing and reporting student achievement. In what ways, if any, have those assessing and reporting methods changed as a result of mandated standardized achievement testing? Share what you find with your classmates. With your classmates, discuss the pros and cons of various systems of assessing and reporting.

2. Other than a paper-and-pencil test, identify alternative techniques for assessing student learning during or after completion of an instructional unit.

3. When using a point system for determining student grades, is it educationally defensible to give a student a higher grade than that student's points call for? A lower grade? Give your rationale for your answers.

4. Describe any student learning activities or situations that you believe should not be graded but should or could be used for assessment of student learning.

5. Do you believe that student scores on state-mandated achievement tests adequately portray the success or failure of a particular school? Of a particular teacher? Explain why or why not.

 Now go to Topic #6: **Assessment** in the MyEducationLab (www.myeducationlab.com) for your course, where you can:

- Find learning outcomes for this topic along with the national standards that connect to these outcomes.
- Complete Assignments and Activities that can help you more deeply understand the chapter content.
- Apply and practice your understanding of the core teaching skills identified in the chapter with the Building Teaching Skills and Dispositions learning units.

EXERCISE 10.1   PREPARING ASSESSMENT ITEMS

INSTRUCTIONS: The purpose of this exercise is to practice your skill in preparing the different types of assessment items discussed previously. You may want to correlate it with your previous work on Exercises 4.12, 5.2A, and 5.3. For use in your own teaching, select one specific instructional objective and write assessment items for it. When completed, share this exercise with your colleagues for their feedback.

Objective: _____

Grade and subject: _____

1. Arrangement item: _____

   _____

   _____

   _____

2. Completion drawing item: _____

   _____

   _____

   _____

   _____

3. Completion statement item: _____

   _____

   _____

   _____

   _____

4. Correction item: _____

   _____

   _____

   _____

   _____

5. Essay item: _____

   _____

   _____

   _____

   _____

6. Grouping item: _____

   _____

   _____

   _____

☞

EXERCISE 10.1 *(continued)*

7. Identification item: _____

_____

_____

_____

8. Matching item: _____

_____

_____

_____

_____

9. Multiple-choice item: _____

_____

_____

_____

_____

10. Performance item: _____

_____

_____

_____

_____

11. Short-explanation item: _____

_____

_____

_____

_____

12. *Modified* true–false item: _____

_____

_____

_____

_____

11

Professional Development:

A Continuing Process

While most of us are not born with innate teaching skills, teaching skills can be learned and steadily improved. Teachers who wish to improve their teaching can do so, and in addition to this book, there are many resources that can help.

This final chapter addresses the assessment and continued development of your effectiveness as a classroom teacher, a process that continues throughout your professional career. Teaching is such an electrifying profession that it is not easy to remain energetic and to stay abreast of changes and trends that result from transformations in society and from research and practice. To become and remain an alert and competent teacher, your effort to do so will need to be unremitting and resolute.

Whether you are a beginning or an experienced teacher, one way to collect data and to improve your effectiveness is through periodic assessment of your teaching performance, either by an evaluation of your teaching in the real classroom or, if you are in a program of teacher preparation, by a technique called micro peer teaching. The latter is the focus of the final section of this chapter and is an example of a type of final performance (authentic) assessment for this resource guide.

Specifically, upon completion of this chapter, you should be able to:

1. Demonstrate knowledge about the field components of teacher preparation.
2. Demonstrate knowledge of how to find a teaching job.
3. Demonstrate knowledge of how to remain an alert and effective classroom teacher throughout your teaching career.

4. Demonstrate competency in lesson planning and implementation of that lesson to peers.
5. Demonstrate ability to self-evaluate and reflect on your teaching.

> It's a big mistake to think that teaching is what we do every day and professional development is an occasional seminar or workshop or institute. No! The job is professional development, and professional development is the job.
>
> Anthony Alvarado (1998)

PROFESSIONAL DEVELOPMENT THROUGH STUDENT TEACHING OR INTERNSHIP

Beginning teachers today enter the profession via one of two ways. Most enter through college or university teacher preparation programs where they experience student teaching. Some new teachers are hired by school districts as teaching interns. Teaching interns may or may not be affiliated with a college or university program of teacher preparation, but just as student teachers, interns too are working on obtaining their permanent teaching credential. Unlike student teachers, interns are being paid to teach. Whether a student teacher or an intern, this section is for you.

You are excited about the prospect of being assigned as a student teacher or as a teaching intern to your first classroom, but you are also concerned. Questions linger in your mind. Will your host (cooperating) teachers like you? Will you get along? Will the students accept you? Will you be assigned to the school, grade level, and subjects you want? What will the students be like? Will there be many classroom management problems? What about special education students and students with limited English proficiency? Your questions will be unending.

Indeed, you should be excited and concerned, for this practical field experience is one of the most significant and important facets of your program of teacher preparation. In some programs, this practical field experience is planned as a co-experience with the college or university theory classes. In other programs, student teaching is the culminating experience. In still other programs, beginning teachers are hired as full- or part-time teaching interns while they are working on their teaching credential. Different sequences are represented in different programs. For example, at some colleges, student teaching extends over two or three semesters. In other programs, teacher candidates first take a theory class followed by a full second semester of student teaching. Regardless of when and how your student teaching or teaching internship occurs, the experience is a bright and shining opportunity to hone your teaching skills in a real classroom. During this time, you will be supported by either a college or a university supervisor or by one or more carefully selected cooperating teachers, or in many instances by both, who will share their expertise.

Everyone concerned in the teacher preparation program—your cooperating teacher, your university instructors, the school administrators, and your university supervisor—realizes that this is your practicum in learning how to teach. During your practical field experience you will no doubt make errors, and with the understanding and guidance of those supervising your work,

you will benefit and learn from those errors. Sometimes your fresh approach to motivation, your creative ideas for learning activities, and your energy and enthusiasm make it possible for the host teacher to learn from you. After all, teaching and learning are always reciprocal processes. What is most important is that the students who are involved with you in the teaching–learning process will benefit from your role as the teacher candidate in the classroom. Whether student teaching or working as a paid intern, the following guidelines are offered to help make this practical experience beneficial to everyone involved.

Whether Student Teaching or Intern Teaching, It Is the Real Thing

Because you have a classroom setting for practicing and honing your teaching skills with active, responsive, young people, student teaching is the real thing. On the other hand, student teaching is not real in the sense that it is your cooperating teacher, not you, who has the ultimate responsibility and authority for the classroom.

Getting Ready for the Beginning Teaching Experience

To prepare yourself, you must study, plan, practice, and reflect. You should become knowledgeable about your students and their developmental backgrounds. In your theory classes, you learned a great deal about students. Review your class notes and textbooks from those courses, or select some readings suggested in previous

Student teaching is perhaps the most significant and important facet of your training.

chapters of this resource guide. Perhaps some of the topics will have greater meaning for you now.

First Impressions

First impressions are often lasting impressions. You have only one chance to make a first impression. You have heard that before, and now, as you prepare for this important phase of your professional preparation, you hear it again. Heed it, for it is crucial to your success. Remember it as you prepare to meet your school principal and cooperating teacher for the first time; remember it as you prepare to meet your students for the first time; remember it as you prepare to meet parents and guardians for the first time; remember it as you prepare for your university supervisor's first observation of your teaching; remember it as you prepare for your school principal's first visit to see you teach; and remember it again as you prepare for each teaching job interview. In each instance, you have only one opportunity to make that memorable first impression.

Continuing to Get Ready

In addition to the aforementioned preparations, you will need to be knowledgeable about your assigned school and the community that surrounds it. Review the subjects you will be teaching and the curriculum content and standards in those subject areas. Carefully discuss with your cooperating teacher and your university supervisor all responsibilities that you will be given.

You may want to run through each lesson verbally, perhaps in front of a mirror, the night before teaching your lesson. Some beginning teachers read through each lesson, recording the lesson, playing it back, and evaluating whether the directions are clear, the instruction is mind grabbing (or at least interesting), the sequence is logical, and the lesson closure is concise. Still another student teacher always has a "plan B" in mind in case "plan A" turns out to be inappropriate.

Student Teaching from the Cooperating Teacher's Point of View

For your consideration, information about student teaching from the viewpoint of a cooperating teacher (or mentor for teaching interns) is presented here in a question-and-answer format. You may wish to share this section with your cooperating teacher (or mentor).

What is my role? As the cooperating teacher, your role is to assist when necessary: to provide guidance, to review lesson plans before they are taught, to facilitate the learning and skill development of your student teacher, and to help your student teacher become and feel like a member of the school faculty and of the profession.

How can I prepare for the experience? Get to know your student teacher before he or she begins teaching. Develop a collegial rapport with the student teacher. If there seems to be a personality clash, resolve it early so your working relationship is productive and enjoyable.

Who is my student teacher? Your student teacher is a person who is making the transition from another career or from the life of a college student to the profession of teaching. Your student teacher may be your age, older, or younger. In any case, your student teacher may be scared to death, anxious, knowledgeable, and, when it comes to teaching philosophy, somewhere between being a romantic idealist and a pragmatic realist. Do not destroy the idealism—help the student teacher to understand and deal with the realism of everyday teaching.

It is important that you learn about the teaching experiences that your student teacher has had prior to this assignment so that together you may build from those experiences. For example, this may be your student teacher's very first teaching experience, or he or she may have substitute teaching experience, experience teaching in another country, or may have had another phase of student teaching at another school prior to this term.

What kind of support, criticism, and supervision should I give? You will have to decide much of this for yourself. On the other hand, some teacher preparation programs include seminars that train the cooperating teachers in techniques for supervising student teachers. Cooperating teachers are often selected not only because of their effectiveness in teaching but also because of their skill in working with other adults. It is likely that you will be working as a member of a team that includes you, the student teacher, and the university supervisor. Your student teacher may have more than one cooperating teacher, who should then also be included as a member of this professional team. Whatever the situation, your student teacher needs support, helpful suggestions, and productive monitoring. It is unprofessional and unacceptable to place a student teacher into a total sink-or-swim situation.

What danger signs should I be alert for? Your student teacher may be quite different from you in both appearance and style of teaching but may potentially be just as effective a teacher. Be slow and cautious in judging your student teacher's effectiveness. Offer suggestions, but do not make demands.

A student teacher who is not preparing well is likely to be heading for trouble. The saying stands: failing to prepare is preparing to fail. Be certain to ask for and to receive lesson plans before they are taught, especially in the beginning and whenever you feel the student teacher is not preparing well.

Another danger signal is when the student teacher seems to show no real interest in the school and the students beyond the classroom. The student teacher should be prompt, eager to spend extra time with you, attend faculty meetings, and be aware of the necessity of performing school clerical tasks. If you feel there is a lurking problem, then let the student teacher or the university supervisor know immediately. Trust your intuition. Poor communication between members of the teaching team is another danger signal.

What else should I know? Your student teacher may be employed elsewhere and have other demands on his or her time. Become aware of these other demands while keeping the educational welfare of your students paramount in your mind.

See that your student teacher is treated as a member of the faculty and invited to faculty functions. Your student teacher should have a personal mailbox (or share yours, with his or her name on it as well) and should understand school policies, procedures, curriculum standards and documents, dates for standardized testing (if any), and other important dates on the school calendar. Be sure to demonstrate your willingness to share both information and teaching materials with your student teacher.

INCREASING RESPONSIBILITY AND ALONE TIME WITH STUDENTS

Once your student teacher is well grounded, he or she should be ready to be gradually left alone with the students for increasingly longer periods of time. It is a good idea, however, to set aside with your student teacher a specified time each week to review plans and to reflect on how it is going. For a specified time, a student teacher's goal is to work toward a competency level that enables the student teacher to assume increasing responsibility for everything and to be the lead teacher for a minimum of 3 weeks (although the exact time will be dependent on the requirements of the particular program of teacher education). This means that you are nearby and on call in case of an emergency, but out of the sight of students.

Comments from the University Supervisor

When is the supervisor coming? Is the supervisor going to be here today? Do you see a university or a college supervisor's observation of your student teaching as a pleasant experience or a painful one? Do you realize that classroom observations of your teaching continue during your beginning years of teaching? Being observed and evaluated does not have to be a painful, nerve-racking experience for you. You do not have to become a bundle of raw nerve endings when you realize the supervisor is coming to see you. Whether you are a student teacher being observed by your university supervisor or a probationary teacher being evaluated by your principal, some professional suggestions may help you turn an evaluating observation into a useful, professionally satisfying experience.

What to Do Before an Observation

Successful teachers seem to be able to ameliorate tension and get through an evaluation with skill and tact. Prepare for your evaluative visit by deciding what you do well and plan to demonstrate your best skills: decorate your room and bulletin boards (especially by displaying student work), make sure your work area is orderly (this shows productive organization), and select an academic aspect of the teaching day that demonstrates some of your best teaching skills. If your university supervisor has previously targeted some areas that need strengthening, plan to demonstrate growth in those teaching abilities.

What to Do During an Observation

Some supervisors and administrators choose to pre-announce their visits. This is certainly true for clinical supervision practices. **Clinical supervision** is based on shared decision making between the supervisor and teacher and is focused on improving, rather than evaluating, teaching behaviors. With the use of clinical supervision, you know when the supervisor or administrator is coming, and you will probably look forward to the visit because of the rapport that has been established between members of your triad (in student teaching situations, your triad is composed of you, your cooperating teacher, and your university or college supervisor).

Features of clinical supervision include a preobservation conference, observation of teaching, and a postobservation conference. In the preobservation conference, the student teacher, cooperating teacher, and supervisor meet to discuss goals, objectives, teaching strategies, and the evaluation process. During the observation of teaching, the supervisor collects data on the classroom students' performance of objectives and on the student teacher's performance of the teaching strategies. In the postobservation conference, the student teacher, cooperating teacher, and the supervisor discuss the performances. They may compare what happened with what was expected, make inferences about students' achievement of objectives, and discuss relationships between teaching performance and student achievement. The supervisor and cooperating teacher act as educational consultants and may discuss alternative strategies for teaching at this conference or at a later one.

Sometimes your supervisor or administrator may drop in unannounced. When that happens, you can take a deep breath, count to 10 (silently), and then proceed with your lesson. You will undoubtedly do just fine if you have been following the guidelines set forth in this book. Additional guidelines for a classroom observation are as follows:

- Allow the observer to sit wherever he or she wishes.
- Do not interrupt your lesson to introduce the observer, unless the observer requests it, but do prepare

your students in advance by letting them know who may be visiting and why.

- Do not put the observer on the spot by suddenly involving him or her in the lesson, but do try to discern in advance the level of participation desired by your observer.

If you have been assigned to a classroom for a student teaching experience, your university supervisor will meet with you and explain some of the tasks you should attend to when the supervisor visits your class. These may vary from the list presented. For instance, some supervisors prefer to walk into a classroom quietly and not interrupt the learning activities. Some prefer not to be introduced to the class or to participate in the activities. Some supervisors are already well known by the students and teaching staff from prior visits to the school. Other supervisors may give you a special form to be completed before he or she arrives for the visit. This form often resembles a lesson plan format and includes space for your objectives, lesson procedures, motivational strategies, related activities, and method of assessing how well the students learned from the lesson. Remember to maintain an open line of communication with your supervisor so you have a clear understanding of what is expected of you when she or he visits your classroom to observe your teaching. Without missing a beat in your lesson, you may walk over and quietly hand the observer a copy of the lesson plan and the textbook (or any other materials being used), complete with a marker showing the appropriate page.

In some teacher preparation programs, the student teacher is expected to maintain a **student teaching binder** in the classroom. (A similar expectation is common in beginning teacher mentor programs.) The binder is stored in a particular location so that the cooperating teacher may refer to it, and also the supervisor (or mentor) can quickly locate it upon entering the classroom and refer to it during the observation. Organized in the binder is the current lesson plan, the current unit plan, previous lessons with reflections, tests and their results, assignments, classroom management plan, and a current seating chart with the students' names. The student teaching binder can, in fact, represent the start of your professional portfolio.

Soon after the observational visit, there should be a conference in which observations are discussed in a nonjudgmental atmosphere. It might be necessary for you to make sure that a conference is scheduled. The purposes of this postobservation conference are for you and the observer to discuss, rather than to evaluate, your teaching and for you to exit the conference with agreements about areas for improvement and how to accomplish those changes. Sometimes, because of conflicting schedules or geographic distances, conferences may be electronic, via email or phone.

What to Do During an Observation Conference

Some supervisors will arrange to have a conference with you to discuss the classroom observation and to begin to resolve any classroom teaching problems. As a teacher or teacher candidate, you should be quite professional during this conference. For instance, one student teacher asks for additional help by requesting resources. Another takes notes and suggests developing a cooperative plan with the supervisor to improve teaching competencies. Still another discusses visiting other classrooms to observe exemplary teachers.

During other conferences, student teachers may ask for assistance in scheduling additional meetings with the supervisor. At such meetings, the teacher (or teacher candidate) views video of selected teaching styles or methods or visits an outside educational consultant or nearby resource center.

Almost all supervisors conclude their conferences by leaving something in writing with the teacher or teacher candidate. This written record usually includes a summary of teaching strengths or weaknesses, with a review of classroom management; the supervisor's recommendations; and, perhaps, steps in an overall plan for the teacher's (or student teacher's) continued professional growth and development.

What to Do After the Supervisor Leaves

In addition to observing the classes of other teachers, attending workshops and conferences, and conferring with college and university authorities, the following are ways to implement your plan for improvement. Be sure you debug your lesson plans by walking through them in advance of implementing them in the classroom. Do what you and your supervisor have agreed on. Document your activities with a record or diary with dated entries. If you maintain a supervisor's binder, this documentation may be kept in the binder along with the supervisor's written comments. If you have a problem with classroom management or organization, review your written classroom management plan and procedures, comparing your plan with the guidelines presented in this resource guide. Review your plan and procedures with your cooperating teacher, a trusted teaching colleague, or your university supervisor. Obtain help when you need it. Write comments to parents or guardians about students' progress, and leave space for a return message from the adult. Keep positive responses that you receive from these adults, and share them with your supervisor at your next conference.

RECOMMENDATIONS FROM YOUR SUPERVISORS

It is important you understand now that in the not to distant future, toward the end of your student teaching or internship, you will be initiating the search for a teaching position (the topic that follows), and prior to job interviews you will be requesting letters of recommendation. The two most important sources of those letters are your cooperating teacher(s) and your university supervisor. Many times these are the only recommendations that truly matter. So it is important you realize from the very beginning of your internship or student teaching experience the importance of those persons in your life. Get them on your side!

FINDING A TEACHING POSITION

As your successful student teaching experience draws to a close, you will embark upon finding your first paid teaching job. The guidelines that follow are provided to help you accomplish your goal.

Guidelines for Locating a Teaching Position

To prepare for finding the position you want, you should focus on (a) letters of recommendation from your cooperating teachers, your college or university supervisor, and, in some instances, the school principal; (b) your professional preparation as evidenced by your letters of recommendation and other items in your professional portfolio; and (c) your job-interviewing skills.

First, consider the recommendations about your teaching. Most colleges and universities have a career center, usually called a job (or career) placement center, where there is probably a counselor who can advise you how to open the job placement file that will hold your professional recommendations. This enables prospective personnel directors or district personnel who are expecting to employ new teachers to review your recommendations. Sometimes there are special forms for writing these recommendations. It is your responsibility to request letters of recommendation and, when appropriate, to supply the person writing the recommendation with the blank form and an appropriately addressed stamped envelope. Sometimes the job placement files are confidential, so your recommendations will be mailed directly to the placement office. The confidentiality of recommendations may be optional, and, when possible, you may want to maintain your own copies of letters of recommendation and include them in your professional portfolio.

The letters of recommendation from educators at the school where you did your student teaching should include the following information: the name of the school and district where you did your student teaching; the grade levels and subjects you taught; your proven skills in managing students of diversity in the classroom; your ability to teach the relevant subjects; your skills in assessing student learning and in reflecting on your teaching performance and learning from that reflection; and your skills in communicating and interacting with students and adults.

Second, consider your preparation as a teacher. Teachers, as you have learned, represent a myriad of specialties. Hiring personnel will want to know how you see yourself—for example, as a specialist in the traditional core subjects typically taught in K–6 grades, as an English/language arts teacher who can also coach soccer, a music teacher, or a social studies teacher who would also like to coach basketball. Perhaps your interest is only in teaching science. You may indicate a special interest or skill, such as competency in skills of soccer or in teaching English as a second language. Or, perhaps, although your teaching field is mathematics, you also are bilingual and have had rich and varied cultural experiences. Have you had varied background experiences so that you will feel comfortable when you are hired and placed in the one assignment in which you were least interested? The hiring personnel who consider your application will be interested in your sincerity and will want to see that you are academically and socially impressive.

Finally, consider your in-person interview with a district official. Sometimes, you will have several interviews, or you will be interviewed simultaneously with other candidates. There may be an initial screening interview by an administrative panel from the district, followed by an interview by a department chairperson or a school principal or by a school team composed of one or more teachers and administrators from the interested school or district. In all interviews, your verbal and nonverbal behaviors will be observed as you respond to various questions, including (a) factual questions about your student teaching or about particular curriculum programs with which you would be expected to work, and (b) hypothetical questions such as "What would you do if ...?" Often these are questions that relate to your philosophy of education, your reasons for wanting to be a teacher or for wanting to teach a particular level of school, your approach to handling a particular classroom situation, and perhaps your reasons for your interest in teaching at this particular school and in this district.

The Professional Career Portfolio (or How to Get Hired by Really Trying)

A way to be proactive in your job search is to create a personal professional portfolio to be shared with persons who are considering your application for employment. The portfolio is now a requirement in most teacher preparation programs.

The professional career portfolio is organized to provide clear evidence of your teaching skills and to make you professionally desirable to a hiring committee. A professional portfolio is not simply a collection of your accomplishments randomly tossed into a folder. It is a deliberate, current, and organized collection of your skills, attributes, experiences, and accomplishments.

A teacher being recorded while teaching in front of a class

ESYR3704   Fulton, New York: March 15, 1999. Newspaper videographe, Dave Bullard, video tapes the music teacher during a music class at Fulton Catholic school. ©Syracuse Newspapers/G. Walts/ The Image Works

Imagine every item in your portfolio collected, organized, and presented electronically on a CD-ROM. With today's technologies, teachers are now doing just that (Bullock & Hawk, 2001).

Resources for Locating Teaching Vacancies

To locate teaching vacancies, you can establish contact with any of the following resources. See also Web site listings in Figure 11.1.

College or university placement office. Establishing a career placement file with your local college or university placement service is an excellent way to begin the process of locating teaching vacancies.

Local school or district personnel office. You can contact school personnel offices to obtain information about teaching vacancies and sometimes about open job interviews.

County educational agency. Contact local county offices of education about job openings.

Figure 11.1 Web sites for teaching job vacancies and related information.

- American Federation of Teachers (AFT) http://www.aft.org
- Credential information state by state http://wdcrobcolp01.ed.gov/Programs/EROD/org_list.cfm?category_ID=SEA
- Education Week http://www.edweek.org
- Educational Placement Service http://www.teacherjob.com
- Employment page at http://www.academploy.com
- European Council of Independent Schools http://www.ecis.org
- International Schools Service http://www.iss.edu
- National Association of Independent Schools http://www.nais.org
- National Education Association (NEA) http://www.nea.org
- National Recruitment Teacher Clearinghouse http://www.recruitingteachers.org
- Overseas Placement Service for Educators http://www.uni.edu/placement/overseas
- Peace Corps www.peacecorps.gov
- Teaching Jobs Overseas http://www.joyjobs.com/center

State departments of education. State departments of education maintain information about job openings statewide. (See Web site listing in Figure 11.1 for state departments of education Internet addresses.)

Independent schools and overseas positions. You can contact non-public-supported schools that interest you, either directly or through Internet sites (such as those listed in Figure 11.1). Perhaps an overseas teaching position might interest you.

Professional journals and other publications. Professional teaching journals (see Figure 2.6 in Chapter 2) and publications such as *Education Week* often advertise teaching vacancies. In addition to the journals, see web listings in Figure 11.1).

If you are interested in the credential requirements for other states and U.S. territories, check at the appropriate office of your own college or university teacher preparation program to see what information is available about requirements for states of interest to you and whether the credential that you are about to receive has reciprocity with other states. Although the National Association of State Directors of Teacher Education and Certification (NASDTEC) publishes an annual listing of requirements and contacts for certification for 50 states, the District of Columbia, the Department of Defense Dependents Schools, 10 Canadian Provinces, and New Zealand, access to their web site (http://NASDTEC.org) is restricted. Your campus, however, may have a copy of the manual for your review.

Addresses and contact numbers for information about state credentials are available on the Internet. See the web site listing in Figure 11.1.

The Professional Résumé

Résumé preparation is the subject of how-to books, computer programs, and commercial services, but a teacher's résumé is specific. Although no one can tell you exactly what résumé will work best for you, a few basic guidelines are especially helpful for the preparation for a teacher's résumé:

- The résumé should be no more than two pages in length.
- The presentation should be neat and uncluttered.
- Page size should be standard $8 \frac{1}{2} \times 11$ inches.
- Stationery color should be white or off-white.
- Do *not* give personal data such as your age, height, weight, marital status, number or names of your children, or a photograph of yourself.
- Sentences should be clear and concise; avoid educational jargon, awkward phrases, abbreviations, long paragraphs, or unfamiliar words.
- Organize the information carefully in this order: your name, address, and contact phone number, followed by your educational and professional data: your professional experience, credential status, location of placement file, professional affiliations, and educational and professional honors.
- When identifying your experiences—academic, teaching, and relevant job or travel experiences—do so in reverse chronological order, listing your most recent degree or your current position first. (See sample résumé in Figure 11.2.)
- Be absolutely truthful; avoid any distortion of facts about your degrees, experiences, or any other information that you provide on your résumé.
- Take time to develop your résumé, and then maintain its currency, producing a most current copy each time you apply for a job.
- Prepare a cover letter to accompany your résumé that is written specifically for the position for which you are applying. Address the letter personally but formally to the personnel director. Limit the cover letter to one page, and emphasize yourself, your teaching experiences and interests, and reasons that you are best qualified for the position. Show a familiarity with the particular school or district. Again, if you maintain a generic application letter in a computer file, you can easily modify it to make it specific for each position.
- Have your résumé and cover letter edited by someone familiar with résumé writing and editing, perhaps an English-teacher friend. A poorly written, poorly typed, or poorly copied résumé fraught with spelling and grammar errors will guarantee that you will not be considered for the job.
- Be sure that your application reaches the personnel director by the announced deadline. If for some reason it will arrive late, then contact the director, explain the circumstances, and request permission to submit your application late.

The In-Person Interview

If your application and résumé are attractive to the personnel director, you will be notified and scheduled for a personal or small-group interview, although in some instances the hiring interview may precede the request for your personal papers. Whichever the case, during the interview you should be honest, and you should be yourself. Practice an interview, perhaps with the aid of a video camera. Request a friend to role-play an interview with you and to ask you some tough questions. Plan your interview wardrobe and ready it the night before. Leave early for your interview so that you arrive promptly or even a bit early so to relax. If possible, long before your scheduled interview, locate someone who works in the school district and discuss curriculum, classroom management policies, popular programs, and district demographics with that person. If you anticipate a professionally embarrassing question during the interview,

Figure 11.2 Sample professional résumé.

Lee Roberson
10 Main St, Weaverville, CA 96093
(916) 552-8996; e-mail Lrob@aol.com

CREDENTIAL

January 2012	California Preliminary Single Subject Credential in English
	Supplemental authorizations in Social Studies and Physical Education
May 2012	CLAD (Culture and Language Academic Development) Certificate
	California State University, Sacramento

EDUCATION

May 2006	Bachelor of Arts Degree in English Literature
	Saint Olaf College, Northfield, Minnesota

TEACHING EXPERIENCE

Fall 2012 (Student Teaching III)	**Douglass Junior High School (Woodland, CA).** *Two 7th-grade 2-hour block* *Language Arts and Social Studies core classes* • Worked with a team to develop interdisciplinary thematic lessons
Spring 2012 (Student Teaching II)	**Davis High School (Davis, CA).** *One period of Jr. Lit* • Developed book clubs, small-group forums for discussing three novels • Developed poetry unit in which students published their poems
Fall 2011 (Student Teaching I)	**Los Cerros Middle School (Danville, CA).** *One period ESL—13 culturally diverse 7th and 8th graders.* • Bilingual stories and activities; reader's theater presentations

RELATED EXPERIENCE

Summer of 2011	• Developed and taught a Summer Writing Workshop for small groups of students, grades 3–10. Met with students and parents to establish goals.
2009–2010	• Reader for English department of Valley High School.

think of diplomatic ways to respond. This means that you should think of ways to turn your weaknesses into strengths. For instance, if your cooperating teacher has mentioned that you need to continue to develop your room environment skills (meaning that you were sloppy), admit that you realize that you need to be more conscientious about keeping supplies and materials neat and tidy, but mention your concern about the students and the learning and that you realize you have a tendency to interact with students more than with objects. Assure someone that you will work on this skill, and then do it. The paragraphs that follow offer additional guidelines for preparing for and handling the in-person interview. As you peruse these guidelines, please know that what may seem trite and obvious to one reader is not necessarily obvious to another.

You will be given a specific time, date, and place for the interview. Regardless of your other activities, accept the time, date, and location suggested, rather than trying to manipulate the interview around a schedule more convenient for you.

As a part of the interview, you may be expected to do a formal but abbreviated (10–15 minutes) teaching demonstration. You may or may not be told in advance of this expectation. So, it is a useful idea to thoughtfully develop and rehearse a model one that you could perform on immediate request. Just in case it might be useful, some candidates carry to the interview a DVD of one of their best real teaching episodes made during student teaching.

Dress for success. Regardless of what else you may be doing for a living, take the time necessary to make a professional and proud appearance.

Avoid arriving at the interview with small children. If necessary, arrange to have them looked after by someone.

Arrive promptly, shake your dry hands firmly with members of the committee, and initiate conversation with a friendly comment, based on your personal knowledge, about the school or district.

Be prepared to answer standard interview questions. Sometimes school districts will send candidates the questions that will be asked during the interview; at other times, these questions are handed to the candidate upon arrival at the interview. The questions that are likely to be asked will cover the following topics:

• *Your experiences with youth of the relevant age.* The committee wants to be reasonably certain that you can effectively manage and teach at this level. You should answer this question by sharing specific successes that demonstrate that you are a decisive and competent teacher.

- *Hobbies and travels.* The committee wants to know more about you as a person to ensure that you will be an interesting and energetic teacher to the students, as well as a congenial member of the faculty.

- *Extracurricular interests and experiences.* The committee wants to know about ways in which you might be helpful in the school and ways in which you will promote the interests and co-curricular activities of students and the school community.

- *Classroom management techniques.* You must convince the committee that you can effectively manage a classroom of diverse learners in a manner that will help the students to develop their self-esteem.

- *Knowledge of the curriculum standards and the subject taught at the level for which you are being considered.* The committee needs to be reasonably certain that you have command of the subject and its place within the developmental stages of learners at this level. This is where you should demonstrate your awareness of national standards and of state and perhaps local curriculum documents.

- *Knowledge of assessment strategies relevant for use in teaching at this level.* This is your place to shine with your professional knowledge about imbedded assessment, about using rubrics and performance assessment, and, if relevant, about standardized assessments.

- *Commitment to teaching at this level.* The committee wants to be assured that you are knowledgeable about and committed to teaching and learning at this level, as opposed to just seeking this job until something better comes along. For example, if you are being interviewed for a middle school teaching position, the interviewing personnel will want to be convinced that you truly look forward to working with middle school youngsters rather than to think you are merely willing to take this job until a high school teaching position comes along.

- *Your ability to reflect on experience and to grow from that reflection.* Demonstrate that you are a reflective decision maker and a lifelong learner.

- *Your perceived weaknesses.* If you are asked about your weaknesses, you have an opportunity to show that you can effectively reflect and self-assess, that you know the value of learning from your own errors and how to do it. Be prepared for this question by identifying a specific error that you have made, perhaps while student teaching, and explain how you turned that error into a profitable learning experience.

Throughout the interview you should maintain eye contact with the interviewer while demonstrating interest, enthusiasm, and self-confidence. When an opportunity arises, ask one or two planned questions that demonstrate your knowledge of and interest in this position and this community and school or district.

When the interview has obviously been brought to a close by the interviewer, that is your signal to leave. Do not hang around; this might be perceived as a sign of your lacking confidence. Follow the interview with a thank you letter addressed to the personnel director or interviewer; even if you do not get the job, you will be better remembered for future reference.

PROFESSIONAL DEVELOPMENT THROUGH REFLECTION AND SELF-ASSESSMENT

Beginning now and continuing throughout your career, you will reflect on your teaching (reflection is inevitable), and you will want to continue to grow as a professional as a result of those reflections (growth is not so inevitable unless self-initiated and systematically planned). The most competent professional is one who is proactive, that is, who takes charge and initiates his or her own continuing professional development. One useful way of continuing to reflect, self-assess, and grow professionally is by maintaining a **professional journal**, much as your students do when they maintain journals reflecting on what they are learning. Another is by continuing to maintain the professional career portfolio that you began assembling early in your preservice program and finalized for your job search.

Some teachers maintain **professional logbooks**, which serve not only as documentations of their specific professional contributions and activities but also as documentation of the breadth of their professional involvement.

Some teachers maintain **research logs** for recording questions that arise during the busy teaching day and for establishing a plan for finding answers. The research log strategy can be of tremendous benefit to you in actively researching and improving your classroom work and also can be of interest to colleagues. Finally, working in teams and sharing your work with team members is still another way of continuing to reflect, self-assess, and grow as a teacher.

PROFESSIONAL DEVELOPMENT THROUGH MENTORING

Mentoring, one teacher facilitating the learning of another, can aid in professional development. In what is sometimes called peer coaching, a mentor teacher volunteers, is selected by the teacher who wishes to improve, or is selected by a school administrator, formally or informally. The mentor observes and coaches (but usually does not participate in formal evaluations of) the teacher to help him or her to improve in teaching. Sometimes the teacher simply wants to learn a new skill. In other instances, the teacher being coached remains with the mentor teacher for an entire school year, developing and improving old and new skills or learning how to teach with a new program. In many districts, as a program of induction, new teachers are automatically assigned to mentor teachers for their first, and sometimes second, year.

It Is Helpful to Have a Mentor, Sometimes More Than One

Learn from those teachers you admire, who have a history of being successful. Whether you have an assigned mentor or not, you should have someone you can confide in and talk with about your work, hopefully someone who has "been there and fought the battles," who can help you develop the self-confidence you will need in order to assume the risks necessary to achieve the goals you set for yourself. Just because a teacher is experienced and successful is no guarantee that he or she will be a good mentor. For that reason alone, and for others as well, it is sometimes beneficial to have several mentors, perhaps one who is your official assigned mentor and then one or two others who are unofficial, and perhaps even, only occasional mentors. To be effective as your mentor, the person doesn't necessarily have to be someone who is older and more experienced than you. For example, it is probably a good idea to establish a collegial relationship with another beginning teacher, perhaps someone not even in the same school as you, but someone with whom you can talk freely and who is likely to be sharing similar experiences and feelings. Another teacher from your school district can be helpful toward guiding your understanding of district and school policies, community relationships, and how best to prepare for special events and other expectations and requirements. It can be useful to maintain a small notebook (perhaps your calendar or diary) of specific questions you want to ask the various members of those who will become your professional network, and then don't hesitate to ask them.

When Should I Seek Help?

Sometimes beginning teachers ask themselves just when they should seek help, exactly how should they go about seeking it, and from whom. My answer to you for the first part is to seek help exactly when you feel a need—don't wait. To the second part, rather than being overly concerned with your wording, ask simple, straightforward questions. And to the final part, don't necessarily keep seeking help from the same person but rather (and as best you can determine) from the right person for the specific question, which is the very reason you need a network of professional friends and mentors rather than just one person.

For example, if you constantly are feeling that there is not enough time in the day for all that you need to do—not at all an uncommon feeling—then seek advice from a colleague who seems to have learned to use time efficiently and effectively, or talk with a member of your teaching team or a school administrator about your concern. After all, 24/7 is identical for each of us; each of us must learn how to best use the time that we have. Talking with a colleague who has apparently achieved effective time management will go a long way in helping you in not only doing your job effectively but also maintaining your physical and mental well-being.

Coping Strategies: Avoiding Feelings of Aloneness

As a first-year teacher, you quickly become aware of the reality, as discussed in Chapter 2, of the myriad responsibilities you have and decisions that you must make each day, many of which are new to you, and of how alone you often seemingly are when carrying out these responsibilities. Life for the first-year teacher can be very lonely, especially if you have no one to approach when you feel frustrated or troubled and burdened by your responsibilities. Thus, as emphasized in the preceding section, you must be proactive about identifying one or more supportive persons with whom you can vent, discuss, and explore your feelings and concerns.

The first few months of the school year seem to be a particularly vital time for the new teacher to have the opportunity to discuss concerns with a mentor or other empathic and knowledgeable person, someone who is more than a "buddy" but is a person who can assist you with acquiring the knowledge, skills, attitudes, and sustained courage you most need.

Incompetent and burned-out teachers simply become aloof to colleagues, staff, and students, and to their professional commitment and responsibilities; effective teachers are able to discover productive ways to cope, such as via self-reflection, deep breathing, mental and physical exercising, and sometimes just plain temporarily getting away from it all.

For example, maintaining your reflections in a journal, even if only a sentence fragment rather than a paragraph, weekly rather than daily, or as a daily email sent to yourself or on a calendar or diary can help provide valuable insight and personal satisfaction regarding your professional growth. To ease the stress of being a beginning teacher and to continue working effectively at what will be a continuing series of challenging tasks requires significant amounts of reflection. Writing your reflections in a personal journal about your work can be useful not only to ease the stress but also in furthering your understanding and effectiveness. And, as an aside, you may find your notes useful in later years, perhaps when assuming new responsibilities or when mentoring others in their initial years of teaching.

In addition to the preceding, and to the stress management techniques discussed in Chapter 10, another very important strategy for coping is that of maintaining and sharing a sense of humor. Students and a school's staff will most often appreciate and work better with teachers who share a sense of humor, who smile and laugh with them. The positive effects of appropriate humor (i.e., humor that is not self-deprecating or disrespectful of others) on learning and living are well established: drop in the pulse rate; reduction of feelings of anxiety, tension, and stress; secretion of endorphins; and an increase in blood oxygen. Humor and laughter cause an increase in immune system activity and a decrease in stress-producing hormones. It causes an increase in the activity of the body's natural cells that attack and kill tumor cells and viruses. It activates T-cells for the immune system, antibodies that fight against harmful microorganisms, and gamma interferon, a hormone that fights viruses and regulates cell growth. Because of these effects, humor relaxes us, helps us stay healthy, and encourages creativity and higher level thinking (Costa, 1991).

Humor is an intelligent behavior that should be cherished, nourished, and modeled by all, especially by those who work with the young. This is true perhaps even more so today, as it seems that so many schools have become so fixated on matters of discipline and safety, standardized test scores, curriculum benchmark objectives, and proficiency that too often they have become depressingly gloomy places. Far too often, we hear of teachers and students commenting that school and learning are not enjoyable—teachers are leaving, students are dropping out, and new principals are becoming steadily more difficult to find. Happy teachers make for good teaching, so please learn to be and to remain happy in your work.

> When teachers develop allies, they remain fresh, committed, and hopeful.
>
> Sonia Nieto

Make Career Plans: A Life Plan Map

Another consideration to help not only with your daily coping but also with your future is to, if you haven't done so already, create for yourself a **life plan map**, which might be kept in your journal but the actual design of which is open. Consider the following suggestions. The purpose of a life plan map is for you to consider and then indicate where you would like to be (personally as well as professionally) down the road, say 5 years from now, 10 years from now, and so forth, perhaps including a listing of rather detailed timelines and actions needed to accomplish your target goals. Then, at planned intervals you should visit the map, make evaluative notes on it, maintaining a list of questions you have encountered, potential answers or sources of answers, books you intend to read and actions you intend to pursue, as well as any adjustments to the targets and additional targets as you deem necessary.

The section that follows addresses specific mechanisms for continued professional development.

PROFESSIONAL DEVELOPMENT THROUGH INSERVICE AND GRADUATE STUDY

Inservice workshops and programs are offered to teachers at the school level by the district and by other agencies, such as a county office of education or a nearby college or university. Inservice workshops and programs are usually designed for specific purposes, such as to train teachers in new teaching skills, to update their knowledge in content, and to introduce them to new teaching materials or programs.

University graduate study is yet another way of continuing your professional development. Some teachers pursue a master's degree in an academic teaching field, and many others pursue master's degrees in curriculum and methods of instruction or in educational administration or counseling.

PROFESSIONAL DEVELOPMENT THROUGH PARTICIPATION IN PROFESSIONAL ORGANIZATIONS

There are many professional organizations—local, state, national, and international. The associations are usually discipline specific, such as the National Council of

---

Teaching in Practice

Caring for Beginning Teachers

Esther entered teaching after a long career as an engineer. Her vast scientific knowledge and professional experience made her a unique asset in the low-income, racially diverse urban vocational high school where she taught.

But Esther found the working conditions intolerable. In her view, student discipline was nonexistent throughout the building. Teachers fought among themselves and openly mocked the principal, who never observed them in their classrooms or provided any form of curricular or instructional leadership. Esther found the school disorderly and unsupportive of good teaching, and she left after only one year. She moved to a suburban school near her home that had strong administrators, supportive colleagues, and an orderly, respectful environment. Looking back at her first job, Esther says, "Maybe if I were a better teacher, more experienced ... maybe I could [have succeeded there]."

But did the responsibility *really* lie with Esther? Are inexperienced teachers—regardless of their talents and subject-area expertise—simply not "good" enough to succeed in urban schools?

Or is there something more to be learned from Esther and the thousands of people like her, new teachers who leave their first schools after only a year or two?

Discuss the case and these questions with your classmates.

Source: Reino Makkonen, "Taking Care of Novice Teachers," *Harvard Education Letter* 29(3): 1–4 (May/June 2004), 1. Copyright © 2004 by the President and Fellows of Harvard College. By permission.

Teachers of Mathematics, the National Council for the Social Studies, the National Council of Teachers of English, and the National Science Teachers Association (see Chapter 4). In most states there is a statewide organization, probably affiliated with a national organization. In addition, there are national teachers organizations, such as the ones shown at the end of this chapter.

Local, district, state, and national organizations have meetings and conferences that include guest speakers, professional development workshops, and publishers' displays. Professional meetings of teachers are educational, enriching, and fulfilling for those who attend. In addition, many other professional associations, such as those for reading teachers, supply speakers and publish articles in their journals that are often of interest to teachers other than the target audience.

Professional organizations publish newsletters and journals (see Chapter 2) for their members, and these will likely be found in your college or university library. Many professional organizations have special membership prices for teachers who are still college or university students, a courtesy that allows for an inexpensive beginning affiliation with a professional association. For information on special membership prices and association services, contact those of interest to you.

PROFESSIONAL DEVELOPMENT THROUGH COMMUNICATIONS WITH TEACHERS

Visiting teachers at other schools; attending inservice workshops, graduate seminars, and programs; participating in teacher study groups and meetings of professional organizations; participating in teacher networks; and sharing with teachers by means of electronic bulletin boards can all be valuable experiences, if for no other reason than talking and sharing with teachers from across the country and around the world. These discussions include a sharing not only of "war stories" but also of ideas and descriptions of new programs, books, materials, and techniques that work.

Talking with other educators about problems you are having can be helpful in discovering new avenues and solutions. Talking with friends and other teachers about a problem is known as **talk therapy** and can be very helpful toward giving you new perspectives and potential solutions. It can also lead to valuable new friendships.

As in other process skills, the teacher practices and models skill in communication, in and out of the classroom. This includes communicating with other teachers to improve one's own repertoire of strategies and knowledge about teaching as well as sharing one's experiences with others. Teaching other teachers about your own special skills and sharing your experiences are important components of the communication and professional development processes.

PROFESSIONAL DEVELOPMENT THROUGH OFF-TEACHING WORK EXPERIENCE

In many areas of the country, there are special programs of short-term employment available to interested teachers. These are offered by public agencies, private industry, foundations, research institutes, and even the school or district in which the teacher is employed. These institutions are interested in disseminating information and providing opportunities for teachers to update their skills and knowledge, with an ultimate hope that the teachers will stimulate in more students a desire to develop their physical fitness, to understand civic responsibilities, and to consider careers in science and technology. Participating industries, foundations, governments, and institutes provide on-the-job training with salaries or stipends to teachers who are selected to participate. During the program of employment and depending on the nature of that work, a variety of people (e.g., scientists, technicians, politicians, businesspersons, social workers, and sometimes university educators) meet with teachers to share experiences and discuss what is being learned and its implications for teaching and curriculum development.

Some of the programs for teachers are government sponsored, field centered, and content specific. For example, a program may concentrate on geology, anthropology, mathematics, or reading. At another location, a program may concentrate on teaching, using a specific new or experimental curriculum. These programs, located around the country, may have university affiliation, which means that university credit may be available. Room and board, travel, and a stipend are sometimes granted to participating teachers.

Sources of information about the availability of programs include school district offices (state, county, and local), professional journals, the local chamber of commerce, and meetings of the local or regional teachers' organization. In areas where there are no organized programs of part-time work experience for teachers, some teachers have had success in initiating their own by establishing contact with management personnel of local businesses or companies.

PROFESSIONAL DEVELOPMENT THROUGH MICRO PEER TEACHING

Micro peer teaching (MPT) is a skill-development strategy used for professional development by both preservice (prior to credentialing) and inservice (credentialed and employed) teachers. Micro peer teaching (to which you were introduced in Exercises 6.7 and 7.2) is a scaled-down teaching experience involving a

- limited objective,
- brief interval for teaching a lesson,
- lesson taught to a few (8–10) peers (as your students), and

- lesson that focuses on the use of one or several instructional strategies.

Micro peer teaching can be a predictor of later teaching effectiveness in a regular classroom. More importantly, it can provide an opportunity to develop and improve specific teaching behaviors. A videotaped MPT allows you to see yourself in action for self-evaluation and diagnosis. Evaluation of an MPT session is based on

- the quality of the teacher's preparation and lesson implementation,
- the quality of the planned and implemented student involvement,
- whether the instructional objectives were reached, and
- the appropriateness of the cognitive level of the lesson.

Whether a preservice or inservice teacher, you are urged to participate in one or more MPT experiences. Formatted differently from previous exercises in this resource guide, Exercise 11.1 can represent a summative performance assessment for the course for which this book is being used.

SUMMARY

This final chapter of this resource guide ushers in an important transition in your professional career, a career that is really only beginning. Throughout your career as a professional educator, you will continue improving and adding to your knowledge and skills in all aspects of teaching and learning. A useful reference you may wish to add to your professional library is *Never Work Harder Than Your Students & Other Principles of Great Teaching* (Jackson, 2009).

> I wish you the very best in what is to be the first chapter in your new career. Be the very best teacher that you can be. Perhaps more than ever before, the nation, indeed the world, and its youth need you.
>
> —Richard Kellough

QUESTIONS FOR CLASS DISCUSSION

1. Discover what professional teacher organizations exist in your geographical area. Share what you find with others in your class. Attend a local, regional, or national meeting of a professional teachers' association, report to your class what it was like and what you learned, and share with your class any free or inexpensive teaching materials you obtained.

2. It has been said "Teaching, alone among the professions, makes the same demands on novices as on experienced practitioners. The moment first-year teachers enter their first classroom, they are held to the same standard and subjected to the same procedures as their more experienced colleagues." Furthermore, in some districts, beginning teachers are assigned "the most preparations, the most difficult students, and the least attractive room (or none at all) and [are left] to 'sink or swim,' [and] when the principal arrives to conduct an observation, he uses the same procedures as those used with experienced teachers" (Danielson & McGreal, 2000, pp. 56–57). Recognizing that, some school districts have developed separate procedures for teacher assessment, one set for beginning teachers, perhaps another for nontenured teachers with limited experience, and yet a third set for those with tenure. Discover the procedures for evaluating teachers used in school districts of interest to you and share your findings with your classmates.

3. Talk with experienced practicing teachers, and find out how they remain current in their teaching fields. Share what you, find with others in your class.

 Now go to Topic #16: **Professional Responsibilities** in the MyEducationLab (www.myeducationlab.com) for your course, where you can:

- Find learning outcomes for this topic along with the national standards that connect to these outcomes.
- Complete Assignments and Activities that can help you more deeply understand the chapter content.
- Apply and practice your understanding of the core teaching skills identified in the chapter with the Building Teaching Skills and Dispositions learning units.

EXERCISE 11.1 PULLING IT ALL TOGETHER—MICRO PEER TEACHING III

INSTRUCTIONS: The purpose of this exercise is to learn how to develop your own MPT experiences. You will prepare and teach a lesson for your peers, at their level of intellectual maturity and understanding (i.e., as opposed to teaching the lesson to peers pretending that they are public school students).

This experience has two components:

1. Your preparation and implementation of a demonstration lesson.
2. Your completion of an analysis of the summative peer assessment and the self-assessment, with statements of how you would change the lesson and your teaching of it were you to repeat the lesson.

You should prepare and carry out a 15- to 20-minute lesson to a group of peers. The exact time limit for the lesson should be set by your group, based on the size of the group and the amount of time available. When the time limit has been set, complete the time-allowed entry (item 1) of Form A of this exercise. Some of your peers will serve as your students; others will be evaluating your teaching. (The process works best when "students" do not evaluate while being students.) Your teaching should be videotaped for self-evaluation.

For your lesson, identify one concept and develop your lesson to teach toward an understanding of that concept. Within the time allowed, your lesson should include both teacher talk and a hands-on activity for the students. Use Form A for the initial planning of your lesson. Then complete a lesson plan, selecting a lesson plan format as discussed in Chapter 5. Then present the lesson to the "students." The peers who are evaluating your presentation should use Form B of this exercise.

After your presentation, collect your peer evaluations (the Form B copies that you gave to the evaluators). Then review your presentation by viewing the videotape. After viewing the tape, prepare the following:

- A tabulation and statistical analysis of the peer evaluations of your lesson.
- A self-evaluation based on your analysis of the peer evaluations, your feelings after having taught the lesson, and your thoughts after viewing the videotape.
- A summary analysis that includes your selection and a description of your teaching strengths and weaknesses, as indicated by this peer-teaching experience, and how you would improve were you to repeat the lesson.

TABULATION OF PEER EVALUATIONS

The procedure for tabulating the completed evaluations received from your peers is as follows:

1. *Use a blank copy of Form B for tabulating.* In the left margin of that copy, place the letters N (number) and σ (total) to prepare for two columns of numbers that will fall below each of those letters. In the far right margin, place the word *Score*.
2. *For each item (a through y) on the peer evaluation form, count the number of evaluators who gave a rating (from 1 to 5) on the item.* Sometimes an evaluator may not rate a particular item, so although 10 peers may have been evaluating your micro-peer teaching, the number of evaluators giving you a rating on any one particular item could be less than 10. For each item, the number of evaluators rating that item we call N. Place this number in the N column at the far left margin on your blank copy of Form B, next to the relevant item.
3. *Using a calculator, obtain the sum of the peer ratings for each item.* For example, for item a, lesson preparation, you add the numbers given by each evaluator for that item. If there were 10 evaluators who gave you a number rating on that item, then your sum on that item will not be more than 50 (5×10). Because individual evaluators will make their X marks differently, you sometimes must estimate an individual evaluator's number rating—that is, rather than a clear rating of 3 or 3.5 on an item, you may have to estimate it as being a 3.2 or a 3.9. In the left margin of your blank copy of Form B, in the σ column, place the sum for each item.
4. *Now obtain a score for each item, a through y.* The score for each item is obtained by dividing σ by N. Your score for each item will range between 1 and 5. Write this dividend in the column in the right margin under the word *Score* on a line parallel to the relevant item. This is the number you will use in the analysis phase.

☞

EXERCISE 11.1 *(continued)*

PROCEDURE FOR ANALYZING THE TABULATIONS

Having completed the tabulation of the peer evaluations of your teaching, you are ready to proceed with your analysis of those tabulations.

1. To proceed, you need a blank copy of Form C of this exercise, your self-analysis form.
2. On the blank copy of Form C, there are five items: Implementation, Personal, Voice, Materials, and Strategies.
3. In the far left margin of Form C, place the letter σ for the sum. To its right, and parallel with it, place the word *Average*. You now have arranged for two columns of five numbers each—a σ column and an *Average* column.
4. For each of the five items, get the total score for that item as follows:
   a. *Implementation.* Add all scores (from the right margin of blank Form B) for the four items a, c, x, and y. The total should be 20 or less (4 × 5). Place this total in the left margin under σ (to the left of "1. Implementation").
   b. *Personal.* Add all scores (from the right margin of blank Form B) for the nine items f, g, m, n, o, p, q, s, and t. The total should be 45 or less (9 × 5). Place this total in the left margin under σ (to the left of "2. Personal").
   c. *Voice.* Add all scores (from the right margin of blank Form B) for the three items h, i, and j. The total should be 15 or less (3 × 5). Place this total in the left margin under σ (to the left of "3. Voice").
   d. *Materials.* Add all "scores" (from the right margin of blank Form B) for item k. The total should be 5 or less (1 × 5). Place this total in the left margin under σ (to the left of "4. Materials").
   e. *Strategies.* Add all "scores" (from the right margin of blank Form B) for the eight items b, d, e, l, r, u, v, and w. The total should be 40 or less (8 × 5). Place this total in the left margin under σ (to the left of "5. Strategies").
5. Now, for each of the five categories, divide the sum by the number of items in the category to get your peer evaluation average score for that category. For item 1 you will divide by 4; for item 2, by 9; for item 3, by 3; for item 4, by 1; and for item 5, by 8. For each category, you should then have a final average peer evaluation score of a number between 1 and 5. If correctly done, you now have average scores for each of the five categories: Implementation, Personal, Voice, Materials, and Strategies. With those scores and evaluators' comments, you can prepare your final summary analysis.

The following table includes three sample analyses of MPT lessons based *only* on the scores— that is, without reference to comments made by individual evaluators, although peer evaluators' comments are important considerations for actual analyses.

Sample Analyses of MPTs Based Only on Peer-Evaluation Scores

Teacher	Category/Rating					Possible Strengths and Weaknesses
	1	*2*	*3*	*4*	*5*	
A	4.2	2.5	2.8	4.5	4.5	Good lesson, weakened by personal items and voice
B	4.5	4.6	5.0	5.0	5.0	Excellent teaching, perhaps needing a stronger start
C	2.5	3.0	3.5	1.0	1.5	Poor strategy choice, lack of student involvement

EXERCISE 11.1 FORM A   MPT PREPARATION

Form A is to be used for initial preparation of your MPT lesson. (For preparation of your lesson, study Form B.) After completing Form A, proceed with the preparation of your MPT lesson using a lesson plan format as discussed in Chapter 5. A copy of the final lesson plan should be presented to the evaluators at the start of your MPT presentation.

1. Time allowed: _____

2. Title or topic of lesson I will teach: _____

3. Concept: _____

4. Specific instructional objectives for the lesson:

   Cognitive: _____

   _____

   Affective: _____

   _____

   Psychomotor: _____

   _____

5. Strategies to be used, including approximate time plan: _____

   Set introduction: _____

   _____

   Transitions: _____

   _____

   Closure: _____

   _____

   Others: _____

   _____

6. Student experiences to be provided (i.e., specify for each—visual, verbal, kinesthetic, and tactile experiences):

   _____

   _____

7. Materials, equipment, and resources needed: _____

   _____

   _____

EXERCISE 11.1 FORM B   PEER EVALUATION

Evaluators use Form B, making an *X* on the continuum between 5 and 1. Far left (5) is the highest rating; far right (1) is the lowest. Completed forms are collected and given to the teacher upon completion of that teacher's MPT and are reviewed by the teacher prior to reviewing his or her videotaped lesson.

To evaluators: Comments as well as marks are useful to the teacher.

To teacher: Give one copy of your lesson plan to the evaluators at the start of your MPT. (Note: It is best if evaluators can be together at a table at the rear of the room.)

Teacher: _____ Date: _____

Topic: _____

Concept: _____

1. *Organization of Lesson*	5	4	3	2	1
a. Lesson preparation evident	very		somewhat		no
b. Lesson beginning effective	yes		somewhat		poor
c. Subject-matter knowledge apparent	yes		somewhat		no
d. Strategies selection effective	yes		somewhat		poor
e. Closure effective	yes		somewhat		poor

Comments:_____

_____

_____

_____

_____

_____

2. *Lesson Implementation*	5	4	3	2	1
f. Eye contact excellent	yes		somewhat		poor
g. Enthusiasm evident	yes		somewhat		no
h. Speech delivery	articulate		minor problems		poor
i. Voice inflection; cueing	effective		minor problems		poor
j. Vocabulary use	wellchosen		minor problems		poor
k. Aids, props, and materials	effective		okay		none
l. Use of examples and analogies	effective		need improvement		none
m. Student involvement	effective		okay		none
n. Use of overlapping skills	good		okay		poor

o. Nonverbal communication	effective	a bit confusing	distracting
p. Use of active listening	effective	okay	poor
q. Responses to students	personal and accepting	passive or indifferent	impersonal and antagonistic
r. Use of questions	effective	okay	poor
s. Use of student names	effective	okay	no
t. Use of humor	effective	okay	poor
u. Directions and refocusing	succinct	a bit vague	confusing
v. Teacher mobility	effective	okay	none
w. Use of transitions	smooth	a bit rough	unclear
x. Motivating presentation	very	somewhat	not at all
y. Momentum (pacing) of lesson	smooth and brisk	okay	too slow or too fast

Comments: _____

_____

_____

_____

_____

_____

_____

_____

_____

_____

_____

_____

_____

_____

_____

_____

_____

EXERCISE 11.1 FORM C   TEACHER'S SUMMATIVE PEER EVALUATION

See instructions within Exercise 11.1 for completing this form.

1. Implementation (items a, c, x, y)		5	4	3	2	1
2. Personal (items f, g, m, n, o, p, q, s, t)		5	4	3	2	1
3. Voice (items h, i, j)		5	4	3	2	1
4. Materials (item k)		5	4	3	2	1
5. Strategies (item b, d, e, l, r, u, v, w)		5	4	3	2	1

Total = _____

Comments: _____

_____

_____

_____

_____

_____

_____

_____

_____

_____

_____

_____

_____

_____

_____

_____

_____

_____

_____

_____

_____

_____

_____

GLOSSARY

ability grouping The assignment of students to separate classrooms or to separate activities within a classroom according to their perceived academic abilities. *Homogeneous grouping* is the grouping of students of similar abilities; *heterogeneous grouping* is the grouping of students of mixed abilities.

acceptable use policy (ACP) Policies adopted by school districts to address student/teacher use of Internet. Also sometimes referred to as IUP, Internet Use Policy.

accountability Reference to the concept that an individual is responsible for his or her behaviors and should be able to demonstrate publicly the worth of the activities carried out.

adolescence The period of life from the onset of puberty to maturity, terminating legally at the age of majority, generally the ages of 12 to 20, although young or early adolescence may start as soon as age 9.

advance organizer Preinstructional cues that encourage a mental set; used to enhance retention of content to be studied.

advisor–advisee Common to many middle schools and increasingly in high schools, the (sometimes referred to as *home base* or *advisory*) program that provides each student with opportunity to interact with peers about school and personal concerns and to develop a meaningful relationship with at least one adult.

affective domain The area of learning related to interests, attitudes, feelings, values, and personal adjustment.

alternative assessment Assessment of learning in ways different from traditional paper-and-pencil objective testing, such as a portfolio, project, or self-assessment. See *authentic assessment.*

anticipatory set See *advance organizer.*

approved curriculum The curriculum that teachers are mandated to teach and that students are expected to learn.

articulation Term used when referring to the connectedness of the various components of the formal curriculum—*vertical articulation* refers to the connectedness of the K–12 curriculum, and *horizontal articulation* refers to the connectedness across a grade level.

assessment The relatively neutral process of finding out what students are or have learned as a result of instruction.

at risk General term given to a student who shows a high potential for not completing school.

audioblog A voice message from a phone that immediately posts to a blog site.

authentic assessment The use of assessment procedures (usually portfolios and projects) that are compatible with the instructional objectives. Also referred to as *accurate, active, aligned, alternative, direct,* and *performance assessment.*

basal reader A reading textbook designed for a specific grade level.

behavioral objective A statement of expectation describing what the learner should be able to do upon completion of the instruction.

behaviorism A theory that equates learning with changes in observable behavior.

blended learning Term used with reference to learning that results from the combination of online and face-to-face approaches.

block scheduling The school programming procedure that provides large blocks of time (e.g., 2 hours) in which individual teachers or teacher teams can organize and arrange groupings of students for varied periods of time, thereby more effectively individualizing the instruction for students with various needs and abilities.

blog Personal space on the Web for the posting of individual commentary.

brainstorming An instructional strategy used to create a flow of new ideas, during which judgments of the ideas of others are forbidden.

bullying Harmful, sometimes violent, practice of verbal and physical abuse, humiliation, and shaming usually done in public by males to males, for the purpose of affirming masculinity, norms of toughness, strength, dominance, and control.

character education Focuses on the development of the values of honesty, kindness, respect, and responsibility.

classroom control   The process of influencing student behavior in the classroom.

classroom management   The teacher's system of establishing a climate for learning, including techniques for preventing and handling student misbehavior.

closure   The means by which a teacher brings the lesson to an end.

coaching   See *mentoring*.

cognition   The process of thinking.

cognitive disequilibrium   The mental state of not yet having made sense out of a perplexing (discrepant) situation.

cognitive domain   The area of learning related to intellectual skills, such as retention and assimilation of knowledge.

cognitive psychology   A branch of psychology devoted to the study of how individuals acquire, process, and use information.

cognitivism   A theory that holds that learning entails the construction or reshaping of mental schemata and that mental processes mediate learning. Also known as *constructivism*.

common planning time   A regularly scheduled time during the school day when teachers who teach the same students meet for joint planning, parent conferences, materials preparation, and student evaluation.

comprehension   A level of cognition that refers to the skill of understanding.

comprehensive high school   A high school that offers college preparatory, general, and vocational programs.

computer-assisted instruction (CAI)   Instruction received by a student when interacting with lessons programmed into a computer system. Known also as computer-assisted learning (CAL).

computer-managed instruction (CMI)   The use of a computer system to manage information about learner performance and learning-resources options in order to prescribe and control individual lessons.

constructionism   See *cognitivism*.

constructivism   See *cognitivism*.

continuous progress   An instructional procedure that allows students to progress at their own pace through a sequenced curriculum.

convergent thinking   Thinking that is directed to a preset conclusion.

cooperative learning   A genre of instructional strategies that use small groups of students working together and helping each other on learning tasks, stressing support for one another rather than competition.

copyright law   Law granting legal right to a copyright holder which requires the permission of the copyright holder to make.

core curriculum   Subject or discipline components of the curriculum considered as being absolutely necessary. Traditionally these are English/language arts, mathematics, science, and social science. However, the *No Child Left Behind Legislation of 2001* includes these as the core subjects: English, reading or language arts, mathematics, science, foreign language, civics and government, economics, arts, history, and geography.

covert behavior   A learner behavior that is not outwardly observable.

criterion   A standard by which behavioral performance is judged.

criterion-referenced assessment   Assessment in which standards are established and behaviors are judged against the present guideline, rather than against the behaviors of others.

critical thinking   The ability to recognize and identify problems, to propose and to test solutions, and to arrive at tentative conclusions based on the data collected.

culturally responsive teaching   Teaching that draws on the experiences, understandings, views, concepts, and ways of knowing of all the students who are in the classroom.

curriculum   Originally derived from a Latin term referring to a racecourse for the chariots, the term still has no widely accepted definition. As used in this text, curriculum is that which is planned and encouraged for teaching and learning. This includes both school and nonschool environments, overt (formal) and hidden (informal) curriculums, and broad as well as narrow notions of content—its development, acquisition, and consequences.

curriculum standards   Statements of the essential knowledge, skills, and attitudes to be learned.

cyberbullying   Use of the Internet to taunt, bully, threaten, or harass another person.

deductive learning   Learning that proceeds from the general to the specific. See also *expository learning*.

detracking   An effort to minimize or eliminate separate classes or programs for students who are of differing abilities.

developmental characteristics   A set of common intellectual, psychological, physical, and social characteristics that, when considered as a whole, indicate an individual's development relative to others during a particular age span.

developmental needs   A set of needs unique and appropriate to the developmental characteristics of a particular age span.

diagnostic assessment   See *preassessment*.

didactic teaching   See *direct instruction*.

differentiated instruction   Varying the methods and content of instruction according to individual student differences and needs.

direct experience   Learning by doing (applying) that which is being learned.

direct instruction   Teacher-centered expository instruction, such as lecturing or a teacher-guided group discussion.

direct intervention   Teacher use of verbal reminders or verbal commands to redirect student behavior, as opposed to nonverbal gestures or cues.

direct teaching   See *direct instruction.*

discipline   The process of controlling student behavior in the classroom. The term has been largely replaced by the terms *classroom control* or *classroom management.* It is also used in reference to the subject taught (e.g., language arts, science, mathematics, and so forth).

discovery learning   Learning that proceeds from identification of a problem, through the development of hypotheses, the testing of the hypotheses, and the arrival at a conclusion. See also *critical thinking.*

divergent thinking   Thinking that expands beyond original thought.

downshifting   Reverting to earlier learned, lower cognitive-level behaviors.

early adolescence   The developmental stage of young people as they approach and begin to experience puberty. This stage usually occurs between 10 and 14 years of age and deals with the successful attainment of the appropriate developmental characteristics for this age span.

eclectic approach   Utilizing the best from a variety of sources.

edblog   Educational blogging sites on the Web.

effective school   A school where students master basic skills, seek academic excellence in all subjects, demonstrate achievement, and display good behavior and attendance. Known also as an *exemplary school.*

elective   High-interest or special-needs courses that are based on student selection from various options.

elemiddle school   Term sometimes used to denote schools with the K–8 grades inclusion.

elementary school   Any school that has been planned and organized especially for children of some combination of grades kindergarten through 6. There are many variations, though; for example, a school might house children of preschool through grade 7 or 8 and still be called an elementary school.

empathy   The ability to understand the feelings of another person.

English language learner (ELL)   A student who has only limited (LEP) or no English proficiency (NEP).

equality   Considered to be same in status or competency level.

equity   Fairness and justice, that is, impartiality.

evaluation   Like assessment, but includes making sense out of the assessment results, usually based on criteria or a rubric. Evaluation is more subjective than is assessment.

exceptional child   A child who deviates from the average in any of the following ways: mental characteristics, sensory ability, neuromotor or physical characteristics, social behavior, communication ability, or multiple handicaps. Also known as a *special-needs student* and/or *student with special needs.*

exemplary school   See *effective school.*

exploratory course   A course designed to help students explore curriculum experiences based on their felt needs, interests, and abilities.

expository learning   The traditional classroom instructional approach that proceeds as follows: presentation of information to the learners, reference to particular examples, and application of the information to the learner's experiences.

extended-year school   Schools that have extended the school-year calendar from the traditional 180 days to a longer period, such as 200 days.

extrinsic motivators   Motivation of learning by rewards outside of the learner, such as parent and teacher expectations, gifts, certificates, stamps, and grades.

facilitating behavior   Teacher behavior that makes it possible for students to learn.

facilitative teaching   See *indirect instruction.*

fair use   A legal principle defining the limitations on exclusive rights of copyright holders that applies to only nonprofit educational institutions and homebound instruction.

family   See *school-within-a-school.*

feedback   Information sent from the receiver to the originator that provides disclosure about the reception of the intended message.

flexible scheduling   Organization of classes and activities in a way that allows for variation from day to day, as opposed to the traditional, fixed schedule that does not vary from day to day.

formative assessment   Assessment of learning in progress.

freeze time   A scheduled time, perhaps an hour, each week of school when all teachers are in their classrooms to help students and meet with parents/guardians, a time during which no other activities, including athletic practices or club meetings, are scheduled.

goal, course   A broad generalized statement about the expected outcomes of a course.

goal, educational   A desired instructional outcome that is broad in scope.

goal, student   A statement about what the student hopes to accomplish.

goal, teacher   A statement about what the teacher hopes to accomplish.

hands-on learning   Learning by actively doing.

Hawthorne effect   Says that no matter what, if you try something new, it will show positive effects at first simply because of the interest demonstrated when something new is tried. Name derived from the first notice of the effect in 1962 at the Hawthorne plant of Western Electric in Cicero, Illinois.

hazing   Any action or situation that coerces the victim into performing any act that degrades, humiliates, and/or causes or creates a substantial risk for mental or physical harm.

heterogeneous grouping   A grouping pattern that does not separate students into groups based on their intelligence, learning achievement, or physical characteristics.

hidden curriculum   Subtle, often unplanned, message systems within a school. Also known as the covert or informal curriculum.

high school   A school that houses students in any combination of grades 9–12.

high-stakes assessment   An assessment is called high stakes if use of the assessment's results carry serious consequences, such as a student's grade promotion rests on the student's performance on one test, or the student's graduation from high school rests on the student's performance on a single test.

heuristic   Any tool used in solving a problem or understanding an idea.

holistic learning   Learning that incorporates emotions with thinking.

home base   See *advisor–advisee*.

homeroom   See *advisor–advisee*.

homogeneous grouping   A grouping pattern that separates students into groups based on common characteristics, such as intelligence, achievement, or physical characteristics.

house   See *school-within-a-school*.

inclusion   The commitment to the education of each learner with special needs, to the maximum extent appropriate, in the school and classroom the student would otherwise attend.

independent study   An instructional strategy that allows a student to select a topic, set the goals, and work alone to attain them.

indirect instruction   Student-centered teaching using discovery and inquiry as learning strategies.

individualized instruction   The self-paced process whereby individual students assume responsibility for learning through study, practice, feedback, and reinforcement with appropriately designed instructional modules.

inductive learning   Learning that proceeds from specifics to the general. See also *discovery learning*.

inquiry learning   Like discovery learning, except the learner designs the processes to be used in resolving the problem.

inservice teacher   Term used when referring to credentialed and employed teachers.

instruction   Planned arrangement of experiences to help a learner develop understanding and to achieve a desirable change in behavior.

instructional module   Any freestanding instructional unit that includes these components: rationale, objectives, pretest, learning activities, comprehension checks with instructive feedback, and posttest.

integrated (interdisciplinary) curriculum   Curriculum organization that combines subject matter traditionally taught independently.

interdisciplinary instruction   Instruction that combines subject-matter disciplines traditionally taught independently.

interdisciplinary team   An organizational pattern of two or more teachers representing different subject areas. The team shares the same students, schedule, areas of the school, and the opportunity for teaching more than one subject.

interdisciplinary thematic unit (ITU)   A thematic unit that crosses boundaries of two or more disciplines.

intermediate grades   Term sometimes used to refer to grades 4–6.

internalization   The extent to which an attitude or value becomes a part of the learner. That is, without having to think about it, the learner's behavior reflects the attitude or value.

International Baccalaureate School   A school with a curriculum approved by the International Baccalaureate Organization (IBO), a worldwide nonprofit educational foundation based in Switzerland.

interscholastic sports   Athletic competition between teams from two or more schools.

intervention   A teacher's interruption to redirect a student's behavior, either by direct intervention (e.g., by a verbal command) or by indirect intervention (e.g., by eye contact or physical proximity).

intramural program   Organized activity program that features events between individuals or teams from within the school.

intrinsic motivation   Motivation of learning through the student's internal sense of accomplishment.

intuition   Knowing without conscious reasoning.

junior high school   A school that houses grades 7–9 or 7–8 and that has a schedule and curriculum that resemble those of the senior high school (grades 9–12 or 10–12) more than they do those of the elementary school.

K–16   Reference to kindergarten through first 2 years of college.

leadership team   A group of teachers and administrators, and sometimes students, designated by the principal or elected by the faculty (and student body) to assist in the leadership of the school.

lead teacher   The member of a teaching team who is designated to facilitate the work and planning of that team.

learning The development of understandings and the change in behavior resulting from experiences. For different interpretations of learning, see *behaviorism* and *cognitivism*.

learning center (LC) An instructional strategy that utilizes activities and materials located at a special place in the classroom and is designed to allow a student to work independently at his or her own pace to learn one area of content. See also *learning station*.

learning modality The way a person receives information. Four modalities are recognized: visual, auditory, tactile (touch), and kinesthetic (movement).

learning resource center The central location in the school where instructional materials and media are stored, organized, and accessed by students and staff.

learning station (LS) Like a learning center, except that each learning center is distinct and unrelated to others, whereas learning stations are sequenced or in some way linked to one another.

learning style The way a person learns best in a given situation.

literacy The ability to read, write, speak, listen, and think critically.

looping An arrangement in which the cohort of students and teachers remain together as a group for several or for all the years a child is at a particular school. Also referred to as multiyear grouping, multiyear instruction, multiyear placement, and teacher–student progression.

magnet school A school that specializes in a particular academic area, such as science, mathematics and technology, the arts, or international relations. Also referred to as a *theme school*.

mainstreaming Placing an exceptional child in regular education classrooms for all (inclusion) or part (partial inclusion) of the school day.

mandala A diagram, usually circular, with spiritual and ritual significance.

mastery learning The concept that a student should master the content of one lesson before moving on to the content of the next.

measurement The process of collecting and interpreting data.

mentoring One-on-one coaching, tutoring, or guidance to facilitate learning.

metacognition Planning, monitoring, and evaluating one's own thinking. Known also as *reflective abstraction*.

micro peer teaching (MPT) Teaching a limited objective for a brief period to a small group of peers for the purpose of evaluation and improvement of particular teaching skills.

middle grades Grades 5–8.

middle-level education Any school unit between elementary and high school.

middle school A school that has been planned and organized especially for young adolescents, that is for students of ages 10–14.

minds-on learning Learning in which the learner is intellectually active, thinking about what is being learned.

misconception Faulty understanding of a major idea or concept. Also known as a *naïve theory* and *conceptual misunderstanding*.

mission statement School or district written statement of its unique beliefs and goals, sometimes referred to as statement of philosophy or vision, although a vision statement is or should be a statement of intention that extends beyond the immediate mission of the school or district, giving future direction to the statement of mission.

modeling The teacher's direct and indirect demonstration, by actions and by words, of the behaviors expected of students.

multicultural education A deliberate attempt to help students understand facts, generalizations, attitudes, and behaviors derived from their own ethnic roots as well as others. In this process, students unlearn racism and biases and recognize the interdependent fabric of society, giving due acknowledgment for contributions made by its members.

multilevel instruction individual students and groups of students are working at different tasks to accomplish the same objective or at different tasks to accomplish different objectives.

multilevel teaching See *multitasking*.

multimedia The combined use of sound, video, and graphics for instruction.

multiple intelligences A theory of several different intelligences, as opposed to just one general intelligence; intelligences that have been described are verbal/linguistic, musical, logical/mathematical, naturalist, visual/spatial, bodily/kinesthetic, interpersonal, and intrapersonal.

multipurpose dry-erase board A writing board with a smooth plastic surface used with special marking pens rather than chalk. Sometimes called a visual aid panel, the board may have a steel backing and then can be used as a magnetic board as well as a screen for projecting visuals.

multitasking The simultaneous use of several levels of teaching and learning in the same classroom, with students working on different objectives or different tasks leading to the same objective. Also called *multilevel teaching*.

naïve theory See *misconception*.

National Education Association (NEA) The nation's oldest professional organization of teachers, founded in 1857 as the National Teachers Association and changed in 1879 to its present name. Recently merged in at least two states (Montana and Minnesota) with the AFT.

No Child Left Behind (NCLB)   Landmark national legislation that promises to improve student achievement and change the culture of U.S. schools while providing equal educational opportunities for all students. It became law on January 8, 2002.

norm referenced   Individual performance is judged relative to overall performance of the group (e.g., grading on a curve), as opposed to being criterion referenced.

orientation set   See *advance organizer*.

overlapping   A teacher behavior where the teacher is able to attend to more than one matter at once.

overt behavior   A behavior that is outwardly observable.

pastoral learning   See *personalized learning*.

peer tutoring   An instructional strategy that places students in a tutorial role in which one student helps another learn.

performance assessment   See *authentic assessment*.

performance-based instruction   Instruction designed around the instruction and assessment of student achievement against specified and predetermined objectives.

performance objective   See *behavioral objective*.

personalized instruction   See *individualized instruction*.

personalized learning   Teaching strategies, school practices, and support mechanisms that take into consideration the unique characteristics and educational needs of each student. Basic components include individualized learning plans (ILPs); consideration of each student's intellectual capacity, interests, and aspirations; involvement of each student in decision making regarding their academic life; and the involvement of committed advisors and mentors for each student.

phonemic awareness   The ability to identify, isolate, and manipulate the individual sounds, or phonemes, in words.

phonics   The application of sound–symbol relationships to the teaching of reading.

phonological awareness   The knowledge of the sounds of language, including the ability to hear syllables in words, hear the parts of the words, hear individual sounds in words, and identify and make rhymes.

portfolio assessment   An alternative approach to evaluation that assembles representative samples of a student's work over time as a basis for assessment.

positive reinforcer   A means of encouraging desired student behaviors by rewarding those behaviors when they occur.

preassessment   Diagnostic assessment of what students know or think they know prior to the instruction.

preservice   Term used when referring to teachers in training, as opposed to inservice teachers, teachers who are employed.

probationary teacher   An untenured teacher. After a designated number of years in the same district, usually three, upon rehire the probationary teacher receives a tenure contract.

procedure   A statement telling the student how to accomplish a task.

professional learning community (PLC)   As traditionally recognized, the PLC is a group of teacher leaders and administrators who work together to seek and share ways of improving student learning in their school. Today's concept of the PLC has broadened to include support staff and the wider community.

psychomotor domain   The domain of learning that involves locomotor behaviors.

punking   See *bullying*.

realia   Real objects used as visual props during instruction, such as political campaign buttons, plants, memorabilia, art, balls, and so forth.

reciprocal teaching   A form of collaborative teaching where the teacher and the students share the teaching responsibility and all are involved in asking questions, clarifying, predicting, and summarizing.

reflection   The conscious process of mentally replaying experiences.

reflective abstraction   See *metacognition*.

reliability   In measurement, the consistency with which an item or instrument is measured over time.

response to intervention (RtI)   Although there are a number of RtI models and programs, the essence of most is based on the practice of instruction and intervention matched to individual student need, monitoring student progress frequently, such as weekly, to make decisions about changes in instruction or goals and applying student response data to education decisions, with the ultimate premise that students should not have to wait and fail in order to receive needed services and support.

rubric   An outline of the criteria used to assess a student's work.

rules   In classroom management, rules are the standards of expectation for classroom behavior.

schema   (plural: schemata) A mental construct by which the learner organizes his or her perceptions of situations and knowledge.

school-within-a-school   Sometimes referred to as a *house, cluster, village, pod,* or *family,* it is a teaching arrangement where one team of teachers is assigned to work with the same group of about 125 students for a common block of time, for the entire school day, or, in some instances, for all the years those students are at that school.

secondary school   Traditionally, any school housing students for any combination of grades 7–12.

self-contained classroom   Commonly used in the primary grades, it is a grouping pattern where one teacher teaches all or most all subjects to one group of children.

self-paced learning   See *individualized instruction*.

senior high school   Usually a high school that houses only students in grades 9–12 or 10–12.

sequencing   Arranging ideas in logical order.

simulation   An abstraction or simplification of a real-life situation.

Socratic questioning   Named for the Athenian teacher Socrates, a questioning strategy in which a teacher asks students a series of questions and encourages students to develop their own conclusions and inferences.

special-needs student   See *exceptional child*.

standards   See *curriculum standards*.

student teaching   A field experience component of teacher preparation, traditionally the culminating experience, where the teacher candidate practices teaching children while under the supervision of a credentialed teacher and a university supervisor.

student with special needs   See *exceptional child*.

summative assessment   Assessment of learning after instruction is completed.

teacher leader   See *lead teacher*.

teaching   See *instruction*.

teaching style   The way teachers teach; their distinctive mannerisms complemented by their choices of teaching behaviors and strategies.

teaching team   A team of two or more teachers who work together to provide instruction to the same group of students, either alternating the instruction or team teaching simultaneously.

team teaching   Two or more teachers working together to provide instruction to a group of students.

tenured teacher   After serving a designated number of years in the same school district (usually three) as a probationary teacher, upon rehire the teacher receives a tenure contract, which means that the teacher is automatically rehired each year thereafter unless the contract is revoked by either the district or the teacher and for specific and legal reasons.

terminal behavior   That which has been learned as a direct result of instruction.

thematic unit   A unit of instruction built on a central theme or concept.

theme school   See *magnet school*.

think time   See *wait time*.

tracking   The practice of the voluntary or involuntary placement of students in different programs or courses according to their ability and prior academic performance. See also *ability grouping*.

traditional teaching   Teacher-centered direct instruction, typically using lectures, discussions, textbooks, and worksheets.

transition   In a lesson, the planned procedures that move student thinking from one idea to the next or that move their actions from one activity to the next. With reference to schooling, transitions are the times when a student moves from one level of school to the next.

untracking   See *detracking*.

validity   In measurement, the degree to which an item or instrument measures that which it is intended to measure.

village   See *school-within-a-school*.

wait time   In the use of questioning, the period of silence between the time a question is asked and the inquirer (teacher) does something, such as repeats the question, rephrases the question, calls on a particular student, answers the question, or asks another question. Also referred to as *think time*.

Weblog   See *blog*.

whole-language learning   A point of view with a focus on seeking or creating meaning that encourages language production, risk taking, independence in producing language, and the use of a wide variety of print materials in authentic reading and writing situations.

withitness   The teacher's timely ability to intervene and redirect a student's inappropriate behavior.

year-round school   A school that operates as is tradition, which is with 180 school days, but the days are spread over 12 months rather than the usual 10. Most common is the 9-weeks on, 3-weeks off format.

young adolescent   The 10- to 14-year-old experiencing the developmental stage of early adolescence.

REFERENCES

Acar, B., & Tarhan, L. (2008). Effects of cooperative learning on students' understanding of metallic bonding. *Research in Science Education, 38*(4), 401–420.

Acker, S., & Halasek, K. (2008). Preparing high school students for college-level writing: Using ePortfolio to support a successful transition. *Journal of General Education, 57*(1), 1–14.

Adam, A., & Mowers, H. (2007). Got the world on a screen. *School Library Journal, 53*(4), 40–42.

Albert, L. (1989). *A teacher's guide to cooperative discipline: How to manage your classroom and promote self-esteem.* Circle Pines, MN: American Guidance Service.

Allen, R. (2003). An early taste of college: Accelerated learning with support motivates urban students. *Education Update, 45*, 1–8.

Allison, B. N., & Rehm, M. L. (2007). Effective teaching strategies for middle school learners in multicultural, multilingual classrooms. *Middle School Journal, 39*(2), 12–18.

Alvarado, A. (1998, Winter). Professional development is the job. *American Educator, 22*(4), 18–23.

Amer, A. (2006). Reflections on Bloom's revised taxonomy. *Electronic Journal of Research in Educational Psychology, 4*(1), 213–230.

Anderson, L. W. (2004). Objectives, evaluation, and the improvement of education. *Studies in Educational Evaluation, 31*(2–3), 102–113.

Annetta, L. A. (2008). Video games in education: Why they should be used and how they are being used. *Theory Into Practice, 47*(3), 229–239.

Armstrong, T. (1998). *Awakening genius in the classroom.* Alexandria, VA: Association for Supervision and Curriculum Development.

Aronson, E., Blaney, N., Stephan, C., Sikes, J., & Snapp, M. (1978). *The jigsaw classroom.* Beverly Hills, CA: Sage.

Arth, A., Ashford, A., Jenkins, J. B., Burns, J., Kane, T., Mitchell, K., et al. (2004). Present imperfect. *Principal Leadership, 4.* Retrieved from http://www.principals.org/publications/pl/pl_present_imperfect_0404.cfm

Ashton, P., & Webb, R. (1986). *Making a difference: Teacher's sense of efficacy and student achievement.* New York, NY: Longman.

Astington, J. W. (1998). Theory of mind goes to school. *Educational Leadership, 56*(3), 46–48.

Ausubel, D. P. (1963). *The psychology of meaningful learning.* New York, NY: Grune & Stratton.

Badke, W. (2009). Stepping beyond Wikipedia. *Educational Leadership, 66*(6), 54–58.

Baker, J. C., & Martin, F. G. (1998). *A neural network guide to teaching. Fastback 431.* Bloomington, IN: Phi Delta Kappa Educational Foundation.

Baldwin, D. (2004). A guide to standardized writing assessment. *Educational Leadership, 62*(2), 72–75.

Banks, J. A. (1999). Multicultural and citizenship education in the new century. *School Administrator, 56*, 8–10. Retrieved from http://www.aasa.org/SA/may9901/htm

Barnes, L. J. (2008). Lecture-free high school biology using an audience response system. *American Biology Teacher, 70*(9), 531–536.

Barojas, J., & Dehesa, N. (2001). Mathematics for social scientists: Learning cycles and teaching strategies. *Industry & Higher Education, 15*, 269–277.

Barrett, H. C. (2007). Researching electronic portfolios and learning engagement. *Journal of Adolescent & Adult Literacy, 50*(6), 436–449.

Barrios, L. C., Jones, S. E., & Gallagher, S. S. (2007). Legal liability: The consequences of school injury. *Journal of School Health, 77*(5), 273–279.

Barron, J. B., & Sternberg, R. J. (Eds.). (1987). *Teaching thinking skills: Theory and practice.* New York, NY: W. H. Freeman.

Battistini, J. (1995). *From theory to practice: Classroom application of outcome-based education.* Bloomington, IN: ERIC Clearinghouse on Reading, English, and Communication.

Beilke, J. R., Stuve, M. J., & Williams-Hawkins, M. A. (2008). "Clubcasting": Educational uses of podcasting in multicultural settings. *Multicultural Education & Technology Journal, 2*(2), 107–117.

Benjamin, A. (2007). *But I'm not a reading teacher: Strategies for literacy instruction in the content areas.* Larchmont, NY: Eye on Education.

Berkeley, S., Bender, W. N., Peaster, L. G., & Saunders, L. (2009). Implementation of response to intervention: A snapshot of progress. *Journal of Learning Disabilities, 42*(1), 85–95.

Berman, S. (2007). *Performance-based learning: Aligning experiential tasks and assessment to increase learning.* Thousand Oaks, CA: Corwin Press.

Bernal, P. (2007). Acting out: Using drama with English learners. *English Journal, 96*(3), 26–28.

Bevevino, M. M., Dengel, J., & Adams, K. (1999). Constructivist theory in the classroom: Internalizing concepts through inquiry learning. *Clearing House, 72,* 275–278.

Bisogno, J., & JeanPierre, B. (2008). Virtual bridge design. *Science Scope, 32*(1), 26–33.

Black, S. (2004). All together now. *American School Board Journal 191*(3), 40–42.

Bloom, B. (1987). *Human characteristics and school learning.* New York, NY: McGraw-Hill.

Bloom, B. S. (Ed.). (1984). *Taxonomy of educational objectives, book 1, cognitive domain.* White Plains, NY: Longman.

Bobek, B. L. (2002). Teacher resiliency: A key to career longevity. *Clearing House, 75,* 202–205.

Bolland, J. M. (2003). Hopelessness and risk behaviour among adolescents living in high-poverty inner-city neighbourhoods. *Journal of Adolescence, 26,* 145–158.

Booker, M. J. (2007). A roof without walls: Benjamin Bloom's taxonomy and the misdirection of American education. *Academic Questions, 20*(4), 347–344.

Boon, R. T., Fore, C. III, & Spencer, V. G. (2007). Teachers' attitudes and perceptions toward the use of Inspiration 6 Software in inclusive world history classes at the secondary level. *Journal of Instructional Psychology, 34*(3), 161–171.

Boston, C. (Ed.). (2002). *Understanding scoring rubrics: A guide for teachers.* College Park, MD: ERIC Clearinghouse on Assessment and Evaluation.

Bowman-Perrott, L. J., Greenwood, C. R., & Tapia, Y. (2007). The efficacy of CWPT used in secondary alternative school classrooms with small teacher/pupil ratios and students with emotional and behavioral disorders. *Education and Treatment of Children, 30*(3), 65–87.

Brand, S., Dunn, R., & Greb, F. (2002). Learning styles of students with attention deficit hyperactivity disorder: Who are they and how can we teach them? *Clearing House, 75,* 268–273.

Brandt, R. (2000). On teaching brains to think: A conversation with Robert Sylwester. *Educational Leadership, 57*(7), 72–75.

Brogan, B. R., & Brogan, W. A. (1995). The Socratic questioner: Teaching and learning in the dialogical classroom. *Educational Forum, 59,* 288–296.

Brookhart, S. M. (2008). *How to give effective feedback to your students.* Alexandria, VA: Association for Supervision and Curriculum Development.

Brooks, J. G., & Brooks, M. G. (1993). *In search of understanding: The case for constructivist classrooms.* Alexandria, VA: Association for Supervision and Curriculum Development.

Brown, D. S. (2003). High school biology: A group approach to concept mapping. *American Biology Teacher, 65*(3), 192–197.

Brown, J. L., & Moffett, C. A. (1999). *The hero's journey.* Alexandria, VA: Association for Supervision and Curriculum Development.

Bruner, J. S. (1960). *Process of education.* Cambridge, MA: Harvard University Press.

Bullock, A. A., & Hawk, P. P. (2001). *Developing a teaching portfolio.* Upper Saddle River, NJ: Merrill Prentice Hall.

Burns, M. (2004). Writing in math. *Educational Leadership, 62*(3), 30–33.

Burrett, K., & Rusnak, T. (1993). *Integrated character education. Fastback 341.* Bloomington, IN: Phi Delta Kappa Educational Foundation.

Caine, R. N. (2000). Building the bridge from research to classroom. *Educational Leadership, 58*(3), 59–61.

Caine, R. N., & Caine, G. (1997). *Education on the edge of possibility.* Alexandria, VA: Association for Supervision and Curriculum Development.

Callahan, C. M. (2001). Beyond the gifted stereotype. *Educational Leadership, 59*(3), 42–46.

Campbell, L., & Campbell, B. (1999). *Multiple intelligences and student achievement: Success stories from six schools.* Alexandria, VA: Association for Supervision and Curriculum Development.

Canter, A., Klotz, M. B., & Cowan, K. (2008). *Principal Leadership, 8*(6), 12–15.

Canter, L., & Canter, M. (2002). *Assertive discipline: Positive behavior management for today's schools* (3rd ed.). Seal Beach, CA: Lee Canter & Associates.

Cardoso, F. S., Dumpel, R., Gomes da Silva, L. B., Rodriques, C. R., Santos, D. O., Cabral, L. M., et al.

(2008). Just working with the cellular machine: A high school game for teaching molecular biology. *Biochemistry and Molecular Biology Education, 36*(2), 120–124.

Carolan, J., & Guinn, A. (2007). Differentiation: Lessons from master teachers. *Educational Leadership, 64*(5), 44–47.

Carrier, K. A. (2005). Key issues for teaching English language learners in academic classrooms. *Middle School Journal, 37*(2), 4–9.

Carroll, J. (1963). A model of school learning. *Teachers College Record, 64,* 723–733.

Carroll, J. (1994). The Copernican plan evaluated. *Phi Delta Kappan, 76*(2), 105–113.

Carter, C. J. (1997). Why reciprocal teaching? *Educational Leadership, 54*(6), 64–68.

Carter, J. B. (2009). Going graphic. *Educational Leadership, 66*(6), 68–72.

Casbarro, J. (2004). Reducing anxiety in the era of high-stakes testing. *Principal, 83*(5), 36–38.

Champeau, R. (2006). Doing advisories. *Principal Leadership, 6*(7), 22–26.

Charsky, D., & Mims, C. (2008). Integrating commercial off-the-shelf video games into school curriculums. *TechTrends: Linking Research and Practice to Improve Learning, 52*(5), 38–44.

Chehayl, L. (2008). Books in action! *Middle School Journal, 40*(1), 26–32.

Chi, M. T. H., Siler, S. A., & Jeong, H. (2004). Can tutors monitor students' understanding accurately? *Cognition & Instruction, 22*(3), 363–387.

Choate, J. S., & Rakes, T. A. (1998). *Inclusive instruction for struggling readers. Fastback 434.* Bloomington, IN: Phi Delta Kappa Educational Foundation.

Ciardiello, A. V. (2000). Student questioning and multidimensional literacy in the 21st century. *Educational Forum, 64,* 215–222.

Clark, G., & Zimmerman, E. (1998). Nurturing the arts in programs for gifted and talented students. *Phi Delta Kappan, 79,* 747–751.

Clark, S. (2009). Using curriculum-based measurement to improve achievement. *Principal, 88*(3), 30–33.

Cobb, C. D., & Rallis, S. F. (2008). District responses to NCLB: Where is the justice? *Leadership and Policy in Schools, 7*(2), 178–201.

Cochran, D., & Conklin, J. (2007). A new Bloom: Transforming learning. *Learning & Leading with Technology, 34*(4), 22–24.

Coelho, E. (1994). *Learning together in the multicultural classroom.* Portsmouth, NH: Heinemann.

Coiro, J. (2009). Rethinking online reading assessment. *Educational Leadership, 66*(6), 59–63.

Combs, A. W. (Ed.). (1962). *Perceiving, behaving, becoming: A new focus for education.* Arlington, VA: Association for Supervision and Curriculum Development.

Conderman, G., Ikan, P. A., & Hatcher, R. E. (2000). Student-led conferences in inclusive settings. *Intervention in School and Clinic, 36*(1), 22–26.

Coney, S., & Kanel, S. (1997, April). *Opening the World of Literature to Children through Interactive Drama Experiences.* Paper presented at the Annual International Conference and Exhibition of the Association for Childhood Education, Portland, OR.

Costa, A. L. (Ed.). (1985). *Developing minds: A resource book for teaching thinking.* Alexandria, VA: Association for Supervision and Curriculum Development.

Costa, A. L. (1991). *The school as a home for the mind.* Palatine, IL: Skylight Publishing.

Costa, A. L., & Kallick, B. (2000). *Discovering and exploring habits of mind, book 1 of habits of mind: A developmental series.* Alexandria, VA: Association for Supervision and Curriculum Development.

Coulter, S. E., & Groenke, S. L. (2008). A differentiated vocabulary unit for John Knowles's "A Separate Peace." *English Journal, 97*(4), 26–32.

Crowe, A., Dirks, C., & Wenderoth, M. P. (2008). Biology in Bloom: Implementing Bloom's taxonomy to enhance student learning in biology. *CBE—Life Sciences Education, 7*(4), 368–381.

Cunningham, J. D., Bradley, K. D., & Osborn, J. (2008). Assessing the impact of "Newton's Universe:" Preliminary findings associated with rural middle school students' and teachers' outcomes linked to inquiry-based physical science. *ERS Spectrum, 26*(1), 39–44.

Curwin, R. L., Mendler, A. N., & Mendler, B. D. (2008). *Discipline with dignity.* Alexandria, VA: Association for Supervision and Curriculum Development.

Danielson, C. (1997). *A collection of performance tasks and rubrics: Middle school mathematics.* Larchmont, NY: Eye on Education.

Danielson, C. (1998). *A collection of performance tasks and rubrics: High school mathematics.* Larchmont, NY: Eye on Education.

Danielson, C., & McGreal, T. I. (2000). *Teacher evaluation to enhance professional practice.* Alexandria, VA: Association for Supervision and Curriculum Development, and Princeton, NJ: Educational Testing Service.

Davidson, J. (2009). Exhibitions: Connecting classroom assessment with culminating demonstrations of mastery. *Theory Into Practice, 48*(1), 36–43.

Davis, A. K. (2001). The politics of barking and the state of our schools. *Phi Delta Kappan, 82,* 786–789.

Davis, A. P., & McGrail, E. (2009). The joy of blogging. *Educational Leadership, 66*(6), 74–77.

De Bono, E. (1970). *Lateral thinking; Creativity step by step.* New York, NY: Harper and Row.

de Mestre, N. (2007). Sudoku. *Australian Mathematics Teacher, 63*(4), 6–7.

Delaney, C. J., & Shafer, F. K. (2007). Teaching to multiple intelligence by following a "slime trail." *Middle School Journal, 39*(1), 38–43.

DeLay, R. (1996). Forming knowledge: Constructivist learning and experiential education. *Journal of Experiential Education, 19*(2), 76–81.

Dewey, J. (1902). *The child and the curriculum.* Chicago, IL: University of Chicago Press.

Dewey, J. (1910). *How we think.* Boston, MA: Heath.

Díaz-Rico, L. T., & Weed, K. Z. (2010). *The crosscultural, language, and academic development handbook* (4th ed.). Boston: Pearson Allyn & Bacon.

Dibley, J., & Parish, J. (2007). Using video games to understand thermoregulation. *Science Scope, 8*(30), 32–35.

Dreikurs, R., & Cassel, P. (1972). *Discipline without tears.* New York, NY: Hawthorne Books.

Dreikurs, R., Grunwald, B. B., & Pepper, F. C. (1982). *Maintaining sanity in the classroom: Classroom management techniques* (2nd ed.). New York, NY: Harper & Row.

Dryfoos, J. (2002). Full service schools: Creating new institutions. *Phi Delta Kappan, 83*(5), 393–399.

Dunn, R. (1995). *Strategies for educating diverse learners. Fastback 384.* Bloomington, IN: Phi Delta Kappa Educational Foundation.

Dweck, C. S. (2007). The perils and promises of praise. *Educational Leadership, 65*(2), 34–39.

Echevarria, J., & Graves, A. (2007). *Sheltered content instruction: Teaching English language learners with diverse abilities* (3rd ed.). Boston, MA: Pearson Allyn & Bacon.

Echevarria, M. (2003). Anomalies as a catalyst for middle school students' knowledge construction and scientific reasoning during science inquiry. *Journal of Educational Psychology, 95,* 357–374.

Educational Leadership. (1999). The constructivist classroom [Entire issue]. *Educational Leadership, 57*(3).

Edwards, C. H. (1997). *Classroom discipline and management* (2nd ed.). Upper Saddle River, NJ: Prentice Hall.

Eilertsen, T. V., & Valdermo, O. (2000). Open-book assessment: A contribution to improved learning? *Studies in Educational Evaluation, 26*(2), 91–103.

Eisner, E. W. (1979). *The educational imagination.* New York, NY: Macmillan.

Eisner, E. W. (2002). The kind of schools we need. *Phi Delta Kappan, 84*(8), 579.

Eisner, E. W. (2004). Preparing for today and tomorrow. *Educational Leadership, 61*(4), 6–10.

Elbow, P. (2004). Writing first! *Educational Leadership, 62*(2), 8–13.

Elias, M. J. (2001). Easing transitions with social-emotional learning. *Principal Leadership, 1,* 1–4. Retrieved from http:// www.nassp.org/news/pl_soc_emo_lrng_ 301.htm

Elliott, J. (2008a). Long Beach's pivotal turn around RTI. *School Administrator, 65*(8), 16.

Elliott, J. (2008b). Response to intervention: What & why? *School Administrator, 65*(8), 10–12.

English, L. (1998). Uncovering students' analytic, practical, and creative intelligences: One school's application of Sternberg's triarchic theory. *School Administrator, 55*(1), 28–29.

Erwin, P. (2009, March). Making grammar improvement enjoyable. *Middle Matters.* Retrieved January 6, 2010, from http:// www.naesp.org/Middle_Matters_ Archives.aspx

Fagan, H., & Sherman, L. (2002). Starting at the end: Alaska project-based learning expert Helena Fagan insists that good projects are designed "backward"— that is, what do we want kids to know when they're done? *Northwest Education, 7*(3), 30–35.

Fahey, K., Lawrence, J., & Paratore, J. (2007). Using electronic portfolios to make learning public. *Journal of Adolescent & Adult Literacy, 50*(6), 460–471.

Fairbanks, E. K., Clark, M., & Barry, J. (2005). Developing a comprehensive homework policy. *Principal, 84*(3), 36–39.

Farber, P. (1999). Speak up: Student-led conference is a real conversation piece. *Middle Ground, 2*(4), 21–24.

Feldhusen, J. F. (1998). Programs for the gifted few or talent development for the many? *Phi Delta Kappan, 79,* 735–738.

Feldman, A. F., & Matjasko, J. L. (2007). Profiles and portfolios of adolescent school-based extracurricular activity participation. *Journal of Adolescence, 30*(2), 313–332.

Ferrandino, V. L., & Tirozzi, G. N. (2001, May 23). Test driven or data driven. *NAESP Principal Online.* Retrieved from http://www.naesp.org

Fersh, S. (1993). *Integrating the trans-national/cultural dimension. Fastback 361.* Bloomington, IN: Phi Delta Kappa Educational Foundation.

Findley, N. (2002). In their own ways. *Educational Leadership, 60*(1), 60–63.

Fiscus, L. (2005). Student voice in school leadership. *Middle Ground, 8*(3), 22–24.

Fisher, D. N. (2008). Take it outside! *Science Scope, 32* (2), 16–19.

Fisher, N. (2002). Teaching accuracy and reliability for student projects. *Physics Education, 37,* 371–375.

Fisher, R. (2008). Debating assessment in music education. *Research and Issues in Music Education, 6*(1), 1–10.

Fitzgerald, J., & Graves, M. F. (2005). Reading supports for all. *Educational Leadership, 62*(4), 68–71.

Fitzgerald, M. (2007). Poster project maps out design process. *Tech Directions, 67*(5), 25–28.

Foreman, J. (2004). Game-based learning: How to delight and instruct in the 21st century. *Educause Review, 39.* Retrieved from http://www.educause.edu/er

Foster, A. S. (2003). Let the dogs out: Using bobble head toys to explore force and motion. *Science Scope, 26*(7), 16–19.

Freiberg, H. J. (Ed.). (1997). *Beyond behaviorism: Changing the classroom management paradigm.* Boston, MA: Allyn & Bacon.

Freiberg, H. J. (Ed.). (1999). *Perceiving behaving becoming: Lessons learned.* Alexandria, VA: Association for Supervision and Curriculum Development.

Frost, R., Olson, E., & Valiquette, L. (2000). The wolf pack: Power shared and power earned—building a middle school nation. *Middle School Journal, 31*(5), 30–36.

Fuchs, D., & Deshler, D. D. (2007). What we need to know about responsiveness to intervention (and shouldn't be afraid to ask). *Learning Disabilities Research & Practice, 22*(2), 129–136.

Fuchs, D., Fuchs, L. S., Thompson, A., Svenson, E., Yen, L., Al Otaiba, S., Saenz, L. (2001). Peer-assisted learning strategies in reading: Extensions for kindergarten, first grade, and high school. *Remedial and Special Education, 22*(1), 15–21.

Fuchs, L. S., & Fuchs, D. (2004). Determining adequate yearly progress from kindergarten through grade 6 with curriculum-based measurement. *Assessment for Effective Intervention, 29*(4), 25–37.

Fuchs, L. S., Fuchs, D., & Courey, S. J. (2005). Curriculum-based measurement of mathematics competence: From computation to concepts and applications to real-life problem solving. *Assessment for Effective Intervention, 30*(2), 33–46.

Fuchs, L. S., Fuchs, D., & Zumeta, R. O. (2008). A curricular-sampling approach to progress monitoring: Mathematics concepts and applications. *Assessment for Effective Instruction, 33*(4), 225–233.

Fulk, B. M. (2003). Concerns about ninth-grade students' poor academic performance: One school's action plan. *American Secondary Education, 31*(2), 8–26.

Gabriel, A. E. (1999). Brain-based learning: The scent of the trail. *Clearing House, 72,* 288–290.

Gagné, R. M., Briggs, L. J., & Wager, W. W. (1994). *Principles of instructional design* (4th ed.). New York, NY: Holt, Rinehart and Winston.

Gardner, H. (1996). Multiple intelligences: Myths and messages. *International Schools Journal, 15*(2), 8–22.

Gathercoal, F. (1997). *Judicious discipline* (4th ed.). San Francisco, CA: Caddo Gap Press.

Gee. J. P., & Levine, M. H. (2009). *Educational Leadership, 66*(6), 48–52.

Geelan, D. R. (1997). Epistemological anarchy and the many forms of constructivism. *Science and Education, 6*(1–2), 14–28.

Gentile, J. R., & Lalley, J. (2003). *Standards and mastery learning: Aligning teaching and assessment so all children can learn.* Thousand Oaks, CA: Corwin Press.

Gibboney, R. A. (2008). Why an undemocratic capitalism has brought public education to its knees: A manifesto. *Phi Delta Kappan, 90*(1), 21–31.

Gibbons, K. (2008). Evaluating RTI's effectiveness over the long term. *School Administrator, 65*(8), 13.

Gillies, R. (2007). *Cooperative learning: Integrating theory and practice.* Los Angeles, CA: SAGE.

Gillies, R. M. (2008). The effects of cooperative learning on junior high school students' behaviors, discourse and learning during a science-based learning activity. *School Psychology International, 29*(3), 328–347.

Ginott, H. G. (1971). *Teacher and child.* New York, NY: Macmillan.

Glasser, W. (1965). *Reality therapy: A new approach to psychiatry.* New York, NY: Harper & Row.

Glasser, W. (1969). *Schools without failure.* New York, NY: Harper & Row.

Glasser, W. (1986). *Control theory in the classroom.* New York, NY: Harper & Row.

Glasser, W. (1990). *The quality school: Managing students without coercion.* New York, NY: Harper & Row.

Glasser, W. (1993). *The quality school teacher.* New York, NY: HarperPerennial.

Glasser, W. (1997). A new look at school failure and school success. *Phi Delta Kappan, 78,* 597–602.

Glover, D., & Miller, D. (2007). Leading changed classroom culture—The impact of interactive whiteboards. *Management in Education, 21*(3), 21–24.

Gold, S. (2006). Right to copy? Three models of copyright training programs your district can emulate. *Technology & Learning, 26*(6), 20.

Goleman, D. (1995). *Emotional intelligence: Why it can matter more than IQ.* New York, NY: Bantam Books.

Goleman, D. (1998). *Working with emotional intelligence.* New York, NY: Bantam Books.

Goleman, D., Boyatzis, R., & McKee, A. (2002). *Primal leadership: Realizing the power of emotional intelligence.* Boston, MA: Harvard Business School Press.

Good, T. L., & Brophy, J. E. (2008). *Looking in classrooms* (10th ed.). Boston, MA: Pearson Allyn & Bacon.

Goos, M., & Galbraith, P. (1996). Do it this way! Metacognitive strategies in collaborative mathematics problem solving. *Educational Studies in Mathematics, 30,* 229–260.

Gordon, T. (1989). *Discipline that works: Promoting self-discipline in the classroom.* New York, NY: Penguin.

Green, M. (1988). *The dialectic of freedom.* New York, NY: Teachers College Press.

Greenwood, S. C., & McCabe, P. P. (2008). How learning contracts motivate students. *Middle School Journal, 39*(5), 13–22.

Gross, M. U. M. (2000). Exceptionally and profoundly gifted students: An underserved population. *Understanding Our Gifted, 12*(2), 3–9.

Guskey, T. R. (Ed.). (1996). *Communicating student learning.* Alexandria, VA: Association for Supervision and Curriculum Development.

Hanna, W. (2007). The new Bloom's taxonomy: Implications for music education. *Arts Education Policy Review, 108*(4), 7–16.

Hannum, W. H., & McCombs, B. L. (2008). *Enhancing distance learning for today's youth with learner-centered principles, 48*(3), 11–21.

Hargardon, S. (2007). A little help from my friends: Classroom 2.0 educators share their experiences. *School Library Journal, 53*(10), 44–48.

Harrington-Lueker, D. (1997). Emotional intelligence. *High Strides, 9*(4), 1, 4–5.

Harris, H. L., & Coy, D. R. (2003). *Helping students cope with test anxiety.* Greensboro, NC: ERIC Clearinghouse on Counseling and Student Services. (ERIC Document Reproduction Service No. ED479355)

Harrison, G., Andrews, J., & Saklofske, D. (2003). Current perspectives on cognitive and learning styles. *Education Canada, 43*(2), 44–47.

Harrow, A. J. (1977). *Taxonomy of the psychomotor domain.* New York, NY: Longman.

Hawken, L. S., Vincent, C. G., & Schumann, J. (2008). Response to intervention for social behavior: Challenges and opportunities. *Journal of Emotional and Behavioral Disorders, 16*(4), 213–225.

Heller, D. A. (2004). *Teachers wanted: Attracting and retaining good teachers.* Alexandria, VA: Association for Supervision and Curriculum Development.

Henriksen, L., Stichter, J., Stone, J., & Wagoner, B. (2008). Senior year experience: Challenges and options. *Principal Leadership, 8*(8), 34–39.

Herman, B. E. (2004). *The revival of K–8 schools. Fastback 519.* Bloomington, IN: Phi Delta Kappa Educational Foundation.

Hoffman, D., & Levak, B. A. (2003). Personalizing schools. *Educational Leadership, 61*(1), 30–34.

Hohlfeld, T. N., Ritzhaupt, A. D., Barron, A. E., & Kemker, K. (2008). Examining the digital divide in K–12 public schools: Four-year trends for supporting ICT literacy in Florida. *Computers & Education, 51*(4), 1648–1663.

Hopping, L. (2000). Multi-age teaming: A real-life approach to the middle school. *Phi Delta Kappan, 82,* 270–272, 292.

Horton, L. (1981). *Mastery learning. Fastback 154.* Bloomington, IN: Phi Delta Kappa Educational Foundation.

Howard, R. M., & Davies, L, J. (2009). *Educational Leadership, 66*(6), 64–67.

Hughes, K., & Golann, J. W. (2008). A virtual world with real results. *Techniques: Connecting Education and Careers, 83*(3), 34–38.

Hyerle, D. (1996). *Visual tools for constructing knowledge.* Alexandria, VA: Association for Supervision and Curriculum Development.

Hyman, L. A., & D'Allessandro, J. (1984). Oversimplifying the discipline problem. *Education Week, 3*(29), 24.

Jackson, A. W., & Davis, G. A. (2000). *Turning points 2000: Educating adolescents in the 21st century.* New York, NY: Teachers College Press.

Jackson, R. R. (2009). *Never work harder than your students & other principles of great teaching.* Alexandria, VA: Association for Supervision and Curriculum Development.

Jacobson, J., Thrope, L., Fisher, D., Lapp, D., Frey, N., & Flood, J. (2001). Cross-age tutoring: A literacy improvement approach for struggling adolescent readers. *Journal of Adolescent & Adult Literacy, 44,* 528–536.

Jensen, E. (1998). *Teaching with the brain in mind.* Alexandria, VA: Association for Supervision and Curriculum Development.

Johnson, D. W., Johnson, R., & Holubec, E. (1998). *Cooperation in the classroom* (3rd ed.). Edina, MN: Interaction Book Co.

Jones, F. (1987). *Positive classroom discipline.* New York, NY: McGraw-Hill.

Jorgenson, O., & Vanosdall, R. (2002). The death of science? What we risk in our rush toward standardized testing and the three R's. *Phi Delta Kappan, 83,* 601–605.

Jung, C. G. (1923). *Psychological types.* New York, NY: Harcourt Brace.

Kagan, S. (1995). Group grades miss the mark. *Educational Leadership, 52*(8), 68–71.

Karplus, R. (1974). *Science curriculum improvement study* (teacher's handbook). Berkeley, CA: University of California.

Kellough, R. D. (1970). The humanistic approach: An experiment in the teaching of biology to slow learners in high school—An experiment in classroom experimentation. *Science Education, 54,* 253–262.

Kellough, R. D. (1994). *A resource guide for teaching: K–12.* New York, NY: Macmillan.

Kellough, R. D. (2008). *A primer for new principals: Guidelines for success.* Lanham, MD: Rowman & Littlefield Education.

Kellough, R. D., & Kellough, N. G. (1999). *Middle school teaching: A guide to methods and resources* (3rd ed.). Upper Saddle River, NJ: Merrill Prentice Hall.

Kellough, R. D., & Roberts, P. L. (1994). *A resource guide for elementary school teaching: Planning for competence* (3rd ed.). New York, NY: Macmillan.

Kelly, E. B. (1994). *Memory enhancement for educators. Fastback 365.* Bloomington, IN: Phi Delta Kappa Educational Foundation.

Kim, E. C., & Kellough, R. D. (1983). *A resource guide for secondary school teaching* (3rd ed.). New York, NY: Macmillan.

Kim, E. C., & Kellough, R. D. (1991). *A resource guide for secondary school teaching* (5th ed.). New York, NY: Macmillan.

Kitsis, S. M. (2008). The Facebook generation: Homework as social networking. *English Journal, 98*(2), 30–36.

Knobel, M., & Wilber, D. (2009). Lets talk 2.0. *Educational Leadership, 66*(6), 20–24.

Koenig, M. (2001). Debating real-world issues. *Science Scope, 24*(5), 19–23.

Kohlberg, I. (1981). *The meaning and measurement of moral development.* Worcester, MA: Clark University Press.

Kohn, A. (1993). *Punished by rewards.* New York, NY: Houghton Mifflin.

Kolb, D. A. (1984). *Experiential learning: Experience as a source of learning and development.* Upper Saddle River, NJ: Prentice Hall.

Kolb, L. (2006). From toy to tool: Audioblogging with cell phones. *Learning & Leading with Technology, 34*(3), 16–20.

Kounin, J. (1970). *Discipline and group management in classroom.* New York, NY: Holt, Rinehart and Winston.

Krathwohl, D. R., Bloom, B. S., & Masia, B. B. (1964). *Taxonomy of educational goals, handbook 2, affective domain.* New York, NY: David McKay.

Kroon, C. D. (2007). Metric madness. *Mathematics Teaching in the Middle School, 13*(3), 172–181.

Lambert, C., DePaepe, J., Lambert, L., & Anderson, D. (2007). e-Portfolios in action. *Kappa Delta Pi Record, 43*(2), 76–81.

Lauer, D. (2008). Responding to RTI in the middle grades. *Breaking Ranks.* Retrieved from http://www.principals.org/s_nassp

Lehnhoff, E., Woolbaugh, W., & Rew, L. (2008). Designing the perfect plant: Activities to investigate plant ecology. *Science Scope, 32*(3), 29–35.

Lemkuhl, M. (2002). Pen-pal letters: The cross-curricular experience. *Reading Teacher, 55,* 720–722.

Lever-Duffy, J., & McDonald, J. B. (2008). *Teaching and learning with technology* (3rd ed.). Boston: Pearson Allyn & Bacon.

Levine, M. (2003). Celebrating diverse minds. *Educational Leadership, 61*(2), 12–18.

Li, Qing. (2006). Cyberbullying in schools: A research of gender differences. *School Psychology International, 27*(2), 157–170.

Linn, R. L., & Gronlund, N. E. (2000). *Measurement and assessment in teaching* (8th ed.). Columbus, OH: Merrill Prentice Hall.

Littky, D. (2004). *The big picture.* Alexandria, VA: Association for Supervision and Curriculum Development.

Livingston, P. (2008). E-learning gets real: Call it virtual, distance, or online education. For today's curricula, it's no longer a question of whether or not to try but when to start. *Technology & Learning, 28*(10), 20.

Lucking, R. A., Christmann, E. P., & Whiting, M. J. (2008). Make your own mashup maps. *Science Scope, 31*(8), 58–61.

Luttrell, W., & Ward, J. (2004). The "n-word" and the racial dynamics of teaching. *Harvard Education Letter, 20*(5), 4–6.

MacBain, D. E. (1996). *Intergenerational education programs. Fastback 402.* Bloomington, IN: Phi Delta Kappa Educational Foundation.

MacBride, R., & Luehmann, A. L. (2008). Capitalizing on emerging technologies: A case study of classroom blogging. *School Science and Mathematics, 108*(5), 173 *RR*–183.

MacPhee, B. C., & Dempesy, C. W. (2003). Science and math for all. *American School Board Journal, 190*(1), 2–25.

Makkonen, R. (2004). Taking care of novice teachers. *Harvard Education Letter, 29*(3), 1–4.

Manning, M. L., & Bucher, K. T. (2001). Revisiting Ginott's congruent communication after thirty years. *Clearing House, 74*(4), 15–18.

Martin, J. (1998). Literature circles. *Thresholds in Education, 24*(3), 15–19.

Marzano, R. J. (1992). *A different kind of classroom: Teaching with dimensions of learning.* Alexandria, VA: Association for Supervision and Curriculum Development.

Marzano, R. J., & Kendall, J. S. (2006). *The new taxonomy of educational objectives.* Thousand Oaks, CA: Corwin Press.

Marzano, R. J., & Marzano, J. S. (2003). The key to classroom management. *Educational Leadership, 61*(1), 6–13.

Marzano, R. J., Pickering, D. J., & Pollock, J. E. (2001). *Classroom instruction that works: Research-based strategies for increasing student achievement.* Alexandria, VA: Association for Supervision and Curriculum Development.

Mastropieri, M. A., & Scruggs, T. E. (1998). Constructing more meaningful relationships in the classroom: Mnemonic research into practice. *Learning Disabilities Research & Practice, 13*(1), 138–145.

Mathews, J. (2008). Contrarian at the helm. *School Administrator, 65*(6), 30–37.

Matthews, M. E. (2008). Selecting and using Mathemagic tricks in the classroom. *Mathematics Teacher, 102*(2), 98–101.

Maxwell, V. L., & Lassak, M. B. (2008). Using an experiment in portfolios in the middle school. *Mathematics Teaching in the Middle School, 13*(7), 404–409.

McCarthy, B. (1997). A tale of four learners: 4MAT's learning styles. *Educational Leadership, 54*(6), 46–51.

McCarty, P., Ostrem, J., & Young, P. (2004). Saving teachers' voices. *Principal, 82*(2), 56–57.

McConachie, S., Hall, M., Resnick, L., Ravi, A. K., Bill, V. L., Bintz, J., & Taylor, J. A. (2006). Task, text, and talk: Literacy for all students. *Educational Leadership, 64*(2), 8–14.

McCullen, C. (2000). In project-based learning, technology adds a new twist to an old idea. *Middle Ground, 3*(5), 7–9.

McEwan, B., & Gathercoal, P. (2000). Creating peaceful classrooms: Judicious discipline and class meetings. *Phi Delta Kappan, 81,* 450–454.

McEwin, C. K., Jenkins, D., & Dickinson, T. S. (1996). *America's middle schools: A 24-year perspective.* Columbus, OH: National Middle Schools Association.

McHale, T. (2008). Tossing out textbooks: How a Tucson high school customized its curriculum around its laptop program. *Technology and Learning, 28*(6), 24.

McHenry, M. (2008). Idea bank: Duct tape note twister. *Music Educators Journal, 95*(2), 26–27.

McIntosh, M. E., & Draper, R. J. (1996). Using the question–answer relationship strategy to improve students' reading of mathematics texts. *Clearing House, 69*(3), 154–162.

McLauchlan, D. (2002). Peers as PALs: Student partnerships in a high school drama class. *Stage of the Art, 14*(2), 9–15.

McNeil, L. M., Coppola, E., Radigan, J., & Heilig, J. V. (2008). Avoidable losses: High-stakes accountability and the dropout crisis. *Education Policy Analysis Archives, 16*(3), 1–48.

McNeil, M. (2008). Benchmarks momentum on increase. *Education Week, 27*(27), 12–13.

Meyer, A., & Rose, D. H. (2000). Universal design for individual differences. *Educational Leadership, 58*(3), 39–43.

Miller, L. (2007). Solve medical mysteries. *Science Scope, 31*(3), 26–29.

Milsom, A., & Gallo, L. L. (2006). Bullying in middle schools: Prevention and intervention. *Middle School Journal, 37*(3), 12–19.

Minicucci, C., Berman, P., McLaughlin, B., McLeod, B., Nelson, B., & Woodworth, K. (1995). School reform and student diversity. *Phi Delta Kappan, 77,* 77–80.

Moskal, B. M. (2003). *Developing classroom performance assessments and scoring rubrics.* College Park, MD: ERIC Clearinghouse on Assessment and Evaluation.

Movitz, A. P., & Holmes, K. P. (2007). Finding center: How learning centers evolved in a secondary student-centered classroom. *English Journal, 96*(3): 68–73.

Murdock, T. B., & Miller, G. (2003). Teachers as sources of middle school students' motivational identity: Variable-centered and person-centered analytic approaches. *Elementary School Journal, 103,* 383–399.

Mustacchi, J. (2009). R U Safe? *Educational Leadership, 66*(6), 78–82.

Nelsen, J. (1987). *Positive discipline* (2nd ed.). New York, NY: Ballantine Books.

Nelsen, J., Lott, L., & Glenn, H. S. (1993). *Positive discipline in the classroom: How to effectively use class meetings and other positive discipline strategies.* Rocklin, CA: Prima Publishing.

Nelson, D. L. (2008). A context-based strategy for teaching vocabulary. *English Journal, 97*(4), 33–37.

Nelson, J. S., Jayanthi, M., Epstein, M. H., & Bursuck, W. D. (2000). Student preferences for adaptations in classroom testing. *Remedial and Special Education, 21*(1), 41–52.

Newmann, F. (Ed.). (1992). *Student engagement and achievement in American secondary schools.* New York, NY: Teachers College Press.

Newton, B. (1978). Theoretical basis for higher cognitive questioning—An avenue to critical thinking. *Education, 98*(3), 286–290.

Novak, J. D. (1990). Concept maps and vee diagrams: Two metacognitive tools to facilitate meaningful learning. *Instructional Science, 19*(1), 29–52.

Novak, J. D. (1998). *Learning, creating, and using knowledge: Concept maps as facilitative tools in schools and corporations.* Mahwah, NJ: Lawrence Erlbaum.

Ohler, J. (2009). Orchestrating the media collage. *Educational Leadership, 66*(6), 9–13.

Oosterhof, A. (2001). *Classroom applications of educational measurement* (3rd ed.). Upper Saddle River, NJ: Merrill Prentice Hall.

Otten, E. H. (2000). *Character education.* Bloomington, IN: ERIC Clearinghouse for Social Studies/Social Science Education. (ERIC Document Reproduction Service No. ED444932).

Overway, K. (2007). Empirical evidence or intuition? An activity involving the scientific method. *Journal of Chemical Education, 84*(4), 606–608.

Palincsar, A. S., & Brown, A. L. (1984). Reciprocal teaching of comprehension-fostering and comprehension-monitoring activities. *Cognition and Instruction, 1*, 117–175.

Pardini, P. (2002). Revival of the K–8 school. *School Administrator, 59*(3), 6–12.

Parkay, F. W., Hass, G., & Anctil, E. J. (2010). *Curriculum leadership: Readings for developing quality educational programs* (9th ed.). Boston, MA: Allyn & Bacon.

Paul, R., & Elder, L. (2006). *The thinkers guide to the art of Socratic questioning.* Dillon Beach, CA: Foundation for Critical Thinking.

Pavio, A. (1971). *Imagery and verbal processing.* New York, NY: Holt, Rinehart & Winston.

Pavio, A. (1990). *Mental representations: A dual coding approach.* New York, NY: Oxford University Press.

Peterson, J. S., & Ray, K. E. (2006). Bullying and the gifted. *Gifted Child Quarterly 50*(2), 148–168.

Peterson, S. S. (2007). Teaching content with the help of writing across the curriculum. *Middle School Journal, 39*(2), 26–33.

Phillips, C. (2000). A sense of wonder: Young philosophers in San Francisco ponder age-old questions. *Teaching Tolerance, 17,* 36–39.

Phillips, D. A. (2007). Punking and bullying: Strategies in middle school, high school, and beyond. *Journal of Interpersonal Violence, 22*(2), 158–178.

Piaget, J. (1970). *Science of education and the psychology of the child.* New York, NY: Orion.

Piaget, J. (1972). *The psychology of intelligence.* Totowa, NJ: Littlefield Adams.

Piaget, J. (1977). *The development of thought: Elaboration of cognitive structures.* New York, NY: Viking.

Pierangelo, R., & Giuliani, G. A. (2007). *Understanding, developing, and writing IEPs: A step-by-step guide for educators.* Thousand Oaks, CA: Corwin Press.

Plotnick, E. (1997). *Concept mapping: A graphical system for understanding the relationship between concepts.* Syracuse, NY: ERIC Clearinghouse on Information and Technology. (ERIC Document Reproduction Service No. ED407938).

Pogash, C. (2009, February). A school-for-scribes program turns kids into novelists. *Edutopia Magazine.* Retrieved January 6, 2010, from http://www.edutopia.org

Porterfield, K. (2006). Preparing for a very bad day. *Principal, 85*(3), 1–3.

Potenza, S. A. (2003). Science buddies. *Science and Children, 40*(4), 40–43.

Potter, R., & Fuller, D. (2008). My new teaching partner? Using the grammar checker in writing instruction. *English Journal, 98*(1), 36–41.

Prasad, V. (2007). FCCLA quilting projects fights bullying. *Journal of Family and Consumer Services, 99*(1), 39–40.

Queen, J. A., Blackwelder, B. B., & Mallen, L. P. (1997). *Responsible classroom management for teachers and students.* Upper Saddle River, NJ: Merrill Prentice Hall.

Rakow, S. J. (1992). Assessment: A driving force. *Science Scope, 15*(6), 3.

Raschke, D., Alper, S., & Eggers, E. (1999). Recalling alphabet letter names: A mnemonic system to facilitate learning. *Preventing School Failure, 4*(2), 80–86.

Ray, K. W. (2004). When kids make books. *Educational Leadership, 62*(2), 14–18.

Rayner, S. (2007). A teaching elixir, learning chimera or just fools' gold? Do learning styles matter? *Support for Learning, 22*(1), 24–30.

Rayneri, L. J., Gerber, B. L., & Wiley, L. P. (2003). Gifted achievers and gifted underachievers: The impact of learning style preference in the classroom. *Journal of Secondary Gifted Education, 14*(4), 197–204.

Redfield, D., & Rousseau, E. (1981). A meta-analysis of experimental research on teacher questioning behavior. *Review of Educational Research, 51*(2), 237–245.

Reents, J. N. (2002). Isolating 9th graders. *School Administrator, 59*(3), 14–19.

Reeves, D. B. (2004). The case against the zero. *Phi Delta Kappan, 85*(4), 749–751.

Reiser, R. A., & Butzin, S. M. (2000). Using teaming, active learning, and technology to improve instruction. *Middle School Journal, 32*(2), 21–29.

Richardson, W. (2009). Becoming network-wise. *Educational Leadership, 66*(6), 26–31.

Robb, L. (2002). Multiple texts: Multiple opportunities for teaching and learning. *Voices from the Middle, 9*(4), 28–32.

Roberts, K. (2000). Conferencing with confidence: Suggestions for using portfolios in student-led conferences. *Ohio Reading Teacher, 34*(2), 34–39.

Ross, P. M., Tronson, D. A., & Ritchie, R. J. (2008). Increasing conceptual understanding of glycolysis & the Krebs cycle using role-play. *American Biology Teacher, 70*(3), 163–168.

Rowe, M. B. (1974). Wait time and reward as instructional variables, their influence on language, logic and fate control: Part I. Wait time. *Journal of Research in Science Teaching, 11*(2), 81–94.

Rozema, R. (2007). The book report, version 2.0: Podcasting on young adult novels. *English Journal, 70*(1), 31–36.

Rutherford, P. M., Rostine, R., Bell, P., & Beugin, A. (2003). High schoolers in motion. *Science Teacher, 70*(5), 35–37.

Saifer, S., & Barton, R. (2007). Promoting culturally responsive standards-based teaching. *Principal Leadership, 8*(1), 24–28.

Salpeter, J. (2008). The new rules of copyright. *Technology & Learning, 29*(3), 33.

Samuels, C. A. (2008). Special education is funding early help. *Education Week, 28*(3), 1, 12–13.

San Antonio, D. M., & Salzfass, E. A. (2007). How we treat one another in school. *Educational Leadership, 64*(8), 32–38.

Saunders, C. L. (2003). Case study: A gifted child at risk. *Journal of Secondary Gifted Education, 14*(2), 100–106.

Scarpaci, R. T. (2006). Bullying: Effective strategies for its prevention. *Kappa Delta Pi Record 42*(4), 170–174.

Schank, R. C. (2000). A vision of education for the 21st century. *T.H.E. Journal, 27*(6), 43–45.

Schneider, E. (2000). Shifting into high gear. *Educational Leadership, 58*(1), 57–60.

Schwab, J. J. (1962). *The teaching of science as enquiry.* Cambridge, MA: Harvard University Press.

Schwartz, S. (1997). *Strategies for identifying the talents of diverse students.* ED410323. New York, NY: ERIC Clearinghouse on Urban Education.

Schwartz, W. (1999). *Preventing violence by elementary school children.* ERIC/CUE Digest Number 149. New York, NY: ERIC Clearinghouse on Urban Education.

Schwartz, W. (Ed.). (2000). *New trends in language education for Hispanic students.* ED442913. New York, NY: ERIC Clearinghouse on Urban Education.

Scott, J. E. (1994). Literature circles in the middle school classroom: Developing reading, responding, and responsibility. *Middle School Journal, 26*(2), 37–41.

Selvidge, E. (2006). Journey to Egypt: A board game. *Montessori Life, 18*(4), 36–39.

Sharan, Y., & Sharan, S. (1992). *Expanding cooperative learning through group investigation.* New York, NY: Teachers College Press.

Simpson, E. J. (1972). *The classification of educational objectives in the psychomotor domain. The psychomotor domain: Vol. 3.* Washington, DC: Gryphon House.

Skinner, B. F. (1968). *The technology of teaching.* New York, NY: Appleton-Century-Crofts.

Skinner, B. F. (1971). *Beyond freedom and dignity.* New York, NY: Knopf.

Slater, W. H., & Horstman, F. R. (2002). Teaching reading and writing to struggling middle school and high school students: The case for reciprocal teaching. *Preventing School Failure, 46*(4), 163–166.

Slavin, R. E. (1980). *Using student team learning* (Rev. ed.). Baltimore, MD: John Hopkins University, Center for Social Organization of Schools.

Slavin, R. E. (1996). Cooperative learning in middle and secondary schools. *Clearing House, 69*, 200–204.

Smerdon, B. A., Burkam, D. T., & Lee, V. E. (1999). Access to constructivist and didactic teaching: Who gets it? Where is it practiced? *Teachers College Record, 101*(1), 5–34.

Smith, T. B. (2008). Teaching vocabulary expeditiously: Three keys to improving vocabulary instruction. *English Journal, 97*(4), 20–25.

Smyth, T. S. (2008). Who is no child left behind leaving behind? *Clearing House, 81*(3), 133–137.

Sosniak, L. (2001). The 9% challenge: Education in school and society. *Teachers College Record.* Retrieved January 6, 2010 from http:// www.tcrecord.org

Sowell, J. E. (1993). Approach to art history in the classroom. *Art Education, 46*(2), 19–24.

Sprick, R. (2009). Doing discipline differently. *Principal Leadership, 9*(5), 18–22.

Stairs, A. J. (2007). Culturally responsive teaching: The Harlem renaissance in an urban English class. *English Journal, 96*(6), 37–42.

Stanley, K. R., & Plucker, J. A. (2008). Improving high school graduation rates. *Center for Evaluation and Education Policy: Education Policy Brief, 6*(7).

Stecker, P. M., Fuchs, L. S., & Fuchs, D. (2005). Using curriculum-based measurement to improve student achievement: Review of research. *Psychology in the Schools, 42*(8), 795–819l.

Stein, S. (2001). The Mural project web site. Available at www.baruch.cuny.edu/spa/community/mural

Steinkuehler, C. (2008). Massively multiplayer online games as an educational technology: An outline for research authors. *Educational Technology Magazine, 48*(1), 10–21.

Sternberg, R. J. (1998). Teaching and assessing for successful intelligence. *School Administrator, 55*(1), 30–31.

Sternberg, R. J. (2008). Excellence for all. *Educational Leadership, 66*(2), 14–19.

Sternberg, R. J., Grigorenko, E. L., & Jarvin, L. (2001). Improving reading instruction: The triarchic model. *Educational Leadership, 58*(6), 48–51.

Stevenson, C., & Carr, J. F. (Eds.). (1993). *Integrated studies in the middle grades.* New York, NY: Teachers College Press.

Stiggins, R. J. (2001). *Student-involved classroom assessment* (3rd ed.). Upper Saddle River, NJ: Prentice Hall.

Stright, S. D., & Supplee, L. H. (2002). Children's self-regulatory behaviors during teacher-directed, seat-work, and small-group instructional contexts. *Journal of Educational Research, 95*(4), 235–244.

Sunderman, G. L., & Kim, J. (2004). Inspiring vision, disappointing results: Four studies on implementing the No Child Left Behind Act. *The Civil Rights Project of Harvard University.* Retrieved from http://www.civilrights-project.harvard.edu

Sylwester, R. (2003). *A biological brain in a cultural classroom* (2nd ed.). Thousand Oaks, CA: Corwin Press.

Sylwester, R. (2007). Skulls and School Boxes: Student Brains that Want out. Retrieved from http://www.designshare.com/index.php/articles/student-brains

Talab, R. S., & Butler, R. P. (2007). Shared electronic spaces in the classroom: Copyright, privacy, and guidelines. *TechTrends, 51*(1), 12–15.

Tanner, H., & Jones, S. (2007). How interactive is your whiteboard? *Mathematics Teaching Incorporating Micromath, 200,* 37–41.

Tassinari, M. (1996). Hands-on projects take students beyond the book. *Social Studies Review, 34*(3), 16–20.

Taylor, R. T. (2006). *Improving reading, writing, and content learning for students in grades 4–12.* Thousand Oaks, CA: Corwin Press.

Thames, D. G., & York, K. C. (2003). Disciplinary border crossing: Adopting a broader, richer view of literacy. *Reading Teacher, 46*(7), 602–610.

Thornton, S. (2001). Subject specific teaching methods: History. In J. Brophy (Ed.), *Subject-specific instructional methods and activities* (pp. 291–313). New York, NY: Elsevier Science.

Thrope, L., & Wood, K. (2000). Cross-age tutoring for young adolescents. *Clearing House, 73,* 239–242.

Tobin, K. G. (1984). The effect of extended wait time on discourse characteristics and achievement in middle school grades. *Journal of Research in Science Teaching, 21,* 779–791.

Tobin, K. G. (1986). The effects of teacher wait time on discourse characteristics in mathematics and language arts classes. *American Educational Research Journal, 23,* 191–200.

Tobin, K. G. (1987). The role of wait time in higher cognitive level learning. *Review of Educational Research, 57*(1), 69–95.

Tomlinson, C. A. (2005). *How to differentiate instruction in mixed-ability classrooms* (2nd ed.). Upper Saddle River, NJ: Pearson Merrill Prentice Hall.

Tomlinson, C., & Strickland, C. (2005). *Differentiation in practice: A resource guide for differentiating curriculum, grades 9–12.* Alexandria, VA: Association for Supervision and Curriculum Development.

Tompkins, G. E., & Hoskisson, K. (1991). *Language arts: Content and teaching strategies.* Upper Saddle River, NJ: Prentice Hall.

United States Department of Education. (1997). *Tried and true: Tested ideas for teaching and learning from the regional educational laboratories.* Washington, DC: Office of Educational Research and Improvement.

Unmuth, K. L. (2009). Keller's Trinity Meadows students use cellphones as classroom computer. *The Dallas Morning News*. Retrieved from www.dallasnews.com

van Boxtel, C., van der Linden, J., Roelofs, E., & Erkens, G. (2002). Collaborative concept mapping: Provoking and supporting meaningful discourse. *Theory Into Practice, 41*(1), 40–46.

van Hell, J. G., & Mahn, A. C. (1997). Keyword mnemonics versus rote rehearsal: Learning concrete and abstract foreign words by experienced and inexperienced learners. *Language Learning, 47*, 507–546.

Vars, G. F., & Beane, J. A. (2000). *Integrative curriculum in a standards-based world.* Champaign, IL: ERIC Clearinghouse on Elementary and Early Childhood Education. (ERIC Document Reproduction Service No. ED4441618).

Vaughn, S., & Bos, C. S. (2009). *Strategies for teaching students with learning and behavior problems* (7th ed.). Upper Saddle River, NJ: Merrill.

Vaughn, S., Fletcher, J. M., Francis, D. J., Denton, C. A., Wanzek, J., Wexler, J., Cirino, P.T., Barth, A. E., & Romain, M. A. (2008). Response to intervention with older students with reading difficulties. *Learning and Individual Differences, 18*(3), 338–345.

Vavilis, B., & Vavilis, S. L. (2004). Why are we learning this? What is this stuff good for, anyway? *Phi Delta Kappan, 84*, 282–287.

Vawter, D. (2009, March). Mining the middle school mind. *Middle School Matters.* Retrieved from http://www.naesp.org/Middle_Matters.aspx

Villa, R. A., & Thousands, J. S. (Eds.). (1995). *Creating an inclusive school.* Alexandria, VA: Association for Supervision and Curriculum Development.

Villano, M. (2007). Building a better podcast. *T.H.E. Journal, 35*(1), 31–33.

Villano, M. (2008a). Point man. *T.H.E. Journal, 35*(3), 48–50, 52–53.

Villano, M. (2008b). When worlds collide: An augmented reality check. *T.H.E. Journal, 35*(2), 33–34, 36, 38.

Vincent, T., & van't Hooft, M. (2007). For kids, by kids: Our city podcast. *Social Education, 71*(3), 125–129.

Vosen, M. A. (2008). Using Bloom's taxonomy to teach students about plagiarism. *English Journal, 97*(6), 43–46.

Vygotsky, L. (1962). *Thought and language.* Cambridge, MA: MIT Press.

Vygotsky, L. (1978). *Mind in society: The development of higher psychological processes.* (Edited by M. Cole, V. John-Steiner, S. Scribner, & E. Souberman). Cambridge: Harvard University Press.

Walach, S. (2008). So far from the bamboo grove: Multiculturalism, historical context, and close reading. *English Journal, 97*(3), 17–20.

Walden, L. M., & Kritsonis, W. A. (2008). The impact of the correlation between the No Child Left Behind Act's high stakes testing and the high drop-out rates of minority students. *National Journal for Publishing and Mentoring Doctoral Student Research, 5*(1). Retrieved from www.nationalforum.com

Want, M. C., Haertel, G. D., & Walberg, H. J. (1993). What helps students learn? *Educational Leadership, 51*(4), 74–79.

Wassermann, S. (1999). Shazam! You're a teacher. *Phi Delta Kappan, 80*, 464, 466–468.

Waters, J. K. (2007). E-portfolios: Making things e-asy. *T.H.E. Journal, 34*(4), 26–33.

Weertz, M. (2002). The benefits of theme schools. *Educational Leadership, 59*(7), 68–71.

Weigel, M., & Gardner, H. (2009). The best of both literacies. *Educational Leadership, 66*(6), 38–41.

Welsh, M. J. (2007). Chemistry of art and color sudoku puzzles. *Journal of Chemical Education, 84*(4), 610–611.

Werderich, D. E. (2002). Individualized responses: Using journal letters as a vehicle for differentiated reading instruction. *Journal of Adolescent & Adult Literacy, 45*(8), 746–754.

Westervelt, M. (2007). Schoolyard inquiry for English language learners. *Science Teacher, 74*(3), 47–51.

Wiggins, G., & McTighe, J. (1998). *Understanding by design.* Alexandria, VA: Association for Supervision and Curriculum Development.

Wiles, J., & Bondi, J. (2001). *The new American middle school* (3rd ed.). Upper Saddle River, NJ: Merrill Prentice Hall.

Willard-Holt, C. (1999). *Dual exceptionalities.* Reston, VA: ERIC Clearinghouse on Disabilities and Gifted Education. (ERIC Document Reproduction Service No. EDE574).

Willard-Holt, C. (2003). Raising expectations for the gifted. *Educational Leadership, 61*(2), 72–75.

Willis, J. (2007). Cooperative group learning is a brain turn-on. *Middle School Journal, 38*(4), 4–13.

Wise, B. (2008). High schools at the tipping point. *Educational Leadership, 65*(8), 8–13.

Wolf, M., & Barzillai, M. (2009). The importance of deep reading. *Educational Leadership, 66*(6), 32–37.

Wolfe, P. (2001). *Brain matters.* Alexandria, VA: Association for Supervision and Curriculum Development.

Wormeli, R. (2006). Accountability: Teaching through assessment and feedback, not grading. *American Secondary Education, 34*(3), 14–27.

Wynne, E. A., & Ryan, K. (1997). *Reclaiming our schools: Teaching character, academics, and discipline* (2nd ed.). Upper Saddle River, NJ: Prentice Hall.

Yancey, K. B. (2004). Using multiple technologies to teach writing. *Educational Leadership, 62*(2), 38–40.

Zhao, Y. (2008). What knowledge has the most worth? *School Administrator, 65*(2), 20–27.

Zimmerman, B. J., & Dibenedetto, M. K. (2008). Mastery learning and assessment. *Psychology in the Schools, 45*(3), 206–216.

Zucker, A. A., & Hug, S. T. (2008). Teaching and learning physics in a 1:1 laptop school. *Journal of Science Education and Technology, 17*(6), 586–594.

NAME INDEX

SUBJECT INDEX

displays, 49
learning log (VLL), 250
learning modality, 177
tools, 249
vocational career dual education, 306

Wahkiakum High School (WA), 304
wait time, 214, 218, 223–224
web sites, 57, 126, 307
West Point Bridge Design, 183
West Salem Middle School (WI),
    185, 187
whiteboards, 46–49

whole
-class discussions, 290–292, 308–313
language, 143
withitness, 39–40, 82
writing
across the curriculum, 297–299
assessment of, 322–323
boards, 46
project-centered learning and, 296–297

year-round education (YRE), 2, 7
YouTube, 56